Multiple-Criteria Decision Making

Multiple-Criteria Decision Making

Editors

Goran Ćirović

Dragan Pamučar

MDPI • Basel • Beijing • Wuhan • Barcelona • Belgrade • Manchester • Tokyo • Cluj • Tianjin

Editors

Goran Ćirović
Faculty of Civil Engineering
Management
University
"UNION–Nikola Tesla"
Belgrade
Serbia

Dragan Pamučar
Department of Logistics
Military Academy
University of Defence
in Belgrade
Belgrade
Serbia

Editorial Office
MDPI
St. Alban-Anlage 66
4052 Basel, Switzerland

This is a reprint of articles from the Special Issue published online in the open access journal *Axioms* (ISSN 2075-1680) (available at: www.mdpi.com/journal/axioms/special_issues/mcdm_I).

For citation purposes, cite each article independently as indicated on the article page online and as indicated below:

LastName, A.A.; LastName, B.B.; LastName, C.C. Article Title. *Journal Name* **Year**, *Volume Number*, Page Range.

ISBN 978-3-0365-2817-5 (Hbk)
ISBN 978-3-0365-2816-8 (PDF)

Contents

About the Editors

Goran Ćirović

Dr. Goran Ćirović was born in Kragujevac and currently lives in Belgrade. He completed his primary and high school education in Belgrade and then finished his undergraduate, master's, and doctoral studies at the Faculty of Civil Engineering, University of Belgrade. He is a professor at the College of Applied Studies of Civil Engineering and Geodesy in Belgrade, full professor at the Faculty of Technical Sciences, the University of Novi Sad, in the department for civil engineering and geodesy, and full professor at the Faculty of Architecture, Civil Engineering, and Geodesy at the University of Banja Luka. He is also a scientific advisor.

Dr. Ćirović has mentored 8 defended doctoral dissertations, 8 master theses, 6 master's papers, over 500 graduation papers, and over 100 specialist papers from the field of civil engineering and investment. He has published 4 monographs and 6 university textbooks; over 200 scientific research papers, books, and publications; and more than 31 papers in international journals on the SCI list. He is involved in the application of operational research in civil engineering, in particular the application of intelligent techniques and optimum management problems. He has been awarded the Charter of Merit for his contribution to the development of operational research in Serbia. In addition, Dr. Ćirović has participated in seven scientific research projects, two technological projects, and five strategic projects.

Dragan Pamučar

Dr. Dragan Pamučar is an Associate Professor at the University of Defence in Belgrade, Department of Logistics, Serbia. Dr. Pamučar received a Ph.D. in Applied Mathematics with a specialization in multi-criteria modeling and soft computing techniques, from the University of Defence in Belgrade, Serbia, in 2013 and an M.Sc. degree from the Faculty of Transport and Traffic Engineering in Belgrade, 2009. His research interest is in the field of computational intelligence; multi-criteria decision-making problems; neuro-fuzzy systems; fuzzy, rough, and intuitionistic fuzzy set theory; and neutrosophic theory. Application areas include a wide range of logistics problems.

Dr. Pamučar has authored/co-authored over 150 papers published in SCI-indexed international journals, including *Expert Systems with Applications, Applied Soft Computing, Soft Computing, Computational Intelligence, Computers and Industrial Engineering Technical Gazette, Sustainability, Symmetry, Water, Asia-Pacific Journal of Operational Research, Operational Research, Journal of Intelligent and Fuzzy Systems, Land use policy, Environmental Impact Assessment Review, International Journal of Physical Sciences, Economic Computation and Economic Cybernetics Studies and Research*, and many more. In the last three years, Prof. Pamučar was awarded top and outstanding reviewer for numerous Elsevier journals such as *Sustainable Production and Consumption, Measurement, Egyptian Informatics Journal, International Journal of Hydrogen Energy*, and so on.

Preface to "Multiple-Criteria Decision Making"

Decision-making in real-world problems, including individual process decisions, requires an appropriate and reliable decision support system. Fuzzy set theory, rough set theory, and neutrosophic set theory, which are MCDM techniques, are useful for modeling complex decision-making problems with imprecise, ambiguous, or vague data. The application of the developed new multi-criteria decision-making (MCDM) methods can be eliminated or decreased by decision-makers' subjectivity, which leads to consistency or symmetry in the weight values of the criteria. Decision making on complex engineering problems, including individual process decisions, requires an appropriate and reliable decision support system. Fuzzy set theory, rough set theory, and neutrosophic set theory that are used for MCDM techniques are very useful for modeling complex engineering problems with imprecise, ambiguous, or vague data. Sustainability in engineering is one of the most discussed topics in recent years and represents one of the key factors in engineering sustainable development and optimization. Sustainable multidisciplinary approaches based on MCDM techniques will enable easier process technology in the future.

This Special Issue on "Multiple-Criteria Decision Making" aims to incorporate recent developments in the area of multiple-criteria decision making. Topics include, but are not limited to, the following:

- MCDM optimization in engineering;
- Environmental sustainability in engineering processes;
- Multi-criteria production and logistics processes planning;
- New trends in the multi-criteria evaluation of sustainable processes;
- Multi-criteria decision making in strategic management based on sustainable criteria.

Engineering is the application of scientific and mathematical principles for practical objectives such as processes, manufacture, design, and operation of products while accounting for constraints invoked by environmental, economic, and social factors. There are various factors that need to be considered in order to address engineering sustainability, which is critical for the overall sustainability of human development and activity. In this regard, in recent decades, decision-making theory has been a subject of intense research activity due to its wide applications in different areas, such as sustainable engineering and environmental sustainability. The decision-making theory approach has become an important means of providing real-time solutions to uncertainty problems, especially for sustainable engineering and environmental sustainability problems in engineering processes. We hope that this Special Issue will stimulate both theoretical and applied research in the related field of multiple-criteria decision making. It is certainly impossible to provide in this short editorial a more comprehensive description for all articles in this Special Issue. However, we sincerely hope that our effort in compiling these articles will enrich our readers and inspire researchers with regard to the common but important issue of decision-making and fuzzy decision-making approaches for sustainable engineering processes.

Goran Ćirović, Dragan Pamučar

Editors

axioms

MDPI

Article

A Single-Valued Neutrosophic Extension of the EDAS Method

Dragiša Stanujkić [1], Darjan Karabašević [2,*], Gabrijela Popović [2], Dragan Pamučar [3], Željko Stević [4], Edmundas Kazimieras Zavadskas [5] and Florentin Smarandache [6]

1 Technical Faculty in Bor, University of Belgrade, Vojske Jugoslavije 12, 19210 Bor, Serbia; dstanujkic@tfbor.bg.ac.rs
2 Faculty of Applied Management, Economics and Finance, University Business Academy in Novi Sad, Jevrejska 24, 11000 Belgrade, Serbia; gabrijela.popovic@mef.edu.rs
3 Department of Logistics, Military Academy, University of Defence in Belgrade, Pavla Jurišića Šturma 33, 11000 Belgrade, Serbia; dragan.pamucar@va.mod.gov.rs
4 Faculty of Transport and Traffic Engineering, University of East Sarajevo, Vojvode Mišića 52, 74000 Doboj, Bosnia and Herzegovina; zeljko.stevic@sf.ues.rs.ba
5 Institute of Sustainable Construction, Vilnius Gediminas Technical University, Sauletekio al. 11, LT-10223 Vilnius, Lithuania; edmundas.zavadskas@vilniustech.lt
6 Mathematics and Science Division, Gallup Campus, University of New Mexico, 705 Gurley Ave., Gallup, NM 87301, USA; smarand@unm.edu
* Correspondence: darjan.karabasevic@mef.edu.rs

Abstract: This manuscript aims to propose a new extension of the EDAS method, adapted for usage with single-valued neutrosophic numbers. By using single-valued neutrosophic numbers, the EDAS method can be more efficient for solving complex problems whose solution requires assessment and prediction, because truth- and falsity-membership functions can be used for expressing the level of satisfaction and dissatisfaction about an attitude. In addition, the indeterminacy-membership function can be used to point out the reliability of the information given with truth- and falsity-membership functions. Thus, the proposed extension of the EDAS method allows the use of a smaller number of complex evaluation criteria. The suitability and applicability of the proposed approach are presented through three illustrative examples.

Keywords: neutrosophic set; single-valued neutrosophic set; EDAS; MCDM

check for updates

Citation: Stanujkić, D.; Karabašević, D.; Popović, G.; Pamučar, D.; Stević, Ž.; Zavadskas, E.K.; Smarandache, F. A Single-Valued Neutrosophic Extension of the EDAS Method. *Axioms* **2021**, *10*, 245. https://doi.org/10.3390/axioms10040245

Academic Editors: Javier Fernandez and Oscar Castillo

Received: 10 June 2021
Accepted: 27 September 2021
Published: 29 September 2021

1. Introduction

Multicriteria decision making facilitates the evaluation of alternatives based on a set of criteria. So far, this technique has been used to solve a number of problems in various fields [1–6].

Notable advancement in solving complex decision-making problems has been made after Bellman and Zadeh [7] introduced fuzzy multiple-criteria decision making, based on fuzzy set theory [8].

In fuzzy set theory, belonging to a set is shown using the membership function $\mu(x) \in [0,1]$. Nonetheless, in some cases, it is not easy to determine the membership to the set using a single crisp number, particularly when solving complex decision-making problems. Therefore, Atanassov [9] extended fuzzy set theory by introducing nonmembership to a set $\nu(x) \in [0,1]$. In Atanassov's theory, intuitionistic sets' indeterminacy is, by default, $1 - \mu(x) - \nu(x)$.

Smarandache [10,11] further extended fuzzy sets by proposing a neutrosophic set. The neutrosophic set includes three independent membership functions, named the truth-membership $T_A(x)$, the falsity-membership $F_A(x)$ and the indeterminacy-membership $I_A(x)$ functions. Smarandache [11] and Wang et al. [12] further proposed a single-valued neutrosophic set, by modifying the conditions $T_A(x)$, $I_A(x)$ and $F_A(x) \in [0, 1]$ and $0 \leq T_A(x) + I_A(x) + F_A(x) \leq 3$, which are more suitable for solving scientific and engineering problems [13].

When solving some kinds of decision-making problems, such as problems related to estimates and predictions, it is not easy to express the ratings of alternatives using crisp values, especially in cases when ratings are collected through surveys. The use of fuzzy sets, intuitionistic fuzzy sets, as well as neutrosophic fuzzy sets can significantly simplify the solving of such types of complex decision-making problems. However, the use of fuzzy sets and intuitionistic fuzzy sets has certain limitations related to the neutrosophic set theory. By using three mutually independent membership functions applied in neutrosophic set theory, the respondent involved in surveys has the possibility of easily expressing their views and preferences. The researchers recognized the potential of the neutrosophic set and involved it in the multiple-criteria decision-making process [14,15].

The Evaluation Based on Distance from Average Solution (EDAS) method was introduced by Keshavarz Ghorabaee et al. [16]. Until now, this method has been applied to solve various problems in different areas, such as: ABC inventory classification [16], facility location selection [17], supplier selection [18–20], third-party logistics provider selection [21], prioritization of sustainable development goals [22], autonomous vehicles selection [23], evaluation of e-learning materials [24], renewable energy adoption [25], safety risk assessment [26], industrial robot selection [27], and so forth.

Several extensions are also proposed for the EDAS method, such as: a fuzzy EDAS [19], an interval type-2 fuzzy extension of the EDAS method [18], a rough EDAS [20], Grey EDAS [28], intuitionistic fuzzy EDAS [29], interval-valued fuzzy EDAS [30], an extension of EDAS method in Minkowski space [23], an extension of the EDAS method under q-rung orthopair fuzzy environment [31], an extension of the EDAS method based on interval-valued complex fuzzy soft weighted arithmetic averaging (IV-CFSWAA) operator and the interval-valued complex fuzzy soft weighted geometric averaging (IV-CFSWGA) operator with interval-valued complex fuzzy soft information [32], and an extension of the EDAS equipped with trapezoidal bipolar fuzzy information [33].

Additionally, part of the EDAS extensions is based on neutrosophic environments, such as refined single-valued neutrosophic EDAS [34], trapezoidal neutrosophic EDAS [35], single-valued complex neutrosophic EDAS [36], single-valued triangular neutrosophic EDAS [37], neutrosophic EDAS [38], an extension of the EDAS method based on multivalued neutrosophic sets [39], a linguistic neutrosophic EDAS [40], the EDAS method under 2-tuple linguistic neutrosophic environment [41], interval-valued neutrosophic EDAS [22,42], interval neutrosophic [43].

In order to enable the usage of the EDAS method for solving complex decision-making problems, a novel extension that enables usage of single-valued neutrosophic numbers is proposed in this article. Therefore, the rest of this paper is organized as follows: In Section 2, some basic definitions related to the single-valued neutrosophic set are given. In Section 3, the computational procedure of the ordinary EDAS method is presented, whereas in Section 3.1, the single-valued neutrosophic extension of the EDAS method is proposed. In Section 4, three illustrative examples are considered with the aim of explaining in detail the proposed methodology. The conclusions are presented in the final section.

2. Preliminaries

Definition 1. *Let X be the universe of discourse, with a generic element in X denoted by x. A Neutrosophic Set (NS) A in X is an object having the following form [11]:*

$$A = \{x < T_A(x), I_A(x), F_A(x) >: x \in X\}, \tag{1}$$

where: $T_A(x)$, $I_A(x)$, and $F_A(x)$ are the truth-membership function, the indeterminacy-membership function and the falsity-membership function, respectively, $T_A(x), I_A(x), F_A(x) : X \to]^-0, 1^+[$, $^-0 \le T_A(x) + I_A(x) + F_A(x) \le 3^+$, and $]^-0, 1^+[$ denotes bounds of NS.

Definition 2. *Let X be a space of points, with a generic element in X denoted by x. A Single-Valued Neutrosophic Set (SVNS) A over X is as follows [12]:*

$$A = \{x < T_A(x), I_A(x), F_A(x) > | x \in X\}, \tag{2}$$

where: $T_A(x)$, $I_A(x)$ and $F_A(x)$ are the truth-membership function, the indeterminacy-membership function and the falsity-membership function, respectively, $T_A(x), I_A(x), F_A(x) : X \to [0, 1]$ and $0 \le T_A(x) + I_A(x) + F_A(x) \le 3$.

Definition 3. *A Single-Valued Neutrosophic Numbera $= \langle t_a, i_a, f_a \rangle$ is a special case of an SVNS on the set of real numbers $\Re$, where $t_a, i_a, f_a \in [0,1]$ and $0 \le t_a + i_a + f_a \le 3$ [12].*

Definition 4. *Let $x_1 = \langle t_1, i_1, f_1 \rangle$ and $x_2 = \langle t_2, i_2, f_2 \rangle$ be two SVNNs and $\lambda > 0$. The basic operations over two SVNNs are as follows:*

$$x_1 + x_2 = < t_1 + t_2 - t_1 t_2, i_1 i_2, f_1 f_2 >, \tag{3}$$

$$x_1 \cdot x_2 = < t_1 t_2, i_1 + i_2 - i_1 i_{2,} f_1 + f_2 - f_1 f_2 > . \tag{4}$$

$$\lambda x_1 = < 1 - (1 - t_1)^\lambda, i_1^\lambda, f_1^\lambda > . \tag{5}$$

$$x_1^\lambda = < t_1^\lambda, i_1^\lambda, 1 - (1 - f_1)^\lambda > . \tag{6}$$

Definition 5. *Let $x = < t_i, i_i, f_i >$ be an SVNN. The score function s_x of x is as follows [44]:*

$$s_i = (1 + t_i - 2i_i - f_i)/2, \tag{7}$$

where $s_i \in [-1, 1]$.

Definition 6. *Let $a_j \le t_j, i_j, f_j > (j = 1, \ldots, n)$ be a collection of SVNSs and $W = (w_1, w_2, \ldots, w_n)^T$ e an associated weighting vector. The Single-Valued Neutrosophic Weighted Average (SVNWA) operator of a_j is as follows [40]:*

$$SVNWA(a_1, a_2, \ldots, a_n) = \sum_{j=1}^{n} w_j a_j = \left(1 - \prod_{j=1}^{n} (1 - t_j)^{w_j}, \prod_{j=1}^{n} (i_j)^{w_j}, \prod_{j=1}^{n} (f_j)^{w_j}\right), \tag{8}$$

where: w_j is the element j of the weighting vector, $w_j \in [0, 1]$ and $\sum_{j=1}^{n} w_j = 1$.

Definition 7. *Let $x = < t_i, i_i, f_i >$ be an SVNN. The reliability r_i of x is as follows [45]:*

$$r_i = \begin{cases} \frac{|t_i - f_i|}{t_i + i_i + f_i} & t_i + i_i + f_i \ne 0 \\ 0 & t_i + i_i + f_i = 0 \end{cases}. \tag{9}$$

Definition 8. *Let D be a decision matrix, dimension m x n, whose elements are SVNNs. The overall reliability of the information contained in the decision matrix is as follows:*

$$r_d = \frac{\sum_{j=1}^{n} r_{ij}}{\sum_{i=1}^{m} \sum_{j=1}^{n} r_{ij}}. \tag{10}$$

3. The EDAS Method

The procedure of solving a decision-making problem with *m* alternatives and *n* criteria using the EDAS method can be presented using the following steps:

Step 1. Determine the average solution according to all criteria, as follows:

$$x_j^* = (x_1, x_2, \cdots, x_n), \tag{11}$$

with:

$$x_j^* = \frac{\sum_{i=1}^{m} x_{ij}}{m}. \tag{12}$$

where: x_{ij} denotes the rating of the alternative i in relation to the criterion j.

Step 2. Calculate the positive distance from average (PDA) d_{ij}^+ and the negative distance from average (NDA) d_{ij}^-, as follows:

$$d_{ij}^+ = \begin{cases} \frac{\max(0,(x_{ij}-x_j^*))}{x_j^*}; & j \in \Omega_{\max} \\ \frac{\max(0,(x_j^*-x_{ij}))}{x_j^*}; & j \in \Omega_{\min} \end{cases}, \tag{13}$$

$$d_{ij}^- = \begin{cases} \frac{\max(0,(x_j^*-x_{ij}))}{x_j^*}; & j \in \Omega_{\max} \\ \frac{\max(0,(x_{ij}-x_j^*))}{x_j^*}; & j \in \Omega_{\min} \end{cases}, \tag{14}$$

where: $\Omega_{\max}$ and $\Omega_{\min}$ denote the set of the beneficial criteria and the nonbeneficial criteria, respectively.

Step 3. Determine the weighted sum of PDA, Q_i^+, and the weighted sum of NDS, Q_i^-, for all alternatives, as follows:

$$Q_i^+ = \sum_{j=1}^{n} w_j d_{ij}^+, \tag{15}$$

$$Q_i^- = \sum_{j=1}^{n} w_j d_{ij}^-, \tag{16}$$

where w_j denotes the weight of the criterion j.

Step 4. Normalize the values of the weighted sum of the PDA and NDA, respectively, for all alternatives, as follows:

$$S_i^+ = \frac{Q_i^+}{\max_k Q_k^+}, \tag{17}$$

$$S_i^- = 1 - \frac{Q_i^-}{\max_k Q_k^-}, \tag{18}$$

where: S_i^+ and S_i^- denote the normalized weighted sum of the PDA and the NDA, respectively.

Step 5. Calculate the appraisal score S_i for all alternatives, as follows:

$$S_i = \frac{1}{2}(S_i^+ + S_i^-). \tag{19}$$

Step 6. Rank the alternatives according to the decreasing values of appraisal score. The alternative with the highest S_i is the best choice among the candidate alternatives.

3.1. The Extension of the EDAS Method Adopted for the Use of Single-Valued Neutrosophic Numbers in a Group Environment

Let us suppose a decision-making problem that include m alternatives, n criteria and k decision makers, where ratings are given using SVNNs. Then, the computational procedure of the proposed extension of the EDAS method can be expressed concisely through the following steps:

Step 1. Construct the single-valued neutrosophic decision-making matrix for each decision maker, as follows:

$$\widetilde{X}^k = \begin{bmatrix} < t_{11}^k, i_{11}^k, f_{11}^k > & < t_{12}^k, i_{12}^k, f_{12}^k > & \cdots & < t_{1n}^k, i_{1n}^k, f_{1n}^k > \\ < t_{21}^k, i_{21}^k, f_{21}^k > & < t_{22}^k, i_{22}^k, f_{22}^k > & \cdots & < t_{2n}^k, i_{2n}^k, f_{2n}^k > \\ \vdots & \vdots & \vdots & \vdots \\ < t_{m1}^k, i_{m1}^k, f_{m1}^k > & < t_{m2}^k, i_{m2}^k, f_{m2}^k > & \cdots & < t_{mn}^k, i_{mn}^k, f_{mn}^k > \end{bmatrix} \tag{20}$$

whose elements $\widetilde{x}_{ij} =< t_{ij}^k, i_{ij}^k, f_{ij}^k >$ are SVNNs.

Step2. Construct the single-valued neutrosophic decision making using Equation (8):

$$\widetilde{X} = \begin{bmatrix} < t_{11}, i_{11}, f_{11} > & < t_{12}, i_{12}, f_{12} > & \cdots & < t_{1n}, i_{1n}, f_{1n} > \\ < t_{21}, i_{21}, f_{21} > & < t_{22}, i_{22}, f_{22} > & \cdots & < t_{2n}, i_{2n}, f_{2n} > \\ \vdots & \vdots & \vdots & \vdots \\ < t_{m1}, i_{m1}, f_{m1} > & < t_{m2}, i_{m2}, f_{m2} > & \cdots & < t_{mn}, i_{mn}, f_{mn} > \end{bmatrix} \tag{21}$$

Step 3. Determine the single-valued average solution (SVAS) $\widetilde{x}_j^*$ according to all criteria, as follows:

$$\widetilde{x}_j^* = (< t_1^*, i_1^*, f_1^* >, < t_2^*, i_2^*, f_2^* >, \cdots, < t_n^*, i_n^*, f_n^* >), \tag{22}$$

where:

$$t_j^* = \frac{\sum_{l=1}^m t_{ij}}{m} \tag{23}$$

$$i_j^* = \frac{\sum_{l=1}^m i_{ij}}{m}, \text{ and} \tag{24}$$

$$f_j^* = \frac{\sum_{l=1}^m f_{ij}}{m} \tag{25}$$

Step 4. Calculate a single-valued neutrosophic PDA (SVNPDA), $\widetilde{d}_{ij}^+ =< t_{ij}^+, i_{ij}^+, f_{ij}^+ >$, and a single-valued neutrosophic NDA (SVNNDA), $\widetilde{d}_{ij}^- =< t_{ij}^-, i_{ij}^-, f_{ij}^- >$, as follows:

$$\widetilde{d}_{ij}^+ =< t_{ij}^+, i_{ij}^+, f_{ij}^+ >= \begin{cases} \left\langle \frac{\max(0,(t_{ij}-t_j^*))}{x_j^*}, \frac{\max(0,(i_{ij}-i_j^*))}{x_j^*}, \frac{\max(0,(f_{ij}-f_j^*))}{x_j^*} \right\rangle & j \in \Omega_{\max} \\ \left\langle \frac{\max(0,(t_j^*-t_{ij}))}{x_j^*}, \frac{\max(0,(i_j^*-i_{ij}))}{x_j^*}, \frac{\max(0,(f_j^*-f_{ij}))}{x_j^*} \right\rangle & j \in \Omega_{\min} \end{cases} \tag{26}$$

$$\widetilde{d}_{ij}^- =< t_{ij}^-, i_{ij}^-, f_{ij}^- >= \begin{cases} \frac{\max(0,(t_j^*-t_{ij}))}{x_j^*}, \frac{\max(0,(i_j^*-i_{ij}))}{x_j^*}, \frac{\max(0,(f_j^*-f_{ij}))}{x_j^*} & j \in \Omega_{\max} \\ \frac{\max(0,(t_{ij}-t_j^*))}{x_j^*}, \frac{\max(0,(i_{ij}-i_j^*))}{x_j^*}, \frac{\max(0,(f_{ij}-f_j^*))}{x_j^*} & j \in \Omega_{\min} \end{cases} \tag{27}$$

where:

$$x_j^* = \max\left(\frac{\sum_{i=1}^m t_{ij}}{m}, \frac{\sum_{i=1}^m i_{ij}}{m}, \frac{\sum_{i=1}^m f_{ij}}{m}\right) \tag{28}$$

For a decision-making problem that includes only beneficial criteria, the SVNPDA and SVNNDA can be determined as follows:

$$\widetilde{d}_{ij}^+ =< t_{ij}^+, i_{ij}^+, f_{ij}^+ >= \left\langle \frac{\max(0,(t_{ij}-t_j^*))}{x_j^*}, \frac{\max(0,(i_{ij}-i_j^*))}{x_j^*}, \frac{\max(0,(f_{ij}-f_j^*))}{x_j^*} \right\rangle \tag{29}$$

$$\widetilde{d}_{ij}^- =< t_{ij}^-, i_{ij}^-, f_{ij}^- >= \left\langle \frac{\max(0,(t_j^*-t_{ij}))}{x_j^*}, \frac{\max(0,(i_j^*-i_{ij}))}{x_j^*}, \frac{\max(0,(f_j^*-f_{ij}))}{x_j^*} \right\rangle \tag{30}$$

Step 5. Determine the weighted sum of the SVNPDA, $\tilde{Q}_i^+ = < t_i^+, i_i^+, f_i^+ >$, and the weighted sum of the SVNNDA, $\tilde{Q}_i^- = < t_i^-, i_i^-, f_i^- >$, for all alternatives. Based on Equations (5) and (8) the weighted sum of the SVNPDA, $\tilde{Q}_i^+$, and the weighted sum of the SVNNDA, $\tilde{Q}_i^-$, can be calculated as follows:

$$\tilde{Q}_i^+ = \sum_{j=1}^{n} w_j \tilde{d}_{ij}^+ = \left\langle 1 - \prod_{j=1}^{n} (1 - t_{ij}^+)^{w_j}, \prod_{j=1}^{n} (i_{ij}^+)^{w_j}, \prod_{j=1}^{n} (f_{ij}^+)^{w_j} \right\rangle, \tag{31}$$

$$\tilde{Q}_i^- = \sum_{j=1}^{n} w_j \tilde{d}_{ij}^- = \left\langle 1 - \prod_{j=1}^{n} (1 - t_{ij}^-)^{w_j}, \prod_{j=1}^{n} (i_{ij}^-)^{w_j}, \prod_{j=1}^{n} (f_{ij}^-)^{w_j} \right\rangle. \tag{32}$$

Step 6. In order to normalize the values of the weighted sum of the single-valued neutrosophic PDA and the weighted sum of the single-valued neutrosophic NDA, these values should be transformed into crisp values. This transformation can be performed using the score function or similar approaches. After that, the following three steps remain the same as in the ordinary EDAS method.

Step 7. Normalize the values of the weighted sum of the SVNPDA and the single-valued neutrosophic SVNNDA for all alternatives, as follows:

$$S_i^+ = \frac{Q_i^+}{\max_k Q_k^+}, \tag{33}$$

$$S_i^- = 1 - \frac{Q_i^-}{\max_k Q_k^-}. \tag{34}$$

Step 8. Calculate the appraisal score S_i for all alternatives, as follows:

$$S_i = \frac{1}{2}(S_i^+ + S_i^-). \tag{35}$$

Step 9. Rank the alternatives according to the decreasing values of the appraisal score. The alternative with the highest S_i is the best choice among the candidate alternatives.

4. A Numerical Illustrations

In this section, three numerical illustrations are presented in order to indicate the applicability of the proposed approach. The first numerical illustration shows in detail the procedure for applying the neutrosophic extension of the EDAS method. The second numerical illustration shows the application of the proposed extension in the case of solving MCDM problems that contain nonbeneficial criteria, while the third numerical illustration shows the application of the proposed approach in combination with the reliability of the information contained in SVNNs.

4.1. The First Numerical Illustration

In this numerical illustration, an example adopted from Biswas et al. [46] is used to demonstrate the proposed approach in detail. Suppose that a team of three IT specialists was formed to select the best tablet from four initially preselected tablets for university students. The purpose of these tablets is to make university e-learning platforms easier to use.

The preselected tablets are evaluated based on the following criteria: Features—C_1, Hardware—C_2, Display—C_3, Communication—C_4, Affordable Price—C_5, and Customer care—C_6. The ratings obtained from three IT specialists are shown in Tables 1–3.

Table 1. The ratings of three tablets obtained from the first of three IT specialist.

	C_1	C_2	C_3	C_4	C_5	C_6
A_1	<1.0, 0.0, 0.0>	<1.0, 0.2, 0.0>	<1.0, 0.0, 0.0>	<0.7, 0.3, 0.0>	<0.8, 0.2, 0.2>	<0.9, 0.1, 0.1>
A_2	<1.0, 0.0, 0.0>	<0.9, 0.0, 0.0>	<1.0, 0.0, 0.0>	<0.7, 0.0, 0.2>	<1.0, 0.0, 0.0>	<0.7, 0.0, 0.0>
A_3	<0.9, 0.0, 0.0>	<0.9, 0.0, 0.0>	<0.7, 0.2, 0.3>	<0.5, 0.0, 0.0>	<0.9, 0.0, 0.0>	<0.7, 2.0, 2.0>
A_4	<0.7, 0.0, 0.3>	<0.7, 0.3, 0.3>	<0.6, 0.4, 0.2>	<0.4, 0.0, 0.0>	<0.9, 0.0, 0.0>	<0.5, 0.0, 0.2>

Table 2. The ratings of three tablets obtained from the second of three IT specialist.

	C_1	C_2	C_3	C_4	C_5	C_6
A_1	<0.8, 0.2, 0.2>	<1.0, 0.0, 0.1>	<0.7, 0.3, 0.2>	<0.7, 0.3, 0.2>	<1.0, 0.0, 0.0>	<0.8, 0.1, 0.1>
A_2	<1.0, 0.0, 0.0>	<1.0, 0.0, 0.0>	<1.0, 0.0, 0.2>	<0.6, 0.0, 0.2>	<1.0, 0.0, 0.0>	<1.0, 0.1, 0.1>
A_3	<0.7, 0.3, 0.2>	<0.9, 0.0, 0.0>	<0.7, 0.2, 0.3>	<0.5, 0.0, 0.0>	<0.9, 0.0, 0.0>	<0.7, 0.2, 0.2>
A_4	<0.7, 0.0, 0.3>	<0.7, 0.3, 0.3>	<0.6, 0.4, 0.2>	<0.4, 0.0, 0.0>	<0.9, 0.0, 0.0>	<0.5, 0.1, 0.2>

Table 3. The ratings of three tablets obtained from the third of three IT specialist.

	C_1	C_2	C_3	C_4	C_5	C_6
A_1	<0.9, 1.0, 1.0>	<0.9, 0.0, 0.2>	<1.0, 0.0, 1.0>	<0.7, 0.3, 0.2>	<1.0, 0.0, 0.0>	<0.9, 0.0, 0.1>
A_2	<1.0, 0.0, 0.0>	<1.0, 0.0, 0.0>	<0.9, 0.2, 0.1>	<0.6, 0.0, 0.2>	<1.0, 0.0, 0.0>	<1.0, 0.1, 0.1>
A_3	<0.6, 0.3, 0.2>	<0.9, 0.0, 0.0>	<0.5, 0.2, 0.2>	<0.5, 0.3, 0.2>	<0.9, 0.2, 0.4>	<0.7, 0.0, 0.0>
A_4	<0.6, 0.0, 0.3>	<0.5, 0.3, 0.4>	<0.4, 0.4, 0.2>	<0.4, 0.0, 0.0>	<0.9, 0.2, 0.3>	<0.7, 0.0, 0.2>

After that, a group evaluation matrix, shown in Table 4, is calculated using Equation (8) and w_k = (0.33, 0.33, 0.33), where w_k denotes the importance of k-th IT specialist.

Table 4. The group evaluation matrix.

	C_1	C_2	C_3	C_4	C_5	C_6
A_1	<1.0, 0.0, 0.0>	<1.0, 0.0, 0.0>	<1.0, 0.0, 0.0>	<0.7, 0.3, 0.0>	<1.0, 0.0, 0.0>	<0.9, 0.0, 0.1>
A_2	<1.0, 0.0, 0.0>	<1.0, 0.0, 0.0>	<1.0, 0.0, 0.0>	<0.6, 0.0, 0.2>	<1.0, 0.0, 0.0>	<1.0, 0.0, 0.0>
A_3	<0.8, 0.0, 0.0>	<0.9, 0.0, 0.0>	<0.6, 0.2, 0.3>	<0.5, 0.0, 0.0>	<0.9, 0.0, 0.0>	<0.7, 0.0, 0.0>
A_4	<0.7, 0.0, 0.3>	<0.6, 0.3, 0.3>	<0.5, 0.4, 0.2>	<0.4, 0.0, 0.0>	<0.9, 0.0, 0.0>	<0.6, 0.0, 0.2>

The SVNPDA and the SVNPDA, shown in Tables 5 and 6, are calculated using Equations (29) and (30).

Table 5. The SVNPDA.

	C_1	C_2	C_3	C_4	C_5	C_6
A_1	<0.2, 0.0, 0.0>	<0.1, 0.0, 0.0>	<0.3, 0.0, 0.0>	<0.3, 0.4, 0.0>	<0.1, 0.0, 0.0>	<0.1, 0.0, 0.0>
A_2	<0.2, 0.0, 0.0>	<0.1, 0.0, 0.0>	<0.3, 0.0, 0.0>	<0.1, 0.0, 0.3>	<0.1, 0.0, 0.0>	<0.3, 0.0, 0.0>
A_3	<0.0, 0.0, 0.0>	<0.0, 0.0, 0.0>	<0.0, 0.1, 0.2>	<0.0, 0.0, 0.0>	<0.0, 0.0, 0.0>	<0.0, 0.0, 0.0>
A_4	<0.0, 0.0, 0.2>	<0.0, 0.3, 0.3>	<0.0, 0.3, 0.1>	<0.0, 0.0, 0.0>	<0.0, 0.0, 0.0>	<0.0, 0.0, 0.1>

Table 6. The SVNNDA.

	C_1	C_2	C_3	C_4	C_5	C_6
A_1	<0.0, 0.0, 0.1>	<0.0, 0.1, 0.1>	<0.0, 0.2, 0.1>	<0.0, 0.0, 0.1>	<0.0, 0.0, 0.0>	<0.0, 0.0, 0.0>
A_2	<0.0, 0.0, 0.1>	<0.0, 0.1, 0.1>	<0.0, 0.2, 0.2>	<0.0, 0.1, 0.0>	<0.0, 0.0, 0.0>	<0.0, 0.0, 0.1>
A_3	<0.1, 0.0, 0.1>	<0.0, 0.1, 0.1>	<0.2, 0.0, 0.0>	<0.1, 0.1, 0.1>	<0.1, 0.0, 0.0>	<0.1, 0.0, 0.1>
A_4	<0.2, 0.0, 0.0>	<0.3, 0.0, 0.0>	<0.3, 0.0, 0.0>	<0.3, 0.1, 0.1>	<0.1, 0.0, 0.0>	<0.3, 0.0, 0.0>

The weighted sum of SVNPDA and the weighted sum of SVNNDA, shown in Table 7, are calculated using Equations (31) and (32), as well as weighting vector w_j = (0.19, 0.19, 0.18, 0.16, 0.14, 0.13). Before calculating the normalized weighted sums of the SVNPDA and SVNNDA, using Equations (33) and (34), as well as appraisal score, using Equation (35), the values of the weighted sum of SVNPDA and SVNNDA are transformed into crisp values using Equation (7).

Table 7. Computational details and ranking order of considered tablets.

	$\tilde{Q}_i^+$		$\tilde{Q}_i^-$		S_i^+	S_i^-	S_i	Rank
	SVNN	**Score**	**SVNN**	**Score**				
A_1	<0.168, 0.000, 0.000>	0.58	<0.000, 0.000, 0.000>	0.50	1.00	0.20	0.597	2
A_2	<0.170, 0.000, 0.000>	0.59	<0.000, 0.027, 0.000>	0.47	1.00	0.24	0.620	1
A_3	<0.003, 0.000, 0.000>	0.50	<0.096, 0.000, 0.000>	0.55	0.86	0.12	0.488	3
A_4	<0.000, 0.000, 0.000>	0.50	<0.245, 0.000, 0.000>	0.62	0.85	0.00	0.427	4

The ranking order of considered alternatives is also shown in Table 7. As it can be seen from Table 7, the most appropriate alternative is the alternative denoted as A_2.

4.2. The Second Numerical Illustration

The second numerical illustration shows the application of the NS extension of the EDAS method in the case of solving MCDM problems that include nonbeneficial criteria.

An example taken from Stanujkic et al. [47] was used for this illustration. In the given example, the evaluation of three comminution circuit designs (CCDs) was performed based on five criteria: Grinding efficiency—C_1, Economic efficiency—C_2, Technological reliability—C_3, Capital investment costs—C_4, and Environmental impact—C_5. The group decision-making matrix, as well as the types of criteria, are shown in Table 8.

Table 8. Group decision-making matrix.

	C_1	C_2	C_3	C_4	C_5
Optimization	**Max**	**Max**	**Max**	**Min**	**Min**
A_1	<0.9, 0.1, 0.2>	<0.7, 0.2, 0.3>	<0.9, 0.1, 0.2>	<0.9, 0.1, 0.2>	<0.9, 0.1, 0.2>
A_2	<0.8, 0.1, 0.3>	<0.8, 0.1, 0.3>	<0.8, 0.1, 0.3>	<0.9, 0.1, 0.2>	<0.8, 0.1, 0.3>
A_3	<1.0, 0.1, 0.3>	<0.9, 0.1, 0.2>	<0.9, 0.1, 0.2>	<0.7, 0.2, 0.5>	<0.7, 0.2, 0.3>

Values of the SVNPDA and SVNPDA, calculated using Equations (26) and (27), are shown in Tables 9 and 10.

Table 9. The SVNPDA.

	C_1	C_2	C_3	C_4	C_5
A_1	<0.2, 0.0, 0.0>	<0.1, 0.0, 0.0>	<0.3, 0.0, 0.0>	<0.3, 0.4, 0.0>	<0.1, 0.0, 0.0>
A_2	<0.2, 0.0, 0.0>	<0.1, 0.0, 0.0>	<0.3, 0.0, 0.0>	<0.1, 0.0, 0.3>	<0.1, 0.0, 0.0>
A_3	<0.0, 0.0, 0.2>	<0.0, 0.3, 0.3>	<0.0, 0.3, 0.1>	<0.0, 0.0, 0.0>	<0.0, 0.0, 0.0>

Table 10. The SVNNDA.

	C_1	C_2	C_3	C_4	C_5
A_1	<0.0, 0.0, 0.1>	<0.0, 0.1, 0.1>	<0.0, 0.2, 0.1>	<0.0, 0.0, 0.1>	<0.0, 0.0, 0.0>
A_2	<0.0, 0.0, 0.1>	<0.0, 0.1, 0.1>	<0.0, 0.2, 0.2>	<0.0, 0.1, 0.0>	<0.0, 0.0, 0.0>
A_3	<0.2, 0.0, 0.0>	<0.3, 0.0, 0.0>	<0.3, 0.0, 0.0>	<0.3, 0.1, 0.1>	<0.1, 0.0, 0.0>

The weighted sum of SVNPDA and the weighted sum of SVNNDA are shown in Table 11. The calculation was performed using the following weighting vector w_j = (0.24, 0.17, 0.24, 0.21, 0.14). The remaining part of the calculation procedure, carried out using formulas Equations (33)–(35) is also summarized in Table 11.

Table 11. Computational details and ranking order of considered GCDs.

	$\tilde{Q}_i^+$		$\tilde{Q}_i^-$		S_i^+	S_i^-	S_i	Rank
	SVNN	**Score**	**SVNN**	**Score**				
A_1	<0.009, 0.000, 0.000>	0.50	<0.057, 0.000, 0.000>	0.53	0.910	0.005	0.458	2
A_2	<0.000, 0.000, 0.000>	0.50	<0.063, 0.000, 0.000>	0.53	0.902	0.000	0.451	3
A_3	<0.109, 0.000, 0.000>	0.55	<0.000, 0.000, 0.000>	0.50	1.000	0.059	0.530	1

As can be seen from Table 11, by applying the proposed extension of the EDAS method, the following ranking order of alternatives is obtained $A_3 > A_1 > A_2$, i.e., the alternative A_3 is selected as the most appropriate.

A similar order of alternatives was obtained in Stanujkic et al. [45] using the Neutrosophic extension of the MULTIMOORA method, where the following order of alternatives was achieved $A_3 > A_2 > A_1$.

4.3. The Third Numerical Illustration

The third numerical illustration shows the use of a newly proposed approach with an approach that allows for determining the reliability of data contained in SVNNs, proposed by Stanujkic et al. [43]. Using this approach, inconsistently completed questionnaires can be identified and, if necessary, eliminated from further evaluation of alternatives.

In order to demonstrate this approach, an example was taken from Stanujkic et al. [48]. In this example, the websites of five wineries were evaluated based on the following five criteria: Content—C_1, Structure and Navigation—C_2, Visual Design—C_3, Interactivity—C_4, and Functionality—C_5.

The ratings obtained from the three respondents are also shown in Tables 12–14.

Table 12. The ratings obtained from the first of three respondents.

	C_1	C_2	C_3	C_4	C_5
A_1	<1.0, 0.0, 0.0>	<1.0, 0.2, 0.0>	<1.0, 0.0, 0.0>	<0.7, 0.3, 0.0>	<0.8, 0.2, 0.2>
A_2	<1.0, 0.0, 0.0>	<1.0, 0.0, 0.0>	<1.0, 0.0, 0.0>	<0.6, 0.0, 0.2>	<1.0, 0.0, 0.0>
A_3	<0.9, 0.0, 0.0>	<0.9, 0.0, 0.0>	<0.7, 0.2, 0.3>	<0.5, 0.0, 0.0>	<0.9, 0.0, 0.0>
A_4	<0.7, 0.0, 0.3>	<0.7, 0.3, 0.3>	<0.6, 0.4, 0.2>	<0.4, 0.0, 0.0>	<0.9, 0.0, 0.0>
A_5	<1.0, 0.0, 0.0>	<1.0, 0.0, 0.0>	<1.0, 0.0, 0.0>	<0.7, 0.0, 0.2>	<1.0, 0.0, 0.0>

Table 13. The ratings obtained from the second of three respondents.

	C_1	C_2	C_3	C_4	C_5
A_1	<0.8, 0.2, 0.2>	<1.0, 0.0, 0.0>	<0.7, 0.3, 0.1>	<0.7, 0.3, 0.2>	<1.0, 0.0, 0.0>
A_2	<1.0, 0.0, 0.0>	<1.0, 0.0, 0.0>	<1.0, 0.0, 0.0>	<0.6, 0.0, 0.2>	<1.0, 0.0, 0.0>
A_3	<0.7, 0.3, 0.2>	<0.9, 0.0, 0.0>	<0.7, 0.2, 0.3>	<0.5, 0.0, 0.0>	<0.9, 0.0, 0.0>
A_4	<0.7, 0.0, 0.3>	<0.7, 0.3, 0.3>	<0.6, 0.4, 0.2>	<0.4, 0.0, 0.0>	<0.9, 0.0, 0.0>
A_5	<1.0, 0.0, 0.0>	<1.0, 0.0, 0.0>	<1.0, 0.0, 0.0>	<0.7, 0.0, 0.2>	<1.0, 0.0, 0.0>

Table 14. The ratings obtained from the third of three respondents.

	C_1	C_2	C_3	C_4	C_5
A_1	<0.9, 1.0, 1.0>	<0.9, 0.0, 0.2>	<1.0, 0.0, 1.0>	<0.7, 0.3, 0.2>	<1.0, 0.0, 0.0>
A_2	<1.0, 0.0, 0.0>	<1.0, 0.0, 0.0>	<1.0, 0.0, 0.0>	<0.6, 0.0, 0.2>	<1.0, 0.0, 0.0>
A_3	<0.6, 0.3, 0.2>	<0.9, 0.0, 0.0>	<0.5, 0.2, 0.3>	<0.5, 0.3, 0.3>	<0.9, 0.3, 0.4>
A_4	<0.6, 0.0, 0.3>	<0.5, 0.3, 0.4>	<0.4, 0.4, 0.2>	<0.4, 0.0, 0.0>	<0.9, 0.3, 0.3>
A_5	<1.0, 0.0, 0.0>	<1.0, 0.0, 0.0>	<1.0, 0.0, 0.0>	<0.7, 0.0, 0.2>	<1.0, 0.0, 0.0>

The reliability of the collected information calculated using Equations (9) and (10) are shown in Tables 15–17. In this case, the lowest value of overall reliability of information was 0.61 which is why all collected questionnaires were used to evaluate alternatives.

Table 15. The reliability of information obtained from the first of three respondents.

	C_1	C_2	C_3	C_4	C_5	*Reliability*
A_1	1.00	0.83	1.00	0.70	0.50	0.81
A_2	1.00	1.00	1.00	0.50	1.00	0.90
A_3	1.00	1.00	0.33	1.00	1.00	0.87
A_4	0.40	0.31	0.33	1.00	1.00	0.61
A_5	1.00	1.00	1.00	0.56	1.00	0.91
				Overall reliability		0.82

Table 16. The reliability of information obtained from the second of three respondents.

	C_1	C_2	C_3	C_4	C_5	*Reliability*
A_1	0.50	1.00	0.55	0.42	1.00	0.69
A_2	1.00	1.00	1.00	0.50	1.00	0.90
A_3	0.42	1.00	0.33	1.00	1.00	0.75
A_4	0.40	0.31	0.33	1.00	1.00	0.61
A_5	1.00	1.00	1.00	0.56	1.00	0.91
				Overall reliability		0.77

Table 17. The reliability of information obtained from the third of three respondents.

	C_1	C_2	C_3	C_4	C_5	*Reliability*
A_1	0.03	0.64	0.00	0.42	1.00	0.42
A_2	1.00	1.00	1.00	0.50	1.00	0.90
A_3	0.36	1.00	0.20	0.18	0.31	0.41
A_4	0.33	0.08	0.20	1.00	0.40	0.40
A_5	1.00	1.00	1.00	0.56	1.00	0.91
				Overall reliability		0.61

The group decision-making matrix formed on the basis of the ratings from Tables 12–14 is shown in Table 18, while the calculation details are summarized in Table 19, using the following weight vector w_j = (0.22, 0.20, 0.25, 0.18, 0.16).

Table 18. The group decision-making matrix.

	C_1	C_2	C_3	C_4	C_5
A_1	<1.0, 0.0, 0.0>	<1.0, 0.0, 0.0>	<1.0, 0.0, 0.0>	<0.7, 0.3, 0.0>	<1.0, 0.0, 0.0>
A_2	<1.0, 0.0, 0.0>	<1.0, 0.0, 0.0>	<1.0, 0.0, 0.0>	<0.6, 0.0, 0.2>	<1.0, 0.0, 0.0>
A_3	<0.8, 0.0, 0.0>	<0.9, 0.0, 0.0>	<0.6, 0.2, 0.3>	<0.5, 0.0, 0.0>	<0.9, 0.0, 0.0>
A_4	<0.7, 0.0, 0.3>	<0.6, 0.3, 0.3>	<0.5, 0.4, 0.2>	<0.4, 0.0, 0.0>	<0.9, 0.0, 0.0>
A_5	<1.0, 0.0, 0.0>	<1.0, 0.0, 0.0>	<1.0, 0.0, 0.0>	<0.7, 0.0, 0.2>	<1.0, 0.0, 0.0>

Table 19. Computational details and ranking order of considered websites.

	$\tilde{Q}_i^+$		$\tilde{Q}_i^-$		S_i^+	S_i^-	S_i	Rank
	SVNN	**Score**	**SVNN**	**Score**				
A_1	<0.141, 0.000, 0.000>	0.57	<0.000, 0.000, 0.000>	0.50	1.00	0.21	0.61	3
A_2	<0.110, 0.000, 0.000>	0.56	<0.000, 0.006, 0.000>	0.47	0.97	0.26	0.62	2
A_3	<0.000, 0.000, 0.000>	0.50	<0.125, 0.000, 0.000>	0.56	0.88	0.11	0.49	4
A_4	<0.000, 0.000, 0.000>	0.50	<0.269, 0.000, 0.000>	0.63	0.88	0.00	0.44	5
A_5	<0.141, 0.000, 0.000>	0.57	<0.000, 0.006, 0.000>	0.47	1.00	0.26	0.63	1

From Table 15 it can be seen that the following order of ranking of alternatives was achieved $A_5 > A_2 > A_1 > A_3 > A_4$, which is similar to the order of alternatives $A_5 = A_2 > A_1 > A_3 > A_4$ given in Stanujkic et al. [48].

5. Conclusions

A novel extension of the EDAS method based on the use of single-valued neutrosophic numbers is proposed in this article. Single-valued neutrosophic numbers enable simultaneous use of truth- and falsity-membership functions, and thus enable expressing the level of satisfaction and the level of dissatisfaction about an attitude. At the same time, using the indeterminacy-membership function, decision makers can express their confidence about already-given satisfaction and dissatisfaction levels.

The evaluation process using the ordinary EDAS method can be considered as simple and easy to understand. Therefore, the primary objective of the development of this extension was the formation of an easy-to-use and easily understandable extension of the EDAS method. By integrating the benefits that can be obtained by using single-valued neutrosophic numbers and simple-to-use and understandable computational procedures of the EDAS method, the proposed extension can be successfully used for solving complex decision-making problems, while the evaluation procedure remains easily understood for decision makers who are not familiar with neutrosophy and multiple-criteria decision making.

Finally, the usability and efficiency of the proposed extension is demonstrated on an example of tablet evaluation.

Author Contributions: Conceptualization, E.K.Z., D.K., Ž.S. and G.P.; methodology, D.K., D.S. and F.S.; validation, D.P.; investigation, D.P.; data curation, G.P.; writing—original draft preparation, D.S. and Ž.S.; writing—review and editing, E.K.Z. and F.S.; supervision, D.K. All authors have read and agreed to the published version of the manuscript.

Funding: This research received no external funding.

Acknowledgments: The research presented in this article was done with the financial support of the Ministry of Education, Science and Technological Development of the Republic of Serbia, within the funding of the scientific research work at the University of Belgrade, Technical Faculty in Bor, according to the contract with registration number 451-03-9/2021-14/200131.

Conflicts of Interest: The authors declare no conflict of interest.

References

1. Karamaşa, Ç.; Demir, E.; Memiş, S.; Korucuk, S. WeIghtIng the factors affectıng logıstıcs outsourcıng. *Decis. Mak. Appl. Manag. Eng.* **2021**, *4*, 19–33. [CrossRef]
2. Valipour, A.; Sarvari, H.; Tamošaitiene, J. Risk Assessment in PPP Projects by Applying Different MCDM Methods and Comparative Results Analysis. *Adm. Sci.* **2018**, *8*, 80. [CrossRef]
3. Ferreira, F.A.; Ilander, G.O.P.-B.; Ferreira, J. MCDM/A in practice: Methodological developments and real-world applications. *Manag. Decis.* **2019**, *57*, 295–299. [CrossRef]
4. Chen, Y.-C.; Lien, H.-P.; Tzeng, G.-H. Measures and evaluation for environment watershed plans using a novel hybrid MCDM model. *Expert Syst. Appl.* **2010**, *37*, 926–938. [CrossRef]
5. Bakır, M.; Atalık, Ö. Application of fuzzy AHP and fuzzy MARCOS approach for the evaluation of e-service quality in the airline industry. *Decis. Mak. Appl. Manag. Eng.* **2021**, *4*, 127–152. [CrossRef]
6. Cakar, T.; Çavuş, B. Supplier selection process in dairy industry using fuzzy TOPSIS method. *Oper. Res. Eng. Sci. Theory Appl.* **2021**, *4*, 82–98. [CrossRef]
7. Bellman, R.E.; Zadeh, L.A. Decision-Making in a Fuzzy Environment. *Manag. Sci.* **1970**, *17*, B141. [CrossRef]
8. Zadeh, L. Fuzzy sets. *Inf. Control.* **1965**, *8*, 338–353. [CrossRef]
9. Atanassov, K.T. Intuitionistic fuzzy sets. *Fuzzy Set. Syst.* **1986**, *20*, 87–96. [CrossRef]
10. Smarandache, F. *Neutrosophy Probability Set and Logic*; American Research Press: Rehoboth, NM, USA, 1998.
11. Smarandache, F. *A Unifying Field in Logics. Neutrosophy: Neutrosophic Probability, Set and Logic*; American Research Press: Rehoboth, NM, USA, 1999.
12. Wang, H.; Smarandache, F.; Zhang, Y.; Sunderraman, R. Single valued neutrosophic sets. *Rev. Air Force Acad.* **2010**, *1*, 10–14.
13. Li, Y.; Liu, P.; Chen, Y. Some Single Valued Neutrosophic Number Heronian Mean Operators and Their Application in Multiple Attribute Group Decision Making. *Informatica* **2016**, *27*, 85–110. [CrossRef]
14. Zavadskas, E.K.; Bausys, R.; Lescauskiene, I.; Omran, J. M-generalised q-neutrosophic MULTIMOORA for Decision Making. *Stud. Inform. Control.* **2020**, *29*, 389–398. [CrossRef]
15. Zavadskas, E.K.; Bausys, R.; Lescauskiene, I.; Usovaite, A. MULTIMOORA under Interval-Valued Neutrosophic Sets as the Basis for the Quantitative Heuristic Evaluation Methodology HEBIN. *Mathematics* **2021**, *9*, 66. [CrossRef]

16. Ghorabaee, M.K.; Zavadskas, E.K.; Olfat, L.; Turskis, Z. Multi-Criteria Inventory Classification Using a New Method of Evaluation Based on Distance from Average Solution (EDAS). *Informatica* **2015**, *26*, 435–451. [CrossRef]
17. Keshavarz Ghorabaee, M.; Zavadskas, E.K.; Amiri, M.; Antucheviciene, J. Evaluation by an area-based method of ranking interval type-2 fuzzy sets (EAMRIT-2F) for multi-criteria group decision-making. *Trans. Bus. Econ.* **2016**, *15*, 76–95.
18. Ghorabaee, M.K.; Amiri, M.; Zavadskas, E.K.; Turskis, Z.; Antucheviciene, J. A new multi-criteria model based on interval type-2 fuzzy sets and EDAS method for supplier evaluation and order allocation with environmental considerations. *Comput. Ind. Eng.* **2017**, *112*, 156–174. [CrossRef]
19. Ghorabaee, M.K.; Zavadskas, E.K.; Amiri, M.; Turskis, Z. Extended EDAS Method for Fuzzy Multi-criteria Decision-making: An Application to Supplier Selection. *Int. J. Comput. Commun. Control.* **2016**, *11*, 358–371. [CrossRef]
20. Stević, Ž.; Pamučar, D.; Vasiljević, M.; Stojić, G.; Korica, S. Novel Integrated Multi-Criteria Model for Supplier Selection: Case Study Construction Company. *Symmetry* **2017**, *9*, 279. [CrossRef]
21. Ecer, F. Third-party logistics (3PLs) provider selection via Fuzzy AHP and EDAS integrated model. *Technol. Econ. Dev. Econ.* **2018**, *24*, 615–634. [CrossRef]
22. Karaşan, A.; Kahraman, C. A novel interval-valued neutrosophic EDAS method: Prioritization of the United Nations national sustainable development goals. *Soft Comput.* **2018**, *22*, 4891–4906. [CrossRef]
23. Zavadskas, E.K.; Stević, Ž.; Turskis, Z.; Tomašević, M. A Novel Extended EDAS in Minkowski Space (EDAS-M) Method for Evaluating Autonomous Vehicles. *Stud. Inform. Control.* **2019**, *28*, 255–264. [CrossRef]
24. Jauković-Jocić, K.; Karabašević, D.; Popović, G. An approach for e-learning courses evaluation based on the EDAS method. *Ekonomika* **2020**, *66*, 47–59. [CrossRef]
25. Asante, D.; He, Z.; Adjei, N.O.; Asante, B. Exploring the barriers to renewable energy adoption utilising MULTIMOORA-EDAS method. *Energy Policy* **2020**, *142*, 111479. [CrossRef]
26. Hou, W.-H.; Wang, X.-K.; Zhang, H.-Y.; Wang, J.-Q.; Li, L. Safety risk assessment of metro construction under epistemic uncertainty: An integrated framework using credal networks and the EDAS method. *Appl. Soft Comput.* **2021**, *108*, 107436. [CrossRef]
27. Rashid, T.; Ali, A.; Chu, Y.-M. Hybrid BW-EDAS MCDM methodology for optimal industrial robot selection. *PLoS ONE* **2021**, *16*, e0246738. [CrossRef]
28. Stanujkic, D.; Zavadskas, E.K.; Ghorabaee, M.K.; Turskis, Z. An Extension of the EDAS Method Based on the Use of Interval Grey Numbers. *Stud. Inform. Control.* **2017**, *26*, 5–12. [CrossRef]
29. Kahraman, C.; Keshavarz-Ghorabaee, M.; Zavadskas, E.K.; Onar, S.C.; Yazdani, M.; Oztaysi, B. Intuitionistic fuzzy EDAS method: An application to solid waste disposal site selection. *J. Environ. Eng. Landsc. Manag.* **2017**, *25*, 1–12. [CrossRef]
30. Peng, X.; Dai, J.; Yuan, H. Interval-valued Fuzzy Soft Decision Making Methods Based on MABAC, Similarity Measure and EDAS. *Fundam. Informaticae* **2017**, *152*, 373–396. [CrossRef]
31. Li, Z.; Wei, G.; Wang, R.; Wu, J.; Wei, C.; Wei, Y. EDAS method for multiple attribute group decision making under q-rung orthopair fuzzy environment. *Technol. Econ. Dev. Econ.* **2020**, *26*, 86–102. [CrossRef]
32. Fan, J.-P.; Cheng, R.; Wu, M.-Q. Extended EDAS Methods for Multi-Criteria Group Decision-Making Based on IV-CFSWAA and IV-CFSWGA Operators with Interval-Valued Complex Fuzzy Soft Information. *IEEE Access* **2019**, *7*, 105546–105561. [CrossRef]
33. Özçelik, G.; Nalkıran, M. An Extension of EDAS Method Equipped with Trapezoidal Bipolar Fuzzy Information: An Application from Healthcare System. *Int. J. Fuzzy Syst.* **2021**. [CrossRef]
34. Tan, R.-P.; Zhang, W.-D. Decision-making method based on new entropy and refined single-valued neutrosophic sets and its application in typhoon disaster assessment. *Appl. Intell.* **2021**, *51*, 283–307. [CrossRef]
35. Abdel-Basset, M.; Gamal, A.; Chakrabortty, R.K.; Ryan, M. Development of a hybrid multi-criteria decision-making approach for sustainability evaluation of bioenergy production technologies: A case study. *J. Clean. Prod.* **2021**, *290*, 125805. [CrossRef]
36. Xu, D.; Cui, X.; Xian, H. An Extended EDAS Method with a Single-Valued Complex Neutrosophic Set and Its Application in Green Supplier Selection. *Mathematics* **2020**, *8*, 282. [CrossRef]
37. Fan, J.; Jia, X.; Wu, M. A new multi-criteria group decision model based on Single-valued triangular Neutrosophic sets and EDAS method. *J. Intell. Fuzzy Syst.* **2020**, *38*, 2089–2102. [CrossRef]
38. Supciller, A.A.; Toprak, F. Selection of wind turbines with multi-criteria decision making techniques involving neutrosophic numbers: A case from Turkey. *Energy* **2020**, *207*, 118237. [CrossRef]
39. Han, L.; Wei, C. An Extended EDAS Method for Multicriteria Decision-Making Based on Multivalued Neutrosophic Sets. *Complexity* **2020**, *2020*, 1–9. [CrossRef]
40. Li, Y.-Y.; Wang, J.-Q.; Wang, T.-L. A Linguistic Neutrosophic Multi-criteria Group Decision-Making Approach with EDAS Method. *Arab. J. Sci. Eng.* **2019**, *44*, 2737–2749. [CrossRef]
41. Wang, P.; Wang, J.; Wei, G. EDAS method for multiple criteria group decision making under 2-tuple linguistic neutrosophic environment. *J. Intell. Fuzzy Syst.* **2019**, *37*, 1597–1608. [CrossRef]
42. Karaşan, A.; Kahraman, C. Interval-Valued Neutrosophic Extension of EDAS Method. In *Advances in Fuzzy Logic and Technology*; Springer: Cham, Switzerland, 2017; pp. 343–357.
43. Peng, X.; Dai, J. Algorithms for interval neutrosophic multiple attribute decision-making based on MABAC, similarity measure, and EDAS. *Int. J. Uncertain. Quantif.* **2017**, *7*, 395–421. [CrossRef]

44. Sahin, R. Multi-criteria neutrosophic decision making method based on score and accuracy functions under neutrosophic environment. *arXiv* **2014**, arXiv:1412.5202.
45. Stanujkic, D.; Karabasevic, D.; Smarandache, F.; Popovic, G. A novel approach for assessing the reliability of data contained in a single valued neutrosophic number and its application in multiple criteria decision making. *Int. J. Neutrosophic. Sci.* **2020**, *11*, 22. [CrossRef]
46. Biswas, P.; Pramanik, S.; Giri, B.C. TOPSIS method for multi-attribute group decision-making under single-valued neutrosophic environment. *Neural Comput. Appl.* **2016**, *27*, 727–737. [CrossRef]
47. Stanujkic, D.; Zavadskas, E.K.; Smarandache, F.; Brauers, W.K.; Karabasevic, D. A neutrosophic extension of the MULTI-MOORA method. *Informatica* **2017**, *28*, 181–192. [CrossRef]
48. Stanujkic, D.; Smarandache, F.; Zavadskas, E.K.; Karabasevic, D. An Approach to Measuring the Website Quality Based on Neutrosophic Sets. In *New Trends in Neutrosophic Theory and Applications*; EU: Brussels, Belgium, 2018; Volume II, pp. 40–50.

axioms

MDPI

Article

Selection of Logistics Service Provider for the E-Commerce Companies in Pakistan Based on Integrated GRA-TOPSIS Approach

Muhammad Hamza Naseem *, **Jiaqi Yang** and **Ziquan Xiang**

School of Transportation and Logistics Engineering, Wuhan University of Technology, Wuhan 430063, China; styjq@whut.edu.cn (J.Y.); xiangziquan@whut.edu.cn (Z.X.)
* Correspondence: Hamzanaseem1a@outlook.com; Tel.: +86-15623623820

Abstract: Recently, the demand for third-party logistics providers has become extremely relevant and the key subject for businesses to enhance their service quality and minimize logistics costs. The key success factor for an e-commerce business is product delivery, and the third-party logistics service provider is responsible for that. Each 3PLP has its own business characteristics, meaning it is important to select the most suitable logistics provider for the e-commerce business. This study uses a combination of grey relational analysis (GRA) and the Technique for Order Preference by Similarity to Ideal Solution (TOPSIS) method, assisting decision makers in choosing the best logistics service provider for their e-business. A case study of an e-commerce company based in Faisalabad, Pakistan, was selected to demonstrate the steps of the proposed methods. In this process, seven criteria of logistics suppliers were considered, and then the best alternatives among four logistics provider companies were selected using the proposed method.

Keywords: logistics provider; outsource; decision making; e-commerce; TOPSIS; GRA

MSC: 90B06; 90B50; 90C29; 90C08

check for updates

Citation: Naseem, M.H.; Yang, J.; Xiang, Z. Selection of Logistics Service Provider for the E-Commerce Companies in Pakistan Based on Integrated GRA-TOPSIS Approach. *Axioms* **2021**, *10*, 208. https://doi.org/10.3390/axioms10030208

Academic Editor: Goran Ćirović

Received: 5 August 2021
Accepted: 25 August 2021
Published: 30 August 2021

1. Introduction

In today's world, traditional businesses are moving towards online businesses. COVID-19 introduced a major change in the buying behavior of consumers. Consumers prefer to buy products online in the comfort of their own home, rather than physically going to make a purchase. E-commerce means buying or selling products and services through the internet (e.g., websites, online stores, social media). It opens a new way of conducting business, particularly for small and medium enterprises (SMEs), because it does not require a physical store or office, and most of the business activities are performed online [1]. Logistics are considered to be the backbone of any business. Logistics in e-commerce involve picking up the order, storing it in the warehouse, sorting, and delivering the order to a specific customer at a certain time and place. In online businesses, all logistics activities are performed by third-party logistics providers (3PLPs). The goal of online businesses is to satisfy their customers. This cannot only be achieved by offering good-quality products; customers must also be provided with a high-quality service, which involves delivering goods on time and to the correct location. There are different third-party logistics providers that are available in the market, each with their own business objectives and services. The evaluation and selection of logistics providers is a complex problem because it includes different alternatives and selection criteria [2–4].

For developing countries such as Pakistan, with a population of 220 million and 183 million active internet users, the penetration of e-commerce business is very fast. Pakistan's Ministry of Commerce revealed that the growth rate of e-commerce business is up to 35%, with the value of Rs being 96 billion in the first four months of 2021. The majority (98%) of e-commerce businesses in Pakistan are small and medium enterprises (SME), meaning they are considered to be very important for Pakistan's economy. In total,

22 third-party logistics companies are working with e-commerce businesses in Pakistan. This makes the selection of the appropriate logistics providers a key issue for e-commerce business because it allows businesses to gain a competitive advantage and achieve operational efficiency and customer satisfaction. Most of the SMEs lack in resources, meaning the evaluation and selection of a logistics service provider (LSP) are key factors, and the area addressed in this study [5]. The aim of this study was to prioritize and select the best third-party logistics provider that meets the criteria and requirements set by e-commerce companies operating in Pakistan. In previous studies, we identified different criteria for the evaluation and selection of 3PLPs, such as low delivery costs, flexibility, customization, operational efficiency, lead time, service quality, reverse logistics, warehousing, order pickup, order delivery, firm reputation, reliability, green technology, and customer satisfaction [6,7]. Due to the fact that the selection and evaluation process consists of decision makers, alternatives, and criteria, it is considered as a multi-criteria decision-making problem (MCDM) that needs to be solved. Different methods have been used before for the selection of 3PL providers, such as the fuzzy TOPSIS, AHP, SWARA, and MOORA methods [1,2,4,8–11].

In previous years, studies have been carried out on the selection of 3PLPs in different industries and countries. For example, Adal et al. [2] checked the application of the proposed approach on a textile company in Turkey. Aggrawal [8] checked the application of the proposed method on a manufacturing company in India. Raut et al. [10] checked the practical application of their approach on a mining firm. Peng [4] used an example of a food company in regard to choosing the right logistics service provider. Ravi et al. [12] checked the application of the proposed approach on a computer company. Bai et al. [13] proposed the use of a model for selecting a 3PLP for an e-commerce company in China. However, to the best of our knowledge, no previous study has focused on the selection of 3PLPs for e-commerce businesses specifically in Pakistan. To fulfill this research gap, this study proposes the use of the integrated TOPSIS and GRA methods for the evaluation and selection of third-party logistics providers for e-commerce businesses in Pakistan. Due to the decision-making process involved, and the subjectivity of qualitative criteria, group MCDM results in uncertainty and vagueness. Grey relational analysis is a part of grey system theory. The GRA method has been successfully used in cases where there is uncertainty or only partial information is available. The TOPSIS method obtains a compromised solution, with the shortest distance from the positive ideal solution and the furthest distance from the negative ideal solution [14]. Moreover, the case of an e-commerce company named Denim Leftover, based in Pakistan, was considered, in order to check the application of the proposed approach. The novelty of this study can be found in its selection criteria, as these criteria are defined by the experience of experts (decision makers) in this field, as well as past studies, particularly regarding Pakistan's e-commerce business perspective. Furthermore, the main contributions of this article are as follows:

(1) This study helps e-commerce businesses, as well as new e-businesses, in Pakistan to choose and select the best third-party logistics service provider company; the one that is compatible with the business's objectives will lead the company to achieving a competitive advantage and suitable customer satisfaction, and minimizing their logistics costs.
(2) This study highlights the 3PLPs that are lacking in regard to each criterion, allowing 3PLPs to improve their business functions, and to attract more e-businesses as their customers.

The structure of this paper is as follows: Section 2 provides a literature review on the selection and evaluation of 3PLPs, as well as the method selection. Section 3 defines the methodology and the framework of the TOPSIS and GRA methods. The results analysis of the case study in Pakistan is presented in Section 4. Finally, Section 5 includes the discussion and conclusion of this study.

2. Literature Review

2.1. Development Status of Third-Party Logistics Suppliers in Pakistan

The third-party logistics provider sector has become a thriving industry over the last decade. Outsourcing logistics activities enables companies to save time and pay more attention to other core business activities. Furthermore, third-party logistics service providers have expertise in their field, enabling companies to minimize their logistics costs, resolve bottleneck problems, promise the delivery of goods, and provide a high-quality service to customers. With the 23rd largest road network in the world and one of the fastest-growing economies in Asia, Pakistan is the key player in global third-party logistics. Modern and advanced transport and logistics infrastructure are the key success factors of a country. During the last two decades, Pakistan has invested a huge amount of money in the development of the country's logistics infrastructure and has been involved in mega development projects under the China–Pakistan Economic Corridor (CPEC) [15]. According to the report issued by the Ministry of Commerce, Pakistan is a country that has more than 98% of businesses that are small and medium enterprises (SMEs). Undoubtedly, they have contracted with 3PLPs. E-commerce development has a direct impact on the economic development of any country. As e-businesses are an interest in Pakistan, these numbers are gradually increasing, and it is estimated that by 2040, 95% of retail sales and purchases will be made online [16]. In e-commerce, almost all companies use the services of 3PLPs which are responsible for collecting, warehousing, sorting, and shipping the parcels to customers. One of the key stakeholders of an e-commerce company is its customers, and customer satisfaction is the top priority of any company as it can only be attained by achieving their expectations such as high-quality products and on-time deliveries. It is important to note that every third-party logistics service provider company has its business model and characteristics, and the choice of the best suitable 3PLP is very important for an e-commerce company. There are different evaluation criteria set by e-commerce companies, and different methods have been used by researchers to evaluate and select the best alternative logistics supplier. The methods and criteria are discussed under the next heading.

2.2. Method Selection

Various noteworthy studies have applied different multi-criteria decision-making (MCDM) techniques according to various decision selection criteria for the evaluation and selection of the appropriate 3PLP. For example, Raut et al. [10] proposed an integrated data envelopment analysis (DEA) and AHP-based decision framework to evaluate and select a 3PLP. They concluded that the DEA coefficient score is very important which should be taken seriously by the management while making decisions on an efficient and effective 3PLP. Ravi et al. [12] used a combination of AHP and TOPSIS methods to solve the problem of selecting a 3PRLP in the computer industry. They considered 10 attributes in their study. Ilgin and Ali [17] proposed an integrated MCDM methodology to solve a problem related to the return of used products which is considered reverse logistics. They designed a 3PRLP network for efficient dealing of used products. In the study of Bali et al. [18], they introduced an integrated DEA-TOPSIS method to evaluate and select a 3PLP for an electrical radiator company. This method can be used for the evaluation of alternatives in different periods. Adal et al. [2] developed a systematic and integrated decision analysis approach for 3PLP evaluation and selection. They used an integrated DEMATEL, ANP, and DEA approach for their study. Datta et al. [19] proposed the six indexes for 3PL providers, which were finance performance, service level, client relationship, management, infrastructure, and enterprise culture, using the fuzzy TOPSIS method. Perçin et al. [20] introduced integrated fuzzy multiple-objective approaches and proposed a model which can be useful for 3PLP selection decisions faced by the Turkish autoparts industry. Raut et al. [21] presented a sustainable relationship framework for 3PLP selection from an environmental sustainability perspective based on data envelopment analysis (DEA) and the analytical network process (ANP). Choudhury et al. [22] suggested the following evaluation indexes that should be considered when selecting a sustainable 3PL provider: response time, transportation cost, operating cost, vehicle rejection, vehicle capacity, corporate social responsibility, and health and safety expenses, based on the DEA methodology. Aggarwal [8] highlighted the 14 major selection criteria for 3PL providers based on the literature and used the DEA-AHP technique to select the most appropriate 3PL provider. Wang et al. [11] adopted the fuzzy analytical hierarchy process (fuzzy AHP) and fuzzy TOPSIS methods to select a 3PRLP for an online business in Vietnam. They found lead time, customer voice, cost, delivery, and service and quality to be the most important factors when selecting a 3PRLP. Xu et al. [23] argued that five factors should be considered by e-commerce companies when selecting a third-party logistics service provider: logistics service quality, logistics service cost, logistics enterprise capability, level of information, and enterprise development prospects, based on the AHP method. Bai et al. [13] proposed an AHP model for the selection and evaluation of third-party logistics providers for e-commerce businesses by considering cost, stability, service level, and sustainability as an evaluation index. Nuengphasuk and Samanchuen [1] found that location, cost, and delivery are the dominant evaluation indexes in the selection process of 3PL providers based on the AHP and TOPSIS methods. Peng et al. [4] established an AHP judgment matrix for third-party logistics provider evaluation with cost, operating efficiency, service quality, and technology level.

In almost every scenario, a reliable decision requires the analysis of different criteria and alternatives, and in more complex cases, it almost becomes difficult to make the optimal decision. To solve these issues, different multi-criteria decision-making (MCDM) methods were proposed in previous studies [14,24]. However, this study uses the combination of TOPSIS and GRA methods for the selection and evaluation of the best alternative logistics provider. The TOPSIS (Technique for Order Preference by Similarity to Ideal Solution) method is a widely used method to solve multi-criteria decision-making problems as it can avoid some flaws of existing multi-attribute methods [25]. It was first proposed in 1981 by Hwang and Yoon [26]. The TOPSIS method is measured by the distance between schemes, where the shortest distance of the object from the ideal solution and the furthest distance from the non-ideal solution are considered to represent the best scheme [27]. When the closeness of the positive and negative ideal schemes at any point in the TOPSIS method is equal, the pros and cons of the schemes cannot be distinguished. TOPSIS is widely used to solve multi-criteria decision-making problems [3,24,28–30]. The grey relational analysis (GRA) method was developed by Deng in 1982, which focuses on the decision-making process, with partial information known and other information yet to be discovered [31]. In this method, the correlation between the reference sequence and comparability sequences is obtained, and thereafter, the ranking is established according to this correlation [9]. Moreover, the GRA method analyzes the changing trend between alternatives and can serialize and present the interrelationships of physical prototypes. However, this method can only analyze the relevance of the same factors and calculate the degree of relevance of the factors in each plan to the same ideal plan factor. Only using grey relational analysis (GRA) as a decision-making problem tool has insufficient comprehensiveness. Therefore, this article integrates the TOPSIS method and GRA method to solve the problem of the selection of a third-party logistics provider.

2.3. Selection of Logistics Service Provider Criteria

The criteria for selecting the third-party logistics service provider were obtained from previous studies; many criteria were provided and studied in previous studies according to the nature of the business. In this study, the seven most important criteria are defined as area of delivery (C1), delivery cost (C2), lead time (C3), payment settlement time (C4), service quality (C5), flexibility (C6), and IT capabilities (C7). These criteria can be used in the evaluation and selection process of third-party logistics service providers for e-commerce businesses. The crucial factors identified through the extensive literature review and experts are presented in Table 1. The definition of each criterion is explained as follows.

Table 1. List of criteria used in third-party logistics provider selection.

Sr. No.	Criteria	Description	References
1	Area of Delivery (C1)	This is an important factor to consider in the 3PLP selection process. It refers to the delivery coverage area in which logistics companies can deliver.	[1,2,6,7,18,22]
2	Delivery Cost (C2)	Cost delivery generally includes the cost for delivery of the product to the customer.	[1,2,6–8,11,13,18,19,23]
3	Lead Time (C3)	This includes the time that is required for the delivery of customer orders. It is also called the transit time.	[2,6,8,10,11,13,18,21–23]
4	Payment Settlement Time (C4)	This is considered an important evaluation criterion for selecting a 3PLP because the Pakistan payment system uses cash on delivery (COD) which means the customer pays after receiving the order. Moreover, payment is first transferred to the 3PLP company's account, and after that, it will be given to an e-commerce company. Therefore, this is the time taken by 3PLPs to give the order payment to the e-commerce company.	[6,13,15,22]
5	Service Quality (C5)	Service quality is related to customer satisfaction. It is the responsibility of the company to deal with customers during the delivery process and provide after-sales services.	[1,4,6,11,18,21,22]
6	Flexibility (C6)	It is the responsibility of an organization to adapt to meet the customers' demands and changing situations of the future. This also includes the ability to respond to the uncertainty of customers.	[1,6–8,10,11,18,19,23]
7	IT Capabilities (C7)	This refers to an information system and tracking system for customers to keep track of their packages and check the delivery status via a mobile application or website.	[1,2,7,8,18,29]

3. Model Building

3.1. Index Assignment

The seven indicators determined in Section 2 are all qualitative indicators, and the expert survey method was used to determine the specific value of each evaluation index. Five experts were used for subjective assignment, and the relative weight of these five experts was determined according to their relative importance:

$$\omega = (\omega_1, \omega_2, \ldots, \omega_5), \text{ and } \sum_{i=1}^{5} \omega_i = 1 \tag{1}$$

Assuming that the five-person expert group's survey concludes on each evaluation index, and each is divided into 7 levels, the corresponding relationship between the 7-level linguistic evaluation value and the degree of membership is established. The specific corresponding relationship is shown in Table 2.

Table 2. Correspondence between linguistic variable values and evaluation values.

Linguistic Variables	Judgment Value
Best (F1)/Highest (W1)	0.95
Very good (F2)/Very high (W2)	0.85
Good (F3)/High (W3)	0.70
Medium (F4)/Medium (W4)	0.50
Poor (F5)/Low (W5)	0.30
Very poor (F6)/Very low (W6)	0.15
Very poor (F7)/Very low (W7)	0.05

If the expert investigation conclusions are x_i, the comprehensive evaluation index y of each evaluation index can be expressed as $y = \sum_{i=1}^{5} \omega_i x_i$.

3.2. Construction of Decision Matrix

After the preliminary screening of experts, there are still m logistics suppliers to choose from, and there are n evaluation indicators to build a decision matrix A.

Among them,

$$A = \begin{bmatrix} a_{11} & a_{12} & \cdots & a_{1n} \\ a_{21} & a_{22} & \cdots & a_{2n} \\ \cdots & \cdots & \cdots & \cdots \\ a_{m1} & a_{m2} & \cdots & a_{mn} \end{bmatrix} \quad (2)$$

In order to eliminate the impact of different evaluation index dimensions on the evaluation results, firstly, the index matrix is normalized.

For the benefit index, the normalization operator is

$$b_{ij} = \frac{a_{ij}}{\min\limits_{1 \le i \le m} a_{ij}}, \ i = 1, 2, \ldots, m; \ j = 1, 2, \ldots, n. \quad (3)$$

For the cost index, the normalization operator is

$$b_{ij} = 1 - \frac{\min\limits_{1 \le i \le m} a_{ij} - a_{ij}}{\max\limits_{1 \le i \le m} a_{ij}}, \ i = 1, 2, \ldots, m; \ j = 1, 2, \ldots, n. \quad (4)$$

After the data are normalized, the normalized decision matrix C can be obtained

$$C = \begin{bmatrix} c_{11} c_{12} \cdots c_{1n} \\ c_{21} c_{22} \cdots C_{2n} \\ \cdots\cdots\cdots \\ c_{m1} c_{m2} \cdots c_{mn} \end{bmatrix} \quad (5)$$

Among them, $c_{ij} = \frac{b_{ij}}{\sum_{i=1}^{m} b_{ij}}$.

3.3. Determination of Evaluation Index Weight

The methods to determine the weight of each index include the subjective method, objective method, and combined subjective and objective method. The subjective evaluation method includes the AHP method and expert evaluation method, which is limited by decision makers' preferences, cognitive level, and experience. The common methods of the objective assignment method include the information entropy method, deviation method, and normal distribution method, which can better retain the objectivity of decision making information, but it is easy to ignore the subjective bias of decision makers. Taking into account the advantages and disadvantages of subjective and objective assignment and improving the reliability of the weight, the combination of the subjective and objective methods is usually used for assignment.

The subjective weight can be evaluated by the decision maker, and therefore the weight of the j index is $\vec{\lambda}_j$.

The entropy weight method is used to determine the objective weight of the wordlist, the information entropy of the j index is

$$H_j = -\frac{1}{In\ m} \sum_{i=1}^{m} c_{ij} In\ c_{ij} \quad (6)$$

and the entropy weight is

$$\overleftarrow{\lambda}_j = \frac{1 - H_j}{\sum\limits_{j=1}^{n} (1 - H_j)} \tag{7}$$

The comprehensive weight is

$$\lambda_j = \frac{\overrightarrow{\lambda}_j \overleftarrow{\lambda}_j}{\sum\limits_{j=1}^{n} \overrightarrow{\lambda}_j \overleftarrow{\lambda}_j}, \ j = 1, 2, \ldots, n \tag{8}$$

The index matrix is weighted to obtain the weighted decision matrix D.

$$D = \begin{bmatrix} d_{11} & d_{12} & \ldots & d_{1n} \\ d_{21} & d_{22} & \ldots & d_{2n} \\ \ldots & \ldots & \ldots & \ldots \\ d_{m1} & d_{m2} & \ldots & d_{mn} \end{bmatrix} \tag{9}$$

Among them, $d_{ij} = \omega_j c_{ij}$, $i = 1, 2, \ldots, m$; $j = 1, 2, \ldots, n$.

3.4. TOPSIS Method

The TOPSIS method realizes comparative analysis through the distance between the alternative scheme and the ideal target. The best and worst hypothetical schemes are drawn up through each scheme, and then the ideal distances between each scheme and the best and worst schemes are compared for selection. The calculation distance is the key point of this method. If a scheme is the furthest away from the unsatisfactory scheme and closest to the optimal scheme, the optimal selection scheme can be deduced. TOPSIS is a commonly used evaluation method of multi-objective decision making. In terms of data processing, it can retain the most original information in each alternative for analysis. The calculation process of this method is simple, and the idea is to achieve a clear, good integrity, adaptability, and reliability. The calculation steps are as follows:

Step 1: Build a decision matrix $A = (a_{ij})_{m \times n}$;

Step 2: Calculate the weight value of the indicator λ;

Step 3: Construct a weighted decision matrix $D = (d_{ij})_{m \times n}$;

Step 4: Determine the ideal plan, and the positive and negative ideal plans; the algorithm formula of the positive and negative ideal plans is as follows:

$$d^+ = (d_1^+, d_2^+, \ldots, d_m^+,)$$
$$d^- = (d_1^-, d_2^-, \ldots, d_m^-,)$$

where $\begin{cases} d_j^+ = \max\limits_{1 \le i \le x} \ d_{ij} \\ d_j^- = \min\limits_{1 \le i \le x} \ d_{ij} \end{cases}$;

Step 5: Calculate the Euclidean distance between each plan and the positive and negative ideal plan:

$$D_i^+ = \sqrt{\sum_{i=1}^{n} \left(d_{ij} - d_j^+\right)^2}$$

$$D_i^- = \sqrt{\sum_{i=1}^{n} \left(d_{ij} - d_j^-\right)^2}$$

Step 6: Calculate the relative closeness:

$$C_j = \frac{D_i^+}{D_i^+ + D_i^-}$$

Step 7: Sort the schemes through the calculated proximity and select the optimal scheme.

3.5. GRA Method

By analyzing the numerical relationship between the indicators of alternative schemes, the grey correlation master calculates the correlation degree between all indicators of each scheme and the ideal scheme. By analyzing the situation of each scheme, the correlation degree of its change state with time is studied. If the change degree of the correlation index is higher, the change degree is higher; on the contrary, the degree of correlation is lower. Therefore, the correlation between schemes can be measured by the grey correlation degree and can be analyzed and compared by comparing the correlation degree between the ideal scheme and other schemes. The steps are as follows:

Step 1: Construct a decision matrix $A = (a_{ij})_{m\times n}$;

Step 2: Calculate the weight value of the indicator w;

Step 3: Construct a weighted normalized decision matrix. Firstly, according to Eqution (5), normalize the decision matrix to obtain $C = (c_{ij})_{x\times m}$, according to the formula $Y = w * c$, the weighted decision matrix $D = (d_{ij})_{x\times m}$ is obtained.

Step 4: Determine the ideal solution.

Through $D = (d_{ij})_{x\times m}$ identifying the ideal solution α^{+}, α^{-}.

Step 5: Calculate the programs with the program over α^{+}, α^{-}. The degree of association is

$$r_{ij} = \frac{\min\limits_{i}\min\limits_{j}|\alpha_{0j} - \alpha_{ij}| + \rho \max\limits_{i}\max\limits_{j}|\alpha_{0j} - \alpha_{ij}|}{|\alpha_{0j} - \alpha_{ij}| + \rho \max\limits_{i}\max\limits_{j}|\alpha_{0j} - \alpha_{ij}|}$$

where r_{ij} and j are the similarities of the points. Research shows that the resolution coefficient $\rho = 0.5$ is the best; therefore, this paper took $\rho = 0.5$.

Step 6: Calculate the overall relevance of each program:

$$R_i = \frac{1}{n}\sum_{j=1}^{n} r_{ij}$$

Step 7: Calculate the closeness:

$$\xi_i = \frac{R_i^{+}}{R_i^{+} + R_i^{-}}$$

Step 8: Calculate the closeness degree by the grey correlation, sort the schemes, and select the optimal scheme.

3.6. Integrated Method Based on GRA-TOPSIS

The TOPSIS method is measured by the distance between the schemes, but when the closeness of the positive and negative ideal schemes at any point in the TOPSIS method is equal, the pros and cons of the schemes cannot be distinguished. The grey correlation method analyzes the changing trend between alternatives and can serialize and present the interrelationships of physical prototypes. However, this method can only analyze the relevance of the same factors and calculate the degree of relevance of the factors in each plan to the same ideal plan factor. Only with the grey correlation as a decision-making problem tool is there a lack of comprehensiveness. Based on the advantages and disadvantages of the two methods in decision analysis, this article combines the TOPSIS method with the GRA method to solve the problem of the comprehensiveness of the single method in the evaluation process and proposes a third-party logistics supplier selection model based on GRA-TOPSIS. The model solving steps are as follows:

Step 1: Build a decision matrix;

Step 2: Determine the weight of the evaluation index and construct a weighted decision matrix;

Step 3: Determine the positive ideal solution and the negative ideal solution:

$$d^+ = \left(d_1^+, d_2^+, \ldots, d_{m'}^+\right) \tag{10}$$

$$d^- = \left(d_1^-, d_2^-, \ldots, d_{m'}^-\right) \tag{11}$$

where $\begin{cases} d_j^+ = \max\limits_{1 \le i \le x} \; d_{ij} \\ d_j^- = \min\limits_{1 \le i \le x} \; d_{ij} \end{cases}$;

Step 4: Calculate the Euclidean distance:

$$D_i^+ = \sqrt{\sum_{i=1}^{n} \left(d_{ij} - d_j^+\right)^2} \tag{12}$$

$$D_i^- = \sqrt{\sum_{i=1}^{n} \left(d_{ij} - d_j^-\right)^2} \tag{13}$$

Step 5: Calculate the grey correlation coefficient of each plan and the ideal plan $R = \left(r_{ij}\right)_{x \times m'}$ where $\rho = 0.5$:

$$g_{ij}^+ = \frac{\min\limits_i \min\limits_j \left|d_j^+ - d_{ij}\right| + \rho \max\limits_i \max\limits_j \left|d_j^+ - d_{ij}\right|}{\left|d_j^+ - d_{ij}\right| + \rho \max\limits_i \max\limits_j \left|d_j^+ - d_{ij}\right|} \tag{14}$$

$$g_{ij}^- = \frac{\min\limits_i \min\limits_j \left|d_j^- - d_{ij}\right| + \rho \max\limits_i \max\limits_j \left|d_j^- - d_{ij}\right|}{\left|d_j^- - d_{ij}\right| + \rho \max\limits_i \max\limits_j \left|d_j^- - d_{ij}\right|} \tag{15}$$

Step 6: Calculate the overall grey correlation degree:

$$g_i^+ = \frac{1}{n} \sum_{j=1}^{n} r_{ij}^+ \tag{16}$$

$$g_i^- = \frac{1}{n} \sum_{j=1}^{n} r_{ij}^- \tag{17}$$

Step 7: Normalize the Euclidean distance and the grey correlation degree:

$$D_i^+ = \frac{d_i^+}{\max d_i^+} \quad D_i^- = \frac{d_i^-}{\max d_i^-} \tag{18}$$

$$G_i^+ = \frac{g_i^+}{\max r_i^+} \quad G_i^- = \frac{g_i^-}{\max r_i^-} \tag{19}$$

Step 8: Calculate the closeness:

$$C_i^+ = \frac{D_i^-}{D_i^+ + D_i^-} \tag{20}$$

$$Q_i^+ = \frac{G_i^+}{G_i^+ + G_i^-} \tag{21}$$

$$T_i^+ = \eta C_i^+ + (1-\eta) Q_i^+ \tag{22}$$

Decision makers can set the value of η according to their preferences.

Moreover, Figure 1 shows the flow chart of the proposed approach used for solving the multi-criteria decision-making problem.

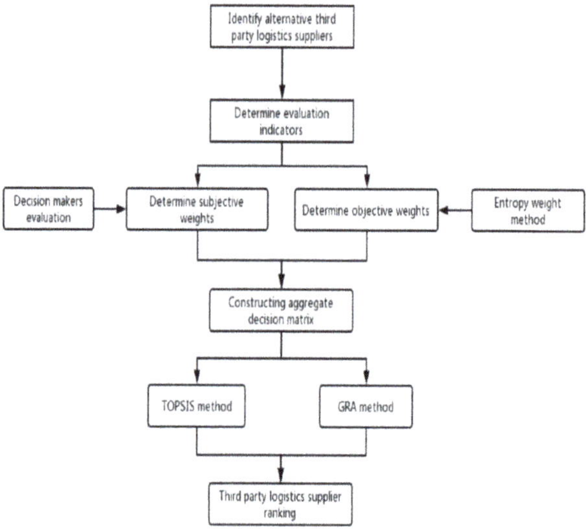

Figure 1. Flow chart of proposed methodology.

4. Case Study

In this section, we present and explain an example by using the methodology explained above. The e-commerce company Denim Leftover, based in Faisalabad, Pakistan, was selected. This is an SME having not more than 50 employees. For SMEs, it is important to select the best 3PLP supplier for their business in order to achieve competitiveness, efficiency, and customer satisfaction. For e-commerce companies, all the logistics activities are performed by third-party logistics providers. This is a complex problem that needs to be solved. This example was chosen to perform the selection of a third-party logistics provider for an e-commerce company (Denim Leftover).

Five experts were selected to determine the evaluation criteria based on their expertise. The evaluation criteria include the area of delivery, delivery costs, service quality, payment schedule, lead time, flexibility, and IT capabilities. According to Section 2.3, the set of evaluation criteria is defined, where C1 represents the area of delivery, C2 represents the delivery cost, C3 represents the lead time, C4 represents the payment settlement time, C5 represents service quality, C6 represents flexibility, and C7 represents IT capabilities. Where C1, C4, C5, C6, and C7 are benefit indicators, the greater the index value, the better; C2 and C3 are cost indicators. The smaller the indicator value, the better. After pre-assessment, a list of potential logistics service providers was developed. A total of four third-party logistics provider alternatives were selected which are Pakistan Post, TCS, M&P, and Leopards. The hierarchical structure for third-party logistics provider selection can be seen in Figure 2.

Step 1: Build a decision matrix and a normalized decision matrix.

The relative weight of the five experts is $\omega = (\omega_1, \omega_2, \ldots, \omega_5)$. The expert survey method was used for assignment, and the relative weight of the five experts is

$$\omega = (0.21,\ 0.16,\ 0.24,\ 0.28,\ 0.11)$$

Five experts obtained the evaluation index assignment table of four candidate logistics suppliers according to Table 2. The results are shown in Table 3. According to Equation (1) and Table 3, the decision matrix is obtained, and the results are shown in Table 4. According to Equations (3) and (4) and Table 3, we can present Table 5.

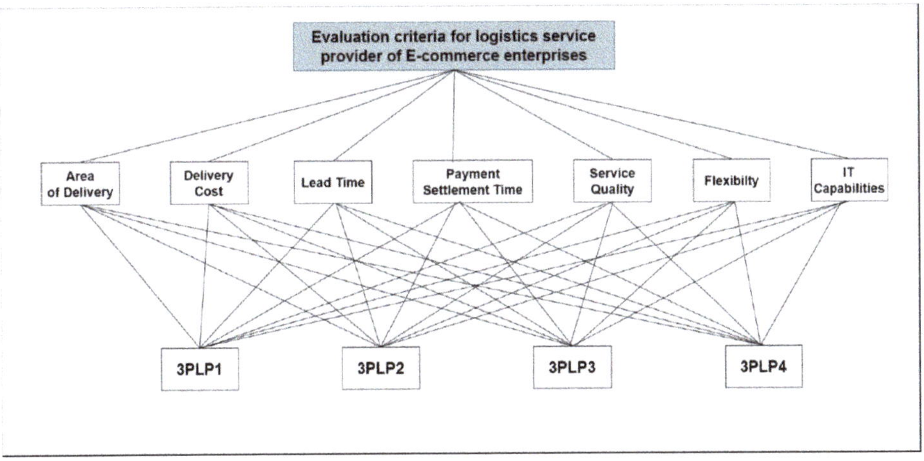

Figure 2. Hierarchical structure for 3PLP selection (source: authors' compilation).

Table 3. Summary table of decision makers' evaluation grades.

	A1					**A2**					**A3**					**A4**				
	E1	**E2**	**E3**	**E4**	**E5**	**E1**	**E2**	**E3**	**E4**	**E5**	**E1**	**E2**	**E3**	**E4**	**E5**	**E1**	**E2**	**E3**	**E4**	**E5**
C1	F1	F2	F1	F2	F1	F2	F3	F3	F1	F1	F2	F3	F3	F3	F4	F1	F1	W2	F2	F4
C2	W5	W5	W4	W6	W5	W4	W5	W5	W5	W5	W3	F5	W5	W4	W4	W6	W4	W5	W5	W4
C3	W4	W5	W5	W6	W6	W6	W5	W5	W5	W6	W5	W5	W5	W4	W5	W4	W5	W5	W5	W4
C4	F2	F2	F2	F2	F1	F1	F2	F2	F1	F3	F2	F2	F2	F1	F3	F5	F3	F3	F4	F3
C5	F3	F6	F4	F4	F3	F1	F2	F3	F3	F2	F2	F2	F3	F1	F2	F4	F4	F4	F3	F5
C6	F4	F4	F3	F3	F4	F2	F3	F2	F3	F2	F3	F4	F4	F3	F3	F5	F3	F3	F3	F4
C7	F2	F2	F2	F2	F2	F1	F1	F1	F1	F1	F1	F1	F2	F1	F1	F1	F1	F3	F2	F3

Table 4. Decision matrix for selecting third-party logistics providers.

	A1	**A2**	**A3**	**A4**
C1	0.9060	0.8290	0.7095	0.8485
C2	0.3063	0.3420	0.4620	0.3225
C3	0.2835	0.2520	0.3550	0.3640
C4	0.8610	0.8825	0.8615	0.5600
C5	0.5080	0.7930	0.8420	0.5340
C6	0.6040	0.7840	0.6200	0.5940
C7	0.8500	0.9500	0.9260	0.8345

Table 5. The normalized decision matrix for selecting a third-party logistics provider.

	A1	**A2**	**A3**	**A4**
C1	0.2751	0.2517	0.2155	0.2577
C2	0.2136	0.2387	0.3225	0.2251
C3	0.2258	0.2007	0.2836	0.2899
C4	0.2720	0.2788	0.2722	0.1769
C5	0.1898	0.2962	0.3145	0.1995
C6	0.2321	0.3013	0.2383	0.2283
C7	0.2387	0.2668	0.2601	0.2344

Step 2: Determine the weight of the evaluation index and construct a weighted normalized decision matrix.

Five decision makers returned the subjective weights for the seven indicators as $\overrightarrow{\omega} = (0.1093, 0.1639, 0.1366, 0.1913, 0.1311, 0.0984, 0.1694)$, and the objective weights calculated by the entropy weight method were $\overleftarrow{\omega} = (0.0492, 0.1781, 0.1483, 0.1967, 0.3210, 0.0874, 0.0193)$ according to Equations (6) and (7). Then, the combined weights $\omega = (0.0367, 0.1994, 0.1383, 0.2571, 0.2874, 0.0587, 0.0223)$ were calculated according to Equation (8). According to the weighted normalized decision matrix, the results are shown in Table 6.

Table 6. The weighted normalized decision matrix for selecting a third-party logistics provider.

	A1	A2	A3	A4
C1	0.0101	0.0092	0.0079	0.0095
C2	0.0426	0.0476	0.0643	0.0449
C3	0.0312	0.0278	0.0392	0.0401
C4	0.0699	0.0717	0.0700	0.0455
C5	0.0545	0.0851	0.0904	0.0573
C6	0.0136	0.0177	0.0140	0.0134
C7	0.0053	0.0060	0.0058	0.0052

Step 3: Determine the positive ideal point and the negative ideal point.

According to Equations (10) and (11), the positive ideal point and the negative ideal point are obtained:

$$d_1^+ = 0.0101,\ d_4^+ = 0.0717,\ d_5^+ = 0.0904, d_6^+ = 0.0177, d_7^+ = 0.0060,$$
$$d_2^- = 0.0426,\ d_3^- = 0.0278$$

Step 4: Calculate the Euclidean distance and the grey correlation degree.

The correlation coefficients were calculated according to Equations (12)–(19), and the results are shown in Table 7.

Table 7. Euclidean distance and grey correlation degree for choosing a third-party logistics provider plan.

	TOPSIS				Grey Relational Analysis Method			
	d^+	d^-	D^+	D^-	g^+	g^-	G^+	G^-
A1	0.0361	0.0035	0.8514	0.1423	0.5289	0.5647	0.6659	0.8489
A2	0.0053	0.0050	0.1250	0.2033	0.6587	0.6652	0.8293	1.0000
A3	0.0046	0.0246	0.1085	1.0000	0.7943	0.5216	1.0000	0.7841
A4	0.0424	0.0126	1.0000	0.5211	0.6621	0.6525	0.8336	0.9809

Step 5: Comprehensive closeness.

The preference factors η are 0, 0.2, 0.4, 0.5, 0.6, 0.8, and 1.0, respectively, and the ranking of the advantages and disadvantages of each alternative is obtained. The results are shown in Table 8.

It can be seen from the table above that when the value changes from 0 to 1, the result of the scheme optimization ranking is relatively stable, which shows that the reliability and stability of the model are maintained. Alternative A3 always ranks first, indicating that it is the best supplier. Alternative A2 holds the second position, which shows that it is the second best alternative. Alternative A4 is the third priority, and Alternative A1 always ranks last, which means that it is the least important; therefore, Alternative A1 is least likely to be chosen.

Table 8. Sorting results of selecting third-party logistics providers.

Preference Factor η	A1	A2	A3	A4
0	4	3	1	2
0.2	4	2	1	3
0.4	4	2	1	3
0.5	4	2	1	3
0.6	4	2	1	3
0.8	4	2	1	3
1.0	4	2	1	3

5. Discussion

In the digital era, where everything is connected through the internet, people are more likely to buy online, especially with the advantage of it being 24/7 and in the comfort of their own home, which allows customers to take as much time as they need rather than leaving unsatisfied and unwillingly wanting to shop in other stores. The e-commerce industry in Pakistan is growing swiftly. The key success factor of e-commerce business is product delivery, which is carried out by 3PLPs. The elevation in e-commerce opens the door for a new business type called third-party logistics providers. Third-party logistics providers have come up with solutions to problems of e-commerce companies related to warehousing, packing, and delivery of goods or services to their customers. As logistics are considered as the backbone of any business, in the case of e-business, choosing the right logistics company is the key. The selection of 3PLPs has become a critical issue that is the roadmap to the success of e-commerce business as this will lead e-commerce companies to achieving a competitive advantage and help to attain customer satisfaction. For a country such as Pakistan, where almost 98% of e-commerce businesses are small and medium enterprises, working with a suitable 3PLP provides them with benefits that ultimately help them to run their business smoothly. There are several key third-party logistics suppliers available in Pakistan's market, and each 3PLP has its business models and objectives. Therefore, there is a big issue for e-commerce companies to choose a compatible 3PLP that can meet their business objectives. Due to the decision makers, different attributes, and alternatives, the selection of 3PLPs is considered an MCDM problem. Moreover, the results of this study have various implications that are as follows:

(1) The proposed model can aid decision makers in selecting the best 3PLP from various assessable options. Moreover, this model enables decision makers to visualize the impact of various criteria on the alternative at the final solution.

(2) The findings of this paper can assist e-commerce businesses in gaining a better understanding of the third-party logistics supplier selection process and in finding the best 3PLP for their business according to their defined selection criteria.

(3) This model can help logistics managers to comprehend the relative relationship and the degree of significance among the criteria and guide them in finding their influence on the 3PLP selection process.

6. Conclusions

Third-party logistics providers are the main part of the logistics process of a company because they help to reduce costs, improve efficiency, and achieve customer satisfaction. Therefore, the evaluation and selection of 3PLPs are important. The main objective of this study was to select the most appropriate third-party logistics provider (3PLP), and throughout the study, MCDM methods were utilized. This paper proposed an evaluation method based on the TOPSIS and grey relational analysis (GRA) methods on the issue of the selection of third-party logistics providers, adopted a more realistic subjective and objective comprehensive weighting method, and introduced preference factors so that the algorithm can be based on the individual factors of the decision maker, which are adjusted to enhance the flexibility of the algorithm and improve the accuracy of decision making. The proposed approach can assist decision makers in systematically evaluating trade-offs among multiple factors and criteria, therefore helping them in settling on more informed decisions when evaluating and selecting a 3PLP. The results show that Alternative A3 (M&P) is the best suitable third-party logistics company because A3 willingly achieved the selection criteria set by the e-commerce company and decision makers.

There are some limitations related to this current study that can be tended to. In future studies, the number of criteria and alternatives may change according to the needs of the company for a 3PLP. Furthermore, other multi-criteria decision-making methods such as AHP, DEMATEL, and DEA can be used for the evaluation and selection process of 3PLPs. Moreover, in the construction of the algorithm model, considering the uncertainty of third-party logistics supplier selection, the combination of fuzzy set theory and multi-criteria decision-making methods is also a future research direction.

Author Contributions: Conceptualization, M.H.N.; Formal analysis, M.H.N.; Funding acquisition, J.Y.; Methodology, Z.X.; Software, Z.X.; Supervision, J.Y.; Writing—original draft, M.H.N.; Writing—review & editing, M.H.N. All authors equally contributed to this paper. All authors have read and agreed to the published version of the manuscript.

Funding: This research work was part of the project named: Cooperative operation organization and management of multiple transportation modes (Grant No: 103-46160101).

Data Availability Statement: Not applicable.

Conflicts of Interest: The authors declare no conflict of interest.

References

1. Nuengphasuk, M.; Samanchuen, T. Selection of logistics service provider for e-commerce using AHP and TOPSIS: A case study of SMEs in Thailand. In Proceedings of the 2019 4th Technology Innovation Management and Engineering Science International Conference (TIMES-iCON), Bangkok, Thailand, 11–13 December 2019; pp. 1–5.
2. Adalı, E.; Işık, A. Integration of DEMATEL, ANP and DEA methods for third party logistics providers' selection. *Manag. Sci. Lett.* **2016**, *6*, 325–340.
3. Muralidhar, P.; Ravindranath, K.; Srihari, V. The influence of GRA and TOPSIS for assortment of green supply chain management strategies in cement industry. *Int. J. Supply Chain Manag.* **2013**, *2*, 49–55.
4. Peng, J.J.E.P. Selection of logistics outsourcing service suppliers based on AHP. *Energy Procedia* **2012**, *17*, 595–601. [CrossRef]
5. Delfmann, W.; Albers, S.; Gehring, M. The impact of electronic commerce on logistics service providers. *Int. J. Phys. Distrib. Logist. Manag.* **2002**, *32*, 203–222. [CrossRef]
6. Memari, A.; Dargi, A.; Jokar, M.R.A.; Ahmad, R.; Rahim, A.R. Sustainable supplier selection: A multi-criteria intuitionistic fuzzy TOPSIS method. *J. Manuf. Syst.* **2019**, *50*, 9–24. [CrossRef]
7. Akman, G.; Baynal, K. Logistics service provider selection through an integrated fuzzy multicriteria decision making approach. *J. Ind. Eng.* **2014**, *2014*, 94918. [CrossRef]
8. Aggarwal, R. Third-party logistics service providers selection using AHP-DEAHP approach. *Int. J. Integr. Supply Manag.* **2019**, *12*, 259–284. [CrossRef]
9. Ertugrul, I.; Oztas, T.; Ozcil, A.; Oztas, G.Z. Grey relational analysis approach in academic performance comparison of university: A case study of Turkish universities. *Eur. Sci. J.* **2016**, *7881*, 128–139.
10. Raut, R.D.; Kharat, M.G.; Kamble, S.S.; Kamble, S.J.; Desai, R. Evaluation and selection of third-party logistics providers using an integrated multi-criteria decision making approach. *Int. J. Serv. Oper. Manag.* **2018**, *29*, 373–392. [CrossRef]
11. Wang, C.-N.; Dang, T.-T.; Nguyen, N.-A. Outsourcing reverse logistics for e-commerce retailers: A two-stage fuzzy optimization approach. *Axioms* **2021**, *10*, 34. [CrossRef]
12. Ravi, V. Selection of third-party reverse logistics providers for End-of-Life computers using TOPSIS-AHP based approach. *Axioms* **2012**, *11*, 24–37. [CrossRef]
13. Bai, J.-F.; Wei, X.-Y.; Yan, J.-C. Research on the selection of business-to-customer e-commerce logistics model based on analytic hierarchy process method. In *Proceedings of the 23rd International Conference on Industrial Engineering and Engineering Management March 8, 2016*; Atlantis Press: Paris, France, 2017; pp. 11–15.
14. Abid, S. Pakistan Logistics and Transport: Problems and Solutions. Available online: https://www.pakistangulfeconomist.com/2019/09/30/pakistan-logistics-and-transport-problems-and-solutions/ (accessed on 30 September 2019).
15. Anjum, S.; Chai, J. Drivers of Cash-on-Delivery Method of Payment in E-Commerce Shopping: Evidence From Pakistan. *Sage Open* **2020**, *10*, 2158244020917392. [CrossRef]
16. Ilgin, M.A. An integrated methodology for the used product selection problem faced by third-party reverse logistics providers. *Int. J. Sustain. Eng.* **2017**, *10*, 399–410. [CrossRef]

17. Bali, Ö.; Gümüş, S.; Kaya, I.; Computing, S. A Multi-Period Decision Making Procedure Based on Intuitionistic Fuzzy Sets for Selection Among Third-Party Logistics Providers. *J. Mult.-Valued Log. Soft Comput.* **2015**, *24*, 1–23.
18. Datta, S.; Samantra, C.; Mahapatra, S.S.; Mandal, G.; Majumdar, G. Appraisement and selection of third party logistics service providers in fuzzy environment. *Benchmarking Int. J.* **2013**, *20*, 537–548. [CrossRef]
19. Perçin, S.; Min, H. A hybrid quality function deployment and fuzzy decision-making methodology for the optimal selection of third-party logistics service providers. *Int. J. Logist. Res. Appl.* **2013**, *16*, 380–397. [CrossRef]
20. Raut, R.; Kharat, M.; Kamble, S.; Kumar, C. Sustainable evaluation and selection of potential third-party logistics (3PL) providers: An integrated MCDM approach. *Benchmarking Int. J.* **2018**, *25*, 76–79. [CrossRef]
21. Choudhury, N.; Raut, R.D.; Gardas, B.B.; Kharat, M.G.; Ichake, S. Evaluation and selection of third party logistics services providers using data envelopment analysis: A sustainable approach. *Int. J. Bus. Excell.* **2018**, *14*, 427–453. [CrossRef]
22. Xu, W.; Li, B. The third party logistics partner selection of B2C E-commerce enterprise. In Proceedings of the MATEC Web of Conferences, Zhengzhou, China, 8 March 2017; p. 02032.
23. Sałabun, W.; Urbaniak, K. A new coefficient of rankings similarity in decision-making problems. In *Proceedings of International Conference on Computational Science June 3*; Springer: Cham, Switzerland, 2020; pp. 632–645.
24. Ziquan, X.; Jiaqi, Y.; Naseem, M.H.; Zuquan, X.; Xueheng, L. Supplier Selection of Shipbuilding Enterprises Based on Intuitionistic Fuzzy Multicriteria Decision. *Math. Probl. Eng.* **2021**, *2021*, 1775053. [CrossRef]
25. Byun, H.; Lee, K. A decision support system for the selection of a rapid prototyping process using the modified TOPSIS method. *Int. J. Adv. Manuf. Technol.* **2005**, *26*, 1338–1347. [CrossRef]
26. Hwang, C.-L.; Yoon, K. Methods for multiple attribute decision making. In *Multiple Attribute Decision Making*; Springer: Berlin/Heidelberg, Germany, 1981; pp. 58–191.
27. Kizielewicz, B.; Shekhovtsov, A.; Sałabun, W. A New Approach to Eliminate Rank Reversal in the MCDA Problems. In Proceedings of the International Conference on Computational Science Jun 16; Springer: Cham, Switzerland, 2021; pp. 338–351.
28. Ayağ, Z.; Özdemir, R.G. Evaluating machine tool alternatives through modified TOPSIS and alpha-cut based fuzzy ANP. *Int. J. Prod. Econ.* **2012**, *140*, 630–636. [CrossRef]
29. Wang, Z.-X.; Wang, Y.-Y. Evaluation of the provincial competitiveness of the Chinese high-tech industry using an improved TOPSIS method. *Expert Syst. Appl.* **2014**, *41*, 2824–2831. [CrossRef]
30. Sałabun, W.; Wątróbski, J.; Shekhovtsov, A. Are mcda methods benchmarkable? a comparative study of topsis, vikor, copras, and promethee ii methods. *Symmetry* **2020**, *12*, 1549. [CrossRef]
31. Patil, A.; Walke Gaurish, A.; Mahesh, G. Grey relation analysis methodology and its application. *Res. Rev. Int. J. Multidiscip.* **2019**, *4*, 409–411.

axioms

Article

Spherical Linear Diophantine Fuzzy Soft Rough Sets with Multi-Criteria Decision Making

Masooma Raza Hashmi [1], **Syeda Tayyba Tehrim** [1], **Muhammad Riaz** [1], **Dragan Pamucar** [2,*] and **Goran Cirovic** [3]

1 Department of Mathematics, University of the Punjab, Lahore 54590, Pakistan; masoomaraza25@gmail.com (M.R.H.); tayyabatehrim126@gmail.com (S.T.T.); mriaz.math@pu.edu.pk (M.R.)
2 Department of Logistics, Military Academy, University of Defence in Belgarde, 11000 Belgarde, Serbia
3 Faculty of Technical Sciences, University of Novi Sad, Trg Dositeja Obradovica 6, 21000 Novi Sad, Serbia; goran.cirovic@uns.ac.rs
* Correspondence: dragan.pamucar@va.mod.gov.rs

Abstract: Modeling uncertainties with spherical linear Diophantine fuzzy sets (SLDFSs) is a robust approach towards engineering, information management, medicine, multi-criteria decision-making (MCDM) applications. The existing concepts of neutrosophic sets (NSs), picture fuzzy sets (PFSs), and spherical fuzzy sets (SFSs) are strong models for MCDM. Nevertheless, these models have certain limitations for three indexes, satisfaction (membership), dissatisfaction (non-membership), refusal/abstain (indeterminacy) grades. A SLDFS with the use of reference parameters becomes an advanced approach to deal with uncertainties in MCDM and to remove strict limitations of above grades. In this approach the decision makers (DMs) have the freedom for the selection of above three indexes in $[0,1]$. The addition of reference parameters with three index/grades is a more effective approach to analyze DMs opinion. We discuss the concept of spherical linear Diophantine fuzzy numbers (SLDFNs) and certain properties of SLDFSs and SLDFNs. These concepts are illustrated by examples and graphical representation. Some score functions for comparison of LDFNs are developed. We introduce the novel concepts of spherical linear Diophantine fuzzy soft rough set (SLDFSRS) and spherical linear Diophantine fuzzy soft approximation space. The proposed model of SLDFSRS is a robust hybrid model of SLDFS, soft set, and rough set. We develop new algorithms for MCDM of suitable clean energy technology. We use the concepts of score functions, reduct, and core for the optimal decision. A brief comparative analysis of the proposed approach with some existing techniques is established to indicate the validity, flexibility, and superiority of the suggested MCDM approach.

Keywords: spherical linear diophantine fuzzy set (SLDFS); spherical linear diophantine fuzzy soft rough set (SLDFSRS); score function; core; reduct; MCDM

Citation: Hashmi, M.R.; Tehrim, S.T.; Riaz, M.; Pamucar, D.; Cirovic, G. Spherical Linear Diophantine Fuzzy Soft Rough Sets with Multi-Criteria Decision Making. *Axioms* **2021**, *10*, 185. https://doi.org/10.3390/axioms10030185

Academic Editor: Faith-Michael E. Uzoka

Received: 17 June 2021
Accepted: 11 August 2021
Published: 13 August 2021

1. Introduction an Literature Review

Conventional Mathematics is not always helpful to tackle real world problems due to hesitations and ambiguities present in their nature. Zadeh [1] established the perception of fuzzy set by assigning the satisfaction grades to alternatives from $[0,1]$. Zadeh [2] established the idea of linguistic variable to relate real world situations and verbal information to Mathematical language and Mathematical modeling. Atanassov [3–6] presented an advanced perception of intuitionistic fuzzy sets (IFSs) by introducing dissatisfaction grades of alternatives with the existing satisfaction grades in fuzzy sets fulfilling the constraint that sum of these two grades are always less than unity. After that Yager initiated the novel perception of Pythagorean fuzzy sets (PyFS) [7,8] with q-rung orthopair fuzzy sets (q-ROFSs) [9] as generalizations of IFSs. Smarandache [10] originated the idea of neutrosophic set with the addition of indeterminacy grades in IFSs, satisfying the constraint that sum of all the three grades less than 3. This structure creates an independency between all the grades to deal real world problems more efficiently. In these applications the information cannot be inadequate between yes or no generally but it can be yes, no, abstain, and refusal. Cuong [11–13] introduced picture fuzzy set (PiFS) in 2013 for these circumstances. In this model, the alternatives can be represented by satisfaction, abstinence, dissatisfaction and refusal degrees. A PiFS to human nature and handle uncertainties of decision-making problems in a better way. Mahmood et al. [14] studied the notion of T-spherical fuzzy set (T-SFS) as an advancement of spherical fuzzy set (SFS). They established these concepts as generalizations of PFSs similar as the extension ideas of PGFSs and q-ROFSs, which were the generalizations of IFSs. Some new AOs on cubic hesitant fuzzy numbers (CHFNs) were introduced by Mahmood et al. [15]. Numerous extensions of fuzzy sets have been originated for solving MCDM problems, medical diagnosis and image processing [16,17], radar images and image segmentation analysis [18–23], fuzzy analysis [24–29], iris image analysis [30,31], image classification [32,33].

Molodtsov [34] invented the new idea of soft sets to deal with the uncertainties by using parameterizations. Maji et al. [35] proposed several results of soft set setting. Rough set was first initiated by Pawlak [36] in 1982. This model gives us a new method to handle vague ideas caused by indiscernibility with incomplete data set. Rough sets replace vagueness with the upper and lower approximations of the assembling under an equivalence relation After that Pawlak and Skowron [37] originated several extensions on rough sets. Various mathematicians considered diverse hybrid fusion of rough sets, fuzzy sets, and soft sets for applications in engineering, information management, medicine, multi-criteria decision-making (MCDM) applications. Ali [38] developed new results of q-ROFSs and their orbits classification. Some logical connectors listed as implications, t-norms and t-conorms was considered by Ali and Shabir [39] for development of fuzzy soft set and soft set as extension of crisp set theory.

Numerous results and applications on generalized IFSSs was established by Agarwal et al. [40]. Garg [41] established various hybrid AOs using Einstein operations in the context of PyFSs with their applications in DM. Chen and Tan [42] studies vague set theory and investigated MCDM methods on it. Tversky and Kahneman [43] established certain fusion in the prospect model for progressive illustration of vagueness. Jose and Kuriaskose [44] studied and investigated some properties of aggregation operators for MCDM. Wang et al. [45] operated on SV-neutrosophic sets and discussed it applications. Peng and Yang [46] introduced certain novel features of PFSs. Peng and Garg [47] developed new algorithms for IVFS-sets in emergency decision-making using new information measure and WDBA and CODAS techniques. Xu [48–50] proposed several AOs for IFSs and HFSs. Ye [51] invented neutrosophic cubic linguistic numbers with applications in MADM problems. In some recent years, various mathematicians established some operations and introduced different aggregations operators on PFSs. Jana et al. [52] established PiF-Dombi's AOs and its applications to MADM problems. Xu et al. [53] established a method to picture fuzzy MADM by using Muirhead mean operators. Wang et al. [54] developed diverse methods for picture fuzzy Muirhead mean operators to solve DM-complication. Wang and Li [55] introduced picture fuzzy hesitant set and presented its applications in MCDM glitches. Khan et al. [56,57] introduced logarithmic aggregation operators for PiFNs for MADM problems. They considered Einstein operations and established aggregation operators based on PiFSs with its applications.

Zhang et al. [58] proposed the idea of covering based IFRSs. They presented various applications related to these ideas in MADM. Zhang et al. [59] proposed the novel perception of IFSRSs with applications. Zhang et al. [60] established a consensus based MAGDM methodology for failure mode and effect analysis. They used linguistics to present effect analysis and failure mode. They introduced a comparative study for consensus efficiency. Zhang et al. [61] established certain Dombi Heronian AOs by using PFSs with applications to MADM problems. Zhang et al. [62–64] defined novel concepts of the priority weights, deriving priority weights, and multiplicative preference relations with MCGDM applications. Zhang et al. [65] created a programmed mechanism under MCGDM method to support consensus reaching. Feng et al. [66] suggested new concepts of generalized intuitionistic fuzzy soft sets. Guo [67] investigated IF-values, information behavior analysis, ranking of IFNs. Liu and Wang [68] introduced several new AOs with q-ROFNs, related properties, numerous results, and advanced approach to MADM.

In 2019, Riaz and Hashmi [69] established the idea of linear Diophantine fuzzy sets (LDFSs) with the accumulation of reference or control parameters. This structure enlarge the valuation space of existing models and categorize the problem with the help of control parameters. Riaz and Hashmi [70] introduced the idea of soft rough Pythagorean m-PFSs. Riaz et al. [71] introduced green supplier chain management approach with q-ROF prioritized aggregation operators. Vashist [72] developed new algorithm for detecting the core and reduct of the consistent dataset. Wang et al. [73] presented some PiF geometric AOs based MADM. Soft rough covering concept and related results introduced by Zhan and Alcantud [74]. Riaz et al. [75] introduced various interesting properties of topological structure on soft multi-sets and their applications in MCDM. Sahu et al. [76] developed a career selection picture fuzzy set and rough set theory method for students with hybridized distance measure measures. Ali et al. [77] introduced Einstein geometric aggregation operators using a novel complex interval-valued pythagorean fuzzy setting. Alosta et al. [78] suggested AHP-RAFSI approach for developing method for the location selection problem. Yorulmaz et al. [79] suggested an approach economic development by using extended TOPSIS technique. Pamucar and Ecer [80] proposed weights prioritizing fuzziness approach for evaluation criterion. Ramakrishnan and Chakraborty [81] presented a green supplier selection criteria with improved TOPSIS model. Kishore et al. [82] developed a framework for subcontractors selection MCDM model for project management. Zararsiz [83] introduced similarity measures of sequence of fuzzy numbers and fuzzy risk analysis. Zararsiz [84] developed entropy measures of QRS-complexes before and after training program of sport horses with ECG.

The objectives and advantages of this research work are expressed as follows.

1. A spherical linear Diophantine fuzzy set (SLDFS) can not deal with the multi-valued parameterizations, roughness of crisp data, and approximation spaces. A rough set with lower and upper approximation spaces is a strong mathematical approach to deal with vagueness in the data. To deal with real-life problems having uncertainties, vagueness, abstinence of the input, lack of information, we introduce novel concept of spherical linear Diophantine fuzzy soft rough set (SLDFSRS).
2. In fact, a SLDFSRS is a robust hybrid model of spherical linear Diophantine fuzzy set, soft set, and rough set. Due to the effectiveness of reference parameters, the proposed models of SLDFSs and SLDFSRSs are more productive and amenable rather than some existing approaches. When we change the physical judgment of reference parameters then the MCDM obstacles generate different categories. Due to the association of reference parameters, SLDFS meets the spaces of certain existing structures and expands the valuation space for satisfaction, abstinence, and dissatisfaction grades.
3. In some real-life circumstances, the total of satisfaction grade, abstinence grade, and dissatisfaction grade of an alternative granted by the decision-maker (DM) may be superior to 1 (e.g., $0.8 + 0.7 + 0.4 > 1$). So PiFSs fail to hold. Likewise, the sum of squares of these grades may also be superior to 1 (e.g., $0.8^2 + 0.7^2 + 0.4^2 > 1$). Then the spherical fuzzy sets (SFSs) fail in such circumstances. The generalized model of T-SFSs overcome these deficiencies by using the condition $0 \leq \ddot{T}^n + \ddot{\mathcal{Z}}^n + \ddot{\mathfrak{S}}^n \leq 1$. For very small values of "n", we cannot deal with these grades independently. In certain practical applications, when all the three degrees are equal to 1 (i.e., $\ddot{T} = \ddot{\mathcal{Z}} = \ddot{\mathfrak{S}} = 1$), we obtain $1^n + 1^n + 1^n > 1$ which opposes the constraint of T-SFS. MCDM techniques with T-SFS fail in these circumstances. It influences the optimum judgment and executes the MCDM restricted. Spherical linear Diophantine fuzzy set (SLDFS) can deal with these circumstances and provides a wide range of applications to the MCDM applications.
4. In decision analysis the membership grades are not enough to analyze objects in the universe. The addition of reference parameters provide freedom to the decision

makers in selecting these grades. SLDFS with associated reference parameter provides a robust approach for modeling uncertainties.

5. Firstly, we fill the research hollow using the intended model of SLDFSs. The alternatives having the characteristics like PF-value, SF-value, T-SF-value, and neutrosophic value can be efficiently supervised by using SLDFSs with the representatives of reference parameters. (For instance for $(0.60 + 0.90 + 0.70 > 1)$, we can propose control parameters such that $(0.60)(0.30) + (0.90)(0.20) + (0.70)(0.10) < 1$, where $\langle 0.30, 0.20, 0.10\rangle$ can be taken as reference parameters for satisfaction, abstinence and dissatisfaction grades).
6. The next purpose is to examine the role of reference parameters in SLDFSs. The PFSs, SFSs, T-SFSs, and neutrosophic sets cannot dispense with parameterizations. The recommended structure intensifies the present methodologies and the decision-maker (DM) can openly select the degrees without any restriction. The feature of the dynamic sense of reference parameters classifies the difficulty.
7. Another objective is to assemble another novel structure with the combination of SLDFSs, soft sets, and rough sets named as SLDFSRSs. This concept can deal with the roughness, vagueness, uncertainty, and ambiguities of information data at the same time. This hybrid idea is strong, valid, and superior as compared to some existing models.
8. Our ultimate objective is to assemble an influential association among suggested models and MCDM obstacles. We generate two innovative algorithms to dispense with the vagueness in the information data following parameterizations. We utilize core, upper and lower reducts, multiple accuracy functions and score functions, and for the selection of feasible alternatives in the MCDM methods. It is fascinating to record that both algorithms generate the identical optimal alternative.

The organization of this manuscript is ordered as follows: Section 2 implements some elementary ideas of fuzzy sets, IFSs, neutrosophic sets, PFSs, SFSs, T-SFSs, soft sets, and rough sets. In Section 3, we originate the contemporary notion of SLDFSs. We exhibit perfection and comparison of the intended model with certain existing structures. We present various examples to relate our structure with the real-life circumstances. In Section 4, we impersonate a comparison by using graphical representations of some existing structures with the SLDFSs. We discuss about the drawbacks of existing operations and AOs on PFSs and establish some new operations on PFNs. We define some operations on SLDFNs. We impersonate multiple score and accuracy functions for the ranking of SLDFNs with distinct classifications. In Section 5, we establish another new idea of SLDFSRSs with its upper and lower approximation operators. We present some results on upper and lower approximation operators. In Section 6, we intend the approach of the MCDM obstacle for the election of clean energy technology with the help of SLDFSRSs and its approximations. We correlate the outcomes received from the suggested two innovative algorithms. We offer a brief association between the intended theories and certain present models. Eventually, the conclusion of this analysis is reviewed in Section 7.

2. Background

Initially, we examine some elementary ideas including fuzzy sets, IFSs, PFSs, SFSs, and T-SFSs. In the entire article, we utilize $\ddot{\mathcal{K}}$ as a fixed reference set.

Definition 1 ([1]). *The mapping $\dot{f} : \ddot{\mathcal{K}} \to [0,1]$ defines a fuzzy set $\mathfrak{F}$ in $\ddot{\mathcal{K}}$, where $\dot{f}(\ddot{\mathscr{D}})$ represents the satisfaction grade to which the alternative $\ddot{\mathscr{D}}$ belongs to $\mathfrak{F}$ for all $\ddot{\mathscr{D}} \in \ddot{\mathcal{K}}$. Alternatively, it can be represented as*

$$\mathfrak{F} = \{(\ddot{\mathscr{D}}, \dot{f}(\ddot{\mathscr{D}})) : \ddot{\mathscr{D}} \in \ddot{\mathcal{K}}\}.$$

The idea of satisfaction with dissatisfaction degrees was suggested by Atanassov [3] satisfying the constraint that the total of both grades cannot be superior to 1.

Definition 2 ([3]). *An IFS $\mathcal{I}$ in $\ddot{\mathcal{K}}$ is scripted as*

$$\mathcal{I} = \{\langle \ddot{\mathscr{D}}, \ddot{\mathscr{T}}_{\mathcal{I}}(\ddot{\mathscr{D}}), \ddot{\mathfrak{S}}_{\mathcal{I}}(\ddot{\mathscr{D}})\rangle : \ddot{\mathscr{D}} \in \ddot{\mathcal{K}}\},$$

where the mappings $\ddot{\mathscr{T}}_{\mathcal{I}} : \ddot{\mathcal{K}} \to [0,1]$ and $\ddot{\mathfrak{S}}_{\mathcal{I}} : \ddot{\mathcal{K}} \to [0,1]$ are called the satisfaction and dissatisfaction functions, respectively. It is required that that $0 \leq \ddot{\mathscr{T}}_{\mathcal{I}}(\ddot{\mathscr{D}}) + \ddot{\mathfrak{S}}_{\mathcal{I}}(\ddot{\mathscr{D}}) \leq 1$ for all $\ddot{\mathscr{D}} \in \ddot{\mathcal{K}}$. The indeterminacy degree of $\ddot{\mathscr{D}}$ to $\mathfrak{I}$ is given by $\dot{\pi}(\ddot{\mathscr{D}}) = 1 - (\ddot{\mathscr{T}}_{\mathcal{I}}(\ddot{\mathscr{D}}) + \ddot{\mathfrak{S}}_{\mathcal{I}}(\ddot{\mathscr{D}}))$. Graphically it can be characterized as Figure 1. This is basically a two dimensional idea and we can observe the behavior of alternatives in a plane (as Figure 1).

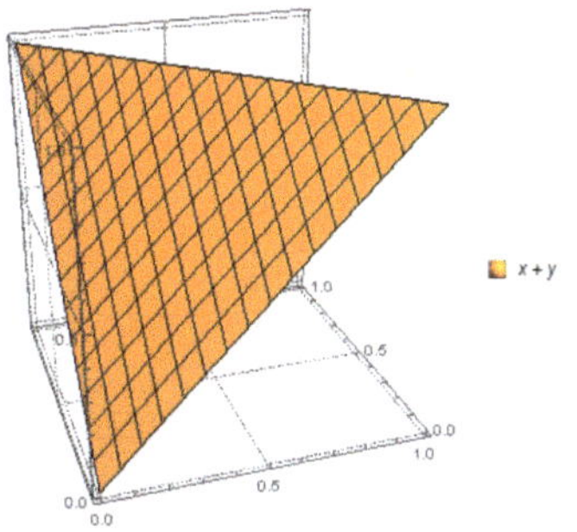

Figure 1. Graph of satisfaction and dissatisfaction grades of IFS.

Definition 3 ([10]). *A neutrosophic set $\mathfrak{N}$ in $\ddot{\mathcal{K}}$ is described by a satisfaction function $\ddot{\mathscr{T}}$, an indeterminacy membership function $\dot{\mathcal{I}}$ and a dissatisfaction function $\ddot{\mathfrak{S}}$. $\ddot{\mathscr{T}}(\ddot{\mathscr{D}}), \dot{\mathcal{I}}(\ddot{\mathscr{D}})$ and $\ddot{\mathfrak{S}}(\ddot{\mathscr{D}})$ are elements of $]0^-, 1^+[$. It can be scripted as*

$$\dot{\mathfrak{N}} = \{(\ddot{\mathscr{D}}, \langle \ddot{\mathscr{T}}(\ddot{\mathscr{D}}), \dot{\mathcal{I}}(\ddot{\mathscr{D}}), \ddot{\mathfrak{S}}(\ddot{\mathscr{D}})\rangle) : \ddot{\mathscr{D}} \in \ddot{\mathcal{K}}\}$$

such that $0^- \leq \ddot{\mathscr{T}}(\ddot{\mathscr{D}}) + \dot{\mathcal{I}}(\ddot{\mathscr{D}}) + \ddot{\mathfrak{S}}(\ddot{\mathscr{D}}) \leq 3+$.

To eradicate the drawbacks of existing models, Cuong [11–13] proposed the idea of picture fuzzy set (PFSs). This concept is closer to human nature and handle real life situations as compared to existing models.

Definition 4 ([11–13]). *A PiFS $\dot{\mathcal{P}}_f$ in $\ddot{\mathcal{K}}$ is scripted as*

$$\dot{\mathcal{P}}_f = \{(\ddot{\mathscr{D}}, \langle \ddot{\mathscr{T}}(\ddot{\mathscr{D}}), \ddot{\mathcal{Z}}(\ddot{\mathscr{D}}), \ddot{\mathfrak{S}}(\ddot{\mathscr{D}})\rangle) : \ddot{\mathscr{D}} \in \ddot{\mathcal{K}}\}$$

where, $0 \leq \ddot{\mathscr{T}}(\ddot{\mathscr{D}}), \ddot{\mathcal{Z}}(\ddot{\mathscr{D}}), \ddot{\mathfrak{S}}(\ddot{\mathscr{D}}) \leq 1$ represents the satisfaction, uncertainty (or abstinence), and dissatisfaction grades respectively, with the constraint $0 \leq \ddot{\mathscr{T}}(\ddot{\mathscr{D}}) + \ddot{\mathcal{Z}}(\ddot{\mathscr{D}}) + \ddot{\mathfrak{S}}(\ddot{\mathscr{D}}) \leq 1$. The value $\dot{\mathcal{R}}(\ddot{\mathscr{D}}) = 1 - (\ddot{\mathscr{T}}(\ddot{\mathscr{D}}) + \ddot{\mathcal{Z}}(\ddot{\mathscr{D}}) + \ddot{\mathfrak{S}}(\ddot{\mathscr{D}}))$ is called refusal grading for $\ddot{\mathscr{D}}$ in $\ddot{\mathcal{K}}$.

A picture fuzzy number can be written as a triplet $\langle \ddot{\mathscr{T}}(\ddot{\mathscr{D}}), \ddot{\mathcal{Z}}(\ddot{\mathscr{D}}), \ddot{\mathfrak{S}}(\ddot{\mathscr{D}})\rangle$, for $\ddot{\mathscr{D}} \in \ddot{\mathcal{K}}$.

Definition 5 ([14]). *A SFS $\dot{\mathcal{S}}$ in $\ddot{\mathcal{K}}$ is defined by*

$$\dot{\mathcal{S}} = \{(\ddot{\mathscr{D}}, \langle \ddot{\mathscr{T}}_s(\ddot{\mathscr{D}}), \ddot{\mathcal{Z}}_s(\ddot{\mathscr{D}}), \ddot{\mathfrak{S}}_s(\ddot{\mathscr{D}})\rangle) : \ddot{\mathscr{D}} \in \ddot{\mathcal{K}}\}$$

where, $0 \leq \langle \ddot{\mathscr{T}}_s(\ddot{\mathscr{D}}), \ddot{\mathcal{Z}}_s(\ddot{\mathscr{D}}), \ddot{\mathfrak{S}}_s(\ddot{\mathscr{D}})\rangle \leq 1$ represents the membership, uncertainty (or abstinence), and dissatisfaction grades, respectively, such that

$$0 \leq \ddot{\mathscr{T}}_s^2(\ddot{\mathscr{D}}) + \ddot{\mathcal{Z}}_s^2(\ddot{\mathscr{D}}) + \ddot{\mathfrak{S}}_s^2(\ddot{\mathscr{D}}) \leq 1$$

The value

$$\dot{\mathcal{R}}_s(\ddot{\mathscr{D}}) = \sqrt{1 - (\ddot{\mathscr{T}}_s^2(\ddot{\mathscr{D}}) + \ddot{\mathcal{Z}}_s^2(\ddot{\mathscr{D}}) + \ddot{\mathfrak{S}}_s^2(\ddot{\mathscr{D}}))}$$

is called refusal grading for $\ddot{\mathscr{D}}$ *in* $\ddot{\mathcal{K}}$ *A spherical fuzzy number (SFN) can be expressed as a triplet* $\langle \ddot{\mathscr{T}}_s(\ddot{\mathscr{D}}), \ddot{\mathcal{Z}}_s(\ddot{\mathscr{D}}), \ddot{\mathfrak{S}}_s(\ddot{\mathscr{D}})\rangle$, *for* $\ddot{\mathscr{D}} \in \ddot{\mathcal{K}}$.

Definition 6 ([14]). *A T-SFS* $\dot{\mathfrak{T}}$ *in* $\ddot{\mathcal{K}}$ *is scripted as*

$$\dot{\mathfrak{T}} = \{(\ddot{\mathscr{D}}, \langle \ddot{\mathscr{T}}_t(\ddot{\mathscr{D}}), \ddot{\mathcal{Z}}_t(\ddot{\mathscr{D}}), \ddot{\mathfrak{S}}_t(\ddot{\mathscr{D}})\rangle) : \ddot{\mathscr{D}} \in \ddot{\mathcal{K}}\}$$

where, $0 \leq \ddot{\mathscr{T}}_t(\ddot{\mathscr{D}}), \ddot{\mathcal{Z}}_t(\ddot{\mathscr{D}}), \ddot{\mathfrak{S}}_t(\ddot{\mathscr{D}}) \leq 1$ *represents the membership, uncertainty (or abstinence), and dissatisfaction grades, respectively, such that*

$$0 \leq \ddot{\mathscr{T}}_t^n(\ddot{\mathscr{D}}) + \ddot{\mathcal{Z}}_t^n(\ddot{\mathscr{D}}) + \ddot{\mathfrak{S}}_t^n(\ddot{\mathscr{D}}) \leq 1; (n = 1, 2, 3, \ldots)$$

The expression

$$\mathcal{R}_t(\ddot{\mathscr{D}}) = \sqrt[n]{1 - (\ddot{\mathscr{T}}_t^n(\ddot{\mathscr{D}}) + \ddot{\mathcal{Z}}_t^n(\ddot{\mathscr{D}}) + \ddot{\mathfrak{S}}_t^n(\ddot{\mathscr{D}}))}$$

gives the refusal grade for $\ddot{\mathscr{D}}$ *in* $\ddot{\mathcal{K}}$. *A T-spherical fuzzy number (T-SFN) can be communicated as a triplet* $\langle \ddot{\mathscr{T}}_t(\ddot{\mathscr{D}}), \ddot{\mathcal{Z}}_t(\ddot{\mathscr{D}}), \ddot{\mathfrak{S}}_t(\ddot{\mathscr{D}})\rangle$, *for* $\ddot{\mathscr{D}} \in \ddot{\mathcal{K}}$.

3. Spherical Linear Diophantine Fuzzy Sets (SLDFSs)

In this section, we inaugurate the novel notion of SLDFSs. In the field of number theory, we have the concept of linear Diophantine equation for three variables given as $ax + by + cz = d$. The intended structure has a correspondence with this equation, so we described it as SLDFS. With a comprehensive comparative study, we found that neutrosophic sets, T-SFSs, PiFSs, and SFSs have various restrictions on satisfaction, abstinence, and dissatisfaction degrees. To eliminate these restrictions, we originate the notion of SLDFS with the extension of reference parameters. Due to the impact of reference parameters a decision-maker (DM) can smoothly take the degrees according to the circumstances and suitable principles. This procedure categorizes the obstacle and provides us a variety of alternatives and attributes. We examine the construction of SLDFS, mathematically and graphically with the help of illustrations. In the entire article, we shall use $\ddot{\mathscr{T}}$, $\ddot{\mathcal{Z}}$ and $\ddot{\mathfrak{S}}$ for satisfaction, uncertainty or abstinence and dissatisfaction degrees, respectively, and α, β, η as reference or control parameters corresponding to $\ddot{\mathscr{T}}$, $\ddot{\mathcal{Z}}$ and $\ddot{\mathfrak{S}}$ respectively.

Definition 7. *A SLDFS* $\mathcal{S}_{\ddot{\mathcal{K}}}$ *in the universe* $\ddot{\mathcal{K}}$ *is defined as*

$$\mathcal{S}_{\ddot{\mathcal{K}}} = \left\{ \left(\ddot{\mathscr{D}}, \langle \ddot{T}_{\ddot{\mathcal{K}}}(\ddot{\mathscr{D}}), \ddot{\mathcal{Z}}_{\ddot{\mathcal{K}}}(\ddot{\mathscr{D}}), \ddot{\mathfrak{S}}_{\ddot{\mathcal{K}}}(\ddot{\mathscr{D}})\rangle, \langle \alpha_{\ddot{\mathcal{K}}}(\ddot{\mathscr{D}}), \beta_{\ddot{\mathcal{K}}}(\ddot{\mathscr{D}}), \eta_{\ddot{\mathcal{K}}}(\ddot{\mathscr{D}})\rangle \right) : \ddot{\mathscr{D}} \in \ddot{\mathcal{K}} \right\}$$

where, $\ddot{T}_{\ddot{\mathcal{K}}}(\ddot{\mathscr{D}}), \ddot{\mathcal{Z}}_{\ddot{\mathcal{K}}}(\ddot{\mathscr{D}}), \ddot{\mathfrak{S}}_{\ddot{\mathcal{K}}}(\ddot{\mathscr{D}}), \alpha_{\ddot{\mathcal{K}}}(\ddot{\mathscr{D}}), \beta_{\ddot{\mathcal{K}}}(\ddot{\mathscr{D}}), \eta_{\ddot{\mathcal{K}}}(\ddot{\mathscr{D}}) \in [0, 1]$ *are membership, uncertainty or abstinence, non-membership and reference parameters corresponding to these grades respectively. These grades satisfy the constraints*

$$0 \leq \alpha_{\ddot{\mathcal{K}}}(\ddot{\mathscr{D}})\ddot{T}_{\ddot{\mathcal{K}}}(\ddot{\mathscr{D}}) + \beta_{\ddot{\mathcal{K}}}(\ddot{\mathscr{D}})\ddot{\mathcal{Z}}_{\ddot{\mathcal{K}}}(\ddot{\mathscr{D}}) + \eta_{\ddot{\mathcal{K}}}(\ddot{\mathscr{D}})\ddot{\mathfrak{S}}_{\ddot{\mathcal{K}}}(\ddot{\mathscr{D}}) \leq 1\,; (\forall \ddot{\mathscr{D}} \in \ddot{\mathcal{K}})$$

$$0 \leq \alpha_{\ddot{\mathcal{K}}}(\ddot{\mathscr{D}}) + \beta_{\ddot{\mathcal{K}}}(\ddot{\mathscr{D}}) + \eta_{\ddot{\mathcal{K}}}(\ddot{\mathscr{D}}) \leq 1.$$

During the scheme of establishing or analyzing a particular system in the input information, the reference parameters play an essential role. The system can be classified by altering the dynamic function of these parameters. Restrictions can be excluded due to the increase in the valuation space. The refusal part can be estimated as

$$\pi_{\ddot{\mathcal{K}}}(\ddot{\mathscr{D}})\mathcal{R}_{\ddot{\mathcal{K}}} = 1 - (\alpha_{\ddot{\mathcal{K}}}(\ddot{\mathscr{D}})\ddot{T}_{\ddot{\mathcal{K}}}(\ddot{\mathscr{D}}) + \beta_{\ddot{\mathcal{K}}}(\ddot{\mathscr{D}})\ddot{\mathcal{Z}}_{\ddot{\mathcal{K}}}(\ddot{\mathscr{D}}) + \eta_{\ddot{\mathcal{K}}}(\ddot{\mathscr{D}})\ddot{\mathfrak{S}}_{\ddot{\mathcal{K}}}(\ddot{\mathscr{D}})),$$

where $\pi_{\ddot{\mathcal{K}}}(\ddot{\mathscr{D}})$ *is the reference parameter related to degree of refusal. Simply*

$$\ddot{\eth} = \left(\langle \ddot{T}_{\ddot{\mathcal{K}}}, \ddot{Z}_{\ddot{\mathcal{K}}}, \ddot{\mathfrak{S}}_{\ddot{\mathcal{K}}} \rangle, \langle \alpha_{\ddot{\mathcal{K}}}, \beta_{\ddot{\mathcal{K}}}, \eta_{\ddot{\mathcal{K}}} \rangle \right)$$

is called SLDFN. Graphically SLDFS can be seen as Figure 2.

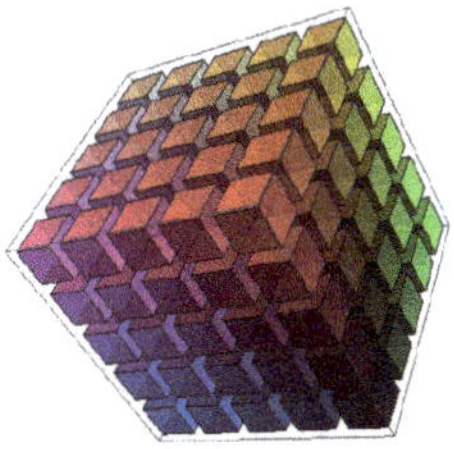

Figure 2. Graph of satisfaction, abstinence, and dissatisfaction grades of SLDFS.

Definition 8. *A SLDFS in* $\ddot{\mathcal{K}}$ *of the form*

$${}^{1}\mathcal{S}_{\ddot{\mathcal{K}}} = \{ (\ddot{\mathscr{D}}, \langle 1,0,0 \rangle, \langle 1,0,0 \rangle) : \ddot{\mathscr{D}} \in \ddot{\mathcal{K}} \}$$

is called absolute SLDFS, and

$${}^{0}\mathcal{S}_{\ddot{\mathcal{K}}} = \{ (\ddot{\mathscr{D}}, \langle 0,1,1 \rangle, \langle 0,0,1 \rangle) : \ddot{\mathscr{D}} \in \ddot{\mathcal{K}} \}$$

is called empty or null SLDFS.

3.1. Digital Image Processing

There are various applications of SLDFSs in diverse fields such as engineering, medical sciences, agriculture, artificial intelligence, business, MADM problems. The wide spectrum of these applications can be examined in this article.

We discuss about the three main levels of image processing given below as:

- Low-Level Processes.
- Mid-Level Processes.
- High-Level Processes.

These three phases correlate to the SLDFS grades of satisfaction, abstinence, and dissatisfaction. The addition of reference parameters improves the procedure's efficiency while also providing specifics on how to deal with the associated grades.

3.2. Medication

Every medication has multi purposes and used to treat different infections due to physical and chemical combinations of salts in it. Consider the assembling of some medicines, which are suitable for different infections given as $Q = \{\ddot{\mathscr{D}}_1, \ddot{\mathscr{D}}_2, \ddot{\mathscr{D}}_3, \ddot{\mathscr{D}}_4, \ddot{\mathscr{D}}_5\}$. These medicines used to cure pneumonia, sinusitis, bronchitis, ear infection and skin infections. We can classify the data on the basis of diseases with good or bad effects of medicines. If we select the reference parameters as:

$$\alpha_{\ddot{\mathcal{K}}} = \text{suitable or effective against bronchitis}$$
$$\beta_{\ddot{\mathcal{K}}} = \text{not highly effected to bronchitis (uneffected or neutral)}$$
$$\eta_{\ddot{\mathcal{K}}} = \text{having some side efffects or bad effects against bronchitis}$$

The Table 1 shows SLDFS.

Table 1. SLDFS.

$\mathcal{S}_{\ddot{\mathcal{K}}}$	$\left(\langle \ddot{T}_{\ddot{\mathcal{K}}}(\ddot{\mathscr{D}}), \ddot{Z}_{\ddot{\mathcal{K}}}(\ddot{\mathscr{D}}), \ddot{\mathfrak{S}}_{\ddot{\mathcal{K}}}(\ddot{\mathscr{D}})\rangle, \langle \alpha_{\ddot{\mathcal{K}}}, \beta_{\ddot{\mathcal{K}}}, \eta_{\ddot{\mathcal{K}}}\rangle\right)$
$\ddot{\mathscr{D}}_1$	$(\langle 0.952, 0.451, 0.413\rangle, \langle 0.64, 0.13, 0.11\rangle)$
$\ddot{\mathscr{D}}_2$	$(\langle 0.873, 0.345, 0.532\rangle, \langle 0.64, 0.11, 0.21\rangle)$
$\ddot{\mathscr{D}}_3$	$(\langle 0.631, 0.234, 0.811\rangle, \langle 0.38, 0.12, 0.11\rangle)$
$\ddot{\mathscr{D}}_4$	$(\langle 0.684, 0.456, 0.715\rangle, \langle 0.29, 0.24, 0.21\rangle)$
$\ddot{\mathscr{D}}_5$	$(\langle 0.882, 0.566, 0.712\rangle, \langle 0.49, 0.11, 0.21\rangle)$

A doctor/conslutant suggests a medicine to the patient that is exactly related to condition or severeness of disease. We can characterize the information system with control parameters which indicate how significant that factor is for the treatment, and their degrees indicate the advantages of keeping those parameters in treatment. If we switch parameter $\alpha_{\ddot{\mathcal{K}}}$ = "best effect against skin infection", $\beta_{\ddot{\mathcal{K}}}$ = "not highly affected or neutral to skin infection", and $\eta_{\ddot{\mathcal{K}}}$ = "side effects against skin infection" or $\alpha_{\ddot{\mathcal{K}}}$ = "less or low side effects", $\beta_{\ddot{\mathcal{K}}}$ = "medium side effects" and $\eta_{\ddot{\mathcal{K}}}$ = "high side effects", etc. then we can establish more SLDFSs on the similar set of alternatives. This arrangement enables a physician in recommending to a patient the most effective and appropriate medicine for his sickness.

3.3. Selection of Best Optimal Choice

The reference parameters can be used to interpret the categories of various object with respect to advantage or disadvantage. A high value of reference parameter indicate high significance. The characteristics of reference parameters in the selection of car, mobile, home appliances, may expressed as follows.

$$\alpha_{\ddot{\mathcal{K}}} = \text{low cost or cheap}$$
$$\beta_{\ddot{\mathcal{K}}} = \text{affordable}$$
$$\eta_{\ddot{\mathcal{K}}} = \text{high cost or expensive}$$

Suppose that a person needs to buy a mobile phone. He wants to choose the most desirable phone with lots of characteristics and having a low price. Let $\ddot{\mathcal{K}} = \{\ddot{\mathscr{D}}_1, \ddot{\mathscr{D}}_2, \ddot{\mathscr{D}}_3, \ddot{\mathscr{D}}_4\}$ be the set of some conventional mobile phones. The SLDFS is indicated as Table 2.

Table 2. SLDFS.

$\mathcal{S}_{\ddot{\mathcal{K}}}$	$\left(\langle \ddot{T}_{\ddot{\mathcal{K}}}(\ddot{\mathscr{D}}), \ddot{Z}_{\ddot{\mathcal{K}}}(\ddot{\mathscr{D}}), \ddot{\mathfrak{S}}_{\ddot{\mathcal{K}}}(\ddot{\mathscr{D}})\rangle, \langle \alpha_{\ddot{\mathcal{K}}}, \beta_{\ddot{\mathcal{K}}}, \eta_{\ddot{\mathcal{K}}}\rangle\right)$
$\ddot{\mathscr{D}}_1$	$(\langle 0.711, 0.452, 0.218\rangle, \langle 0.42, 0.11, 0.34\rangle)$
$\ddot{\mathscr{D}}_2$	$(\langle 0.933, 0.653, 0.522\rangle, \langle 0.31, 0.11, 0.47\rangle)$
$\ddot{\mathscr{D}}_3$	$(\langle 0.374, 0.677, 0.611\rangle, \langle 0.29, 0.24, 0.27\rangle)$
$\ddot{\mathscr{D}}_4$	$(\langle 0.516, 0.345, 0.474\rangle, \langle 0.31, 0.21, 0.33\rangle)$

If we alter the dynamical denotation of reference parameters, then we can classify the information data in another sense in the form of SLDFS. For second SLDFS we can utilize the reference parameters as:

$$\alpha_{\ddot{\mathcal{K}}} = \text{high battery timing}$$
$$\beta_{\ddot{\mathcal{K}}} = \text{average or medium battery timing}$$
$$\eta_{\ddot{\mathcal{K}}} = \text{low battery timing}$$

For the selected data the SLDF input information can be represented as Table 3.

Table 3. SLDFS.

$\mathcal{S}_{\ddot{\mathcal{K}}}$	$\left(\langle \dot{T}_{\ddot{\mathcal{K}}}(\ddot{\mathscr{D}}), \ddot{Z}_{\ddot{\mathcal{K}}}(\ddot{\mathscr{D}}), \ddot{\mathfrak{S}}_{\ddot{\mathcal{K}}}(\ddot{\mathscr{D}}) \rangle, \langle \alpha_{\ddot{\mathcal{K}}}, \beta_{\ddot{\mathcal{K}}}, \eta_{\ddot{\mathcal{K}}} \rangle\right)$
$\ddot{\mathscr{D}}_1$	$(\langle 0.932, 0.234, 0.411\rangle, \langle 0.54, 0.12, 0.11\rangle)$
$\ddot{\mathscr{D}}_2$	$(\langle 0.793, 0.435, 0.532\rangle, \langle 0.34, 0.23, 0.21\rangle)$
$\ddot{\mathscr{D}}_3$	$(\langle 0.531, 0.456, 0.811\rangle, \langle 0.38, 0.32, 0.11\rangle)$
$\ddot{\mathscr{D}}_4$	$(\langle 0.782, 0.236, 0.714\rangle, \langle 0.29, 0.34, 0.21\rangle)$

In this application, the control parameters present an essential role. They describe certain particular features about phones like it is cheap, affordable, expensive, high, medium or low battery timings, easy to learn, medium to learn or difficult to learn, etc. The grades $\dot{T}_{\ddot{\mathcal{K}}}(\ddot{\mathscr{D}})$, $\ddot{Z}_{\ddot{\mathcal{K}}}(\ddot{\mathscr{D}})$ and $\ddot{\mathfrak{S}}_{\ddot{\mathcal{K}}}(\ddot{\mathscr{D}})$ describe the grades of phone $\ddot{\mathscr{D}}$, which determines that how much a phone is cheap, affordable or expensive, while parameters represent that how much a machine should be cheap, affordable or expensive.

In SLDFSs three grades/indexes are assigned by the decision makers and estimated from the uncertain data/information about alternatives while the reference parameters are used to further analyze decision-makers opinion about three grades/indexes.

4. Graphical Representation of SLDFS

In this section, We present the graphical description of SLDFSs with reference or control parameters. We graphically examine that how its space is larger than the space of PFSs, SFSs, and T-SFSs. Figures 3–5 gives us the geometrical representation of PiFS, SFS and SLDFS. Figures 6–10 shows the grap of PiFS, SFS, T-SFS with some values of "n" and SLDFS.

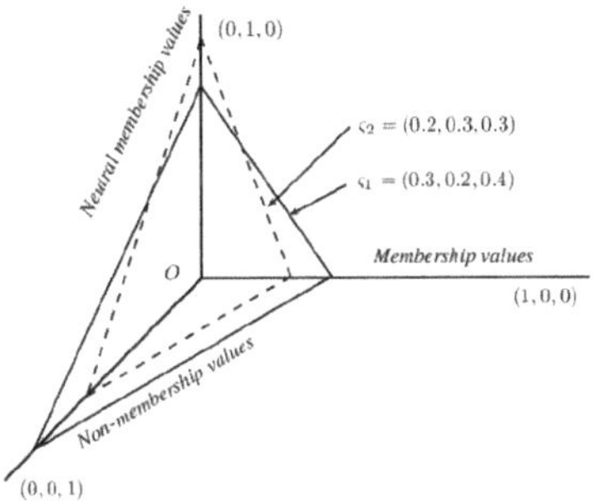

Figure 3. Graph of three indexes of PiFS.

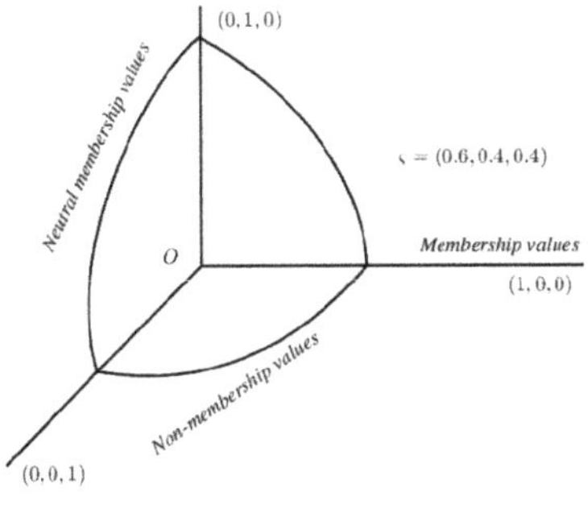

Figure 4. Graph of three indexes of SFS.

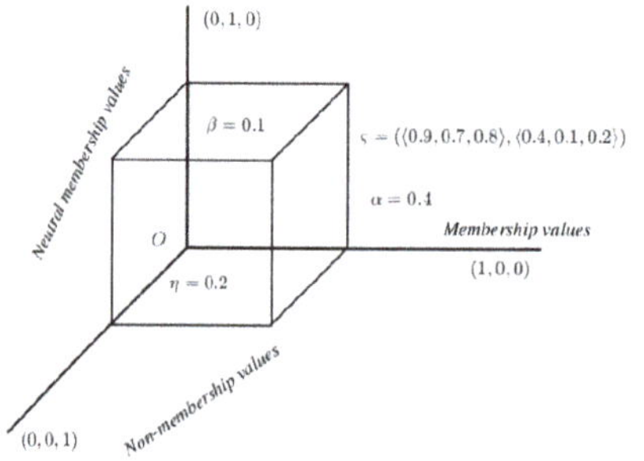

Figure 5. Graph of three indexes of SLDFS.

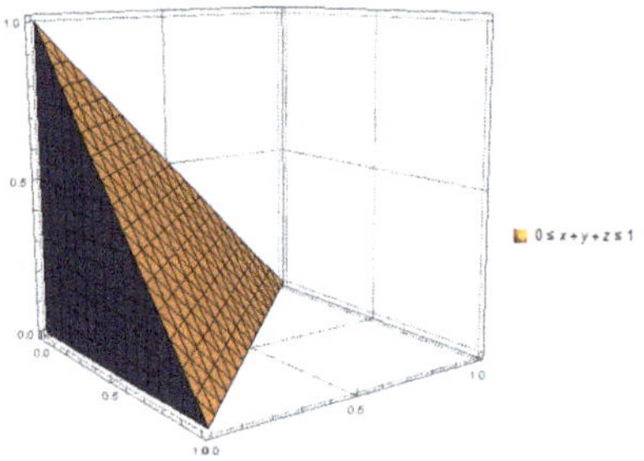

Figure 6. Graph of three indexes of PFS.

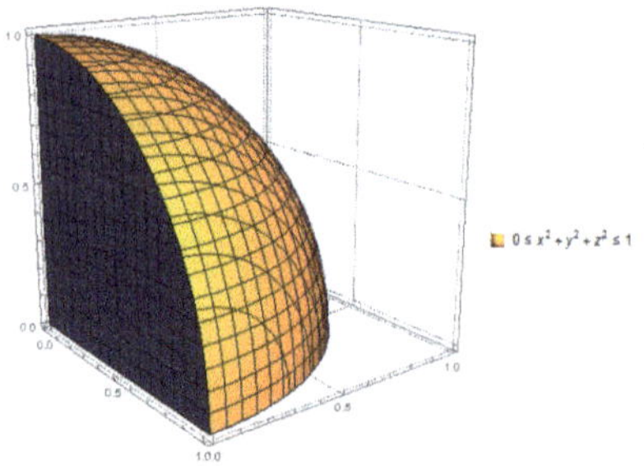

Figure 7. Graph of three indexes of SFS.

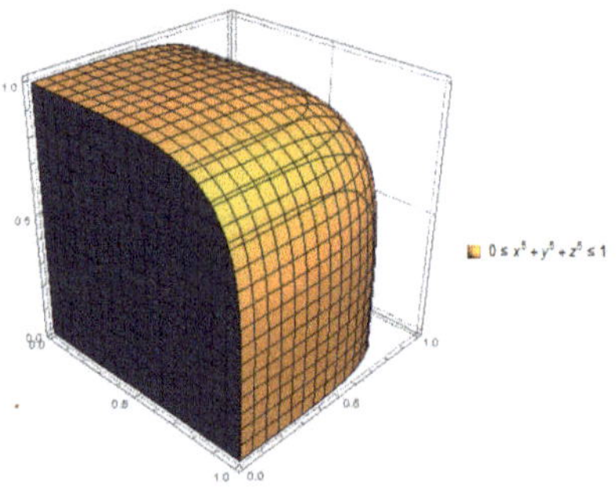

Figure 8. Graph of three indexes of T-SFS with n = 5.

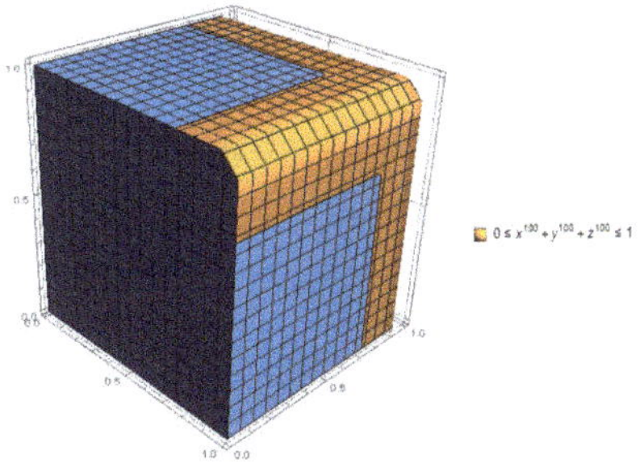

Figure 9. Graph of three indexes of T-SFS with n = 100.

It can be observed form Figure 10 and the graph of three grades/indexes in SLDFS provides a larger space than PiFS, SFS, and T-SFS. The addition of reference parameters provide freedom to the decision makers in selecting three grades/indexes. Thus a SLDFS with addition of reference parameter provides a robust approach for modeling uncertainties.

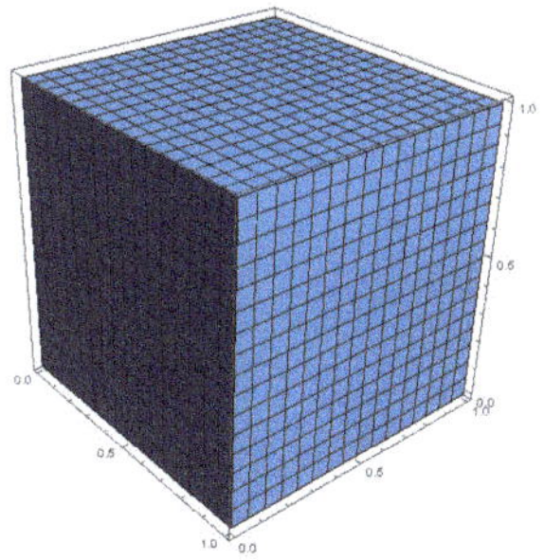

Figure 10. Graph of three indexes of SLDFS for reference parameters $\alpha_{\ddot{K}}, \beta_{\ddot{K}}, \eta_{\ddot{K}} \in [0,1]$.

Operations on Spherical Linear Diophantine Fuzzy Numbers (SLDFNs)

In this subsection, we define some operations on SLDFNs. For the comparison of SLDFNs, we develop various score functions and accuracy functions.

Definition 9. *Let us consider* $\ddot{\eth}_{\wp} = (\langle {}^{\wp}\ddot{T}_{\ddot{K}}, {}^{\wp}\ddot{Z}_{\ddot{K}}, {}^{\wp}\ddot{\mathfrak{S}}_{\ddot{K}} \rangle, \langle {}^{\wp}\alpha_{\ddot{K}}, {}^{\wp}\beta_{\ddot{K}}, {}^{\wp}\eta_{\ddot{K}} \rangle)$ *for* $\wp \in \Delta$ *(indexing set) be an assembling of SLDFNs over the reference set* $\ddot{K}$ *and* $\mathfrak{X} > 0$ *then the fundamental operations on SLDNFNs are the following*

- $\ddot{\eth}^c_{\wp} = (\langle {}^{\wp}\ddot{\mathfrak{S}}_{\ddot{K}}, 1 - {}^{\wp}\ddot{Z}_{\ddot{K}}, {}^{\wp}\ddot{T}_{\ddot{K}} \rangle, \langle {}^{\wp}\eta_{\ddot{K}}, {}^{\wp}\beta_{\ddot{K}}, {}^{\wp}\alpha_{\ddot{K}} \rangle),$
- $\ddot{\eth}_1 = \ddot{\eth}_2 \Leftrightarrow {}^1\ddot{T}_{\ddot{K}} = {}^2\ddot{T}_{\ddot{K}}, {}^1\ddot{Z}_{\ddot{K}} = {}^2\ddot{Z}_{\ddot{K}}, {}^1\ddot{\mathfrak{S}}_{\ddot{K}} = {}^2\ddot{\mathfrak{S}}_{\ddot{K}}, {}^1\alpha_{\ddot{K}} = {}^2\alpha_{\ddot{K}}, {}^1\beta_{\ddot{K}} = {}^2\beta_{\ddot{K}}, {}^1\eta_{\ddot{K}} = {}^2\eta_{\ddot{K}},$
- $\ddot{\eth}_1 \subseteq \ddot{\eth}_2 \Leftrightarrow {}^1\ddot{T}_{\ddot{K}} \leq {}^2\ddot{T}_{\ddot{K}}, {}^1\ddot{Z}_{\ddot{K}} \geq {}^2\ddot{Z}_{\ddot{K}}, {}^1\ddot{\mathfrak{S}}_{\ddot{K}} \geq {}^2\ddot{\mathfrak{S}}_{\ddot{K}}, {}^1\alpha_{\ddot{K}} \leq {}^2\alpha_{\ddot{K}}, {}^1\beta_{\ddot{K}} \geq {}^2\beta_{\ddot{K}}, {}^1\eta_{\ddot{K}} \geq {}^2\eta_{\ddot{K}},$
- $\bigcup_{\wp \in \Delta} \ddot{\eth}_{\wp} = \Big(\langle \sup_{\wp \in \Delta} {}^{\wp}\ddot{T}_{\ddot{K}}, \inf_{\wp \in \Delta} {}^{\wp}\ddot{Z}_{\ddot{K}}, \inf_{\wp \in \Delta} {}^{\wp}\ddot{\mathfrak{S}}_{\ddot{K}} \rangle, \langle \sup_{\wp \in \Delta} {}^{\wp}\alpha_{\ddot{K}}, \inf_{\wp \in \Delta} {}^{\wp}\beta_{\ddot{K}}, \inf_{\wp \in \Delta} {}^{\wp}\eta_{\ddot{K}} \rangle \Big),$
- $\bigcap_{\wp \in \Delta} \ddot{\eth}_{\wp} = \Big(\langle \inf_{\wp \in \Delta} {}^{\wp}\ddot{T}_{\ddot{K}}, \sup_{\wp \in \Delta} {}^{\wp}\ddot{Z}_{\ddot{K}}, \sup_{\wp \in \Delta} {}^{\wp}\ddot{\mathfrak{S}}_{\ddot{K}} \rangle, \langle \inf_{\wp \in \Delta} {}^{\wp}\alpha_{\ddot{K}}, \sup_{\wp \in \Delta} {}^{\wp}\beta_{\ddot{K}}, \sup_{\wp \in \Delta} {}^{\wp}\eta_{\ddot{K}} \rangle \Big),$
- $\ddot{\eth}_1 \oplus \ddot{\eth}_2 = \Big(\langle {}^1\ddot{T}_{\ddot{K}} + {}^2\ddot{T}_{\ddot{K}} - {}^1\ddot{T}_{\ddot{K}}{}^2\ddot{T}_{\ddot{K}}, {}^1\ddot{Z}_{\ddot{K}}{}^2\ddot{Z}_{\ddot{K}}, {}^1\ddot{\mathfrak{S}}_{\ddot{K}}{}^2\ddot{\mathfrak{S}}_{\ddot{K}} \rangle, \langle 1 - (1 - {}^1\alpha_{\ddot{K}})(1 - {}^2\alpha_{\ddot{K}}), {}^1\beta_{\ddot{K}}{}^2\beta_{\ddot{K}}, ({}^1\eta_{\ddot{K}} + {}^1\beta_{\ddot{K}})({}^2\eta_{\ddot{K}} + {}^2\beta_{\ddot{K}}) - {}^1\beta_{\ddot{K}}{}^2\beta_{\ddot{K}} \rangle \Big),$
- $\ddot{\eth}_1 \otimes \ddot{\eth}_2 = \Big(\langle {}^1\ddot{T}_{\ddot{K}}{}^2\ddot{T}_{\ddot{K}}, {}^1\ddot{Z}_{\ddot{K}} + {}^2\ddot{Z}_{\ddot{K}} - {}^1\ddot{Z}_{\ddot{K}}{}^2\ddot{Z}_{\ddot{K}}, {}^1\ddot{\mathfrak{S}}_{\ddot{K}} + {}^2\ddot{\mathfrak{S}}_{\ddot{K}} - {}^1\ddot{\mathfrak{S}}_{\ddot{K}}{}^2\ddot{\mathfrak{S}}_{\ddot{K}} \rangle, \langle ({}^1\alpha_{\ddot{K}} + {}^1\beta_{\ddot{K}})({}^2\alpha_{\ddot{K}} + {}^2\beta_{\ddot{K}}) - {}^1\beta_{\ddot{K}}{}^2\beta_{\ddot{K}}, {}^1\beta_{\ddot{K}}{}^2\beta_{\ddot{K}}, 1 - (1 - {}^1\eta_{\ddot{K}})(1 - {}^2\eta_{\ddot{K}}) \rangle \Big),$

- $\mathfrak{X}\ddot{\eth}_1 = \Big(\langle 1-(1-{}^1\ddot{T}_{\dot{\mathcal{K}}})^{\mathfrak{X}}, {}^1\ddot{\mathcal{Z}}_{\dot{\mathcal{K}}}^{\mathfrak{X}}, {}^1\ddot{\mathfrak{S}}_{\dot{\mathcal{K}}}^{\mathfrak{X}}\rangle, \langle 1-(1-{}^1\alpha_{\dot{\mathcal{K}}})^{\mathfrak{X}}, {}^1\beta_{\dot{\mathcal{K}}}{}^{\mathfrak{X}}, ({}^1\eta_{\dot{\mathcal{K}}}+{}^1\beta_{\dot{\mathcal{K}}})^{\mathfrak{X}} - {}^1\beta_{\dot{\mathcal{K}}}{}^{\mathfrak{X}}\rangle\Big)$; $\mathfrak{X} > 0$,
- $\ddot{\eth}_1^{\mathfrak{X}} = \Big(\langle {}^1\ddot{T}_{\dot{\mathcal{K}}}^{\mathfrak{X}}, 1-(1-{}^1\ddot{\mathcal{Z}}_{\dot{\mathcal{K}}})^{\mathfrak{X}}, 1-(1-{}^1\ddot{\mathfrak{S}}_{\dot{\mathcal{K}}})^{\mathfrak{X}}\rangle, \langle ({}^1\alpha_{\dot{\mathcal{K}}}+{}^1\beta_{\dot{\mathcal{K}}})^{\mathfrak{X}} - {}^1\beta_{\dot{\mathcal{K}}}{}^{\mathfrak{X}}, {}^1\beta_{\dot{\mathcal{K}}}{}^{\mathfrak{X}}, 1-(1-{}^1\eta_{\dot{\mathcal{K}}})^{\mathfrak{X}}\rangle\Big)$; $\mathfrak{X} > 0$.

Proposition 1. *Let* $\ddot{\eth}_1 = (\langle {}^1\ddot{T}_{\dot{\mathcal{K}}}, {}^1\ddot{\mathcal{Z}}_{\dot{\mathcal{K}}}, {}^1\ddot{\mathfrak{S}}_{\dot{\mathcal{K}}}\rangle, \langle {}^1\alpha_{\dot{\mathcal{K}}}, {}^1\beta_{\dot{\mathcal{K}}}, {}^1\eta_{\dot{\mathcal{K}}}\rangle)$ *and* $\ddot{\eth}_2 = (\langle {}^2\ddot{T}_{\dot{\mathcal{K}}}, {}^2\ddot{\mathcal{Z}}_{\dot{\mathcal{K}}}, {}^2\ddot{\mathfrak{S}}_{\dot{\mathcal{K}}}\rangle, \langle {}^2\alpha_{\dot{\mathcal{K}}}, {}^2\beta_{\dot{\mathcal{K}}}, {}^2\eta_{\dot{\mathcal{K}}}\rangle)$ *be two SLDFNs and* $\mathfrak{X} > 0$, *then* $\ddot{\eth}_1^c, \ddot{\eth}_1 \cup \ddot{\eth}_2, \ddot{\eth}_1 \cap \ddot{\eth}_2, \ddot{\eth}_1 \oplus \ddot{\eth}_2, \ddot{\eth}_1 \otimes \ddot{\eth}_2, \mathfrak{X}\ddot{\eth}_1$ *and* $\ddot{\eth}_1^{\mathfrak{X}}$ *are also SLDFNs.*

Proof. The proof follows by using Definition 9. □

Example 1. *Let* $\ddot{\eth}_1 = (\langle 0.93, 0.25, 0.31\rangle, \langle 0.38, 0.21, 0.34\rangle)$ *and* $\ddot{\eth}_2 = (\langle 0.83, 0.38, 0.32\rangle, \langle 0.25, 0.26, 0.41\rangle)$ *be two SLDFNs, then*

- $\ddot{\eth}_1^c = (\langle 0.31, 0.75, 0.93\rangle, \langle 0.34, 0.21, 0.38\rangle)$
- *Clearly by using Definition 9* $\ddot{\eth}_2 \subseteq \ddot{\eth}_1$
- $\ddot{\eth}_1 \cup \ddot{\eth}_2 = (\langle 0.93, 0.25, 0.31\rangle, \langle 0.38, 0.21, 0.34\rangle) = \ddot{\eth}_1$
- $\ddot{\eth}_1 \cap \ddot{\eth}_2 = (\langle 0.83, 0.38, 0.32\rangle, \langle 0.25, 0.26, 0.41\rangle) = \ddot{\eth}_2$
- $\ddot{\eth}_1 \oplus \ddot{\eth}_2 = (\langle 0.9881, 0.095, 0.0992\rangle, \langle 0.535, 0.0546, 0.3139\rangle)$
- $\ddot{\eth}_1 \otimes \ddot{\eth}_2 = (\langle 0.7719, 0.535, 0.5308\rangle, \langle 0.2463, 0.0546, 0.6106\rangle)$

  If $\mathfrak{X} = 0.1$ *then*
- $\mathfrak{X}\ddot{\eth}_1 = (\langle 0.2335, 0.7578, 0.8894\rangle, \langle 0.0466, 0.8555, 0.0864\rangle)$
- $\ddot{\eth}_1^{\mathfrak{X}} = (\langle 0.9927, 0.0283, 0.0364\rangle, \langle 0.0931, 0.8555, 0.0407\rangle)$

Proposition 2. *For two SLDFNs* $\ddot{\eth}_1$ *and* $\ddot{\eth}_2$ *with* $\mathfrak{X} > 0$ *then* $\ddot{\eth}_1^c, \ddot{\eth}_1 \cup \ddot{\eth}_2, \ddot{\eth}_1 \cap \ddot{\eth}_2, \ddot{\eth}_1 \oplus \ddot{\eth}_2, \ddot{\eth}_1 \otimes \ddot{\eth}_2, \mathfrak{X}\ddot{\eth}_1$ *and* $\ddot{\eth}_1^{\mathfrak{X}}$ *are also SLDFNs.*

Proof. Proof follows by using Definition 9. □

Chen and Tan [42] invented the idea of score functions for IFSs. Before that Tversky and Kahneman [43] proposed the same concept. We extend this idea for hybrid structures and SLDFNs. We invented different mappings to calculate the scores due to different strategies of approximation operators used in the proposed algorithms. These different score and accuracy functions determine the behavior of SLDFNs and provide us an appropriate optimal decision.

Definition 10. *Let* $\ddot{\eth} = (\langle \ddot{T}_{\dot{\mathcal{K}}}, \ddot{\mathcal{Z}}_{\dot{\mathcal{K}}}, \ddot{\mathfrak{S}}_{\dot{\mathcal{K}}}\rangle, \langle \alpha_{\dot{\mathcal{K}}}, \beta_{\dot{\mathcal{K}}}, \eta_{\dot{\mathcal{K}}}\rangle)$ *be a SLDFN, then the mapping* $\mathfrak{P} : SLDFN(\dot{\mathcal{K}}) \to [-1, 1]$ *define a score function (SF) on* $\ddot{\eth}$ *scripted as*

$$\mathfrak{P}_{\ddot{\eth}} = \mathfrak{P}(\ddot{\eth}) = \frac{1}{2}[(\ddot{T}_{\dot{\mathcal{K}}} - \ddot{\mathcal{Z}}_{\dot{\mathcal{K}}} - \ddot{\mathfrak{S}}_{\dot{\mathcal{K}}}) + (\alpha_{\dot{\mathcal{K}}} - \beta_{\dot{\mathcal{K}}} - \eta_{\dot{\mathcal{K}}})]$$

where $SLDFN(\dot{\mathcal{K}})$ *is an assembling of SLDFNs over* $\dot{\mathcal{K}}$.

Definition 11. *The mapping* $\psi : SLDFN(\dot{\mathcal{K}}) \to [0, 1]$ *defines an accuracy function (AF) scripted as*

$$\psi_{\ddot{\eth}} = \psi(\ddot{\eth}) = \frac{1}{2}\Big[\Big(\frac{\ddot{T}_{\dot{\mathcal{K}}} + \ddot{\mathcal{Z}}_{\dot{\mathcal{K}}} + \ddot{\mathfrak{S}}_{\dot{\mathcal{K}}}}{3}\Big) + (\alpha_{\dot{\mathcal{K}}} + \beta_{\dot{\mathcal{K}}} + \eta_{\dot{\mathcal{K}}})\Big]$$

Definition 12. *The mapping* $\mathfrak{J} : SLDFN(\dot{\mathcal{K}}) \to [-1, 1]$ *defines a quadratic score function (QSF) for SLDFN defined as*

$$\mathfrak{J}_{\ddot{\eth}} = \mathfrak{J}(\ddot{\eth}) = \frac{1}{2}[(\ddot{T}_{\dot{\mathcal{K}}}^2 - \ddot{\mathcal{Z}}_{\dot{\mathcal{K}}}^2 - \ddot{\mathfrak{S}}_{\dot{\mathcal{K}}}^2) + (\alpha_{\dot{\mathcal{K}}}^2 - \beta_{\dot{\mathcal{K}}}^2 - \eta_{\dot{\mathcal{K}}}^2)]$$

Definition 13. *The mapping* $\phi : SLDFN(\ddot{\mathcal{K}}) \rightarrow [0,1]$ *expresses the quadratic accuracy function (QAF) for SLDFN scripted as*

$$\phi_{\ddot{\eth}} = \phi(\ddot{\eth}) = \frac{1}{2}\Big[\Big(\frac{\ddot{T}^2_{\ddot{\mathcal{K}}} + \ddot{Z}^2_{\ddot{\mathcal{K}}} + \ddot{\mathfrak{S}}^2_{\ddot{\mathcal{K}}}}{3}\Big) + (\alpha^2_{\ddot{\mathcal{K}}} + \beta^2_{\ddot{\mathcal{K}}} + \eta^2_{\ddot{\mathcal{K}}})\Big]$$

Definition 14. *The expectation score function (ESF) on* $SLDFN(\ddot{\mathcal{K}})$ *and scripted by the mapping* $\mathfrak{M} : SLDFN(\ddot{\mathcal{K}}) \rightarrow [0,1]$ *such that*

$$\mathfrak{M}_{\ddot{\eth}} = \mathfrak{M}(\ddot{\eth}) = \frac{1}{3}\Big[\frac{(\ddot{T}_{\ddot{\mathcal{K}}} - \ddot{Z}_{\ddot{\mathcal{K}}} - \ddot{\mathfrak{S}}_{\ddot{\mathcal{K}}} + 2)}{2} + \frac{(\alpha_{\ddot{\mathcal{K}}} - \beta_{\ddot{\mathcal{K}}} - \eta_{\ddot{\mathcal{K}}} + 2)}{2}\Big]$$

This is modified form of SF.

Definition 15. *Let* $\ddot{\eth}_1$ *and* $\ddot{\eth}_2$ *be SLDFNs. The binary relation* $\leq_{(\ddot{T},\mathfrak{M})}$ *on* $SLDFN(\ddot{\mathcal{K}})$ *can be expressed as* $\ddot{\eth}_1 \leq_{(\ddot{T},\mathfrak{M})} \ddot{\eth}_2 \Leftrightarrow ((^1\ddot{T}_{\ddot{\mathcal{K}}} < {}^2\ddot{T}_{\ddot{\mathcal{K}}}) \wedge (^1\alpha_{\ddot{\mathcal{K}}} < {}^2\alpha_{\ddot{\mathcal{K}}})) \vee ((^1\ddot{T}_{\ddot{\mathcal{K}}} = {}^2\ddot{T}_{\ddot{\mathcal{K}}}) \wedge (^1\alpha_{\ddot{\mathcal{K}}} = {}^2\alpha_{\ddot{\mathcal{K}}}) \wedge (\mathfrak{M}_{\ddot{\eth}_1} \leq \mathfrak{M}_{\ddot{\eth}_2}))$.

Definition 16. *Let* $\ddot{\eth}_1$ *and* $\ddot{\eth}_2$ *be SLDFNs. The binary relation* $\leq_{(\mathfrak{M},\ddot{T})}$ *on* $SLDFN(\ddot{\mathcal{K}})$ *can be expressed as* $\ddot{\eth}_1 \leq_{(\mathfrak{M},\ddot{T})} \ddot{\eth}_2 \Leftrightarrow (\mathfrak{M}_{\ddot{\eth}_1} < \mathfrak{M}_{\ddot{\eth}_2}) \vee ((\mathfrak{M}_{\ddot{\eth}_1} = \mathfrak{M}_{\ddot{\eth}_2}) \wedge (^1\ddot{T}_{\ddot{\mathcal{K}}} \leq {}^2\ddot{T}_{\ddot{\mathcal{K}}}) \wedge (^1\alpha_{\ddot{\mathcal{K}}} \leq {}^2\alpha_{\ddot{\mathcal{K}}}))$.

5. Spherical Linear Diophantine Fuzzy Soft Rough Sets (SLDFSRSs)

Definition 17. *Let* $\ddot{\mathcal{K}}$ *be any set of objects,* $\ddot{\mathcal{G}}$ *be the set of attributes, and take* $\ddot{\mathcal{O}} \subseteq \ddot{\mathcal{G}}$*. A spherical linear Diophantine fuzzy soft set (SLDFSS)* $(\ddot{\delta}, \ddot{\mathcal{O}})$ *can be expressed by the mapping*

$$\ddot{\delta} : \ddot{\mathcal{O}} \rightarrow SLDFS(\ddot{\mathcal{K}})$$

where $SLDFS(\ddot{\mathcal{K}})$ *is an assembling of all SLDF-subsets of* $\ddot{\mathcal{K}}$*. A SLDFSS can be expressed as*

$$(\ddot{\delta}, \ddot{\mathcal{O}}) = \Big\{(\dot{\wp}, \ddot{\delta}(\dot{\wp})) : \dot{\wp} \in \ddot{\mathcal{O}}, \ddot{\delta}(\dot{\wp}) \in SLDFS(\ddot{\mathcal{K}})\Big\}$$

Definition 18. *Let* $(\ddot{\delta}, \ddot{\mathcal{O}})$ *be a SLDFSS in* $\ddot{\mathcal{K}}$*. Then a SLDF-subset* $\ddot{\mathscr{E}}$ *of* $\ddot{\mathcal{K}} \times \ddot{\mathcal{G}}$ *is called spherical linear Diophantine fuzzy soft relation (SLDFSR) from* $\ddot{\mathcal{K}}$ *to* $\ddot{\mathcal{G}}$ *scripted as*

$$\ddot{\mathscr{E}} = \Big\{((\ddot{\mathscr{D}}, \dot{\wp}), \langle \ddot{T}_{\ddot{\mathscr{E}}}(\ddot{\mathscr{D}}, \dot{\wp}), \ddot{Z}_{\ddot{\mathscr{E}}}(\ddot{\mathscr{D}}, \dot{\wp}), \ddot{\mathfrak{S}}_{\ddot{\mathscr{E}}}(\ddot{\mathscr{D}}, \dot{\wp})\rangle, \langle \alpha_{\ddot{\mathscr{E}}}(\ddot{\mathscr{D}}, \dot{\wp}), \beta_{\ddot{\mathscr{E}}}(\ddot{\mathscr{D}}, \dot{\wp}), \eta_{\ddot{\mathscr{E}}}(\ddot{\mathscr{D}}, \dot{\wp})\rangle) : (\ddot{\mathscr{D}}, \dot{\wp}) \in \ddot{\mathcal{K}} \times \ddot{\mathcal{G}}\Big\}$$

where ${}^{\alpha}\ddot{T}_{\ddot{\mathscr{E}}}(\ddot{\mathscr{D}}, \dot{\wp}), {}^{\alpha}\ddot{Z}_{\ddot{\mathscr{E}}}(\ddot{\mathscr{D}}, \dot{\wp}), {}^{\alpha}\ddot{\mathfrak{S}}_{\ddot{\mathscr{E}}}(\ddot{\mathscr{D}}, \dot{\wp}) \in [0,1]$ *are satisfaction, uncertainty or abstinence and dissatisfaction grades respectively, with the corresponding reference parameters* $\alpha_{\ddot{\mathscr{E}}}(\ddot{\mathscr{D}}, \dot{\wp}), \beta_{\ddot{\mathscr{E}}}(\ddot{\mathscr{D}}, \dot{\wp})$, $\eta_{\ddot{\mathscr{E}}}(\ddot{\mathscr{D}}, \dot{\wp}) \in [0,1]$ *satisfying the constraints*

$$0 \leq \alpha_{\ddot{\mathscr{E}}}(\ddot{\mathscr{D}}, \dot{\wp})^{\alpha}\ddot{T}_{\ddot{\mathscr{E}}}(\ddot{\mathscr{D}}, \dot{\wp}) + \beta_{\ddot{\mathscr{E}}}(\ddot{\mathscr{D}}, \dot{\wp})^{\alpha}\ddot{Z}_{\ddot{\mathscr{E}}}(\ddot{\mathscr{D}}, \dot{\wp}) + \eta_{\ddot{\mathscr{E}}}(\ddot{\mathscr{D}}, \dot{\wp})^{\alpha}\ddot{\mathfrak{S}}_{\ddot{\mathscr{E}}}(\ddot{\mathscr{D}}, \dot{\wp}) \leq 1$$

$$0 \leq \alpha_{\ddot{\mathscr{E}}}(\ddot{\mathscr{D}}, \dot{\wp}) + \beta_{\ddot{\mathscr{E}}}(\ddot{\mathscr{D}}, \dot{\wp}) + \eta_{\ddot{\mathscr{E}}}(\ddot{\mathscr{D}}, \dot{\wp}) \leq 1$$

If $\ddot{\mathcal{K}} = \{\ddot{\mathscr{D}}_1, \ddot{\mathscr{D}}_2, \ldots, \ddot{\mathscr{D}}_n\}$ *and* $\ddot{\mathcal{G}} = \{\dot{\wp}_1, \dot{\wp}_2, \ldots, \dot{\wp}_m\}$*, then SLDFSR* $\ddot{\mathscr{E}}$ *on* $\ddot{\mathcal{K}} \times \ddot{\mathcal{G}}$ *can be represented in tabular form as Table 4.*

Table 4. Spherical linear Diophantine fuzzy soft relation (SLDFSR).

$\ddot{\mathscr{E}}$	$\dot{\wp}_1$	...	$\dot{\wp}_m$
$\ddot{\mathscr{D}}_1$	$(\langle \dot{T}_{\ddot{\mathscr{E}}}(\ddot{\mathscr{D}}_1, \dot{\wp}_1), \dot{Z}_{\ddot{\mathscr{E}}}(\ddot{\mathscr{D}}_1, \dot{\wp}_1) \ddot{\mathfrak{S}}_{\ddot{\mathscr{E}}}(\ddot{\mathscr{D}}_1, \dot{\wp}_1)\rangle, \langle \alpha_{\ddot{\mathscr{E}}}(\ddot{\mathscr{D}}_1, \dot{\wp}_1), \beta_{\ddot{\mathscr{E}}}(\ddot{\mathscr{D}}_1, \dot{\wp}_1), \eta_{\ddot{\mathscr{E}}}(\ddot{\mathscr{D}}_1, \dot{\wp}_1)\rangle)$	...	$(\langle \dot{T}_{\ddot{\mathscr{E}}}(\ddot{\mathscr{D}}_1, \dot{\wp}_m), \dot{Z}_{\ddot{\mathscr{E}}}(\ddot{\mathscr{D}}_1, \dot{\wp}_m) \ddot{\mathfrak{S}}_{\ddot{\mathscr{E}}}(\ddot{\mathscr{D}}_1, \dot{\wp}_m)\rangle, \langle \alpha_{\ddot{\mathscr{E}}}(\ddot{\mathscr{D}}_1, \dot{\wp}_m), \beta_{\ddot{\mathscr{E}}}(\ddot{\mathscr{D}}_1, \dot{\wp}_m), \eta_{\ddot{\mathscr{E}}}(\ddot{\mathscr{D}}_1, \dot{\wp}_m)\rangle)$
$\ddot{\mathscr{D}}_2$	$(\langle \dot{T}_{\ddot{\mathscr{E}}}(\ddot{\mathscr{D}}_2, \dot{\wp}_1), \dot{Z}_{\ddot{\mathscr{E}}}(\ddot{\mathscr{D}}_2, \dot{\wp}_1) \ddot{\mathfrak{S}}_{\ddot{\mathscr{E}}}(\ddot{\mathscr{D}}_2, \dot{\wp}_1)\rangle, \langle \alpha_{\ddot{\mathscr{E}}}(\ddot{\mathscr{D}}_2, \dot{\wp}_1), \beta_{\ddot{\mathscr{E}}}(\ddot{\mathscr{D}}_2, \dot{\wp}_1), \eta_{\ddot{\mathscr{E}}}(\ddot{\mathscr{D}}_2, \dot{\wp}_1)\rangle)$	...	$(\langle \dot{T}_{\ddot{\mathscr{E}}}(\ddot{\mathscr{D}}_2, \dot{\wp}_m), \dot{Z}_{\ddot{\mathscr{E}}}(\ddot{\mathscr{D}}_2, \dot{\wp}_m) \ddot{\mathfrak{S}}_{\ddot{\mathscr{E}}}(\ddot{\mathscr{D}}_2, \dot{\wp}_m)\rangle, \langle \alpha_{\ddot{\mathscr{E}}}(\ddot{\mathscr{D}}_2, \dot{\wp}_m), \beta_{\ddot{\mathscr{E}}}(\ddot{\mathscr{D}}_2, \dot{\wp}_m), \eta_{\ddot{\mathscr{E}}}(\ddot{\mathscr{D}}_2, \dot{\wp}_m)\rangle)$
$\ddot{\mathscr{D}}_n$	$(\langle \dot{T}_{\ddot{\mathscr{E}}}(\ddot{\mathscr{D}}_n, \dot{\wp}_1), \dot{Z}_{\ddot{\mathscr{E}}}(\ddot{\mathscr{D}}_n, \dot{\wp}_1) \ddot{\mathfrak{S}}_{\ddot{\mathscr{E}}}(\ddot{\mathscr{D}}_n, \dot{\wp}_1)\rangle, \langle \alpha_{\ddot{\mathscr{E}}}(\ddot{\mathscr{D}}_n, \dot{\wp}_1), \beta_{\ddot{\mathscr{E}}}(\ddot{\mathscr{D}}_n, \dot{\wp}_1), \eta_{\ddot{\mathscr{E}}}(\ddot{\mathscr{D}}_n, \dot{\wp}_1)\rangle)$	...	$(\langle \dot{T}_{\ddot{\mathscr{E}}}(\ddot{\mathscr{D}}_n, \dot{\wp}_m), \dot{Z}_{\ddot{\mathscr{E}}}(\ddot{\mathscr{D}}_n, \dot{\wp}_m) \ddot{\mathfrak{S}}_{\ddot{\mathscr{E}}}(\ddot{\mathscr{D}}_n, \dot{\wp}_m)\rangle, \langle \alpha_{\ddot{\mathscr{E}}}(\ddot{\mathscr{D}}_n, \dot{\wp}_m), \beta_{\ddot{\mathscr{E}}}(\ddot{\mathscr{D}}_n, \dot{\wp}_m), \eta_{\ddot{\mathscr{E}}}(\ddot{\mathscr{D}}_n, \dot{\wp}_m)\rangle)$

Definition 19. *For the reference set $\ddot{\mathcal{K}}$ and set of decision variables $\dot{\mathcal{G}}$, if we define a SLDFSR $\ddot{\mathscr{E}}$ over $\ddot{\mathcal{K}} \times \dot{\mathcal{G}}$, then $(\ddot{\mathcal{K}}, \dot{\mathcal{G}}, \ddot{\mathscr{E}})$ is called a spherical linear Diophantine fuzzy soft approximation space (SLDFS-approximation space). If $\ddot{\mathcal{Y}} \in SLDFS(\dot{\mathcal{G}})$, then $\ddot{\mathscr{E}}^\star(\ddot{\mathcal{Y}})$ and $\ddot{\mathscr{E}}_\star(\ddot{\mathcal{Y}})$ are called upper and lower approximations of $\ddot{\mathcal{Y}}$ about $(\ddot{\mathcal{K}}, \dot{\mathcal{G}}, \ddot{\mathscr{E}})$ respectively and scripted as*

$$\ddot{\mathscr{E}}^\star(\ddot{\mathcal{Y}}) = \{(\ddot{\mathscr{D}}, \langle \dot{T}_{\ddot{\mathscr{E}}^\star(\ddot{\mathcal{Y}})}(\ddot{\mathscr{D}}), \dot{Z}_{\ddot{\mathscr{E}}^\star(\ddot{\mathcal{Y}})}(\ddot{\mathscr{D}}), \ddot{\mathfrak{S}}_{\ddot{\mathscr{E}}^\star(\ddot{\mathcal{Y}})}(\ddot{\mathscr{D}})\rangle, \langle \alpha_{\ddot{\mathscr{E}}^\star(\ddot{\mathcal{Y}})}(\ddot{\mathscr{D}}), \beta_{\ddot{\mathscr{E}}^\star(\ddot{\mathcal{Y}})}(\ddot{\mathscr{D}}), \eta_{\ddot{\mathscr{E}}^\star(\ddot{\mathcal{Y}})}(\ddot{\mathscr{D}})\rangle) : \ddot{\mathscr{D}} \in \ddot{\mathcal{K}}\}$$

$$\ddot{\mathscr{E}}_\star(\ddot{\mathcal{Y}}) = \{(\ddot{\mathscr{D}}, \langle \dot{T}_{\ddot{\mathscr{E}}_\star(\ddot{\mathcal{Y}})}(\ddot{\mathscr{D}}), \dot{Z}_{\ddot{\mathscr{E}}_\star(\ddot{\mathcal{Y}})}(\ddot{\mathscr{D}}), \ddot{\mathfrak{S}}_{\ddot{\mathscr{E}}_\star(\ddot{\mathcal{Y}})}(\ddot{\mathscr{D}})\rangle, \langle \alpha_{\ddot{\mathscr{E}}_\star(\ddot{\mathcal{Y}})}(\ddot{\mathscr{D}}), \beta_{\ddot{\mathscr{E}}_\star(\ddot{\mathcal{Y}})}(\ddot{\mathscr{D}}), \eta_{\ddot{\mathscr{E}}_\star(\ddot{\mathcal{Y}})}(\ddot{\mathscr{D}})\rangle) : \ddot{\mathscr{D}} \in \ddot{\mathcal{K}}\}$$

where

$$\dot{T}_{\ddot{\mathscr{E}}^\star(\ddot{\mathcal{Y}})}(\ddot{\mathscr{D}}) = \bigvee_{\dot{\wp} \in \dot{\mathcal{G}}} [\dot{T}_{\ddot{\mathscr{E}}}(\ddot{\mathscr{D}}, \dot{\wp}) \wedge \dot{T}_{\mathcal{Y}}(\dot{\wp})], \qquad \dot{Z}_{\ddot{\mathscr{E}}^\star(\ddot{\mathcal{Y}})}(\ddot{\mathscr{D}}) = \bigwedge_{\dot{\wp} \in \dot{\mathcal{G}}} [(1 - \dot{Z}_{\ddot{\mathscr{E}}}(\ddot{\mathscr{D}}, \dot{\wp})) \vee \dot{Z}_{\mathcal{Y}}(\dot{\wp})]$$

$$\ddot{\mathfrak{S}}_{\ddot{\mathscr{E}}^\star(\ddot{\mathcal{Y}})}(\ddot{\mathscr{D}}) = \bigwedge_{\dot{\wp} \in \dot{\mathcal{G}}} [(1 - \ddot{\mathfrak{S}}_{\ddot{\mathscr{E}}}(\ddot{\mathscr{D}}, \dot{\wp})) \vee \ddot{\mathfrak{S}}_{\mathcal{Y}}(\dot{\wp})], \qquad \alpha_{\ddot{\mathscr{E}}^\star(\ddot{\mathcal{Y}})}(\ddot{\mathscr{D}}) = \bigvee_{\dot{\wp} \in \dot{\mathcal{G}}} [\alpha_{\ddot{\mathscr{E}}}(\ddot{\mathscr{D}}, \dot{\wp}) \wedge \alpha_{\mathcal{Y}}(\dot{\wp})]$$

$$\beta_{\ddot{\mathscr{E}}^\star(\ddot{\mathcal{Y}})}(\ddot{\mathscr{D}}) = \bigwedge_{\dot{\wp} \in \dot{\mathcal{G}}} [\beta_{\ddot{\mathscr{E}}}(\ddot{\mathscr{D}}, \dot{\wp}) \vee \beta_{\mathcal{Y}}(\dot{\wp})], \qquad \eta_{\ddot{\mathscr{E}}^\star(\ddot{\mathcal{Y}})}(\ddot{\mathscr{D}}) = \bigwedge_{\dot{\wp} \in \dot{\mathcal{G}}} [\eta_{\ddot{\mathscr{E}}}(\ddot{\mathscr{D}}, \dot{\wp}) \vee \eta_{\mathcal{Y}}(\dot{\wp})]$$

$$\dot{T}_{\ddot{\mathscr{E}}_\star(\ddot{\mathcal{Y}})}(\ddot{\mathscr{D}}) = \bigwedge_{\dot{\wp} \in \dot{\mathcal{G}}} [(1 - \dot{T}_{\ddot{\mathscr{E}}}(\ddot{\mathscr{D}}, \dot{\wp})) \vee \dot{T}_{\mathcal{Y}}(\dot{\wp})], \qquad \dot{Z}_{\ddot{\mathscr{E}}_\star(\ddot{\mathcal{Y}})}(\ddot{\mathscr{D}}) = \bigvee_{\dot{\wp} \in \dot{\mathcal{G}}} [\dot{Z}_{\ddot{\mathscr{E}}}(\ddot{\mathscr{D}}, \dot{\wp}) \wedge \dot{Z}_{\mathcal{Y}}(\dot{\wp})]$$

$$\ddot{\mathfrak{S}}_{\ddot{\mathscr{E}}_\star(\ddot{\mathcal{Y}})}(\ddot{\mathscr{D}}) = \bigvee_{\dot{\wp} \in \dot{\mathcal{G}}} [\ddot{\mathfrak{S}}_{\ddot{\mathscr{E}}}(\ddot{\mathscr{D}}, \dot{\wp}) \wedge \ddot{\mathfrak{S}}_{\mathcal{Y}}(\dot{\wp})], \qquad \alpha_{\ddot{\mathscr{E}}_\star(\ddot{\mathcal{Y}})}(\ddot{\mathscr{D}}) = \bigwedge_{\dot{\wp} \in \dot{\mathcal{G}}} [\alpha_{\ddot{\mathscr{E}}}(\ddot{\mathscr{D}}, \dot{\wp}) \vee \alpha_{\mathcal{Y}}(\dot{\wp})]$$

$$\beta_{\ddot{\mathscr{E}}_\star(\ddot{\mathcal{Y}})}(\ddot{\mathscr{D}}) = \bigvee_{\dot{\wp} \in \dot{\mathcal{G}}} [\beta_{\ddot{\mathscr{E}}}(\ddot{\mathscr{D}}, \dot{\wp}) \wedge \beta_{\mathcal{Y}}(\dot{\wp})], \qquad \eta_{\ddot{\mathscr{E}}_\star(\ddot{\mathcal{Y}})}(\ddot{\mathscr{D}}) = \bigvee_{\dot{\wp} \in \dot{\mathcal{G}}} [\eta_{\ddot{\mathscr{E}}}(\ddot{\mathscr{D}}, \dot{\wp}) \wedge \eta_{\mathcal{Y}}(\dot{\wp})]$$

The pair $(\ddot{\mathscr{E}}_\star(\ddot{\mathcal{Y}}), \ddot{\mathscr{E}}^\star(\ddot{\mathcal{Y}}))$ is called SLDFSRS in $(\ddot{\mathcal{K}}, \dot{\mathcal{G}}, \ddot{\mathscr{E}})$. The lower and upper approximation operators are represented as $\ddot{\mathscr{E}}_\star(\ddot{\mathcal{Y}})$ and $\ddot{\mathscr{E}}^\star(\ddot{\mathcal{Y}})$, respectively. If $\ddot{\mathscr{E}}_\star(\ddot{\mathcal{Y}}) = \ddot{\mathscr{E}}^\star(\ddot{\mathcal{Y}})$, then $\ddot{\mathcal{Y}}$ is said to be definable.

Example 2. *Let $\ddot{\mathcal{K}} = \{\ddot{\mathscr{D}}_1, \ddot{\mathscr{D}}_2\}$ be the set of some famous shoe brands and $\dot{\mathcal{G}} = \{\dot{\wp}_1, \dot{\wp}_2, \dot{\wp}_3\}$ be the collection of some attributes, where*

$\dot{\wp}_1 =$ *Product quality,*

$\dot{\wp}_2 =$ *affordable,*

$\dot{\wp}_3 =$ *Recovery service.*

We consider the SLDFSR, $\ddot{\mathscr{E}} : \ddot{\mathcal{K}} \to \dot{\mathcal{G}}$ given by Table 5.

Table 5. SLDFSR.

$\ddot{\mathscr{E}}$	Numeric Values of SLDFNs
$\ddot{\mathscr{D}}_1$	$\wp_1$:($\langle 0.684, 0.355, 0.356\rangle, \langle 0.221, 0.325, 0.311\rangle$) $\wp_2$:($\langle 0.825, 0.836, 0.546\rangle, \langle 0.226, 0.123, 0.421\rangle$) $\wp_3$:($\langle 0.826, 0.265, 0.489\rangle, \langle 0.122, 0.323, 0.345\rangle$)
$\ddot{\mathscr{D}}_2$	$\wp_1$:($\langle 0.973, 0.543, 0.478\rangle, \langle 0.246, 0.614, 0.112\rangle$) $\wp_2$:($\langle 0.822, 0.642, 0.789\rangle, \langle 0.223, 0.524, 0.124\rangle$) $\wp_3$:($\langle 0.752, 0.275, 0.788\rangle, \langle 0.122, 0.233, 0.574\rangle$)

Consider a SLDF-subset $\ddot{\mathcal{Y}}$ of $\ddot{\mathcal{G}}$ given as

$$\ddot{\mathcal{Y}} = \{(\wp_1, \langle 0.837, 0.535, 0.785\rangle, \langle 0.242, 0.242, 0.478\rangle), (\wp_2, \langle 0.833, 0.635, 0.784\rangle, \langle 0.634, 0.121, 0.211\rangle), (\wp_3, \langle 0.725, 0.526, 0.478\rangle, \langle 0.625, 0.211, 111\rangle)\}$$

By using Definition 19, we find the upper and lower approximations of $\ddot{\mathcal{Y}}$ given by

$$\ddot{T}_{\ddot{\mathscr{E}}^\star(\ddot{\mathcal{Y}})}(\ddot{\mathscr{D}}_1) = \bigvee_{\wp}[0.684, 0.825, 0.725] = 0.825, \quad \ddot{Z}_{\ddot{\mathscr{E}}^\star(\ddot{\mathcal{Y}})}(\ddot{\mathscr{D}}_1) = \bigwedge_{\wp}[0.645, 0.635, 0.735] = 0.635,$$

$$\ddot{\mathfrak{S}}_{\ddot{\mathscr{E}}^\star(\ddot{\mathcal{Y}})}(\ddot{\mathscr{D}}_1) = \bigwedge_{\wp}[0.785, 0.784, 0.511] = 0.511, \quad \alpha_{\ddot{\mathscr{E}}^\star(\ddot{\mathcal{Y}})}(\ddot{\mathscr{D}}_1) = \bigvee_{\wp}[0.221, 0.226, 0.122] = 0.226,$$

$$\beta_{\ddot{\mathscr{E}}^\star(\ddot{\mathcal{Y}})}(\ddot{\mathscr{D}}_1) = \bigwedge_{\wp}[0.325, 0.123, 0.323] = 0.123, \quad \eta_{\ddot{\mathscr{E}}^\star(\ddot{\mathcal{Y}})}(\ddot{\mathscr{D}}_1) = \bigwedge_{\wp}[0.478, 0.421, 0.345] = 0.345$$

Now we can find other approximations of $\ddot{\mathcal{Y}}$ as follows.

$$\ddot{\mathscr{E}}^\star(\ddot{\mathcal{Y}}) = \{(\ddot{\mathscr{D}}_1, \langle 0.825, 0.635, 0.511\rangle, \langle 0.226, 0.123, 0.345\rangle), (\ddot{\mathscr{D}}_2, \langle 0.837, 0.535, 0.478\rangle, \langle 0.242, 0.233, 0.211\rangle)\}$$
$$\ddot{\mathscr{E}}_\star(\ddot{\mathcal{Y}}) = \{(\ddot{\mathscr{D}}_1, \langle 0.725, 0.635, 0.546\rangle, \langle 0.242, 0.242, 0.311\rangle), (\ddot{\mathscr{D}}_2, \langle 0.752, 0.635, 0.784\rangle, \langle 0.246, 0.242, 0.124\rangle)\}$$

Thus $(\ddot{\mathscr{E}}_\star(\ddot{\mathcal{Y}}), \ddot{\mathscr{E}}^\star(\ddot{\mathcal{Y}}))$ is called SLDFSRS.

Theorem 1. *For arbitrary $\ddot{\mathcal{Y}}, \mathcal{B} \in SLDFS(\mathcal{G})$, the upper and lower approximation operators $\ddot{\mathscr{E}}_\star(\ddot{\mathcal{Y}}), \ddot{\mathscr{E}}_\star(\mathcal{B}), \ddot{\mathscr{E}}^\star(\ddot{\mathcal{Y}})$ and $\ddot{\mathscr{E}}^\star(\mathcal{B})$ on SLDFS-approximation space $(\ddot{\mathcal{K}}, \ddot{\mathcal{G}}, \ddot{\mathscr{E}})$ satisfy the following axioms:*

(1) $\ddot{\mathscr{E}}_\star(\ddot{\mathcal{Y}}) = \sim \ddot{\mathscr{E}}^\star(\sim \ddot{\mathcal{Y}})$,
(2) $\ddot{\mathcal{Y}} \subseteq \mathcal{B} \Rightarrow \ddot{\mathscr{E}}_\star(\ddot{\mathcal{Y}}) \subseteq \ddot{\mathscr{E}}_\star(\mathcal{B})$,
(3) $\ddot{\mathscr{E}}_\star(\ddot{\mathcal{Y}} \cap \mathcal{B}) = \ddot{\mathscr{E}}_\star(\ddot{\mathcal{Y}}) \cap \ddot{\mathscr{E}}_\star(\mathcal{B})$,
(4) $\ddot{\mathscr{E}}_\star(\ddot{\mathcal{Y}} \cup \mathcal{B}) \supseteq \ddot{\mathscr{E}}_\star(\ddot{\mathcal{Y}}) \cup \ddot{\mathscr{E}}_\star(\mathcal{B})$,
(5) $\ddot{\mathscr{E}}^\star(\ddot{\mathcal{Y}}) = \sim \ddot{\mathscr{E}}_\star(\sim \ddot{\mathcal{Y}})$,
(6) $\ddot{\mathcal{Y}} \subseteq \mathcal{B} \Rightarrow \ddot{\mathscr{E}}^\star(\ddot{\mathcal{Y}}) \subseteq \ddot{\mathscr{E}}^\star(\mathcal{B})$,
(7) $\ddot{\mathscr{E}}^\star(\ddot{\mathcal{Y}} \cup \mathcal{B}) = \ddot{\mathscr{E}}^\star(\ddot{\mathcal{Y}}) \cup \ddot{\mathscr{E}}^\star(\mathcal{B})$,
(8) $\ddot{\mathscr{E}}^\star(\ddot{\mathcal{Y}} \cap \mathcal{B}) \subseteq \ddot{\mathscr{E}}^\star(\ddot{\mathcal{Y}}) \cup \ddot{\mathscr{E}}^\star(\mathcal{B})$.

The complement of $\ddot{\mathcal{Y}}$ is represented by $\sim \ddot{\mathcal{Y}}$.

Proof. (1) From Definition 19,

$$\begin{aligned}
\sim \ddot{\mathscr{E}}^\star(\sim \ddot{\mathscr{Y}}) &= \{(\ddot{\mathscr{D}}, \langle \ddot{\mathfrak{S}}_{\ddot{\mathscr{E}}^\star(\sim\ddot{\mathscr{Y}})}(\ddot{\mathscr{D}}), 1-\ddot{Z}_{\ddot{\mathscr{E}}^\star(\sim\ddot{\mathscr{Y}})}(\ddot{\mathscr{D}}), \ddot{T}_{\ddot{\mathscr{E}}^\star(\sim\ddot{\mathscr{Y}})}(\ddot{\mathscr{D}})\rangle, \langle \eta_{\ddot{\mathscr{E}}^\star(\sim\ddot{\mathscr{Y}})}(\ddot{\mathscr{D}}), \beta_{\ddot{\mathscr{E}}^\star(\sim\ddot{\mathscr{Y}})}(\ddot{\mathscr{D}}), \alpha_{\ddot{\mathscr{E}}^\star(\sim\ddot{\mathscr{Y}})}(\ddot{\mathscr{D}})\rangle) : \ddot{\mathscr{D}} \in \ddot{\mathcal{K}}\} \\
&= \{(\ddot{\mathscr{D}}, \langle \bigwedge_{\dot{\wp}\in\ddot{\mathcal{G}}} [(1-\ddot{\mathfrak{S}}_{\ddot{\mathscr{E}}}(\ddot{\mathscr{D}},\dot{\wp})) \vee \ddot{\mathfrak{S}}_{(\sim\ddot{\mathscr{Y}})}(\dot{\wp})], 1-\bigwedge_{\dot{\wp}\in\ddot{\mathcal{G}}} [(1-\ddot{Z}_{\ddot{\mathscr{E}}}(\ddot{\mathscr{D}},\dot{\wp})) \vee \ddot{Z}_{(\sim\ddot{\mathscr{Y}})}(\dot{\wp})], \bigvee_{\dot{\wp}\in\ddot{\mathcal{G}}} [\ddot{T}_{\ddot{\mathscr{E}}}(\ddot{\mathscr{D}},\dot{\wp}) \wedge \ddot{T}_{(\sim\ddot{\mathscr{Y}})}(\dot{\wp})]\rangle, \\
&\langle \bigwedge_{\dot{\wp}\in\ddot{\mathcal{G}}} [(\eta_{\ddot{\mathscr{E}}}(\ddot{\mathscr{D}},\dot{\wp})) \vee \eta_{(\sim\ddot{\mathscr{Y}})}(\dot{\wp})], \bigwedge_{\dot{\wp}\in\ddot{\mathcal{G}}} [(\beta_{\ddot{\mathscr{E}}}(\ddot{\mathscr{D}},\dot{\wp})) \vee \beta_{(\sim\ddot{\mathscr{Y}})}(\dot{\wp})], \bigvee_{\dot{\wp}\in\ddot{\mathcal{G}}} [\alpha_{\ddot{\mathscr{E}}}(\ddot{\mathscr{D}},\dot{\wp}) \wedge \alpha_{(\sim\ddot{\mathscr{Y}})}(\dot{\wp})]\rangle)\} \\
&= \{(\ddot{\mathscr{D}}, \langle \bigwedge_{\dot{\wp}\in\ddot{\mathcal{G}}} [(1-\ddot{T}_{\ddot{\mathscr{E}}}(\ddot{\mathscr{D}},\dot{\wp})) \vee \ddot{T}_{(\ddot{\mathscr{Y}})}(\dot{\wp})], \bigvee_{\dot{\wp}\in\ddot{\mathcal{G}}} [(\ddot{Z}_{\ddot{\mathscr{E}}}(\ddot{\mathscr{D}},\dot{\wp})) \vee \ddot{Z}_{(\ddot{\mathscr{Y}})}(\dot{\wp})], \bigvee_{\dot{\wp}\in\ddot{\mathcal{G}}} [\ddot{\mathfrak{S}}_{\ddot{\mathscr{E}}}(\ddot{\mathscr{D}},\dot{\wp}) \wedge \ddot{\mathfrak{S}}_{(\ddot{\mathscr{Y}})}(\dot{\wp})]\rangle, \\
&\langle \bigwedge_{\dot{\wp}\in\ddot{\mathcal{G}}} [(\alpha_{\ddot{\mathscr{E}}}(\ddot{\mathscr{D}},\dot{\wp})) \vee \alpha_{(\ddot{\mathscr{Y}})}(\dot{\wp})], \bigvee_{\dot{\wp}\in\ddot{\mathcal{G}}} [(\beta_{\ddot{\mathscr{E}}}(\ddot{\mathscr{D}},\dot{\wp})) \vee \beta_{(\ddot{\mathscr{Y}})}(\dot{\wp})], \bigvee_{\dot{\wp}\in\ddot{\mathcal{G}}} [\eta_{\ddot{\mathscr{E}}}(\ddot{\mathscr{D}},\dot{\wp}) \wedge \eta_{(\ddot{\mathscr{Y}})}(\dot{\wp})]\rangle)\} \\
&= \{(\ddot{\mathscr{D}}, \langle \ddot{T}_{\ddot{\mathscr{E}}_\star(\ddot{\mathscr{Y}})}(\ddot{\mathscr{D}}), \ddot{Z}_{\ddot{\mathscr{E}}_\star(\ddot{\mathscr{Y}})}(\ddot{\mathscr{D}}), \ddot{\mathfrak{S}}_{\ddot{\mathscr{E}}_\star(\ddot{\mathscr{Y}})}(\ddot{\mathscr{D}})\rangle, \langle \alpha_{\ddot{\mathscr{E}}_\star(\ddot{\mathscr{Y}})}(\ddot{\mathscr{D}}), \beta_{\ddot{\mathscr{E}}_\star(\ddot{\mathscr{Y}})}(\ddot{\mathscr{D}}), \eta_{\ddot{\mathscr{E}}_\star(\ddot{\mathscr{Y}})}(\ddot{\mathscr{D}})\rangle) : \ddot{\mathscr{D}} \in \ddot{\mathcal{K}}\}
\end{aligned}$$

(2) We can prove this by Definition 19.

(3) By Definition 19, we consider that

$$\begin{aligned}
\ddot{\mathscr{E}}_\star(\ddot{\mathscr{Y}} \cap \mathcal{B}) &= \{(\ddot{\mathscr{D}}, \langle \ddot{T}_{\ddot{\mathscr{E}}_\star(\ddot{\mathscr{Y}}\cap\mathcal{B})}(\ddot{\mathscr{D}}), \ddot{Z}_{\ddot{\mathscr{E}}_\star(\ddot{\mathscr{Y}}\cap\mathcal{B})}(\ddot{\mathscr{D}}), \ddot{\mathfrak{S}}_{\ddot{\mathscr{E}}_\star(\ddot{\mathscr{Y}}\cap\mathcal{B})}(\ddot{\mathscr{D}})\rangle, \langle \alpha_{\ddot{\mathscr{E}}_\star(\ddot{\mathscr{Y}}\cap\mathcal{B})}(\ddot{\mathscr{D}}), \beta_{\ddot{\mathscr{E}}_\star(\ddot{\mathscr{Y}}\cap\mathcal{B})}(\ddot{\mathscr{D}}), \eta_{\ddot{\mathscr{E}}_\star(\ddot{\mathscr{Y}}\cap\mathcal{B})}(\ddot{\mathscr{D}})\rangle) : \ddot{\mathscr{D}} \in \ddot{\mathcal{K}}\} \\
&= \{(\ddot{\mathscr{D}}, \langle \bigwedge_{\dot{\wp}\in\ddot{\mathcal{G}}} [(1-\ddot{T}_{\ddot{\mathscr{E}}}(\ddot{\mathscr{D}},\dot{\wp})) \vee \ddot{T}_{(\ddot{\mathscr{Y}}\cap\mathcal{B})}(\dot{\wp})], \bigvee_{\dot{\wp}\in\ddot{\mathcal{G}}} [\ddot{Z}_{\ddot{\mathscr{E}}}(\ddot{\mathscr{D}},\dot{\wp}) \wedge \ddot{Z}_{(\ddot{\mathscr{Y}}\cap\mathcal{B})}(\dot{\wp})], \bigvee_{\dot{\wp}\in\ddot{\mathcal{G}}} [\ddot{\mathfrak{S}}_{\ddot{\mathscr{E}}}(\ddot{\mathscr{D}},\dot{\wp}) \wedge \ddot{\mathfrak{S}}_{(\ddot{\mathscr{Y}}\cap\mathcal{B})}(\dot{\wp})]\rangle, \\
&\langle \bigwedge_{\dot{\wp}\in\ddot{\mathcal{G}}} [(\alpha_{\ddot{\mathscr{E}}}(\ddot{\mathscr{D}},\dot{\wp})) \vee \alpha_{(\ddot{\mathscr{Y}}\cap\mathcal{B})}(\dot{\wp})], \bigvee_{\dot{\wp}\in\ddot{\mathcal{G}}} [\beta_{\ddot{\mathscr{E}}}(\ddot{\mathscr{D}},\dot{\wp}) \wedge \beta_{(\ddot{\mathscr{Y}}\cap\mathcal{B})}(\dot{\wp})], \bigvee_{\dot{\wp}\in\ddot{\mathcal{G}}} [\eta_{\ddot{\mathscr{E}}}(\ddot{\mathscr{D}},\dot{\wp}) \wedge \eta_{(\ddot{\mathscr{Y}}\cap\mathcal{B})}(\dot{\wp})]\rangle)\} \\
&= \{(\ddot{\mathscr{D}}, \langle \bigwedge_{\dot{\wp}\in\ddot{\mathcal{G}}} [(1-\ddot{T}_{\ddot{\mathscr{E}}}(\ddot{\mathscr{D}},\dot{\wp})) \vee (\ddot{T}_{\mathcal{Y}}(\dot{\wp}) \wedge \ddot{T}_{\mathcal{B}}(\dot{\wp}))], \bigvee_{\dot{\wp}\in\ddot{\mathcal{G}}} [\ddot{Z}_{\ddot{\mathscr{E}}}(\ddot{\mathscr{D}},\dot{\wp}) \wedge (\ddot{Z}_{\mathcal{Y}}(\dot{\wp}) \vee \ddot{Z}_{\mathcal{B}}(\dot{\wp}))], \\
&\bigvee_{\dot{\wp}\in\ddot{\mathcal{G}}} [\ddot{\mathfrak{S}}_{\ddot{\mathscr{E}}}(\ddot{\mathscr{D}},\dot{\wp}) \wedge (\ddot{\mathfrak{S}}_{\mathcal{Y}}(\dot{\wp}) \vee \ddot{\mathfrak{S}}_{\mathcal{B}}(\dot{\wp}))]\rangle, \langle \bigwedge_{\dot{\wp}\in\ddot{\mathcal{G}}} [(\alpha_{\ddot{\mathscr{E}}}(\ddot{\mathscr{D}},\dot{\wp})) \vee (\alpha_{\mathcal{Y}}(\dot{\wp}) \wedge \alpha_{\mathcal{B}}(\dot{\wp}))], \\
&\bigvee_{\dot{\wp}\in\ddot{\mathcal{G}}} [\beta_{\ddot{\mathscr{E}}}(\ddot{\mathscr{D}},\dot{\wp}) \wedge (\beta_{\mathcal{Y}}(\dot{\wp}) \vee \beta_{\mathcal{B}}(\dot{\wp}))], \bigvee_{\dot{\wp}\in\ddot{\mathcal{G}}} [\eta_{\ddot{\mathscr{E}}}(\ddot{\mathscr{D}},\dot{\wp}) \wedge (\eta_{\mathcal{Y}}(\dot{\wp}) \vee \eta_{\mathcal{B}}(\dot{\wp}))]\rangle)\} \\
&= \{(\ddot{\mathscr{D}}, \langle (\ddot{T}_{\ddot{\mathscr{E}}_\star(\mathcal{Y})}(\ddot{\mathscr{D}}) \wedge \ddot{T}_{\ddot{\mathscr{E}}_\star(\mathcal{B})}(\ddot{\mathscr{D}})), (\ddot{Z}_{\ddot{\mathscr{E}}_\star(\mathcal{Y})}(\ddot{\mathscr{D}}) \vee \ddot{Z}_{\ddot{\mathscr{E}}_\star(\mathcal{B})}(\ddot{\mathscr{D}})), (\ddot{\mathfrak{S}}_{\ddot{\mathscr{E}}_\star(\mathcal{Y})}(\ddot{\mathscr{D}}) \vee \ddot{\mathfrak{S}}_{\ddot{\mathscr{E}}_\star(\mathcal{B})}(\ddot{\mathscr{D}}))\rangle, \\
&\langle (\alpha_{\ddot{\mathscr{E}}_\star(\mathcal{Y})}(\ddot{\mathscr{D}}) \wedge \alpha_{\ddot{\mathscr{E}}_\star(\mathcal{B})}(\ddot{\mathscr{D}})), (\beta_{\ddot{\mathscr{E}}_\star(\mathcal{Y})}(\ddot{\mathscr{D}}) \vee \beta_{\ddot{\mathscr{E}}_\star(\mathcal{B})}(\ddot{\mathscr{D}})), (\eta_{\ddot{\mathscr{E}}_\star(\mathcal{Y})}(\ddot{\mathscr{D}}) \vee \eta_{\ddot{\mathscr{E}}_\star(\mathcal{B})}(\ddot{\mathscr{D}}))\rangle) : \ddot{\mathscr{D}} \in \ddot{\mathcal{K}}\} \\
&= \ddot{\mathscr{E}}_\star(\ddot{\mathscr{Y}}) \cap \ddot{\mathscr{E}}_\star(\mathcal{B})
\end{aligned}$$

(4) By following the Definition 19, we can write that

$$\begin{aligned}
\ddot{\mathscr{E}}_\star(\ddot{\mathscr{Y}} \cup \mathcal{B}) &= \{(\ddot{\mathscr{D}}, \langle \ddot{T}_{\ddot{\mathscr{E}}_\star(\ddot{\mathscr{Y}}\cup\mathcal{B})}(\ddot{\mathscr{D}}), \ddot{Z}_{\ddot{\mathscr{E}}_\star(\ddot{\mathscr{Y}}\cup\mathcal{B})}(\ddot{\mathscr{D}}), \ddot{\mathfrak{S}}_{\ddot{\mathscr{E}}_\star(\ddot{\mathscr{Y}}\cup\mathcal{B})}(\ddot{\mathscr{D}})\rangle, \langle \alpha_{\ddot{\mathscr{E}}_\star(\ddot{\mathscr{Y}}\cup\mathcal{B})}(\ddot{\mathscr{D}}), \beta_{\ddot{\mathscr{E}}_\star(\ddot{\mathscr{Y}}\cup\mathcal{B})}(\ddot{\mathscr{D}}), \eta_{\ddot{\mathscr{E}}_\star(\ddot{\mathscr{Y}}\cup\mathcal{B})}(\ddot{\mathscr{D}})\rangle) : \ddot{\mathscr{D}} \in \ddot{\mathcal{K}}\} \\
&= \{(\ddot{\mathscr{D}}, \langle \bigwedge_{\dot{\wp}\in\ddot{\mathcal{G}}} [(1-\ddot{T}_{\ddot{\mathscr{E}}}(\ddot{\mathscr{D}},\dot{\wp})) \vee \ddot{T}_{(\ddot{\mathscr{Y}}\cup\mathcal{B})}(\dot{\wp})], \bigvee_{\dot{\wp}\in\ddot{\mathcal{G}}} [\ddot{Z}_{\ddot{\mathscr{E}}}(\ddot{\mathscr{D}},\dot{\wp}) \wedge \ddot{Z}_{(\ddot{\mathscr{Y}}\cup\mathcal{B})}(\dot{\wp})], \bigvee_{\dot{\wp}\in\ddot{\mathcal{G}}} [\ddot{\mathfrak{S}}_{\ddot{\mathscr{E}}}(\ddot{\mathscr{D}},\dot{\wp}) \wedge \ddot{\mathfrak{S}}_{(\ddot{\mathscr{Y}}\cup\mathcal{B})}(\dot{\wp})]\rangle, \\
&\langle \bigwedge_{\dot{\wp}\in\ddot{\mathcal{G}}} [(\alpha_{\ddot{\mathscr{E}}}(\ddot{\mathscr{D}},\dot{\wp})) \vee \alpha_{(\ddot{\mathscr{Y}}\cup\mathcal{B})}(\dot{\wp})], \bigvee_{\dot{\wp}\in\ddot{\mathcal{G}}} [\beta_{\ddot{\mathscr{E}}}(\ddot{\mathscr{D}},\dot{\wp}) \wedge \beta_{(\ddot{\mathscr{Y}}\cup\mathcal{B})}(\dot{\wp})], \bigvee_{\dot{\wp}\in\ddot{\mathcal{G}}} [\eta_{\ddot{\mathscr{E}}}(\ddot{\mathscr{D}},\dot{\wp}) \wedge \eta_{(\ddot{\mathscr{Y}}\cup\mathcal{B})}(\dot{\wp})]\rangle)\} \\
&\supseteq \{(\ddot{\mathscr{D}}, \langle \bigwedge_{\dot{\wp}\in\ddot{\mathcal{G}}} [(1-\ddot{T}_{\ddot{\mathscr{E}}}(\ddot{\mathscr{D}},\dot{\wp})) \vee (\ddot{T}_{\mathcal{Y}}(\dot{\wp}) \vee \ddot{T}_{\mathcal{B}}(\dot{\wp}))], \bigvee_{\dot{\wp}\in\ddot{\mathcal{G}}} [\ddot{Z}_{\ddot{\mathscr{E}}}(\ddot{\mathscr{D}},\dot{\wp}) \wedge (\ddot{Z}_{\mathcal{Y}}(\dot{\wp}) \wedge \ddot{Z}_{\mathcal{B}}(\dot{\wp}))], \\
&\bigvee_{\dot{\wp}\in\ddot{\mathcal{G}}} [\ddot{\mathfrak{S}}_{\ddot{\mathscr{E}}}(\ddot{\mathscr{D}},\dot{\wp}) \wedge (\ddot{\mathfrak{S}}_{\mathcal{Y}}(\dot{\wp}) \wedge \ddot{\mathfrak{S}}_{\mathcal{B}}(\dot{\wp}))]\rangle, \langle \bigwedge_{\dot{\wp}\in\ddot{\mathcal{G}}} [(\alpha_{\ddot{\mathscr{E}}}(\ddot{\mathscr{D}},\dot{\wp})) \vee (\alpha_{\mathcal{Y}}(\dot{\wp}) \vee \alpha_{\mathcal{B}}(\dot{\wp}))], \\
&\bigvee_{\dot{\wp}\in\ddot{\mathcal{G}}} [\beta_{\ddot{\mathscr{E}}}(\ddot{\mathscr{D}},\dot{\wp}) \wedge (\beta_{\mathcal{Y}}(\dot{\wp}) \wedge \beta_{\mathcal{B}}(\dot{\wp}))], \bigvee_{\dot{\wp}\in\ddot{\mathcal{G}}} [\eta_{\ddot{\mathscr{E}}}(\ddot{\mathscr{D}},\dot{\wp}) \wedge (\eta_{\mathcal{Y}}(\dot{\wp}) \wedge \beta_{\mathcal{B}}(\dot{\wp}))]\rangle)\} \\
&= \{(\ddot{\mathscr{D}}, \langle (\ddot{T}_{\ddot{\mathscr{E}}_\star(\mathcal{Y})}(\ddot{\mathscr{D}}) \vee \ddot{T}_{\ddot{\mathscr{E}}_\star(\mathcal{B})}(\ddot{\mathscr{D}})), (\ddot{Z}_{\ddot{\mathscr{E}}_\star(\mathcal{Y})}(\ddot{\mathscr{D}}) \wedge \ddot{Z}_{\ddot{\mathscr{E}}_\star(\mathcal{B})}(\ddot{\mathscr{D}})), (\ddot{\mathfrak{S}}_{\ddot{\mathscr{E}}_\star(\mathcal{Y})}(\ddot{\mathscr{D}}) \wedge \ddot{\mathfrak{S}}_{\ddot{\mathscr{E}}_\star(\mathcal{B})}(\ddot{\mathscr{D}}))\rangle, \\
&\langle (\alpha_{\ddot{\mathscr{E}}_\star(\mathcal{Y})}(\ddot{\mathscr{D}}) \vee \alpha_{\ddot{\mathscr{E}}_\star(\mathcal{B})}(\ddot{\mathscr{D}})), (\beta_{\ddot{\mathscr{E}}_\star(\mathcal{Y})}(\ddot{\mathscr{D}}) \wedge \beta_{\ddot{\mathscr{E}}_\star(\mathcal{B})}(\ddot{\mathscr{D}})), (\eta_{\ddot{\mathscr{E}}_\star(\mathcal{Y})}(\ddot{\mathscr{D}}) \wedge \eta_{\ddot{\mathscr{E}}_\star(\mathcal{B})}(\ddot{\mathscr{D}}))\rangle) : \ddot{\mathscr{D}} \in \ddot{\mathcal{K}}\} \\
&= \ddot{\mathscr{E}}_\star(\ddot{\mathscr{Y}}) \cup \ddot{\mathscr{E}}_\star(\mathcal{B})
\end{aligned}$$

Thus $\ddot{\mathscr{E}}_\star(\ddot{\mathscr{Y}} \cup \mathcal{B}) \supseteq \ddot{\mathscr{E}}_\star(\ddot{\mathscr{Y}}) \cup \ddot{\mathscr{E}}_\star(\mathcal{B})$.

The other axioms follows similar way. □

Proposition 3. *For arbitrary* $\ddot{\mathcal{Y}}, \mathcal{B} \in SLDFS(\mathcal{G})$, *the upper and lower approximation operators* $\ddot{\mathscr{E}}_{\star}(\ddot{\mathcal{Y}}), \ddot{\mathscr{E}}_{\star}(\mathcal{B}), \ddot{\mathscr{E}}^{\star}(\ddot{\mathcal{Y}})$ *and* $\ddot{\mathscr{E}}^{\star}(\mathcal{B})$ *on SLDFS-approximation space* $(\breve{\mathcal{K}}, \ddot{\mathcal{G}}, \ddot{\mathscr{E}})$ *satisfy the following axioms:*

(1) $\sim(\ddot{\mathscr{E}}_{\star}(\ddot{\mathcal{Y}}) \cup \ddot{\mathscr{E}}_{\star}(\mathcal{B})) = \ddot{\mathscr{E}}^{\star}(\sim \ddot{\mathcal{Y}}) \cap \ddot{\mathscr{E}}^{\star}(\sim \mathcal{B})$,
(2) $\sim(\ddot{\mathscr{E}}_{\star}(\ddot{\mathcal{Y}}) \cup \ddot{\mathscr{E}}^{\star}(\mathcal{B})) = \ddot{\mathscr{E}}^{\star}(\sim \ddot{\mathcal{Y}}) \cap \ddot{\mathscr{E}}_{\star}(\sim \mathcal{B})$,
(3) $\sim(\ddot{\mathscr{E}}^{\star}(\ddot{\mathcal{Y}}) \cup \ddot{\mathscr{E}}_{\star}(\mathcal{B})) = \ddot{\mathscr{E}}_{\star}(\sim \ddot{\mathcal{Y}}) \cap \ddot{\mathscr{E}}^{\star}(\sim \mathcal{B})$,
(4) $\sim(\ddot{\mathscr{E}}^{\star}(\ddot{\mathcal{Y}}) \cup \ddot{\mathscr{E}}^{\star}(\mathcal{B})) = \ddot{\mathscr{E}}_{\star}(\sim \ddot{\mathcal{Y}}) \cap \ddot{\mathscr{E}}_{\star}(\sim \mathcal{B})$,
(5) $\sim(\ddot{\mathscr{E}}_{\star}(\ddot{\mathcal{Y}}) \cap \ddot{\mathscr{E}}_{\star}(\mathcal{B})) = \ddot{\mathscr{E}}^{\star}(\sim \ddot{\mathcal{Y}}) \cup \ddot{\mathscr{E}}^{\star}(\sim \mathcal{B})$,
(6) $\sim(\ddot{\mathscr{E}}_{\star}(\ddot{\mathcal{Y}}) \cap \ddot{\mathscr{E}}^{\star}(\mathcal{B})) = \ddot{\mathscr{E}}^{\star}(\sim \ddot{\mathcal{Y}}) \cup \ddot{\mathscr{E}}_{\star}(\sim \mathcal{B})$,
(7) $\sim(\ddot{\mathscr{E}}^{\star}(\ddot{\mathcal{Y}}) \cap \ddot{\mathscr{E}}_{\star}(\mathcal{B})) = \ddot{\mathscr{E}}_{\star}(\sim \ddot{\mathcal{Y}}) \cup \ddot{\mathscr{E}}^{\star}(\sim \mathcal{B})$,
(8) $\sim(\ddot{\mathscr{E}}^{\star}(\ddot{\mathcal{Y}}) \cap \ddot{\mathscr{E}}^{\star}(\mathcal{B})) = \ddot{\mathscr{E}}_{\star}(\sim \ddot{\mathcal{Y}}) \cup \ddot{\mathscr{E}}_{\star}(\sim \mathcal{B})$.

Proof. Proof is obvious. □

Theorem 2. *For SLDFS-approximation space* $(\breve{\mathcal{K}}, \mathcal{G}, \ddot{\mathscr{E}})$, *if* $\ddot{\mathscr{E}}$ *is serial, then* $\ddot{\mathscr{E}}_{\star}(\ddot{\mathcal{Y}})$ *and* $\ddot{\mathscr{E}}^{\star}(\ddot{\mathcal{Y}})$ *satisfy the following:*

(1) $\ddot{\mathscr{E}}_{\star}(\varnothing) = \varnothing, \ddot{\mathscr{E}}^{\star}(\ddot{\mathcal{G}}) = \ddot{\mathcal{G}}$,
(2) $\ddot{\mathscr{E}}_{\star}(\ddot{\mathcal{Y}}) \subseteq \ddot{\mathscr{E}}^{\star}(\ddot{\mathcal{Y}}), \ \forall \ \ddot{\mathcal{Y}} \in SLDFS(\mathcal{G})$.

Proof. Proof is obvious by following Definition 19. □

Definition 20. *Let* $\ddot{\mathcal{Y}} \in SLDFS(\breve{\mathcal{K}})$ *and let* $\ddot{\mathscr{E}}_{\star}(\ddot{\mathcal{Y}}), \ddot{\mathscr{E}}^{\star}(\ddot{\mathcal{Y}})$ *are lower and upper SLDFSR-approximation operators. Then ring sum operation of* $\ddot{\mathscr{E}}_{\star}(\ddot{\mathcal{Y}})$ *and* $\ddot{\mathscr{E}}^{\star}(\ddot{\mathcal{Y}})$ *is scripted as*

$$\begin{aligned}
\ddot{\mathscr{E}}_{\star}(\ddot{\mathcal{Y}}) \oplus \ddot{\mathscr{E}}^{\star}(\ddot{\mathcal{Y}}) = \{(\ddot{\mathscr{D}}, \langle \ddot{T}_{\ddot{\mathscr{E}}_{\star}(\ddot{\mathcal{Y}})}(\ddot{\mathscr{D}}) + \ddot{T}_{\ddot{\mathscr{E}}^{\star}(\ddot{\mathcal{Y}})}(\ddot{\mathscr{D}}) - (\ddot{T}_{\ddot{\mathscr{E}}_{\star}(\ddot{\mathcal{Y}})}(\ddot{\mathscr{D}}) \times \ddot{T}_{\ddot{\mathscr{E}}^{\star}(\ddot{\mathcal{Y}})}(\ddot{\mathscr{D}})), \ddot{Z}_{\ddot{\mathscr{E}}_{\star}(\ddot{\mathcal{Y}})}(\ddot{\mathscr{D}}) \times \ddot{Z}_{\ddot{\mathscr{E}}^{\star}(\ddot{\mathcal{Y}})}(\ddot{\mathscr{D}}), \\
\ddot{\mathfrak{S}}_{\ddot{\mathscr{E}}_{\star}(\ddot{\mathcal{Y}})}(\ddot{\mathscr{D}}) \times \ddot{\mathfrak{S}}_{\ddot{\mathscr{E}}^{\star}(\ddot{\mathcal{Y}})}(\ddot{\mathscr{D}}) \rangle, \langle 1 - (1 - \alpha_{\ddot{\mathscr{E}}_{\star}(\ddot{\mathcal{Y}})}(\ddot{\mathscr{D}}))(1 - \alpha_{\ddot{\mathscr{E}}^{\star}(\ddot{\mathcal{Y}})}(\ddot{\mathscr{D}})), \beta_{\ddot{\mathscr{E}}_{\star}(\ddot{\mathcal{Y}})}(\ddot{\mathscr{D}}) \times \beta_{\ddot{\mathscr{E}}^{\star}(\ddot{\mathcal{Y}})}(\ddot{\mathscr{D}}), \\
(\eta_{\ddot{\mathscr{E}}_{\star}(\ddot{\mathcal{Y}})}(\ddot{\mathscr{D}}) + \beta_{\ddot{\mathscr{E}}_{\star}(\ddot{\mathcal{Y}})}(\ddot{\mathscr{D}}))(\eta_{\ddot{\mathscr{E}}^{\star}(\ddot{\mathcal{Y}})}(\ddot{\mathscr{D}}) + \beta_{\ddot{\mathscr{E}}^{\star}(\ddot{\mathcal{Y}})}(\ddot{\mathscr{D}})) - \beta_{\ddot{\mathscr{E}}_{\star}(\ddot{\mathcal{Y}})}(\ddot{\mathscr{D}}) \times \beta_{\ddot{\mathscr{E}}^{\star}(\ddot{\mathcal{Y}})}(\ddot{\mathscr{D}}) \rangle) : \ddot{\mathscr{D}} \in \breve{\mathcal{K}}\}
\end{aligned}$$

6. Application of SLDFSRSs towards the Selection of Appropriate Clean Energy Technology

Ocean energy, biomass energy, wind energy, geothermal energy, and hydropower energy are all examples of clean energy technologies. These innovations are massive and are used to provide energy to the entire globe. In this section, we present an application that uses SLDFSRSs to select the most reliable and appropriate clean energy technology. We intended to develop two new algorithms.

6.1. Numerical Example

We suppose that a country wants to initiate an appropriate clean energy technology program for the development and to reach the industrial and social needs. They set a committee consisting on some energy and economical experts to construct a list of some clean energy technologies systems. The board of committee construct the set of feasible elements given as $\breve{\mathcal{K}} = \{\ddot{\mathscr{D}}_1, \ddot{\mathscr{D}}_2, \ddot{\mathscr{D}}_3, \ddot{\mathscr{D}}_4, \ddot{\mathscr{D}}_5, \ddot{\mathscr{D}}_6\}$, where

$\ddot{\mathscr{D}}_1 =$ "Wave power plant",
$\ddot{\mathscr{D}}_2 =$ "Solar power plant",
$\ddot{\mathscr{D}}_3 =$ "Biomass power plant",
$\ddot{\mathscr{D}}_4 =$ "hydro power plant",
$\ddot{\mathscr{D}}_4 =$ "Geothermal power plant",
$\ddot{\mathscr{D}}_4 =$ "Wind power plant".

Let $\ddot{\mathcal{G}} = \{\wp_1, \wp_2, \wp_3, \wp_4\}$ be the set of attributes or decision parameters, where

$\wp_1$ = "Environmental: pollutant emission, land requirement, requirement for waste disposal",
$\wp_2$ = "Socio-political: Government policy, labor impact, social acceptance",
$\wp_3$ = "Economic: implementation cost, economic value, affordability",
$\wp_4$ = "Technological and quality of energy resource: continuity and predictability of the performance, risk, local technical knowledge, sustainability, durability".

The sub-criterion for attributes can be further categorized as follows:

- "Environmental: pollutant emission, land requirement, requirement for waste disposal" means that the alternative is "friendly", "average" or may be "not-friendly" for the environment.
- "Socio-political: Government policy, labor impact, social acceptance" means that the alternative has "maximum", "average" or "minimum" acceptance.
- "Economic: implementation cost, economic value, affordability" means that the alternative is "expensive", "affordable" or may be "cheap".
- "Technological and quality of energy resource: continuity and predictability of the performance risk, local technical knowledge, sustainability, durability" means that the alternative is "highly", "medium" or may be "low" technical.

The tabular representation of these sub-criteria can be seen in Table 6.

Table 6. characteristics of selected decision variables.

Decision Variables	Characteristics for SLDFSR
Environmental: land requirement, pollutant emission, requirement for waste disposal	$(\langle \text{membership, abstinence, non-membership} \rangle, \langle \text{friendly, average, not-friendly} \rangle)$
Socio-political: Government policy, social acceptance, labor impact	$(\langle \text{membership, abstinence, non-membership} \rangle, \langle \text{maximum, average, minimum} \rangle)$
Economic: implementation cost, economic value, affordability	$(\langle \text{membership, abstinence, non-membership} \rangle, \langle \text{expensive, affordable, cheap} \rangle)$
Technological and quality of energy resource: continuity and predictability of the performance risk, sustainability, local technical knowledge, durability	$(\langle \text{membership, abstinence, non-membership} \rangle, \langle \text{high, medium, low} \rangle)$

We proposed two new algorithms (Algorithms 1 and 2) by using SLDFSRSs for the selection of best clean energy technology. The graphical view of both algorithms is given in Figure 11.

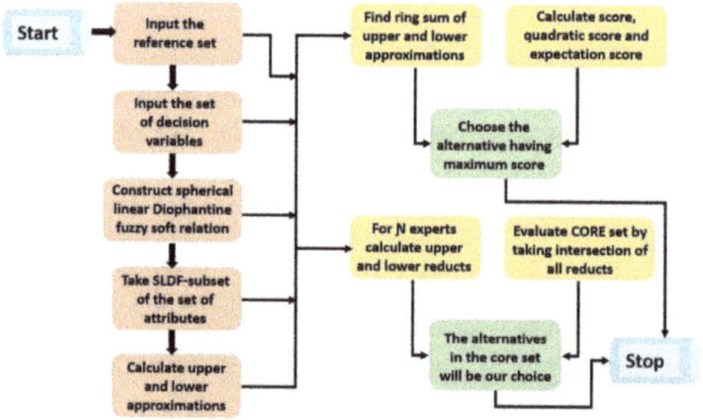

Figure 11. Flow chart diagram of Algorithms 1 and 2.

Algorithm 1 Selection of a best clean energy technology by using SLDFSRSs

Input:
1. Consider $\ddot{\mathcal{K}}$ as an initial universe.
2. Consider $\ddot{\mathcal{G}}$ as a set of attributes.

Construction:
3. Executing the efficiency of DMs, build a SLDFSR $\ddot{\mathscr{E}} : \ddot{\mathcal{K}} \to \ddot{\mathcal{G}}$.
4. Compute SLDF-subset $\mathcal{B}$ of $\ddot{\mathcal{G}}$ as an optimal normal decision set.

Calculation:
5. Find the SLDFSR-approximation operators $\ddot{\mathscr{E}}_{\star}(\mathcal{B})$ and $\ddot{\mathscr{E}}^{\star}(\mathcal{B})$ as lower and upper approximations with the help of Definition 19.
6. Find the ring sum $\ddot{\mathscr{E}}_{\star}(\mathcal{B}) \oplus \ddot{\mathscr{E}}^{\star}(\mathcal{B})$ and the choice SLDFS.

Output:
7. By using Definitions 10, 12, 14, calculate score, quadratic score and expectation score of every alternative in $\ddot{\mathscr{E}}_{\star}(\mathcal{B}) \oplus \ddot{\mathscr{E}}^{\star}(\mathcal{B})$.
8. By using Definition 16, find the ranking of alternatives.

Final decision:
9. An alternative with highest score function value is the required optimal alternative.

Algorithm 2 Selection of a best clean energy technology by using SLDFSRSs

Input:
1. Consider $\ddot{\mathcal{K}}$ as a universe of discourse.
2. Consider $\ddot{\mathcal{G}}$ as a set of attributes.

Construction:
3. Executing the efficiency of DMs, construct a SLDFSR $\ddot{\mathscr{E}} : \ddot{\mathcal{K}} \to \ddot{\mathcal{G}}$.
4. Find SLDF-subset $\mathcal{B}$ of $\ddot{\mathcal{G}}$ as an optimal normal decision set.

Calculation:
5. Find the SLDFSR-approximation operators $\ddot{\mathscr{E}}_{\star}(\mathcal{B})$ and $\ddot{\mathscr{E}}^{\star}(\mathcal{B})$ as lower and upper approximations by using Definition 19.
6. For "$\mathscr{N}$" number of experts, estimate upper and lower reducts, respectively.

Output:
7. Form calculated "$2\mathscr{N}$" reducts, we get "$2\mathscr{N}$" crisp subsets of the reference set $\ddot{\mathcal{K}}$. The subsets can be constructed by using the "YES" and "NO" logic. Then "YES" gives the optimal object.
8. Find the core by calculating the intersection of all reducts.

Final decision:
9. An alternative with highest score function value is the required optimal alternative.

6.1.1. Calculations by Algorithm 1

According to the environment of land and considering some important factors, the experts of committee give their preferences to the alternatives corresponding to the selected criteria. The verbal information can be converted into the SLDFNs by using linguistic term logic. The indiscernibility relation is "the selection of best clean energy technology". This relation can be observed by SLDFSR, $\ddot{\mathscr{E}} : \ddot{\mathcal{K}} \to \ddot{\mathcal{G}}$ given as Table 7.

Thus $\ddot{\mathscr{E}}$ be a SLDFSR on $\ddot{\mathcal{K}} \times \ddot{\mathcal{G}}$. This relation gives us the numeric values in the form of SLDFNs of each alternative corresponding to every decision variable. For example, for the alternative $\ddot{\mathscr{D}}_1$ the decision variable $\wp_1$ ("Environmental: pollutant emission, land requirement, requirement for waste disposal") has numeric value $(\langle 0.738, 0.381.0.421\rangle, \langle 0.431, 0.211, 0.178\rangle)$. This value shows that the alternative $\ddot{\mathscr{D}}_1$ is 73.8% suitable for the environment, 38.1% is abstinence and 42.1% is its falsity value. The triplet $\langle 0.431, 0.211, 0.178\rangle$ represents the reference parameters for the satisfaction, abstinence and dissatisfaction grades, where we can observe that alternative $\ddot{\mathscr{D}}_1$ is 43.1% friendly, 21.1% average and 17.8% is not friendly for environment.

Table 7. SLDFSR.

$\ddot{\mathscr{E}}$	SLDFNs	SLDFNs
$\ddot{\mathscr{D}}_1$	$\wp_1 : (\langle 0.738, 0.381, 0.421\rangle, \langle 0.431, 0.211, 0.178\rangle)$ $\wp_3 : (\langle 0.652, 0.456, 0.531\rangle, \langle 0.317, 0.312, 0.217\rangle)$ $\wp_5 : (\langle 0.731, 0.457, 0.431\rangle, \langle 0.412, 0.213, 0.118\rangle)$	$\wp_2 : (\langle 0.631, 0.521, 0.438\rangle, \langle 0.318, 0.214, 0.314\rangle)$ $\wp_4 : (\langle 0.748, 0.638, 0.456\rangle, \langle 0.217, 0.318, 0.231\rangle)$
$\ddot{\mathscr{D}}_2$	$\wp_1 : (\langle 0.218, 0.891, 0.731\rangle, \langle 0.117, 0.213, 0.417\rangle)$ $\wp_3 : (\langle 0.117, 0.687, 0.734\rangle, \langle 0.121, 0.238, 0.247\rangle)$ $\wp_5 : (\langle 0.231, 0.891, 0.896\rangle, \langle 0.213, 0.378, 0.312\rangle)$	$\wp_2 : (\langle 0.231, 0.873, 0.731\rangle, \langle 0.213, 0.317, 0.319\rangle)$ $\wp_4 : (\langle 0.218, 0.787, 0.634\rangle, \langle 0.118, 0.413, 0.312\rangle)$
$\ddot{\mathscr{D}}_3$	$\wp_1 : (\langle 0.456, 0.431, 0.567\rangle, \langle 0.238, 0.241, 0.268\rangle)$ $\wp_3 : (\langle 0.451, 0.532, 0.511\rangle, \langle 0.241, 0.238, 0.211\rangle)$ $\wp_5 : (\langle 0.548, 0.471, 0.436\rangle, \langle 0.247, 0.253, 0.261\rangle)$	$\wp_2 : (\langle 0.576, 0.513, 0.417\rangle, \langle 0.238, 0.241, 0.273\rangle)$ $\wp_4 : (\langle 0.518, 0.417, 0.519\rangle, \langle 0.311, 0.217, 0.218\rangle)$
$\ddot{\mathscr{D}}_4$	$\wp_1 : (\langle 0.731, 0.341, 0.421\rangle, \langle 0.238, 0.347, 0.238\rangle)$ $\wp_3 : (\langle 0.643, 0.456, 0.321\rangle, \langle 0.311, 0.213, 0.238\rangle)$ $\wp_5 : (\langle 0.638, 0.411, 0.311\rangle, \langle 0.213, 0.217, 0.231\rangle)$	$\wp_2 : (\langle 0.678, 0.431, 0.373\rangle, \langle 0.341, 0.231, 0.241\rangle)$ $\wp_4 : (\langle 0.731, 0.431, 0.321\rangle, \langle 0.343, 0.231, 0.211\rangle)$
$\ddot{\mathscr{D}}_5$	$\wp_1 : (\langle 0.917, 0.211, 0.118\rangle, \langle 0.421, 0.117, 0.115\rangle)$ $\wp_3 : (\langle 0.915, 0.113, 0.114\rangle, \langle 0.631, 0.113, 0.112\rangle)$ $\wp_5 : (\langle 0.999, 0.112, 0.121\rangle, \langle 0.711, 0.113, 0.112\rangle)$	$\wp_2 : (\langle 0.998, 0.321, 0.211\rangle, \langle 0.537, 0.117, 0.113\rangle)$ $\wp_4 : (\langle 0.912, 0.321, 0.211\rangle, \langle 0.541, 0.211, 0.114\rangle)$
$\ddot{\mathscr{D}}_6$	$\wp_1 : (\langle 0.513, 0.538, 0.641\rangle, \langle 0.213, 0.341, 0.347\rangle)$ $\wp_3 : (\langle 0.613, 0.438, 0.541\rangle, \langle 0.217, 0.343, 0.331\rangle)$ $\wp_5 : (\langle 0.438, 0.561, 0.437\rangle, \langle 0.321, 0.218, 0.117\rangle)$	$\wp_2 : (\langle 0.432, 0.546, 0.538\rangle, \langle 0.341, 0.348, 0.211\rangle)$ $\wp_4 : (\langle 0.447, 0.577, 0.589\rangle, \langle 0.331, 0.238, 0.341\rangle)$

The set $\mathcal{B}$ is SLDF-subset of $\ddot{\mathcal{G}}$ and scripted as follows

$$\begin{aligned}\mathcal{B} = \{&(\wp_1, \langle 0.738, 0.421, 0.337\rangle, \langle 0.421, 0.213, 0.318\rangle), (\wp_2, \langle 0.918, 0.211, 0.238\rangle, \langle 0.631, 0.113, 0.117\rangle),\\ &(\wp_3, \langle 0.213, 0.891, 0.793\rangle, \langle 0.117, 0.438, 0.321\rangle), (\wp_4, \langle 0.541, 0.538, 0.477\rangle, \langle 0.218, 0.347, 0.321\rangle),\\ &(\wp_5, \langle 0.638, 0.432, 0.337\rangle, \langle 0.321, 0.211, 0.118\rangle)\}.\end{aligned}$$

The lower and upper approximations of LDFS $\mathcal{B}$ on LDFSR $\ddot{\mathscr{E}}$ are as follows.

$$\begin{aligned}\ddot{\mathscr{E}}^{\star}(\mathcal{B}) = \{&(\ddot{\mathscr{D}}_1, \langle 0.738, 0.421, 0.337\rangle, \langle 0.421, 0.213, 0.118\rangle), (\ddot{\mathscr{D}}_2, \langle 0.231, 0.211, 0.269\rangle, \langle 0.213, 0.213, 0.312\rangle),\\ &(\ddot{\mathscr{D}}_3, \langle 0.576, 0.487, 0.433\rangle, \langle 0.247, 0.241, 0.261\rangle), (\ddot{\mathscr{D}}_4, \langle 0.731, 0.569, 0.579\rangle, \langle 0.341, 0.217, 0.231\rangle),\\ &(\ddot{\mathscr{D}}_5, \langle 0.918, 0.679, 0.789\rangle, \langle 0.537, 0.117, 0.117\rangle, (\ddot{\mathscr{D}}_6, \langle 0.513, 0.439, 0.359\rangle, \langle 0.341, 0.218, 0.118\rangle)\}\end{aligned}$$

$$\begin{aligned}\ddot{\mathscr{E}}_{\star}(\mathcal{B}) = \{&(\ddot{\mathscr{D}}_1, \langle 0.348, 0.538, 0.531\rangle, \langle 0.218, 0.318, 0.231\rangle), (\ddot{\mathscr{D}}_2, \langle 0.769, 0.687, 0.734\rangle, \langle 0.121, 0.347, 0.318\rangle),\\ &(\ddot{\mathscr{D}}_3, \langle 0.541, 0.532, 0.511\rangle, \langle 0.241, 0.238, 0.268\rangle), (\ddot{\mathscr{D}}_4, \langle 0.357, 0.456, 0.337\rangle, \langle 0.311, 0.231, 0.238\rangle),\\ &(\ddot{\mathscr{D}}_5, \langle 0.213, 0.321, 0.211\rangle, \langle 0.421, 0.211, 0.115\rangle, (\ddot{\mathscr{D}}_6, \langle 0.387, 0.538, 0.541\rangle, \langle 0.217, 0.343, 0.321\rangle)\}\end{aligned}$$

$$\begin{aligned}\ddot{\mathscr{E}}_{\star}(\mathcal{B}) \oplus \ddot{\mathscr{E}}^{\star}(\mathcal{B}) = \{&(\ddot{\mathscr{D}}_1, \langle 0.829, 0.257, 0.288\rangle, \langle 0.547, 0.067, 0.114\rangle), (\ddot{\mathscr{D}}_2, \langle 0.822, 0.144, 0.197\rangle, \langle 0.308, 0.073, 0.276\rangle),\\ &(\ddot{\mathscr{D}}_3, \langle 0.805, 0.259, 0.221\rangle, \langle 0.428, 0.057, 0.197\rangle), (\ddot{\mathscr{D}}_4, \langle 0.827, 0.259, 0.195\rangle, \langle 0.545, 0.050, 0.197\rangle),\\ &(\ddot{\mathscr{D}}_5, \langle 0.935, 0.217, 0.166\rangle, \langle 0.731, 0.024, 0.140\rangle, (\ddot{\mathscr{D}}_6, \langle 0.701, 0.236, 0.194\rangle, \langle 0.484, 0.074, 0.149\rangle)\}\end{aligned}$$

Now we calculate the score values, quadratic score values and expectation score values of alternatives in $\ddot{\mathscr{E}}_{\star}(\mathcal{B}) \oplus \ddot{\mathscr{E}}^{\star}(\mathcal{B})$ by using Definitions 10, 12 and 14. The calculated data with final ranking is given in Table 8.

Table 8. Ranking of alternatives for different score values.

LDFS	$\ddot{\mathscr{D}}_1$	$\ddot{\mathscr{D}}_2$	$\ddot{\mathscr{D}}_3$	$\ddot{\mathscr{D}}_4$	$\ddot{\mathscr{D}}_5$	$\ddot{\mathscr{D}}_6$	Ranking	Rank Orders	Final Decision
$\mathfrak{P}$ (SF)	0.325	0.259	0.249	0.354	0.559	0.266	$\ddot{\mathscr{D}}_5 \succ \ddot{\mathscr{D}}_4 \succ \ddot{\mathscr{D}}_1 \succ \ddot{\mathscr{D}}_6 \succ \ddot{\mathscr{D}}_2 \succ \ddot{\mathscr{D}}_3$	$\leq_{(\mathfrak{P},\psi)}$	$\ddot{\mathscr{D}}_5$
$\mathfrak{J}$ (QSF)	0.409	0.314	0.336	0.423	0.656	0.302	$\ddot{\mathscr{D}}_5 \succ \ddot{\mathscr{D}}_4 \succ \ddot{\mathscr{D}}_1 \succ \ddot{\mathscr{D}}_3 \succ \ddot{\mathscr{D}}_2 \succ \ddot{\mathscr{D}}_6$	$\leq_{(\mathfrak{J},\phi)}$	$\ddot{\mathscr{D}}_5$
$\mathfrak{M}$ (ESF)	0.775	0.739	0.749	0.784	0.853	0.755	$\ddot{\mathscr{D}}_5 \succ \ddot{\mathscr{D}}_4 \succ \ddot{\mathscr{D}}_1 \succ \ddot{\mathscr{D}}_6 \succ \ddot{\mathscr{D}}_3 \succ \ddot{\mathscr{D}}_2$	$\leq_{(\mathfrak{M},\mathfrak{A})}$	$\ddot{\mathscr{D}}_5$

From Table 8 we can observe that the alternative $\ddot{\mathscr{D}}_5$, which is "geothermal power plant" is most suitable alternative for the final decision. The bar chart of ranking results for alternatives is given in Figure 12.

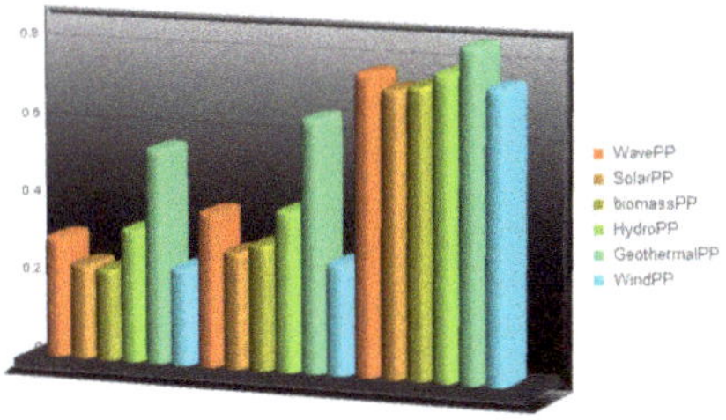

Figure 12. Bar chart of alternatives under SLDFSRS for SF ($\mathfrak{P}$), QSF ($\mathfrak{J}$) and ESF ($\mathfrak{M}$).

6.1.2. Calculations by Algorithm 2

The initial 5 steps of Algorithm 1 are same as Algorithm 2. Now we compute the upper and lower reducts from upper and lower approximations of SLDFS. Consider a committee of three experts given as

Expert X
Expert Y
Expert Z

The reducts from approximations can be constructed by using the following terms.

$\dot{T}_{\ddot{K}}$ = Satisfaction grade,
$\dot{Z}_{\ddot{K}}$ = Abstinence grade,
$\ddot{\mathfrak{S}}_{\ddot{K}}$ = Dissatisfaction grade,
$\alpha_{\ddot{K}}$ = Reference parameter corresponding to the satisfaction grade,
$\beta_{\ddot{K}}$ = Reference parameter corresponding to the abstinence grade,
$\eta_{\ddot{K}}$ = Reference parameter corresponding to the dissatisfaction grade,
$\mathfrak{M}$ = Expectation score function value of SLDFN,
$\widehat{\mathscr{L}}$ = Ranking given by experts to the alternatives from crisp set {0, 1}
$\mathscr{L}^*$ = Selection of alternative by using "YES" or "NO".

The final decision is based on the $\widehat{\mathscr{L}}$ and $\mathscr{L}^*$ given in Table 9

Table 9. The criteria for the final decision (F.D).

$\widehat{\mathscr{L}}$	$\mathscr{L}^*$	F.D
0	NO	NO
1	YES	YES
0	YES	NO
1	NO	NO

For expert-X, the upper reduct of upper approximation $\ddot{\mathscr{E}}^*(\mathcal{B})$ (calculated in Algorithm 1) of SLDFS $\mathcal{B}$ is given as Table 10. The average of score values of all the alternatives for $\ddot{\mathscr{E}}^*(\mathcal{B})$ is 0.599.

Table 10. Upper reduct for expert-X $(\mathcal{U}_X)$ from $\ddot{\mathscr{E}}^{\star}(\mathcal{B})$.

$(\mathcal{U}_X)$	$\ddot{T}_{\ddot{K}}$	$\ddot{Z}_{\ddot{K}}$	$\ddot{\mathfrak{S}}_{\ddot{K}}$	$\alpha_{\ddot{K}}$	$\beta_{\ddot{K}}$	$\eta_{\ddot{K}}$	$\mathfrak{M}$	$\widehat{\mathscr{L}}$	$\mathscr{L}^*$	F.D
$\ddot{\mathscr{D}}_1$	0.738	0.479	0.544	0.421	0.213	0.118	0.634	1	$\mathfrak{M} > 0.599 \rightarrow$ YES	YES
$\ddot{\mathscr{D}}_2$	0.231	0.211	0.269	0.213	0.213	0.312	0.573	0	$\mathfrak{M} < 0.599 \rightarrow$ NO	NO
$\ddot{\mathscr{D}}_3$	0.576	0.487	0.433	0.247	0.241	0.261	0.566	1	$\mathfrak{M} < 0.599 \rightarrow$ NO	NO
$\ddot{\mathscr{D}}_4$	0.731	0.569	0.579	0.341	0.217	0.231	0.579	0	$\mathfrak{M} < 0.599 \rightarrow$ NO	NO
$\ddot{\mathscr{D}}_5$	0.918	0.679	0.789	0.537	0.117	0.117	0.625	1	$\mathfrak{M} > 0.599 \rightarrow$ YES	YES
$\ddot{\mathscr{D}}_6$	0.513	0.439	0.359	0.341	0.218	0.118	0.619	1	$\mathfrak{M} > 0.599 \rightarrow$ YES	YES

This implies that $\mathcal{U}_X = \{\ddot{\mathscr{D}}_1, \ddot{\mathscr{D}}_5, \ddot{\mathscr{D}}_6\}$. For expert-X, the lower reduct of lower approximation $\ddot{\mathscr{E}}_{\star}(\mathcal{B})$ (calculated in Algorithm 1) of SLDFS $\mathcal{B}$ is given as Table 11. The average of score values of all the alternatives for $\ddot{\mathscr{E}}_{\star}(\mathcal{B})$ is 0.528.

Table 11. Lower reduct for expert-X (L_X) from $\ddot{\mathscr{E}}^{\star}(\mathcal{B})$.

$(\mathcal{U}_X)$	$\ddot{T}_{\ddot{K}}$	$\ddot{Z}_{\ddot{K}}$	$\ddot{\mathfrak{S}}_{\ddot{K}}$	$\alpha_{\ddot{K}}$	$\beta_{\ddot{K}}$	$\eta_{\ddot{K}}$	$\mathfrak{M}$	$\widehat{\mathscr{L}}$	$\mathscr{L}^*$	F.D
$\ddot{\mathscr{D}}_1$	0.348	0.538	0.531	0.218	0.318	0.231	0.491	1	$\mathfrak{M} < 0.528 \rightarrow$ NO	NO
$\ddot{\mathscr{D}}_2$	0.769	0.687	0.734	0.121	0.347	0.318	0.467	0	$\mathfrak{M} < 0.528 \rightarrow$ NO	NO
$\ddot{\mathscr{D}}_3$	0.541	0.532	0.511	0.241	0.238	0.268	0.538	1	$\mathfrak{M} > 0.528 \rightarrow$ YES	YES
$\ddot{\mathscr{D}}_4$	0.357	0.456	0.337	0.311	0.231	0.238	0.567	0	$\mathfrak{M} > 0.528 \rightarrow$ YES	NO
$\ddot{\mathscr{D}}_5$	0.213	0.321	0.211	0.421	0.211	0.115	0.629	1	$\mathfrak{M} > 0.528 \rightarrow$ YES	YES
$\ddot{\mathscr{D}}_6$	0.387	0.538	0.541	0.217	0.343	0.321	0.476	1	$\mathfrak{M} < 0.528 \rightarrow$ NO	NO

This implies that $L_X = \{\ddot{\mathscr{D}}_3, \ddot{\mathscr{D}}_5\}$. For expert-Y, the upper reduct of upper approximation $\ddot{\mathscr{E}}^{\star}(\mathcal{B})$ (calculated in Algorithm 1) of SLDFS $\mathcal{B}$ is given as Table 12.

Table 12. Upper reduct for expert-Y $(\mathcal{U}_Y)$ from $\ddot{\mathscr{E}}^{\star}(\mathcal{B})$.

$(\mathcal{U}_X)$	$\ddot{T}_{\ddot{K}}$	$\ddot{Z}_{\ddot{K}}$	$\ddot{\mathfrak{S}}_{\ddot{K}}$	$\alpha_{\ddot{K}}$	$\beta_{\ddot{K}}$	$\eta_{\ddot{K}}$	$\mathfrak{M}$	$\widehat{\mathscr{L}}$	$\mathscr{L}^*$	F.D
$\ddot{\mathscr{D}}_1$	0.738	0.479	0.544	0.421	0.213	0.118	0.634	0	$\mathfrak{M} > 0.599 \rightarrow$ YES	NO
$\ddot{\mathscr{D}}_2$	0.231	0.211	0.269	0.213	0.213	0.312	0.573	1	$\mathfrak{M} < 0.599 \rightarrow$ NO	NO
$\ddot{\mathscr{D}}_3$	0.576	0.487	0.433	0.247	0.241	0.261	0.566	0	$\mathfrak{M} < 0.599 \rightarrow$ NO	NO
$\ddot{\mathscr{D}}_4$	0.731	0.569	0.579	0.341	0.217	0.231	0.579	1	$\mathfrak{M} < 0.599 \rightarrow$ NO	NO
$\ddot{\mathscr{D}}_5$	0.918	0.679	0.789	0.537	0.117	0.117	0.625	1	$\mathfrak{M} > 0.599 \rightarrow$ YES	YES
$\ddot{\mathscr{D}}_6$	0.513	0.439	0.359	0.341	0.218	0.118	0.619	1	$\mathfrak{M} > 0.599 \rightarrow$ YES	YES

This implies that $\mathcal{U}_Y = \{\ddot{\mathscr{D}}_5, \ddot{\mathscr{D}}_6\}$. For expert-Y, the lower reduct of lower approximation $\ddot{\mathscr{E}}_{\star}(\mathcal{B})$ (calculated in Algorithm 1) of SLDFS $\mathcal{B}$ is given as Table 13.

Table 13. Lower reduct for expert-Y (L_Y) from $\ddot{\mathscr{E}}^{\star}(\mathcal{B})$.

$(\mathcal{U}_X)$	$\ddot{T}_{\ddot{K}}$	$\ddot{Z}_{\ddot{K}}$	$\ddot{\mathfrak{S}}_{\ddot{K}}$	$\alpha_{\ddot{K}}$	$\beta_{\ddot{K}}$	$\eta_{\ddot{K}}$	$\mathfrak{M}$	$\widehat{\mathscr{L}}$	$\mathscr{L}^*$	F.D
$\ddot{\mathscr{D}}_1$	0.348	0.538	0.531	0.218	0.318	0.231	0.491	0	$\mathfrak{M} < 0.528 \rightarrow$ NO	NO
$\ddot{\mathscr{D}}_2$	0.769	0.687	0.734	0.121	0.347	0.318	0.467	1	$\mathfrak{M} < 0.528 \rightarrow$ NO	NO
$\ddot{\mathscr{D}}_3$	0.541	0.532	0.511	0.241	0.238	0.268	0.538	0	$\mathfrak{M} > 0.528 \rightarrow$ YES	NO
$\ddot{\mathscr{D}}_4$	0.357	0.456	0.337	0.311	0.231	0.238	0.567	1	$\mathfrak{M} > 0.528 \rightarrow$ YES	YES
$\ddot{\mathscr{D}}_5$	0.213	0.321	0.211	0.421	0.211	0.115	0.629	1	$\mathfrak{M} > 0.528 \rightarrow$ YES	YES
$\ddot{\mathscr{D}}_6$	0.387	0.538	0.541	0.217	0.343	0.321	0.476	1	$\mathfrak{M} < 0.528 \rightarrow$ NO	NO

This implies that $L_Y = \{\ddot{\mathscr{D}}_4, \ddot{\mathscr{D}}_5\}$. For expert-Z, the upper reduct of upper approximation $\ddot{\mathscr{E}}^{\star}(\mathcal{B})$ (calculated in Algorithm 1) of SLDFS $\mathcal{B}$ is given as Table 14.

Table 14. Upper reduct for expert-Z (U_Z) from $\ddot{\mathscr{E}}^{\star}(\mathcal{B})$.

(U_X)	$\ddot{T}_{\ddot{K}}$	$\ddot{Z}_{\ddot{K}}$	$\ddot{\mathfrak{S}}_{\ddot{K}}$	$\alpha_{\ddot{K}}$	$\beta_{\ddot{K}}$	$\eta_{\ddot{K}}$	$\mathfrak{M}$	$\widehat{\mathscr{L}}$	$\mathscr{L}^*$	F.D
$\ddot{\mathscr{D}}_1$	0.738	0.479	0.544	0.421	0.213	0.118	0.634	1	$\mathfrak{M} > 0.599 \to$ YES	YES
$\ddot{\mathscr{D}}_2$	0.231	0.211	0.269	0.213	0.213	0.312	0.573	0	$\mathfrak{M} < 0.599 \to$ NO	NO
$\ddot{\mathscr{D}}_3$	0.576	0.487	0.433	0.247	0.241	0.261	0.566	1	$\mathfrak{M} < 0.599 \to$ NO	NO
$\ddot{\mathscr{D}}_4$	0.731	0.569	0.579	0.341	0.217	0.231	0.579	1	$\mathfrak{M} < 0.599 \to$ NO	NO
$\ddot{\mathscr{D}}_5$	0.918	0.679	0.789	0.537	0.117	0.117	0.625	1	$\mathfrak{M} > 0.599 \to$ YES	YES
$\ddot{\mathscr{D}}_6$	0.513	0.439	0.359	0.341	0.218	0.118	0.619	0	$\mathfrak{M} > 0.599 \to$ YES	NO

This implies that $U_Z = \{\ddot{\mathscr{D}}_1, \ddot{\mathscr{D}}_5\}$. For expert-Z, the lower reduct of lower approximation $\ddot{\mathscr{E}}_{\star}(\mathcal{B})$ (calculated in Algorithm 1) of SLDFS $\mathcal{B}$ is given as Table 15.

Table 15. Lower reduct for expert-Z (L_Z) from $\ddot{\mathscr{E}}^{\star}(\mathcal{B})$.

(U_X)	$\ddot{T}_{\ddot{K}}$	$\ddot{Z}_{\ddot{K}}$	$\ddot{\mathfrak{S}}_{\ddot{K}}$	$\alpha_{\ddot{K}}$	$\beta_{\ddot{K}}$	$\eta_{\ddot{K}}$	$\mathfrak{M}$	$\widehat{\mathscr{L}}$	$\mathscr{L}^*$	F.D
$\ddot{\mathscr{D}}_1$	0.348	0.538	0.531	0.218	0.318	0.231	0.491	1	$\mathfrak{M} < 0.528 \to$ NO	NO
$\ddot{\mathscr{D}}_2$	0.769	0.687	0.734	0.121	0.347	0.318	0.467	0	$\mathfrak{M} < 0.528 \to$ NO	NO
$\ddot{\mathscr{D}}_3$	0.541	0.532	0.511	0.241	0.238	0.268	0.538	1	$\mathfrak{M} > 0.528 \to$ YES	YES
$\ddot{\mathscr{D}}_4$	0.357	0.456	0.337	0.311	0.231	0.238	0.567	1	$\mathfrak{M} > 0.528 \to$ YES	YES
$\ddot{\mathscr{D}}_5$	0.213	0.321	0.211	0.421	0.211	0.115	0.629	1	$\mathfrak{M} > 0.528 \to$ YES	YES
$\ddot{\mathscr{D}}_6$	0.387	0.538	0.541	0.217	0.343	0.321	0.476	0	$\mathfrak{M} < 0.528 \to$ NO	NO

This implies that $L_Z = \{\ddot{\mathscr{D}}_3, \ddot{\mathscr{D}}_4, \ddot{\mathscr{D}}_5\}$. Now we calculate the core by taking the intersection of all upper and lower reducts for all three experts.

$$\text{Core} = U_X \cap L_X \cap U_Y \cap L_Y \cap U_Z \cap L_Z = \{\ddot{\mathscr{D}}_5\}$$

This means that "$\ddot{\mathscr{D}}_5$" (geothermal power plant) is the most suitable alternative for the final decision.

6.2. Advantages, Superiority, and Novelty of Proposed Algorithms

In this subsection, we discuss the advantages, superiority, and novelty of proposed algorithms.

1. Proposed Algorithms 1 and 2 are designed to deal with real-life problems based on novel hybrid approach of spherical linear Diophantine fuzzy soft rough sets (SLDFSRSs) and to utilize the characteristics of existing models like soft sets, rough sets, and spherical linear Diophantine fuzzy sets. A hybrid model is always more efficient, powerful and reliable to deal with uncertain real-life problems. A hybrid model can be utilized to handle multiple issues, multiple criterion, and multiple paradigms.
2. Algorithms 1 and 2 are developed to examine the role of reference parameters in spherical linear Diophantine fuzzy sets. The existing algorithms based on PFSs, SFSs, T-SFSs, and neutrosophic sets cannot deal with parameterizations. The proposed algorithm provide freedom to the decision-maker(DM) to select grades/indexes without any restriction. The dynamic features of reference parameters can classify and effectively resolve uncertain multi-criteria decision-making (MCDM) problems.
3. The proposed approach is efficient and suitable for any kind of uncertain information. The space of existing theories such as PFSs, SFSs, T-SFSs, and neutrosophic sets can be enhanced by proposed model of spherical linear Diophantine fuzzy sets. This model increases the valuation space of three (satisfaction, abstinence, and dissatisfaction) indexes/degrees. The algorithms are simple to understand, easy to apply, and efficient on diverse kinds of alternatives and attributes.
4. Various score functions has been established by Feng et al. [66] for IFSs. We developed three different kinds of score functions named as "score function" (SF), "quadratic

score function" (QSF), and "expectation score function" (ESF). We also establish their associated accuracy functions to compare the SLDFNs. The slight difference in ordering of optimal results is due to diverse strategies of score functions in the calculations. Table 8 implies the difference in ordering for the worst alternatives. Although it is fascinating to examine that final result from both algorithms are equivalent for all varieties of score functions.

6.3. Comparison Analysis

The comparison of proposed model SLDFSRSs and Algorithms 1 and 2 with some existing models and algorithms is given to discuss advantage, superiority, and validity of proposed approach. Table 16 represents the characteristics of suggested SLDFSRSs and ranking of alternatives computed by different techniques.

For two proposed algorithms based on SLDFSRSs and its SLDFS-approximation spaces, the final results for the decision-making problem of clean energy technique selection is given in Table 17.

The optimal alternative computed by the both algorithms is exactly same. Hence the alternative $\ddot{\mathscr{D}}_1$ (geothermal power plant) is the optimal selected alternative.

Table 16. Comparison analysis of proposed concepts with existing ideas.

Concepts	Satisfaction Grade	Abstinence Grade	Dissatisfaction Grade	Refusal Grade
Fuzzy set [1]	✓	×	×	×
Neutrosophic set [10]	✓	✓	✓	×
Rough set [36]	×	×	×	×
Soft set [34]	×	×	×	×
Picture fuzzy set [11–13]	✓	✓	✓	✓
Spherical fuzzy set [14]	✓	✓	✓	✓
T-spherical fuzzy set [14]	✓	✓	✓	✓
LDFS [69]	✓	✓	✓	×
SLDFS (proposed)	✓	✓	✓	✓
SLDFSS (proposed)	✓	✓	✓	✓
SLDFSRS (proposed)	✓	✓	✓	✓
Concepts	**Reference Parameterizations**	**Upper and Lower Approximations**	**Boundary Region**	**Multi-Valued Parameterizations**
Fuzzy set [1]	×	×	×	×
Neutrosophic set [10]	×	×	×	×
Rough set [36]	×	✓	✓	×
Soft set [34]	×	×	×	✓
Picture fuzzy set [11–13]	×	×	×	×
Spherical fuzzy set [14]	×	×	×	×
T-spherical fuzzy set [14]	×	×	×	×
LDFS [69]	✓	×	×	×
SLDFS (proposed)	✓	×	×	×
SLDFSS (proposed)	✓	×	×	✓
SLDFSRS (proposed)	✓	✓	✓	✓

Table 17. Comparison of results obtained from proposed algorithms.

Proposed Algorithm	Score Function	Core	Optimal Decision
Algorithm 1	$\mathfrak{P}$	×	$\ddot{\mathscr{D}}_5$
Algorithm 1	$\mathfrak{I}$	×	$\ddot{\mathscr{D}}_5$
Algorithm 1	$\mathfrak{M}$	×	$\ddot{\mathscr{D}}_5$
Algorithm 2	×	✓	$\ddot{\mathscr{D}}_5$

7. Conclusions

We studied certain fuzzy sets including PiFSs, SFSs, T-SFSs, and NSs. These extension have a large number of applications in solving real-life problems, and many researchers have been successfully applied these extensions. Unfortunately, these extensions have some strict limitations on indexes/grades. In order to deal with such problems, we introduced a robust hybrid model named as spherical linear diophantine fuzzy set which fusion of spherical linear Diophantine fuzzy set (SLDFS), soft set, and rough set. The addition of reference parameters in SLDFS provide freedom to the decision makers (DMs) for the selection of indexes/grades. A SLDFS is an efficient model to deal with uncertainties due to addition of reference parameters $\alpha_{\mathcal{K}}, \beta_{\mathcal{K}}$ and $\eta_{\mathcal{K}}$. We presented the graphical representation of SLDFS to compare it with some existing extensions of fuzzy sets. We introduced various score functions and accuracy functions to compare SLDFNs. We prolonged the idea of SLDFSs to SLDFSRSs by joining SLDFSs, rough sets, and soft sets. We investigated some new results for upper and lower approximation operators of SLDFSRSs. We developed two new algorithms for multi-criteria decision making (MCDM) based on SLDFSRSs. We presented a brief association among the recommended and existing theories and examined the strong impact of proposed structures to the MCDM problems. To resolve the real-world problems these findings will be fruitful and supportive for the scholars and decision-makers. In future, we will investigate the real-life problems associated with the ideas based on SLDF-graphs, SLDF-topology, and SLDF-information measures.

Author Contributions: M.R.H., S.T.T., M.R., D.P. and G.C., originated the research plan and started to work together to write this manuscript, M.R., G.C. and D.P., developed the algorithms for data analysis and design the model of the manuscript, M.R.H., S.T.T. and D.P., processed the data collection and wrote the paper. All authors have read and agreed to the published version of the manuscript.

Funding: This research received no external funding.

Institutional Review Board Statement: Not applicable.

Informed Consent Statement: Not applicable.

Data Availability Statement: Not applicable.

Conflicts of Interest: The authors declare no conflict of interest.

References

1. Zadeh, L.A. Fuzzy sets. *Inf. Control* **1965**, *8*, 338–353. [CrossRef]
2. Zadeh, L.A. The concept of a linguistic variable and its application to approximate reasoning—I. *Inf. Sci.* **1975**, *8*, 199–249. [CrossRef]
3. Atanassov, K.T. Intuitionistic fuzzy sets. In *VII ITKRs Session*; Sgurev, V., Ed.; Central Sci. and Techn. Library, Bulg. Academy of Sciences: Sofia, Bulgaria, 1984; reprinted in *Int. J. Bioautom.* **2016**, *20*, S1–S6.
4. Atanassov, K.T.; Stoeva, S. Intuitionistic fuzzy sets. In Proceedings of the Polish Symposium on Interval and Fuzzy Mathematics, Poznan, Poland, 23–26 August 1983.
5. Atanassov, K.T. Intuitionistic fuzzy sets. *Fuzzy Sets Syst.* **1986**, *20*, 87–96. [CrossRef]
6. Atanassov, K.T. Geometrical interpretation of the elemets of the intuitionistic fuzzy objects. *Int. J. Bio-Autom.* **2016**, *20* (Suppl. 1), S27–S42.
7. Yager, R.P. Pythagorean fuzzy subsets. In Proceedings of the IFSA World Congress and NAFIPS Annual Meeting, Edmonton, AB, Canada, 24–28 June 2013; pp. 57–61.

8. Yager, R.P. Pythagorean membership grades in multi criteria decision-making. *IEEE Trans. Fuzzy Syst.* **2014**, *22*, 958–965. [CrossRef]
9. Yager, R.P. Generalized orthopair fuzzy sets. *IEEE Trans. Fuzzy Syst.* **2017**, *25*, 1222–1230. [CrossRef]
10. Smarandache, F. *A Unifying Field in Logics: Neutrosophic Logic. Neutrosophy, Neutrosophic Set, Neutrosophic Probability and Statistics*, 5th ed.; American Research Press: Rehoboth, DE, USA, 2006; pp. 1–155.
11. Cuong, B.C. Picture fuzzy sets-first results. In *Preprint of Seminar on Neuro-Fuzzy Systems with Applications*; Institute of Mathematics: Hanoi, Vietnam, May 2013; Part 1.
12. Cuong, B.C. Picture fuzzy sets-first results. In *Preprint of Seminar on Neuro-Fuzzy Systems with Applications*; Institute of Mathematics: Hanoi, Vietnam, June 2013; Part 2.
13. Cuong, B.C.; Kreinovich, V. Picture fuzzy sets—A new concept for computational intelligence problems. In Proceedings of the 3rd World Congress on Information and Communication Technologies (WICT), Hanoi, Vietnam, 15–18 December 2013.
14. Mahmood, T.; Ullah, K.; Khan, Q.; Jan, N. An approach toward decision-making and medical diagnosis problems using the concept of spherical fuzzy sets. *Neural Comput. Appl.* **2019**, *31*, 7041–7053. [CrossRef]
15. Mahmood, T.; Mehmood, F.; Khan, Q. Some generalized aggregation operators for cubic hesitant fuzzy sets and their application to multi criteria decision making. *Punjab Univ. J. Math.* **2017**, *49*, 31–49.
16. Suapang, P.; Dejhan, K.; Yimmun, S. Medical image processing and analysis for nuclear medicine diagnosis. In Proceedings of the International Conference on Control Automation and Systems (ICCAS), Gyeonggi-do, Korea, 27–30 October 2010. [CrossRef]
17. Akbarizadeh, G.; Moghaddam, A.E. Detection of lung nodes in CT scans based on unsupervised feature learning and fuzzy inference. *J. Med Imaging Health Inform.* **2016**, *6*, 477–483. [CrossRef]
18. Akbarizadeh, G. A new statistical-based kurtosis wavelet energy feature for texture recognition of SAR images. *IEEE Trans. Geosci. Remote Sens.* **2012**, *50*, 4358–4368. [CrossRef]
19. Akbarizadeh, G. Segmentation of SAR satellite images unsing cellular learning automata and adaptive chains. *J. Remote Sens. Technol.* **2013**, *1*, 44. [CrossRef]
20. Akbarizadeh, G.; Rahmani, M. A new ensemble clustering method for PolSAR image segmentation. In Proceedings of the 7th Conference on Information Knowledge and Technology (IKT), Urmia, Iran, 26–28 May 2015; A New Computer Vision Algorithm for Classification of POLSAR Images. [CrossRef]
21. Akbarizadeh, G.; Tirandaz, Z.; Kooshesh, M. A new curvelet-based texture classification approach for land cover recognition of SAR satellite images. *Malays. J. Comput. Sci.* **2014**, *27*, 218–239.
22. Akbarizadeh, G.; Tirandaz, Z. Segmentation parameter estimation algorithm based on curvelet transform coefficients energy for feature extraction and texture description of SAR images. In Proceedings of the 7th Conference on Information and Knowledge Technology (IKT), Urmia, Iran, 26–28 May 2015. [CrossRef]
23. Akbarizadeh, G.; Rahmani, M. Efficient combination of texture and color features in a new spectral clustering method for PolSAR image segmentation. *Natl. Acad. Sci. Lett.* **2017**, *40*, 117–120. [CrossRef]
24. Benz, U.C.; Hofmann, P.; Willhauck, G.; Lingenfelder, I.; Heynen, M. Multi-resolution object-oriented fuzzy analysis of remote sensing data for GIS-ready information. *ISPRS J. Photogramm. Remote Sens.* **2004**, *58*, 239–258. [CrossRef]
25. Gong, M.; Zhou, Z.; Ma, J. Change detection in synthetic aperture redar images based on image fusion and fuzzy clustering. *IEEE Trans. Image Process.* **2012**, *21*, 2141–2151. [CrossRef] [PubMed]
26. Modava, M.; Akbarizadeh, G. Coastline extraction from SAR images using spatial fuzzy clustering and the active contour method. *Int. J. Remote Sens.* **2017**, *38*, 355–370. [CrossRef]
27. Modava, M.; Akbarizadeh, G. A level set based method for coastline detection of SAR images. In Proceedings of the 3rd International Conference on Patteren Recognition and Image Analysis (IPRIA), Shahrekord, Iran, 19–20 April 2017. [CrossRef]
28. Shanmugan, K.S.; Narayanan, V.; Frost, V.S.; Stiles, J.A.; Holtzman, J.C. Textural features for redar image analysis. *IEEE Trans. Geosci. Remote Sens.* **1981**, *3*, 153–156. [CrossRef]
29. Tirandaz, Z.; Akbarizadeh, G. A two-phased algorithm based on kurtosis curvelet energy and unsupervised spectral regression for segmentation for SAR images. *IEEE J. Sel. Top. Appl. Earth Obs. Remote Sens.* **2016**, *9*, 1244–1264. [CrossRef]
30. Ahmadi, N.; Akbarizadeh, G. Hybrid robust iris recognition approach using iris image pre-processing, two-dimensional gabor features and multi-layer perceptron neural network/PSO. *IET Biom.* **2018**, *7*, 153–162. [CrossRef]
31. Duagman, J. How iris recognition works. In *The Essential Guide to Image Processing*; Academic Press: Cambridge, MA, USA, 2009; pp. 715–739. [CrossRef]
32. Andekah, Z.A.; Naderan, M.; Akbarizadeh, G. Semi-supervised Hyperspectral image classification using spatial-spectral features and superpixel-based sparse codes. In Proceedings of the Iranian Conference of Electrical Engineering (ICEE), Tehran, Iran, 2–4 May 2017. [CrossRef]
33. Perić, N. Fuzzy logic and fuzzy set theory based edge detection algorithm. *Serbian J. Electr. Eng.* **2015**, *12*, 109–116. [CrossRef]
34. Molodtsov, D. Soft set theory-first results. *Comput. Math. Appl.* **1999**, *37*, 19–31. [CrossRef]
35. Maji, P.K.; Biswas, R.; Roy, A.R. Soft set theory. *Comput. Math. Appl.* **2003**, *45*, 555–562. [CrossRef]
36. Pawlak, Z. Rough sets. *Int. J. Comput. Inf. Sci.* **1982**, *2*, 145–172. [CrossRef]
37. Pawlak, Z.; Skowron, A. Rough sets: Some extensions. *Inf. Sci.* **2007**, *177*, 28–40. [CrossRef]
38. Ali, M.I. Another view on q-rung orthopair fuzzy sets. *Int. J. Intell. Syst.* **2018**, *33*, 2139–2153. [CrossRef]
39. Ali, M.I.; Shabir, M. Logic connectives for soft sets and fuzzy soft sets. *IEEE Trans. Fuzzy Syst.* **2014**, *22*, 1431–1442. [CrossRef]

40. Agarwal, M.; Biswas, K.K.; Hanmandlu, M. Generalized intuitionitic fuzzy soft sets with applications in decision-making. *Appl. Soft Comput.* **2013**, *20*, 3552–3566. [CrossRef]
41. Garg, H. A new generalized Pythagorean fuzzy information aggregation using Einstein operations and its application to decision making. *Int. J. Intell. Syst.* **2016**, *31*, 886–920. [CrossRef]
42. Chen, S.M.; Tan, M.J. Handling multi-criteria fuzzy decision-makling problems based on vague set theory. *Fuzzy Sets Syst.* **1994**, *67*, 163–172. [CrossRef]
43. Tversky, A.; Kahneman, D. Advances in prospect theory: Cumulative representation of uncertainity. *J. Risk Uncertain.* **1992**, *5*, 297–323. [CrossRef]
44. Jose, S.; Kuriaskose, S. Aggregation operators, score function and accuracy function for multi criteria decision making in intuitionistic fuzzy context. *Notes Intuitionist Fuzzy Sets* **2014**, *20*, 40–44.
45. Wang, H.; Smarandache, F.; Zhang, Y.Q.; Sunderraman, R. Single valued neutrosophic sets. *Multispace Multistruct.* **2010**, *4*, 410–413.
46. Peng, X.; Yang, Y. Some results for pythagorean fuzzy sets. *Int. J. Intell. Syst.* **2015**, *30*, 1133–1160. [CrossRef]
47. Peng, X.; Garg, H. Algorithms for interval-valued fuzzy soft sets in emergency decision-making based on WDBA and CODAS with new information measure. *Comput. Ind. Eng.* **2018**, *119*, 439–452. [CrossRef]
48. Xu, Z.S. Intuitionistic fuzzy aggregation operators. *IEEE Trans. Fuzzy Syst.* **2007**, *15*, 1179–1187.
49. Xu, Z.; Cai, X. *Intuitionistic Fuzzy Information Aggregation: Theory and Applications*; Science Press: Beijing, China; Springer: Berlin/Heidelberg, Germany, 2012.
50. Xu, Z. *Studies in Fuzziness and Soft Computing: Hesitant Fuzzy Sets Theory*; Springer International Publishing: Cham, Switzerland, 2014.
51. Ye, J. Linguistic neutrosophic cubic numbers and their multiple attribute decision-making method. *Information* **2017**, *8*, 110. [CrossRef]
52. Jana, C.; Senapati, T.; Pal, M.; Yager, R.R. Picture fuzzy Dombi aggreegation operators: Application to MADM process. *Appl. Soft Comput. J.* **2019**, *74*, 99–109. [CrossRef]
53. Xu, Y.; Shang, X.; Wang, J.; Zhang, R.; Li, W.; Xing, Y. A method to multi-attribute decision-making with picture fuzzy information based on Muirhead mean. *J. Intell. Fuzzy Syst.* **2018**, *36*, 1–17. [CrossRef]
54. Wang, R.; Wang, J.; Gao, H.; Wei, G. Methods for MADM with picture fuzzy Muirhead mean operators and their applications for evaluating the financial investment risk. *Symmetry* **2019**, *11*, 6. [CrossRef]
55. Wang, R.; Li, Y. Picture hesitant fuzzy set and its applications to multiple criteria decision-making. *Symmetry* **2018**, *10*, 259. [CrossRef]
56. Khan, S.; Abdullah, S.; Abdullah, L.; Ashraf, S. Logarithmic aggregation operators of picture fuzzy numbers for multi-attribute decision-making problems. *Mathematics* **2019**, *7*, 608. [CrossRef]
57. Khan, S.; Abdullah, S.; Ashraf, S. Picture fuzzy aggregation information based on Einstein operations and their application in decision-making. *Math. Sci.* **2019**, *13*, 213–229. [CrossRef]
58. Zhang, L.; Zhan, J.; Xu, Z.X. Covering-based generalized IF rough sets with applications to multi-attribute decision-making. *Inf. Sci.* **2019**, *478*, 275–302. [CrossRef]
59. Zhang, H.; Shu, L.; Liao, S. Intuitionistic fuzzy soft rough set and its applications in decision-making. *Abstr. Appl. Anal.* **2014**, *2014*, 287314. [CrossRef]
60. Zhang, H.; Dong, Y.; Carrascosa, I.P.; Zhou, H. Failure mode and effect analysis in a linguistic context: A consensus-based multi-attribute group decision-making approach. *IEEE Trans. Reliab.* **2019**, *68*, 566–582. [CrossRef]
61. Zhang, H.; Zhang, R.; Huang, H.; Wang, J. Some picture fuzzy Dombi Heronian mean operators with their applications to multi-attribute decision-making. *Symmetry* **2018**, *10*, 593. [CrossRef]
62. Zhang, Z.; Kou, X.; Yu, W.; Guo, C. On priority weights and consistency for incomplete hesitant fuzzy preference relations. *Knowl. Based Syst.* **2018**, *143*, 115–126. [CrossRef]
63. Zhang, Z.; Guo, C. Deriving priority weights from intuitionistic multiplicative preference relations under group decision-making settings. *J. Oper. Res. Soc.* **2017**, *68*, 1582–1599. [CrossRef]
64. Zhang, Z.; Guo, C.; Martine, L. Managing multigranular linguistic distribution assessments in large-scale multiattribute group decision-making. *IEEE Trans. Syst. Man Cybern. Syst.* **2017**, *47*, 3063–3076. [CrossRef]
65. Zhang, B.; Dong, Y.; Viedma, E.H. Group decision making with heterogeneous preference structures: An automatic mechanism to support consensus reaching. *Nigotiation* **2019**, *28*, 585–617. [CrossRef]
66. Feng, F.; Fujita, H.; Ali, M.I.; Yager, R.R.; Liu, X. Another view on generalized intuitionistic fuzzy soft sets and related multi-attribute decision making methods. *IEEE Trans. Fuzzy Syst.* **2019**, *27*, 474–488. [CrossRef]
67. Guo, K. Amount of information and attitudinal-based method for ranking Atanassov's intuitionistic fuzzy values. *IEEE Trans. Fuzzy Syst.* **2014**, *22*, 177–188. [CrossRef]
68. Liu, P.; Wang, P. Some q-rung orthopair fuzzy aggregation operators and their applications to multiple-attribute decision-making. *Int. J. Intell. Syst.* **1983**, *33*, 259–280. [CrossRef]
69. Riaz, M.; Hashmi, M.R. Linear Diophantine fuzzy set and its applications towards multi-attribute decision making problems. *J. Intell. Fuzzy Syst.* **2019**, *37*, 5417–5439. [CrossRef]
70. Riaz, M.; Hashmi, M.R. Soft rough Pythagorean m-polar fuzzy sets and Pythagorean m-polar fuzzy soft rough sets with application to decision-making. *Comput. Appl. Math.* **2020**, *39*, 1–36. [CrossRef]

71. Riaz, M.; Pamucar, D.; Farid, H.M.A.; Hashmi, M.R. q-Rung orthopair fuzzy prioritized aggregation operators and their application towards green supplier chain management. *Symmetry* **2020**, *12*, 976. [CrossRef]
72. Vashist, R. An algorithm for finding the reduct and core of the consistent dataset. In Proceedings of the International Conference on Computational Intelligence and Communications Networks, Jabalpur, India, 12–14 December 2015. [CrossRef]
73. Wang, C.; Zhou, X.; Tu, H.; Tao, S. Some geometric aggregation operators based on picture fuzzy sets and their applications in multiple-attribute decision-making. *Iran. J. Pure Appl. Math.* **2017**, *37*, 477–492.
74. Zhan, J.; Alcantud, J.C.R. A novel type of soft rough covering and its application to multi-criteria group decision-making. *Artif. Intell. Rev.* **2018**, *52*, 2381–2410. [CrossRef]
75. Riaz, M.; Çagman, N.; Wali, N.; Mushtaq, A. Certain properties of soft multi-set topology with applications in multi-criteria decision making. *Decis. Mak. Appl. Manag. Eng.* **2020**, *3*, 70–96. [CrossRef]
76. Sahu, R.; Dash, S.R.; Das, S. Career selection of students using hybridized distance measure based on picture fuzzy set and rough set theory. *Decis. Mak. Appl. Manag. Eng.* **2021**, *4*, 104–126. [CrossRef]
77. Ali, Z.; Mahmood, T.; Ullah, K.; Khan, Q. Einstein Geometric Aggregation Operators using a Novel Complex Interval-valued Pythagorean Fuzzy Setting with Application in Green Supplier Chain Management. *Rep. Mech. Eng.* **2021**, *2*, 105–134. [CrossRef]
78. Alosta, A.; Elmansuri, O.; Badi, I. Resolving a location selection problem by means of an integrated AHP-RAFSI approach. *Rep. Mech. Eng.* **2021**, *2*, 135–142. [CrossRef]
79. Yorulmaz, Ö; Kuzu Yildirim, S.; Yildirim, B.F. Robust Mahalanobis Distance based TOPSIS to Evaluate the Economic Development of Provinces. *Oper. Res. Eng. Sci. Theory Appl.* **2021**, *4*, 102–123. [CrossRef]
80. Pamucar, D.; Ecer, F. Prioritizing the weights of the evaluation criteria under fuzziness: The fuzzy full consistency method—FUCOM-F. *Facta Univ. Ser. Mech. Eng.* **2020**, *18*, 419–437. [CrossRef]
81. Ramakrishnan, K.R.; Chakraborty, S. A cloud TOPSIS model for green supplier selection. *Facta Univ. Ser. Mech. Eng.* **2020**, *18*, 375–397.
82. Kishore, R.; Mousavi Dehmourdi, S.A.; Naik, M.G.; Hassanpour, M. Designing a framework for Subcontractor's selection in construction projects using MCDM model. *Oper. Res. Eng. Sci. Theory Appl.* **2020**, *3*, 48–64. [CrossRef]
83. Zararsiz, Z. Similarity measures of sequence of fuzzy numbers and fuzzy risk analysis. *Adv. Math. Phys.* **2015**, *2015*, 724647. [CrossRef]
84. Zararsiz, Z. Measuring entropy values of QRS-complexes before and after training program of sport horses with ECG. *Ann. Fuzzy Math. Inform.* **2018**, *15*, 243–251. [CrossRef]

axioms

MDPI

Article

Social Network Group Decision-Making Method Based on Q-Rung Orthopair Fuzzy Set and Its Application in the Evaluation of Online Teaching Quality

Yingjie Hu [1], Shouzhen Zeng [1,2,*], Llopis-Albert Carlos [3], Kifayat Ullah [4] and Yuqi Yang [5]

1 School of Business, Ningbo University, Ningbo 315211, China; a17858955393@163.com
2 College of Statistics and Mathematics, Zhejiang Gongshang University, Hangzhou 310018, China
3 Centro de Investigación en Ingeniería Mecánica (CIIM), Universitat Politècnica de València, Camino de Vera s/n, 46022 Valencia, Spain; cllopisa@upvnet.upv.es
4 Department of Mathematics, Riphah Institute of Computing & Applied Sciences (RICAS), Riphah International University (Lahore Campus), Lahore 54000, Pakistan; kifayat.khan.dr@gmail.com
5 School of Mathematics, Southwest Jiaotong University, Chengdu 611756, China; yyq1234678@163.com
* Correspondence: zszzxl@163.com

Abstract: As q-rung orthopair fuzzy set (q-ROFS) theory can effectively express complex fuzzy information, this study explores its application to social network environments and proposes a social network group decision-making (SNGDM) method based on the q-ROFS. Firstly, the q-rung orthopair fuzzy value is used to represent the trust relationships between experts in the social network, and a trust q-rung orthopair fuzzy value is defined. Secondly, considering the decreasing and multipath of trust in the process of trust propagation, this study designs a trust propagation mechanism by using its multiplication operation in the q-ROFS environment and proposes a trust q-ROFS aggregation approach. Moreover, based on the trust scores and confidence levels of experts, a new integration operator called q-rung orthopair fuzzy-induced ordered weighted average operator is proposed to fuse experts' evaluation information. Additionally, considering the impact of consensus interaction on decision-making results, a consensus interaction model based on the q-ROF distance measure and trust relationship is proposed, including consistency measurement, identification of inconsistent expert decision-making opinions and a personalized adjustment mechanism. Finally, the SNGDM method is applied to solve the problem of evaluating online teaching quality.

Keywords: q-ROFS; trust propagation model; confidence level; consensus interaction model; evaluation of online teaching quality

MSC: 03B52; 47S40; 90B50

Citation: Hu, Y.; Zeng, S.; Carlos, L.-A.; Ullah, K.; Yang, Y. Social Network Group Decision-Making Method Based on Q-Rung Orthopair Fuzzy Set and Its Application in the Evaluation of Online Teaching Quality. *Axioms* **2021**, *10*, 168. https://doi.org/10.3390/axioms10030168

Academic Editor: Goran Ćirović

Received: 27 June 2021
Accepted: 21 July 2021
Published: 28 July 2021

1. Introduction

Online teaching is a new Internet-based teaching mode that can achieve the purpose of teaching through online teaching platforms without face-to-face interactions. Although online teaching is not currently the main method of teaching, it can be used as an alternative emergency teaching mode. For example, the COVID-19 pandemic that occurred at the end of 2019 forced many schools to suspend the traditional classroom-based teaching mode to prevent the spread of the virus. At this point, the online teaching mode largely solves the problem of delays in teaching and ensures the progress of instruction. However, online teaching has its own problems. For example, too many students in the class will cause network freezes and instability of the teaching platform. At the same time, teachers and students cannot communicate face-to-face, and teachers cannot address students' questions in a timely manner. The evaluation of classroom teaching quality can help teachers to fully understand the problems existing in the teaching process and can enhance teachers' teaching ability and improve the quality of teaching. Therefore, it is necessary to propose a scientific and effective method to evaluate the quality of online teaching. The problem of evaluating teaching quality is essentially a multi-attribute group decision-making (MAGDM) problem, because the evaluation process involves multiple evaluation indices, multiple decision-making experts, and multiple decision-making experts that provide the corresponding evaluation information that is used to arrive at a final conclusion regarding the quality level. At present, many scholars have studied the problem of evaluating teaching quality and have proposed various evaluation methods, including offline and online assessment methods. Targeting the imperfect evaluation system used to measure the quality of teaching in the social sports specialty, Liu [1] proposed a novel MAGDM method based on the intuitionistic fuzzy (IF)-TOPSIS method. Carlucci et al. [2] proposed a framework for teaching and curriculum quality evaluation combining u-control chart and fuzzy weight ABC analysis to assess students' evaluation of higher education teaching quality. Using a fuzzy comprehensive evaluation method and combining a fuzzy analytic hierarchy process (AHP) to put forward a new teaching performance evaluation framework, Chen et al. [3] proposed five sub-evaluation factors: planning and preparation, communication and interaction, teaching for learning, managing learning environment, student evaluation, and professionalism. Zhang et al. [4] proposed a new evaluation method based on heterogeneous linguistic information for the MAGDM problem faced in the evaluation of classroom teaching quality. Yu [5] considered teaching attitude, teaching ability, teaching content, and teaching feedback as evaluation indices and proposed a group decision-making (GDM) method based on triangular IF to deal with the evaluation of teaching quality in colleges and universities. Yang and Xiang [6] proposed a multi-attribute decision-making (MADM) method based on the power aggregation operator of fuzzy uncertain linguistic information to solve the problem of assessing teaching quality in higher education. Specifically, the quality of music teaching in colleges and universities was evaluated on four factors: education and teaching services, education and teaching management services, logistics management services, and students' further development services. Considering that the nature of evaluating the quality of teaching is very fuzzy and imprecise, Peng and Dai [7] used q-rung orthopair fuzzy value (q-ROFV) to deal with its uncertainty, and used teaching attitude, teaching ability, teaching content, teaching method and teaching effect as evaluation indices; two algorithms based on distance evaluation and multi-parameter similarity measure based on q-rung orthopair fuzzy set (q-ROFS) were proposed to solve the MADM problem of evaluating classroom teaching quality. Yu [8] improved AprioriTid algorithm and constructed an online evaluation model of teaching quality according to teaching needs and evaluated English online teaching quality through data mining. Liu et al. [9] proposed a new MAGDM method based on the Choquet integral operator and multi-granularity probabilistic linguistic term set, and used it to solve the problem of evaluating the quality of online teaching. Lin et al. [10] proposed an extended linguistic MAGDM framework to solve the problem of evaluating the quality of online teaching. Thus, we can see that existing research mainly used MAGDM/MADM method to solve the problem. As a scientific and effective decision-making method in a complex environment, the MAGDM considers the backgrounds and experiences of multiple decision-making experts, which avoids the subjectivity and one-sidedness presented by a single decision-making expert [11–13].

The traditional evaluation of offline teaching quality has gained increasing attention; however, few studies have focused on the evaluation of online teaching quality. Moreover, in the process of evaluating teaching quality, the influence of the social network relationships between decision-making experts on the evaluation results should be considered. The emergence of the Web2.0 mode has brought decision-making experts closer, and the corresponding social network relationships among experts have also become increasingly prominent. The influence of the Web2.0 on GDM cannot be ignored. Thus, this study combines the social network analysis (SNA) method with GDM method and proposes a new q-ROFS social network group decision-making (SNGDM) method to solve the problem of evaluating online teaching quality.

At present, GDM methods based on social networks mainly focus on the representation of trust, the propagation/aggregation operator of trust, the method of obtaining expert weights, and consensus interaction models (CIMs). The first study focused on the representation of trust. There are discrete values [14–16], continuous values [17,18], fuzzy logic values (including interval values [19–21], intuitionistic fuzzy values (IFVs) [22–25], Pythagorean fuzzy values (PFVs) [26], interval-valued Pythagorean fuzzy values (IVPFVs) [27]), and other trust representations. The second is the trust propagation method. At present, T-norm and T-conorm are used to design trust propagation operators to ensure a decrease in trust and an increase in distrust during the propagation process [24,28,29]. Some authors have designed trust propagation operators based on the Uninorm (U) operator [30,31]. This research on trust aggregation operators is mainly focused on studying the trust relationship integration of multiple propagation paths and the selection of the shortest path. Most researchers select the shortest path trust relationship as the final trust aggregation result, or assign different weights to paths of different lengths, or assign the same weights to paths of the same length, and then integrate the trust relationship on the corresponding paths to obtain the final trust evaluation value [24,30,32,33]. The third research field is on the method of obtaining the weights of experts, which is based mainly on the linguistic quantifier Q [30,32,34] and the SNA method [24,28,35,36] (centrality theory, etc.) to compute the weights of experts. The fourth research topic is the CIM; at present, the CIM focuses mainly on the identification of inconsistent experts and the adjustment of inconsistent expert decision-making opinions [28,32,34,37,38]. In considering of the differences in backgrounds and experience among experts, it is difficult for them to reach an agreement on the initial opinions of the GDM process. In other words, experts do not reach a consensus on decision-making opinions, which will affect the final evaluation and decision-making results, so experts must reach a consensus before making a final decision.

However, there are some defects in the above-mentioned social network decision-making methods: (1) using discrete values, continuous values, and interval values to describe trust information does not consider the fuzziness, uncertainty, and subjectivity of trust. Although IFV and PFV can describe the fuzziness and uncertainty of trust information, they express that the scope of fuzzy information is limited (i.e., the membership and non-membership grades are satisfied: $0 \leq \mu + v \leq 1$ or $0 \leq \mu^2 + v^2 \leq 1$); (2) using the U operator to design trust propagation operators will increase the trust value after propagation, which violates the principle of trust decreasing during trust propagation. At the same time, when integrating trust information, the selection of the shortest propagation path will cause a loss of trust information. Assigning the same path weight to the same length of path will reduce the accuracy of the trust value after propagation; (3) solving for the weights of experts ignores the importance of the confidence levels of experts. According to the results of Guha and Chakraborty [39], the evaluation of alternatives by experts is related to the confidence levels of experts. Therefore, in the real decision-making process, we cannot ignore the confidence levels of experts; (4) in the current research on the CIM, the adjustment of expert opinions tends to be based on group preferences, without considering the impact of trust relationships among experts on the adjustment of expert opinions in the social networks. In fact, the experts who need to adjust their opinions are more willing to believe the experts who have direct trust relationships with them than the others. In the study of social network relationships, consider the social network of trust relationships between individuals as a trust relationship network [24,29,32]. The emergence of this network of trust relationships in decision-making has a significant impact on the consensus among experts.

Therefore, according to the analysis of the above four defects, this study proposes a new SNGDM method within the q-ROFS situation to solve the problem of evaluating online teaching quality. Its innovation is reflected in the following four aspects:

(1) In view of the superiority of q-ROFV in expressing fuzzy information, this study uses the q-ROFV to describe the trust relationship among experts in the process of

evaluating online teaching quality, which compensates for the limitations of other data to express trust information, to improve the reliability of decision-making results.
(2) In view of the diminishing principle of trust in the process of propagation, this study uses the multiplication operation of q-ROFS to design the trust propagation operator to ensure a decline in trust.
(3) Considering the importance of the confidence levels of experts in evaluating information, this study introduces the concept of confidence level in the q-ROF environment and uses it to obtain the weights of experts.
(4) A CIM based on trust relationships is proposed to better reflect experts' acceptance of opinion adjustment.

The remainder of this study is organized as follows: Section 2 presents the proposed methods. It mainly introduces the theoretical knowledge of q-ROFS, including the definition of q-ROFS, operation rules, distance measure, score function, and q-rung orthopair fuzzy weighted averaging operator (q-ROFWA). The representation of trust relations, trust networks, and the operators of trust propagation and aggregation are also provided in this section. Section 3 presents the results of this study; it develops a q-ROF aggregation operator based on trust scores and confidence levels of experts, CIM, and decision-making analysis, and a comparison with other methods. Section 4 discusses the results of this study and presents the conclusions.

2. Theoretical Fundamentals

2.1. Theoretical Knowledge of Q-ROFSs

This section briefly reviews the relevant theoretical knowledge of the q-ROFSs.

Definition 1 ([40]). *Let $\aleph = \{Y_1, Y_2, \cdots, Y_n\}$ be a discourse, a q-ROFS defined on $\aleph$ can then be expressed as:*

$$G = \{\langle Y, \mu_G(Y), v_G(Y)\rangle | Y \in \aleph\}, \quad (1)$$

where $\mu_G(Y)$ and $v_G(Y)$ are the membership and non-membership grades of the element $Y \in \aleph$ respectively, and $\mu_G(Y)$ and $v_G(Y)$ satisfy the constraint $\mu_G^q(Y) + v_G^q(Y) \leq 1$ $(\mu_G(Y) \in [0,1], v_G(Y) \in [0,1])$ for all $q \geq 1$. The hesitation grade is expressed as: $\pi_G(Y) = \sqrt[q]{(1 - (\mu_G(Y))^q - (v_G(Y))^q)}$.

In addition, for the convenience of application, Liu and Wang [41] called $\langle \mu_G(Y), v_G(Y)\rangle$ a q-ROFV and denoted it as $G = \langle \mu_G, v_G\rangle$.

Definition 2 ([41]). *Let $G_1 = \langle \mu_1, v_1\rangle$, $G_2 = \langle \mu_2, v_2\rangle$ and $G = \langle \mu, v\rangle$ be three q-ROFVs. Then their operation rules are defined as:*

(i) $G_1 \oplus G_2 = \left(\sqrt[q]{\left(\mu_1^q + \mu_2^q - \mu_1^q\mu_2^q\right)}, v_1 v_2\right)$,

(ii) $G_1 \otimes G_2 = \left(\mu_1\mu_2, \sqrt[q]{\left(v_1^q + v_2^q - v_1^q v_2^q\right)}\right)$,

(iii) $\lambda G = \left(\sqrt[q]{1 - (1 - \mu^q)^\lambda}, v^\lambda\right), \lambda > 0$.

(iv) $G^\lambda = \left(\mu^\lambda, \sqrt[q]{1 - (1 - v^q)^\lambda}\right), \lambda > 0$.

Definition 3 ([42]). *Given any two q-ROFVs $G_1 = \langle \mu_1, v_1\rangle$ and $G_2 = \langle \mu_2, v_2\rangle$, their distances are computed as follows:*

$$d(G_1, G_2) = \frac{1}{2}\left(\left|\mu_1^q - \mu_2^q\right| + \left|v_1^q - v_2^q\right| + \left|\pi_1^q - \pi_2^q\right|\right). \quad (2)$$

Definition 4 ([43]). *Given a q-ROFV $G = \langle \mu, v \rangle$, its score and accuracy functions are defined as $SV(G) = \frac{1+\mu^q - v^q}{2}$ and $AV(G) = \mu^q + v^q$ respectively, and*

(i) *If $SV(G_1) > SV(G_2)$, then $G_1 \succ G_2$;*
(ii) *If $SV(G_1) = SV(G_2)$, then their accuracy function should be further compared as follows:*
  (a) *If $AV(G_1) > AV(G_2)$, then $G_1 \succ G_2$;*
  (b) *If $AV(G_1) = AV(G_2)$, then $G_1 \sim G_2$.*

Definition 5 ([41]). *Let a series of q-ROFVs be $G_t = \langle \mu_t, v_t \rangle (t = 1, 2, \cdots, n)$, where $\omega = (\omega_1, \omega_2, \cdots, \omega_n)^T$ is the weight vector, such that $\omega_t \in [0,1]$, $\sum_{t=1}^{n} \omega_t = 1$. The q-rung orthopair fuzzy weighted average (q-ROFWA) operator is then defined as:*

$$\text{q} - \text{ROFWA}(G_1, G_2, \cdots, G_n) = \overset{n}{\underset{t=1}{\oplus}} \omega_t G_t = \omega_1 G_1 \oplus \omega_2 G_2 \oplus \cdots \oplus \omega_n G_n. \quad (3)$$

2.2. Representation of Trust Relationships

In light of the limitations of crisp value, IFV, and PFV in expressing fuzzy information, this study proposes a trust q-rung orthopair fuzzy value (Tq-ROFV) to represent the complex trust relationships, defined as follows:

Definition 6. *The Tq-ROFV refers to a q-ROFV $G = \langle \mu_G, v_G \rangle$ to represent the trust relationships between experts in a social network, where μ_G represents the membership grade, i.e., the trust degree. v_G represents the non-membership grade, i.e., the distrust degree. $\pi_G = \sqrt[q]{(1 - (\mu_G)^q - (v_G)^q)}$ then represents the uncertainty of trust.*

It follows that when $q = 1$, the Tq-ROFV degenerates into the trust IF value (TIFV) [44].

Definition 7. *Given a Tq-ROFV $G = \langle \mu, v \rangle$, its trust score is defined as: $TS = \frac{\mu^q - v^q + 1}{2}$, where $0 \leq TS \leq 1$.*

2.3. Q-ROF Trust Network and Trust Propagation Operator

A trust network is composed of nodes and directed edges, where in the GDM process, nodes represent experts, and the directed edges represent the trust relationships between experts. Therefore, the trust network based on GDM can be regarded as being composed of expert sets and trust relationships. In this study, the q-ROFV is introduced into the trust network, and a q-ROF trust network is constructed, a representation of which is shown in Figure 1.

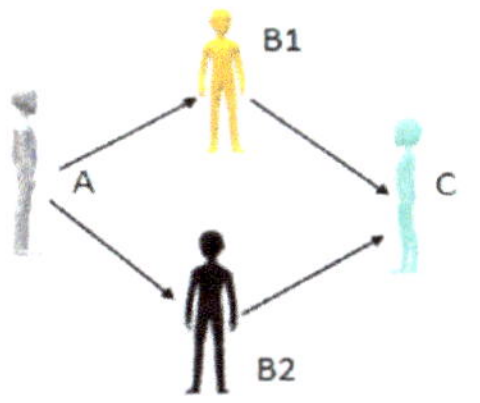

Figure 1. Trust network graph.

In Figure 1, A, B1, B2, and C denote expert nodes, and the directed arrows denote directed edges. For example, A → B1 indicates that there is a trust relationship between expert A and expert B1, which is represented by a q-ROFV. It can be seen that there is no directed arrow directly connecting expert A with expert C, but there are directed arrows directly connecting expert A with experts B1 and B2, and experts B1 and B2 with expert C. We call the trust relationships between experts who are directly connected as direct trust, and those who are not directly connected (but indirectly connected through other experts) as indirect trust. In other words, trust relationships between experts can be divided into direct and indirect trust [45].

As shown in Figure 1, there is no direct trust relationship between expert A and expert C, but there is an indirect trust relationship; that is, it is propagated through experts B1 and B2, so we need to calculate the trust relationship between expert A and expert C. Considering the principle that trust does not increase and distrust does not decrease in the process of trust propagation [46], and based on the multiplication operation of q-ROFS, we propose a new trust propagation operator to calculate the indirect trust among experts.

Definition 8. *Let $e_0, e_1, e_2, \cdots, e_{n-1}, e_n$ be the $n+1$ experts, and $G_1, G_2, \cdots, G_{n-1}, G_n$ be the n Tq-ROFVs. The trust evaluation value of expert e_0 to expert e_1 is represented by a Tq-ROFV G_1, the trust evaluation value of expert e_1 to expert e_2 is represented by a Tq-ROFV G_2, and so on. It follows that the trust evaluation value of expert e_{n-1} to expert e_n is expressed by a Tq-ROFV G_n, and the trust evaluation value of expert e_0 to expert e_n is expressed as:*

$$\dot{q}(e_0, e_1, \cdots e_{n-1}, e_n) = G_1 \otimes G_2 \otimes \cdots \otimes G_n. \tag{4}$$

In particular, when $n = 2$, we have $G_1 \otimes G_2 = \left(\mu_1\mu_2, \sqrt[q]{v_1^q + v_2^q - v_1^q v_2^q}\right)$. When $n = 3$, $G_1 \otimes G_2 \otimes G_3 = \left(\mu_1\mu_2\mu_3, \sqrt[q]{1 + \left(v_1^q - 1\right)\left(v_2^q - 1\right)\left(v_3^q - 1\right)}\right)$. Thus, according to the recursive method, we can obtain:

$$\dot{q}(e_0, e_1, \cdots e_{n-1}, e_n) = G_1 \otimes G_2 \otimes \cdots \otimes G_n = \left(\prod_{t=1}^{n} \mu_t, \sqrt[q]{1 + (-1)^{n-1} \prod_{t=1}^{n} \left(v_t^q - 1\right)}\right). \tag{5}$$

It can be proved that $\prod_{t=1}^{n} \mu_t \le \min(\mu_t)$, and $\sqrt[q]{1 + (-1)^{n-1} \prod_{t=1}^{n} \left(v_t^q - 1\right)} \ge \max(v_t)$, i.e., the designed trust propagation operator $\dot{q}$ satisfies the principle that trust does not increase and distrust does not decrease in the process of trust propagation.

Some special cases of the trust propagation operator can be achieved as follows:

(1) When all $G_t = (1, 0)$, then $G_1 \otimes G_2 \otimes \cdots \otimes G_n = (1, 0)$.

(2) If $\exists G_t = (0, 1)$, then $G_1 \otimes G_2 \otimes \cdots \otimes G_n = (0, 1)$. This shows that as long as there is a complete distrust relationship on the propagation path, the final result after propagation is complete distrust, regardless of the other trust relationships.

(3) If $G_1 = G_2 = G_3 = (0.8, 0.2)$, without loss of generality, suppose that $q = 1$, then $G_1 \otimes G_2 \otimes G_3 = (0.51, 0.49)$. The trust value after trust propagation is $0.51 < 0.8$, and the distrust value is $0.49 > 0.2$, which means that the principle of decreasing trust and increasing distrust is satisfied in the process of trust propagation.

(4) If $G_1 = (0.2, 0.8)$, $G_2 = (0.8, 0.2)$, $G_3 = (0.8, 0.1)$, and suppose that $q = 1$, then $G_1 \otimes G_2 \otimes G_3 = (0.13, 0.86)$. Although the trust values of G_2 and G_3 are very high, the trust value of G_1 is low (only 0.2), and so the final trust value after propagation is also low.

The above special cases also show that the trust propagation operator based on the q-ROF multiplication operation is reasonable.

2.4. Trust Aggregation Operator Based on q-ROFS

In the trust network shown in Figure 1, there are two propagation paths for the indirect trust of expert A to expert C. Therefore, it is necessary to integrate the trust relationships of these two propagation paths in order to obtain the final trust evaluation value of expert A with expert C. This study uses the following path weighting method:

$$\mathrm{T} = \sum_{i=1}^{n} w_i G_i = w_1 G_1 \oplus w_2 G_2 \oplus \cdots \oplus w_n G_n, \tag{6}$$

where G_i is a Tq-ROFV, and T is a Tq-ROF weighted average operator. $w_i = Q\left(\frac{i}{n}\right) - Q\left(\frac{i-1}{n}\right)$ is the path weight, and i is the i-th path. In order from shortest to longest, the shorter the path is, the closer to the front it is, and the longer the path, the further back it is. The path with the larger trust score is at the front when the path lengths are the same. The linguistic quantifiers $Q(r) = r^a (a \geq 0)$, and $Q : [0,1] \to [0,1]$, $Q(0) = 0$, $Q(1) = 1$. Among them, $a = 0.5$ is the fuzzy quantifier for "most" [34].

Example 1. *By the end of 2019, with the emergence of COVID-19, most universities had to terminate their teaching tasks offline. According to the principle of "stopping classes without stopping teaching, and stopping classes without stopping school", universities changed from a traditional offline teaching mode to an online teaching mode. The evaluation of the classroom teaching quality of large-scale online teaching is beneficial for teachers to realize a deficiency in the teaching process, and to improve the quality of teaching. This study evaluates the online teaching quality of teachers in four colleges and universities* $\{Z_1, Z_2, Z_3, Z_4\}$ *during the pandemic. Based on the analysis of the teaching quality evaluation index system in the literature* [7,10,47], *and by considering the three factors of before class, during class, and after class, this study introduces five evaluation indices to comprehensively evaluate the online teaching quality of teachers in colleges and universities: the stability of teaching platforms* C_1, *the pertinence of teaching resources* C_2, *the timeliness of answering questions and feedback* C_3, *the strictness of teaching attitude* C_4, *the rationality of teaching content* C_5, *and their corresponding index weights* $W = (0.20, 0.25, 0.10, 0.15, 0.30)^T$. *The five attributes are described as follows:*

Stability of teaching platforms C_1: Whether the online teaching platforms used by schools, such as Tencent Classroom and Zoom, are stable, e.g., whether they are stuck, etc.

Pertinence of teaching resources C_2: Whether the PPT courseware and teaching materials provided by teachers before the class are aimed at teaching content in the class, i.e., whether there are differences between the two.

Timeliness of answering questions and feedback C_3: Whether the teacher solves the students' questions in time during and after class.

Strictness of teaching attitude C_4: Whether the teacher has rational and scientific teaching, e.g., whether the words and actions are appropriate, whether the preparation is sufficient, etc.

Rationality of teaching content C_5: Whether the content taught in the class is based mainly on basic knowledge and supplemented by difficult knowledge.

Taking a major of four universities as an example to evaluate the online teaching quality of teachers, we consulted some of the students who had the highest academic achievements in this major as experts. Therefore, the evaluation problem can be regarded as an SNGDM problem. There are five experts $\{e_1, e_2, e_3, e_4, e_5\}$ with a social matrix T_L based on the trust relationships between them. The listed trust values indicate that there is direct trust among the experts, and the unlisted trust value indicates that there is no direct trust between the experts.

$$T_L = \begin{pmatrix} - & (0.6,0.2) & & & (0.7,0.1) \\ & - & & (0.6,0.1) & \\ (0.6,0.1) & (0.8,0.1) & - & (0.7,0.2) & \\ & & (0.5,0.4) & - & (0.6,0.3) \\ & & (0.5,0.2) & & - \end{pmatrix}.$$

In this study, we complete the missing values of the trust evaluation T_L based on the proposed trust propagation operator $\overset{\bullet}{q}$. Taking the missing value of trust evaluation between experts e_1 and e_3 as an example, for the sake of generality, we take $q = 1$. There is no direct trust between experts e_1 and e_3, but there are three indirect trust propagation paths, namely $l_1 : e_1 \to e_5 \to e_3$, $l_2 : e_1 \to e_2 \to e_4 \to e_3$ and $l_3 : e_1 \to e_2 \to e_4 \to e_5 \to e_3$. Considering the importance of each path trust information, this study uses the above path weighting method to solve the indirect trust between experts e_1 and e_3, namely:

$$\begin{aligned} \overset{\bullet l_1}{q}((0.7,0.1),(0.5,0.2)) &= (0.35,0.28), \\ \overset{\bullet l_2}{q}((0.6,0.2),(0.6,0.1),(0.5,0.4)) &= (0.18,0.57), \\ \overset{\bullet l_3}{q}((0.6,0.2),(0.6,0.1),(0.6,0.3),(0.5,0.2)) &= (0.11,0.60), \end{aligned}$$

where the weights of three paths are given by $w_i = Q\left(\frac{i}{n}\right) - Q\left(\frac{i-1}{n}\right)$, and $w_1 = 0.58$, $w_2 = 0.24, w_3 = 0.18$.

Therefore, according to Equation (6), the indirect trust of expert e_1 to expert e_3 is:

$$\mathrm{T}(e_1 \to e_3) = 0.58 \cdot (0.35,0.28) \oplus 0.24 \cdot (0.18,0.57) \oplus 0.18 \cdot (0.11,0.60) = (0.27,0.38).$$

Other missing trust evaluation values can be calculated similarly, so the final social matrix T_L is:

$$T_L = \begin{pmatrix} - & (0.60,0.20) & (0.27,0.38) & (0.30,0.33) & (0.70,0.10) \\ (0.16,0.52) & - & (0.27,0.47) & (0.60,0.10) & (0.30,0.42) \\ (0.60,0.10) & (0.80,0.10) & - & (0.70,0.20) & (0.40,0.27) \\ (0.27,0.47) & (0.30,0.50) & (0.50,0.40) & - & (0.60,0.30) \\ (0.30,0.28) & (0.34,0.32) & (0.50,0.20) & (0.29,0.38) & - \end{pmatrix}.$$

Simultaneously, the trust score matrix TS_{hk} can be obtained according to the matrix T_L:

$$TS_{hk} = \begin{pmatrix} - & 0.70 & 0.45 & 0.49 & 0.80 \\ 0.32 & - & 0.40 & 0.75 & 0.44 \\ 0.75 & 0.85 & - & 0.75 & 0.57 \\ 0.40 & 0.40 & 0.55 & - & 0.65 \\ 0.51 & 0.51 & 0.65 & 0.46 & - \end{pmatrix}.$$

Therefore, according to the matrix TS_{hk} and equation $TS_k = \frac{1}{n-1}\sum_{h=1}^{n} TS_{hk}$, the trust scores TS_k of each expert can be obtained, thus:

$$TS_1 = 0.495,\ TS_2 = 0.615,\ TS_3 = 0.513,\ TS_4 = 0.613,\ TS_5 = 0.615.$$

3. Results

3.1. Q-ROF Aggregation Operator Based on Trust Scores and Confidence Levels of Experts

To integrate the evaluation information of the experts, we propose a new q-rung orthopair fuzzy induced ordered weighted average (q-ROFIOWA) operator based on the trust scores and confidence levels (CL) of experts.

Definition 9. *Let a series of q-ROFVs be* $G_t = \langle \mu_t, \nu_t \rangle\ (t = 1,2,\cdots,n)$, *where* $\omega = (\omega_1, \omega_2, \cdots, \omega_n)^T$ *is the weight vector, and* $\omega_t \in [0,1]$, $\sum_{t=1}^{n} \omega_t = 1$. *The q-ROFIOWA operator is then defined as:*

$$\mathrm{q-ROFIOWA}\left(\left(TL^1, G_1\right), \left(TL^2, G_2\right), \cdots, \left(TL^n, G_n\right)\right) = \overset{n}{\underset{t=1}{\oplus}} \omega_t G_{\sigma(t)} = \omega_1 G_{\sigma(1)} \oplus \omega_2 G_{\sigma(2)} \oplus \cdots \oplus \omega_n G_{\sigma(n)}, \quad (7)$$

where $G_{\sigma(t)}$ *is arranged by* $TL^{\sigma(t)}$ *from largest to smallest, and* $TL^{\sigma(t-1)} \geq TL^{\sigma(t)}$.

Suppose that there are n experts $e_t\,(t = 1,2,\cdots,n)$, m alternatives $Z_i\,(i = 1,2,\cdots,m)$, s attributes $C_j\,(j = 1,2,\cdots,s)$ and the experts' evaluation matrix is $L_t\,(t = 1,2,\cdots,n) = \left(G_{ij}^t\right)_{m\times s}$, then the integrated q-ROF matrix is $L^{TL} = \left(G_{ij}^{TL}\right) = \left(\mu_{ij}^{TL}, v_{ij}^{TL}\right)$, where μ_{ij}^{TL}, v_{ij}^{TL}, TL are calculated by the following equations, respectively:

$$\mu_{ij}^{TL} = \varphi_{\omega}^{TL}\left(\left(TL^1,\mu_{ij}^1\right),\cdots,\left(TL^n,\mu_{ij}^n\right)\right) = \sqrt[q]{1-\prod_{t=1}^{n}\left(1-\mu_{ij\sigma(t)}^{q}\right)^{\omega_t}}, \tag{8}$$

$$v_{ij}^{TL} = \psi_{\omega}^{TL}\left(\left(TL^1,v_{ij}^1\right),\cdots,\left(TL^n,v_{ij}^n\right)\right) = \prod_{t=1}^{n} v_{ij\sigma(t)}^{\omega_t}, \tag{9}$$

$$TL = \eta TS + (1-\eta)CL, \tag{10}$$

where $\omega_{\sigma(t-1)} \geq \omega_{\sigma(t)}\,(t = 2,\cdots,n)$, and

$$\omega_t = Q\left(\frac{TL(\sigma(t))}{TL(\sigma(n))}\right) - Q\left(\frac{TL(\sigma(t-1))}{TL(\sigma(n))}\right). \tag{11}$$

The above TL solution also needs to calculate the CL of experts, which is characterized by attributes, alternatives, and experts.

Level 1. Attribute level: the confidence level of the expert e_t on the alternative Z_i under attribute C_j is:

$$CL_{ij}^t = 1 - \pi_{ij}. \tag{12}$$

where $\pi_{ij} = \sqrt[q]{\left(1-(\mu_{ij})^q-(v_{ij})^q\right)}$.

Level 2. Alternative level: the confidence level of the expert e_t on the alternative Z_i is:

$$CL_i^t = \frac{1}{s}\sum_{j=1}^{s} CL_{ij}^t. \tag{13}$$

Level 3. Expert level: the confidence level of the expert e_t is:

$$CL^t = \frac{1}{m}\sum_{i=1}^{m} CL_i^t. \tag{14}$$

Thus, the confidence level of the expert e_t is:

$$CL^t = \frac{1}{ms}\sum_{i=1}^{m}\sum_{j=1}^{s} CL_{ij}^t. \tag{15}$$

From Equation (12), we can see that the confidence level of the expert e_t is based on the grade of hesitation when the expert e_t evaluates information. When $\pi_{ij} = 0$ and $CL_{ij}^t = 1$, there is no hesitation. When the q value increases, the hesitation grade increases, and the corresponding confidence level of the expert e_t decreases.

Example 2 (Continuation of Example 1). *Suppose that for teachers of a particular major in four universities, there are five experts' evaluation matrices:*

$$A^1 = \begin{pmatrix} [0.7,0.1] & [0.3,0.5] & [0.4,0.5] & [0.5,0.3] & [0.5,0.1] \\ [0.5,0.4] & [0.4,0.2] & [0.6,0.1] & [0.6,0.2] & [0.5,0.2] \\ [0.4,0.3] & [0.5,0.3] & [0.4,0.2] & [0.5,0.3] & [0.4,0.4] \\ [0.6,0.4] & [0.3,0.4] & [0.3,0.6] & [0.6,0.2] & [0.3,0.6] \end{pmatrix}$$

$$A^2 = \begin{pmatrix} [0.3,0.4] & [0.5,0.2] & [0.4,0.6] & [0.7,0.1] & [0.8,0.1] \\ [0.7,0.2] & [0.6,0.4] & [0.3,0.5] & [0.4,0.3] & [0.5,0.2] \\ [0.5,0.1] & [0.3,0.6] & [0.8,0.2] & [0.6,0.3] & [0.5,0.3] \\ [0.4,0.3] & [0.7,0.2] & [0.6,0.3] & [0.3,0.4] & [0.9,0.1] \end{pmatrix}$$

$$A^3 = \begin{pmatrix} [0.5,0.2] & [0.6,0.1] & [0.3,0.5] & [0.4,0.1] & [0.4,0.5] \\ [0.8,0.1] & [0.3,0.2] & [0.6,0.2] & [0.5,0.3] & [0.5,0.2] \\ [0.4,0.2] & [0.2,0.5] & [0.5,0.4] & [0.3,0.4] & [0.6,0.1] \\ [0.7,0.1] & [0.5,0.3] & [0.4,0.2] & [0.8,0.1] & [0.3,0.3] \end{pmatrix}$$

$$A^4 = \begin{pmatrix} [0.5,0.4] & [0.4,0.3] & [0.3,0.6] & [0.2,0.4] & [0.5,0.4] \\ [0.3,0.5] & [0.5,0.2] & [0.2,0.5] & [0.7,0.1] & [0.5,0.3] \\ [0.6,0.2] & [0.7,0.1] & [0.4,0.5] & [0.3,0.6] & [0.7,0.2] \\ [0.4,0.2] & [0.6,0.1] & [0.5,0.3] & [0.7,0.2] & [0.5,0.2] \end{pmatrix}$$

$$A^5 = \begin{pmatrix} [0.5,0.3] & [0.6,0.2] & [0.3,0.5] & [0.7,0.1] & [0.5,0.4] \\ [0.6,0.3] & [0.5,0.2] & [0.4,0.6] & [0.8,0.2] & [0.7,0.2] \\ [0.4,0.5] & [0.8,0.1] & [0.5,0.5] & [0.6,0.2] & [0.4,0.5] \\ [0.3,0.4] & [0.7,0.1] & [0.6,0.3] & [0.4,0.4] & [0.5,0.1] \end{pmatrix}$$

Then the corresponding confidence levels of experts are:

$$CL^1 = 0.78,\ CL^2 = 0.83,\ CL^3 = 0.73,\ CL^4 = 0.79,\ CL^5 = 0.85.$$

By combining the above TS and CL, and setting $\eta = 0.5$, TL can be obtained:

$$TL_1 = 0.64,\ TL_2 = 0.72,\ TL_3 = 0.62,\ TL_4 = 0.70,\ TL_5 = 0.73.$$

Therefore, the weights of the experts can be obtained according to Equation (11):

$$\omega_1 = 0.111,\ \omega_2 = 0.189,\ \omega_3 = 0.095,\ \omega_4 = 0.142,\ \omega_5 = 0.463.$$

Combined with Equation (7), the comprehensive evaluation matrix $\overline{A}$ can be given as:

$$\overline{A} = \begin{pmatrix} (0.497,0.281) & (0.530,0.220) & (0.332,0.531) & (0.610,0.138) & (0.572,0.270) \\ (0.606,0.278) & (0.495,0.228) & (0.408,0.417) & (0.693,0.203) & (0.605,0.212) \\ (0.453,0.281) & (0.661,0.185) & (0.560,0.372) & (0.532,0.282) & (0.495,0.334) \\ (0.423,0.301) & (0.641,0.148) & (0.543,0.312) & (0.518,0.294) & (0.605,0.149) \end{pmatrix}.$$

3.2. *CIM and Decision-Making Analysis Based on Q-ROF with the Paragraphs*

Considering the influence of the CIM on the final results, this study proposes a CIM based on q-ROF distance measure and trust relationships between experts, including consistency measurement, identification of inconsistent expert decision-making opinions, and a personalized adjustment mechanism (based on direct trust relationships between experts).

3.2.1. Calculation of Consistency Degree

The consistency index is divided into three levels:

Level 1. Attribute level: the consistency degree of the expert e_t on the alternative Z_i under attribute C_j is:

$$CE_{ij}^{t} = 1 - d(G_{ij}^{t}, \overline{G}_{ij}) = 1 - \frac{1}{2}\left(\left|\left(\mu_{ij}^{t}\right)^{q} - \left(\overline{\mu}_{ij}\right)^{q}\right| + \left|\left(v_{ij}^{t}\right)^{q} - \left(\overline{v}_{ij}\right)^{q}\right| + \left|\left(\pi_{ij}^{t}\right)^{q} - \left(\overline{\pi}_{ij}\right)^{q}\right|\right). \quad (16)$$

Level 2. Alternative level: the consistency degree of the expert e_t on the alternative Z_i is:

$$CA_i^t = \frac{1}{s}\sum_{j=1}^{s} CE_{ij}^t. \quad (17)$$

Level 3. Expert level: the consistency degree of the expert e_t is:

$$CI^t = \frac{1}{m}\sum_{i=1}^{m} CA_i^t. \quad (18)$$

Example 3 (Continuation of Example 2). *The evaluation matrix for each expert is known. According to Equations (16)–(18), the degree of consistency at the attribute level is calculated as:*

$$CE^1 = \begin{pmatrix} 0.797 & 0.720 & 0.932 & 0.838 & 0.758 \\ 0.878 & 0.877 & 0.683 & 0.904 & 0.883 \\ 0.947 & 0.839 & 0.669 & 0.968 & 0.906 \\ 0.724 & 0.660 & 0.712 & 0.906 & 0.549 \end{pmatrix}, CE^2 = \begin{pmatrix} 0.804 & 0.951 & 0.863 & 0.910 & 0.772 \\ 0.906 & 0.723 & 0.892 & 0.707 & 0.883 \\ 0.820 & 0.585 & 0.760 & 0.914 & 0.966 \\ 0.976 & 0.887 & 0.943 & 0.782 & 0.705 \end{pmatrix},$$

$$CE^3 = \begin{pmatrix} 0.919 & 0.880 & 0.937 & 0.752 & 0.770 \\ 0.806 & 0.777 & 0.783 & 0.807 & 0.883 \\ 0.867 & 0.539 & 0.940 & 0.768 & 0.766 \\ 0.723 & 0.848 & 0.745 & 0.718 & 0.695 \end{pmatrix}, CE^4 = \begin{pmatrix} 0.878 & 0.870 & 0.931 & 0.590 & 0.870 \\ 0.694 & 0.972 & 0.792 & 0.897 & 0.895 \\ 0.853 & 0.915 & 0.840 & 0.682 & 0.795 \\ 0.876 & 0.913 & 0.945 & 0.818 & 0.895 \end{pmatrix},$$

$$CE^5 = \begin{pmatrix} 0.978 & 0.930 & 0.937 & 0.910 & 0.870 \\ 0.978 & 0.972 & 0.817 & 0.893 & 0.905 \\ 0.781 & 0.861 & 0.872 & 0.918 & 0.834 \\ 0.877 & 0.940 & 0.943 & 0.882 & 0.846 \end{pmatrix}.$$

The degree of consistency at the alternative level:

$$CA^1 = (0.809, 0.845, 0.866, 0.710),\ CA^2 = (0.860, 0.822, 0.809, 0.859),$$
$$CA^3 = (0.852, 0.811, 0.776, 0.746),\ CA^4 = (0.828, 0.850, 0.817, 0.889),$$
$$CA^5 = (0.925, 0.913, 0.853, 0.898).$$

And the consistency at the expert level:

$$CI^1 = 0.807,\ CI^2 = 0.837,\ CI^3 = 0.796,\ CI^4 = 0.846,\ CI^5 = 0.897.$$

3.2.2. Identification of Inconsistent Expert Decision-Making Opinions and a Personalized Adjustment Mechanism

After obtaining the consistency degree of the above three levels, we need to identify the decision-making information of inconsistent experts and then modify their corresponding decision-making opinions. According to the literature [34], a three-level recognition method is proposed:

Level 1. Determine all experts whose consistency is lower than the consensus threshold δ, which is defined as:

$$EXPCH = \{t | CI^t < \delta\}.$$

Level 2. On the basis of obtaining all inconsistent experts, determine all alternatives whose consistency is lower than the consensus threshold δ, which is defined as:

$$ALT = \{(t,i) | t \in EXPCH \wedge CA_i^t < \delta\}.$$

Level 3. Determine all attribute evaluation information with a degree of consistency lower than the consensus threshold δ:

$$APS = \left\{(t,i,j)\middle|(t,i) \in ALT \wedge CE_{ij}^{t} < \delta\right\}.$$

As mentioned above, the experts who need to adjust their opinions are more willing to trust the decision-making opinions of the experts who have a direct trust relationship with them. Therefore, this study modifies the expert's decision-making opinions according to the following adjustment advice:

$$GG_{ij}^{t} = (1-\vartheta)\cdot G_{ij}^{t} + \vartheta \cdot \widetilde{G}, \tag{19}$$

where $\widetilde{G} = (\widetilde{\mu}_{ij}, \widetilde{v}_{ij})$, $\widetilde{\mu}_{ij} = \frac{1}{l}\sum_{r=1}^{l}\widetilde{\mu}_{ij}^{r}$, $\widetilde{v}_{ij} = \frac{1}{l}\sum_{r=1}^{l}\widetilde{v}_{ij}^{r}$, and $r = 1,2,\cdots,l$ means the expert e_t has l directly trusted experts.

Example 4 (Continuation of Example 3). *Assuming $\delta = 0.8$, the expert e_3 needs to be adjusted. The specific evaluation opinions that need to be adjusted at the attribute level are:*

$$G_{32}^{3}, G_{34}^{3}, G_{35}^{3}, G_{41}^{3}, G_{43}^{3}, G_{44}^{3}, G_{45}^{3}.$$

Let $\vartheta = 0.5$, then the opinions of the expert e_3 are modified to become:
$G_{32}^{3} = (0.39, 0.36)$, $G_{34}^{3} = (0.40, 0.39)$, $G_{35}^{3} = (0.58, 0.17)$, $G_{41}^{3} = (0.60, 0.17)$, $G_{43}^{3} = (0.44, 0.27)$, $G_{44}^{3} = (0.70, 0.16)$, $G_{45}^{3} = (0.52, 0.26)$.

3.2.3. Decision-Making Analysis after Reaching Consensus (Alternatives Ranking)

After adjusting the evaluation opinions, the new consistency degrees of the experts are calculated as follows:

$$CI^1 = 0.806,\ CI^2 = 0.838,\ CI^3 = 0.836,\ CI^4 = 0.844,\ CI^5 = 0.900.$$

The corresponding weights of experts are:

$$\omega_1 = 0.110,\ \omega_2 = 0.189,\ \omega_3 = 0.097,\ \omega_4 = 0.142,\ \omega_5 = 0.462.$$

Therefore, the adjusted aggregation evaluation matrix is:

$$\overline{A} = \begin{pmatrix} (0.496, 0.281) & (0.530, 0.219) & (0.332, 0.531) & (0.610, 0.137) & (0.572, 0.270) \\ (0.607, 0.277) & (0.495, 0.228) & (0.408, 0.417) & (0.692, 0.204) & (0.605, 0.212) \\ (0.453, 0.280) & (0.669, 0.179) & (0.560, 0.372) & (0.538, 0.282) & (0.493, 0.350) \\ (0.408, 0.316) & (0.640, 0.148) & (0.546, 0.321) & (0.499, 0.307) & (0.619, 0.147) \end{pmatrix}.$$

According to Equation (3) and attribute weights, we can get

$$G_{Z_1} = [0.533, 0.250],\ G_{Z_2} = [0.579, 0.242],\ G_{Z_3} = [0.550, 0.276],\ G_{Z_4} = [0.565, 0.207].$$

The trust scores are thus calculated as:

$$TS_1 = 0.642,\ TS_2 = 0.669,\ TS_3 = 0.637,\ TS_4 = 0.679.$$

Therefore, the ranking of alternatives is: $Z_4 \succ Z_2 \succ Z_1 \succ Z_3$.

In summary, the specific steps of the proposed SNGDM method based on q-ROFS are as follows.

Step 1: Based on the proposed trust propagation and aggregation operators in Equations (4) and (6), the missing q-ROF trust social matrix is completed, and the corresponding trust score matrix and the trust score of each expert have been calculated.

Step 2: Calculate the confidence levels of experts based on Equations (12)–(15) and calculate the weights of experts combined with the trust scores of experts. Based on Equation (7), a comprehensive decision-making matrix is obtained by integrating the expert evaluation matrices.

Step 3: Calculate the consistency degree of the three levels based on Equations (16)–(18). If the consistency of all experts is greater than the threshold, we skip to Step 4. Otherwise, identify the inconsistent experts and their decision-making opinions, adjust the inconsistent decision-making opinions according to Equation (19), and then return to Step 2.

Step 4: Calculate the evaluation value of each alternative based on Equation (3) and attribute weight and sort the alternatives according to Definition 4.

Accordingly, the SNGDM method can be represented by the following flow chart (Figure 2):

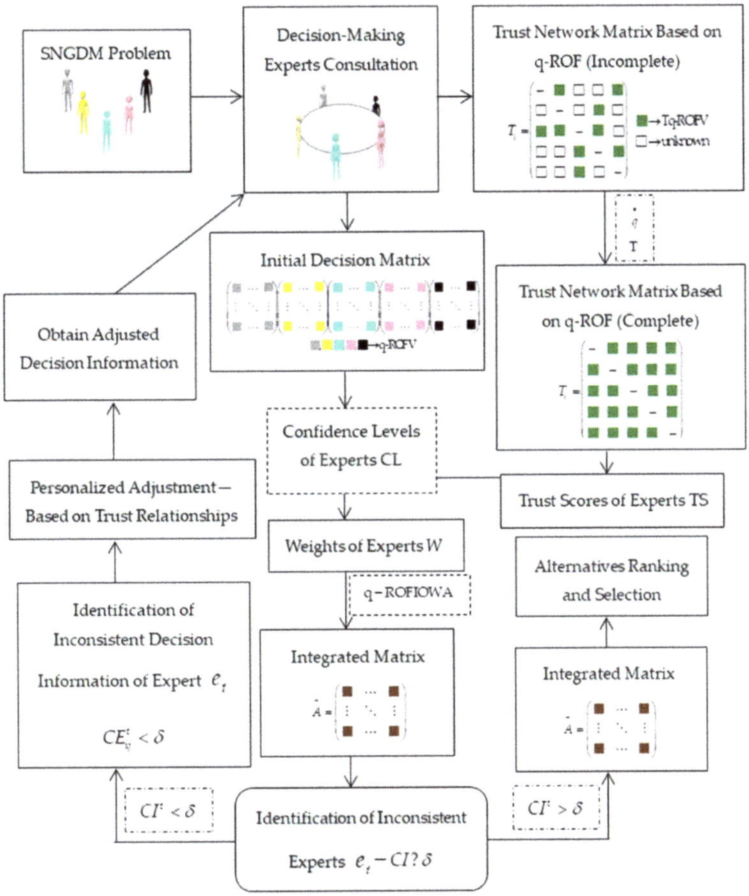

Figure 2. Framework of SNGDM method based on q-ROFS.

3.2.4. Analysis of the Influence of the Parameter q on Alternative Ranking

In this study, we consider the influence of the change in parameter q on the ranking of alternatives and take $q = 1, 2, 3, 5, 10$ and 20, respectively. The trust scores and ranking results of the alternatives are presented in Table 1; it can be seen that with the increase in the parameter q, the trust score TS of each alternative Z_i presents a decreasing trend. Moreover, when q takes different values, the ranking results of the alternatives are not the same. Specifically, when $q = 1$, the ranking of the alternatives is $Z_4 \succ Z_2 \succ Z_1 \succ Z_3$; when $q = 2, 3$ and 5, the ranking of the alternatives is $Z_4 \succ Z_1 \succ Z_2 \succ Z_3$; when $q = 10$ and 20, the ranking of the alternatives is $Z_4 \succ Z_1 \succ Z_3 \succ Z_2$. Therefore, the value of q has a definite influence on the trust scores and ranking of the alternatives. However, regardless of how q changes, the optimal alternative does not change, that is, the alternative Z_4, which indicates that the operator q-ROFIOWA is relatively stable. At the same time, the decision-making experts can choose an appropriate value of q to express their preferences according to the actual situation, which highlights the flexibility of the proposed method.

Table 1. Alternative ranking under parameter q.

q	TS	Ranking
1	$TS_1 = 0.642, TS_2 = 0.669$ $TS_3 = 0.637, TS_4 = 0.679$	$Z_4 \succ Z_2 \succ Z_1 \succ Z_3$
2	$TS_1 = 0.638, TS_2 = 0.628$ $TS_3 = 0.613, TS_4 = 0.686$	$Z_4 \succ Z_1 \succ Z_2 \succ Z_3$
3	$TS_1 = 0.596, TS_2 = 0.588$ $TS_3 = 0.579, TS_4 = 0.643$	$Z_4 \succ Z_1 \succ Z_2 \succ Z_3$
5	$TS_1 = 0.545, TS_2 = 0.538$ $TS_3 = 0.536, TS_4 = 0.584$	$Z_4 \succ Z_1 \succ Z_2 \succ Z_3$
10	$TS_1 = 0.510, TS_2 = 0.506$ $TS_3 = 0.507, TS_4 = 0.532$	$Z_4 \succ Z_1 \succ Z_3 \succ Z_2$
20	$TS_1 = 0.501, TS_2 = 0.500$ $TS_3 = 0.501, TS_4 = 0.509$	$Z_4 \succ Z_1 \succ Z_3 \succ Z_2$

Note: when $q = 20$, $TS_1 = TS_3$, and $H_1 > H_3$, so $Z_1 \succ Z_3$.

3.3. *Comparative Analysis*

3.3.1. Feasibility Analysis

It can be seen in Table 2 that the ranking results of the existing methods are not the same as the method proposed in this study. For example, based on IFVs and Frank operators, Zheng and Xu [24] proposed a new trust propagation operator that contains an IF trust weighted average (IFTWA) operator and length (L-IFTWA) operator. The final result was the same as that of the proposed method ($q = 1$), but different from that obtained by $q = 2$ and 10. Wu et al. [30] used representable uninorm U to propagate trust, and the final result was the same as that obtained by the proposed method ($q = 2$), but different from that obtained by $q = 1$ and 10. Although the ranking of alternatives is different, the optimal alternative is Z_4, which shows that the proposed method is feasible.

Table 2. Different methods of alternative ranking.

Methods	Ranking
IFTWA/L-IFTWA [24]	$Z_4 \succ Z_2 \succ Z_1 \succ Z_3$
Uninorm [30]	$Z_4 \succ Z_1 \succ Z_2 \succ Z_3$
q-ROFIOWA [the proposed method, $q = 1$]	$Z_4 \succ Z_2 \succ Z_1 \succ Z_3$
q-ROFIOWA [the proposed method, $q = 2$]	$Z_4 \succ Z_1 \succ Z_2 \succ Z_3$
q-ROFIOWA [the proposed method, $q = 10$]	$Z_4 \succ Z_1 \succ Z_3 \succ Z_2$

3.3.2. Superiority Analysis

To demonstrate the advantages of the proposed method, we carry out a detailed comparative analysis using the methods in literatures [24,30]; the results are given in Table 3.

Table 3. Comparative analysis.

Methods	Method of Literature [24]	Method of Literature [30]	The Proposed Method
Problems Solved	SNGDM	SNGDM	SNGDM
The Representation of Trust	IFVs	Trust decision space	q-ROFVs
Trust Paopagation (Diminishing Trust)	Frank operator (Decrease)	Uninorm (Increase)	$\dot{q}$ (Decrease)
Trust Aggregation	L-IFTWA	Shortest path	T
Experts' Weights	Centrality theory	Q(TS)	Q(TS + CL)
CIM	No considered	No considered	Considered

(1) Comparison with the method proposed in [24]. First, the condition $0 \leq \mu + v \leq 1$ must always be maintained in the range of IFVs expressing the trust relationship, but in reality, the situation of $\mu + v > 1$ often appears. This study proposes a Tq-ROFV, which uses q-ROFV to represent the trust relationships among experts and express trust information over a wider range. Naturally, the TIFV is a special case of the Tq-ROFV; i.e., when $q = 1$, the Tq-ROFV degenerates into the TIFV.

Second, when integrating the trust information of multiple propagation paths, Zheng and Xu [24] make full use of each path, but it falls short when the lengths of the paths are the same and the weights are the same. When the lengths of the paths are the same, the greater the trust score, and the greater the weight. Therefore, the method for determination of the experts' weights based on a Q quantifier in this study is more reasonable. Moreover, the method proposed in [24] does not consider the impact of the CIM on the decision-making results.

(2) Comparison with the method proposed in [30]. First, the distrust values of the previous trust relationships are not considered in [30], and only the distrust value of the last trust relationship is considered. Simultaneously, the values of trust increase during the trust propagation process. For example, if there are two direct trust relationships $G_1 = (0.55, 0.35)$ and $G_2 = (0.75, 0.20)$ on the propagation path, then the U operator is used for trust propagation, and we get:

$$U(G_1, G_2) = \left(\frac{0.55 \times 0.75}{0.55 \times 0.75 + 0.45 \times 0.25}, \frac{0.55 \times 0.20}{0.55 \times 0.20 + 0.45 \times 0.80}\right) = (0.79, 0.23).$$

It is clear that the trust value after propagation is $0.79 > 0.75$, $0.79 > 0.55$; the trust value increases, which does not conform to the principle of trust diminishing in the process of trust propagation. Moreover, the distrust value of G_1 is not used in the process of trust propagation, and only the distrust value of G_2 is considered. This study proposes a trust propagation operator based on q-ROF multiplication operation to compensate for this defect, that is, (assuming $q = 1$):

$$q(G_1, G_2) = (0.55 \times 0.75, 0.35 + 0.20 - 0.35 \times 0.20) = (0.41, 0.48).$$

Given $0.41 < 0.75$, $0.41 < 0.55$ and $0.48 > 0.35$, $0.48 > 0.20$, the trust relationship after propagation satisfies the principles of diminishing trust and increasing distrust. At the same time, the distrust value of each trust relationship was considered.

Second, when integrating the trust information of multiple paths, Wu et al. [30] directly selects the trust relationship of the shortest path as the ultimate indirect trust relationship, ignoring the trust information of other paths. However, in this study, we use the trust information of each path, taking into account and assigning the corresponding weights. The shorter the path, the greater the weight, and the longer the path, the smaller the weight, and when the path length is the same, the greater the trust score, the greater the weight of the path, and so the path weighting method in this study is more reasonable.

Third, Wu et al. [30] use the TS as the guidance to solve the weights of experts, and the importance of experts' confidence level in the process of GDM is ignored. This study not only considers the trust score TS, but also considers the confidence level CL of experts, and further enables solving for the weights of experts through the combination of the two.

Fourth, considering the difference in professional backgrounds among experts, it is difficult to reach an agreement on the initial opinion, and a consensus needs to be reached through mutual coordination and adjustment of opinion. Therefore, considering the importance of consensus building, this study proposes a CIM based on the q-ROF distance measure and trust relationship, whereas the literature [30] does not consider the CIM.

4. Discussion and Conclusions

At present, there are many GDM methods for teaching quality evaluation [1,4,5,9,10], but most of them do not consider the influence of trust networks among experts on the evaluation results. This study extends the SNA method to the GDM method and proposes a new SNGDM method based on q-ROFS for the evaluation of online teaching quality, which makes the evaluation results more reasonable. At the same time, considering the subjectivity, fuzziness, and uncertainty of trust and the vagueness of evaluation indices, this study uses q-ROFV to describe them in a more comprehensive and detailed manner. Thus, decision-makers can choose the appropriate value of the parameter q to evaluate the indices according to the actual situation in order to minimize the loss of information. The example presented in this study shows that the alternative ranking of different methods varies greatly, but the optimal alternative remains unchanged. Additionally, a comparison with the existing SNGDM methods in [24] and [30] verifies that the proposed method is more advantageous and feasible. Specifically, the advantages and contributions of the proposed SNGDM method can be summarized as follows:

First, this study combines q-ROF theory with the SNA method and proposes a Tq-ROFV to express the trust relationships between experts, which can describe the subjectivity, ambiguity, and uncertainty of trust more comprehensively. Second, a trust propagation operator based on the q-ROF multiplication operator is proposed to obtain an indirect trust between experts, which fully considers the principle of diminishing trust values in the process of trust propagation. In view of the flexibility of the trust propagation operator (including varying parameter q), decision-makers can choose the appropriate parameters according to the actual situation, and the greater the value of q, the greater the uncertainty. Moreover, considering the existence of multiple trust paths, a trust aggregation operator based on q-ROFS is proposed to integrate the trust relationships of multiple paths. Additionally, to integrate the evaluation information of experts, a q-ROFIOWA operator is proposed, which considers the confidence levels of experts when evaluating the information. Finally, given the impact of the CIM and the trust relationships among experts on decision-making results, a CIM based on q-ROF distance measure and trust relationships among experts is introduced.

The SNGDM method not only provides a new method for the evaluation of online teaching quality, but also enables teachers to discover issues in the teaching process in time and make improvements. However, the SNGDM method has some limitations. First, the evaluation information of experts in the process of evaluating online teaching quality is known, and there is no missing evaluation information. In fact, some or all experts involved in the evaluation process may not have a thorough understanding of the issues involved, so it is often impossible to give all the evaluation information. Therefore, we will consider the situation in which evaluation information is missing in future work. Second, the SNGDM method is implemented in a multi-attribute environment, and whether it can be extended to other decision-making environments remains to be seen, such as fuzzy preference relationships [22,48–50]. At the same time, it is yet to be determined as to whether the SNGDM method can be extended to solve evaluation decision-making problems in other industries, such as venture capital evaluation, green supply chain management, e-learning course selection, selection of the best substitutes for biopesticides, site assessment, digitalization in logistics and retail, and weapon selection decisions [27,51–57]. Third, when adjusting expert opinions, this study takes the decision-making opinions of trusted experts as a simple weighted average. In fact, among all trusted experts, inconsistent decision-makers have different trust levels for different experts. That is, when the expert's opinions are adjusted, the adjustment of weights should be different for different levels of trust, which is our future avenue of research.

Author Contributions: Conceptualization, Y.H. and S.Z.; Funding acquisition, S.Z.; Investigation, Y.H., S.Z. and Y.Y.; Methodology, Y.H., S.Z., L.-A.C. and K.U.; Project administration, Y.H., S.Z., and K.U.; Software, Y.H., S.Z., L.-A.C., K.U. and Y.Y.; Validation, Y.H., S.Z. and Y.Y.; Writing—original draft, Y.H., and Y.Y.; Writing—review and editing, S.Z., L.-A.C., and K.U. All authors have read and agreed to the published version of the manuscript.

Funding: This work is supported by the Social Sciences Planning Projects of Zhejiang (21QNYC11ZD), Statistical Scientific Key Research Project of China (2021LZ33), Major Humanities and Social Sciences Research Projects in Zhejiang Universities (2018QN058), Fundamental Research Funds for the Provincial Universities of Zhejiang (SJWZ2020002), Longyuan Construction Financial Research Project of Ningbo University (LYYB2002), Statistical Scientifific Key Research Project of China and the First Class Discipline of Zhejiang-A (Zhejiang Gongshang University-Statistics).

Institutional Review Board Statement: Not applicable.

Informed Consent Statement: Not applicable.

Data Availability Statement: Not applicable.

Acknowledgments: The authors are extremely grateful for the editorial team's valuable comments on improving the quality of this article.

Conflicts of Interest: The authors declare no conflict of interest.

References

1. Liu, S. Research on the teaching quality evaluation of physical education with intuitionistic fuzzy TOPSIS method. *J. Intell. Fuzzy Syst.* **2021**, *40*, 9227–9236. [CrossRef]
2. Carlucci, D.; Renna, P.; Izzo, C.; Schiuma, G. Assessing teaching performance in higher education: A framework for continuous improvement. *Manag. Decis.* **2019**, *57*, 461–479. [CrossRef]
3. Chen, J.F.; Hsieh, H.N.; Do, Q.H. Evaluating teaching performance based on fuzzy AHP and comprehensive evaluation approach. *Appl. Soft. Comput.* **2015**, *28*, 100–108. [CrossRef]
4. Zhang, X.; Wang, J.; Zhang, H.; Hu, J. A heterogeneous linguistic MAGDM framework to classroom teaching quality evaluation. *Eurasia J. Math. Sci. Technol. Educ.* **2017**, *13*, 4929–4956. [CrossRef]
5. Yu, D. Prioritized information fusion method for triangular intuitionistic fuzzy set and its application to teaching quality evaluation. *Int. J. Intell. Syst.* **2013**, *28*, 411–435. [CrossRef]
6. Yang, H.; Xiang, C. Approaches to multiple attribute decision making based on the hesitant fuzzy uncertain linguistic information and their applications to teaching quality evaluation in higher education. In Proceedings of the National Academy of Sciences, New Delhi, India, 8–9 March 2018; pp. 577–583.
7. Peng, X.; Dai, J. Research on the assessment of classroom teaching quality with q-rung orthopair fuzzy information based on multiparametric similarity measure and combinative distance-based assessment. *Int. J. Intell. Syst.* **2019**, *34*, 1588–1630. [CrossRef]
8. Yu, H. Online teaching quality evaluation based on emotion recognition and improved AprioriTid algorithm. *J. Intell. Fuzzy Syst.* **2021**, *40*, 7037–7047. [CrossRef]
9. Liu, P.; Wang, X.; Teng, F. Online teaching quality evaluation based on multi-granularity probabilistic linguistic term sets. *J. Intell. Fuzzy Syst.* **2021**, *40*, 9915–9935. [CrossRef]
10. Lin, H.; You, J.; Xu, T. Evaluation of online teaching quality: An extended linguistic MAGDM framework based on risk preferences and unknown weight information. *Symmetry* **2021**, *13*, 192. [CrossRef]
11. Ali, Z.; Mahmood, T.; Ullah, K.; Khan, Q. Einstein geometric aggregation operators using a novel complex interval-valued Pythagorean fuzzy setting with application in green supplier chain management. *Rep. Mech. Eng.* **2021**, *2*, 105–134. [CrossRef]
12. Bu, F.; He, J.; Li, H.; Fu, Q. Interval-valued intuitionistic fuzzy MADM method based on TOPSIS and grey correlation analysis. *Math. Biosci. Eng.* **2020**, *17*, 5584–5603. [CrossRef] [PubMed]
13. Senapati, T.; Chen, G. Some novel interval-valued Pythagorean fuzzy aggregation operator based on Hamacher triangular norms and their application in MADM issues. *Comput. Appl. Math.* **2021**, *40*, 109. [CrossRef]

14. Abdul-Rahman, A.; Hailes, S. Supporting trust in virtual communities. In Proceedings of the 33rd Annual Hawaii International Conference on System Sciences, Maui, HI, USA, 7 January 2000; pp. 4–7.
15. Guha, R.; Kumar, R.; Raghavan, R.; Tomkins, A. Propagation of trust and distrust. In Proceedings of the 13th international conference on World Wide Web. *ACM* **2004**, 403–412. [CrossRef]
16. Kim, Y.A.; Song, H.S. Strategies for predicting local trust based on trust propagation in social networks. *Knowl. Based Syst.* **2011**, *24*, 1360–1371. [CrossRef]
17. Wang, Y.; Hang, C.; Singh, M.P. A Probabilistic Approach for Maintaining Trust Based on Evidence. *J. Artif. Intell. Res.* **2011**, *40*, 221–267. [CrossRef]
18. Wang, G.; Wu, J. Multi-dimensional evidence-based trust management with multi-trusted paths. *Futur. Gener. Comp. Syst.* **2011**, *27*, 529–538. [CrossRef]
19. Ma, H.; Hu, Z. Cloud service recommendation based on trust measurement using ternary interval numbers. In Proceedings of the 2014 International Conference on Smart Computing (SMARTCOMP), Hong Kong, China, 3–5 November 2014; pp. 21–24.
20. Shakeri, H.; Bafghi, A.G. Propagation of trust and confidence using intervals. In Proceedings of the 2011 International Conference for Internet Technology and Secured Transactions, Abu Dhabi, United Arab Emirates, 11–14 December 2011; pp. 436–441.
21. Shakeri, H.; Bafghi, A.G. A confidence-aware interval-based trust model. *J. Inf. Secur.* **2012**, *4*, 1–15.
22. Taghavi, A.; Eslami, E.; Herrera-Viedma, E.; Urena, R. Trust based group decision making in environments with extreme uncertainty. *Knowl. Based Syst.* **2020**, *191*, 105168. [CrossRef]
23. Pei, F.; He, Y.; Yan, A.; Zhou, M.; Chen, Y.; Wu, J. A Consensus Model for Intuitionistic Fuzzy Group Decision-Making Problems Based on the Construction and Propagation of Trust/Distrust Relationships in Social Networks. *Int. J. Fuzzy Syst.* **2020**, *22*, 2664–2679. [CrossRef]
24. Zheng, Y.; Xu, J. A trust transitivity model for group decision making in social network with intuitionistic fuzzy information. *Filomat* **2018**, *32*, 1937–1945. [CrossRef]
25. Wang, H.; Jin, M.; Ren, P. Intuitionistic fuzzy social network position and role analysis. *Cluster Comput. J. Netw. Softw. Tools Appl.* **2019**, *22*, S8099–S8108. [CrossRef]
26. Liang, D.; Yi, B.; Xu, Z. Opinion dynamics based on infectious disease transmission model in the non-connected context of Pythagorean fuzzy trust relationship. *J. Operational Res. Soc.* **2020**, 1–21. [CrossRef]
27. Ji, Y.; Xu, Y.; Qu, S.; Xu, Z.; Wu, Z.; Nabe, M. A Novel Two-Stage Multi-Criteria Decision-Making Method Based on Interval-Valued Pythagorean Fuzzy Aggregation Operators with Self-Confdence Levels. *Arab J. Sci Eng.* **2021**, *46*, 1561–1584. [CrossRef]
28. Tian, Z.; Nie, R.; Wang, J.; Zhang, H. A two-fold feedback mechanism to support consensus-reaching in social network group decision-making. *Knowl. Based Syst.* **2018**, *162*, 74–91. [CrossRef]
29. Wu, J.; Chiclana, F.; Herrera-Viedma, E. Trust based consensus model for social network in an incomplete linguistic information context. *Appl. Soft. Comput.* **2015**, *35*, 827–839. [CrossRef]
30. Wu, J.; Xiong, R.; Chiclana, F. Uninorm trust propagation and aggregation methods for group decision making in social network with four tuple information. *Knowl. Based Syst.* **2016**, *96*, 29–39. [CrossRef]
31. Wang, H.; Huang, L.; Ren, P.; Zhao, R.; Luo, Y. Dynamic incomplete uninorm trust propagation and aggregation methods in social network. *J. Intell. Fuzzy Syst.* **2017**, *33*, 3027–3039. [CrossRef]
32. Wu, J.; Chiclana, F.; Fujita, H.; Herrera-Viedma, E. A visual interaction consensus model for social network group decision making with trust propagation. *Knowl. Based Syst.* **2017**, *122*, 39–50. [CrossRef]
33. Verbiest, N.; Cornelis, C.; Victor, P.; Herrera-Viedma, E. Trust and distrust aggregation enhanced with path length incorporation. *Fuzzy Sets Syst.* **2012**, *202*, 61–74. [CrossRef]
34. Liu, Y.; Liang, C.; Chiclana, F.; Wu, J. A trust induced recommendation mechanism for reaching consensus in group decision making. *Knowl. Based Syst.* **2017**, *119*, 221–231. [CrossRef]
35. Hu, R.; Li, Q.; Zhang, G.; Ma, W. Centrality measures in directed fuzzy social networks. *Fuzzy Inf. Eng.* **2015**, *7*, 115–128. [CrossRef]
36. Wu, J.; Chiclana, F. A social network analysis trust-consensus based approach to group decision-making problems with interval-valued fuzzy reciprocal preference relations. *Knowl. Based Syst.* **2014**, *59*, 97–107. [CrossRef]
37. Wu, J.; Chiclana, F. Visual information feedback mechanism and attitudinal prioritisation method for group decision making with triangular fuzzy complementary preference relations. *Inf. Sci.* **2014**, *279*, 716–734. [CrossRef]
38. Xu, Z. An automatic approach to reaching consensus in multiple attribute group decision making. *Comput. Ind. Eng.* **2009**, *56*, 1369–1374. [CrossRef]
39. Guha, D.; Chakraborty, D. A new approach to fuzzy distance measure and similarity measure between two generalized fuzzy numbers. *Appl. Soft. Comput.* **2010**, *10*, 90–99. [CrossRef]
40. Yager, R.R. Generalized orthopair fuzzy sets. *IEEE Trans. Fuzzy Syst.* **2017**, *25*, 1222–1230. [CrossRef]
41. Liu, P.; Wang, P. Some q-rung orthopair fuzzy aggregation operators and their applications to multiple-attribute decision making. *Int. J. Intell. Syst.* **2018**, *33*, 259–280. [CrossRef]
42. Liu, P.; Chen, S.M.; Wang, P. The q-rung orthopair fuzzy power maclaurin symmetric mean operators. In Proceedings of the 2018 10th International Conference on Advanced Computational Intelligence (ICACI), Xiamen, China, 29–31 March 2018; pp. 156–161.
43. Wei, G.; Wei, C.; Wang, J.; Gao, H.; Wei, Y. Some q-rung orthopair fuzzy maclaurin symmetric mean operators and their applications to potential evaluation of emerging technology commercialization. *Int. J. Intell. Syst.* **2019**, *34*, 50–81. [CrossRef]

44. Xu, J. Study on Trust Evaluation Method Based on Intuitionistic Fuzzy Theory. Ph.D. Dissertation, Jiangxi University of Finance and Economics, Nanchang, China, 2015.
45. Beth, T.; Borcherding, M.; Klein, B. *Valuation of Trust in Open Networks*; Springer: Berlin/Heidelberg, Germany, 1994; pp. 1–18.
46. Sun, Y.L.; Yu, W.; Han, Z.; Liu, K.J.R. Information theoretic framework of trust modeling and evaluation for ad hoc networks. *IEEE J. Sel. Areas Commun.* **2006**, *24*, 305–317.
47. Luo, W.; Liu, B.; He, H.; Xu, Y.; Hu, C. Construction andempirical study of comprehensive evaluation index system of online teaching in the period of COVID-19. *J. Wuhan Polytech. Univ.* **2020**, *39*, 109–114.
48. Liu, P.; Ali, A.; Rehman, N.; Shah, S.I.A. Another view on intuitionistic fuzzy preference relation-based aggregation operators and their applications. *Int. J. Fuzzy Syst.* **2020**, *22*, 1786–1800. [CrossRef]
49. Luo, S.; Zhang, H.; Wang, J.; Li, L. Group decision-making approach for evaluating the sustainability of constructed wetlands with probabilistic linguistic preference relations. *J. Oper. Res. Soc.* **2019**, *70*, 2039–2055. [CrossRef]
50. Mandal, P.; Ranadive, A.S. Pythagorean fuzzy preference relations and their applications in group decision-making systems. *Int. J. Intell. Syst.* **2019**, *34*, 1700–1717. [CrossRef]
51. Fu, S.; Xiao, Y.; Zhou, H.; Liu, S. Venture capital project selection based on interval number grey target decision model. *Soft Comput.* **2021**, *25*, 4685–4874. [CrossRef]
52. Zhang, C.; Hu, Q.; Zeng, S.; Su, W. IOWLAD-based MCDM model for the site assessment of a household waste processing plant under a Pythagorean fuzzy environment. *Environ. Impact Assess. Rev.* **2021**, *89*, 106579. [CrossRef]
53. Dagdeviren, M.; Yavuz, S.; Kilinc, N. Weapon selection decision-making based on expert trust network under incomplete information. *Expert Syst. Appl.* **2009**, *36*, 8143–8151.
54. Riaz, M.; Agman, N.; Wali, N.; Mushtaq, A. Certain Properties of Soft multi-set topology with applications in multi-criteria decision making. *Decis. Mak. Appl. Manag. Eng.* **2020**, *3*, 70–96. [CrossRef]
55. Barykin, S.Y.; Smirnova, E.A.; Sharapaev, P.A.; Mottaeva, A.B. Development of the Kazakhstan digital retail chains within the EAEU E-commerce. *Acad. Strateg. Manag. J.* **2021**, *20*, 1–18.
56. Jocic, K.J.; Jocic, G.; Karabasevic, D.; Popovic, G.; Stanujkic, D.; Zavadskas, E.K.; Nguyen, P.T. A Novel Integrated PIPRECIA–Interval-Valued Triangular Fuzzy ARAS Model: E-Learning Course Selection. *Symmetry.* **2020**, *12*, 928. [CrossRef]
57. Xie, X.Y.; Liu, H.W.; Zeng, S.Z.; Lin, L.B.; Li, W. A novel progressively undersampling method based on the density peaks sequence for imbalanced data. *Knowl. Based Syst.* **2021**, *213*, 106689. [CrossRef]

axioms

MDPI

Article

Approach to Multi-Attribute Decision-Making Methods for Performance Evaluation Process Using Interval-Valued T-Spherical Fuzzy Hamacher Aggregation Information

Yun Jin [1], Zareena Kousar [2], Kifayat Ullah [2,*], Tahir Mahmood [3], Nimet Yapici Pehlivan [4] and Zeeshan Ali [3]

1 Tourism Department, Wuxi Vocational College of Science and Technology, Wuxi 214028, China; yjin@nuaa.edu.cn

2 Department of Mathematics, Riphah Institute of Computing & Applied Sciences (RICAS), Riphah International University (Lahore Campus), Lahore 54000, Pakistan; zarinakausar046@gmail.com or 15662@students.riu.edu.pk

3 Department of Mathematics & Statistics, International Islamic University Islamabad, Islamabad 44000, Pakistan; tahirbakhat@iiu.edu.pk (T.M.); zeeshan.phdma102@iiu.edu.pk (Z.A.)

4 Department of Statistics, Science Faculty, Selçuk University, Konya 42031, Turkey; nimet@selcuk.edu.tr

* Correspondence: kifayat.khan.dr@gmail.com; Tel.: +92-334-909-0225

Abstract: Interval-valued T-spherical fuzzy set (IVTSFS) handles uncertain and vague information by discussing their membership degree (MD), abstinence degree (AD), non-membership degree (NMD), and refusal degree (RD). MD, AD, NMD, and RD are defined in terms of closed subintervals of [0, 1] that reduce information loss compared to the T-spherical fuzzy set (TSFS), which takes crisp values from [0, 1] intervals; hence, some information may be lost. The purpose of this manuscript is to develop some Hamacher aggregation operators (HAOs) in the environment of IVTSFSs. To do so, some Hamacher operational laws based on Hamacher t-norms (HTNs) and Hamacher t-conorms (HTCNs) are introduced. Using Hamacher operational laws, we develop some aggregation operators (AOs), including an interval-valued T-spherical fuzzy Hamacher (IVTSFH) weighted averaging (IVTSFHWA) operator, an IVTSFH-ordered weighted averaging (IVTSFHOWA) operator, an IVTSFH hybrid averaging (IVTSFHHA) operator, an IVTSFH-weighted geometric (IVTSFHWG) operator, an IVTSFH-ordered weighted geometric (IVTSFHOWG) operator, and an IVTSFH hybrid geometric (IVTSFHHG) operator. The validation of the newly developed HAOs is investigated, and their basic properties are examined. In view of some restrictions, the generalization and proposed HAOs are shown, and a multi-attribute decision-making (MADM) procedure is explored based on the HAOs, which are further exemplified. Finally, a comparative analysis of the proposed work is also discussed with previous literature to show the superiority of our work.

Keywords: T-spherical fuzzy set; interval-valued T-spherical fuzzy set; Hamacher aggregation operators; multi-attribute decision-making methods

MSC: 03B52; 47S40; 90B50

Citation: Jin, Y.; Kousar, Z.; Ullah, K.; Mahmood, T.; Yapici Pehlivan, N.; Ali, Z. Approach to Multi-Attribute Decision-Making Methods for Performance Evaluation Process Using Interval-Valued T-Spherical Fuzzy Hamacher Aggregation Information. *Axioms* **2021**, *10*, 145. https://doi.org/10.3390/axioms10030145

Academic Editors: Goran Ćirović and Dragan Pamučar

Received: 21 May 2021
Accepted: 26 June 2021
Published: 1 July 2021

Publisher's Note: MDPI stays neutral with regard to jurisdictional claims in published maps and institutional affiliations.

1. Introduction

Multi-attribute decision making (MADM) is the most well-known branch of decision making that aims to select the most suitable alternative from a set of alternatives in the presence of multiple criteria that often conflict with each other. With the indecisiveness of decision-making (DM) topics and the fuzziness of DM conditions, MADM is accepted as an important technique due to its easy applicability. To solve such problems, where information is uncertain, Zadeh [1] put forward the theory of fuzzy sets (FSs), which describe (MD) information on a scale of [0, 1] and provide a flexible platform to handle uncertainties. Atanassov [2] discovered intuitionistic FS (IFS) by coupling MD with an NMD under a restriction that the sum of both lies in [0, 1]. Although IFS provides better ground for handling uncertain information, it still restricts the decision-makers to a certain range and provides very little flexibility. Therefore, Yager [3,4] proposed the theories of Pythagorean FS (PyFS) and q-rung Orthopair FS (q-ROPFS), which improve the restrictions of IFSs and, hence, provide more flexible grounds in taking the MDs and NMDs. Keeping the advantages of expressing MD and NMD in terms of intervals instead of crisp values from $[0, 1]$, the theory of interval-valued IFS (IVIFS) was elaborated by Atanassov and Gargov [5] by improving the theory of interval-valued FS (IVFS), which was explored by Zadeh [6]. Moreover, the theory of interval-valued PyFS (IVPyFS) was elaborated by Peng and Yang [7], and the idea of interval-valued q-ROPFS (IVq-ROPFS) was introduced by Joshi et al. [8]. Garg and Rani [9,10] and Garg and Kumar [11] established some fruitful AOs of PyFSs and IFSs and investigated their applications in MADM. For a study on the theory and application of these concepts, one is referred to [12–18].

Theories of IFS, PyFS, and q-ROPFS cope with uncertain and complicated information in many practical situations of MADM and pattern recognition, but these duplets discussed only two phases of human opinion, i.e., MD and NMD, and AD and RD are ignored, which leads to the loss of information. To handle such issues, Cuong and Kreinovich [19] put forward the theory of picture FS (PFS), which is based on the MD, AD, NMD, and RD of information, with the condition that the sum of MD, AD, and NMD must lie in the $[0, 1]$ interval. Moreover, the theory of interval-valued PFS (IVPFS) was elaborated by Cuong and Kreinovich [19] and was further studied by Liu et al. [20]. Several scholars have applied the theory of IVPFS in numerous fields [21–23]. Mahmoud et al. [24] relaxed the strict condition of PFS and introduced the notion of spherical FS (SFS) and TSFS, where the range for assigning MD, AD, and NMD is limitless. Moreover, the theory of interval-valued TSFS (IVTSFS) was elaborated by Ullah et al. [25], where the closed subintervals of $[0, 1]$ are taken as MD, AD, NMD, and RD instead of crisp numbers from $[0, 1]$. Several scholars have applied the theory of TSFSs to numerous fields [26–31].

HAOs are among the most influential AOs that are discussed in fuzzy frameworks, and a wide range of studies has been conducted on the theory of HAOs, which are based on HTN and HTCN [32] in different fuzzy environments. Numerous HAOs have been introduced and all these have different applications in different fields. Huang [33] introduced HAOs in IFS. Garg [34] introduced intuitionistic fuzzy HAOs with entropy weight and investigated their applications in MADM. Liu [35] studied the applications of HAOs of IVIFSs in MADM problems. Gao [36] familiarized prioritized Pythagorean fuzzy HAOs for MADM problems. Wei [37] established Pythagorean power HAOs and explored their applications in MADM. Darko and Liang [38] presented the notion of HAOs for q-ROPFs, while the HAOs of IVq-ROPFS were introduced by Donyatalab et al. [39]. A study of enterprise selection using MADM techniques was established by Jana and Pal [40]. The problems related to search and rescue robots was discussed using TSF HAOs by Ullah et al. [41]. Some other recent work on HAOs can be found in [42–46].

Ullah et al. [25] observed that processing uncertain and ambiguous information using IVTSFSs instead of TSFSs and defining MD, AD, NMD, and RD as an interval rather than crisp numbers taken from [0, 1] greatly reduced information loss. The aim of this paper is to introduce the notion of HAOs in the environment of IVTSFSs. The motivation for doing so is that the HAOs proposed in [32–38] can describe only two aspects of human opinion and lead to information loss. Further, the HAOs of PFSs and TSFSs proposed by Jana and Pal [39] and Ullah et al. [40] discuss the four aspects of human opinion but the MD, AD, NMD, and RD are described in terms of crisp numbers and, hence, lead to information loss. The paper focuses on the following points.

1. To introduce some novel Hamacher operational laws based on IVTSFSs.
2. By using Hamacher operational laws, novel IVTSFHWA and IVTSFHWG operators are developed.
3. An MADM procedure is explored based on the proposed HAOs using IVTSFSs.
4. To observe the consistency and validity of the presented approaches, some examples are examined.

5. A comparative analysis of the current and previous studies is developed.

This manuscript is organized as in Section 2; we recall some ideas like TSFS, IVTSFS, and some relevant concepts, including HTN and HTCN. In Section 3, we investigate some Hamacher operational laws for IVTSFSs. In Section 4, we explore the idea of an IVTSFHWA operator, an IVTSFHOWA operator, and an IVTSFHHA operator. In Section 5, the idea of IVTSFHWG, IVTSFHOWG, and IVTSFHHG operators is investigated and their properties are discussed. In Section 6, the superiority of the proposed HAOs is analyzed in view of some special cases. Section 7 is based on the MADM procedure and a comprehensive example, where the impact of the variable parameters is examined. A comparative study of the current and previous HAOs is set up in Section 8, while a thorough summary of the paper is presented in Section 9.

2. Preliminaries

Some basic definitions of TSFS and IVTSFS over set X, through some remarks, are defined in this section. Definitions of HTN and HTCN are also discussed.

Definition 1 ([26]). *A TSFS on set X is defined by* $I = (m(x), i(x), n(x) : x \in X)$*, where* $m(x)$*,* $i(x)$ *and* $n(x)$ *are mappings from X to* $[0, 1]$*, denoting MD, AD, and NMD with the condition* $0 \leq m^q(x) + i^q(x) + n^q(x) \leq 1$ *for* $q \in \mathbb{Z}^+$*. RD is defined by* $r(x) = (1 - (m^q(x) + i^q(x) + n^q(x)))^{\frac{1}{q}}$ and the triplet $(m(x),\ i(x),\ n(x))$ is known as the T-spherical fuzzy number (TSFN).

The superiority of TSFS can be understood from Remark 1.

Remark 1 ([27]). *From Definition 1, some existing special fuzzy sets can be derived from TSFS as follows:*

1. *q −ROPFS for* $i(x) = 0$.
2. *SFS for* $q = 2$.
3. *PyFS for* $q = 2$ *and* $i(x) = 0$.
4. *PFS for* $q = 1$.
5. *IFS for* $q = 1$ *and* $i(x) = 0$.
6. *FS for* $q = 1$ *and* $i(x) = 0 = n(x)$.

Definition 2 ([27]). *An IVTSFS on set X is defined by* $I = \left(\left[m^l(x), m^u(x)\right], \left[i^l(x), i^u(x)\right], \left[n^l(x), n^u(x)\right] : x \in X\right)$*, where* $m(x), i(x)$ *and* $n(x)$ *are mappings from X to closed subintervals of* $[0, 1]$*, denoting the MD, AD and NMD with the condition* $0 \leq (m^u)^q(x) + (i^u)^q(x) + (n^u)^q(x) \leq 1$ *for* $q \in \mathbb{Z}^+$*. RD can be defined as:*

$$r(x) = \left(\left[r^l(x), r^u(x)\right]\right) = \left(\left[\begin{array}{c} (1 - ((m^u)^q(x) + (i^u)^q(x) + (n^u)^q(x)))^{\frac{1}{q}}, \\ \left(1 - \left(m^l\right)^q(x) + \left(i^l\right)^q(x) + \left(n^l\right)^q(x)\right)\right)^{\frac{1}{q}} \end{array}\right]\right)$$

and the triplet $\left(\left[m^l(x), m^u(x)\right], \left[i^l(x), i^u(x)\right], \left[n^l(x), n^u(x)\right]\right)$ *is defined as an interval-valued T-spherical fuzzy number (IVTSFN).*

From Definition 2, it is quite clear that existing fuzzy frameworks are derived from IVTSFS under some restrictions, given as follows:

Theorem 1 ([27]). *From Definition 2, an IVTSFS can be reduced to the following special fuzzy sets:*

1. *TSFS for* $m^l = m^u,\ i^l = i^u,\ n^l = n^u$.
2. *Interval-valued SFS (IVSFS) for* $q = 2$.

3. *SFS for* $q = 2$ *and* $m^l = m^u, i^l = i^u, n^l = n^u$.
4. *IVPFS for* $q = 1$.
5. *PFS for* $q = 1$ *and* $m^l = m^u, i^l = i^u, n^l = n^u$.
6. *IVq-ROPFS for* $i^l = i^u = 0$.
7. q *−ROPFS* $m^l = m^u, i^l = i^u = 0, n^l = n^u$.
8. *IVPyFS for* $q = 2$ *and* $i^l = i^u = 0$.
9. *PyFS for* $q = 2$ *and* $m^l = m^u, i^l = i^u = 0, n^l = n^u$.
10. *IVIFS for* $q = 1$ *and* $i^l = i^u = 0$.
11. *IFS for* $q = 1$ *and* $m^l = m^u, i^l = i^u = 0, n^l = n^u$.
12. *IVFS for* $q = 1$ *and* $n^l = n^u = i^l = i^u = 0$.
13. *FS for* $q = 1$ *and* $n^l = n^u = i^l = i^u = 0$ *and* $m^l = m^u$.

Proof. Trivial. □

In order to rank two or more IVTSFNs, the score function can be used given in Definition 3.

Definition 3 ([25]). *For an IVTSFN* $I = \left(\left[m^l, m^u\right], \left[i^l, i^u\right], \left[n^l, n^u\right]\right)$, *the score function is defined by:*

$$SC(I) = \frac{\left(m^l\right)^q\left(1 - \left(i^l\right)^q - \left(n^l\right)^q\right) + (m^u)^q(1 - (i^u)^q - (n^u)^q)}{3}, \ SC(I) \in [0, 1]$$

Definition 4 ([32]). *HTN and HTCN are defined as follows, respectively:*

$$T_{hn}(a, b) = \frac{a.b}{\gamma + (1-\gamma)(a + b - ab)}, \ \gamma > 0, (a,\ b) \in [0,\ 1]^2$$

$$T_{hcn}(a,\ b) = \frac{a + b - ab - (1-\gamma)ab}{1 - (1-\gamma)ab}, \ \gamma > 0, (a,\ b) \in [0,\ 1]^2$$

Further, $T_{hn}(a, b)$ *is also considered a Hamacher product and* $T_{hcn}(a,\ b)$ *is known as the Hamacher sum.* $T_{hn}(a, b)$ *and* $T_{hcn}\ (a,\ b)$ *can be stated as follows, respectively:*

$$a \otimes b = \frac{a.b}{\gamma + (1-\gamma)(a + b - ab)}, \ \gamma > 0\ (a,\ b) \in [0,\ 1]^2$$

$$a \oplus b = \frac{a + b - ab - (1-\gamma)ab}{1 - (1-\gamma)ab}, \ \gamma > 0\ (a,\ b) \in [0,\ 1]^2$$

Remark 2. *Hamacher product and Hamacher sum are given in Definition 4; they are converted into algebraic product and algebraic sum for* $\gamma = 1$, *while they are converted into Einstein product and Einstein sum for* $\gamma = 2$.

3. Interval-Valued T-Spherical Fuzzy Hamacher Operations

The aim of this section is to develop some Hamacher operations in the framework of IVTSFSs. The Hamacher operations, including Hamacher sum and Hamacher product, are proposed. Then, some special cases of the TSF Hamacher operations are investigated.

Definition 5. *Let* $A = \left(\left[m^{l}_{A}, m^{u}_{A}\right], \left[i^{l}_{A}, i^{u}_{B}\right], \left[n^{l}_{A}, n^{u}_{A}\right]\right)$ *and* $B = \left(\left[m^{l}_{B}, m^{u}_{B}\right], \left[i^{l}_{B}, i^{u}_{B}\right], \left[n^{l}_{B}, n^{u}_{B}\right]\right)$ be two IVTSFNs for $\lambda, \gamma > 0$. The novel interval-valued T-spherical fuzzy Hamacher operations are expressed as:

$$A \oplus B = \begin{pmatrix} \begin{bmatrix} \sqrt[q]{\dfrac{m^{l\,q}_{A} + m^{l\,q}_{B} - m^{l\,q}_{A} m^{l\,q}_{B} - (1-\gamma) m^{l\,q}_{A} m^{l\,q}_{B}}{1-(1-\gamma) m^{l\,q}_{A} m^{l\,q}_{B}}}, \\ \sqrt[q]{\dfrac{m^{u\,q}_{A} + m^{u\,q}_{B} - m^{u\,q}_{A} m^{u\,q}_{B} - (1-\gamma) m^{u\,q}_{A} m^{u\,q}_{B}}{1-(1-\gamma) m^{u\,q}_{A} m^{u\,q}_{B}}} \end{bmatrix} \\ \begin{bmatrix} \dfrac{i^{l}_{A} i^{l}_{B}}{\sqrt[q]{\gamma + (1-\gamma)(i^{l\,q}_{A} + i^{l\,q}_{B} - i^{l\,q}_{A} i^{l\,q}_{B})}}, \\ \dfrac{i^{u}_{A} i^{u}_{B}}{\sqrt[q]{\gamma + (1-\gamma)(i^{u\,q}_{A} + i^{u\,q}_{B} - i^{u\,q}_{A} i^{u\,q}_{B})}} \end{bmatrix} \\ \begin{bmatrix} \dfrac{n^{l}_{A} n^{l}_{B}}{\sqrt[q]{\gamma + (1-\gamma)(n^{l\,q}_{A} + n^{l\,q}_{B} - n^{l\,q}_{A} n^{l\,q}_{B})}}, \\ \dfrac{n^{u}_{A} n^{u}_{B}}{\sqrt[q]{\gamma + (1-\gamma)(n^{u\,q}_{A} + n^{u\,q}_{B} - n^{u\,q}_{A} n^{u\,q}_{B})}} \end{bmatrix} \end{pmatrix} \tag{1}$$

$$A \oplus B = \begin{pmatrix} \begin{bmatrix} \dfrac{m^{l}_{A} m^{l}_{B}}{\sqrt[q]{\gamma + (1-\gamma)\left(m^{l\,q}_{A} + m^{l\,q}_{B} - m^{l\,q}_{A} m^{l\,q}_{B}\right)}}, \\ \dfrac{m^{u}_{A} m^{u}_{B}}{\sqrt[q]{\gamma + (1-\gamma)\left(m^{u\,q}_{A} + m^{u\,q}_{B} - m^{u\,q}_{A} m^{u\,q}_{B}\right)}} \end{bmatrix} \\ \begin{bmatrix} \sqrt[q]{\dfrac{i^{l\,q}_{A} + i^{l\,q}_{B} - i^{l\,q}_{A} i^{l\,q}_{B} - (1-\gamma) i^{l\,q}_{A} i^{l\,q}_{B}}{1-(1-\gamma) i^{l\,q}_{A} i^{l\,q}_{B}}}, \\ \sqrt[q]{\dfrac{i^{u\,q}_{A} + i^{u\,q}_{B} - i^{u\,q}_{A} i^{u\,q}_{B} - (1-\gamma) i^{u\,q}_{A} i^{u\,q}_{B}}{1-(1-\gamma) i^{u\,q}_{A} i^{u\,q}_{B}}} \end{bmatrix} \\ \begin{bmatrix} \sqrt[q]{\dfrac{n^{l\,q}_{A} + n^{l\,q}_{B} - n^{l\,q}_{A} n^{l\,q}_{B} - (1-\gamma) n^{l\,q}_{A} n^{l\,q}_{B}}{1-(1-\gamma) n^{l\,q}_{A} n^{l\,q}_{B}}}, \\ \sqrt[q]{\dfrac{n^{u\,q}_{A} + n^{u\,q}_{B} - n^{u\,q}_{A} n^{u\,q}_{B} - (1-\gamma) n^{u\,q}_{A} n^{u\,q}_{B}}{1-(1-\gamma) n^{u\,q}_{A} n^{u\,q}_{B}}} \end{bmatrix} \end{pmatrix} \tag{2}$$

$$\lambda A = \begin{pmatrix} \begin{bmatrix} \sqrt[q]{\dfrac{\left(1+(\gamma-1) m^{l\,q}_{A}\right)^{\lambda} - \left(1-m^{l\,q}_{A}\right)^{\lambda}}{\left(1+(\gamma-1) m^{l\,q}_{A}\right)^{\lambda} + (\gamma-1)\left(1-m^{l\,q}_{A}\right)^{\lambda}}}, \\ \sqrt[q]{\dfrac{\left(1+(\gamma-1) m^{u\,q}_{A}\right)^{\lambda} - \left(1-m^{u\,q}_{A}\right)^{\lambda}}{\left(1+(\gamma-1) m^{u\,q}_{A}\right)^{\lambda} + (\gamma-1)\left(1-m^{u\,q}_{A}\right)^{\lambda}}} \end{bmatrix} \\ \begin{bmatrix} \dfrac{\sqrt[q]{\gamma}\left(i^{l}_{A}\right)^{\lambda}}{\sqrt[q]{\left(1+(\gamma-1)(1-i^{l\,q}_{A})\right)^{\lambda} + (\gamma-1)\left(i^{l\,q}_{A}\right)^{\lambda}}}, \\ \dfrac{\sqrt[q]{\gamma}\left(i^{u}_{A}\right)^{\lambda}}{\sqrt[q]{\left(1+(\gamma-1)(1-i^{u\,q}_{A})\right)^{\lambda} + (\gamma-1)\left(i^{u\,q}_{A}\right)^{\lambda}}} \end{bmatrix} \\ \begin{bmatrix} \dfrac{\sqrt[q]{\gamma}\left(n^{l}_{A}\right)^{\lambda}}{\sqrt[q]{\left(1+(\gamma-1)(1-n^{l\,q}_{A})\right)^{\lambda} + (\gamma-1)\left(n^{l\,q}_{A}\right)^{\lambda}}}, \\ \dfrac{\sqrt[q]{\gamma}\left(n^{u}_{A}\right)^{\lambda}}{\sqrt[q]{\left(1+(\gamma-1)(1-n^{u\,q}_{A})\right)^{\lambda} + (\gamma-1)\left(n^{u\,q}_{A}\right)^{\lambda}}} \end{bmatrix} \end{pmatrix} \tag{3}$$

$$A^{\lambda}=\left(\begin{array}{c}\left[\begin{array}{c}\frac{\sqrt[q]{\gamma}\left(m_{A}^{l}\right)^{\lambda}}{\sqrt[q]{\left(1+(\gamma-1)\left(1-m_{A}^{l\,q}\right)\right)^{\lambda}+(\gamma-1)\left(m_{A}^{l\,q}\right)^{\lambda}}},\\ \frac{\sqrt[q]{\gamma}\left(m_{A}^{u}\right)^{\lambda}}{\sqrt[q]{\left(1+(\gamma-1)\left(1-m_{A}^{u\,q}\right)\right)^{\lambda}+(\gamma-1)\left(m_{A}^{u\,q}\right)^{\lambda}}}\end{array}\right]\\ \left[\begin{array}{c}\sqrt[q]{\frac{\left(1+(\gamma-1)i_{A}^{l\,q}\right)^{\lambda}-\left(1-i_{A}^{l\,q}\right)^{\lambda}}{\left(1+(\gamma-1)i_{A}^{l\,q}\right)^{\lambda}+(\gamma-1)\left(1-i_{A}^{l\,q}\right)^{\lambda}}},\\ \sqrt[q]{\frac{\left(1+(\gamma-1)i_{A}^{u\,q}\right)^{\lambda}-\left(1-i_{A}^{u\,q}\right)^{\lambda}}{\left(1+(\gamma-1)i_{A}^{u\,q}\right)^{\lambda}+(\gamma-1)\left(1-i_{A}^{u\,q}\right)^{\lambda}}}\end{array}\right]\\ \left[\begin{array}{c}\sqrt[q]{\frac{\left(1+(\gamma-1)n_{A}^{l\,q}\right)^{\lambda}-\left(1-n_{A}^{l\,q}\right)^{\lambda}}{\left(1+(\gamma-1)n_{A}^{l\,q}\right)^{\lambda}+(\gamma-1)\left(1-n_{A}^{l\,q}\right)^{\lambda}}},\\ \sqrt[q]{\frac{\left(1+(\gamma-1)n_{A}^{u\,q}\right)^{\lambda}-\left(1-n_{A}^{u\,q}\right)^{\lambda}}{\left(1+(\gamma-1)n_{A}^{u\,q}\right)^{\lambda}+(\gamma-1)\left(1-n_{A}^{u\,q}\right)^{\lambda}}}\end{array}\right]\end{array}\right) \quad (4)$$

The Hamacher operations defined in Equations (1)–(4) are more effective than earlier Hamacher operations of IVIFSs, IVPyFSs, IVq-ROPFSs, and PFSs. The novel interval-valued T-spherical fuzzy Hamacher (IVTSFH) operations explain MD, AD, NMD, and RD with no restrictions because for every triplet $\left(\left[m_{A}^{l}, m_{A}^{u}\right], \left[i_{A}^{l}, i_{A}^{u}\right], \left[n_{A}^{l}, n_{A}^{u}\right]\right)$, there exist some $q \in \mathbb{Z}^{+}$ for which the triplet becomes an IVTSFN.

The Hamacher operations defined in Equations (1)–(4) can be reduced to some existing fuzzy sets, which can be described as:

1. For $q = 2$, IVTSFH operations become the Hamacher operations of the IVSFSs.
2. For $q = 1$, IVTSFH operations become the Hamacher operations of the IVPFSs.
3. For $i = 0$, IVTSFH operations become the Hamacher operations of the IVq-ROPFSs.
4. For $q = 2$, and $i = 0$, IVTSFH operations become the Hamacher operations of the PyFSs.
5. For $q = 1$ and $i = 0$, IVTSFH operations become the Hamacher operations of the IVIFSs.

4. Interval Valued T-Spherical Fuzzy Hamacher Weighted Averaging (IVTSFHWA) Operators

The aim of this section is to develop IVTSFHWA operators based on the Hamacher operation introduced in Section 3. Note that from this section onward, $w_j = (w_1, w_2, \ldots, w_l)^T$ represents the weight vector, where $w_j > 0$, and $\sum_{1}^{l} w_j = 1$, where $j, k \in J = \{1, 2, 3 \ldots l\}$.

Definition 6. *Suppose* $T_j = \left(\left[m_j^l, m_j^u\right], \left[i_j^l, i_j^u\right], \left[n_j^l, n_j^u\right]\right)$ $\forall j = 1, 2, 3, \ldots, l$ *are some IVTSFNs. Then, the IVTSFHWA operator* $T^l \rightarrow T$ *is defined as:*

$$IVTSFHWA\ (T_1, T_2, T_3, \ldots T_l) = \sum_{j=1}^{l} w_j T_j \quad (5)$$

By using previous results defined in Definition 5, we can obtain the subsequent result, as given in Theorem 2.

Theorem 2. *Consider* $T_j = \left(\left[m_j^l, m_j^u\right], \left[i_j^l, i_j^u\right], \left[n_j^l, n_j^u\right]\right)$ $\forall\, j = 1, 2, 3, \ldots, l$ *are some IVTSFNs. Then, the IVTSFHWA operator is an IVTSFN and given by:*

$$IVTSFHWA(T_1, T_2, T_3, \ldots T_l) = \left(\begin{array}{c} \left[\begin{array}{c} \sqrt[q]{\dfrac{\prod_{j=1}^{l}\left(1+(\gamma-1)m_j^{lq}\right)^{w_j}-\prod_{j=1}^{l}\left(1-m_j^{lq}\right)^{w_j}}{\prod_{j=1}^{l}\left(1+(\gamma-1)m_j^{lq}\right)^{w_j}+(\gamma-1)\prod_{j=1}^{l}\left(1-m_j^{lq}\right)^{w_j}}} \\ ,\sqrt[q]{\dfrac{\prod_{j=1}^{l}\left(1+(\gamma-1)m_j^{uq}\right)^{w_j}-\prod_{j=1}^{l}\left(1-m_j^{uq}\right)^{w_j}}{\prod_{j=1}^{l}\left(1+(\gamma-1)m_j^{uq}\right)^{w_j}+(\gamma-1)\prod_{j=1}^{l}\left(1-m_j^{uq}\right)^{w_j}}} \end{array}\right] \\ \left[\begin{array}{c} \dfrac{\sqrt[q]{\gamma}\prod_{j=1}^{l}\left(i_j^l\right)^{w_j}}{\sqrt[q]{\prod_{j=1}^{l}\left(1+(\gamma-1)\left(1-i_j^{lq}\right)\right)^{w_j}+(\gamma-1)\prod_{j=1}^{l}\left(i_j^{lq}\right)^{w_j}}} \\ ,\dfrac{\sqrt[q]{\gamma}\prod_{j=1}^{l}\left(i_j^u\right)^{w_j}}{\sqrt[q]{\prod_{j=1}^{l}\left(1+(\gamma-1)\left(1-i_j^{uq}\right)\right)^{w_j}+(\gamma-1)\prod_{j=1}^{l}\left(i_j^{uq}\right)^{w_j}}} \end{array}\right] \\ \left[\begin{array}{c} \dfrac{\sqrt[q]{\gamma}\prod_{j=1}^{l}\left(n_j^l\right)^{w_j}}{\sqrt[q]{\prod_{j=1}^{l}\left(1+(\gamma-1)\left(1-n_j^{lq}\right)\right)^{w_j}+(\gamma-1)\prod_{j=1}^{l}\left(n_j^{lq}\right)^{w_j}}} \\ ,\dfrac{\sqrt[q]{\gamma}\prod_{j=1}^{l}\left(n_j^u\right)^{w_j}}{\sqrt[q]{\prod_{j=1}^{l}\left(1+(\gamma-1)\left(1-n_j^{uq}\right)\right)^{w_j}+(\gamma-1)\prod_{j=1}^{l}\left(n_j^{uq}\right)^{w_j}}} \end{array}\right] \end{array}\right) \tag{6}$$

Proof. To prove, the mathematical induction method is used.

Let $j = 2$

$$w_1 T_1 \oplus w_2 T_2 = \left(\begin{array}{c} \left[\begin{array}{c} \sqrt[q]{\dfrac{\left(1+(\gamma-1)m_1^{lq}\right)^{w_1}-\left(1-m_1^{lq}\right)^{w_1}}{\left(1+(\gamma-1)m_1^{lq}\right)^{w_1}+(\gamma-1)\left(1-m_1^{lq}\right)^{w_1}}}, \\ \sqrt[q]{\dfrac{\left(1+(\gamma-1)m_1^{uq}\right)^{w_1}-\left(1-m_1^{uq}\right)^{w_1}}{\left(1+(\gamma-1)m_1^{uq}\right)^{w_1}+(\gamma-1)\left(1-m_1^{uq}\right)^{w_1}}} \end{array}\right] \\ \left[\begin{array}{c} \dfrac{\sqrt[q]{\gamma}\left(i_1^l\right)^{w_1}}{\sqrt[q]{\left(1+(\gamma-1)\left(1-i_1^{lq}\right)\right)^{w_1}+(\gamma-1)\left(i_1^{lq}\right)^{w_1}}} \\ \dfrac{\sqrt[q]{\gamma}\left(i_1^u\right)^{w_1}}{\sqrt[q]{\left(1+(\gamma-1)\left(1-i_1^{uq}\right)\right)^{w_1}+(\gamma-1)\left(i_1^{uq}\right)^{w_1}}} \end{array}\right] \\ \left[\begin{array}{c} \dfrac{\sqrt[q]{\gamma}\left(n_1^l\right)^{w_1}}{\sqrt[q]{\left(1+(\gamma-1)\left(1-n_1^{lq}\right)\right)^{w_1}+(\gamma-1)\left(n_1^{lq}\right)^{w_1}}} \\ \dfrac{\sqrt[q]{\gamma}\left(n_1^u\right)^{w_1}}{\sqrt[q]{\left(1+(\gamma-1)\left(1-n_1^{uq}\right)\right)^{w_1}+(\gamma-1)\left(n_1^{uq}\right)^{w_1}}} \end{array}\right] \end{array}\right) \oplus \left(\begin{array}{c} \left[\begin{array}{c} \sqrt[q]{\dfrac{\left(1+(\gamma-1)m_2^{lq}\right)^{w_2}-\left(1-m_2^{lq}\right)^{w_2}}{\left(1+(\gamma-1)m_2^{lq}\right)^{w_2}+(\gamma-1)\left(1-m_2^{lq}\right)^{w_2}}}, \\ \sqrt[q]{\dfrac{\left(1+(\gamma-1)m_2^{uq}\right)^{w_2}-\left(1-m_2^{uq}\right)^{w_2}}{\left(1+(\gamma-1)m_2^{uq}\right)^{2}+(\gamma-1)\left(1-m_1^{uq}\right)^{w_2}}} \end{array}\right] \\ \left[\begin{array}{c} \dfrac{\sqrt[q]{\gamma}\left(i_2^l\right)^{w_2}}{\sqrt[q]{\left(1+(\gamma-1)\left(1-i_2^{lq}\right)\right)^{w_2}+(\gamma-1)\left(i_2^{lq}\right)^{w_2}}} \\ \dfrac{\sqrt[q]{\gamma}\left(i_2^u\right)^{w_2}}{\sqrt[q]{\left(1+(\gamma-1)\left(1-i_2^{uq}\right)\right)^{w_2}+(\gamma-1)\left(i_2^{uq}\right)^{w_2}}} \end{array}\right] \\ \left[\begin{array}{c} \dfrac{\sqrt[q]{\gamma}\left(n_2^l\right)^{w_2}}{\sqrt[q]{\left(1+(\gamma-1)\left(1-n_2^{lq}\right)\right)^{w_2}+(\gamma-1)\left(n_2^{lq}\right)^{w_2}}} \\ \dfrac{\sqrt[q]{\gamma}\left(n_2^u\right)^{w_2}}{\sqrt[q]{\left(1+(\gamma-1)\left(1-n_2^{uq}\right)\right)^{w_2}+(\gamma-1)\left(n_2^{uq}\right)^{w_2}}} \end{array}\right] \end{array}\right)$$

$$= \left(\begin{array}{c} \left[\sqrt[q]{\frac{\prod_{j=1}^{2}(1+(\gamma-1)m_j^{lq})^{w_j}-\prod_{j=1}^{2}(1-m_j^{lq})^{w_j}}{\prod_{j=1}^{2}(1+(\gamma-1)m_j^{lq})^{w_j}+(\gamma-1)\prod_{j=1}^{2}(1-m_j^{lq})^{w_j}}}, \sqrt[q]{\frac{\prod_{j=1}^{2}(1+(\gamma-1)m_j^{uq})^{w_j}-\prod_{j=1}^{2}(1-m_j^{uq})^{w_j}}{\prod_{j=1}^{2}(1+(\gamma-1)m_j^{uq})^{w_j}+(\gamma-1)\prod_{j=1}^{2}(1-m_j^{uq})^{w_j}}} \right] \\ \left[\frac{\sqrt[q]{\gamma}\prod_{j=1}^{2}(i_j^{l})^{w_j}}{\sqrt[q]{\prod_{j=1}^{2}(1+(\gamma-1)(1-i_j^{lq}))^{w_j}+(\gamma-1)\prod_{j=1}^{2}(i_j^{lq})^{w_j}}}, \frac{\sqrt[q]{\gamma}\prod_{j=1}^{2}(i_j^{u})^{w_j}}{\sqrt[q]{\prod_{j=1}^{2}(1+(\gamma-1)(1-i_j^{uq}))^{w_j}+(\gamma-1)\prod_{j=1}^{2}(i_j^{uq})^{w_j}}} \right] \\ \left[\frac{\sqrt[q]{\gamma}\prod_{j=1}^{2}(n_j^{l})^{w_j}}{\sqrt[q]{\prod_{j=1}^{2}(1+(\gamma-1)(1-n_j^{lq}))^{w_j}+(\gamma-1)\prod_{j=1}^{2}(n_j^{lq})^{w_j}}}, \frac{\sqrt[q]{\gamma}\prod_{j=1}^{2}(n_j^{u})^{w_j}}{\sqrt[q]{\prod_{j=1}^{2}(1+(\gamma-1)(1-n_j^{uq}))^{w_j}-(\gamma-1)\prod_{j=1}^{2}(n_j^{uq})^{w_j}}} \right] \end{array} \right)$$

Hence, this result is true for $l = 2$.

Now, let us assume that it is true for $l = k$ and we have to prove that it is true for $l = k + 1$

$$IVTSFHWA(\text{Ꚍ}_1, \text{Ꚍ}_2, \text{Ꚍ}_3, \ldots \text{Ꚍ}_k) =$$

$$\left(\begin{array}{c} \left[\sqrt[q]{\frac{\prod_{j=1}^{k}(1+(\gamma-1)m_j^{lq})^{w_j}-\prod_{j=1}^{k}(1-m_j^{lq})^{w_j}}{\prod_{j=1}^{k}(1+(\gamma-1)m_j^{lq})^{w_j}+(\gamma-1)\prod_{j=1}^{k}(1-m_j^{lq})^{w_j}}}, \sqrt[q]{\frac{\prod_{j=1}^{k}(1+(\gamma-1)m_j^{uq})^{w_j}-\prod_{j=1}^{k}(1-m_j^{uq})^{w_j}}{\prod_{j=1}^{k}(1+(\gamma-1)m_j^{uq})^{w_j}+(\gamma-1)\prod_{j=1}^{k}(1-m_j^{uq})^{w_j}}} \right] \\ \left[\frac{\sqrt[q]{\gamma}\prod_{j=1}^{k}(i_j^{l})^{w_j}}{\sqrt[q]{\prod_{j=1}^{k}(1+(\gamma-1)(1-i_j^{lq}))^{w_j}+(\gamma-1)\prod_{j=1}^{k}(i_j^{lq})^{w_j}}}, \frac{\sqrt[q]{\gamma}\prod_{j=1}^{k}(i_j^{u})^{w_j}}{\sqrt[q]{\prod_{j=1}^{k}(1+(\gamma-1)(1-i_j^{uq}))^{w_j}+(\gamma-1)\prod_{j=1}^{k}(i_j^{uq})^{w_j}}} \right] \\ \left[\frac{\sqrt[q]{\gamma}\prod_{j=1}^{k}(n_j^{l})^{w_j}}{\sqrt[q]{\prod_{j=1}^{k}(1+(\gamma-1)(1-n_j^{lq}))^{w_j}+(\gamma-1)\prod_{j=1}^{k}(n_j^{lq})^{w_j}}}, \frac{\sqrt[q]{\gamma}\prod_{j=1}^{k}(n_j^{u})^{w_j}}{\sqrt[q]{\prod_{j=1}^{k}(1+(\gamma-1)(1-n_j^{uq}))^{w_j}+(\gamma-1)\prod_{j=1}^{k}(n_j^{uq})^{w_j}}} \right] \end{array} \right)$$

$$IVTSFHWA(\text{Ꚍ}_1, \text{Ꚍ}_2, \ldots, \text{Ꚍ}_k, \text{Ꚍ}_{k+1}) = IVTSFHWA(\text{Ꚍ}_1, \text{Ꚍ}_2, \ldots, \text{Ꚍ}_k) \oplus \text{Ꚍ}_{k+1}$$

$$= \left(\begin{array}{c} \left[\sqrt[q]{\frac{\prod_{j=1}^{k}(1+(\gamma-1)m_j^{lq})^{w_j}-\prod_{j=1}^{k}(1-m_j^{lq})^{w_j}}{\prod_{j=1}^{k}(1+(\gamma-1)m_j^{lq})^{w_j}+(\gamma-1)\prod_{j=1}^{k}(1-m_j^{lq})^{w_j}}}, \sqrt[q]{\frac{\prod_{j=1}^{k}(1+(\gamma-1)m_j^{uq})^{w_j}-\prod_{j=1}^{k}(1-m_j^{uq})^{w_j}}{\prod_{j=1}^{k}(1+(\gamma-1)m_j^{uq})^{w_j}+(\gamma-1)\prod_{j=1}^{k}(1-m_j^{uq})^{w_j}}} \right] \\ \left[\frac{\sqrt[q]{\gamma}\prod_{j=1}^{k}(i_j^{l})^{w_j}}{\sqrt[q]{\prod_{j=1}^{k}(1+(\gamma-1)(1-i_j^{lq}))^{w_j}+(\gamma-1)\prod_{j=1}^{k}(i_j^{lq})^{w_j}}}, \frac{\sqrt[q]{\gamma}\prod_{j=1}^{k}(i_j^{u})^{w_j}}{\sqrt[q]{\prod_{j=1}^{k}(1+(\gamma-1)(1-i_j^{uq}))^{w_j}+(\gamma-1)\prod_{j=1}^{k}(i_j^{uq})^{w_j}}} \right] \\ \left[\frac{\sqrt[q]{\gamma}\prod_{j=1}^{k}(n_j^{l})^{w_j}}{\sqrt[q]{\prod_{j=1}^{k}(1+(\gamma-1)(1-n_j^{lq}))^{w_j}+(\gamma-1)\prod_{j=1}^{k}(n_j^{lq})^{w_j}}}, \frac{\sqrt[q]{\gamma}\prod_{j=1}^{k}(n_j^{u})^{w_j}}{\sqrt[q]{\prod_{j=1}^{k}(1+(\gamma-1)(1-n_j^{uq}))^{w_j}+(\gamma-1)\prod_{j=1}^{k}(n_j^{uq})^{w_j}}} \right] \end{array} \right)$$

$$\oplus\left(\begin{array}{c}\left[\begin{array}{c}\sqrt[q]{\frac{(1+(\gamma-1)m^{l}_{k+1}{}^{q})^{w_{k+1}}-(1-m^{l}_{k+1}{}^{q})^{w_{k+1}}}{(1+(\gamma-1)m^{l}_{k+1}{}^{q})^{w_{k+1}}+(\gamma-1)(1-m^{l}_{k+1}{}^{q})^{w_{k+1}}}},\\ \sqrt[q]{\frac{(1+(\gamma-1)m^{u}_{k+1}{}^{q})^{w_{k+1}}-(1-m^{u}_{k+1}{}^{q})^{w_{k+1}}}{(1+(\gamma-1)m^{u}_{k+1}{}^{q})^{w_{k+1}}+(\gamma-1)(1-m^{u}_{k+1}{}^{q})^{w_{k+1}}}}\end{array}\right]\\ \left[\begin{array}{c}\frac{\sqrt[q]{\gamma}(i^{l}_{k+1})^{w_{k+1}}}{\sqrt[q]{(1+(\gamma-1)(1-i^{l}_{k+1}{}^{q}))^{w_{k+1}}+(\gamma-1)(i^{l}_{k+1}{}^{q})^{w_{k+1}}}},\\ \frac{\sqrt[q]{\gamma}(i^{u}_{k+1})^{w_{k+1}}}{\sqrt[q]{(1+(\gamma-1)(1-i^{u}_{k+1}{}^{q}))^{w_{k+1}}+(\gamma-1)(i^{u}_{k+1}{}^{q})^{w_{k+1}}}}\end{array}\right]\\ \left[\begin{array}{c}\frac{\sqrt[q]{\gamma}(n^{l}_{k+1})^{w_{k+1}}}{\sqrt[q]{(1+(\gamma-1)(1-n^{l}_{k+1}{}^{q}))^{w_{k+1}}+(\gamma-1)(n^{l}_{k+1}{}^{q})^{w_{k+1}}}},\\ \frac{\sqrt[q]{\gamma}(n^{u}_{k+1})^{w_{k+1}}}{\sqrt[q]{(1+(\gamma-1)(1-n^{u}_{k+1}{}^{q}))^{w_{k+1}}+(\gamma-1)(n^{u}_{k+1}{}^{q})^{w_{k+1}}}}\end{array}\right]\end{array}\right)$$

$$IVTSFHWA(\text{Ꞇ}_1,\text{Ꞇ}_2,\text{Ꞇ}_3,\ldots\text{Ꞇ}_{k+1})=$$

$$\left(\begin{array}{c}\left[\begin{array}{c}\sqrt[q]{\frac{\prod_{j=1}^{k+1}(1+(\gamma-1)m_j^{lq})^{w_j}-\prod_{j=1}^{k+1}(1-m_j^{lq})^{w_j}}{\prod_{j=1}^{k+1}(1+(\gamma-1)m_j^{lq})^{w_j}+(\gamma-1)\prod_{j=1}^{k+1}(1-m_j^{lq})^{w_j}}},\\ \sqrt[q]{\frac{\prod_{j=1}^{k+1}(1+(\gamma-1)m_j^{uq})^{w_j}-\prod_{j=1}^{k+1}(1-m_j^{uq})^{w_j}}{\prod_{j=1}^{k+1}(1+(\gamma-1)m_j^{uq})^{w_j}+(\gamma-1)\prod_{j=1}^{k+1}(1-m_j^{uq})^{w_j}}}\end{array}\right]\\ \left[\begin{array}{c}\frac{\sqrt[q]{\gamma}\prod_{j=1}^{k+1}(i_j^l)^{w_j}}{\sqrt[q]{\prod_{j=1}^{k+1}(1+(\gamma-1)(1-i_j^{lq}))^{w_j}+(\gamma-1)\prod_{j=1}^{k+1}(i_j^{lq})^{w_j}}},\\ \frac{\sqrt[q]{\gamma}\prod_{j=1}^{k+1}(i_j^u)^{w_j}}{\sqrt[q]{\prod_{j=1}^{k+1}(1+(\gamma-1)(1-i_j^{uq}))^{w_j}+(\gamma-1)\prod_{j=1}^{k+1}(i_j^{uq})^{w_j}}}\end{array}\right]\\ \left[\begin{array}{c}\frac{\sqrt[q]{\gamma}\prod_{j=1}^{k+1}(n_j^l)^{w_j}}{\sqrt[q]{\prod_{j=1}^{k+1}(1+(\gamma-1)(1-n_j^{lq}))^{w_j}+(\gamma-1)\prod_{j=1}^{k+1}(n_j^{lq})^{w_j}}},\\ \frac{\sqrt[q]{\gamma}\prod_{j=1}^{k+1}(n_j^u)^{w_j}}{\sqrt[q]{\prod_{j=1}^{k+1}(1+(\gamma-1)(1-n_j^{uq}))^{w_j}+(\gamma-1)\prod_{j=1}^{k+1}(n_j^{uq})^{w_j}}}\end{array}\right]\end{array}\right)$$

It shows that it is true for $l = k + 1$, and, hence, it holds for all values of l. □

Here, we define some main characteristics of the IVTSFHWA operator in Theorem 3.

Theorem 3. *The HAOs of IVTSFNs satisfy the following properties:*

1. ***Idempotency.*** *If* $\text{Ꞇ}_j = \text{Ꞇ} = \left(\left[m_j^l, m_j^u\right], \left[i_j^l, i_j^u\right], \left[n_j^l, n_j^u\right]\right)\ \forall\ j = 1, 2, 3, \ldots l$. Then, $IVTSFHWA(\text{Ꞇ}_1, \text{Ꞇ}_2, \text{Ꞇ}_3, \ldots \text{Ꞇ}_l) = \text{Ꞇ}$
2. ***Boundedness.*** *If* $\text{Ꞇ}^- = \left(\left[\overset{l}{\min}_j m_j^l, \overset{u}{\min}_j m_j^u\right], \left[\overset{l}{\max}_j i_j^l, \overset{u}{\max}_j i_j^u\right], \left[\overset{l}{\max}_j n_j^l, \overset{u}{\max}_j n_j^u\right]\right)$ *and* $\text{Ꞇ}^+ = \left(\left[\overset{l}{\max}_j m_j^l, \overset{u}{\max}_j m_j^u\right], \left[\overset{l}{\min}_j i_j^l, \overset{u}{\min}_j i_j^u\right], \left[\overset{l}{\min}_j n_j^l, \overset{u}{\min}_j n_j^u\right]\right)$. *Then,* $\text{Ꞇ}^- \leq IVTSFHWA(\text{Ꞇ}_1, \text{Ꞇ}_2, \text{Ꞇ}_3, \ldots \text{Ꞇ}_l) \leq \text{Ꞇ}^+$
3. **Monotonicity.** *Let* Ꞇ_j *and* P_j *IVTSFNs such that* $\text{Ꞇ}_j \leq P_j\ \forall\ j$. *Then,* $IVTSFHWA(\text{Ꞇ}_1, \text{Ꞇ}_2, \text{Ꞇ}_3, \ldots \text{Ꞇ}_l) \leq IVTSFHWA(P_1, P_2, P_3, \ldots P_l)$

Proof. Trivial. □

The IVTSFHWA operator only evaluates IVTSFNs. To address situations where the ordering status of IVTSFNs is important in MADM problems, the IVTSFHOWA operator is defined as follows:

Definition 7. *Suppose that* $T_j = \left(\left[m_j^l, m_j^u\right], \left[i_j^l, i_j^u\right], \left[n_j^l, n_j^u\right]\right)\ \forall\ j = 1, 2, 3, \ldots, l$ *are some IVTSFNs. Then, the IVTSFHOWA operator* $T^l \rightarrow T$ *is defined as:*

$$IVTSFHOWA(\text{T}_1,\ \text{T}_2,\ \text{T}_3,\ \ldots \text{T}_l) = \sum_{j=1}^{l} w_j \text{T}_{\sigma(j)} \tag{7}$$

where $\text{T}_{\sigma(j-1)} \geq \text{T}_{\sigma(j)}\ \forall\ j$ *is satisfied.*

Theorem 4. *Consider that* $T_j = \left(\left[m_j^l, m_j^u\right], \left[i_j^l, i_j^u\right], \left[n_j^l, n_j^u\right]\right)\ \forall\ j = 1, 2, 3, \ldots, l$ *are IVTSFNs. Then, the IVTSFHOWA operator is an IVTSFN and given by:*

$$\begin{gathered} IVTSFHOWA(\text{T}_1, \text{T}_2, \text{T}_3, \ldots \text{T}_l) = \sum_{j=1}^{l} w_j \text{T}_{\sigma(j)} = \\ \left(\begin{array}{c} \left[\begin{array}{c} \sqrt[q]{\frac{\prod_{j=1}^{l}\left(1+(\gamma-1){m^l_{\sigma(j)}}^q\right)^{w_j}-\prod_{j=1}^{l}\left(1-{m^l_{\sigma(j)}}^q\right)^{w_j}}{\prod_{j=1}^{l}\left(1+(\gamma-1){m^l_{\sigma(j)}}^q\right)^{w_j}+(\gamma-1)\prod_{j=1}^{l}\left(1-{m^l_{\sigma(j)}}^q\right)^{w_j}}} \\ ,\sqrt[q]{\frac{\prod_{j=1}^{l}\left(1+(\gamma-1){m^u_{\sigma(j)}}^q\right)^{w_j}-\prod_{j=1}^{l}\left(1-{m^u_{\sigma(j)}}^q\right)^{w_j}}{\prod_{j=1}^{l}\left(1+(\gamma-1){m^u_{\sigma(j)}}^q\right)^{w_j}+(\gamma-1)\prod_{j=1}^{l}\left(1-{m^u_{\sigma(j)}}^q\right)^{w_j}}} \end{array} \right] \\ \left[\begin{array}{c} \frac{\sqrt[q]{\gamma}\prod_{j=1}^{k}\left(i^l_{\sigma(j)}\right)^{w_j}}{\sqrt[q]{\prod_{j=1}^{l}\left(1+(\gamma-1)\left(1-{i^l_{\sigma(j)}}^q\right)\right)^{w_j}+(\gamma-1)\prod_{j=1}^{l}\left({i^l_{\sigma(j)}}^q\right)^{w_j}}} \\ ,\frac{\sqrt[q]{\gamma}\prod_{j=1}^{k}\left(i^u_{\sigma(j)}\right)^{w_j}}{\sqrt[q]{\prod_{j=1}^{l}\left(1+(\gamma-1)\left(1-{i^u_{\sigma(j)}}^q\right)\right)^{w_j}+(\gamma-1)\prod_{j=1}^{l}\left({i^u_{\sigma(j)}}^q\right)^{w_j}}} \end{array} \right] \\ \left[\begin{array}{c} \frac{\sqrt[q]{\gamma}\prod_{j=1}^{k}\left(n^l_{\sigma(j)}\right)^{w_j}}{\sqrt[q]{\prod_{j=1}^{l}\left(1+(\gamma-1)\left(1-{n^l_{\sigma(j)}}^q\right)\right)^{w_j}+(\gamma-1)\prod_{j=1}^{l}\left({n^l_{\sigma(j)}}^q\right)^{w_j}}} \\ ,\frac{\sqrt[q]{\gamma}\prod_{j=1}^{k}\left(n^u_{\sigma(j)}\right)^{w_j}}{\sqrt[q]{\prod_{j=1}^{l}\left(1+(\gamma-1)\left(1-{n^u_{\sigma(j)}}^q\right)\right)^{w_j}+(\gamma-1)\prod_{j=1}^{l}\left({n^u_{\sigma(j)}}^q\right)^{w_j}}} \end{array} \right] \end{array} \right) \end{gathered} \tag{8}$$

Proof. Trivial. □

Remark 3. *The IVTSFHOWA operator satisfies the three conditions of Idempotency, Monotonicity, and Boundedness, as defined in Theorem 3.*

The IVTSFHWA operator only evaluates IVTSFNs, while the IVTSFHOWA operator only aggregates the ordered position of IVTSFNs. When the ordered position and weight of the argument are important, the IVTSFHHA operator is proposed as follows:

Definition 8. *Suppose that* $T_j = \left(\left[m_j^l, m_j^u\right], \left[i_j^l, i_j^u\right], \left[n_j^l, n_j^u\right]\right)\ \forall\ j = 1, 2, 3, \ldots, l$ *are IVTSFNs. Then, the IVTSFHHA operator* $T^l \rightarrow T$ *is defined as:*

$$IVTSFHHA(\text{T}_1,\ \text{T}_2,\ \text{T}_3,\ \ldots \text{T}_l) = \sum_{j=1}^{l} w_j \dot{\text{T}}_{\sigma(j)} \tag{9}$$

where $\dot{\text{T}}_{\sigma(j)}$ *is the* jth *largest value of the IVTSFNs* $\dot{\text{T}}_j = l\varpi_j \text{T}_j$ *with* ϖ_j *as the weight of interval-valued T-Spherical fuzzy aϖrguments* T_j *such that* $\varpi_j \in [0, 1]$ *and* $\sum_1^n \varpi_j = 1$ *and the balancing coefficient is denoted by* l.

Theorem 5. *Consider that* $T_j = \left(\left[m_j^l, m_j^u\right], \left[i_j^l, i_j^u\right], \left[n_j^l, n_j^u\right]\right)$ $\forall\, j = 1, 2, 3, \ldots, l$ *are IVTSFNs. Then, the IVTSFHHA operator is an IVTSFN and given by:*

$$IVTSFHHA(\mathrm{T}_1, \mathrm{T}_2, \mathrm{T}_3, \ldots \mathrm{T}_l) =$$
$$\left(\begin{array}{c}\left[\sqrt[q]{\frac{\prod_{j=1}^{l}\left(1+(\gamma-1)\dot{m}_{\sigma(j)}^{l}{}^{q}\right)^{w_j}-\prod_{j=1}^{l}\left(1-\dot{m}_{\sigma(j)}^{l}{}^{q}\right)^{w_j}}{\prod_{j=1}^{l}\left(1+(\gamma-1)\dot{m}_{\sigma(j)}^{l}{}^{q}\right)^{w_j}+(\gamma-1)\prod_{j=1}^{l}\left(1-\dot{m}_{\sigma(j)}^{l}{}^{q}\right)^{w_j}}}, \sqrt[q]{\frac{\prod_{j=1}^{l}\left(1+(\gamma-1)\dot{m}_{\sigma(j)}^{u}{}^{q}\right)^{w_j}-\prod_{j=1}^{l}\left(1-\dot{m}_{\sigma(j)}^{u}{}^{q}\right)^{w_j}}{\prod_{j=1}^{l}\left(1+(\gamma-1)\dot{m}_{\sigma(j)}^{u}{}^{q}\right)^{w_j}+(\gamma-1)\prod_{j=1}^{l}\left(1-\dot{m}_{\sigma(j)}^{u}{}^{q}\right)^{w_j}}}\right] \\ \left[\frac{\sqrt[q]{\gamma}\prod_{j=1}^{k}\left(i_{\sigma(j)}^{l}\right)^{w_j}}{\sqrt[q]{\prod_{j=1}^{l}\left(1+(\gamma-1)\left(1-i_{\sigma(j)}^{l}{}^{q}\right)\right)^{w_j}+(\gamma-1)\prod_{j=1}^{l}\left(i_{\sigma(j)}^{l}{}^{q}\right)^{w_j}}}, \frac{\sqrt[q]{\gamma}\prod_{j=1}^{k}\left(i_{\sigma(j)}^{u}\right)^{w_j}}{\sqrt[q]{\prod_{j=1}^{l}\left(1+(\gamma-1)\left(1-i_{\sigma(j)}^{u}{}^{q}\right)\right)^{w_j}+(\gamma-1)\prod_{j=1}^{l}\left(i_{\sigma(j)}^{u}{}^{q}\right)^{w_j}}}\right] \\ \left[\frac{\sqrt[q]{\gamma}\prod_{j=1}^{k}\left(\dot{n}_{\sigma(j)}^{l}\right)^{w_j}}{\sqrt[q]{\prod_{j=1}^{l}\left(1+(\gamma-1)\left(1-\dot{n}_{\sigma(j)}^{l}{}^{q}\right)\right)^{w_j}+(\gamma-1)\prod_{j=1}^{l}\left(\dot{n}_{\sigma(j)}^{l}{}^{q}\right)^{w_j}}}, \frac{\sqrt[q]{\gamma}\prod_{j=1}^{k}\left(\dot{n}_{\sigma(j)}^{u}\right)^{w_j}}{\sqrt[q]{\prod_{j=1}^{l}\left(1+(\gamma-1)\left(1-\dot{n}_{\sigma(j)}^{u}{}^{q}\right)\right)^{w_j}+(\gamma-1)\prod_{j=1}^{l}\left(\dot{n}_{\sigma(j)}^{u}{}^{q}\right)^{w_j}}}\right]\end{array}\right) \quad (10)$$

Proof. Trivial. □

Remark 4. *Theorem 5 reduces to the IVTSFHWA operator for* $w_j = \left(\frac{1}{l}, \frac{1}{l}, \frac{1}{l}, \ldots \frac{1}{l}\right)^T$. *Then, it reduces into the IVTSFHOWA operator for* $w_j = \left(\frac{1}{l}, \frac{1}{l}, \frac{1}{l}, \ldots \frac{1}{l}\right)^T$.

Remark 5. *The IVTSFHOWA operator satisfies the three conditions of Idempotency, Monotonicity, and Boundedness defined in Theorem 3.*

5. Interval-Valued T-Spherical fuzzy Hamacher Weighted Geometric (IVTSFHWG) Operators

The aim of this section is to develop IVTSFHWG operators based on the Hamacher operations introduced in Section 3. Some basic characteristics of the IVTSFHWG operators are also investigated.

Definition 9. *Suppose that* $T_j = \left(\left[m_j^l, m_j^u\right], \left[i_j^l, i_j^u\right], \left[n_j^l, n_j^u\right]\right)$ $\forall\, j = 1, 2, 3, \ldots, l$ *are IVTSFNs. Then, the IVTSFHWG operator* $T^l \rightarrow T$ *is defined as:*

$$IVTSFHWG\,(\mathrm{T}_1, \mathrm{T}_2, \mathrm{T}_3, \ldots \mathrm{T}_l) = \sum_{j=1}^{l} \mathrm{T}_j^{w_j} \quad (11)$$

By using previous results defined in Definition 5, we can obtain the subsequent result, as given in Theorem 6.

Theorem 6. *Consider that* $T_j = \left(\left[m_j^l, m_j^u\right], \left[i_j^l, i_j^u\right], \left[n_j^l, n_j^u\right]\right)\ \forall\ j = 1,2,3,\ldots,l$ *are IVTSFNs. Then, the IVTSFHWG operator is an IVTSFN and given by:*

$$IVTSFHWG(T_1, T_2, T_3, \ldots T_l) = \left(\begin{array}{c} \left[\frac{\sqrt[q]{\gamma}\prod_{j=1}^{l}(m_j^l)^{w_j}}{\sqrt[q]{\prod_{j=1}^{l}(1+(\gamma-1)(1-m_j^{l\,q}))^{w_j}+(\gamma-1)\prod_{j=1}^{l}(m_j^{l\,q})^{w_j}}}, \frac{\sqrt[q]{\gamma}\prod_{j=1}^{l}(m_j^u)^{w_j}}{\sqrt[q]{\prod_{j=1}^{l}(1+(\gamma-1)(1-m_j^{u\,q}))^{w_j}+(\gamma-1)\prod_{j=1}^{l}(m_j^{u\,q})^{w_j}}} \right] \\ \left[\sqrt[q]{\frac{\prod_{j=1}^{l}(1+(\gamma-1)i_j^{l\,q})^{w_j}-\prod_{j=1}^{l}(1-i_j^{l\,q})^{w_j}}{\prod_{j=1}^{l}(1+(\gamma-1)i_j^{l\,q})^{w_j}+(\gamma-1)\prod_{j=1}^{l}(1-i_j^{l\,q})^{w_j}}}, \sqrt[q]{\frac{\prod_{j=1}^{l}(1+(\gamma-1)i_j^{u\,q})^{w_j}-\prod_{j=1}^{l}(1-i_j^{u\,q})^{w_j}}{\prod_{j=1}^{l}(1+(\gamma-1)i_j^{u\,q})^{w_j}+(\gamma-1)\prod_{j=1}^{l}(1-i_j^{u\,q})^{w_j}}} \right] \\ \left[\sqrt[q]{\frac{\prod_{j=1}^{l}(1+(\gamma-1)n_j^{l\,q})^{w_j}-\prod_{j=1}^{l}(1-n_j^{l\,q})^{w_j}}{\prod_{j=1}^{l}(1+(\gamma-1)n_j^{l\,q})^{w_j}+(\gamma-1)\prod_{j=1}^{l}(1-n_j^{l\,q})^{w_j}}}, \sqrt[q]{\frac{\prod_{j=1}^{l}(1+(\gamma-1)n_j^{u\,q})^{w_j}-\prod_{j=1}^{l}(1-n_j^{u\,q})^{w_j}}{\prod_{j=1}^{l}(1+(\gamma-1)n_j^{u\,q})^{w_j}+(\gamma-1)\prod_{j=1}^{l}(1-n_j^{u\,q})^{w_j}}} \right] \end{array} \right) \quad (12)$$

Proof. This result can be proven similar to Theorem 2. It can be noted that this operator also fulfilled the conditions of Monotonicity, Idempotency, and Boundedness. □

Definition 10. *Suppose that* $T_j = \left(\left[m_j^l, m_j^u\right], \left[i_j^l, i_j^u\right], \left[n_j^l, n_j^u\right]\right)\ \forall\ j = 1,2,3,\ldots,l$ *are IVTSFNs. Then, the IVTSFHWG operator* $T^l \to T$ *is defined as:*

$$IVTSFHOWG(T_1,\ T_2,\ T_3,\ \ldots T_l) = \sum_{j=1}^{l} T_{\sigma(j)}^{w_j} \quad (13)$$

where $T_{\sigma(j-1)} \geq T_{\sigma(j)}\ \forall\ j$ *is satisfied.*

Theorem 7. *Consider that* $T_j = \left(\left[m_j^l, m_j^u\right], \left[i_j^l, i_j^u\right], \left[n_j^l, n_j^u\right]\right)\ \forall\ j = 1,2,3,\ldots,l$ *are IVTSFNs. Then, the IVTSFHOWG operator is an IVTSFN and given by:*

$$IVTSFHOWG(T_1, T_2, T_3, \ldots T_l) = \sum_{j=1}^{l} T_{\sigma(j)}^{w_j} = \left(\begin{array}{c} \left[\frac{\sqrt[q]{\gamma}\prod_{j=1}^{l}(m_{\sigma(j)}^l)^{w_j}}{\sqrt[q]{\prod_{j=1}^{l}(1+(\gamma-1)(1-m_{\sigma(j)}^{l}{}^{q}))^{w_j}+(\gamma-1)\prod_{j=1}^{l}(m_{\sigma(j)}^{l}{}^{q})^{w_j}}}, \frac{\sqrt[q]{\gamma}\prod_{j=1}^{l}(m_{\sigma(j)}^u)^{w_j}}{\sqrt[q]{\prod_{j=1}^{l}(1+(\gamma-1)(1-m_{\sigma(j)}^{u}{}^{q}))^{w_j}+(\gamma-1)\prod_{j=1}^{l}(m_{\sigma(j)}^{u}{}^{q})^{w_j}}} \right] \\ \left[\sqrt[q]{\frac{\prod_{j=1}^{l}(1+(\gamma-1)i_{\sigma(j)}^{l}{}^{q})^{w_j}-\prod_{j=1}^{l}(1-i_{\sigma(j)}^{l}{}^{q})^{w_j}}{\prod_{j=1}^{l}(1+(\gamma-1)i_{\sigma(j)}^{l}{}^{q})^{w_j}+(\gamma-1)\prod_{j=1}^{l}(1-i_{\sigma(j)}^{l}{}^{q})^{w_j}}}, \sqrt[q]{\frac{\prod_{j=1}^{l}(1+(\gamma-1)i_{\sigma(j)}^{u}{}^{q})^{w_j}-\prod_{j=1}^{l}(1-i_{\sigma(j)}^{u}{}^{q})^{w_j}}{\prod_{j=1}^{l}(1+(\gamma-1)i_{\sigma(j)}^{u}{}^{q})^{w_j}+(\gamma-1)\prod_{j=1}^{l}(1-i_{\sigma(j)}^{u}{}^{q})^{w_j}}} \right] \\ \left[\sqrt[q]{\frac{\prod_{j=1}^{l}(1+(\gamma-1)n_{\sigma(j)}^{l}{}^{q})^{w_j}-\prod_{j=1}^{l}(1-n_{\sigma(j)}^{l}{}^{q})^{w_j}}{\prod_{j=1}^{l}(1+(\gamma-1)n_{\sigma(j)}^{l}{}^{q})^{w_j}+(\gamma-1)\prod_{j=1}^{l}(1-n_{\sigma(j)}^{l}{}^{q})^{w_j}}}, \sqrt[q]{\frac{\prod_{j=1}^{l}(1+(\gamma-1)n_{\sigma(j)}^{u}{}^{q})^{w_j}-\prod_{j=1}^{l}(1-n_{\sigma(j)}^{u}{}^{q})^{w_j}}{\prod_{j=1}^{l}(1+(\gamma-1)n_{\sigma(j)}^{u}{}^{q})^{w_j}+(\gamma-1)\prod_{j=1}^{l}(1-n_{\sigma(j)}^{u}{}^{q})^{w_j}}} \right] \end{array} \right) \quad (14)$$

Proof. Trivial. □

Remark 6. *The IVTSFHOWG operator satisfies the three conditions of Idempotency, Monotonicity, and Boundedness defined in Theorem 3.*

The IVTSFHWG operator only evaluates the IVTSFNs, while the IVTSFHOWG operator only aggregates the ordered position of the IVTSFNs. When both ordered position and weight of the argument becomes important, the IVTSFHHG operator is as follows:

Definition 11. *Suppose that* $T_j = \left(\left[m_j^l, m_j^u\right], \left[i_j^l, i_j^u\right], \left[n_j^l, n_j^u\right]\right) \forall j = 1,2,3,\ldots,l$ *are IVTSFNs. Then, the IVTSFHHG operator* $T^l \rightarrow T$ *is defined as:*

$$IVTSFHHG(\text{T}_1,\ \text{T}_2,\ \text{T}_3,\ \ldots \text{T}_j) = \sum_{j=1}^{l} \dot{\text{T}}_{\sigma(j)}^{w_j} \tag{15}$$

where $\dot{\text{T}}_{\sigma(j)}$ *is the* jth *largest of the IVTSFNs* $\dot{\text{T}}_j = l\mathcal{w}_j\text{T}_j$, *with* $\mathcal{w}_j$ *as the weight of interval-valued T-Spherical fuzzy arguments* T_j *such that* $\mathcal{w}_j \in [0,1]$ *and* $\sum_1^n \mathcal{w}_j = 1$ *and the balancing coefficient is denoted by* l.

Theorem 8. *Consider that* $T_j = \left(\left[m_j^l, m_j^u\right], \left[i_j^l, i_j^u\right], \left[n_j^l, n_j^u\right]\right) \forall j = 1,2,3,\ldots,l$ *are IVTSFNs. Then, the IVTSFHHG operator is an IVTSFN and given by:*

$$\begin{aligned} &IVTSFHHG(\text{T}_1, \text{T}_2, \text{T}_3, \ldots \text{T}_l) \\ &= \left(\begin{array}{c} \left[\frac{\sqrt[q]{\gamma}\prod_{j=1}^{l}\left(\dot{m}_{\sigma(j)}^{l}\right)^{w_j}}{\sqrt[q]{\prod_{j=1}^{l}\left(1+(\gamma-1)\left(1-\dot{m}_{\sigma(j)}^{l}{}^{q}\right)\right)^{w_j}+(\gamma-1)\prod_{j=1}^{l}\left(\dot{m}_{\sigma(j)}^{l}{}^{q}\right)^{w_j}}}, \frac{\sqrt[q]{\gamma}\prod_{j=1}^{l}\left(\dot{m}_{\sigma(j)}^{u}\right)^{w_j}}{\sqrt[q]{\prod_{j=1}^{l}\left(1+(\gamma-1)\left(1-\dot{m}_{\sigma(j)}^{u}{}^{q}\right)\right)^{w_j}+(\gamma-1)\prod_{j=1}^{l}\left(\dot{m}_{\sigma(j)}^{u}{}^{q}\right)^{w_j}}} \right] \\ \left[\sqrt[q]{\frac{\prod_{j=1}^{l}\left(1+(\gamma-1)i_{\sigma(j)}^{l}{}^{q}\right)^{w_j}-\prod_{j=1}^{l}\left(1-i_{\sigma(j)}^{l}{}^{q}\right)^{w_j}}{\prod_{j=1}^{l}\left(1+(\gamma-1)i_{\sigma(j)}^{l}{}^{q}\right)^{w_j}+(\gamma-1)\prod_{j=1}^{l}\left(1-i_{\sigma(j)}^{l}{}^{q}\right)^{w_j}}}, \sqrt[q]{\frac{\prod_{j=1}^{l}\left(1+(\gamma-1)i_{\sigma(j)}^{u}{}^{q}\right)^{w_j}-\prod_{j=1}^{l}\left(1-i_{\sigma(j)}^{u}{}^{q}\right)^{w_j}}{\prod_{j=1}^{l}\left(1+(\gamma-1)i_{\sigma(j)}^{u}{}^{q}\right)^{w_j}+(\gamma-1)\prod_{j=1}^{l}\left(1-i_{\sigma(j)}^{u}{}^{q}\right)^{w_j}}} \right] \\ \left[\sqrt[q]{\frac{\prod_{j=1}^{l}\left(1+(\gamma-1)\dot{n}_{\sigma(j)}^{l}{}^{q}\right)^{w_j}-\prod_{j=1}^{l}\left(1-\dot{n}_{\sigma(j)}^{l}{}^{q}\right)^{w_j}}{\prod_{j=1}^{l}\left(1+(\gamma-1)\dot{n}_{\sigma(j)}^{l}{}^{q}\right)^{w_j}+(\gamma-1)\prod_{j=1}^{l}\left(1-\dot{n}_{\sigma(j)}^{l}{}^{q}\right)^{w_j}}}, \sqrt[q]{\frac{\prod_{j=1}^{l}\left(1+(\gamma-1)\dot{n}_{\sigma(j)}^{u}{}^{q}\right)^{w_j}-\prod_{j=1}^{l}\left(1-\dot{n}_{\sigma(j)}^{u}{}^{q}\right)^{w_j}}{\prod_{j=1}^{l}\left(1+(\gamma-1)\dot{n}_{\sigma(j)}^{u}{}^{q}\right)^{w_j}+(\gamma-1)\prod_{j=1}^{l}\left(1-\dot{n}_{\sigma(j)}^{u}{}^{q}\right)^{w_j}}} \right] \end{array} \right) \end{aligned} \tag{16}$$

Proof. Trivial. □

Remark 7. *Equation (11) is reduced to the IVTSFHWG operator for* $w_j = \left(\frac{1}{l}, \frac{1}{l}, \frac{1}{l}, \ldots \frac{1}{l}\right)^T$. *Then, it is reduced into the IVTSFHOWG operator for* $\mathcal{w}_j = \left(\frac{1}{l}, \frac{1}{l}, \frac{1}{l}, \ldots \frac{1}{l}\right)^T$.

6. Special Cases

It can be noticed that the AOs defined for some existing fuzzy sets, such as IVIFSs, IVPyFSs, IVq-ROPFSs, IVPFSs, and IVSFSs, can be reduced from the proposed operators. It means that the earlier defined HAOs become special cases of the proposed IVTSFHWA and IVTSFHWG operators. Proposed IVTSFHWA and IVTSFHWG operators are defined as following, respectively:

$$IVTSFHWA(\text{T}_1, \text{T}_2, \text{T}_3, \ldots \text{T}_l) = \begin{pmatrix} \left[\sqrt[q]{\frac{\prod_{j=1}^{l}(1+(\gamma-1)m_j^{lq})^{w_j} - \prod_{j=1}^{l}(1-m_j^{lq})^{w_j}}{\prod_{j=1}^{l}(1+(\gamma-1)m_j^{lq})^{w_j} + (\gamma-1)\prod_{j=1}^{l}(1-m_j^{lq})^{w_j}}}, \sqrt[q]{\frac{\prod_{j=1}^{l}(1+(\gamma-1)m_j^{uq})^{w_j} - \prod_{j=1}^{l}(1-m_j^{uq})^{w_j}}{\prod_{j=1}^{l}(1+(\gamma-1)m_j^{uq})^{w_j} + (\gamma-1)\prod_{j=1}^{l}(1-m_j^{uq})^{w_j}}} \right] \\ \left[\frac{\sqrt[q]{\gamma}\prod_{j=1}^{l}(i_j^{l})^{w_j}}{\sqrt[q]{\prod_{j=1}^{l}(1+(\gamma-1)(1-i_j^{lq}))^{w_j} + (\gamma-1)\prod_{j=1}^{l}(i_j^{lq})^{w_j}}}, \frac{\sqrt[q]{\gamma}\prod_{j=1}^{l}(i_j^{u})^{w_j}}{\sqrt[q]{\prod_{j=1}^{l}(1+(\gamma-1)(1-i_j^{uq}))^{w_j} + (\gamma-1)\prod_{j=1}^{l}(i_j^{uq})^{w_j}}} \right] \\ \left[\frac{\sqrt[q]{\gamma}\prod_{j=1}^{l}(n_j^{l})^{w_j}}{\sqrt[q]{\prod_{j=1}^{l}(1+(\gamma-1)(1-n_j^{lq}))^{w_j} + (\gamma-1)\prod_{j=1}^{l}(n_j^{lq})^{w_j}}}, \frac{\sqrt[q]{\gamma}\prod_{j=1}^{l}(n_j^{u})^{w_j}}{\sqrt[q]{\prod_{j=1}^{l}(1+(\gamma-1)(1-n_j^{uq}))^{w_j} + (\gamma-1)\prod_{j=1}^{l}(n_j^{uq})^{w_j}}} \right] \end{pmatrix}$$

$$IVTSFHWG(\text{T}_1, \text{T}_2, \text{T}_3, \ldots \text{T}_l) = \begin{pmatrix} \left[\frac{\sqrt[q]{\gamma}\prod_{j=1}^{l}(m_j^{l})^{w_j}}{\sqrt[q]{\prod_{j=1}^{l}(1+(\gamma-1)(1-m_j^{lq}))^{w_j} + (\gamma-1)\prod_{j=1}^{l}(m_j^{lq})^{w_j}}}, \frac{\sqrt[q]{\gamma}\prod_{j=1}^{l}(m_j^{u})^{w_j}}{\sqrt[q]{\prod_{j=1}^{l}(1+(\gamma-1)(1-m_j^{uq}))^{w_j} + (\gamma-1)\prod_{j=1}^{l}(m_j^{uq})^{w_j}}} \right] \\ \left[\sqrt[q]{\frac{\prod_{j=1}^{l}(1+(\gamma-1)i_j^{lq})^{w_j} - \prod_{j=1}^{l}(1-i_j^{lq})^{w_j}}{\prod_{j=1}^{l}(1+(\gamma-1)i_j^{lq})^{w_j} + (\gamma-1)\prod_{j=1}^{l}(1-i_j^{lq})^{w_j}}}, \sqrt[q]{\frac{\prod_{j=1}^{l}(1+(\gamma-1)i_j^{uq})^{w_j} - \prod_{j=1}^{l}(1-i_j^{uq})^{w_j}}{\prod_{j=1}^{l}(1+(\gamma-1)i_j^{uq})^{w_j} + (\gamma-1)\prod_{j=1}^{l}(1-i_j^{uq})^{w_j}}} \right] \\ \left[\sqrt[q]{\frac{\prod_{j=1}^{l}(1+(\gamma-1)n_j^{lq})^{w_j} - \prod_{j=1}^{l}(1-n_j^{lq})^{w_j}}{\prod_{j=1}^{l}(1+(\gamma-1)n_j^{lq})^{w_j} + (\gamma-1)\prod_{j=1}^{l}(1-n_j^{lq})^{w_j}}}, \sqrt[q]{\frac{\prod_{j=1}^{l}(1+(\gamma-1)n_j^{uq})^{w_j} - \prod_{j=1}^{l}(1-n_j^{uq})^{w_j}}{\prod_{j=1}^{l}(1+(\gamma-1)n_j^{uq})^{w_j} + (\gamma-1)\prod_{j=1}^{l}(1-n_j^{uq})^{w_j}}} \right] \end{pmatrix}$$

1. If $m^l = m^u = m$, $i^l = i^u = i$ and $n^l = n^u = n$, then the IVTSFHWA and IVTSFHWG operators are converted into TSFHWA and TSFHWG, given as follows:

$$TSFHWA(\text{T}_1, \text{T}_2, \text{T}_3, \ldots \text{T}_l) = \begin{pmatrix} \sqrt[q]{\frac{\prod_{j=1}^{l}(1+(\gamma-1)m_j^{q})^{w_j} - \prod_{j=1}^{l}(1-m_j^{q})^{w_j}}{\prod_{j=1}^{l}(1+(\gamma-1)m_j^{q})^{w_j} + (\gamma-1)\prod_{j=1}^{l}(1-m_j^{q})^{w_j}}} \\ \frac{\sqrt[q]{\gamma}\prod_{j=1}^{l} i_j^{w_j}}{\sqrt[q]{\prod_{j=1}^{l}(1+(\gamma-1)(1-i_j^{q}))^{w_j} + (\gamma-1)\prod_{j=1}^{l}(i_j^{q})^{w_j}}} \\ \frac{\sqrt[q]{\gamma}\prod_{j=1}^{l} n_j^{w_j}}{\sqrt[q]{\prod_{j=1}^{l}(1+(\gamma-1)(1-n_j^{q}))^{w_j} + (\gamma-1)\prod_{j=1}^{l}(n_j^{q})^{w_j}}} \end{pmatrix} \quad (17)$$

$$
\begin{aligned}
&TSFHWG(\daleth_1, \daleth_2, \daleth_3, \ldots \daleth_l) \\
&= \left(\begin{array}{c}
\frac{\sqrt[q]{\gamma}\prod_{j=1}^{l}(m_j^{w_j})}{\sqrt[q]{\prod_{j=1}^{l}(1+(\gamma-1)(1-m_j^q))^{w_j}+(\gamma-1)\prod_{j=1}^{l}(m_j^q)^{w_j}}} \\
\sqrt[q]{\frac{\prod_{j=1}^{l}(1+(\gamma-1)i_j^q)^{w_j}-\prod_{j=1}^{l}(1-i_j^q)^{w_j}}{\prod_{j=1}^{l}(1+(\gamma-1)i_j^q)^{w_j}+(\gamma-1)\prod_{j=1}^{l}(1-i_j^q)^{w_j}}} \\
\sqrt[q]{\frac{\prod_{j=1}^{l}(1+(\gamma-1)n_j^q)^{w_j}-\prod_{j=1}^{l}(1-n_j^q)^{w_j}}{\prod_{j=1}^{l}(1+(\gamma-1)n_j^q)^{w_j}+(\gamma-1)\prod_{j=1}^{l}(1-n_j^q)^{w_j}}}
\end{array} \right)
\end{aligned} \tag{18}
$$

2. If $q = 2$, then aggregated operators (AOs) of the IVTSFHWA and IVTSFHWG are converted to IVSFHWA and IVSFWG, given as follows:

$$
\begin{aligned}
&IVSFHWA(\daleth_1, \daleth_2, \daleth_3, \ldots \daleth_l) = \\
&\left(\begin{array}{c}
\left[\begin{array}{c}
\sqrt{\frac{\prod_{j=1}^{l}(1+(\gamma-1)m_j^{l2})^{w_j}-\prod_{j=1}^{l}(1-m_j^{l2})^{w_j}}{\prod_{j=1}^{l}(1+(\gamma-1)m_j^{l2})^{w_j}+(\gamma-1)\prod_{j=1}^{l}(1-m_j^{l2})^{w_j}}} \\
,\sqrt{\frac{\prod_{j=1}^{l}(1+(\gamma-1)m_j^{u2})^{w_j}-\prod_{j=1}^{l}(1-m_j^{u2})^{w_j}}{\prod_{j=1}^{l}(1+(\gamma-1)m_j^{u2})^{w_j}+(\gamma-1)\prod_{j=1}^{l}(1-m_j^{u2})^{w_j}}}
\end{array} \right] \\
\left[\begin{array}{c}
\frac{\sqrt{\gamma}\prod_{j=1}^{l}(i_j^l)^{w_j}}{\sqrt{\prod_{j=1}^{l}(1+(\gamma-1)(1-i_j^{l2}))^{w_j}+(\gamma-1)\prod_{j=1}^{l}(i_j^{l2})^{w_j}}} \\
,\frac{\sqrt{\gamma}\prod_{j=1}^{l}(i_j^u)^{w_j}}{\sqrt{\prod_{j=1}^{l}(1+(\gamma-1)(1-i_j^{u2}))^{w_j}+(\gamma-1)\prod_{j=1}^{l}(i_j^{u2})^{w_j}}}
\end{array} \right] \\
\left[\begin{array}{c}
\frac{\sqrt{\gamma}\prod_{j=1}^{l}(n_j^l)^{w_j}}{\sqrt{\prod_{j=1}^{l}(1+(\gamma-1)(1-n_j^{l2}))^{w_j}+(\gamma-1)\prod_{j=1}^{l}(n_j^{l2})^{w_j}}} \\
,\frac{\sqrt{\gamma}\prod_{j=1}^{l}(n_j^u)^{w_j}}{\sqrt{\prod_{j=1}^{l}(1+(\gamma-1)(1-n_j^{u2}))^{w_j}+(\gamma-1)\prod_{j=1}^{l}(n_j^{u2})^{w_j}}}
\end{array} \right]
\end{array} \right)
\end{aligned} \tag{19}
$$

$$
\begin{aligned}
&IVSFHWG(\daleth_1, \daleth_2, \daleth_3, \ldots \daleth_l) \\
&= \left(\begin{array}{c}
\left[\begin{array}{c}
\frac{\sqrt{\gamma}\prod_{j=1}^{l}(m_j^l)^{w_j}}{\sqrt{\prod_{j=1}^{l}(1+(\gamma-1)(1-m_j^{l2}))^{w_j}+(\gamma-1)\prod_{j=1}^{l}(m_j^{l2})^{w_j}}} \\
,\frac{\sqrt{\gamma}\prod_{j=1}^{l}(m_j^u)^{w_j}}{\sqrt{\prod_{j=1}^{l}(1+(\gamma-1)(1-m_j^{u2}))^{w_j}+(\gamma-1)\prod_{j=1}^{l}(m_j^{u2})^{w_j}}}
\end{array} \right] \\
\left[\begin{array}{c}
\sqrt{\frac{\prod_{j=1}^{l}(1+(\gamma-1)m_j^{l2})^{w_j}-\prod_{j=1}^{l}(1-m_j^{l2})^{w_j}}{\prod_{j=1}^{l}(1+(\gamma-1)m_j^{l2})^{w_j}+(\gamma-1)\prod_{j=1}^{l}(1-m_j^{l2})^{w_j}}}, \\
\sqrt{\frac{\prod_{j=1}^{l}(1+(\gamma-1)m_j^{u2})^{w_j}-\prod_{j=1}^{l}(1-m_j^{u2})^{w_j}}{\prod_{j=1}^{l}(1+(\gamma-1)m_j^{u2})^{w_j}+(\gamma-1)\prod_{j=1}^{l}(1-m_j^{u2})^{w_j}}}
\end{array} \right] \\
\left[\begin{array}{c}
\sqrt{\frac{\prod_{j=1}^{l}(1+(\gamma-1)n_j^{l2})^{w_j}-\prod_{j=1}^{l}(1-n_j^{l2})^{w_j}}{\prod_{j=1}^{l}(1+(\gamma-1)n_j^{l2})^{w_j}+(\gamma-1)\prod_{j=1}^{l}(1-n_j^{l2})^{w_j}}} \\
,\sqrt{\frac{\prod_{j=1}^{l}(1+(\gamma-1)n_j^{u2})^{w_j}-\prod_{j=1}^{l}(1-n_j^{u2})^{w_j}}{\prod_{j=1}^{l}(1+(\gamma-1)n_j^{u2})^{w_j}+(\gamma-1)\prod_{j=1}^{l}(1-n_j^{u2})^{w_j}}}
\end{array} \right]
\end{array} \right)
\end{aligned} \tag{20}
$$

3. If $q = 2$, $m^l = m^u = m$, $i^l = i^u = i$ and $n^l = n^u = n$, then the IVTSFHWA and IVTSFHWG operators are converted into a spherical fuzzy environment.

$$SFHWA(Ꚋ_1, Ꚋ_2, Ꚋ_3, \ldots Ꚋ_l) = \begin{pmatrix} \sqrt{\frac{\prod_{j=1}^{l}(1+(\gamma-1)m_j^2)^{w_j}-\prod_{j=1}^{l}(1-m_j^2)^{w_j}}{\prod_{j=1}^{l}(1+(\gamma-1)m_j^2)^{w_j}+(\gamma-1)\prod_{j=1}^{l}(1-m_j^2)^{w_j}}} \\ \frac{\sqrt{\gamma}\prod_{j=1}^{l} i_j^{w_j}}{\sqrt{\prod_{j=1}^{l}(1+(\gamma-1)(1-i_j^2))^{w_j}+(\gamma-1)\prod_{j=1}^{l}(i_j^2)^{w_j}}} \\ \frac{\sqrt{\gamma}\prod_{j=1}^{l} n_j^{w_j}}{\sqrt{\prod_{j=1}^{l}(1+(\gamma-1)(1-n_j^2))^{w_j}+(\gamma-1)\prod_{j=1}^{l}(n_j^2)^{w_j}}} \end{pmatrix} \quad (21)$$

$$SFHWG(Ꚋ_1, Ꚋ_2, Ꚋ_3, \ldots Ꚋ_l) = \begin{pmatrix} \frac{\sqrt{\gamma}\prod_{j=1}^{l}(m_j^{w_j})}{\sqrt{\prod_{j=1}^{l}(1+(\gamma-1)(1-m_j^2))^{w_j}+(\gamma-1)\prod_{j=1}^{l}(m_j^2)^{w_j}}} \\ \sqrt{\frac{\prod_{j=1}^{l}(1+(\gamma-1)i_j^2)^{w_j}-\prod_{j=1}^{l}(1-i_j^2)^{w_j}}{\prod_{j=1}^{l}(1+(\gamma-1)i_j^2)^{w_j}+(\gamma-1)\prod_{j=1}^{l}(1-i_j^2)^{w_j}}} \\ \sqrt{\frac{\prod_{j=1}^{l}(1+(\gamma-1)n_j^2)^{w_j}-\prod_{j=1}^{l}(1-n_j^2)^{w_j}}{\prod_{j=1}^{l}(1+(\gamma-1)n_j^2)^{w_j}+(\gamma-1)\prod_{j=1}^{l}(1-n_j^2)^{w_j}}} \end{pmatrix} \quad (22)$$

4. If $q = 1$, then A the IVTSFHWA and IVTSFHWG are converted into interval-valued picture fuzzy settings and can be defined as:

$$IVPFHWA(Ꚋ_1, Ꚋ_2, Ꚋ_3, \ldots Ꚋ_l) = \begin{pmatrix} \begin{bmatrix} \frac{\prod_{j=1}^{l}(1+(\gamma-1)m_j^l)^{w_j}-\prod_{j=1}^{l}(1-m_j^l)^{w_j}}{\prod_{j=1}^{l}(1+(\gamma-1)m_j^l)^{w_j}+(\gamma-1)\prod_{j=1}^{l}(1-m_j^l)^{w_j}}, \\ \frac{\prod_{j=1}^{l}(1+(\gamma-1)m_j^u)^{w_j}-\prod_{j=1}^{l}(1-m_j^u)^{w_j}}{\prod_{j=1}^{l}(1+(\gamma-1)m_j^u)^{w_j}+(\gamma-1)\prod_{j=1}^{l}(1-m_j^u)^{w_j}} \end{bmatrix} \\ \begin{bmatrix} \frac{\gamma\prod_{j=1}^{l}(i_j^l)^{w_j}}{\prod_{j=1}^{l}(1+(\gamma-1)(1-i_j^l))^{w_j}+(\gamma-1)\prod_{j=1}^{l}(i_j^l)^{w_j}} \\ ,\frac{\gamma\prod_{j=1}^{l}(i_j^u)^{w_j}}{\prod_{j=1}^{l}(1+(\gamma-1)(1-i_j^u))^{w_j}+(\gamma-1)\prod_{j=1}^{l}(i_j^u)^{w_j}} \end{bmatrix} \\ \begin{bmatrix} \frac{\gamma\prod_{j=1}^{l}(n_j^l)^{w_j}}{\prod_{j=1}^{l}(1+(\gamma-1)(1-n_j^l))^{w_j}+(\gamma-1)\prod_{j=1}^{l}(n_j^l)^{w_j}} \\ ,\frac{\gamma\prod_{j=1}^{l}(n_j^u)^{w_j}}{\prod_{j=1}^{l}(1+(\gamma-1)(1-n_j^u))^{w_j}+(\gamma-1)\prod_{j=1}^{l}(n_j^u)^{w_j}} \end{bmatrix} \end{pmatrix} \quad (23)$$

$$IVPSFHWG(Ꚋ_1, Ꚋ_2, Ꚋ_3, \ldots Ꚋ_l) = \begin{pmatrix} \begin{bmatrix} \frac{\gamma\prod_{j=1}^{l}(m_j^l)^{w_j}}{\prod_{j=1}^{l}(1+(\gamma-1)(1-m_j^l))^{w_j}+(\gamma-1)\prod_{j=1}^{l}(m_j^l)^{w_j}} \\ ,\frac{\gamma\prod_{j=1}^{l}(m_j^u)^{w_j}}{\prod_{j=1}^{l}(1+(\gamma-1)(1-m_j^u))^{w_j}+(\gamma-1)\prod_{j=1}^{l}(m_j^u)^{w_j}} \end{bmatrix} \\ \begin{bmatrix} \frac{\prod_{j=1}^{l}(1+(\gamma-1)i_j^l)^{w_j}-\prod_{j=1}^{l}(1-i_j^l)^{w_j}}{\prod_{j=1}^{l}(1+(\gamma-1)i_j^l)^{w_j}+(\gamma-1)\prod_{j=1}^{l}(1-i_j^l)^{w_j}}, \\ \frac{\prod_{j=1}^{l}(1+(\gamma-1)i_j^u)^{w_j}-\prod_{j=1}^{l}(1-i_j^u)^{w_j}}{\prod_{j=1}^{l}(1+(\gamma-1)i_j^u)^{w_j}+(\gamma-1)\prod_{j=1}^{l}(1-i_j^u)^{w_j}} \end{bmatrix} \\ \begin{bmatrix} \frac{\prod_{j=1}^{l}(1+(\gamma-1)n_j^l)^{w_j}-\prod_{j=1}^{l}(1-n_j^l)^{w_j}}{\prod_{j=1}^{l}(1+(\gamma-1)n_j^l)^{w_j}+(\gamma-1)\prod_{j=1}^{l}(1-n_j^l)^{w_j}}, \\ \frac{\prod_{j=1}^{l}(1+(\gamma-1)n_j^u)^{w_j}-\prod_{j=1}^{l}(1-n_j^u)^{w_j}}{\prod_{j=1}^{l}(1+(\gamma-1)n_j^u)^{w_j}+(\gamma-1)\prod_{j=1}^{l}(1-n_j^u)^{w_j}} \end{bmatrix} \end{pmatrix} \quad (24)$$

5. If $q = 1$ and $m^l = m^u = m$, $i^l = i^u = i$, $n^l = n^u = n$, then IVTSFHWA and IVTSFHWG are converted into picture fuzzy settings, given as follows:

$$PFHWA(\text{Ꞇ}_1, \text{Ꞇ}_2, \text{Ꞇ}_3, \ldots \text{Ꞇ}_l) = \left(\begin{array}{c} \frac{\prod_{j=1}^{l}(1+(\gamma-1)m_j)^{w_j} - \prod_{j=1}^{l}(1-m_j)^{w_j}}{\prod_{j=1}^{l}(1+(\gamma-1)m_j)^{w_j} + (\gamma-1)\prod_{j=1}^{l}(1-m_j)^{w_j}} \\ \frac{\gamma \prod_{j=1}^{l} i_j^{w_j}}{\prod_{j=1}^{l}(1+(\gamma-1)(1-i_j))^{w_j} + (\gamma-1)\prod_{j=1}^{l}(i_j)^{w_j}} \\ \frac{\gamma \prod_{j=1}^{l} n_j^{w_j}}{\prod_{j=1}^{l}(1+(\gamma-1)(1-n_j))^{w_j} + (\gamma-1)\prod_{j=1}^{l}(n_j)^{w_j}} \end{array} \right) \quad (25)$$

$$PFHWG(\text{Ꞇ}_1, \text{Ꞇ}_2, \text{Ꞇ}_3, \ldots \text{Ꞇ}_l) = \left(\begin{array}{c} \frac{\gamma \prod_{j=1}^{l}(m_j^{w_j})}{\prod_{j=1}^{l}(1+(\gamma-1)(1-m_j))^{w_j} + (\gamma-1)\prod_{j=1}^{l}(m_j)^{w_j}} \\ \frac{\prod_{j=1}^{l}(1+(\gamma-1)i_j)^{w_j} - \prod_{j=1}^{l}(1-i_j)^{w_j}}{\prod_{j=1}^{l}(1+(\gamma-1)i_j)^{w_j} + (\gamma-1)\prod_{j=1}^{l}(1-i_j)^{w_j}} \\ \frac{\prod_{j=1}^{l}(1+(\gamma-1)n_j)^{w_j} - \prod_{j=1}^{l}(1-n_j)^{w_j}}{\prod_{j=1}^{l}(1+(\gamma-1)n_j)^{w_j} + (\gamma-1)\prod_{j=1}^{l}(1-n_j)^{w_j}} \end{array} \right) \quad (26)$$

6. If $i^l = i^u = i = 0$, then IVTSFHWA and IVTSFHWG are converted into interval-valued q-ROPFSs, given as follows:

$$IVq - ROPFHWA(\text{Ꞇ}_1, \text{Ꞇ}_2, \text{Ꞇ}_3, \ldots \text{Ꞇ}_l) = \left(\begin{array}{c} \left[\begin{array}{c} \sqrt[q]{\frac{\prod_{j=1}^{l}(1+(\gamma-1)m_j^{lq})^{w_j} - \prod_{j=1}^{l}(1-m_j^{lq})^{w_j}}{\prod_{j=1}^{l}(1+(\gamma-1)m_j^{lq})^{w_j} + (\gamma-1)\prod_{j=1}^{l}(1-m_j^{lq})^{w_j}}}, \\ \sqrt[q]{\frac{\prod_{j=1}^{l}(1+(\gamma-1)m_j^{uq})^{w_j} - \prod_{j=1}^{l}(1-m_j^{uq})^{w_j}}{\prod_{j=1}^{l}(1+(\gamma-1)m_j^{uq})^{w_j} + (\gamma-1)\prod_{j=1}^{l}(1-m_j^{uq})^{w_j}}} \end{array} \right] \\ \left[\begin{array}{c} \frac{\sqrt[q]{\gamma}\prod_{j=1}^{l}(n_j^l)^{w_j}}{\sqrt[q]{\prod_{j=1}^{l}(1+(\gamma-1)(1-n_j^{lq}))^{w_j} + (\gamma-1)\prod_{j=1}^{l}(n_j^{lq})^{w_j}}} \\ , \frac{\sqrt[q]{\gamma}\prod_{j=1}^{l}(n_j^u)^{w_j}}{\sqrt[q]{\prod_{j=1}^{l}(1+(\gamma-1)(1-n_j^{uq}))^{w_j} + (\gamma-1)\prod_{j=1}^{l}(n_j^{uq})^{w_j}}} \end{array} \right] \end{array} \right) \quad (27)$$

$$IVq - ROPFHWG(\text{Ꞇ}_1, \text{Ꞇ}_2, \text{Ꞇ}_3, \ldots \text{Ꞇ}_l) = \left(\begin{array}{c} \left[\begin{array}{c} \frac{\sqrt[q]{\gamma}\prod_{j=1}^{l}(m_j^l)^{w_j}}{\sqrt[q]{\prod_{j=1}^{l}(1+(\gamma-1)(1-m_j^{lq}))^{w_j} + (\gamma-1)\prod_{j=1}^{l}(m_j^{lq})^{w_j}}} \\ , \frac{\sqrt[q]{\gamma}\prod_{j=1}^{l}(m_j^u)^{w_j}}{\sqrt[q]{\prod_{j=1}^{l}(1+(\gamma-1)(1-m_j^{uq}))^{w_j} + (\gamma-1)\prod_{j=1}^{l}(n_j^{uq})^{w_j}}} \end{array} \right] \\ \left[\begin{array}{c} \sqrt[q]{\frac{\prod_{j=1}^{l}(1+(\gamma-1)n_j^{lq})^{w_j} - \prod_{j=1}^{l}(1-n_j^{lq})^{w_j}}{\prod_{j=1}^{l}(1+(\gamma-1)n_j^{lq})^{w_j} + (\gamma-1)\prod_{j=1}^{l}(1-n_j^{lq})^{w_j}}}, \\ \sqrt[q]{\frac{\prod_{j=1}^{l}(1+(\gamma-1)n_j^{uq})^{w_j} - \prod_{j=1}^{l}(1-n_j^{uq})^{w_j}}{\prod_{j=1}^{l}(1+(\gamma-1)n_j^{uq})^{w_j} + (\gamma-1)\prod_{j=1}^{l}(1-n_j^{uq})^{w_j}}} \end{array} \right] \end{array} \right) \quad (28)$$

7. If $m^l = m^u = m$, $i^l = i^u = i = 0$ and $n^l = n^u = n$, then the IVTSFHWA and IVTSFHWG operators are converted into q-ring orthpair fuzzy layouts, given as follows:

$$q - ROPFHWA(\text{Ꞇ}_1, \text{Ꞇ}_2, \text{Ꞇ}_3, \ldots \text{Ꞇ}_l) = \left(\begin{array}{c} \sqrt[q]{\frac{\prod_{j=1}^{l}(1+(\gamma-1)m_j^q)^{w_j} - \prod_{j=1}^{l}(1-m_j^q)^{w_j}}{\prod_{j=1}^{l}(1+(\gamma-1)m_j^q)^{w_j} + (\gamma-1)\prod_{j=1}^{l}(1-m_j^q)^{w_j}}} \\ \frac{\sqrt[q]{\gamma}\prod_{j=1}^{l} n_j^{w_j}}{\sqrt[q]{\prod_{j=1}^{l}(1+(\gamma-1)(1-n_j^q))^{w_j} + (\gamma-1)\prod_{j=1}^{l}(n_j^q)^{w_j}}} \end{array} \right) \quad (29)$$

$$q - ROPFHWG(\text{Ț}_1, \text{Ț}_2, \text{Ț}_3, \ldots \text{Ț}_l) = \left(\begin{array}{c} \frac{\sqrt[q]{\gamma}\prod_{j=1}^{l}(m_j^{w_j})}{\sqrt[q]{\prod_{j=1}^{l}(1+(\gamma-1)(1-m_j^q))^{w_j}+(\gamma-1)\prod_{j=1}^{l}(m_j^q)^{w_j}}} \\ \sqrt[q]{\frac{\prod_{j=1}^{l}(1+(\gamma-1)n_j^q)^{w_j}-\prod_{j=1}^{l}(1-n_j^q)^{w_j}}{\prod_{j=1}^{l}(1+(\gamma-1)n_j^q)^{w_j}+(\gamma-1)\prod_{j=1}^{l}(1-n_j^q)^{w_j}}} \end{array} \right) \tag{30}$$

8. If $q = 2$ and $i^l = i^u = i = 0$, then IVTSFHWA and IVTSFHWG are converted into interval-valued Pythagorean fuzzy layouts, given as follows:

$$IVPyFHWA(\text{Ț}_1, \text{Ț}_2, \text{Ț}_3, \ldots \text{Ț}_l) = \left(\begin{array}{c} \left[\begin{array}{c} \sqrt{\frac{\prod_{j=1}^{l}(1+(\gamma-1)m_j^{l2})^{w_j}-\prod_{j=1}^{l}(1-m_j^{l2})^{w_j}}{\prod_{j=1}^{l}(1+(\gamma-1)m_j^{l2})^{w_j}+(\gamma-1)\prod_{j=1}^{l}(1-m_j^{l2})^{w_j}}}, \\ \sqrt{\frac{\prod_{j=1}^{l}(1+(\gamma-1)m_j^{u2})^{w_j}-\prod_{j=1}^{l}(1-m_j^{u2})^{w_j}}{\prod_{j=1}^{l}(1+(\gamma-1)m_j^{u2})^{w_j}+(\gamma-1)\prod_{j=1}^{l}(1-m_j^{u2})^{w_j}}} \end{array} \right] \\ \left[\begin{array}{c} \frac{\sqrt{\gamma}\prod_{j=1}^{l}(n_j^l)^{w_j}}{\sqrt{\prod_{j=1}^{l}(1+(\gamma-1)(1-n_j^{l2}))^{w_j}+(\gamma-1)\prod_{j=1}^{l}(n_j^{l2})^{w_j}}} \\ , \frac{\sqrt{\gamma}\prod_{j=1}^{l}(n_j^u)^{w_j}}{\sqrt{\prod_{j=1}^{l}(1+(\gamma-1)(1-n_j^{u2}))^{w_j}+(\gamma-1)\prod_{j=1}^{l}(n_j^{u2})^{w_j}}} \end{array} \right] \end{array} \right) \tag{31}$$

$$IVPyFHWG(\text{Ț}_1, \text{Ț}_2, \text{Ț}_3, \ldots \text{Ț}_l) = \left(\begin{array}{c} \left[\begin{array}{c} \frac{\sqrt{\gamma}\prod_{j=1}^{l}(m_j^l)^{w_j}}{\sqrt{\prod_{j=1}^{l}(1+(\gamma-1)(1-m_j^{l2}))^{w_j}+(\gamma-1)\prod_{j=1}^{l}(m_j^{l2})^{w_j}}} \\ , \frac{\sqrt{\gamma}\prod_{j=1}^{l}(m_j^u)^{w_j}}{\sqrt{\prod_{j=1}^{l}(1+(\gamma-1)(1-m_j^{u2}))^{w_j}+(\gamma-1)\prod_{j=1}^{l}(m_j^{u2})^{w_j}}} \end{array} \right] \\ \left[\begin{array}{c} \sqrt{\frac{\prod_{j=1}^{l}(1+(\gamma-1)n_j^{l2})^{w_j}-\prod_{j=1}^{l}(1-n_j^{l2})^{w_j}}{\prod_{j=1}^{l}(1+(\gamma-1)n_j^{l2})^{w_j}+(\gamma-1)\prod_{j=1}^{l}(1-n_j^{l2})^{w_j}}} \\ , \sqrt{\frac{\prod_{j=1}^{l}(1+(\gamma-1)n_j^{u2})^{w_j}-\prod_{j=1}^{l}(1-n_j^{u2})^{w_j}}{\prod_{j=1}^{l}(1+(\gamma-1)n_j^{u2})^{w_j}+(\gamma-1)\prod_{j=1}^{l}(1-n_j^{u2})^{w_j}}} \end{array} \right] \end{array} \right) \tag{32}$$

9. If $q = 2$ and $m^l = m^u = m$, $i^l = i^u = 0$, $n^l = n^u = n$, then IVTSFHWA and IVTSFHWG are converted into PyFSs, given as follows:

$$PyFHWA(\text{Ț}_1, \text{Ț}_2, \text{Ț}_3, \ldots \text{Ț}_l) = \left(\begin{array}{c} \sqrt{\frac{\prod_{j=1}^{l}(1+(\gamma-1)m_j^2)^{w_j}-\prod_{j=1}^{l}(1-m_j^2)^{w_j}}{\prod_{j=1}^{l}(1+(\gamma-1)m_j^2)^{w_j}+(\gamma-1)\prod_{j=1}^{l}(1-m_j^2)^{w_j}}} \\ \frac{\sqrt{\gamma}\prod_{j=1}^{l}n_j^{w_j}}{\sqrt{\prod_{j=1}^{l}(1+(\gamma-1)(1-n_j^2))^{w_j}+(\gamma-1)\prod_{j=1}^{l}(n_j^2)^{w_j}}} \end{array} \right) \tag{33}$$

$$PyFHWG(\text{Ț}_1, \text{Ț}_2, \text{Ț}_3, \ldots \text{Ț}_l) = \left(\begin{array}{c} \frac{\sqrt{\gamma}\prod_{j=1}^{l}(m_j^{w_j})}{\sqrt{\prod_{j=1}^{l}(1+(\gamma-1)(1-m_j^2))^{w_j}+(\gamma-1)\prod_{j=1}^{l}(m_j^2)^{w_j}}} \\ \sqrt{\frac{\prod_{j=1}^{l}(1+(\gamma-1)n_j^2)^{w_j}-\prod_{j=1}^{l}(1-n_j^2)^{w_j}}{\prod_{j=1}^{l}(1+(\gamma-1)n_j^2)^{w_j}+(\gamma-1)\prod_{j=1}^{l}(1-n_j^2)^{w_j}}} \end{array} \right) \tag{34}$$

10. If $q = 1$ and, $i^l = i^u = i = 0$, then IVTSFHWA and IVTSFHWG are converted to interval-valued IFSs, given as follows:

$$IVIFHWA(\text{Ϯ}_1, \text{Ϯ}_2, \text{Ϯ}_3, \ldots \text{Ϯ}_l) = \left(\begin{array}{c} \left[\begin{array}{c} \frac{\prod_{j=1}^{l}(1+(\gamma-1)m_j^l)^{w_j} - \prod_{j=1}^{l}(1-m_j^l)^{w_j}}{\prod_{j=1}^{l}(1+(\gamma-1)m_j^l)^{w_j} + (\gamma-1)\prod_{j=1}^{l}(1-m_j^l)^{w_j}}, \\ \frac{\prod_{j=1}^{l}(1+(\gamma-1)m_j^u)^{w_j} - \prod_{j=1}^{l}(1-m_j^u)^{w_j}}{\prod_{j=1}^{l}(1+(\gamma-1)m_j^u)^{w_j} + (\gamma-1)\prod_{j=1}^{l}(1-m_j^u)^{w_j}} \end{array} \right] \\ \left[\begin{array}{c} \frac{\gamma\prod_{j=1}^{l}(n_j^l)^{w_j}}{\prod_{j=1}^{l}(1+(\gamma-1)(1-n_j^l))^{w_j} + (\gamma-1)\prod_{j=1}^{l}(n_j^l)^{w_j}}, \\ \frac{\gamma\prod_{j=1}^{l}(n_j^u)^{w_j}}{\prod_{j=1}^{l}(1+(\gamma-1)(1-n_j^u))^{w_j} + (\gamma-1)\prod_{j=1}^{l}(n_j^u)^{w_j}} \end{array} \right] \end{array} \right) \quad (35)$$

$$IVIFHWG(\text{Ϯ}_1, \text{Ϯ}_2, \text{Ϯ}_3, \ldots \text{Ϯ}_l) = \left(\begin{array}{c} \left[\begin{array}{c} \frac{\gamma\prod_{j=1}^{l}(m_j^l)^{w_j}}{\prod_{j=1}^{l}(1+(\gamma-1)(1-m_j^l))^{w_j} + (\gamma-1)\prod_{j=1}^{l}(m_j^l)^{w_j}} \\ , \frac{\gamma\prod_{j=1}^{l}(m_j^u)^{w_j}}{\prod_{j=1}^{l}(1+(\gamma-1)(1-m_j^u))^{w_j} + (\gamma-1)\prod_{j=1}^{l}(m_j^u)^{w_j}} \end{array} \right] \\ \left[\begin{array}{c} \frac{\prod_{j=1}^{l}(1+(\gamma-1)n_j^l)^{w_j} - \prod_{j=1}^{l}(1-n_j^l)^{w_j}}{\prod_{j=1}^{l}(1+(\gamma-1)n_j^l)^{w_j} + (\gamma-1)\prod_{j=1}^{l}(1-n_j^l)^{w_j}}, \\ \frac{\prod_{j=1}^{l}(1+(\gamma-1)n_j^u)^{w_j} - \prod_{j=1}^{l}(1-n_j^u)^{w_j}}{\prod_{j=1}^{l}(1+(\gamma-1)n_j^u)^{w_j} + (\gamma-1)\prod_{j=1}^{l}(1-n_j^u)^{w_j}} \end{array} \right] \end{array} \right) \quad (36)$$

11. If $q = 1$ and $m^l = m^u = m$, $i^l = i^u = 0$, $n^l = n^u = n$, then IVTSFHWA and IVTSFHWG are converted into intuitionistic fuzzy settings, given as follows.

$$IFHWA(\text{Ϯ}_1, \text{Ϯ}_2, \text{Ϯ}_3, \ldots \text{Ϯ}_l) = \left(\begin{array}{c} \frac{\prod_{j=1}^{l}(1+(\gamma-1)m_j)^{w_j} - \prod_{j=1}^{l}(1-m_j)^{w_j}}{\prod_{j=1}^{l}(1+(\gamma-1)m_j)^{w_j} + (\gamma-1)\prod_{j=1}^{l}(1-m_j)^{w_j}} \\ \frac{\gamma\prod_{j=1}^{l}n_j^{w_j}}{\prod_{j=1}^{l}(1+(\gamma-1)(1-n_j))^{w_j} + (\gamma-1)\prod_{j=1}^{l}(n_j)^{w_j}} \end{array} \right) \quad (37)$$

$$IFHWG(\text{Ϯ}_1, \text{Ϯ}_2, \text{Ϯ}_3, \ldots \text{Ϯ}_l) = \left(\begin{array}{c} \frac{\gamma\prod_{j=1}^{l}(m_j^{w_j})}{\prod_{j=1}^{l}(1+(\gamma-1)(1-m_j))^{w_j} + (\gamma-1)\prod_{j=1}^{l}(m_j)^{w_j}} \\ \frac{\prod_{j=1}^{l}(1+(\gamma-1)n_j)^{w_j} - \prod_{j=1}^{l}(1-n_j)^{w_j}}{\prod_{j=1}^{l}(1+(\gamma-1)n_j)^{w_j} + (\gamma-1)\prod_{j=1}^{l}(1-n_j)^{w_j}} \end{array} \right) \quad (38)$$

7. Multi-Attribute Decision Making

The aim of this section is to utilize the HAOs of TSFSs defined in Sections 4 and 5 in a MADM problem. We propose an algorithm for MADM based on HAOs of IVTSFSs. A numerical example to demonstrate the applicability of the HAOs and the effect of parameters γ and q is also studied.

In MADM problems, the aim is to choose the most preferred alternative from a set of alternatives by AOs using score functions. The information used in this process is based on the human opinion that can be represented by IVTSFNs. IVTSFNs are enabled to discuss four aspects of evaluations provided by experts, including MD, NMD, AD, and RD, of an uncertain environment. Let $A = \{A_1, A_2, \ldots, A_k\}$ be a set of alternatives and a set of attributes $G = \{G_1, G_2, \ldots, G_j\}$ where j is finite, with weight vector w_j. $D_{k\times j} = (T)_{k\times j} = \left(\left[m^l, m^u\right], \left[i^l, i^u\right], \left[n^l, n^u\right]\right)$ represents the decision matrix containing information on the alternatives concerning the attributes in the form of IVTSFNs. The algorithm of the MADM process based on HAOs is given below, followed by a flowchart in Figure 1.

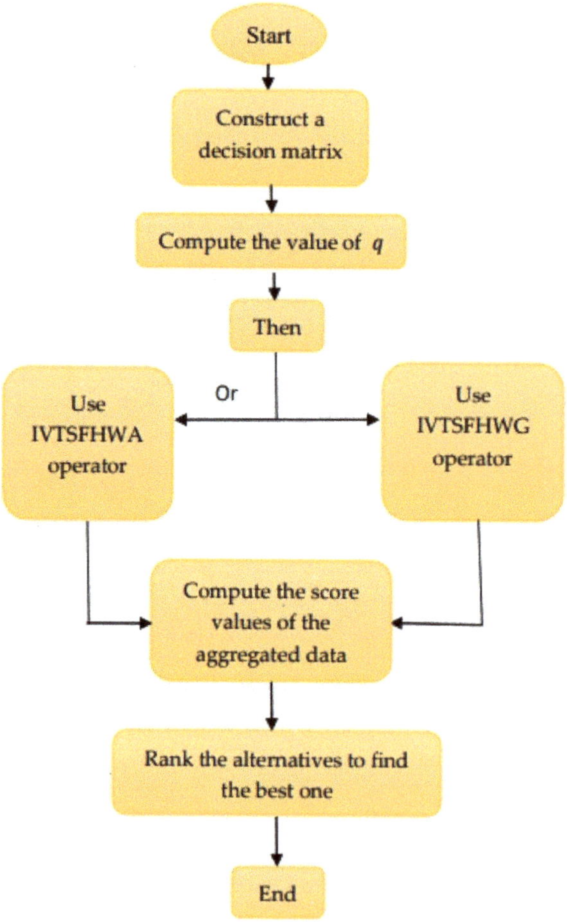

Figure 1. Flowchart of the MADM algorithm.

Step 1. A decision matrix is formed from the data gathered from the decision-makers about alternatives based on attributes. The q-values are also considered IVTSFNs.

Step 2. The decision matrix is aggregated using the IVTSFHWA and IVTSFHWG operators.

Step 3. The score values of aggregated IVTSFNs are calculated using

$$SC(I) = \frac{\left(m^l\right)^q\left(1-\left(i^l\right)^q-\left(n^l\right)^q\right)+(m^u)^q(1-(i^u)^q-(n^u)^q)}{3}, \; SC(I) \in [-1,1]$$

Step 4. The score values of the alternative are examined to find the optimum one.

7.1. Numerical Example

This subsection aims to take a practical example for utilizing MADM based on the HAOs of IVTSFNs. We adapt an example from [33], where the selection of optimum enterprise is carried out using the MADM algorithm.

In this example, we take the problem of evaluating enterprise financial performance, where we analyze some enterprises under some attributes to get the most optimum enterprise using the HAOs based on IVTSF information. The four possible enterprises denoted by A_j $(1 \leq j \leq 4)$*, according to four attributes, are denoted by* G_i $(1 \leq i \leq 4)$*, where* G_1 *is the debt-paying ability,* G_2 *is the operation capability,* G_3 *is the earning capacity, and* G_4 *is the development capability. The four possible enterprises* (A_1, A_2, A_3, A_4) *are to be evaluated using the IVTSFHWA and IVTSFHWG operators by the decision-maker under the four attributes with weights* $w_j = (0.2, 0.5, 0.25, 0.05)^T$.

The decision matrix is formed by IVTSFNs.

Step 1. The evaluations about enterprises are provided by the experts in Table 1. Note that in this problem, evaluations are represented by IVTSFNs for $q = 5$.

Table 1. Decision matrix.

	G_1	G_2	G_3	G_4
A_1	([0.6, 0.8], [0.3, 0.5], [0.3, 0.6])	([0.4, 0.5], [0.1, 0.6], [0.5, 0.9])	([0.5, 0.7], [0.4, 0.8], [0.1, 0.3])	([0.3, 0.6], [0.1, 0.6], [0.4, 0.7])
A_2	([0.7, 0.9], [0.1, 0.8], [0.3, 0.4])	([0.3, 0.6], [0.3, 0.5], [0.4, 0.8])	([0.1, 0.6], [0.1, 0.5], [0.1, 0.9])	([0.4, 0.6], [0.2, 0.5], [0.5, 0.6])
A_3	([0.3, 0.5], [0.2, 0.3], [0.2, 0.8])	([0.2, 0.5], [0.6, 0.7], [0.2, 0.9])	([0.2, 0.4], [0.3, 0.4], [0.3, 0.6])	([0.2, 0.7], [0.4, 0.6], [0.1, 0.4])
A_4	([0.2, 0.4], [0.1, 0.3], [0.7, 0.9])	([0.7, 0.8], [0.3, 0.5], [0.1, 0.2])	([0.5, 0.8], [0.4, 0.9], [0.2, 0.4])	([0.4, 0.7], [0.5, 0.6], [0.3, 0.7])

Step 2. The IVTSFHWA and IVTSFHWG operators are applied to get aggregated information, given as in Table 2. Note that while using IVTSFHWA and IVTSFHWG operators, we take $q = 5$, $\gamma = 2$ and $w = (0.2, 0.5, 0.25, 0.05)^T$.

Table 2. Aggregated values of IVTSFHWA and IVTSFHWG operators.

	IVTSFHWA Operator	IVTSFHWG Operator
A_1	([0.491328, 0.664195], [0.1762, 0.6243], [0.2990, 0.63395])	([0.4526, 0.6061], [0.005313, 0.230905], [0.02895, 0.586139])
A_2	([0.513349, 0.721466], [0.179335, 0.5518], [0.270219, 0.7183])	([0.274969, 0.6558], [0.0022, 0.160593], [0.012486, 0.568143])
A_3	([0.236636 , 0.505216], [0.3981 , 0.5128], [0.213815 , 0.7738])	([0.21691, 0.4812], [0.069814, 0.158957], [0.001449, 0.684677])
A_4	([0.621815 , 0.763604], [0.265618, 0.5357], [0.186066 , 0.3471])	([0.4904, 0.6991], [0.009297, 0.316949], [0.059314, 0.247336])

Step 3. The scores of the aggregated value of data in Table 2 are computed. The score values for each alternative are computed and shown in Table 3.

Table 3. Score values of IVTSFHWA and IVTSFHWG operators.

	IVTSFHWA Operator	IVTSFHWG Operator
A_1	0.0439	0.03169
A_2	0.0612	0.03856
A_3		0.0075
A_4	0.1132	0.06489

Step 4. Alternatives are ranked using score values in decreasing order. The ranking is handled as $A_4 > A_2 > A_1 > A_3$. Thus, the best enterprise from different companies is A_4. The comparison between the results using the IVTSFHWA and IVTSFHWG operators is discussed in Table 3.

7.2. Effect of "γ" on Ranking of Alternatives

Ullah et al. [41] observed a significant change in the ranking results while dealing with TSF HAOs for various values of q and γ. Therefore, we examined the consequence of deviations in γ on the ranking result. Hence, we solved the MADM problem discussed in Section 7.2 for different γ values, and the effect on the ranking of the alternatives is given in Table 4.

Table 4. Impact of γ on the ranking results.

γ	Operators	Score Values of IVTSFHWA Operator and IVTSFHWG Operator	Resulting Pattern
2	IVTSFHWA	$S_1 = 0.0439,\ S_2 = 0.0612,\ S_3 = 0.0078, S_4 = 0.1132$	$A_4 > A_2 > A_1 > A_3$
	IVTSFHWG	$S_1 = 0.0317, S_2 = 0.0386,\ S_3 = 0.0075,\ S_4 = 0.0649$	$A_4 > A_2 > A_1 > A_3$
4	IVTSFHWA	$S_1 = 0.0342,\ S_2 = 0.0456,\ S_3 = 0.0074,\ S_4 = 0.0824$	$A_4 > A_2 > A_1 > A_3$
	IVTSFHWG	$S_1 = 0.0336,\ S_2 = 0.0415,\ S_3 = 0.0084,\ S_4 = 0.0669$	$A_4 > A_2 > A_1 > A_3$
5	IVTSFHWA	$S_1 = 0.0334,\ S_2 = 0.04398,\ S_3 = 0.0073,\ S_4 = 0.0809$	$A_4 > A_2 > A_1 > A_3$
	IVTSFHWG	$S_1 = 0.0338,\ S_2 = 0.0418,\ S_3 = 0.0085,\ S_4 = 0.0673$	$A_4 > A_2 > A_1 > A_3$
6	IVTSFHWA	$S_1 = 0.0328,\ S_2 = 0.0428,\ S_3 = 0.0073,\ S_4 = 0.0798$	$A_4 > A_2 > A_1 > A_3$
	IVTSFHWG	$S_1 = 0.0339,\ S_2 = 0.0421,\ S_3 = 0.0085,\ S_4 = 0.0676$	$A_4 > A_2 > A_1 > A_3$
8	IVTSFHWA	$S_1 = 0.0319,\ S_2 = 0.0412,\ S_3 = 0.0072,\ S_4 = 0.0783$	$A_4 > A_2 > A_1 > A_3$
	IVTSFHWG	$S_1 = 0.0341,\ S_2 = 0.0424,\ S_3 = 0.0086,\ S_4 = 0.0679$	$A_4 > A_2 > A_1 > A_3$
9	IVTSFHWA	$S_1 = 0.0316,\ S_2 = 0.0406,\ S_3 = 0.0071,\ S_4 = 0.0777$	$A_4 > A_2 > A_1 > A_3$
	IVTSFHWG	$S_1 = 0.0341, S_2 = 0.0425, S_3 = 0.0086,\ S_4 = 0.0680$	$A_1 > A_4 > A_3 > A_2$
12	IVTSFHWA	$S_1 = 0.0306,\ S_2 = 0.0393,\ S_3 = 0.0070,\ S_4 = 0.0760$	$A_4 > A_2 > A_1 > A_3$
	IVTSFHWG	$S_1 = 0.03424,\ S_2 = 0.0427,\ S_3 = 0.0086, S_4 = 0.0683$	$A_1 > A_3 > A_4 > A_2$

From Table 4, we noticed that there is no significant change in the ranking results in the case of the IVTSFHWA operator and the IVTSFHWG operator for various values of γ. This whole scenario can be observed from Figure 2.

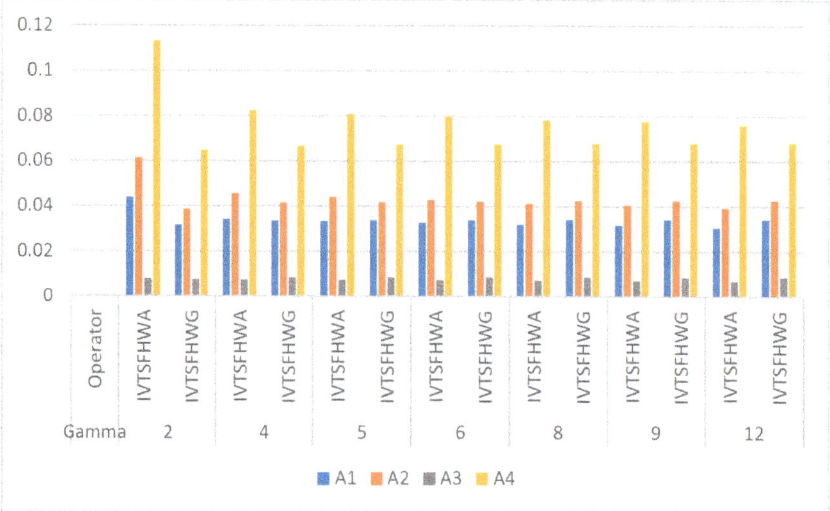

Figure 2. Graphical view of Table 4.

7.3. Effect of Variations in "q" on Ranking Results

As we have observed the impact of variations in "γ" on the ranking result in Section 7.3, here, we aim to analyze the effect of variations in "q" using IVTSFHWA and IVTSFHWG operators on ranking results. In the measured problem studied in Section 7.2, if we differentiate the values of "q" from 5 onward, then the variable ranking order of the given alternative is as displayed in Table 5 below.

Table 5. Ranking result for various values of "q" when $\gamma = 2$.

q	Operators	Score Values of IVTSFHWA and IVTSFHWG	Resulting Pattern
5	IVTSFHWA	$S_1 = 0.0439$, $S_2 = 0.0612$, $S_3 = 0.0078$, $S_4 = 0.1132$	$A_4 > A_2 > A_1 > A_3$
	IVTSFHWG	$S_1 = 0.0317$, $S_2 = 0.0386$, $S_3 = 0.0075$, $S_4 = 0.0649$	$A_4 > A_2 > A_1 > A_3$
7	IVTSFHWA	$S_1 = 0.0238$, $S_2 = 0.0429$, $S_3 = 0.0028$, $S_4 = 0.0679$	$A_4 > A_2 > A_1 > A_3$
	IVTSFHWG	$S_1 = 0.0111$, $S_2 = 0.0171$, $S_3 = 0.0020$, $S_4 = 0.0287$	$A_4 > A_2 > A_1 > A_3$
9	IVTSFHWA	$S_1 = 0.0134$, $S_2 = 0.0310$, $S_3 = 0.0010$, $S_4 = 0.0411$	$A_4 > A_2 > A_1 > A_3$
	IVTSFHWG	$S_1 = 0.0038$, $S_2 = 0.0072$, $S_3 = 0.00046$, $S_4 = 0.0130$	$A_4 > A_2 > A_1 > A_3$
11	IVTSFHWA	$S_1 = 0.0077$, $S_2 = 0.0233$, $S_3 = 0.0004$, $S_4 = 0.0251$	$A_4 > A_2 > A_1 > A_3$
	IVTSFHWG	$S_1 = 0.0013$, $S_2 = 0.0030$, $S_3 = 0.00011$, $S_4 = 0.0061$	$A_4 > A_2 > A_1 > A_3$
12	IVTSFHWA	$S_1 = 0.0059$, $S_2 = 0.0205$, $S_3 = 0.00028$, $S_4 = 0.0197$	$A_2 > A_4 > A_1 > A_3$
	IVTSFHWG	$S_1 = 0.0041$, $S_2 = 0.00198$, $S_3 = 0.0008$, $S_4 = 5.1E-05$	$A_4 > A_2 > A_1 > A_3$

It can be noted that the ranking array is changed at $q = 12$ in the case of the IVTSFHWA operator, but the final ranking order does not change in the case of the IVTSFHWG operator. However, the ranking array does not change after $q = 12$ in both cases. This demonstrates the consistency in ranking consequences at $q = 12$. The whole scenario can be seen at a glance in Figure 3 below.

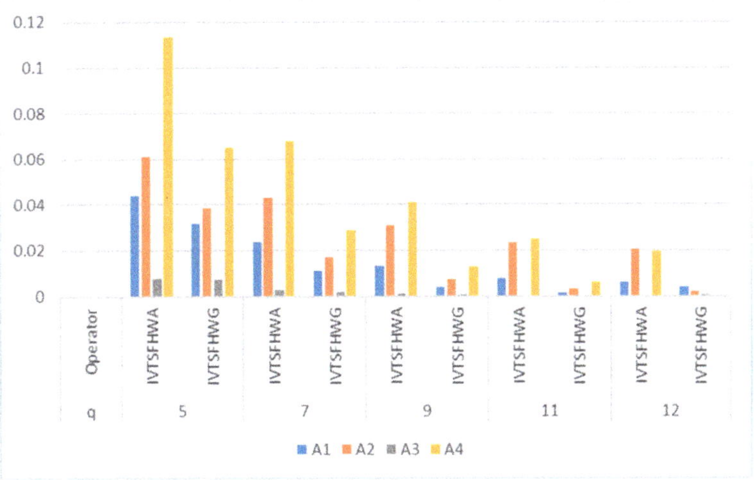

Figure 3. Graphical view of Table 5.

8. A Comparison of the Result Obtained Using Proposed and Existing Methods

The goal of this section is to set up a comparative analysis of the IVTSFHWA and IVTSFHWG operators with existing HAOs.

To examine the reliability and effectiveness of the presented approaches, we choose the information of the example studied in Section 7.1 and solve it by using some previously defined operators of IVTSFSs by Ullah et al. [25]. We further show the HAOs established in the environment of IFSs, PyFSs, q-ROPFSs, PFSs, and TSFSs cannot be applied to the problem where information is in the form of IVTSFNs. The relative analysis of the presented approaches with some current approaches is discussed in Table 6 below.

Table 6. Ranking of alternatives using existing and proposed methods.

Method	Reference	Score Values	Ranking
IVTSFWA	Ullah et al. [25]	$S_1 = 0.0463, S_2 = 0.0683, S_3 = 0.0081, S_4 = 0.1164$	$A_4 > A_2 > A_1 > A_3$
IVTSFWG	Ullah et al. [25]	$S_1 = 0.0203, S_2 = 0.0239, S_3 = 0.0048, S_4 = 0.0503$	$A_4 > A_2 > A_1 > A_3$
Proposed work WA	This paper	$S_1 = 0.0439, S_2 = 0.0612, S_3 = 0.0078, S_4 = 0.1132$	$A_4 > A_2 > A_1 > A_3$
Proposed work WG	This paper	$S_1 = 0.0317, S_2 = 0.0386, S_3 = 0.0075, S_4 = 0.0649$	$A_4 > A_2 > A_1 > A_3$
HAOs of IFSs	Huang [33]	Failed	Cannot be specified
HAOs of IVIFSs	Liu [35]	Failed	Cannot be specified
HAOs of PyFSs	Gao [36]	Failed	Cannot be specified
HAOs of IVPyFSs	Peng and Yang [38]	Failed	Cannot be specified
HAOs of q-ROPFSs	Darko and Liang [39]	Failed	Cannot be specified
HAOS of PFSs	Jana & Pal [40]	Failed	Cannot be specified
HAOs of TSFSs	Ullah et al. [41]	Failed	Cannot be specified

From the above analysis, we observed that the results obtained in this paper are compatible with that of previous work. Moreover, it is shown that the HAOs developed in Huang et al. [33], Liu [35], Gao [36], Peng and Yang [38], Darko and Liang [39], Jana and Pal [40], and Ullah et al. [41] cannot be applied to the problem. The comparison results are portrayed in Figure 4.

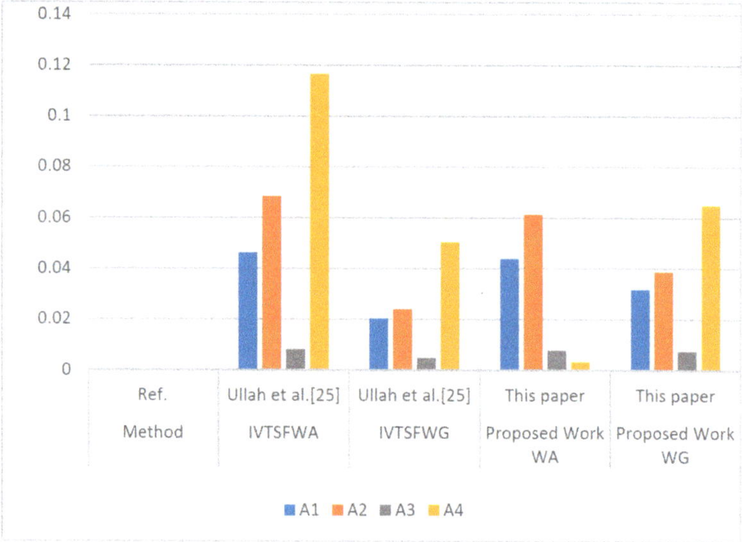

Figure 4. Interpretation of the information in Table 6.

9. Conclusions

In this paper, first, we discussed the importance of working in the setting of interval-valued fuzzy frameworks, as such fuzzy frameworks, which reduces the loss of information and ensures the effective modeling of human opinion. Based on this fact, we developed the notion of IVTSFHWA and IVTSFHWG operators that can aggregate the information given in the form of IVTSFNs. We exemplified each newly developed operator and studied its monotonicity, boundedness, and idempotency properties for newly defined HAOs. Some further study based on the HAOs of IVTSFNs is as follows:

1. To meet the situations where the ordered position and weights of the information matters, we proposed the IVTSFHOWA, IVTSFHHA, IVTSFHOWG, and IVTSFHHG operators.
2. We comprehensively studied the special cases of the newly developed HAOs.
3. A MADM algorithm based on the HAOs of IVTSFNs was produced and applied to the problem of the evaluation of the performance of enterprises.
4. The impact of parameters q and γ on the ranking pattern was analyzed and geometrically portrayed, where it was observed that severe fluctuations may occur by varying the values of γ and q.
5. A comparative study of the newly developed HAOs and previously established HAOs was set up, where the advantage of using the proposed HAOs became prominent as all the existing HAOs failed to handle some situations without information loss.

The key advantage of the proposed HAOs is that they reduce information loss due to their ability to describe the information in terms of the closed subintervals of $[0, 1]$. Another advantage of the HAOs of IVTSFSs is that they describe the AD and RD of the information along with the MD and NMD, unlike the HAOs of IFSs, PyFSs, and QROFSs. However, these HAOs can be further generalized to the frame of complex TSFSs, so their ability to handle uncertain information would be increased.

Author Contributions: Conceptualization, Y.J. and Z.K.; Formal analysis, K.U., T.M. and N.Y.P.; Funding acquisition, Y.J.; Investigation, Z.K., K.U., T.M., N.Y.P. and Z.A.; Methodology, N.Y.P. and Z.A.; Project administration, Y.J., K.U. and T.M.; Software, Y.J., Z.K., K.U., T.M., N.Y.P. and Z.A.; Validation, K.U., T.M., N.Y.P. and Z.A.; Writing—original draft, Y.J., Z.K. and K.U.; Writing—review and editing, Z.K., N.Y.P. and Z.A. All authors have read and agreed to the published version of the manuscript.

Funding: This paper is funded by the Qinglan Project of Jiangsu Province.

Institutional Review Board Statement: Not applicable.

Informed Consent Statement: Not applicable.

Data Availability Statement: Not applicable.

Acknowledgments: The corresponding author is thankful to the office of Research, Innovation and Commercialization (ORIC) of Riphah International University Lahore for supporting this research under the project: R-ORIC-21/FEAS-09.

Conflicts of Interest: The authors declare no conflict of interest.

References

1. Zadeh, L.A. Fuzzy sets. *Inf. Control* **1965**, *8*, 338–353. [CrossRef]
2. Atanassov, K. Intuitionistic fuzzy sets. *Fuzzy Set Syst.* **1986**, *20*, 87–96. [CrossRef]
3. Yager, R.R. Pythagorean fuzzy subsets. In Proceedings of the 2013 Joint IFSA World Congress and NAFIPS Annual Meeting (IFSA/NAFIPS), Edmonton, AB, Canada, 24–28 June 2013; pp. 57–61.
4. Yager, R.R. Generalized Orthopair fuzzy sets. *IEEE Trans. Fuzzy Syst.* **2016**, *25*, 1222–1230. [CrossRef]
5. Atanassov, K.; Gargov, G. Interval valued intuitionistic fuzzy sets. *Fuzzy Set Syst.* **1989**, *31*, 343–349. [CrossRef]
6. Zadeh, L.A. The concept of a linguistic variable and its application to approximate reasoning—I. *Inf. Sci.* **1975**, *8*, 199–249. [CrossRef]
7. Peng, X.; Yang, Y. Fundamental properties of interval-valued Pythagorean fuzzy aggregation operators. *Int. J. Intell. Syst.* **2016**, *31*, 444–487. [CrossRef]
8. Joshi, B.P.; Singh, A.; Bhatt, P.K.; Vaisla, K.S. Interval valued q-rung orthopair fuzzy sets and their properties. *J. Intell. Fuzzy Syst.* **2018**, *35*, 5225–5230. [CrossRef]
9. Garg, H.; Rani, D. Complex interval-valued intuitionistic fuzzy sets and their aggregation operators. *Fundam. Inform.* **2019**, *164*, 61–101. [CrossRef]
10. Garg, H.; Rani, D. Novel aggregation operators and ranking method for complex intuitionistic fuzzy sets and their applications to decision-making process. *Artif. Intell. Rev.* **2020**, *53*, 3595–3620. [CrossRef]
11. Garg, H.; Kumar, K. Linguistic interval-valued Atanassov intuitionistic fuzzy sets and their applications to group decision making problems. *IEEE Trans. Fuzzy Syst.* **2019**, *27*, 2302–2311. [CrossRef]

12. Sharma, H.K.; Kumari, K.; Kar, S. A rough set approach for forecasting models. *Decis. Mak. Appl. Manag. Eng.* **2020**, *3*, 1–21. [CrossRef]
13. Garg, H. A linear programming method based on an improved score function for interval-valued Pythagorean fuzzy numbers and its application to decision-making. *Int. J. Uncertain. Fuzziness Knowl. Based Syst.* **2018**, *26*, 67–80. [CrossRef]
14. Riaz, M.; Çagman, N.; Wali, N.; Mushtaq, A. Certain properties of soft multi-set topology with applications in multi-criteria decision making. *Decis. Mak. Appl. Manag. Eng.* **2020**, *3*, 70–96. [CrossRef]
15. Ullah, K.; Mahmood, T.; Ali, Z.; Jan, N. On some distance measures of complex Pythagorean fuzzy sets and their applications in pattern recognition. *Complex Intell. Syst.* **2020**, *6*, 15–27. [CrossRef]
16. Wei, G.; Gao, H.; Wei, Y. Some q-rung orthopair fuzzy Heronian mean operators in multiple attribute decision making. *Int. J. Intell. Syst.* **2018**, *33*, 1426–1458. [CrossRef]
17. Liu, D.; Chen, X.; Peng, D. Some cosine similarity measures and distance measures between q-rung orthopair fuzzy sets. *Int. J. Intell. Syst.* **2019**, *34*, 1572–1587. [CrossRef]
18. Kushwaha, D.K.; Panchal, D.; Sachdeva, A. Risk analysis of cutting system under intuitionistic fuzzy environment. *Rep. Mech. Eng.* **2020**, *1*, 162–173. [CrossRef]
19. Cuong, B.C.; Kreinovich, V. Picture fuzzy sets. *J. Comput. Sci. Cybern.* **2014**, *30*, 409–420.
20. Liu, P.; Munir, M.; Mahmood, T.; Ullah, K. Some similarity measures for interval-valued picture fuzzy sets and their applications in decision making. *Information* **2019**, *10*, 369. [CrossRef]
21. Jan, N.; Ali, Z.; Mahmood, T.; Ullah, K. Some Generalized Distance and Similarity Measures for Picture Hesitant Fuzzy Sets and Their Applications in Building Material Recognition and Multi-Attribute Decision Making. *Punjab Univ. J. Math.* **2019**, *51*, 51–70.
22. Ullah, K.; Ali, Z.; Jan, N.; Mahmood, T.; Maqsood, S. Multi-attribute decision making based on averaging aggregation operators for picture hesitant fuzzy sets. *Tech. J.* **2018**, *23*, 84–95.
23. Mahmood, T.; Ali, Z. The Fuzzy Cross-Entropy for Picture Hesitant Fuzzy Sets and Their Application in Multi Criteria Decision Making. *Punjab Univ. J. Math.* **2020**, *52*, 55–82.
24. Mahmood, T.; Ullah, K.; Khan, Q.; Jan, N. An approach toward decision-making and medical diagnosis problems using the concept of spherical fuzzy sets. *Neural. Comput. Appl.* **2019**, *31*, 7041–7053. [CrossRef]
25. Ullah, K.; Hassan, N.; Mahmood, T.; Jan, N.; Hassan, M. Evaluation of investment policy based on multi-attribute decision-making using interval valued T-spherical fuzzy aggregation operators. *Symmetry* **2019**, *11*, 357. [CrossRef]
26. Ullah, K.; Mahmood, T.; Jan, N. Similarity measures for T-spherical fuzzy sets with applications in pattern recognition. *Symmetry* **2018**, *10*, 193. [CrossRef]
27. Garg, H.; Munir, M.; Ullah, K.; Mahmood, T.; Jan, N. Algorithm for T-spherical fuzzy multi-attribute decision making based on improved interactive aggregation operators. *Symmetry* **2018**, *10*, 670. [CrossRef]
28. Ullah, K.; Garg, H.; Mahmood, T.; Jan, N.; Ali, Z. Correlation coefficients for T-spherical fuzzy sets and their applications in clustering and multi-attribute decision making. *Soft Comput.* **2020**, *24*, 1647–1659. [CrossRef]
29. Wu, M.Q.; Chen, T.Y.; Fan, J.P. Divergence measure of T-Spherical Fuzzy Sets and its applications in Pattern Recognition. *IEEE Access* **2019**, *8*, 10208–10221. [CrossRef]
30. Pamucar, D. Normalized weighted Geometric Dombi Bonferoni Mean Operator with interval grey numbers: Application in multicriteria decision making. *Rep. Mech. Eng.* **2020**, *1*, 44–52. [CrossRef]
31. Munir, M.; Kalsoom, H.; Ullah, K.; Mahmood, T.; Chu, Y.M. T-spherical fuzzy Einstein hybrid aggregation operators and their applications in smulti-attribute decision making problems. *Symmetry* **2020**, *12*, 365. [CrossRef]
32. Oussalah, M. On the use of Hamacher's t-norms family for information aggregation. *Inform. Sci.* **2003**, *153*, 107–154. [CrossRef]
33. Huang, J.Y. Intuitionistic fuzzy Hamacher aggregation operators and their application to multiple attribute decision making. *J. Intell. Fuzzy Syst.* **2014**, *27*, 505–513. [CrossRef]
34. Garg, H. Intuitionistic fuzzy hamacher aggregation operators with entropy weight and their applications to multi-criteria decision-making problems. *Iran. J. Sci. Tech. Trans. Electr. Eng.* **2019**, *43*, 597–613. [CrossRef]
35. Liu, P. Some Hamacher aggregation operators based on the interval-valued intuitionistic fuzzy numbers and their application to group decision making. *IEEE Trans. Fuzzy Syst.* **2013**, *22*, 83–97. [CrossRef]
36. Gao, H. Pythagorean fuzzy Hamacher prioritized aggregation operators in multiple attribute decision making. *J. Intell. Fuzzy Syst.* **2018**, *35*, 2229–2245. [CrossRef]
37. Wei, G.W. Pythagorean fuzzy Hamacher power aggregation operators in multiple attribute decision making. *Fundam. Inform.* **2019**, *166*, 57–85. [CrossRef]
38. Darko, A.P.; Liang, D. Some q-rung Orthopair fuzzy Hamacher aggregation operators and their application to multiple attribute group decision making with modified EDAS method. *Eng. Appl. Artif. Intell.* **2020**, *87*, 103259. [CrossRef]
39. Donyatalab, Y.; Farrokhizadeh, E.; Shishavan, S.A.S.; Seifi, S.H. Hamacher Aggregation Operators Based on Interval-Valued q-Rung Orthopair Fuzzy Sets and Their Applications to Decision Making Problems. In *International Conference on Intelligent and Fuzzy Systems*; Springer: Cham, Switzerland, 2020; pp. 466–474.
40. Jana, C.; Pal, M. Assessment of enterprise performance based on picture fuzzy Hamacher aggregation operators. *Symmetry* **2019**, *11*, 75. [CrossRef]
41. Ullah, K.; Mahmood, T.; Garg, H. Evaluation of the Performance of Search and Rescue Robots Using T-spherical Fuzzy Hamacher Aggregation Operators. *Int. J. Fuzzy Syst.* **2020**, *22*, 570–582. [CrossRef]

42. Wang, L.; Garg, H.; Li, N. Pythagorean fuzzy interactive Hamacher power aggregation operators for assessment of express service quality with entropy weight. *Soft Comput.* **2020**, *25*, 1–21. [CrossRef]
43. Zhu, W.B.; Shuai, B.; Zhang, S.H. The Linguistic Interval-Valued Intuitionistic Fuzzy Aggregation Operators Based on Extended Hamacher T-Norm and S-Norm and Their Application. *Symmetry* **2020**, *1*, 668. [CrossRef]
44. Gao, H.; Lu, M.; Wei, Y. Dual hesitant bipolar fuzzy Hamacher aggregation operators and their applications to multiple attribute decision making. *J. Intell. Fuzzy Syst.* **2019**, *37*, 5755–5766. [CrossRef]
45. Zeng, S.Z.; Hu, Y.J.; Balezentis, T.; Streimikiene, D. A multi-criteria sustainable supplier selection framework based on neutrosophic fuzzy data and entropy weighting. *Sustain. Dev.* **2020**, *28*, 1431–1440. [CrossRef]
46. Tang, J.; Meng, F. Linguistic intuitionistic fuzzy Hamacher aggregation operators and their application to group decision making. *Granul. Comput.* **2019**, *4*, 109–124. [CrossRef]

axioms

Article

An Innovative Grey Approach for Group Multi-Criteria Decision Analysis Based on the Median of Ratings by Using Python

Dragiša Stanujkić [1], Darjan Karabašević [2,*], Gabrijela Popović [2], Predrag S. Stanimirović [3], Florentin Smarandache [4], Muzafer Saračević [5], Alptekin Ulutaş [6] and Vasilios N. Katsikis [7]

1 Technical Faculty in Bor, University of Belgrade, Vojske Jugoslavije 12, 19210 Bor, Serbia; dstanujkic@tfbor.bg.ac.rs
2 Faculty of Applied Management, Economics and Finance, University Business Academy in Novi Sad, Jevrejska 24, 11000 Belgrade, Serbia; gabrijela.popovic@mef.edu.rs
3 Faculty of Sciences and Mathematics, University of Niš, Višegradska 33, 18000 Niš, Serbia; pecko@pmf.ni.ac.rs
4 Mathematics and Science Division, Gallup Campus, University of New Mexico, 705 Gurley Ave., Gallup, NM 87301, USA; smarand@unm.edu
5 Department of Computer Sciences, University of Novi Pazar, Dimitrija Tucovića bb, 36300 Novi Pazar, Serbia; muzafers@uninp.edu.rs
6 Department of International Trade and Logistics, Faculty of Economics and Administrative Sciences, Sivas Cumhuriyet University, Sivas 58140, Turkey; aulutas@cumhuriyet.edu.tr
7 Division of Mathematics and Informatics, Department of Economics, National and Kapodistrian University of Athens, Panepistimiopolis, 15784 Ilissia, Greece; vaskatsikis@econ.uoa.gr
* Correspondence: darjan.karabasevic@mef.edu.rs

Citation: Stanujkić, D.; Karabašević, D.; Popović, G.; Stanimirović, P.S.; Smarandache, F.; Saračević, M.; Ulutaş, A.; Katsikis, V.N. An Innovative Grey Approach for Group Multi-Criteria Decision Analysis Based on the Median of Ratings by Using Python. *Axioms* **2021**, *10*, 124. https://doi.org/10.3390/axioms10020124

Academic Editors: Goran Ćirović and Dragan Pamučar

Received: 24 May 2021
Accepted: 16 June 2021
Published: 19 June 2021

Abstract: Some decision-making problems, i.e., multi-criteria decision analysis (MCDA) problems, require taking into account the attitudes of a large number of decision-makers and/or respondents. Therefore, an approach to the transformation of crisp ratings, collected from respondents, in grey interval numbers form based on the median of collected scores, i.e., ratings, is considered in this article. In this way, the simplicity of collecting respondents' attitudes using crisp values, i.e., by applying some form of Likert scale, is combined with the advantages that can be achieved by using grey interval numbers. In this way, a grey extension of MCDA methods is obtained. The application of the proposed approach was considered in the example of evaluating the websites of tourism organizations by using several MCDA methods. Additionally, an analysis of the application of the proposed approach in the case of a large number of respondents, done in Python, is presented. The advantages of the proposed method, as well as its possible limitations, are summarized.

Keywords: MCDA; grey interval numbers; group decision-making; Python

1. Introduction

Multi-criteria decision-making (MCDM), or multi-criteria decision analysis (MCDA), has so far been used for solving a large number of numerous different decision-making problems [1–4]. Therefore, MCDA is dealing with solving complex real-world problems of the greatest interest to the organization that cannot be solved by conventional methods [5–8]. In due course of time, many multi-criteria analysis (MCA) methods were proposed, primarily due to the dynamic and rapid development of the field of operational research. The following can be mentioned as some of the most cited articles from this area: Hajkowicz and Collins [9], Hajkowicz and Higgins [10], Kaklauskas et al. [11], Kostreva et al. [12], and Belton and Vickers [13].

Besides this research, there are many studies in this area, such as: research and development project portfolio selection [14] (Mavrotas and Makryvelios, 2021), assessing national energy sustainability [15], energy consumption analysis of high-speed trains [16], evaluation of transport emissions reduction policies [17], planning renewable energy use and carbon saving [18], and so forth.

MCDA has also been used successfully for solving decision-making problems that are related to uncertainties or require a group decision-making approach for solving them [19–25]. As some examples of such approaches, the following can be mentioned: a grey absolute decision analysis [26], a multiple criteria decision analysis framework for the dispersed group [27], a fuzzy multi-criteria analysis [28–30], and collaborative decision-making in the multi-actor multi-criteria analysis [31].

From the aforestated, it is clear that some decision-making problems can be more adequately solved if a larger number of respondents take part in solving them. In such cases, the question that arises is how to transform the attitudes collected from respondents into group attitudes.

The approach based on the use of a five-point Liker's scale, or similar, can be mentioned as one of the probably simplest approaches for collecting the respondents' attitudes. So far, in numerous articles published in scientific journals, numerous approaches have been proposed for the transformation of individual attitudes acquired in this way into group attitudes. The results obtained, the advantages, as well as the weaknesses of these approaches, are also presented in these journals.

In this article, an approach to the transformation of crisp ratings, collected from respondents, as grey interval numbers form based on the median of collected scores, i.e., ratings, is considered. Therefore, the article proposes the transformation of individual ratings collected from respondents into grey intervals with the aim of performing MCDA with minimal loss of information in relation to cases when crisp ratings are transformed into crisp group ratings. The application of the proposed approach was considered on the example of evaluating the websites of tourism organizations by using several MCDA methods, and also an analysis of the application of the proposed approach in the case of a large number of respondents was done in Python and described. Additionally, the main idea of the article was to propose a simple procedure for gathering respondent's attitudes instead of a complex procedure that is sometimes difficult to understand by ordinary respondents/decision-makers who are not familiar with MCDM and fuzzy logic.

Therefore, the rest of this article is organized as follows: In Section 2, some basic definitions about grey numbers are given, while a new approach is proposed in Section 3. In Section 4, a numerical illustration is presented in order to highlight the basic characteristics of the proposed approach, while in Section 5 an analysis of the obtained results is performed. Finally, conclusions are given at the end of the article.

2. Preliminaries

Definition 1. *Grey number [32]. A grey number $\otimes x$ is such a number whose exact value is unknown, but the range in which value can lie is known.*

Definition 2. *Interval grey number [32]. An interval grey number is a grey number with a known lower bound $\underline{x}$ and upper bound $\overline{x}$, but with the unknown value of x, and it is shown as follows:*

$$\otimes x \in [\underline{x}, \overline{x}] = [\underline{x} \leq x \leq \overline{x}]. \tag{1}$$

Definition 3. *The whitening function [33–35]. The whitening function transforms an interval grey number into a crisp number whose possible values lie between the bounds of the interval grey number. For the given interval grey number, the whitened value $x_{(\lambda)}$ of interval grey number $\otimes x$ is defined as*

$$x_{(\lambda)} = (1-\lambda)\underline{x} + \lambda\overline{x}, \tag{2}$$

where $\in [0,1]$ denotes the whitening coefficient.

In the particular case $\lambda = 0.5$, the whitened value becomes the mean of the interval grey number, as follows:

$$x_{(0.5)} = 0.5(\underline{x} + \overline{x}). \tag{3}$$

3. The Newly Proposed Approach

Suppose that the decision matrix is presented in the form

$$D = [x_{ij}^k], \tag{4}$$

where: x_{ij}^k denotes the evaluation of alternative i to criterion j stated by the decision-maker k; $i = 1, \ldots, m$, and m denotes the number of alternatives; $j = 1, \ldots, n$, and n denotes the number of criteria; $k = 1 \ldots K$, and K denotes the number of decision-makers.

Such a three-dimensional matrix can be transformed into a group two-dimensional matrix as follows:

$$D = [x'_{ij}], \tag{5}$$

with

$$x'_{ij} = \left(\sum_{k=1}^{K} x_{ij}^k \right) / K. \tag{6}$$

Essentially, x'_{ij} denotes rating of alternative i to criterion j. Such defined x'_{ij} is actually the mean value of all assessments of the alternative i in relation to the criterion j.

However, the matrix shown using Equation (4) can be also transformed into a grey group decision matrix, as follows:

$$D = ([\underline{x}_{ij}, \overline{x}_{ij}]), \tag{7}$$

with

$$\underline{x}_{ij} = \left(\sum_{k \in k^-} x_{ij}^k \right) / n^-; \tag{8}$$

$$\overline{x}_{ij} = \left(\sum_{k \in k+} x_{ij}^k \right) / n^+. \tag{9}$$

In (8), k^- denotes the set of elements whose values are less than or equal to the median value of x_{ij}^k, and n^- denotes the number of elements in this set. Similarly, k^+ in (9) denotes a set of elements whose values are greater than or equal to the median value of x_{ij}^k and n^+ denotes the number of elements in this set.

Example

Let S be a sequence of 10 integers from interval [1, 5] and $S = (1, 2, 3, 1, 5, 3, 3, 1, 4, 5)$.

Then, the mean and median of S are as follows: $mean = 2.80$ and $median = 3.00$. The mean value of a number which is less than or equal to the median (1, 2, 3, 1, 3, 3, 1) is $x_l = 2.00$ and the mean value of a number greater or equal to the median (3, 5, 3, 3, 4, 5) is $x_u = 3.83$.

The mean value of such interval [2.00, 3.83], determined using Equation (3), is 2.915, and the distance between it and the mean is $2.915 - 2.80 = 0.115$, that is in percentages 4.11%.

The results obtained based on several sequences of randomly generated numbers from interval [1, 10] are shown in Table 1. The calculation was done in Python using the seed (1).

Table 1. Difference between the mean value of the sequence of numbers and the value obtained by the proposed approach.

Sample	*Mean*	*Median*	x_l	x_u	$x_m = (x_u - x_l)/2$	d = abs(*Mean* $- x_m$)	d (%)
5	5.60	5.00	4.00	7.00	5.50	0.10	1.79
10	7.10	7.50	5.40	8.80	7.10	0.00	0.00
15	5.13	6.00	2.88	7.50	5.19	0.05	1.06
20	6.50	7.00	5.08	8.00	6.54	0.04	0.64
25	4.52	4.00	2.43	6.50	4.46	0.06	1.23
50	5.20	5.00	3.07	7.14	5.11	0.09	1.81
100	5.01	5.00	2.93	7.09	5.01	0.00	0.02
150	5.16	5.00	3.05	6.91	4.98	0.18	3.45

From Table 1, it can be seen that the difference between the mean value of the sequence of numbers and the value obtained by the proposed approach is not large.

4. A Numerical Illustration

In this section, the use of the proposed approach is presented in the case of evaluating websites of tourist organizations from Eastern Serbia. The evaluation was performed on the websites of 5 tourist organizations from the Timok frontier, or more precisely tourist organizations of the Municipalities of Boljevac, Bor, Majdanpek, Negotin and Kladovo (It is important to state that the order of municipalities does not correspond to the order of alternatives, because the aim of this article is not to favor any of the above-mentioned tourist organizations.). The evaluation is performed based on the following criteria: Visual design—C_1, Structure and navigability—C_2, Content—C_3, Innovation—C_4, Personalization—C_5.

The evaluation was performed using ARAS [36], WASPAS [37], CoCoSo [38] and WISP [39] methods. In the first case, the evaluation was performed using ordinary MCDA methods and the mean value of the collected ratings, while in the first case, the evaluation was performed using the proposed approach.

This illustration does not show all the possibilities that the proposed approach provides in terms of analysis. The main goal was to compare the results obtained by applying the mean value of all assessments and the proposed approach, where the transformation of grey numbers was performed using Equation (3) and $\lambda = 0.5$.

The rating obtained from 10 respondents is shown in Tables 2–6.

Table 2. Ratings of alternative A_1 in relation to the evaluation criteria obtained from 10 respondents.

A_1	I	II	III	IV	V	VI	VII	VIII	IX	X
C_1	1	2	3	3	5	3	3	4	3	2
C_2	3	3	4	5	3	4	4	4	2	4
C_3	3	3	4	3	3	4	4	5	5	4
C_4	1	1	2	3	4	4	5	2	3	2
C_5	2	1	2	2	1	2	3	4	3	2

Table 3. Ratings of alternative A_2 in relation to the evaluation criteria obtained from 10 respondents.

A_2	I	II	III	IV	V	VI	VII	VIII	IX	X
C_1	3	5	4	4	4	4	5	3	2	2
C_2	5	5	4	5	4	5	5	4	3	4
C_3	2	4	4	4	3	4	5	3	3	3
C_4	4	4	5	4	2	2	5	3	5	3
C_5	4	4	5	3	4	3	4	3	2	4

Table 4. Ratings of alternative A_3 in relation to the evaluation criteria obtained from 10 respondents.

A_3	I	II	III	IV	V	VI	VII	VIII	IX	X
C_1	1	2	2	2	2	2	2	3	2	1
C_2	3	5	5	4	2	2	3	4	4	4
C_3	1	4	4	2	2	2	4	3	2	2
C_4	1	1	3	3	1	1	4	2	1	1
C_5	3	5	5	3	4	4	3	4	4	4

Table 5. Ratings of alternative A_4 in relation to the evaluation criteria obtained from 10 respondents.

A_4	I	II	III	IV	V	VI	VII	VIII	IX	X
C_1	4	4	4	5	4	4	4	4	5	4
C_2	5	5	4	5	3	3	4	5	5	3
C_3	5	5	4	4	3	3	4	5	5	5
C_4	4	4	5	5	5	3	5	5	4	3
C_5	4	4	5	3	4	4	3	5	4	4

Table 6. Ratings of alternative A_5 in relation to the evaluation criteria obtained from 10 respondents.

A_4	I	II	III	IV	V	VI	VII	VIII	IX	X
C_1	4	3	5	5	5	3	5	3	4	3
C_2	4	4	4	5	4	3	5	4	4	4
C_3	5	4	4	4	3	3	4	4	3	5
C_4	4	4	5	3	2	4	3	5	3	3
C_5	3	4	4	4	4	3	4	5	4	4

The group decision matrix, formed on the basis of the responses of all respondents, is shown in Table 7. The elements of this matrix represent the mean value of the ratings obtained from the respondents.

Table 7. Group decision-making matrix.

Criteria Alternatives	C_1	C_2	C_3	C_4	C_5
A_1	2.90	3.60	3.80	2.70	2.20
A_2	3.60	4.40	3.50	3.70	3.60
A_3	1.90	3.60	2.60	1.80	3.90
A_4	4.20	4.20	4.30	4.30	4.00
A_5	4.00	4.10	3.90	3.60	3.90

A similar decision matrix is shown in Table 8, where the elements of that matrix represent the median of ratings obtained from the respondents.

Table 8. The median of ratings obtained from the respondents.

Criteria Alternatives	C_1	C_2	C_3	C_4	C_5
A_1	2.96	3.81	3.92	2.70	2.11
A_2	3.79	4.40	3.50	3.82	3.81
A_3	1.95	3.79	2.31	1.40	3.96
A_4	4.10	4.20	4.30	4.30	4.00
A_5	4.00	4.05	3.96	3.60	3.95

The results of the evaluation performed using ordinary ARAS, WASPAS, CoCoSo and WISP methods, weighting vector w_i = (0.25, 0.24, 0.22, 0.20, 0.10), and the data from Table 7, are shown in Table 9.

Table 9. Ranking of alternatives using ordinary ARAS, WASPAS, CoCoSo and WISP methods.

	ARAS		WASPAS		CoCoSo		WISP	
Alternatives	S_i	Rank	S_i	Rank	S_i	Rank	S_i	Rank
A_1	0.73	4	0.73	4	1.80	4	0.87	4
A_2	0.88	3	0.88	3	2.17	3	0.95	3
A_3	0.61	5	0.60	5	1.49	5	0.81	5
A_4	0.99	1	0.99	1	2.43	1	1.00	1
A_5	0.92	2	0.92	2	2.25	2	0.96	2

In the second case, based on data from Table 8 as well as ratings from Tables 2–6, a grey decision matrix was formed as shown in Table 10.

Table 10. Grey group decision-making matrix.

Criteria Alternatives	C_1	C_2	C_3	C_4	C_5
A_1	[2.50, 3.43]	[3.44, 4.17]	[3.50, 4.33]	[1.60, 3.80]	[1.71, 2.50]
A_2	[3.25, 4.33]	[3.80, 5.00]	[2.80, 4.20]	[3.14, 4.50]	[3.44, 4.17]
A_3	[1.78, 2.13]	[3.25, 4.33]	[1.83, 2.78]	[1.00, 1.80]	[3.62, 4.29]
A_4	[4.00, 4.20]	[3.40, 5.00]	[3.60, 5.00]	[3.60, 5.00]	[3.75, 4.25]
A_5	[3.33, 4.67]	[3.88, 4.22]	[3.63, 4.29]	[2.80, 4.40]	[3.78, 4.13]

The evaluation results generated using the grey ARAS, WASPAS, CoCoSo and WISP methods, and the data from Table 10, are shown in Table 11. It should be noted again that the grey numbers from Table 10 were transformed into crisp values, using Equation (3) and $\lambda = 0.5$, before the evaluation.

Table 11. Ranking of alternatives using grey WS, WP, WASPAS and CoCoSo methods.

	ARAS		WASPAS		CoCoSo		WISP	
Alternatives	S_i	Rank	S_i	Rank	S_i	Rank	S_i	Rank
A_1	0.76	4	0.46	4	1.90	4	0.74	4
A_2	0.91	3	0.55	3	2.29	3	0.89	3
A_3	0.59	5	0.36	5	1.47	5	0.62	5
A_4	0.99	1	0.60	1	2.48	1	0.99	1
A_5	0.92	2	0.56	2	2.32	2	0.92	2

From Tables 9 and 11, it can be seen that differences in ranking orders of alternatives achieved on the basis of the mean value of all assessments and the proposed approach were not observed. Of course, it should be reiterated here that the proposed approach provides significantly greater opportunities in terms of analyzing various scenarios, such as pessimistic or optimistic.

5. Analysis and Discussion

In order to verify the proposed approach, this section presents the results of the evaluation based on the assessments of a number of virtual respondents. For easier evaluation, the scores were generated as random numbers from the interval [1, 10], using a program written in the Python programming language, in which all calculations were also performed. In this analysis, random numbers are generated with the seed (1). The results obtained on the basis of series of 10, 50, 100 and 150 virtual respondents are shown in Tables 12–20. The weighting vector $w_i = (0.2, 0.2, 0.2, 0.2, 0.2)$ is used in this evaluation.

The calculation details obtained on the basis of 10 virtual respondents are shown in Tables 12 and 13. As can be seen from Tables 12 and 13, in this case, the same ranking orders are obtained by applying all methods and approaches.

Table 12. Ranking of alternatives on the basis of 10 virtual respondents and crisp approach.

	WS		WP		WASPAS		CoCoSo		WISP	
Alternatives	S_i	Rank	P_i	Rank	Q_i	Rank	K_i	Rank	S_i	Rank
A_1	0.83	5	0.75	5	0.75	5	1.77	5	0.59	5
A_2	1.00	1	0.91	1	0.91	1	2.16	1	1.00	1
A_3	0.98	2	0.87	2	0.88	2	2.09	2	0.88	2
A_4	0.84	4	0.75	4	0.76	4	1.79	4	0.61	4
A_5	0.89	3	0.80	3	0.81	3	1.91	3	0.71	3

Table 13. Ranking of alternatives on the basis of 10 virtual respondents and the proposed grey approach.

	WS		WP		WASPAS		CoCoSo		WISP	
Alternatives	S_i	Rank	P_i	Rank	Q_i	Rank	K_i	Rank	S_i	Rank
A_1	0.82	5	0.74	5	0.75	5	1.78	5	0.58	5
A_2	1.00	1	0.92	1	0.92	1	2.18	1	1.00	1
A_3	0.95	2	0.84	2	0.86	2	2.04	2	0.80	2
A_4	0.83	4	0.75	4	0.75	4	1.79	4	0.59	4
A_5	0.88	3	0.80	3	0.81	3	1.91	3	0.69	3

Table 14. Ranking of alternatives on the basis of 50 virtual respondents and crisp approach.

	WS		WP		WASPAS		CoCoSo		WISP	
Alternatives	S_i	Rank	P_i	Rank	S_i	S_i	K_i	Rank	S_i	Rank
A_1	0.97	3	0.94	3	0.94	3	1.90	3	0.91	3
A_2	0.92	4	0.89	4	0.89	4	1.80	4	0.78	4
A_3	1.00	1	0.97	1	0.97	1	1.97	1	1.00	1
A_4	0.91	5	0.88	5	0.89	5	1.79	5	0.77	5
A_5	0.97	2	0.94	2	0.95	2	1.91	2	0.91	2

Table 15. Ranking of alternatives on the basis of 50 virtual respondents and the proposed grey approach.

	WS		WP		WASPAS		CoCoSo		WISP	
Alternatives	S_i	Rank	P_i	Rank	Q_i	Rank	K_i	Rank	S_i	Rank
A_1	0.98	2	0.94	2	0.94	2	1.90	2	0.94	2
A_2	0.92	5	0.89	5	0.89	5	1.79	5	0.80	5
A_3	1.00	1	0.96	1	0.96	1	1.94	1	1.00	1
A_4	0.93	4	0.89	4	0.89	4	1.81	4	0.82	4
A_5	0.97	3	0.93	3	0.93	3	1.87	3	0.90	3

Table 16. Ranking orders of alternatives obtained on the basis of 50 virtual respondents.

	Crisp					Grey Approach				
Alternatives	WS	WP	WASPAS	CoCoSo	WISP	WS	WP	WASPAS	CoCoSo	WISP
A_1	3	3	3	3	3	2	2	2	2	2
A_2	4	4	4	4	4	5	5	5	5	5
A_3	1	1	1	1	1	1	1	1	1	1
A_4	5	5	5	5	5	4	4	4	4	4
A_5	2	2	2	2	2	3	3	3	3	3

Table 17. Ranking orders of alternatives obtained on the basis of 100 virtual respondents.

	Crisp					Grey Approach				
Alternatives	WS	WP	WASPAS	CoCoSo	WISP	WS	WP	WASPAS	CoCoSo	WISP
A_1	4	4	4	4	4	4	4	4	4	4
A_2	3	3	3	3	3	2	2	2	2	2
A_3	2	2	2	2	2	3	3	3	3	3
A_4	1	1	1	1	1	1	1	1	1	1
A_5	5	5	5	5	5	5	5	5	5	5

Table 18. Ranking of alternatives on the basis of 150 virtual respondents and crisp methods.

	WS		WP		WASPAS		CoCoSo		WISP	
Alternatives	S_i	Rank	P_i	Rank	S_i	S_i	K_i	Rank	S_i	Rank
A_1	0.993	2	0.960	2	0.961	2	1.840	2	0.977	2
A_2	0.975	3	0.944	3	0.944	3	1.808	3	0.927	3
A_3	0.971	5	0.938	5	0.939	5	1.799	5	0.914	5
A_4	1.000	1	0.968	1	0.968	1	1.854	1	1.000	1
A_5	0.973	4	0.942	4	0.942	4	1.805	4	0.923	4

Table 19. Ranking of alternatives on the basis of 150 virtual respondents and grey methods.

	WS		WP		WASPAS		CoCoSo		WISP	
Alternatives	S_i	Rank	P_i	Rank	Q_i	Rank	K_i	Rank	S_i	Rank
A_1	0.988	2	0.954	2	0.955	2	1.806	2	0.965	2
A_2	0.988	3	0.953	3	0.954	3	1.805	3	0.963	3
A_3	0.987	4	0.952	4	0.953	4	1.804	4	0.960	4
A_4	1.000	1	0.966	1	0.966	1	1.828	1	1.000	1
A_5	0.985	5	0.952	5	0.952	5	1.801	5	0.958	5

Table 20. Ranking orders of alternatives obtained on the basis of 150 virtual respondents.

	Crisp					Grey Approach				
Alternatives	WS	WP	WASPAS	CoCoSo	WISP	WS	WP	WASPAS	CoCoSo	WISP
A_1	2	2	2	2	2	2	2	2	2	2
A_2	3	3	3	3	3	3	3	3	3	3
A_3	5	5	5	5	5	4	4	4	4	4
A_4	1	1	1	1	1	1	1	1	1	1
A_5	4	4	4	4	4	5	5	5	5	5

The calculation details obtained on the basis of 50 virtual respondents are shown in Tables 14–16. In this case, there were some discrepancies in the order of the second and third-placed alternatives, which can be clearly seen in Figure 1.

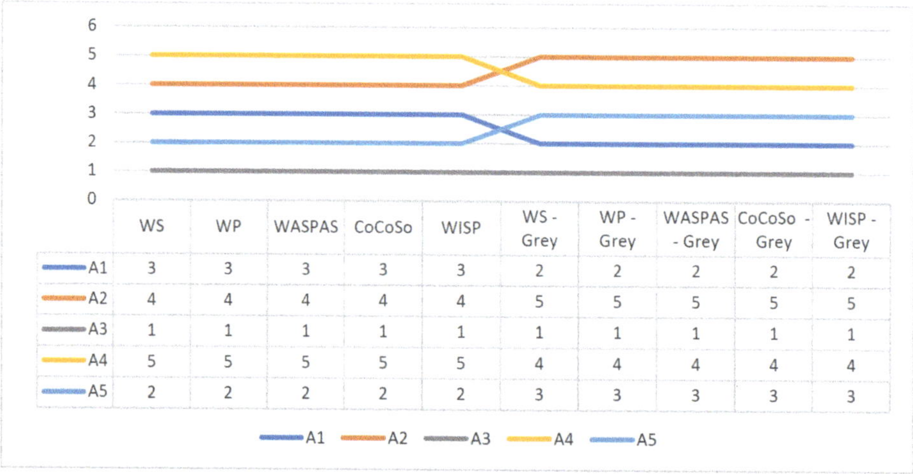

Figure 1. Ranking orders of alternatives obtained on the basis of 50 virtual respondents.

It can be seen from Tables 14 and 15 that differences between second-placed and third-placed alternatives are not high, which is why it can be expected that the same ranking order of alternatives could be obtained by using another weight vector.

Ranking orders of alternatives, obtained on the basis of 100 virtual respondents, are shown in Tabe 17, and presented in Figure 2. This case is similar to the previous one.

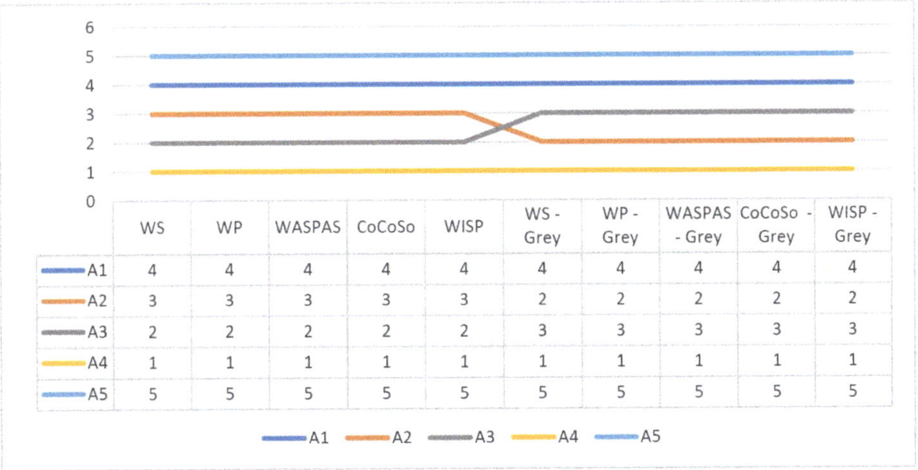

	WS	WP	WASPAS	CoCoSo	WISP	WS - Grey	WP - Grey	WASPAS - Grey	CoCoSo - Grey	WISP - Grey
A1	4	4	4	4	4	4	4	4	4	4
A2	3	3	3	3	3	2	2	2	2	2
A3	2	2	2	2	2	3	3	3	3	3
A4	1	1	1	1	1	1	1	1	1	1
A5	5	5	5	5	5	5	5	5	5	5

Figure 2. Ranking orders of alternatives obtained on the basis of 100 virtual respondents.

From Table 17 and Figure 2 it can be observed that in this case, the differences occur only in the case of the second and third-placed alternatives.

Ranking orders of alternatives that arise from 150 virtual respondents are arranged in Tables 18–20 and presented in Figure 3.

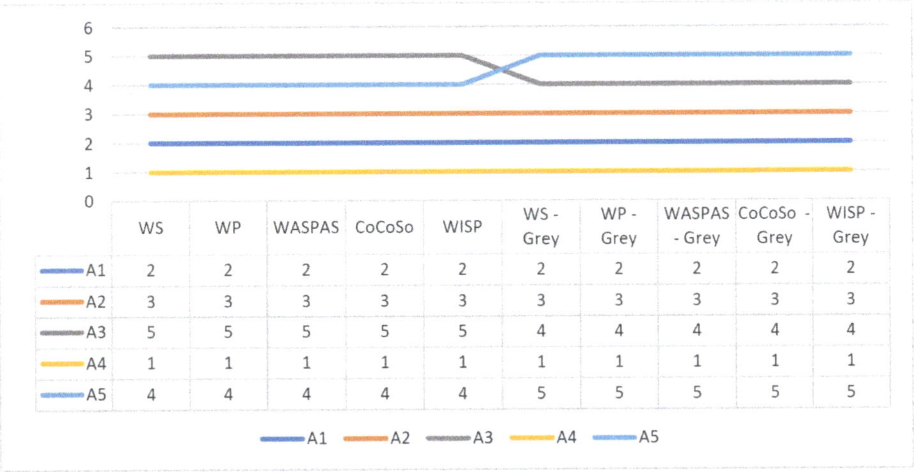

	WS	WP	WASPAS	CoCoSo	WISP	WS - Grey	WP - Grey	WASPAS - Grey	CoCoSo - Grey	WISP - Grey
A1	2	2	2	2	2	2	2	2	2	2
A2	3	3	3	3	3	3	3	3	3	3
A3	5	5	5	5	5	4	4	4	4	4
A4	1	1	1	1	1	1	1	1	1	1
A5	4	4	4	4	4	5	5	5	5	5

Figure 3. Ranking orders of alternatives obtained on the basis of 150 virtual respondents.

Table 20 and Figure 3 clearly show that the alternative A_4 is best ranked according to all methods, with all crisp methods gave the same order of ranking A_4, A_1, A_2, A_5, A_3, while the proposed grey approach gave the following rankings order A_4, A_1, A_2, A_3, A_5. However, from Table 20 it is observable that there are very small differences in overall performance between the second-placed, third-placed and fourth-placed alternatives, which is why it can be expected that different ranking orders of alternatives could be obtained by using another weighting vector.

6. Conclusions

The advantages of using grey instead of crisp numbers in multi-criteria decision analysis have been considered and proven in a number of previously published studies. One of the advantages which should be emphasized using grey numbers is the possibility of considering various scenarios, such as: pessimistic, realistic, and optimistic. The proposed approach allows the transformation of crisp ratings, collected by employing surveys based on the use of the Likert scale, into grey numbers and thus considering different scenarios. The proposed approach may be suitable when it is necessary to collect and analyze the realistic attitudes of a larger number of respondents. Moreover, the proposed transformation enables greater robustness and further possibility of analysis and consideration of different scenarios.

The results of the website evaluation based on the mean value of the ratings obtained from all respondents and the proposed approach did not indicate a difference in the ranking orders of alternatives. However, the results of the conducted analysis indicate that differences may arise between the two approaches, especially in the case of the lower-ranked alternatives.

Some differences in the results are expected because the proposed approach is not a substitute for applying the mean value of the scores obtained from all respondents, but an approach that further allows the possibility of analysis. Certain differences in the ranking results using the newly proposed approach and applying the mean of the scores obtained in all respondents can be cited as a weakness of this approach.

Finally, consideration of the transformation of a larger number of crisp ratings into corresponding triangular fuzzy numbers or interval-valued triangular fuzzy numbers can be mentioned as one of the possible directions for the further development of the proposed approach.

Author Contributions: Conceptualization, P.S.S., D.K., V.N.K. and G.P.; methodology, D.K., D.S. and F.S.; validation, A.U.; investigation, A.U.; data curation, G.P.; writing—original draft preparation, D.S., V.N.K. and M.S.; writing—review and editing, P.S.S. and M.S.; supervision, D.K.; funding acquisition, F.S. All authors have read and agreed to the published version of the manuscript.

Funding: The research presented in this article was done with the financial support of the Ministry of Education, Science and Technological Development of the Republic of Serbia, within the funding of the scientific research work at the University of Belgrade, Technical Faculty in Bor, according to the contract with registration number 451-03-9/2021-14/200131.

Conflicts of Interest: The authors declare no conflict of interest.

References

1. Ulutaş, A.; Stanujkic, D.; Karabasevic, D.; Popovic, G.; Zavadskas, E.K.; Smarandache, F.; Brauers, W.K. Developing of a Novel Integrated MCDM MULTIMOOSRAL Approach for Supplier Selection. *Informatica* **2021**, *32*, 145–161. [CrossRef]
2. Karabasevic, D.; Radanov, P.; Stanujkic, D.; Popovic, G.; Predic, B. Going green: Strategic evaluation of green ICT adoption in the textile industry by using bipolar fuzzy Multimoora method. *Ind. Text.* **2021**, *72*, 3–10. [CrossRef]
3. Jaukovic Jocic, K.; Jocic, G.; Karabasevic, D.; Popovic, G.; Stanujkic, D.; Zavadskas, E.K.; Thanh Nguyen, P. A novel integrated piprecia–interval-valued triangular fuzzy aras model: E-learning course selection. *Symmetry* **2020**, *12*, 928. [CrossRef]
4. Karabašević, D.; Stanujkić, D.; Zavadskas, E.K.; Stanimirović, P.; Popović, G.; Predić, B.; Ulutaş, A. A Novel Extension of the TOPSIS Method Adapted for the Use of Single-Valued Neutrosophic Sets and Hamming Distance for E-Commerce Development Strategies Selection. *Symmetry* **2020**, *12*, 1263. [CrossRef]
5. Amiri, M.; Hashemi-Tabatabaei, M.; Ghahremanloo, M.; Keshavarz-Ghorabaee, M.; Zavadskas, E.K.; Antucheviciene, J. A novel model for multi-criteria assessment based on BWM and possibilistic chance-constrained programming. *Comput. Ind. Eng.* **2021**, *156*, 107287. [CrossRef]
6. Lu, K.; Liao, H.; Zavadskas, E.K. An overview of fuzzy techniques in supply chain management: Bibliometrics, methodologies, applications and future directions. *Technol. Econ. Dev. Econ.* **2021**, *27*, 402–458. [CrossRef]

7. Stanujkic, D.; Zavadskas, E.K.; Liu, S.; Karabasevic, D.; Popovic, G. Improved OCRA method based on the use of interval grey numbers. *J. Grey Syst.* **2017**, *29*, 49–60.
8. Popovic, G.; Stanujkic, D.; Brzakovic, M.; Karabasevic, D. A multiple-criteria decision-making model for the selection of a hotel location. *Land Use Policy* **2019**, *84*, 49–58. [CrossRef]
9. Hajkowicz, S.; Collins, K. A review of multiple criteria analysis for water resource planning and management. *Water Resour. Manag.* **2007**, *21*, 1553–1566. [CrossRef]
10. Hajkowicz, S.; Higgins, A. A comparison of multiple criteria analysis techniques for water resource management. *Eur. J. Oper. Res.* **2008**, *184*, 255–265. [CrossRef]
11. Kaklauskas, A.; Zavadskas, E.K.; Raslanas, S. Multivariant design and multiple criteria analysis of building refurbishments. *Energy Build.* **2005**, *37*, 361–372. [CrossRef]
12. Kostreva, M.M.; Ogryczak, W.; Wierzbicki, A. Equitable aggregations and multiple criteria analysis. *Eur. J. Oper. Res.* **2004**, *158*, 362–377. [CrossRef]
13. Belton, V.; Vickers, S.P. Demystifying DEA—A visual interactive approach based on multiple criteria analysis. *J. Oper. Res. Soc.* **1993**, *44*, 883–896.
14. Mavrotas, G.; Makryvelios, E. Combining multiple criteria analysis, mathematical programming and Monte Carlo simulation to tackle uncertainty in Research and Development project portfolio selection: A case study from Greece. *Eur. J. Oper. Res.* **2021**, *291*, 794–806. [CrossRef]
15. Phillis, A.; Grigoroudis, E.; Kouikoglou, V.S. Assessing national energy sustainability using multiple criteria decision analysis. *Int. J. Sustain. Dev. World Ecol.* **2021**, *28*, 18–35. [CrossRef]
16. Peng, Y.; Zhang, H.; Wang, T.; Yang, M.; Wang, K.; Meng, W.; Wang, D. Energy consumption analysis and multiple-criteria evaluation of high-speed trains with different marshaled forms in China. *Sci. Total Environ.* **2021**, *759*, 143678. [CrossRef]
17. Hasan, M.A.; Chapman, R.; Frame, D.J. Acceptability of transport emissions reduction policies: A multi-criteria analysis. *Renew. Sustain. Energy Rev.* **2020**, *133*, 110298. [CrossRef]
18. Ahmed, A.; Sutrisno, S.W.; You, S. A two-stage multi-criteria analysis method for planning renewable energy use and carbon saving. *Energy* **2020**, *199*, 117475. [CrossRef]
19. Huang, H.; Mommens, K.; Lebeau, P.; Macharis, C. The Multi-Actor Multi-Criteria Analysis (MAMCA) for Mass-Participation Decision Making. In *International Conference on Decision Support System Technology*; Springer International Publishing: Cham, Switzerland, 2021; pp. 3–17.
20. Salo, A.; Hämäläinen, R.; Lahtinen, T. Multicriteria Methods for Group Decision Processes: An Overview. In *Handbook of Group Decision and Negotiation*; Kilgour, D.M., Eden, C., Eds.; Springer Science & Business Media: Berlin/Heidelberg, Germany, 2021.
21. Tao, R.; Liu, Z.; Cai, R.; Cheong, K.H. A dynamic group MCDM model with intuitionistic fuzzy set: Perspective of alternative queuing method. *Inf. Sci.* **2021**, *555*, 85–103. [CrossRef]
22. Hsu, W.C.J.; Liou, J.J.; Lo, H.W. A group decision-making approach for exploring trends in the development of the healthcare industry in Taiwan. *Decis. Support Syst.* **2021**, *141*, 113447. [CrossRef]
23. Zhan, J.; Zhang, K.; Wu, W.Z. An investigation on Wu-Leung multi-scale information systems and multi-expert group decision-making. *Expert Syst. Appl.* **2021**, *170*, 114542. [CrossRef]
24. Liu, S.; Yu, W.; Chan, F.T.; Niu, B. A variable weight-based hybrid approach for multi-attribute group decision making under interval-valued intuitionistic fuzzy sets. *Int. J. Intell. Syst.* **2021**, *36*, 1015–1052. [CrossRef]
25. Biswas, S.; Pamucar, D. Facility location selection for b-schools in indian context: A multi-criteria group decision based analysis. *Axioms* **2020**, *9*, 77. [CrossRef]
26. Javed, S.A.; Mahmoudi, A.; Liu, S. Grey Absolute Decision Analysis (GADA) Method for multiple criteria group decision-making under uncertainty. *Int. J. Fuzzy Syst.* **2020**, *22*, 1073–1090. [CrossRef]
27. Carneiro, J.; Martinho, D.; Alves, P.; Conceição, L.; Marreiros, G.; Novais, P. A multiple criteria decision analysis framework for dispersed group decision-making contexts. *Appl. Sci.* **2020**, *10*, 4614. [CrossRef]
28. Al Asbahi, A.A.M.H.; Fang, Z.; Chandio, Z.A.; Tunio, M.K.; Ahmed, J.; Abbas, M. Assessing barriers and solutions for Yemen energy crisis to adopt green and sustainable practices: A fuzzy multi-criteria analysis. *Environ. Sci. Pollut. Res.* **2020**, *27*, 36765–36781. [CrossRef]
29. Musaad, O.A.S.; Zhuo, Z.; Musaad, O.A.O.; Ali Siyal, Z.; Hashmi, H.; Shah, S.A.A. A fuzzy multi-criteria analysis of barriers and policy strategies for small and medium enterprises to adopt green innovation. *Symmetry* **2020**, *12*, 116. [CrossRef]
30. Durmić, E.; Stević, Ž.; Chatterjee, P.; Vasiljević, M.; Tomašević, M. Sustainable supplier selection using combined FUCOM—Rough SAW model. *Rep. Mech. Eng.* **2020**, *1*, 34–43. [CrossRef]
31. Huang, H.; De Smet, Y.; Macharis, C.; Doan, N.A.V. Collaborative decision-making in sustainable mobility: Identifying possible consensuses in the multi-actor multi-criteria analysis based on inverse mixed-integer linear optimization. *Int. J. Sustain. Dev. World Ecol.* **2021**, *28*, 64–74. [CrossRef]
32. Deng, J.L. Introduction to Grey System Theory. *J. Grey Syst.* **1989**, *1*, 1–24.
33. Liu, S.F.; Yang, Y.J.; Forrest, J.Y.L. *Grey Data Analysis: Methods, Models and Applications*; Springer: Berlin/Heidelberg, Germany, 2016.
34. Liu, S.F.; Forrest, J.Y.L. *Grey Systems: Theory and Applications*; Springer: Berlin/Heidelberg, Germany, 2010.

35. Liu, S.; Rui, H.; Fang, Z.; Yang, Y.; Forrest, J. Explanation of terms of grey numbers and its operations. *Grey Syst. Theory Appl.* **2016**, *6*, 436–441. [CrossRef]
36. Turskis, Z.; Zavadskas, E.K. A novel method for multiple criteria analysis: Grey additive ratio assessment (ARAS-G) method. *Informatica* **2010**, *21*, 597–610. [CrossRef]
37. Zavadskas, E.K.; Turskis, Z.; Antucheviciene, J. Selecting a Contractor by Using a Novel Method forMultiple Attribute Analysis: Weighted Aggregated SumProduct Assessment with Grey Values (WASPAS-G). *Stud. Inform. Control.* **2015**, *24*, 141–150. [CrossRef]
38. Yazdani, M.; Wen, Z.; Liao, H.; Banaitis, A.; Turskis, Z. A grey combined compromise solution (COCOSO-G) method for supplier selection in construction management. *J. Civ. Eng. Manag.* **2019**, *25*, 858–874. [CrossRef]
39. Stanujkic, D.; Popovic, G.; Karabasevic, D.; Meidute-Kavaliauskiene, I.; Ulutas, A. An Integrated Simple Weighted Sum Product Method—WISP. *IEEE Trans. Eng. Manag.* **2021**, 1–12. [CrossRef]

axioms

Article

A Decision-Making Approach Based on New Aggregation Operators under Fermatean Fuzzy Linguistic Information Environment

Rajkumar Verma

Department of Management Control and Information Systems, University of Chile, Av. Diagonal Paraguay 257, Santiago 8330015, Chile; rkver83@gmail.com or rverma@fen.uchile.cl

Abstract: Fermatean fuzzy linguistic (FFL) set theory provides an efficient tool for modeling a higher level of uncertain and imprecise information, which cannot be represented using intuitionistic fuzzy linguistic (IFL)/Pythagorean fuzzy linguistic (PFL) sets. On the other hand, the linguistic scale function (LSF) is the better way to consider the semantics of the linguistic terms during the evaluation process. It is worth noting that the existing operational laws and aggregation operators (AOs) for Fermatean fuzzy linguistic numbers (FFLNs) are not valid in many situations, which can generate errors in real-life applications. The present study aims to define new robust operational laws and AOs under Fermatean fuzzy linguistic environment. To do so, first, we define some new modified operational laws for FFLNs based on LSF and prove some important mathematical properties of them. Next, the work defines several new AOs, namely, the FFL-weighted averaging (FFLWA) operator, the FFL-weighted geometric (FFLWG) operator, the FFL-ordered weighted averaging (FFLOWA) operator, the FFL-ordered weighted geometric (FFLOWG) operator, the FFL-hybrid averaging (FFLHA) operator and the FFL-hybrid geometric (FFLHG) operator under Fermatean fuzzy linguistic environment. Several properties of these AOs are investigated in detail. Further, based on the proposed AOs, a new decision-making approach with Fermatean fuzzy linguistic information is developed to solve group decision-making problems with multiple attributes. Finally, to illustrate the effectiveness of the present approach, a real-life supplier selection problem is presented where the evaluation information of the alternatives is given in terms of FFLNs. Compared to the existing methods, the salient features of the developed approach are (1) it can solve decision-making problems with qualitative information data using FFLNs; (2) It can consider the attitudinal character of the decision-makers during the solution process; (3) It has a solid ability to distinguish the optimal alternative.

Keywords: Fermatean fuzzy set; Fermatean fuzzy linguistic set; Fermatean fuzzy linguistic number; MAGDM; supplier selection

MSC: 03E72; 62A86; 90B50

Citation: Verma, R. A Decision-Making Approach Based on New Aggregation Operators under Fermatean Fuzzy Linguistic Information Environment. *Axioms* **2021**, *10*, 113. https://doi.org/10.3390/axioms10020113

Academic Editors: Dragan Pamučar and Goran Ćirović

Received: 10 April 2021
Accepted: 31 May 2021
Published: 4 June 2021

1. Introduction

The intuitionistic fuzzy set (IFS) theory was introduced by Atanassov [1] in 1983 to accommodate uncertain and vague concepts more precisely in complex real-life situations. An IFS assigns each element a degree of membership (DM) and a degree of non-membership (DNM), whose sum is always less than or equal to one. It has become an important and widely studied generalization of fuzzy sets [2]. Due to the applicability and effectiveness of the IFS theory, several researchers started work in this direction and established many significant results. For aggregating different intuitionistic fuzzy numbers (IFNs), a large number of AOs have been defined by considering various aspects of available information [3–6]. The Bonferroni mean operators were studied in [7–10] to capture the interrelationship between aggregated IFNs. Verma [11] proposed prioritized weighted aggregation operators with intuitionistic fuzzy information based on Einstein t-norms. Zhenghai and Xu [12–14] undertook a detailed study on intuitionistic fuzzy calculus and explored its utility in decision-making problems. Besides, several information measures have been proposed under an intuitionistic fuzzy environment, including distance measure [15–18], similarity measure [19–22], entropy measure [23–26], divergence measure [27–29], and inaccuracy measure [30] and applied them in different application areas including pattern recognition, medical diagnosis, and decision making.

1.1. Literature Review

In 2013, Yager [31] and Yager and Abbasov [32] proposed the notion of the Pythagorean fuzzy sets (PFSs) as a new generalization to IFSs. PFSs are more effective in modeling imperfect or vague information, which cannot be represented in terms of IFSs. For example: suppose an expert provides the DM of an alternative corresponding to a criterion as 0.8 and the DNM as 0.5. As we see, the sum of both degrees is 1.3, which does not satisfy the essential condition of IFS. Further, if we consider the sum of the squares of both the degrees, i.e., $0.8^2 + 0.5^2$ then we obtain $0.89 < 1$; hence, this information can be represented in the form of PFS, not in IFS. In a short span, the PFS theory has become an efficient tool for solving various real-life problems. Zhang and Xu [33] extended the TOPSIS method under the Pythagorean fuzzy environment. Yager [34] proposed some novel AOs for aggregating Pythagorean fuzzy numbers (PFNs). The power AOs were studied by Wei and Lu [35] under a Pythagorean fuzzy environment. Yang et al. [36] defined some Pythagorean fuzzy Bonferroni mean operators using t-norms. Akram et al. [37] developed a two-phase group decision-making approach using the ELECTRE III method with Pythagorean fuzzy information. Ejegwa [38] defined a modified Zhang and Xu's distance measure for solving pattern recognition problems with Pythagorean fuzzy information. Molla et al. [39] extended the PROMETHEE method with PFSs and utilized them in medical diagnosis. Bakioglu and Atahan [40] conducted a detailed study on prioritizing risks in self-driving vehicles based on hybrid approaches with Pythagorean fuzzy information.

Again, let us assume the DM as 0.9 and the DNM as 0.6 in the above-discussed example. It is clear that we do not express this information by using IFS and PFS. To cope with this problem, Senapati and Yager [41] proposed the concept of Fermatean fuzzy set (FFS), where the DM and DNM are both real numbers that lie between 0 and 1 and satisfy the condition $0 \leq (\text{DM})^3 + (\text{DNM})^3 \leq 1$. The main advantage of the FFS is that it provides a better tool than IFS and PFS for handling the higher level of uncertainties arising in many real-life decision-making problems. As we obtain $0.9^3 + 0.6^3 < 1$, hence FFS is an appropriate tool to capture this uncertain information. Later on, Senapati and Yager [42] defined some operations on FFSs and discussed their application in decision-making. To aggregate different Fermatean fuzzy numbers (FFNs), Senapati and Yager [43] developed some weighted averaging/geometric AOs and utilized them to solve decision-making problems with multiple criteria. Aydemir and Yilmaz Gunduz [44] used the TOPSIS method with Dombi AOs for solving decision-making problems with Fermatean fuzzy information. Mishra et al. [45] formulated a Fermatean fuzzy CRITIC-EDAS approach to select sustainable logistics providers.

In many real-life situations, due to the increase in complexities and uncertainties in practical decision problems, an expert feels difficulty expressing his/her preference information by exact numerical values. Besides, many attributes and criteria can be evaluated quickly and effectively in terms of linguistic values. Firstly, Zadeh [46,47] developed the idea of the linguistic term set (LTS) in 1975. For example—suppose an expert evaluates the performance of a motorbike, then he/she may use the terms "good", "excellent", etc., to express his/her evaluation information because linguistic terms (LTs) are very close to human cognition. In 2010, Wang and Li [48] developed a hybrid set theory by combining the notions of LTS and IFS in a single formulation, which is known as the intuitionistic linguistic fuzzy sets (ILFSs). In the literature, several research studies have been conducted under the intuitionistic linguistic fuzzy environment. Liu [49] proposed some generalized dependent AOs with intuitionistic linguistic fuzzy numbers (ILFNs) and studied their application in decision-making. Liu and Wang [50] defined some intuitionistic linguistic generalized power aggregation operators. Su et al. [51] studied ordered weighted distance averaging operators with intuitionistic linguistic fuzzy information. Yu et al. [52] presented an extended TODIM method for solving MAGDM problems with ILFNs.

Recently, Liu et al. [53] generalized the notion of ILFSs and introduced Fermatean fuzzy linguistic sets (FFLS) by integrating the idea of LTS with FFS. Besides, a MCDM approach was formulated for solving decision problems with Fermatean fuzzy linguistic information. Further, Liu et al. [54] defined some new distance and similarity measures between FFLSs based on linguistic scale function (LSF) and utilized them in the development of TODIM and TOPSIS methods. In conclusion, Fermatean fuzzy linguistic set theory has a broader scope of applications in different practical areas. However, a limited investigation has been conducted on FFLSs and their applications. It is also worth noting that the operational laws defined by Liu et al. [54] for FFLNs are not valid in general. Therefore, it is significant to pay attention to the research studies under the Fermatean fuzzy linguistic environment.

1.2. Objective and Contributions of the Work

The main objective of this work is to define the modified operational laws for Fermatean fuzzy linguistic numbers (FFLNs) and study different AOs based on them to aggregate Fermatean fuzzy linguistic information. To fulfill the aim of the proposed study, firstly, the work defines some new modified operational laws for FFLNs based on LSF, which overcome the drawbacks of the existing operational laws. We also study several essential properties of the proposed modified operational laws. Then, the paper develops several new AOs for aggregating different FFLNs and discusses several properties associated with them. Finally, a decision-making approach is formulated to solve MAGDM problems under the Fermatean fuzzy linguistic environment. The contributions of this paper can be summarized as follows:

1. New and improved operational laws are introduced for FFLNs with their properties.
2. Several new AOs such as the FFL-weighted averaging (FFLWA) operator, the FFL-weighted geometric (FFLWG) operator, the FFL-ordered weighted averaging (FFLOWA) operator, the FFL-ordered weighted geometric (FFLOWG) operator, the FFL-hybrid averaging (FFLHA) operator and the FFL-hybrid geometric (FFLHG) operator are defined for aggregating Fermatean fuzzy linguistic information.
3. A MAGDM method based on the proposed AOs is constructed to support the decision-making problems under Fermatean fuzzy linguistic environment.
4. A sensitivity analysis is also conducted to analyze the impact of different AOs on the ranking of the alternatives.

1.3. Organization of the Paper

The rest of the manuscript is organized as follows: In Section 2 we briefly review some preliminary results on linguistic variables (LVs), LSF, FFS, FFLS and discuss some significant drawbacks of the Fermatean fuzzy linguistic operational laws defined by Liu et al. [54]. Section 3 presents modified algebraic operational laws for FFLNs based on LSF and proves several important properties of FFLNs using proposed operation laws. Then, we define the FFLWA, FFLWG, FFLOWA, FFLOWG, FFLHA, and FFLHG AOs to aggregate different FFLNs. In Section 4, based on the developed AOs, a MAGDM approach is formulated for solving real-life decision problems with Fermatean fuzzy linguistic information. Then, a real-life supplier selection problem is given to illustrate the decision-making steps and effectiveness of the developed approach. In Section 5 we conclude the paper and discuss some future works.

2. Preliminaries

2.1. Linguistic Variables

The linguistic variable provides a useful tool to represent qualitative information in terms of linguistic values. According to Herrera and Martínez [55], the linguistic variable can be defined as follows:

Definition 1 ([55]). *Let $\hat{L} = \{\ell_d | d = 0, 1 \ldots, 2t\}$ be a totally ordered discrete LTS with the odd cardinality. Any level ℓ_d denotes a possible value for a linguistic variable and t is a positive integer. The LTS should meet the following properties:*

i. $\ell_i \leq \ell_j \Leftrightarrow i \leq j$;
ii. $neg(\ell_d) = \ell_{2t-d}$;
iii. $\max(\ell_i, \ell_j) = \ell_i \Leftrightarrow i \geq j$;
iv. $\min(\ell_i, \ell_j) = \ell_i \Leftrightarrow i \leq j$;
where neg denotes the negation operator.

For example, a well-known set of seven linguistic terms can be defined as:

$$\hat{L} = \left\{ \begin{array}{r} \ell_0 = \mathrm{N(none)}, \ell_1 = \mathrm{VL(very\ low)}, \ell_2 = \mathrm{L(low)}, \ell_3 = \mathrm{M(medium)}, \\ \ell_4 = \mathrm{H(\ high\ )}, \ell_5 = \mathrm{VH(very\ high)}, \ell_6 = \mathrm{P(perfect)} \end{array} \right\}.$$

Further, Xu [56] defined the extended continuous LTS $\overset{\frown}{L}_{[0,2t]} = \{\ell_d | \ell_0 \leq \ell_d \leq \ell_{2t}, d \in [0, 2t]\}$, where, if $\ell_d \in \overset{\frown}{L}$, then ℓ_d is called the original linguistic term (OLT), otherwise ℓ_d is called the virtual linguistic term (VLT). However, $\ell_d \in \overset{\frown}{L}$ is usually used by the decision-makers to evaluate attributes/alternatives while $\ell_d \in \overset{\frown}{L}_{[0,2t]}$ only appears in the calculation process.

Definition 2 ([56]). *Let $\ell_\alpha, \ell_\beta \in \overset{\frown}{L}_{[0,2t]}$ and $\lambda, \lambda_1, \lambda_2 \in [0, 1]$, then some operational laws are given as follows:*

(i) $\ell_\alpha \oplus \ell_\beta = \ell_{\alpha+\beta}$;
(ii) $\ell_\alpha \otimes \ell_\beta = \ell_{\alpha\times\beta}$;
(iii) $\lambda\ell_\alpha = \ell_{\lambda\alpha}$;
(iv) $\lambda(\ell_\alpha \oplus \ell_\beta) = \lambda\ell_\alpha \oplus \lambda\ell_\beta$;

2.2. Linguistic Scale Function

In the evaluation process, an expert uses LTs directly rather than their corresponding semantics. In general, the simplest way to deal with LTs is to use the levels of LTs directly. However, in different semantics decision-making environments, LTs have some differences in expressing evaluations. To resolve these issues, Wang et al. [57] defined the LSF to deal with linguistic information. According to the decision-making environment, experts can consider different LSFs, which express available linguistic information more flexibly and precisely in different semantic situations.

Definition 3 ([57]). *Let $\hat{L} = \{\ell_d | d = 0, 1, 2, \ldots, 2t\}$ be a discrete LTSs with the odd cardinality and $\kappa_d \in [0, 1]$ be a real number, then the LSF φ can be defined as*

$$\varphi : \ell_d \to \kappa_d,\ d = 0, 1, 2, \ldots, 2t. \tag{1}$$

where φ is a strictly monotonically increasing function with respect to subscript d.

In general, there are three different linguistic scaling functions, given as

LSF 1 ([58]). *When the semantics of linguistic terms are uniformly (balanced) distributed, i.e., the absolute semantic gap (ASG) between any adjacent LTs is always equal.*

$$\varphi_1(\ell_d) = \kappa_d = \frac{d}{2t}, d = 0,1,2,\ldots,2t. \tag{2}$$

LSF 2 ([58]). *When the ASG between two semantics of the adjacent LTs increases with the extension from ℓ_t to both ends of LTS.*

$$\varphi_2(\ell_d) = \kappa_d = \begin{cases} \frac{\theta^t - \theta^{t-d}}{2(\theta^t - 1)}, & d = 0,1,2,\ldots,t, \\ \frac{\theta^t + \theta^{d-t} - 2}{2(\theta^t - 1)}, & d = t+1, t+2, \ldots, 2t, \end{cases} \tag{3}$$

where θ is a threshold, which can be determined by a subjective method according to the specific problem, and it should be greater than or equal to 1. If the LTS is a set of seven terms, then $\theta \in [1.37, 1.40]$.

LSF 3 ([58]). *When the ASG between two semantics of the adjacent LTs decreases with the extension from ℓ_t to both ends of LTS.*

$$\varphi_3(\ell_d) = \kappa_d = \begin{cases} \frac{t^\rho - (t-d)^\rho}{2t^\rho}, & d = 0,1,2,\ldots,t, \\ \frac{t^\tau + (d-t)^\tau}{2t^\tau}, & d = t+1, t+2, \ldots, 2t, \end{cases} \tag{4}$$

where $\rho, \tau \in [0,1]$ are determined according to the specific problem. If the LTS is a set of seven terms, then $\rho = \tau = 0.8$.

Example 1. *Let* $\hat{L} = \left\{ \begin{array}{c} \ell_0 = \text{N(none)}, \ell_1 = \text{VL(very low)}, \ell_2 = \text{L(low)}, \ell_3 = \text{M(medium)}, \\ \ell_4 = \text{H(high)}, \ell_5 = \text{VH(very high)}, \ell_6 = \text{P(perfect)} \end{array} \right\}$ *be a LTS with seven terms. Figures 1–3 show the balanced distribution of $\hat{L}$, unbalanced distribution of $\hat{L}$ in an increasing trend and the unbalanced distribution of $\hat{L}$ in a decreasing trend, respectively. Besides, Figure 4 represents the relationships between LTs of $\hat{L}$ and their corresponding semantics under different situations.*

Meanwhile, to avoid an information loss and to facilitate the calculation process, the LSF φ can be further generalized to an extended continuous LTS as follows:

Definition 4 ([57]). *Let $\hat{L}_{[0,2t]} = \{\ell_d | \ell_0 \le \ell_d \le \ell_{2t}, d \in [0,2t]\}$ be an extended continuous LTS and $\kappa_d \in [0,1]$ be a real number, then the LSF φ^* is defined as*

$$\varphi^* : \hat{L}_{[0,2t]} \to \kappa_d \tag{5}$$

where φ^* is also a strictly monotonically increasing function, and its inverse is expressed as φ^{*-1}.

Example 2. *Let $\hat{L}_{[0,6]} = \{\ell_d | d \in [0,6]\}$ be a continuous LTS, then the inverse corresponding to the LSFs φ_1^*, φ_2^* and φ_3^* can be obtained as follows:*

(1) *If* $\varphi_1^*(\ell_d) = \kappa_d = \frac{d}{6}\ (d = [0,6])$, *then* $\varphi_1^{*-1}(\kappa_d) = \ell_{6\times\kappa_d} (\kappa_d \in [0,1])$.

(2) *If* $\varphi_2^*(\ell_d) = \kappa_d = \begin{cases} \frac{\theta^3 - \theta^{3-d}}{2(\theta^3 - 1)}, & 0 \le d \le 3 \\ \frac{\theta^3 + \theta^{d-3} - 2}{2(\theta^3 - 1)}, & 3 < d \le 6 \end{cases}$, *then* $\varphi_2^{*-1}(\kappa_d) = \begin{cases} \ell_{3 - \log_\theta [\theta^3 - (2\theta^3 - 2)\kappa_d]}, & \kappa_d \in [0, 0.5], \\ \ell_{3 + \log_\theta [(2\theta^3 - 2)\kappa_d - \theta^3 + 2]}, & \kappa_d \in (0.5, 1]. \end{cases}$

(3) *If* $\varphi_3^*(\ell_d) = \kappa_d = \begin{cases} \frac{3^\rho - (3-d)^\rho}{2\times 3^\rho}, & 0 \le d \le 3 \\ \frac{3^\tau + (d-3)^\tau}{2\times 3^\tau}, & 3 < d \le 6 \end{cases}$, *then* $\varphi_3^{*-1}(\kappa_d) = \begin{cases} \ell_{3 - [3^\rho - 2\times 3^\rho \times \kappa_d]^{1/\rho}}, & \kappa_d \in [0, 0.5], \\ \ell_{3 + [2\times 3^\tau \times \kappa_d - 3^\tau]^{1/\tau}}, & \kappa_d \in (0.5, 1]. \end{cases}$

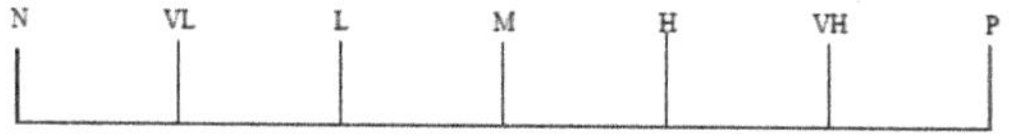

Figure 1. The uniformly distributed linguistic terms set.

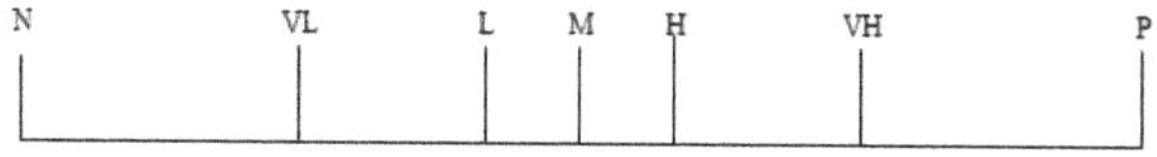

Figure 2. The semantics of the unbalanced distributed LTS in ASG increasing trend.

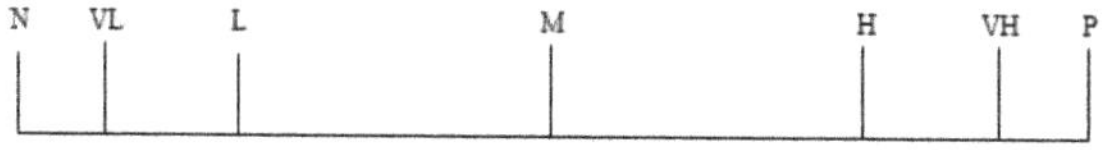

Figure 3. The unbalanced distributed LTS in ASG decreasing trend.

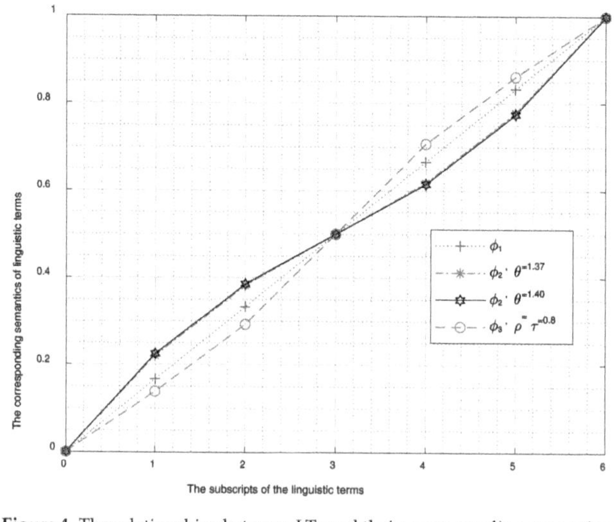

Figure 4. The relationships between LTs and their corresponding semantics under different situations.

2.3. *Fermatean Fuzzy Linguistic Set*

Definition 5 ([41]). *A FFS $\hat{F}$ in a fixed set $X = \{x_1, x_2, \ldots, x_n\}$ is given by*

$$\hat{F} = \{\langle x_j, \xi_{\hat{F}}(x_j), \psi_{\hat{F}}(x_j)\rangle | x_j \in X\} \tag{6}$$

where $\xi_{\hat{F}}(x_j)$ and $\psi_{\hat{F}}(x_j)$ denote, respectively, the DM and DNM of $x_j \in X$ to the set $\hat{F}$, with the conditions $\xi_{\hat{F}} : X \to [0,1]$, $\psi_{\hat{F}} : X \to [0,1]$ and $0 \leq (\xi_{\hat{F}}(x_j))^3 + (\psi_{\hat{F}}(x_j))^3 \leq 1 \; \forall \, x \in X$.

For all $x_j \in X$, the corresponding degree of hesitancy (DH) is defined as $\zeta_{\hat{F}}(x_j) = \sqrt[3]{1 - (\xi_{\hat{F}}(x_j))^3 - (\psi_{\hat{F}}(x_j))^3}$. In the interest of simplicity, Senapati and Yager [41] called the pair $\langle \xi_{\hat{F}}(x_j), \psi_{\hat{F}}(x_j)\rangle$ a FFLN and denoted by $\alpha = \langle \xi_\alpha, \psi_\alpha \rangle$, which satisfies the conditions $\xi_\alpha \in [0,1]$, $\psi_\alpha \in [0,1]$ and $0 \leq (\xi_\alpha)^3 + (\psi_\alpha)^3 \leq 1$.

Definition 6 ([53]). *Let $X = \{x_1, x_2, \ldots, x_n\}$ be a fixed set and $\hat{L}_{[0,2t]} = \{\ell_d | \ell_0 \leq \ell_d \leq \ell_{2t}, d \in [0,2t]\}$ be an extended continuous LTS, then a FFLS can be defined as*

$$F = \left\{ \left\langle x_j, \ell_{\sigma_F(x_j)}, \xi_F(x_j), \psi_F(x_j) \right\rangle | x_j \in X \right\} \tag{7}$$

where $\ell_{\sigma_F(x_j)} \in \hat{L}_{[0,2t]}$, $\xi_F : X \rightarrow [0,1]$ *and* $\psi_F : X \rightarrow [0,1]$, *satisfying* $0 \leq (\xi_F(x_j))^3 + (\psi_F(x_j))^3 \leq 1 \; \forall \; x_j \in X$. *The numbers* $\xi_F(x_j)$ *and* $\psi_F(x_j)$ *represent, respectively, the DM and DNM of* $x_j \in X$ *to the linguistic term* $\ell_{\sigma_F(x_j)}$. *For all* $x_j \in X$, *if* $\zeta_F(x_j) = \sqrt[3]{1 - (\xi_F(x_j))^3 - (\psi_F(x_j))^3}$, *then* $\zeta_F(x_j)$ *is called the DH of* $x_j \in X$ *to* $\ell_{\sigma_F(x_j)}$.

Note that when $\xi_F(x_j) = 1$ and $\psi_F(x_j) = 0 \; \forall \; x_j \in X$, the FFLS reduces to the LTS. In particular, when X has only one element, the FFLS is reduced into $\left\langle \ell_{\sigma_F(x)}, \xi_F(x), \psi_F(x) \right\rangle$. For convenience, the triplet $\left\langle \ell_{\sigma_F(x)}, \xi_F(x), \psi_F(x) \right\rangle$ is called a FFLN and simply denoted by $\wp = \left\langle \ell_{\sigma(\wp)}, \xi_\wp, \psi_\wp \right\rangle$, which meets the conditions $\xi_\wp \in [0,1], \psi_\wp \in [0,1]$ and $0 \leq (\xi_\wp)^3 + (\psi_\wp)^3 \leq 1$. We indicate the collection of all FFLNs by Ω.

Definition 7 ([54]). *Let* $\hat{L}_{[0,2t]}$ *be an extended continuous LTS,* $\wp = \left\langle \ell_{\sigma(\wp)}, \xi_\wp, \psi_\wp \right\rangle$, $\wp_1 = \left\langle \ell_{\sigma(\wp_1)}, \xi_{\wp_1}, \psi_{\wp_1} \right\rangle$ *and* $\wp_2 = \left\langle \ell_{\sigma(\wp_2)}, \xi_{\wp_2}, \psi_{\wp_2} \right\rangle$ *be any three FFLNs, where* $\ell_{\sigma(\wp)}, \ell_{\sigma(\wp_1)}, \ell_{\sigma(\wp_2)} \in \hat{L}_{[0,2t]}$. *Further, consider that* φ^* *and* φ^{*-1} *denote a linguistic scale function and its inverse function, respectively. Then, by using the LSF, some algebraic operational laws on FFLNs were defined by Liu et al. [54] as follows:*

(i). $\wp_1 \oplus \wp_2 = \left\langle \varphi^{*-1}\left(\varphi^*\left(\ell_{\sigma(\wp_1)}\right) + \varphi^*\left(\ell_{\sigma(\wp_2)}\right)\right), \sqrt[3]{\xi_{\wp_1}^3 + \xi_{\wp_2}^3 - \xi_{\wp_1}^3 \xi_{\wp_2}^3}, \psi_{\wp_1}\psi_{\wp_2} \right\rangle$;

(ii). $\wp_1 \otimes \wp_2 = \left\langle \varphi^{*-1}\left(\varphi^*\left(\ell_{\sigma(\wp_1)}\right)\varphi^*\left(\ell_{\sigma(\wp_2)}\right)\right), \xi_{\wp_1}\xi_{\wp_2}, \sqrt[3]{\psi_{\wp_1}^3 + \psi_{\wp_2}^3 - \psi_{\wp_1}^3 \psi_{\wp_2}^3} \right\rangle$;

(iii). $\lambda\wp = \left\langle \varphi^{*-1}\left(\lambda\varphi^*\left(\ell_{\sigma(\wp)}\right)\right), \sqrt[3]{1 - (1 - \xi_\wp^3)^\lambda}, (\psi_\wp)^\lambda \right\rangle$, $\lambda \geq 0$;

(iv). $\wp^\lambda = \left\langle \varphi^{*-1}\left(\left(\varphi^*\left(\ell_{\sigma(\wp)}\right)\right)^\lambda\right), (\xi_\wp)^\lambda, \sqrt[3]{1 - (1 - \psi_\wp^3)^\lambda} \right\rangle$, $\lambda \geq 0$;

(v). $neg(\wp) = \left\langle \varphi^{*-1}\left(\varphi^*(\ell_{2t}) - \varphi^*\left(\ell_{\sigma(\wp)}\right)\right), \psi_\wp, \xi_\wp \right\rangle$.

Definition 8 ([54]). *Let* $\wp = \left\langle \ell_{\sigma(\wp)}, \xi_\wp, \psi_\wp \right\rangle$ *be a FFLN and* φ^* *be a LSF, the score and accuracy functions of* $\wp$ *are defined as*

$$\mathfrak{S}(\wp) = \varphi^*\left(\ell_{\sigma(\wp)}\right) \times \left(\frac{\xi_\wp^3 + 1 - \psi_\wp^3}{2}\right) \text{ and } \mathfrak{A}(\wp) = \varphi^*\left(\ell_{\sigma(\wp)}\right) \times \left(\xi_\wp^3 + \psi_\wp^3\right) \quad (8)$$

For any two FFLNs $\wp_1 = \left\langle \ell_{\sigma(\wp_1)}, \xi_{\wp_1}, \psi_{\wp_1} \right\rangle$ and $\wp_2 = \left\langle \ell_{\sigma(\wp_2)}, \xi_{\wp_2}, \psi_{\wp_2} \right\rangle$, the comparison rules between $\wp_1$ and $\wp_2$ are given as

(i). If $\mathfrak{S}(\wp_1) > \mathfrak{S}(\wp_2)$, then $\wp_1 \succ \wp_2$;

(ii). If $\mathfrak{S}(\wp_1) = \mathfrak{S}(\wp_2)$, then: (a) $\mathfrak{A}(\wp_1) > \mathfrak{A}(\wp_2)$, then $\wp_1 \succ \wp_2$; (b) $\mathfrak{A}(\wp_1) = \mathfrak{A}(\wp_2)$, then $\wp_1 = \wp_2$.

Some shortcomings of the operational laws given in Definition 7

Here, we consider a numerical example in order to show the shortcomings of the operations on FFLNs defined by Liu et al. [54].

Example 3. *Let* $\hat{L}_{[0,6]} = \{\ell_d | d \in [0,6]\}$ *be an extended continuous LTS,* $\wp_1 = \langle \ell_3, 0.3, 0.6 \rangle$, $\wp_2 = \langle \ell_5, 0.5, 0.7 \rangle$ $\wp_3 = \langle \ell_1, 0, 0.5 \rangle$, $\wp_4 = \langle \ell_3, 0, 0.7 \rangle$, $\wp_5 = \langle \ell_4, 0.8, 0 \rangle$ *and* $\wp_6 = \langle \ell_6, 0.6, 0 \rangle$ *be six FFLNs. If* $\varphi^*\left(\ell_{\sigma(a)}\right) = \varphi_2^*\left(\ell_{\sigma(a)}\right) (\theta = 1.4)$ *and* $\lambda = 4$, *then according to the operational laws given in Definition 7, we have*

(i). $\wp_1 \oplus \wp_2 = \left\langle \varphi_2^{*-1}(\varphi_2^*(\ell_3) + \varphi_2^*(\ell_5)), \sqrt[3]{0.3^3 + 0.5^3 - 0.3^3 0.5^3}, 0.6 \times 0.7 \right\rangle = \langle \varphi_2^{*-1}(0.5000 + 0.7752), 0.5279, 0.4200 \rangle = \langle \varphi_2^{*-1}(1.2752), 0.5279, 0.4200 \rangle$. *Here, we* *see that* $\varphi_2^*(\ell_3) + \varphi_2^*(\ell_5) = 1.2752 > 1$, *therefore*, $\varphi_2^{*-1}(\varphi_2^*(\ell_3) + \varphi_2^*(\ell_5)) = \varphi_2^{*-1}(1.2752)$ is undefined.

(ii). $\wp_1 \otimes \wp_3 = \left\langle \varphi_2^{*-1}(\varphi_2^*(\ell_3)\varphi_2^*(\ell_1)), 0.3 \times 0, \sqrt[3]{0.6^3 + 0.5^3 - 0.6^3 \times 0.5^3} \right\rangle$

$$= \left\langle \varphi_2^{*-1}(0.5000 \times 0.2248), 0.0000, 0.6797 \right\rangle = \langle \ell_{0.4619}, 0.0000, 0.6797 \rangle \quad (9)$$

and

$$\begin{aligned} \wp_1 \otimes \wp_4 &= \left\langle \varphi_2^{*-1}(\varphi_2^*(\ell_3)\varphi_2^*(\ell_3)), 0.3 \times 0, \sqrt[3]{0.6^3 + 0.7^3 - 0.6^3 \times 0.7^3} \right\rangle \\ &= \langle \varphi_2^{*-1}(0.5000 + 0.5000), 0.0000, 0.7856 \rangle = \langle \ell_6, 0.0000, 0.7856 \rangle \end{aligned} \quad (10)$$

From Equations (9) and (10), it is clear that there is no effect of nonmembership values on the membership values of $\wp_1 \otimes \wp_3$ *and* $\wp_1 \otimes \wp_4$. *In general, if* $\wp_1 = \left\langle \ell_{\sigma(\wp_1)}, \xi_{\wp_1}, \psi_{\wp_1} \right\rangle$, $\wp_2 = \left\langle \ell_{\sigma(\wp_2)}, \xi_{\wp_2}, \psi_{\wp_2} \right\rangle$ *and* $\wp_3 = \left\langle \ell_{\sigma(\wp_3)}, \xi_{\wp_3}, \psi_{\wp_3} \right\rangle$ *are three different FFLNs satisfying,* $\xi_{\wp_2} = \xi_{\wp_3} = 0, \psi_{\wp_2} \neq \psi_{\wp_3}$ *then we always obtain* $\xi_{\wp_1 \otimes \wp_2} = \xi_{\wp_1 \otimes \wp_3} = 0$. *This outcome does not match our intuition.*

(iii). $\wp_2 \oplus \wp_5 = \left\langle \varphi_2^{*-1}(\varphi_2^*(\ell_5) + \varphi_2^*(\ell_4)), \sqrt[3]{0.5^3 + 0.8^3 - 0.5^3 \times 0.8^3}, 0.7 \times 0, \right\rangle$

$$= \left\langle \varphi_2^{*-1}(0.7752 + 0.6147), 0.8306, 0.0000 \right\rangle = \left\langle \varphi_2^{*-1}(1.3899), 0.8306, 0.0000 \right\rangle \quad (11)$$

and

$$\begin{aligned} &\wp_2 \oplus \wp_6 = \left\langle \varphi_2^{*-1}(\varphi_2^*(\ell_5) + \varphi_2^*(\ell_6)), \sqrt[3]{0.5^3 + 0.6^3 - 0.5^3 \times 0.6^3}, 0.7 \times 0 \right\rangle \\ &= \langle \varphi_2^{*-1}(0.7752 + 1.0000), 0.6797, 0.0000 \rangle = \langle \varphi_2^{*-1}(1.7752), 0.6797, 0.0000 \rangle \end{aligned} \quad (12)$$

The obtained resulting values in Equations (11) and (12) indicate that there is no effect of the membership values on the nonmembership values of $\wp_2 \oplus \wp_5$ *and* $\wp_2 \oplus \wp_6$. *In general, if* $\wp_1 = \left\langle \ell_{\sigma(\wp_1)}, \xi_{\wp_1}, \psi_{\wp_1} \right\rangle$, $\wp_2 = \left\langle \ell_{\sigma(\wp_2)}, \xi_{\wp_2}, \psi_{\wp_2} \right\rangle$ *and* $\wp_3 = \left\langle \ell_{\sigma(\wp_3)}, \xi_{\wp_3}, \psi_{\wp_3} \right\rangle$ *are three different FFLNs satisfying,* $\xi_{\wp_2} \neq \xi_{\wp_3}, \psi_{\wp_2} = \psi_{\wp_3} = 0$ *then we always obtain* $\psi_{\wp_1 \oplus \wp_2} = \psi_{\wp_1 \oplus \wp_3} = 0$. *Additionally,* $\varphi_2^{*-1}(1.3899)$ *and* $\varphi_2^{*-1}(1.7752)$ *are undefined.*

$$4\wp_1 = \left\langle \varphi_2^{*-1}(4 \times \varphi_2^*(\ell_3)), \sqrt[3]{1 - (1 - 0.3^3)^4}, (0.6)^4 \right\rangle = \left\langle \varphi_2^{*-1}(2.0000), 0.4698, 0.1296 \right\rangle, \quad (13)$$

$$4\wp_2 = \left\langle \varphi_2^{*-1}(4 \times \varphi_2^*(\ell_5)), \sqrt[3]{1 - (1 - 0.5^3)^4}, (0.7)^4 \right\rangle = \left\langle \varphi_2^{*-1}(3.1008), 0.7452, 0.2401 \right\rangle \quad (14)$$

From Equations (13) and (14), we can see that $\varphi_2^{*-1}(2.0000)$ *and* $\varphi_2^{*-1}(3.1008)$ *are undefined because here* $\kappa_d > 1$. Hence, $4\wp_1$ *and* $4\wp_2$ *are not FFLNs.*

Based on the above analysis, we conclude that the operational laws defined in Definition 7 are not suitable for FFLNs. Therefore, in order to nullify the above shortcomings, it is necessary to modify these operational laws. In the next section, we first define some new modified operational laws for FFLNs based on LSF and discuss their properties in detail. Then, we introduce some aggregation operators for aggregating different FFLNs.

3. Fermatean Fuzzy Aggregation Operators

3.1. Improved Operational Laws for FFLNs Based on LSF

Here, we define some improved operational laws for FFLNs, which overcome the shortcomings of the existing operations.

Definition 9. *Let* $\hat{L}_{[0,2t]}$ *be an extended continuous LTS,* $\wp = \left\langle \ell_{\sigma(\wp)}, \xi_{\wp}, \psi_{\wp} \right\rangle$, $\wp_1 = \left\langle \ell_{\sigma(\wp_1)}, \xi_{\wp_1}, \psi_{\wp_1} \right\rangle$ *and* $\wp_2 = \left\langle s_{\sigma(\wp_2)}, \xi_{\wp_2}, \psi_{\wp_2} \right\rangle$ *be three FFLNs, where* $\ell_{\sigma(\wp)}, \ell_{\sigma(\wp_1)}, \ell_{\sigma(\wp_2)}$

$\in \hat{L}_{[0,2t]}$. *Further, consider that* φ^* and φ^{*-1} *denote a linguistic scale function and its inverse function, respectively. The improved operational laws between them based on LSFs are defined as*

(i) $\wp_1 \widetilde{\oplus} \wp_2 = \left\langle \varphi^{*-1}\left(\varphi^*\left(\ell_{\sigma(\wp_1)}\right) + \varphi^*\left(\ell_{\sigma(\wp_2)}\right) - \varphi^*\left(\ell_{\sigma(\wp_1)}\right)\varphi^*\left(\ell_{\sigma(\wp_2)}\right)\right), \sqrt[3]{\xi_{\wp_1}^3 + \xi_{\wp_2}^3 - \xi_{\wp_1}^3\xi_{\wp_2}^3}, \sqrt[3]{\psi_{\wp_1}^3 + \psi_{\wp_2}^3 - \psi_{\wp_1}^3\psi_{\wp_2}^3 - \psi_{\wp_1}^3\xi_{\wp_2}^3 - \xi_{\wp_1}^3\psi_{\wp_2}^3} \right\rangle$
$= \left\langle \varphi^{*-1}\left(1 - \left(1 - \varphi^*\left(\ell_{\sigma(\wp_1)}\right)\right)\left(1 - \varphi^*\left(\ell_{\sigma(\wp_2)}\right)\right)\right), \sqrt[3]{1 - (1 - \xi_{\wp_1}^3)(1 - \xi_{\wp_2}^3)}, \sqrt[3]{(1 - \xi_{\wp_1}^3)(1 - \xi_{\wp_2}^3) - (1 - (\xi_{\wp_1}^3 + \psi_{\wp_1}^3))(1 - (\xi_{\wp_2}^3 + \psi_{\wp_2}^3))} \right\rangle$;

(ii) $\wp_1 \widetilde{\otimes} \wp_2 = \left\langle \varphi^{*-1}\left(\varphi^*\left(\ell_{\sigma(\wp_1)}\right)\varphi^*\left(\ell_{\sigma(\wp_2)}\right)\right), \sqrt[3]{\xi_{\wp_1}^3 + \xi_{\wp_2}^3 - \xi_{\wp_1}^3\xi_{\wp_2}^3 - \xi_{\wp_1}^3\psi_{\wp_2}^3 - \psi_{\wp_1}^3\xi_{\wp_2}^3}, \sqrt[3]{\psi_{\wp_1}^3 + \psi_{\wp_2}^3 - \psi_{\wp_1}^3\psi_{\wp_2}^3} \right\rangle$
$= \left\langle \varphi^{*-1}\left(\varphi^*\left(\ell_{\sigma(\wp_1)}\right)\varphi^*\left(\ell_{\sigma(\wp_2)}\right)\right), \sqrt[3]{(1 - \psi_{\wp_1}^3)(1 - \psi_{\wp_2}^3) - (1 - (\xi_{\wp_1}^3 + \psi_{\wp_1}^3))(1 - (\xi_{\wp_2}^3 + \psi_{\wp_2}^3))}, \sqrt[3]{1 - (1 - \psi_{\wp_1}^3)(1 - \psi_{\wp_2}^3)} \right\rangle$;

(iii) $\lambda \widetilde{*} \wp = \left\langle \varphi^{*-1}\left(1 - \left(1 - \varphi^*\left(\ell_{\sigma(\wp)}\right)\right)^\lambda\right), \sqrt[3]{1 - (1 - \xi_\wp^3)^\lambda}, \sqrt[3]{(1 - \xi_\wp^3)^\lambda - (1 - (\xi_\wp^3 + \psi_\wp^3))^\lambda} \right\rangle$, $\lambda > 0$;

(iv) $\wp \widetilde{\wedge} \lambda = \left\langle \varphi^{*-1}\left(\left(\varphi^*\left(\ell_{\sigma(\wp)}\right)\right)^\lambda\right), \sqrt[3]{(1 - \psi_\wp^3)^\lambda - (1 - (\xi_\wp^3 + \psi_\wp^3))^\lambda}, \sqrt[3]{1 - (1 - \psi_\wp^3)^\lambda} \right\rangle$, $\lambda > 0$.

Theorem 1. *The numbers* $\wp_1 \widetilde{\oplus} \wp_2$, $\wp_1 \widetilde{\otimes} \wp_2$, $\lambda \widetilde{*} \wp$, *and* $\wp \widetilde{\wedge} \lambda$ *are also FFLNs.*

Proof. Here, we shall prove only $\wp_1 \widetilde{\oplus} \wp_2$ and $\lambda \widetilde{*} \wp$ are FFLNs, while others can be shown similarly. Since $\wp_i = \left\langle \ell_{\sigma(\wp_i)}, \xi_{\wp_i}, \psi_{\wp_i} \right\rangle (i = 1, 2)$ are two FFLNs, where $\ell_{\sigma(\wp_i)} \in \hat{L}_{[0,2t]}$, $\xi_{\wp_i}, \psi_{\wp_i} \in [0, 1]$ and $0 \le \xi_{\wp_i}^3 + \psi_{\wp_i}^3 \le 1$, $i = 1, 2$. For $\ell_{\sigma(\wp_1)}, \ell_{\sigma(\wp_2)} \in \hat{L}_{[0,2t]}$, based on the definition of the LSFs, we know $0 \le \varphi^*\left(\ell_{\sigma(\wp_1)}\right), \varphi^*\left(\ell_{\sigma(\wp_2)}\right) \le 1$. Then, $0 \le 1 - \left(1 - \varphi^*\left(\ell_{\sigma(\wp_1)}\right)\right)\left(1 - \varphi^*\left(\ell_{\sigma(\wp_2)}\right)\right) \le 1 \Rightarrow \varphi^{*-1}\left(1 - \left(1 - \varphi^*\left(\ell_{\sigma(\wp_1)}\right)\right)\left(1 - \varphi^*\left(\ell_{\sigma(\wp_2)}\right)\right)\right) \in \hat{L}_{[0,2t]}$. Now $0 \le \xi_{\wp_1}, \xi_{\wp_2} \le 1$, which implies $0 \le (1 - \xi_{\wp_1}^3)(1 - \xi_{\wp_2}^3) \le 1 \Leftrightarrow 0 \le \sqrt[3]{1 - (1 - \xi_{\wp_1}^3)(1 - \xi_{\wp_2}^3)} \le 1$. Moreover, because $1 - \xi_{\wp_1}^3 \ge 1 - \xi_{\wp_1}^3 - \psi_{\wp_1}^3$ and $1 - \xi_{\wp_2}^3 \ge 1 - \xi_{\wp_2}^3 - \psi_{\wp_2}^3$, then $0 \le \sqrt[3]{(1 - \xi_{\wp_1}^3)(1 - \xi_{\wp_2}^3) - (1 - (\xi_{\wp_1}^3 + \psi_{\wp_1}^3))(1 - (\xi_{\wp_2}^3 + \psi_{\wp_2}^3))} \le 1$.

Further $\left(\sqrt[3]{1 - \begin{pmatrix} (1 - \xi_{\wp_1}^3) \\ (1 - \xi_{\wp_2}^3) \end{pmatrix}}\right)^3 + \left(\sqrt[3]{\begin{pmatrix} (1 - \xi_{\wp_1}^3) \\ (1 - \xi_{\wp_2}^3) \end{pmatrix} - \begin{pmatrix} (1 - (\xi_{\wp_1}^3 + \psi_{\wp_1}^3)) \\ (1 - (\xi_{\wp_2}^3 + \psi_{\wp_2}^3)) \end{pmatrix}}\right)^3$ $= 1 - (1 - (\xi_{\wp_1}^3 + \psi_{\wp_1}^3))(1 - (\xi_{\wp_2}^3 + \psi_{\wp_2}^3)) \le 1$. Thus, it shows that the $a_1 \widetilde{\oplus} a_2$ is a FFLN.

For any $\lambda > 0$, $0 \le 1 - \left(1 - \varphi^*\left(\ell_{\sigma(\wp)}\right)\right)^\lambda \le 1$, which gives $\varphi^{*-1}\left(1 - \left(1 - \varphi^*\left(\ell_{\sigma(\wp)}\right)\right)^\lambda\right) \in \hat{L}_{[0,2t]}$. Additionally, $0 \le \xi_{\wp_1}, \xi_{\wp_2}, \psi_{\wp_1}, \psi_{\wp_2} \le 1$, which implies $0 \le \sqrt[3]{1 - (1 - \xi_\wp^3)^\lambda} \le 1$ and $0 \le \sqrt[3]{(1 - \xi_\wp^3)^\lambda - (1 - (\xi_\wp^3 + \psi_\wp^3))^\lambda} \le 1$.

Further $\left(\sqrt[3]{1 - (1 - \xi_\wp^3)^\lambda}\right)^3 + \left(\sqrt[3]{(1 - \xi_\wp^3)^\lambda - (1 - (\xi_\wp^3 + \psi_\wp^3))^\lambda}\right)^3$ $= 1 - (1 - (\xi_\wp^3 + \psi_\wp^3))^\lambda \le 1$. Hence, $\lambda \widetilde{*} \wp$ is also a FFLN.

This completes the proof. □

Example 4. *Let* $\hat{L}_{[0,6]} = \{\ell_d | d \in [0, 6]\}$ *be an extended continuous LTS,* $\wp = \langle \ell_2, 0.4, 0.5 \rangle$, $\wp_1 = \langle \ell_3, 0.3, 0.6 \rangle$, $\wp_2 = \langle \ell_5, 0.5, 0.7 \rangle$ *be three FFLNs and* $\lambda = 5$. *Then, according to the modified operation laws, we obtained the following results as shown in Table 1:*

Table 1. Values of different operations.

Operation	$\varphi^* = \varphi_1^*$	$\varphi^* = \varphi_2^*$ and $\theta = 1.4$	$\varphi^* = \varphi_3^*$ and $\rho = \tau = 0.8$
$\wp_1 \widetilde{\oplus} \wp_2$	$\langle \ell_{5.4996}, 0.5297, 0.7655 \rangle$	$\langle \ell_{5.5418}, 0.5297, 0.7655 \rangle$	$\langle \ell_{5.4896}, 0.5297, 0.7655 \rangle$
$\wp_1 \widetilde{\otimes} \wp_2$	$\langle \ell_{2.5002}, 0.4826, 0.7856 \rangle$	$\langle \ell_{2.0169}, 0.4826, 0.7856 \rangle$	$\langle \ell_{2.7468}, 0.4826, 0.7856 \rangle$
$\lambda \widetilde{*} \wp$	$\langle \ell_{5.2098}, 0.6149, 0.6945 \rangle$	$\langle \ell_{5.6483}, 0.6149, 0.6945 \rangle$	$\langle \ell_{4.7348}, 0.6149, 0.6945 \rangle$
$\wp \widetilde{\wedge} \lambda$	$\langle \ell_{0.0246}, 0.5355, 0.7452 \rangle$	$\langle \ell_{0.0323}, 0.5355, 0.7452 \rangle$	$\langle \ell_{0.0157}, 0.5355, 0.7452 \rangle$

Further, if we consider Example 3 again and utilize the improved operational laws summarized in Definition 9, Table 2 presents the obtained results.

Table 2. Calculation results of Example 3 based on the proposed operational laws.

Operation	$\varphi^* = \varphi_2^*$ and $\theta = 1.4$
$\wp_1 \widetilde{\oplus} \wp_2$	$\langle \ell_{5.5418}, 0.5279, 0.7655 \rangle$
$\wp_1 \widetilde{\otimes} \wp_3$	$\langle \ell_{0.4582}, 0.2869, 0.6797 \rangle$
$\wp_1 \widetilde{\otimes} \wp_4$	$\langle \ell_{1.1365}, 0.2608, 0.7856 \rangle$
$\wp_2 \widetilde{\oplus} \wp_5$	$\langle \ell_{5.6534}, 0.8306, 0.5511 \rangle$
$\wp_2 \widetilde{\oplus} \wp_6$	$\langle \ell_{6.0000}, 0.6797, 0.6455 \rangle$
$4 \widetilde{*} \wp_1$	$\langle \ell_{5.7540}, 0.4698, 0.8281 \rangle$
$4 \widetilde{*} \wp_2$	$\langle \ell_{5.9902}, 0.7452, 0.7969 \rangle$

The obtained calculation results verify that the improved operational laws are more reasonable and realistic as per our intuition.

Theorem 2. *Let $\hat{L}_{[0,2t]}$ be an extended continuous LTS, and $\wp_1 = \left\langle \ell_{\sigma(\wp_1)}, \xi_{\wp_1}, \psi_{\wp_1} \right\rangle$, $\wp_2 = \left\langle \ell_{\sigma(\wp_2)}, \xi_{\wp_2}, \psi_{\wp_2} \right\rangle$ and $\wp_3 = \left\langle \ell_{\sigma(\wp_3)}, \xi_{\wp_3}, \psi_{\wp_3} \right\rangle$ be three FFLNs, where $\ell_{\sigma(\wp_1)}, \ell_{\sigma(\wp_2)}, \ell_{\sigma(\wp_3)} \in \hat{L}_{[0,2t]}$. The following results hold:*

(i). $\wp_1 \widetilde{\oplus} \wp_2 = \wp_2 \widetilde{\oplus} \wp_1$;
(ii). $\wp_1 \widetilde{\otimes} \wp_2 = \wp_2 \widetilde{\otimes} \wp_1$;
(iii). $(\wp_1 \widetilde{\oplus} \wp_2) \widetilde{\oplus} \wp_3 = \wp_1 \widetilde{\oplus} (\wp_2 \widetilde{\oplus} \wp_3)$;
(iv). $(\wp_1 \widetilde{\otimes} \wp_2) \widetilde{\otimes} \wp_3 = \wp_1 \widetilde{\otimes} (\wp_2 \widetilde{\otimes} \wp_3)$.

Proof. The results follow directly from Definition 9, so we omit the proofs of them. □

Theorem 3. *Let $\hat{L}_{[0,2t]}$ be an extended continuous LTS, $\wp = \left\langle \ell_{\sigma(\wp)}, \xi_{\wp}, \psi_{\wp} \right\rangle$ $\wp_1 = \left\langle \ell_{\sigma(\wp_1)}, \xi_{\wp_1}, \psi_{\wp_1} \right\rangle$, and $\wp_2 = \left\langle \ell_{\sigma(\wp_2)}, \xi_{\wp_2}, \psi_{\wp_2} \right\rangle$ be three FFLNs and $\lambda, \lambda_1, \lambda_2 > 0$, where $\ell_{\sigma(\wp)}, \ell_{\sigma(\wp_2)}, \ell_{\sigma(\wp_2)} \in \hat{L}_{[0,2t]}$, then*

(i). $(\lambda \widetilde{*} \wp_1) \widetilde{\oplus} (\lambda \widetilde{*} \wp_2) = \lambda \widetilde{*} (\wp_1 \widetilde{\oplus} \wp_2)$;
(ii). $(\lambda_1 \widetilde{*} \wp) \widetilde{\oplus} (\lambda_2 \hat{*} \wp) = (\lambda_1 + \lambda_2) \widetilde{*} \wp$
(iii). $\left(\wp_1 \widetilde{\wedge} \lambda\right) \widetilde{\otimes} \left(\wp_2 \widetilde{\wedge} \lambda\right) = (\wp_1 \widetilde{\otimes} \wp_2) \widetilde{\wedge} \lambda$;
(iv). $\left(\wp \widetilde{\wedge} \lambda_1\right) \widetilde{\otimes} \left(\wp \widetilde{\wedge} \lambda_2\right) = \wp \widetilde{\wedge} (\lambda_1 + \lambda_2)$;
(v). $\lambda_1 \widetilde{*} (\lambda_2 \widetilde{*} \wp) = (\lambda_1 \lambda_2) \widetilde{*} \wp$;
(vi). $\left(\wp \widetilde{\wedge} \lambda_1\right) \widetilde{\wedge} \lambda_2 = \wp \widetilde{\wedge} (\lambda_1 \lambda_2)$.
(vii). $neg(\wp_1 \widetilde{\oplus} \wp_2) = neg(\wp_1) \widetilde{\otimes} neg(\wp_2)$
(viii). $neg(\wp_1 \widetilde{\otimes} \wp_2) = neg(\wp_1) \widetilde{\oplus} neg(\wp_2)$;
(ix). $(neg(\wp)) \widetilde{\wedge} \lambda = neg(\lambda \widetilde{*} \wp)$;
(x). $\lambda \widetilde{*} (neg(\wp)) = neg\left(\wp \widetilde{\wedge} \lambda\right)$.

Proof. Here, we only prove the parts (i), (iii), (v), (vii), and (ix); the others can be proved similarly.

(i) From Definition 9, we have

$$\lambda \widetilde{*} \wp_1 = \left\langle \varphi^{*-1}\left(1 - \left(1 - \varphi^*\left(\ell_{\sigma(\wp_1)}\right)\right)^{\lambda}\right), \sqrt[3]{1 - (1 - \xi_{\wp_1}^3)^{\lambda}}, \sqrt[3]{(1 - \xi_{\wp_1}^3)^{\lambda} - (1 - (\xi_{\wp_1}^3 + \psi_{\wp_1}^3))^{\lambda}} \right\rangle, \tag{15}$$

and

$$\lambda \widetilde{*} \wp_2 = \left\langle \varphi^{*-1}\left(1 - \left(1 - \varphi^*\left(\ell_{\sigma(\wp_2)}\right)\right)^{\lambda}\right), \sqrt[3]{1 - (1 - \xi_{\wp_2}^3)^{\lambda}}, \sqrt[3]{(1 - \xi_{\wp_2}^3)^{\lambda} - (1 - (\xi_{\wp_2}^3 + \psi_{\wp_2}^3))^{\lambda}} \right\rangle, \tag{16}$$

Using Equations (15) and (16), we obtain

$$
\begin{aligned}
&(\lambda\tilde{*}\wp_1)\tilde{\oplus}(\lambda\tilde{*}\wp_2)\\
&=\left\langle\begin{array}{c}
\varphi^{*-1}\left(\begin{array}{c}1-\left(1-\varphi^*\left(\varphi^{*-1}\left(1-\left(1-\varphi^*\left(\ell_{\sigma(\wp_1)}\right)\right)^{\lambda}\right)\right)\right)\\ \left(1-\varphi^*\left(\varphi^{*-1}\left(1-\left(1-\varphi^*\left(\ell_{\sigma(\wp_2)}\right)\right)^{\lambda}\right)\right)\right)\end{array}\right), \sqrt[3]{1-\left(1-\left(\sqrt[3]{1-(1-\xi^3_{\wp_1})^{\lambda}}\right)^3\right)\left(1-\left(\sqrt[3]{1-(1-\xi^3_{\wp_1})^{\lambda}}\right)^3\right)},\\
\sqrt[3]{\begin{array}{c}\left(1-\left(\sqrt[3]{1-(1-\xi^3_{\wp_1})^{\lambda}}\right)^3\right)\left(1-\left(\sqrt[3]{1-(1-\xi^3_{\wp_2})^{\lambda}}\right)^3\right)\\
-\left(1-\left(\left(\sqrt[3]{1-(1-\xi^3_{\wp_1})^{\lambda}}\right)^3+\left(\sqrt[3]{(1-\xi^3_{\wp_1})^{\lambda}-(1-(\xi^3_{\wp_1}+\psi^3_{\wp_1}))^{\lambda}}\right)^3\right)\right)\\
\left(1-\left(\left(\sqrt[3]{1-(1-\xi^3_{\wp_2})^{\lambda}}\right)^3+\left(\sqrt[3]{(1-\xi^3_{\wp_2})^{\lambda}-(1-(\xi^3_{\wp_2}+\psi^3_{\wp_2}))^{\lambda}}\right)^3\right)\right)\end{array}}
\end{array}\right\rangle\\
&=\left\langle\begin{array}{c}\varphi^{*-1}\left(1-\left(\left(1-\varphi^*\left(\ell_{\sigma(\wp_1)}\right)\right)\left(1-\varphi^*\left(\ell_{\sigma(\wp_2)}\right)\right)\right)^{\lambda}\right), \sqrt[3]{1-((1-\xi^3_{\wp_1})(1-\xi^3_{\wp_2}))^{\lambda}},\\
\sqrt[3]{((1-\xi^3_{\wp_1})(1-\xi^3_{\wp_2}))^{\lambda}-((1-(\xi^3_{\wp_1}+\psi^3_{\wp_1}))(1-(\xi^3_{\wp_2}+\psi^3_{\wp_2})))^{\lambda}}\end{array}\right\rangle=\lambda\tilde{*}(\wp_1\tilde{\oplus}\wp_2).
\end{aligned}
$$

(iii) According to Definition 9, we have

$$
\wp_1\tilde{\wedge}\lambda=\left\langle\varphi^{*-1}\left(\left(\varphi^*\left(\ell_{\sigma(\wp_1)}\right)\right)^{\lambda}\right), \sqrt[3]{(1-\psi^3_{\wp_1})^{\lambda}-(1-(\xi^3_{\wp_1}+\psi^3_{\wp_1}))^{\lambda}}, \sqrt[3]{1-(1-\psi^3_{\wp_1})^{\lambda}}\right\rangle, \tag{17}
$$

and

$$
\wp_2\tilde{\wedge}\lambda=\left\langle\varphi^{*-1}\left(\left(\varphi^*\left(\ell_{\sigma(\wp_2)}\right)\right)^{\lambda}\right), \sqrt[3]{(1-\psi^3_{\wp_2})^{\lambda}-(1-(\xi^3_{\wp_2}+\psi^3_{\wp_2}))^{\lambda}}, \sqrt[3]{1-(1-\psi^3_{\wp_2})^{\lambda}}\right\rangle. \tag{18}
$$

By Equations (17) and (18), we obtain

$$
\begin{aligned}
&\left(\wp_1\tilde{\wedge}\lambda\right)\tilde{\otimes}\left(\wp_2\tilde{\wedge}\lambda\right)=\left\langle\begin{array}{c}
\varphi^{*-1}\left(\varphi^*\left(\varphi^{*-1}\left(\left(\varphi^*\left(\ell_{\sigma(\wp_1)}\right)\right)^{\lambda}\right)\right)\varphi^*\left(\varphi^{*-1}\left(\left(\varphi^*\left(\ell_{\sigma(\wp_2)}\right)\right)^{\lambda}\right)\right)\right),\\
\sqrt[3]{\left(\begin{array}{c}\left(1-\left(\sqrt[3]{1-(1-\psi^3_{\wp_1})^{\lambda}}\right)^3\right)\\ \left(1-\left(\sqrt[3]{1-(1-\psi^3_{\wp_2})^{\lambda}}\right)^3\right)\end{array}\right)-\left(\begin{array}{c}\left(1-\left(\begin{array}{c}\left(\sqrt[3]{(1-\psi^3_{\wp_1})^{\lambda}-(1-(\xi^3_{\wp_1}+\psi^3_{\wp_1}))^{\lambda}}\right)^3\\ +\left(\sqrt[3]{1-(1-\psi^3_{\wp_1})^{\lambda}}\right)^3\end{array}\right)\right)\\ \left(1-\left(\begin{array}{c}\left(\sqrt[3]{(1-\psi^3_{\wp_2})^{\lambda}-(1-(\xi^3_{\wp_2}+\psi^3_{\wp_2}))^{\lambda}}\right)^3\\ +\left(\sqrt[3]{1-(1-\psi^3_{\wp_2})^{\lambda}}\right)^3\end{array}\right)\right)\end{array}\right)},\\
\sqrt[3]{1-\left(1-\left(\sqrt[3]{1-(1-\psi^3_{\wp_1})^{\lambda}}\right)^3\right)\left(1-\left(\sqrt[3]{1-(1-\psi^3_{\wp_2})^{\lambda}}\right)^3\right)}
\end{array}\right\rangle\\
&=\left\langle\begin{array}{c}\varphi^{*-1}\left(\left(\varphi^*\left(\ell_{\sigma(\wp_1)}\right)\varphi^*\left(\ell_{\sigma(\wp_2)}\right)\right)^{\lambda}\right), \sqrt[3]{((1-\psi^3_{\wp_1})(1-\psi^3_{\wp_2}))^{\lambda}-((1-(\xi^3_{\wp_1}+\psi^3_{\wp_1}))(1-(\xi^3_{\wp_2}+\psi^3_{\wp_2})))^{\lambda}},\\ \sqrt[3]{1-((1-\psi^3_{\wp_1})(1-\psi^3_{\wp_2}))^{\lambda}}\end{array}\right\rangle=(\wp_1\tilde{\otimes}\wp_2)\tilde{\wedge}\lambda.
\end{aligned}
$$

(v) For two positive real numbers λ_1 and λ_2, we have

$$
\begin{aligned}
&\lambda_1\tilde{*}(\lambda_2\tilde{*}\wp)=\lambda_1\left(\left\langle\varphi^{*-1}\left(1-\left(1-\varphi^*\left(\ell_{\sigma(\wp)}\right)\right)^{\lambda_2}\right), \sqrt[3]{1-(1-\xi^3_{\wp})^{\lambda_2}}, \sqrt[3]{(1-\xi^3_{\wp})^{\lambda_2}-(1-(\xi^3_{\wp}+\psi^3_{\wp}))^{\lambda_2}}\right\rangle\right),\\
&=\left\langle\begin{array}{c}\varphi^{*-1}\left(1-\left(1-\varphi^*\left(\varphi^{*-1}\left(1-\left(1-\varphi^*\left(\ell_{\sigma(\wp)}\right)\right)^{\lambda_2}\right)\right)\right)^{\lambda_1}\right), \sqrt[3]{1-\left(1-\left(\sqrt[3]{1-(1-\xi^3_{\wp})^{\lambda_2}}\right)^3\right)^{\lambda_1}},\\
\sqrt[3]{\left(1-\left(\sqrt[3]{1-(1-\xi^3_{\wp})^{\lambda_2}}\right)^3\right)^{\lambda_1}-\left(1-\left(\left(\sqrt[3]{1-(1-\xi^3_{\wp})^{\lambda_2}}\right)^3+\left(\sqrt[3]{(1-\xi^3_{\wp})^{\lambda_2}-(1-(\xi^3_{\wp}+\psi^3_{\wp}))^{\lambda_2}}\right)^3\right)\right)^{\lambda_1}}\end{array}\right\rangle\\
&=\left\langle\varphi^{*-1}\left(1-\left(1-\varphi^*\left(\ell_{\sigma(\wp)}\right)\right)^{\lambda_1\lambda_2}\right), \sqrt[3]{1-(1-\xi^3_{\wp})^{\lambda_1\lambda_2}}, \sqrt[3]{(1-\xi^3_{\wp})^{\lambda_1\lambda_2}-(1-(\xi^3_{\wp}+\psi^3_{\wp}))^{\lambda_1\lambda_2}}\right\rangle=(\lambda_1\lambda_2)\tilde{*}\wp
\end{aligned}
$$

(vii) From Definitions 7 and 9, we have

$$neg(\wp_1 \widetilde{\oplus} \wp_2) = \left\langle \begin{array}{c} \varphi^{*-1}\left(\varphi^*(\ell_{2t}) - \varphi^*\left(\varphi^{*-1}\left(1-\left(1-\varphi^*\left(\ell_{\sigma(\wp_1)}\right)\right)\left(1-\varphi^*\left(\ell_{\sigma(\wp_2)}\right)\right)\right)\right)\right), \\ \sqrt[3]{(1-\xi^3_{\wp_1})(1-\xi^3_{\wp_2}) - (1-(\xi^3_{\wp_1}+\psi^3_{\wp_1}))(1-(\xi^3_{\wp_2}+\psi^3_{\wp_2}))}, \sqrt[3]{1-(1-\xi^3_{\wp_1})(1-\xi^3_{\wp_2})} \end{array} \right\rangle$$

$$= \left\langle \begin{array}{c} \varphi^{*-1}\left(\varphi^*(\ell_{2t}) - \left(1-\left(1-\varphi^*\left(\ell_{\sigma(\wp_1)}\right)\right)\left(1-\varphi^*\left(\ell_{\sigma(\wp_2)}\right)\right)\right)\right), \\ \sqrt[3]{(1-\xi^3_{\wp_1})(1-\xi^3_{\wp_2}) - (1-(\xi^3_{\wp_1}+\psi^3_{\wp_1}))(1-(\xi^3_{\wp_2}+\psi^3_{\wp_2}))}, \sqrt[3]{1-(1-\xi^3_{\wp_1})(1-\xi^3_{\wp_2})} \end{array} \right\rangle$$

$$= \left\langle \begin{array}{c} \varphi^{*-1}\left(\left(\varphi^*(\ell_{2t}) - \varphi^*\left(\ell_{\sigma(\wp_1)}\right)\right)\left(\varphi^*(\ell_{2t}) - \varphi^*\left(\ell_{\sigma(\wp_2)}\right)\right)\right), \\ \sqrt[3]{(1-\xi^3_{\wp_1})(1-\xi^3_{\wp_2}) - (1-(\psi^3_{\wp_1}+\xi^3_{\wp_1}))(1-(\psi^3_{\wp_2}+\xi^3_{\wp_2}))}, \sqrt[3]{1-(1-\xi^3_{\wp_1})(1-\xi^3_{\wp_2})} \end{array} \right\rangle := neg(\wp_1)\widetilde{\otimes} neg(\wp_2)$$

(ix) $(neg(\wp))\widetilde{\wedge}\lambda = \left(\left\langle \varphi^{*-1}\left(\varphi^*(\ell_{2t}) - \varphi^*\left(\ell_{\sigma(\wp)}\right)\right), \psi_\wp, \xi_\wp \right\rangle\right)^\lambda$

$$= \left\langle \varphi^{*-1}\left(\left(\varphi^*(\ell_{2t}) - \varphi^*\left(\ell_{\sigma(\wp)}\right)\right)^\lambda\right), \sqrt[3]{(1-\xi^3_\wp)^\lambda - (1-(\xi^3_\wp+\psi^3_\wp))^\lambda}, \sqrt[3]{1-(1-\xi^3_\wp)^\lambda} \right\rangle$$
$$= \left\langle \varphi^{*-1}\left(\varphi^*(\ell_{2t}) - \varphi^*\left(\varphi^{*-1}\left(1-\left(1-\varphi^*\left(\ell_{\sigma(\wp)}\right)\right)^\lambda\right)\right)\right), \sqrt[3]{(1-\xi^3_\wp)^\lambda - (1-(\xi^3_\wp+\psi^3_\wp))^\lambda}, \sqrt[3]{1-(1-\xi^3_\wp)^\lambda} \right\rangle$$
$$= neg\left(\left\langle \varphi^{*-1}\left(1-\left(1-\varphi^*\left(\ell_{\sigma(\wp)}\right)\right)^\lambda\right), \sqrt[3]{1-(1-\xi^3_\wp)^\lambda}, \sqrt[3]{(1-\xi^3_\wp)^\lambda - (1-(\xi^3_\wp+\psi^3_\wp))^\lambda} \right\rangle\right)$$
$$= neg(\lambda \widetilde{*} \wp).$$

This completes the proof. □

Next, by utilizing proposed improved operational laws on FFLNs, we propose some arithmetic and geometric aggregation operators for fusing a collection of FFLNs $\wp_i = \left\langle \ell_{\sigma(\wp_i)}, \xi_{\wp_i}, \psi_{\wp_i} \right\rangle (i = 1, 2, \ldots, n)$.

3.2. FFL-Weighted Average (FFLWA) Operator

The weighted average (WA) is the most commonly used mean operator in a wide range of application areas. Here, we extend the idea of WA to the Fermetean fuzzy linguistic information environment and propose the following formal definition.

Definition 10. *Let* $\wp_i = \left\langle \ell_{\sigma(\wp_i)}, \xi_{\wp_i}, \psi_{\wp_i} \right\rangle (i = 1, 2, \ldots, n)$ *be a collection of FFLNs. The FFL-weighted average (FFLWA) operator is a mapping* $\text{FFLWA} : \Omega^n \to \Omega$, *such that*

$$\text{FFLWA}(\wp_1, \wp_2, \ldots, \wp_n) = \widetilde{\bigoplus_{i=1}^{n}} (w_i \widetilde{*} \wp_i), \tag{19}$$

where $w = (w_1, w_2, \ldots, w_n)^T$ *is the weight vector of* $\wp_i$ *with* $w_i \in [0,1]$, $\sum_{i=1}^{n} w_i = 1$. *Especially when* $w = \left(\frac{1}{n}, \frac{1}{n}, \ldots, \frac{1}{n}\right)^T$, *the* FFLWA *operator reduces to FFL-average (FFLA) operator, which is defined as*

$$\text{FFLWA}(\wp_1, \wp_2, \ldots, \wp_n) = \frac{1}{n} \widetilde{*} \left(\widetilde{\bigoplus_{i=1}^{n}} \wp_i \right). \tag{20}$$

Theorem 4. *Let* $\wp_i = \left\langle \ell_{\sigma(\wp_i)}, \xi_{\wp_i}, \psi_{\wp_i} \right\rangle (i = 1, 2, \ldots, n)$ *be a collection of n FFLNs and* $w = (w_1, w_2, \ldots, w_n)^T$ *be the weight vector of* $\wp_i$ *with* $w_i \in [0,1]$, $\sum_{i=1}^{n} w_i = 1$, *then the aggregated value by using the FFLWA operator is also a FFLN and*

$$\mathrm{FFLWA}(\wp_1, \wp_2, \ldots, \wp_n) = \left\langle \begin{array}{c} \varphi^{*-1}\left(1 - \prod_{i=1}^{n}\left(1 - \varphi^*\left(\ell_{\sigma(\wp_i)}\right)\right)^{w_i}\right), \sqrt[3]{1 - \prod_{i=1}^{n}\left(1 - \xi_{\wp_i}^3\right)^{w_i}}, \\ \sqrt[3]{\prod_{i=1}^{n}\left(1 - \xi_{\wp_i}^3\right)^{w_i} - \prod_{i=1}^{n}\left(1 - \left(\xi_{\wp_i}^3 + \psi_{\wp_i}^3\right)\right)^{w_i}} \end{array} \right\rangle. \tag{21}$$

Proof. The first result directly holds from Theorem 1. Using the principle of mathematical induction, we shall prove the result stated in Equation (21). Firstly, for $n = 2$, by Definition 9, we obtain

$$\left.\begin{array}{l} w_1\widetilde{*}\wp_1 = \left\langle \varphi^{*-1}\left(1 - \left(1 - \varphi^*\left(\ell_{\sigma(\wp_1)}\right)\right)^{w_1}\right), \sqrt[3]{1 - (1 - \xi_{\wp_1}^3)^{w_1}}, \sqrt[3]{(1 - \xi_{\wp_1}^3)^{w_1} - (1 - (\xi_{\wp_1}^3 + \psi_{\wp_1}^3))^{w_1}} \right\rangle, \\ w_2\widetilde{*}\wp_2 = \left\langle \varphi^{*-1}\left(1 - \left(1 - \varphi^*\left(\ell_{\sigma(\wp_2)}\right)\right)^{w_2}\right), \sqrt[3]{1 - (1 - \xi_{\wp_2}^3)^{w_2}}, \sqrt[3]{(1 - \xi_{\wp_2}^3)^{w_2} - (1 - (\xi_{\wp_2}^3 + \psi_{\wp_2}^3))^{w_2}} \right\rangle \end{array}\right\}. \tag{22}$$

Hence,

$$\mathrm{FFLWA}(\wp_1, \wp_2) = \left\langle \begin{array}{c} \varphi^{*-1}\left(1 - \prod_{i=1}^{2}\left(1 - \varphi^*\left(\ell_{\sigma(\wp_i)}\right)\right)^{w_i}\right), \sqrt[3]{1 - \prod_{i=1}^{2}\left(1 - \xi_{\wp_i}^3\right)^{w_i}}, \\ \sqrt[3]{\prod_{i=1}^{2}\left(1 - \xi_{\wp_i}^3\right)^{w_i} - \prod_{i=1}^{2}\left(1 - \left(\xi_{\wp_i}^3 + \psi_{\wp_i}^3\right)\right)^{w_i}} \end{array} \right\rangle \tag{23}$$

Hence, the result is valid for $n = 2$.

Next, assume that Equation (21) is true for $n = k$, i.e.,

$$\mathrm{FFLWA}(\wp_1, \wp_2, \ldots, \wp_k) = \left\langle \begin{array}{c} \varphi^{*-1}\left(1 - \prod_{i=1}^{k}\left(1 - \varphi^*\left(\ell_{\sigma(\wp_i)}\right)\right)^{w_i}\right), \sqrt[3]{1 - \prod_{i=1}^{k}\left(1 - \xi_{\wp_i}^3\right)^{w_i}}, \\ \sqrt[3]{\prod_{i=1}^{k}\left(1 - \xi_{\wp_i}^3\right)^{w_i} - \prod_{i=1}^{k}\left(1 - \left(\xi_{\wp_i}^3 + \psi_{\wp_i}^3\right)\right)^{w_i}} \end{array} \right\rangle. \tag{24}$$

Then, for $n = k + 1$, by Definition 10, we have

$$\begin{aligned} &\mathrm{FFLWA}(\wp_1, \wp_2, \ldots, \wp_k, \wp_{k+1}) = \mathrm{FFLWA}(\wp_1, \wp_2, \ldots, \wp_k)\widetilde{\oplus}(w_{k+1}\widetilde{*}\wp_{k+1}) \\ &= \left\langle \begin{array}{c} \varphi^{*-1}\left(1 - \prod_{i=1}^{k}\left(1 - \varphi^*\left(\ell_{\sigma(\wp_i)}\right)\right)^{w_i}\right), \sqrt[3]{1 - \prod_{i=1}^{k}\left(1 - \xi_{\wp_i}^3\right)^{w_i}}, \\ \sqrt[3]{\prod_{i=1}^{k}\left(1 - \xi_{\wp_i}^3\right)^{w_i} - \prod_{i=1}^{k}\left(1 - \left(\xi_{\wp_i}^3 + \psi_{\wp_i}^3\right)\right)^{w_i}} \end{array} \right\rangle \widetilde{\oplus} \left\langle \ell_{\sigma(\wp_{k+1})}, \xi_{\wp_{k+1}}, \psi_{\wp_{k+1}} \right\rangle \\ &= \left\langle \begin{array}{c} \varphi^{*-1}\left(1 - \prod_{i=1}^{k}\left(1 - \varphi^*\left(\ell_{\sigma(\wp_i)}\right)\right)^{w_i}\left(1 - \varphi^*\left(\ell_{\sigma(\wp_{k+i})}\right)\right)^{w_{k+i}}\right), \sqrt[3]{1 - \prod_{i=1}^{k}\left(1 - \xi_{\wp_i}^3\right)^{w_i}\left(1 - \xi_{\wp_{k+1}}^3\right)^{w_{k+1}}}, \\ \sqrt[3]{\prod_{i=1}^{k}\left(1 - \xi_{\wp_i}^3\right)^{w_i}\left(1 - \xi_{\wp_{k+1}}^3\right)^{w_{k+1}} - \prod_{i=1}^{k}\left(1 - \left(\xi_{\wp_i}^3 + \psi_{\wp_i}^3\right)\right)^{w_i}\left(1 - \left(\xi_{\wp_{k+1}}^3 + \psi_{\wp_{k+1}}^3\right)\right)^{w_{k+1}}} \end{array} \right\rangle \\ &= \left\langle \begin{array}{c} \varphi^{*-1}\left(1 - \prod_{i=1}^{k+1}\left(1 - \varphi^*\left(\ell_{\sigma(a_i)}\right)\right)^{w_i}\right), \sqrt[3]{1 - \prod_{i=1}^{k+1}\left(1 - \xi_{\wp_i}^3\right)^{w_i}}, \\ \sqrt[3]{\prod_{i=1}^{k+1}\left(1 - \xi_{\wp_i}^3\right)^{w_i} - \prod_{i=1}^{k+1}\left(1 - \left(\xi_{\wp_i}^3 + \psi_{\wp_i}^3\right)\right)^{w_i}} \end{array} \right\rangle \end{aligned} \tag{25}$$

i.e., the Equation (21) holds for $n = k + 1$.

This proves the theorem. □

Theorem 5. *The FFLWA operator, defined in Equation (21), holds the following properties:*

(P1) *(Idempotency): If* $\wp_i = \wp = \left\langle \ell_{\sigma(\wp)}, \xi_{\wp}, \psi_{\wp} \right\rangle$ $\forall\, i$, *then*

$$\text{FFLWA}(\wp_1, \wp_2, \ldots, \wp_n) = \wp. \tag{26}$$

(P2) *(Monotonicity): Let* $\wp_i = \left\langle \ell_{\sigma(\wp_i)}, \xi_{\wp_i}, \psi_{\wp_i} \right\rangle$ *and* $\aleph_i = \left\langle \ell_{\sigma(\aleph_i)}, \xi_{\aleph_i}, \psi_{\aleph_i} \right\rangle$ $(i = 1, 2, \ldots, n)$ *be two collections of FFLNs such that* $\ell_{\sigma(\wp_i)} \leq \ell_{\sigma(\aleph_i)}, \xi^3_{\wp_i} \leq \xi^3_{\aleph_i}, \xi^3_{\wp_i} + \psi^3_{\wp_i} \geq \xi^3_{\aleph_i} + \psi^3_{\aleph_i} \forall\, i$, *then*

$$\text{FFLWA}(\wp_1, \wp_2, \ldots, \wp_n) \leq \text{FFLWA}(\aleph_1, \aleph_2, \ldots, \aleph_n). \tag{27}$$

(P3) *(Boundedness): Let*

$$\wp^- = \left\langle \min\left(\ell_{\sigma(\wp_1)}, \ell_{\sigma(\wp_2)}, \ldots, \ell_{\sigma(\wp_n)}\right), \min\left(\xi^3_{\wp_1}, \xi^3_{\wp_2}, \ldots, \xi^3_{\wp_n}\right), \max\left\{0, \left(\begin{array}{c} \max\left(\xi^3_{\wp_1} + \psi^3_{\wp_1}, \xi^3_{\wp_2} + \psi^3_{\wp_2}, \ldots, \xi^3_{\wp_n} + \psi^3_{\wp_n}\right) \\ -\min\left(\xi^3_{\wp_1}, \xi^3_{\wp_2}, \ldots, \xi^3_{\wp_n}\right) \end{array} \right)\right\} \right\rangle,$$

and

$$\wp^+ = \left\langle \max\left(\ell_{\sigma(\wp_1)}, \ell_{\sigma(\wp_2)}, \ldots, \ell_{\sigma(\wp_n)}\right), \max\left(\xi^3_{\wp_1}, \xi^3_{\wp_2}, \ldots, \xi^3_{\wp_n}\right), \left(\begin{array}{c} \min\left(\xi^3_{\wp_1} + \psi^3_{\wp_1}, \xi^3_{\wp_2} + \psi^3_{\wp_2}, \ldots, \xi^3_{\wp_n} + \psi^3_{\wp_n}\right) \\ -\max\left(\xi^3_{\wp_1}, \xi^3_{\wp_2}, \ldots, \xi^3_{\wp_n}\right) \end{array} \right) \right\rangle,$$

then

$$\wp^- \leq \text{FFLWA}(\wp_1, \wp_2, \ldots, \wp_n) \leq \wp^+.$$

(P4)*: If* $\aleph = \left\langle s_{\sigma(\aleph)}, \xi_{\aleph}, \psi_{\aleph} \right\rangle$ *is another FFLN, then*

$$\text{FFLWA}(\wp_1 \widetilde{\oplus} \aleph, \wp_2 \widetilde{\oplus} \aleph, \ldots, \wp_n \widetilde{\oplus} \aleph) = \text{FFLWA}(\wp_1, \wp_2, \ldots, \wp_n) \widetilde{\oplus} \aleph. \tag{28}$$

(P5)*: Let* $\vartheta > 0$ *be a real number, then*

$$\text{FFLWA}(\vartheta \widetilde{*} \wp_1, \vartheta \widetilde{*} \wp_2, \ldots, \vartheta \widetilde{*} \wp_n) = \vartheta \widetilde{*} (\text{FFLWA}(\wp_1, \wp_2, \ldots, \wp_n)). \tag{29}$$

(P6)*: Let* $\aleph = \left\langle s_{\sigma(\aleph)}, \xi_{\aleph}, \psi_{\aleph} \right\rangle$ *be another FFLN and* $\vartheta > 0$ *be a real number, then*

$$\text{FFLWA}((\vartheta \widetilde{*} \wp_1) \widetilde{\oplus} \aleph, (\vartheta \widetilde{*} \wp_2) \widetilde{\oplus} \aleph, \ldots, (\vartheta \widetilde{*} \wp_n) \widetilde{\oplus} \aleph) = (\vartheta \widetilde{*} (\text{FFLWA}(\wp_1, \wp_2, \ldots, \wp_n))) \widetilde{\oplus} b. \tag{30}$$

(P7)*: Let* $\wp_i = \left\langle \ell_{\sigma(\wp_i)}, \xi_{\wp_i}, \psi_{\wp_i} \right\rangle$ *and* $\aleph_i = \left\langle s_{\sigma(\aleph_i)}, \xi_{\aleph_i}, \psi_{\aleph_i} \right\rangle$, $(i = 1, 2, \ldots, n)$ *be two collections of FFLNs, then*

$$\text{FFLWA}(\wp_1 \widetilde{\oplus} \aleph_1, \wp_2 \widetilde{\oplus} \aleph_2, \ldots, \wp_n \widetilde{\oplus} \aleph_n) = \text{FFLWA}(\wp_1, \wp_2, \ldots, \wp_n) \widetilde{\oplus} \text{FFLWA}(\aleph_1, \aleph_2, \ldots, \aleph_n). \tag{31}$$

Proof. **(P1)** Assume that $\wp_i = \wp = \left\langle \ell_{\sigma(\wp)}, \xi_{\wp}, \psi_{\wp} \right\rangle$ $\forall\, i$, then

$$
\begin{aligned}
&\mathrm{FFLWA}(\wp_1,\wp_2,\ldots,\wp_n)=\mathrm{FFLWA}(\wp,\wp,\ldots,\wp)\\
&=\left\langle\begin{array}{c}\varphi^{*-1}\left(1-\prod_{i=1}^{n}\left(1-\varphi^{*}\left(\ell_{\sigma(\wp)}\right)\right)^{w_i}\right),\sqrt[3]{1-\prod_{i=1}^{n}(1-\xi_{\wp}^{3})^{w_i}},\\ \sqrt[3]{\prod_{i=1}^{n}(1-\xi_{\wp}^{3})^{w_i}-\prod_{i=1}^{n}(1-(\xi_{\wp}^{3}+\psi_{\wp}^{3}))^{w_i}}\end{array}\right\rangle\\
&=\left\langle\begin{array}{c}\varphi^{*-1}\left(1-\left(1-\varphi^{*}\left(\ell_{\sigma(\wp)}\right)\right)^{w_1+w_2+\cdots+w_n}\right),\sqrt[3]{1-(1-\xi_{\wp}^{3})^{w_1+w_2+\cdots+w_n}},\\ \sqrt[3]{(1-\xi_{\wp}^{3})^{w_1+w_2+\cdots+w_n}-(1-(\xi_{\wp}^{3}+\psi_{\wp}^{3}))^{w_1+w_2+\cdots+w_n}}\end{array}\right\rangle\\
&=\left\langle\ell_{\sigma(\wp)},\xi_{\wp},\psi_{\wp}\right\rangle=\wp.
\end{aligned}
$$

(P2) Since $\ell_{\sigma(\wp_i)}\le\ell_{\sigma(\aleph_i)}$ and φ^{*} is a strictly monotonically increasing function, then

$$
\left.\begin{array}{l}\ell_{\sigma(\wp_i)}\le\ell_{\sigma(\aleph_i)}\Leftrightarrow 1-\varphi^{*}\left(\ell_{\sigma(\wp_i)}\right)\ge 1-\varphi^{*}\left(\ell_{\sigma(\aleph_i)}\right)\\ \Leftrightarrow\varphi^{*-1}\left(1-\prod_{i=1}^{n}\left(1-\varphi^{*}\left(\ell_{\sigma(\wp_i)}\right)\right)^{w_i}\right)\le\varphi^{*-1}\left(1-\prod_{i=1}^{n}\left(1-\varphi^{*}\left(\ell_{\sigma(\aleph_i)}\right)\right)^{w_i}\right)\end{array}\right\}. \tag{32}
$$

As $\xi_{\wp_i}^{3}\le\xi_{\aleph_i}^{3}(i=1,2,\ldots,n)$ and $\xi_{\wp_i}^{3}+\psi_{\wp_i}^{3}\ge\xi_{\aleph_i}^{3}+\psi_{\aleph_i}^{3}(i=1,2,\ldots,n)$, we have

$$
\left.\begin{array}{c}\sqrt[3]{1-\prod_{i=1}^{n}\left(1-\xi_{\wp_i}^{3}\right)^{w_i}}\le\sqrt[3]{1-\prod_{i=1}^{n}\left(1-\xi_{\aleph_i}^{3}\right)^{w_i}}\\ \sqrt[3]{\prod_{i=1}^{n}\left(1-\xi_{\wp_i}^{3}\right)^{w_i}-\prod_{i=1}^{n}\left(1-\left(\xi_{\wp_i}^{3}+\psi_{\wp_i}^{3}\right)\right)^{w_i}}\ge\sqrt[3]{\prod_{i=1}^{n}\left(1-\xi_{\aleph_i}^{3}\right)^{w_i}-\prod_{i=1}^{n}\left(1-\left(\xi_{\aleph_i}^{3}+\psi_{\aleph_i}^{3}\right)\right)^{w_i}}\end{array}\right\}. \tag{33}
$$

According to Definition 10, we have

$$
\mathrm{FFLWA}(\wp_1,\wp_2,\ldots,\wp_n)=\left\langle\begin{array}{c}\varphi^{*-1}\left(1-\prod_{i=1}^{n}\left(1-\varphi^{*}\left(\ell_{\sigma(\wp_i)}\right)\right)^{w_i}\right),\sqrt[3]{1-\prod_{i=1}^{n}\left(1-\xi_{\wp_i}^{3}\right)^{w_i}},\\ \sqrt[3]{\prod_{i=1}^{n}\left(1-\xi_{\wp_i}^{3}\right)^{w_i}-\prod_{i=1}^{n}\left(1-\left(\xi_{\wp_i}^{3}+\psi_{\wp_i}^{3}\right)\right)^{w_i}}\end{array}\right\rangle,
$$

and

$$
\mathrm{FFLWA}(\aleph_1,\aleph_2,\ldots,\aleph_n)=\left\langle\begin{array}{c}\varphi^{*-1}\left(1-\prod_{i=1}^{n}\left(1-\varphi^{*}\left(\ell_{\sigma(\aleph_i)}\right)\right)^{w_i}\right),\sqrt[3]{1-\prod_{i=1}^{n}\left(1-\xi_{\aleph_i}^{3}\right)^{w_i}},\\ \sqrt[3]{\prod_{i=1}^{n}\left(1-\xi_{\aleph_i}^{3}\right)^{w_i}-\prod_{i=1}^{n}\left(1-\left(\xi_{\aleph_i}^{3}+\psi_{\aleph_i}^{3}\right)\right)^{w_i}}\end{array}\right\rangle
$$

Now, using Definition 8, we obtain $\mathfrak{S}(\mathrm{FFLWA}(\wp_1,\wp_2,\ldots,\wp_n))\le\mathfrak{S}(\mathrm{FFLWA}(\aleph_1,\aleph_2,\ldots,\aleph_n))$, which gives

$$
\mathrm{FFLWA}(\wp_1,\wp_2,\ldots,\wp_n)\le\mathrm{FFLWA}(\aleph_1,\aleph_2,\ldots,\aleph_n).
$$

(P3) It directly follows from Property 2.
(P4) Since, so

$$
\wp_i\widetilde{\oplus}\aleph=\left\langle\begin{array}{c}\varphi^{*-1}\left(1-\left(1-\varphi^{*}\left(\ell_{\sigma(\wp_i)}\right)\right)\left(1-\varphi^{*}\left(\ell_{\sigma(\aleph)}\right)\right)\right),\sqrt[3]{1-\left(1-\xi_{\wp_i}^{3}\right)(1-\xi_{\aleph}^{3})},\\ \sqrt[3]{\left(1-\xi_{\wp_i}^{3}\right)(1-\xi_{\aleph}^{3})-\left(1-\left(\xi_{\wp_i}^{3}+\psi_{\wp_i}^{3}\right)\right)(1-(\xi_{\aleph}^{3}+\psi_{\aleph}^{3}))}\end{array}\right\rangle \tag{34}
$$

Therefore,

$$\mathrm{FFLWA}(\wp_1\widetilde{\oplus}\aleph, \wp_2\widetilde{\oplus}\aleph, \ldots, \wp_n\widetilde{\oplus}\aleph)$$
$$= \left\langle \begin{array}{c} \varphi^{*-1}\left(1-\prod_{i=1}^{n}\left(\left(1-\varphi^*\left(\ell_{\sigma(\wp_i)}\right)\right)\left(1-\varphi^*\left(\ell_{\sigma(\aleph)}\right)\right)\right)^{w_i}\right), \sqrt[3]{1-\prod_{i=1}^{n}\left(\left(1-\xi_{\wp_i}^3\right)\left(1-\xi_{\aleph}^3\right)\right)^{w_i}}, \\ \sqrt[3]{\prod_{i=1}^{n}\left(\left(1-\xi_{\wp_i}^3\right)\left(1-\xi_{\aleph}^3\right)\right)^{w_i} - \prod_{i=1}^{n}\left(\left(1-\left(\xi_{\wp_i}^3+\psi_{\wp_i}^3\right)\right)\left(1-\left(\xi_{\aleph}^3+\psi_{\aleph}^3\right)\right)\right)^{w_i}} \end{array} \right\rangle$$
$$= \left\langle \begin{array}{c} \varphi^{*-1}\left(1-\left(\prod_{i=1}^{n}\left(\left(1-\varphi^*\left(\ell_{\sigma(\wp_i)}\right)\right)\right)^{w_i}\right)\left(1-\varphi^*\left(\ell_{\sigma(\aleph)}\right)\right)\right), \sqrt[3]{1-\left(\prod_{i=1}^{n}\left(1-\xi_{\wp_i}^3\right)^{w_i}\right)\left(1-\xi_{\aleph}^3\right)}, \\ \sqrt[3]{\left(\prod_{i=1}^{n}\left(1-\xi_{\wp_i}^3\right)^{w_i}\right)\left(1-\xi_{\aleph}^3\right) - \left(\prod_{i=1}^{n}\left(1-\left(\xi_{\wp_i}^3+\psi_{\wp_i}^3\right)\right)^{w_i}\right)\left(1-\left(\xi_{\aleph}^3+\psi_{\aleph}^3\right)\right)} \end{array} \right\rangle$$
$$= \left\langle \begin{array}{c} \varphi^{*-1}\left(1-\prod_{i=1}^{n}\left(1-\varphi^*\left(\ell_{\sigma(\wp_i)}\right)\right)^{w_i}\right), \sqrt[3]{1-\prod_{i=1}^{n}\left(1-\xi_{\wp_i}^3\right)^{w_i}}, \\ \sqrt[3]{\prod_{i=1}^{n}\left(1-\xi_{\wp_i}^3\right)^{w_i} - \prod_{i=1}^{n}\left(1-\left(\xi_{\wp_i}^3+\psi_{\wp_i}^3\right)\right)^{w_i}} \end{array} \right\rangle \widetilde{\oplus}\left\langle \ell_{\sigma(\aleph)}, \xi_{\aleph}, \psi_{\aleph}\right\rangle$$
$$= \mathrm{FFLWA}(\wp_1, \wp_2, \ldots, \wp_n)\widetilde{\oplus}\aleph.$$

(P5) For any $\vartheta > 0$, we have

$$\vartheta\widetilde{*}\wp_i = \left\langle \varphi^{*-1}\left(1-\left(1-\varphi^*\left(\ell_{\sigma(\wp_i)}\right)\right)^{\vartheta}\right), \sqrt[3]{1-\left(1-\xi_{\wp_i}^3\right)^{\vartheta}}, \sqrt[3]{\left(1-\xi_{\wp_i}^3\right)^{\vartheta} - \left(1-\left(\xi_{\wp_i}^3+\psi_{\wp_i}^3\right)\right)^{\vartheta}} \right\rangle. \tag{35}$$

Therefore,

$$\mathrm{FFLWA}(\vartheta\widetilde{*}\wp_1, \vartheta\widetilde{*}\wp_2, \ldots, \vartheta\widetilde{*}\wp_n) = \left\langle \begin{array}{c} \varphi^{*-1}\left(1-\prod_{i=1}^{n}\left(\left(1-\varphi^*\left(\ell_{\sigma(\wp_i)}\right)\right)^{\vartheta}\right)^{w_i}\right), \sqrt[3]{1-\prod_{i=1}^{n}\left(\left(1-\xi_{\wp_i}^3\right)^{\vartheta}\right)^{w_i}}, \\ \sqrt[3]{\prod_{i=1}^{n}\left(\left(1-\xi_{\wp_i}^3\right)^{\vartheta}\right)^{w_i} - \prod_{i=1}^{n}\left(\left(1-\left(\xi_{\wp_i}^3+\psi_{\wp_i}^3\right)\right)^{\vartheta}\right)^{w_i}} \end{array} \right\rangle$$
$$= \left\langle \begin{array}{c} \varphi^{*-1}\left(1-\prod_{i=1}^{n}\left(\left(1-\varphi^*\left(\ell_{\sigma(\wp_i)}\right)\right)^{w_i}\right)^{\vartheta}\right), \sqrt[3]{1-\prod_{i=1}^{n}\left(\left(1-\xi_{\wp_i}^3\right)^{w_i}\right)^{\vartheta}}, \\ \sqrt[3]{\prod_{i=1}^{n}\left(\left(1-\xi_{\wp_i}^3\right)^{w_i}\right)^{\vartheta} - \prod_{i=1}^{n}\left(\left(1-\left(\xi_{\wp_i}^3+\psi_{\wp_i}^3\right)\right)^{w_i}\right)^{\vartheta}} \end{array} \right\rangle$$
$$= \vartheta\widetilde{*}(\mathrm{FFLWA}(\wp_1, \wp_2, \ldots, \wp_n)).$$

(P6) From Property 4, we know

$$\mathrm{FFLWA}(\wp_1\widetilde{\oplus}\aleph, \wp_2\widetilde{\oplus}\aleph, \ldots, \wp_n\widetilde{\oplus}\aleph) = \mathrm{FFLWA}(\wp_1, \wp_2, \ldots, \wp_n)\widetilde{\oplus}\aleph, \tag{36}$$

and according to Property 5, we have

$$\mathrm{FFLWA}(\vartheta\widetilde{*}\wp_1, \vartheta\widetilde{*}\wp_2, \ldots, \vartheta\widetilde{*}\wp_n) = \vartheta\widetilde{*}(\mathrm{FFLWA}(\wp_1, \wp_2, \ldots, \wp_n)).,\tag{37}$$

From Equations (36) and (37), we obtain the desired results.

(P7) Since $\wp_i, \aleph_i \in \Omega$, then

$$\wp_i\widetilde{\oplus}\aleph_i = \left\langle \begin{array}{c} \varphi^{*-1}\left(1-\left(1-\varphi^*\left(\ell_{\sigma(\wp_i)}\right)\right)\left(1-\varphi^*\left(\ell_{\sigma(\aleph_i)}\right)\right)\right), \sqrt[3]{1-\left(1-\xi_{\wp_i}^3\right)\left(1-\xi_{\aleph_i}^3\right)}, \\ \sqrt[3]{\left(1-\xi_{\wp_i}^3\right)\left(1-\xi_{\aleph_i}^3\right) - \left(1-\left(\xi_{\wp_i}^3+\psi_{\aleph_i}^3\right)\right)\left(1-\left(\xi_{\wp_i}^3+\psi_{\aleph_i}^3\right)\right)} \end{array} \right\rangle. \tag{38}$$

Therefore,

$$\begin{aligned}
&\text{FFLWA}\left(\wp_1\tilde{\oplus}\aleph_1, \wp_2\tilde{\oplus}\aleph_2, \ldots, \wp_n\tilde{\oplus}\aleph_n\right)\\
&= \left\langle \begin{array}{c} \varphi^{*-1}\left(1-\prod_{i=1}^{n}\left(\left(1-\varphi^*\left(\ell_{\sigma(\wp_i)}\right)\right)\left(1-\varphi^*\left(\ell_{\sigma(\aleph_i)}\right)\right)\right)^{w_i}\right), \sqrt[3]{1-\prod_{i=1}^{n}\left(\left(1-\xi_{\wp_i}^3\right)\left(1-\xi_{\aleph_i}^3\right)\right)^{w_i}}, \\ \sqrt[3]{\prod_{i=1}^{n}\left(\left(1-\xi_{\wp_i}^3\right)\left(1-\xi_{\aleph_i}^3\right)\right)^{w_i} - \prod_{i=1}^{n}\left(\left(1-\left(\xi_{\wp_i}^3+\psi_{\aleph_i}^3\right)\right)\left(1-\left(\xi_{\wp_i}^3+\psi_{\aleph_i}^3\right)\right)\right)^{w_i}} \end{array} \right\rangle\\
&= \left\langle \begin{array}{c} \varphi^{*-1}\left(1-\prod_{i=1}^{n}\left(1-\varphi^*\left(\ell_{\sigma(\wp_i)}\right)\right)^{w_i}\prod_{i=1}^{n}\left(1-\varphi^*\left(\ell_{\sigma(\aleph_i)}\right)\right)^{w_i}\right), \sqrt[3]{1-\prod_{i=1}^{n}\left(1-\xi_{\wp_i}^3\right)^{w_i}\prod_{i=1}^{n}\left(1-\xi_{\aleph_i}^3\right)^{w_i}}, \\ \sqrt[3]{\prod_{i=1}^{n}\left(1-\xi_{\wp_i}^3\right)^{w_i}\prod_{i=1}^{n}\left(1-\xi_{\aleph_i}^3\right)^{w_i} - \prod_{i=1}^{n}\left(1-\left(\xi_{\wp_i}^3+\psi_{\wp_i}^3\right)\right)^{w_i}\prod_{i=1}^{n}\left(1-\left(\xi_{\aleph_i}^3+\psi_{\aleph_i}^3\right)\right)^{w_i}} \end{array} \right\rangle\\
&= \left\langle \begin{array}{c} \varphi^{*-1}\left(1-\prod_{i=1}^{n}\left(1-\varphi^*\left(\ell_{\sigma(\wp_i)}\right)\right)^{w_i}\right), \sqrt[3]{1-\prod_{i=1}^{n}\left(1-\xi_{\wp_i}^3\right)^{w_i}}, \\ \sqrt[3]{\prod_{i=1}^{n}\left(1-\xi_{\wp_i}^3\right)^{w_i} - \prod_{i=1}^{n}\left(1-\left(\xi_{\wp_i}^3+\psi_{\wp_i}^3\right)\right)^{w_i}} \end{array} \right\rangle \tilde{\oplus} \left\langle \begin{array}{c} \varphi^{*-1}\left(1-\prod_{i=1}^{n}\left(1-\varphi^*\left(\ell_{\sigma(\wp_i)}\right)\right)^{w_i}\right), \sqrt[3]{1-\prod_{i=1}^{n}\left(1-\xi_{\wp_i}^3\right)^{w_i}}, \\ \sqrt[3]{\prod_{i=1}^{n}\left(1-\xi_{\wp_i}^3\right)^{w_i} - \prod_{i=1}^{n}\left(1-\left(\xi_{\wp_i}^3+\psi_{\wp_i}^3\right)\right)^{w_i}} \end{array} \right\rangle\\
&= \text{FFLWA}(\wp_1, \wp_2, \ldots, \wp_n)\tilde{\oplus}\text{FFLWA}(\aleph_1, \aleph_2, \ldots, \aleph_n).
\end{aligned}$$

This proves the theorem. □

3.3. FFL-Ordered Weighted Average (FFLOWA) Operator

The ordered weighted averaging (OWA) operator [59] is an aggregation operator that provides a parameterized family of aggregation operators between the minimum and the maximum. In this subsection, we extend the idea of the FFLWA operator into the FFLOWA operator based on the OWA operator.

Definition 11. *Let* $\wp_i = \left\langle \ell_{\sigma(\wp_i)}, \xi_{\wp_i}, \psi_{\wp_i} \right\rangle (i = 1, 2, \ldots, n)$ *be a collection of FFLNs, the FFLOWA operator of dimension n is a mapping* FFLOWA : $\Omega^n \to \Omega$, *that has an associated weight vector* $\omega = (\omega_1, \omega_2, \ldots, \omega_n)^T$ *such that* $\omega_i \in [0, 1]$ *and* $\sum_{i=1}^{n} \omega_i = 1$, *then*

$$\text{FFLOWA}(\wp_1, \wp_2, \ldots, \wp_n) = \tilde{\oplus}_{i=1}^{n}\left(\omega_i \tilde{*} \wp_{\phi(i)}\right), \tag{39}$$

where $\wp_{\phi(i)}$ *is the* i^{th} *largest value of* $\wp_i (i = 1, 2, \ldots, n)$.

Theorem 6. *Let* $\wp_i = \left\langle \ell_{\sigma(\wp_i)}, \xi_{\wp_i}, \psi_{\wp_i} \right\rangle (i = 1, 2, \ldots, n)$ *be a collection of FFLNs, then the aggregated value by using the FFLOWA operator is also a FFLN and*

$$\text{FFLOWA}(\wp_1, \wp_2, \ldots, \wp_n) = \left\langle \begin{array}{c} \varphi^{*-1}\left(1-\prod_{i=1}^{n}\left(1-\varphi^*\left(\ell_{\sigma(\wp_{\phi(i)})}\right)\right)^{\omega_i}\right), \sqrt[3]{1-\prod_{i=1}^{n}\left(1-\xi_{\wp_{\phi(i)}}^3\right)^{\omega_i}}, \\ \sqrt[3]{\prod_{i=1}^{n}\left(1-\xi_{\wp_{\phi(i)}}^3\right)^{\omega_i} - \prod_{i=1}^{n}\left(1-\left(\xi_{\wp_{\phi(i)}}^3+\psi_{\wp_{\phi(i)}}^3\right)\right)^{\omega_i}} \end{array} \right\rangle. \tag{40}$$

Proof. The proof of this theorem is similar to Theorem 4, so it is omitted here. □

It can be easily proved that the FFLOWA operator holds the following properties.

(P1) (*Idempotency*): If $\wp_i = \wp = \left\langle \ell_{\sigma(\wp)}, \xi_{\wp}, \psi_{\wp} \right\rangle \forall\, i$, then

$$\text{FFLOWA}(\wp_1, \wp_2, \ldots, \wp_n) = \wp. \tag{41}$$

(P2) (*Monotonicity*): Let $\wp_i = \left\langle \ell_{\sigma(\wp_i)}, \xi_{\wp_i}, \psi_{\wp_i} \right\rangle$ and $\aleph_i = \left\langle \ell_{\sigma(\wp_i)}, \xi_{\wp_i}, \psi_{\wp_i} \right\rangle (i = 1, 2, \ldots, n)$ be two collections of FFLNs such that $\ell_{\sigma(\wp_i)} \leq \ell_{\sigma(\aleph_i)}, \xi_{\wp_i} \leq \xi_{\aleph_i}, \xi_{\wp_i} + \psi_{\wp_i} \geq \xi_{\aleph_i} + \psi_{\aleph_i} \forall\, i$, then

$$\text{FFLOWA}(\wp_1, \wp_2, \ldots, \wp_n) \leq \text{FFLOWA}(\aleph_1, \aleph_2, \ldots, \aleph_n). \tag{42}$$

(P3) (*Boundedness*): Let

$$\wp^{-}=\left\langle \min\left(\ell_{\sigma(\wp_1)},\ell_{\sigma(\wp_2)},\ldots,\ell_{\sigma(\wp_n)}\right),\min\left(\xi^3_{\wp_1},\xi^3_{\wp_2},\ldots,\xi^3_{\wp_n}\right),\max\left\{0,\left(\begin{array}{c}\max\left(\xi^3_{\wp_1}+\psi^3_{\wp_1},\xi^3_{\wp_2}+\psi^3_{\wp_2},\ldots,\xi^3_{\wp_n}+\psi^3_{\wp_n}\right)\\-\min\left(\xi^3_{\wp_1},\xi^3_{\wp_2},\ldots,\xi^3_{\wp_n}\right)\end{array}\right)\right\}\right\rangle,$$

and

$$\wp^{+}=\left\langle \max\left(\ell_{\sigma(\wp_1)},\ell_{\sigma(\wp_2)},\ldots,\ell_{\sigma(\wp_n)}\right),\max\left(\xi^3_{\wp_1},\xi^3_{\wp_2},\ldots,\xi^3_{\wp_n}\right),\left(\begin{array}{c}\min\left(\xi^3_{\wp_1}+\psi^3_{\wp_1},\xi^3_{\wp_2}+\psi^3_{\wp_2},\ldots,\xi^3_{\wp_n}+\psi^3_{\wp_n}\right)\\-\max\left(\xi^3_{\wp_1},\xi^3_{\wp_2},\ldots,\xi^3_{\wp_n}\right)\end{array}\right)\right\rangle$$

then

$$\wp^{-}\leq \text{FFLOWA}(\wp_1,\wp_2,\ldots,\wp_n)\leq \wp^{+}. \tag{43}$$

P4 (*Commutativity*): Let $(\wp'_1,\wp'_2,,\ldots,\wp'_n)$ be any permutation of $(\wp_1,\wp_2,\ldots,\wp_n)$, then

$$\text{FFLOWA}(\wp_1,\wp_2,\ldots,\wp_n)=\text{FFLOWA}(\wp'_1,\wp'_2,,\ldots,\wp'_n). \tag{44}$$

Further, motivated by the idea of geometric mean and ordered weighted geometric operator [60], we develop the FFLWG operator and the FFLOWG operator.

3.4. FFL-Weighted Geometric (FFLWG) Operator

This subsection extends the notion of weighted geometric mean to the Fermetean fuzzy linguistic information environment and defines the FFL-weighted geometric operator as follows:

Definition 12. *Let* $\wp_i=\left\langle \ell_{\sigma(\wp_i)},\xi_{\wp_i},\psi_{\wp_i}\right\rangle$, $(i=1,2,\ldots,n)$ *be a collection of FFLNs. The FFL-weighted geometric (FFLWG) operator is a mapping* $\text{FFLWG}:\Omega^n\to\Omega$, *such that*

$$\text{FFLWG}(\wp_1,\wp_2,\ldots,\wp_n)=\mathop{\tilde{\otimes}}_{i=1}^{n}\left(\wp_i\tilde{^}w_i\right), \tag{45}$$

where $w=(w_1,w_2,\ldots,w_n)^T$ *denotes the weight vector of* $\wp_i$ *with* $w_i\in[0,1]$, $\sum_{i=1}^{n}w_i=1$. *Especially, in the case of* $w=\left(\frac{1}{n},\frac{1}{n},\ldots,\frac{1}{n}\right)^T$, *the FFLWG operator is reduced into FFLG operator expressed as*

$$\text{FFLG}(a_1,a_2,\ldots,a_n)=\mathop{\tilde{\otimes}}_{i=1}^{n}\left(\wp_i\tilde{^}\frac{1}{n}\right). \tag{46}$$

Theorem 7. *Let* $\wp_i=\left\langle \ell_{\sigma(\wp_i)},\xi_{\wp_i},\psi_{\wp_i}\right\rangle$, $(i=1,2,\ldots,n)$ *be a collection of FFLNs, then the aggregated value by using the FFLWG operator is also a FFLN and*

$$\text{FFLWG}(\wp_1,\wp_2,\ldots,\wp_n)=\left\langle\begin{array}{c}\varphi^{*-1}\left(\prod_{i=1}^{n}\left(\varphi^{*}\left(\ell_{\sigma(\wp_i)}\right)\right)^{w_i}\right),\sqrt[3]{\prod_{i=1}^{n}\left(1-\psi^3_{\wp_i}\right)^{w_i}-\prod_{i=1}^{n}\left(1-\left(\xi^3_{\wp_i}+\psi^3_{\wp_i}\right)\right)^{w_i}},\\ \sqrt[3]{1-\prod_{i=1}^{n}\left(1-\psi^3_{\wp_i}\right)^{w_i}}\end{array}\right\rangle. \tag{47}$$

Proof. Based on improved operational laws on FFLNs mentioned in Definition 9, Theorem 6 is evident from Theorems 4. □

Theorem 8. *The FFLWG operator satisfies the following properties:*

(P1) *(Idempotency): If* $\wp_i = \wp = \left\langle \ell_{\sigma(\wp)}, \xi_\wp, \psi_\wp \right\rangle \forall\, i$, *then*

$$\text{FFLWG}(\wp_1, \wp_2, \ldots, \wp_n) = \wp. \tag{48}$$

(P2) *(Monotonicity): Let* $\wp_i = \left\langle \ell_{\sigma(\wp_i)}, \xi_{\wp_i}, \psi_{\wp_i} \right\rangle$ and $\aleph_i = \left\langle \ell_{\sigma(\aleph_i)}, \xi_{\aleph_i}, \psi_{\aleph_i} \right\rangle (i = 1, 2, \ldots, n)$ *be two collections of FFLNs such that* $\ell_{\sigma(\wp_i)} \leq \ell_{\sigma(\aleph_i)}, \psi_{\wp_i} \geq \psi_{\aleph_i}, \xi_{\wp_i} + \psi_{\wp_i} \leq \xi_{\aleph_i} + \psi_{\aleph_i} \forall\, i$, *then*

$$\text{FFLWG}(\wp_1, \wp_2, \ldots, \wp_n) \leq \text{FFLWG}(\aleph_1, \aleph_2, \ldots, \aleph_n). \tag{49}$$

(P3) *(Boundedness): Let*

$$\wp^- = \left\langle \min\left(\ell_{\sigma(\wp_1)}, \ell_{\sigma(\wp_2)}, \ldots, \ell_{\sigma(\wp_n)}\right), \max\left\{0, \left(\begin{array}{c} \min(\xi^3_{\wp_1} + \psi^3_{\wp_1}, \xi^3_{\wp_2} + \psi^3_{\wp_2}, \ldots, \xi^3_{\wp_n} + \psi^3_{\wp_n}) \\ -\max(\psi_{\wp_1}, \psi_{\wp_2}, \ldots, \psi_{\wp_n}) \end{array} \right)\right\}, \max(\psi_{\wp_1}, \psi_{\wp_2}, \ldots, \psi_{\wp_n}) \right\rangle$$

and

$$\wp^+ = \left\langle \max\left(\ell_{\sigma(\wp_1)}, \ell_{\sigma(\wp_2)}, \ldots, \ell_{\sigma(\wp_n)}\right), \left(\begin{array}{c} \max(\xi^3_{\wp_1} + \psi^3_{\wp_1}, \xi^3_{\wp_2} + \psi^3_{\wp_2}, \ldots, \xi^3_{\wp_n} + \psi^3_{\wp_n}) \\ -\min(\psi^3_{\wp_1}, \psi^3_{\wp_1}, \ldots, \psi^3_{\wp_1}) \end{array} \right), \min\left(\psi^3_{\wp_1}, \psi^3_{\wp_1}, \ldots, \psi^3_{\wp_1}\right) \right\rangle,$$

then

$$\wp^- \leq \text{FFLWG}(\wp_1, \wp_2, \ldots, \wp_n) \leq \wp^+. \tag{50}$$

(P4): *If* $\aleph = \left\langle \ell_{\sigma(\aleph)}, \xi_\aleph, \psi_\aleph \right\rangle$ *is another FFLN, then*

$$\text{FFLWG}(\wp_1 \widetilde{\otimes} \aleph, \wp_2 \widetilde{\otimes} \aleph, \ldots, \wp_n \widetilde{\otimes} \aleph) = \text{FFLWG}(\wp_1, \wp_2, \ldots, \wp_n) \widetilde{\otimes} \aleph. \tag{51}$$

(P5): *If* $\vartheta > 0$ *is a real number, then*

$$\text{FFLWG}\left(\wp_1 \widetilde{\vartheta}, \wp_2 \widetilde{\vartheta}, \ldots, \wp_n \widetilde{\vartheta}\right) = (\text{FFLWFG}(\wp_1, \wp_2, \ldots, \wp_n)) \widetilde{\wedge} \vartheta. \tag{52}$$

(P6): *Let* $\aleph = \left\langle \ell_{\sigma(\aleph)}, \xi_\aleph, \psi_\aleph \right\rangle$ *be another FFLN and* $\vartheta > 0$ *be a real number, then*

$$\text{FFLWG}\left(\left(\wp_1 \widetilde{\vartheta}\right) \widetilde{\otimes} \aleph, \left(\wp_2 \widetilde{\vartheta}\right) \widetilde{\otimes} \aleph, \ldots, \left(\wp_n \widetilde{\vartheta}\right) \widetilde{\otimes} \aleph\right) = \left((\text{FFLWG}(\wp_1, \wp_2, \ldots, \wp_n)) \widetilde{\wedge} \vartheta\right) \widetilde{\otimes} \aleph. \tag{53}$$

(P7): *Let* $\wp_i = \left\langle \ell_{\sigma(\wp_i)}, \xi_{\wp_i}, \psi_{\wp_i} \right\rangle$ *and* $\aleph_i = \left\langle \ell_{\sigma(\aleph_i)}, \xi_{\aleph_i}, \psi_{\aleph_i} \right\rangle$, $(i = 1, 2, \ldots, n)$ *be two collections of FFLNs, then*

$$\text{FFLWG}(\wp_1 \widetilde{\otimes} \aleph_1, \wp_2 \widetilde{\otimes} \aleph_2, \ldots, \wp_n \widetilde{\otimes} \aleph_n) = \text{FFLWG}(\wp_1, \wp_2, \ldots, \wp_n) \widetilde{\otimes} \text{FFLWG}(\aleph_1, \aleph_2, \ldots, \aleph_n). \tag{54}$$

Proof. Here, we prove the properties 4 and 5 only, and others can proceed likewise. □

(P4) From Definition 9, we have

$$\wp_i \widetilde{\otimes} \aleph = \left\langle \begin{array}{c} \varphi^{*-1}\left(\varphi^*\left(\ell_{\sigma(\wp_i)}\right) \varphi^*\left(\ell_{\sigma(\aleph)}\right)\right), \sqrt[3]{\left(1 - \psi^3_{\wp_i}\right)(1 - \psi^3_\aleph) - \left(1 - \left(\xi^3_{\wp_i} + \psi^3_{\wp_i}\right)\right)(1 - (\xi^3_\aleph + \psi^3_\aleph))}, \\ \sqrt[3]{1 - \left(1 - \psi^3_{\wp_i}\right)(1 - \psi^3_\aleph)} \end{array} \right\rangle \tag{55}$$

Therefore

$$\mathrm{FFLWG}(\wp_1\tilde{\otimes}\aleph, \wp_2\tilde{\otimes}\aleph, \ldots, \wp_n\tilde{\otimes}\aleph)$$
$$= \left\langle \varphi^{*-1}\left(\prod_{i=1}^{n}\left(\varphi^*\left(\ell_{\sigma(\wp_i)}\right)\varphi^*\left(\ell_{\sigma(\aleph)}\right)\right)^{w_i}\right), \sqrt[3]{\begin{array}{c}\prod_{i=1}^{n}\left(\left(1-\psi_{\wp_i}^3\right)\left(1-\psi_{\aleph}^3\right)\right)^{w_i} \\ -\prod_{i=1}^{n}\left(\left(1-\left(\xi_{\wp_i}^3+\psi_{\wp_1}^3\right)\right)\left(1-\left(\xi_{\aleph}^3+\psi_{\aleph}^3\right)\right)\right)^{w_i}\end{array}}, \sqrt[3]{1-\prod_{i=1}^{n}\left(\left(1-\psi_{\wp}^3\right)\left(1-\psi_{\aleph}^3\right)\right)^{w_i}} \right\rangle$$
$$= \left\langle \varphi^{*-1}\left(\prod_{i=1}^{n}\left(\varphi^*\left(\ell_{\sigma(\wp_i)}\right)\right)^{w_i}\varphi^*\left(\ell_{\sigma(\aleph)}\right)\right), \sqrt[3]{\begin{array}{c}\left(\prod_{i=1}^{n}\left(1-\psi_{\wp_i}^3\right)^{w_i}\right)\left(1-\psi_{\aleph_i}^3\right) \\ -\left(\prod_{i=1}^{n}\left(1-\left(\xi_{\wp_i}^3+\psi_{\wp_1}^3\right)\right)^{w_i}\right)\left(1-\left(\xi_{\aleph_i}^3+\psi_{\aleph_i}^3\right)\right)\end{array}}, \sqrt[3]{1-\left(\prod_{i=1}^{n}\left(1-\psi_{\wp_i}^3\right)^{w_i}\right)\left(1-\psi_{\aleph_i}^3\right)} \right\rangle$$
$$= \left\langle \varphi^{*-1}\left(\prod_{i=1}^{n}\left(\varphi^*\left(\ell_{\sigma(\wp_i)}\right)\right)^{w_i}\right), \sqrt[3]{\prod_{i=1}^{n}\left(1-\psi_{\wp_i}^3\right)^{w_i}-\prod_{i=1}^{n}\left(1-\left(\xi_{\wp_i}^3+\psi_{\wp_i}^3\right)\right)^{w_i}}, \sqrt[3]{1-\prod_{i=1}^{n}\left(1-\psi_{\wp_i}^3\right)^{w_i}} \right\rangle \tilde{\otimes}\left\langle \ell_{\sigma(\aleph)}, \xi_{\aleph}, \psi_{\aleph}\right\rangle$$
$$= \mathrm{FFLWG}(\wp_1, \wp_2, \ldots, \wp_n)\tilde{\otimes}\aleph$$

(P5) Using Definition 9, we obtain

$$\wp_i\tilde{\vartheta} = \left\langle \varphi^{*-1}\left(\left(\varphi^*\left(\ell_{\sigma(\wp_i)}\right)\right)^{\vartheta}\right), \sqrt[3]{\left(1-\psi_{\wp_i}^3\right)^{\vartheta}-\left(1-\left(\xi_{\wp_i}^3+\psi_{\wp_i}^3\right)\right)^{\vartheta}}, \sqrt[3]{1-\left(1-\psi_{\wp_i}^3\right)^{\vartheta}} \right\rangle \tag{56}$$

Therefore

$$\mathrm{FFLWG}\left(\wp_1\tilde{\vartheta}, \wp_2\tilde{\vartheta}, \ldots, \wp_n\tilde{\vartheta}\right)$$
$$= \left\langle \varphi^{*-1}\left(\prod_{i=1}^{n}\left(\left(\varphi^*\left(\ell_{\sigma(\wp_i)}\right)\right)^{\vartheta}\right)^{w_i}\right), \sqrt[3]{\prod_{i=1}^{n}\left(\left(1-\psi_{\wp_i}^3\right)^{\vartheta}\right)^{w_i}-\prod_{i=1}^{n}\left(\left(1-\left(\xi_{\wp_i}^3+\psi_{\wp_i}^3\right)\right)^{\vartheta}\right)^{w_i}}, \sqrt[3]{1-\prod_{i=1}^{n}\left(\left(1-\psi_{\wp_i}^3\right)^{\vartheta}\right)^{w_i}} \right\rangle$$
$$= \left\langle \varphi^{*-1}\left(\prod_{i=1}^{n}\left(\left(\varphi^*\left(\ell_{\sigma(\wp_i)}\right)\right)^{w_i}\right)\right)^{\vartheta}, \sqrt[3]{\prod_{i=1}^{n}\left(\left(1-\psi_{\wp_i}^3\right)^{w_i}\right)^{\vartheta}-\prod_{i=1}^{n}\left(\left(1-\left(\xi_{\wp_i}^3+\psi_{\wp_i}^3\right)\right)^{w_i}\right)^{\vartheta}}, \sqrt[3]{1-\prod_{i=1}^{n}\left(\left(1-\psi_{\wp_i}^3\right)^{w_i}\right)^{\vartheta}} \right\rangle$$
$$= (\mathrm{FFLWFG}(\wp_1, \wp_2, \ldots, \wp_n))\tilde{\vartheta}.$$

3.5. FFL-Ordered Weighted Geometric (FFLOWG) Operator

The ordered weighted geometric (OWG) operator [60] is a common aggregation operator in the field of information fusion. However, the existing OWG operator cannot aggregate FFLNs. Now, we define the FFLOWG operator based on the notion of the OWG operator to aggregate FFLNs.

Definition 13. *Let* $\wp_i = \left\langle \ell_{\sigma(\wp_i)}, \xi_{\wp_i}, \psi_{\wp_i}\right\rangle$, $(i = 1,2,\ldots,n)$ *be a collection of FFLNs, the FFLOWG operator of dimension n is a mapping* FFLOWG : $\Omega^n \to \Omega$, *that has an associated weight vector* $\omega = (\omega_1, \omega_2, \ldots, \omega_n)^T$ *such that* $\omega_i \in [0,1]$ *and* $\sum_{i=1}^{n}\omega_i = 1$, *then*

$$\mathrm{FFLOWG}(\wp_1, \wp_2, \ldots, \wp_n) = \tilde{\otimes}_{i=1}^{n}\left(\wp_{\phi(i)}\tilde{\omega}_i\right), \tag{57}$$

where $\wp_{\phi(i)}$ *is the* i^{th} *largest value of* $\wp_i(i = 1, 2, \ldots, n)$.

Theorem 9. *Let* $\wp_i = \left\langle \ell_{\sigma(\wp_i)}, \xi_{\wp_i}, \psi_{\wp_i} \right\rangle (i = 1, 2, \ldots, n)$ *be a collection of FFLNs, then the aggregated value by the FFLOWG operator is also a FFLN and*

$$\begin{aligned} &\text{FFLOWG}(\wp_1, \wp_2, \ldots, \wp_n) \\ &= \left\langle \varphi^{*-1}\left(\prod_{i=1}^{n}\left(\varphi^*\left(\ell_{\sigma(\wp_{\phi(i)})}\right)\right)^{\omega_i}\right), \frac{\sqrt[3]{\prod_{i=1}^{n}\left(1-\psi^3_{\wp_{\phi(i)}}\right)^{\omega_i} - \prod_{i=1}^{n}\left(1-\left(\xi^3_{\wp_{\phi(i)}}+\psi^3_{\wp_{\phi(i)}}\right)\right)^{\omega_i}}}{\sqrt[3]{1-\prod_{i=1}^{n}\left(1-\psi^3_{\wp_{\phi(i)}}\right)^{\omega_i}}} \right\rangle \end{aligned} \tag{58}$$

Proof. We can derive the proof similar to Theorem 4, so we omit it here. □

Moreover, the FFLOWG operator also satisfies properties such as idempotency, monotonicity, boundedness, and commutativity.

3.6. FFL-Hybrid Average (FFLHA) Operator and FFL-Hybrid Geometric (FFLHG) Operator

From Definitions 10 to 13, we know that the FFLWA and FFLWG AOs only weight the FFLNs, while the FFLOWA and FFLOWG AOs weight the ordered position of the FFLNs instead of weighting the FFLNs itself. In both cases, the weights address different aspects during the aggregation process of the FFLNs. However, the developed aggregation operators for FFLNs consider only one of them. The hybrid averaging (HA) operator [61] is an aggregation operator that uses the weighted average (WA) and the ordered weighted averaging (OWA) operator in the same formulation. In the following, we propose the FFL-hybrid average (FFLHA) operator and the FFL-hybrid geometric (FFLHG) operator.

Definition 14. *Let* $\wp_i = \left\langle \ell_{\sigma(\wp_i)}, \xi_{\wp_i}, \psi_{\wp_i} \right\rangle (i = 1, 2, \ldots, n)$ *be a collection of FFLNs, the FFL-hybrid average (FFLHA) operator of dimension n is a mapping* FFLHA : $\Omega^n \to \Omega$, *that has an associated weight vector* $\omega = (\omega_1, \omega_2, \ldots, \omega_n)^T$ *such that* $\omega_i \in [0, 1]$ *and* $\sum_{i=1}^{n} \omega_i = 1$, *then*

$$\text{FFLHA}(\wp_1, \wp_2, \ldots, \wp_n) = \tilde{\bigoplus}_{i=1}^{n}\left(\omega_i \tilde{*} \dot{\wp}_{\phi(i)}\right) \tag{59}$$

where $\dot{\wp}_{\phi(i)}$ *is the* i^{th} *largest number of the weighted FFLNs* $\dot{\wp}_i (\dot{\wp}_i = (nw_i)\tilde{*}\wp_i,\ i = 1, 2, \ldots, n)$, $w = (w_1, w_2, \ldots, w_n)^T$ *is the weight vector of* $\wp_i$ $(i = 1, 2, \ldots, n)$ *such that* $w_i \in [0, 1]$, $\sum_{i=1}^{n} w_i = 1$ *and n is the balancing coefficient.*

Theorem 10. *Let* $\wp_i = \left\langle \ell_{\sigma(\wp_i)}, \xi_{\wp_i}, \psi_{\wp_i} \right\rangle$, $(i = 1, 2, \ldots, n)$ *be a collection of FFLNs, then the aggregated value by using the FFLHA operator is also a FFLN and*

$$\text{FFLHA}(\wp_1, \wp_2, \ldots, \wp_n) = \left\langle \varphi^{*-1}\left(1-\prod_{i=1}^{n}\left(1-\varphi^*\left(\ell_{\sigma(\dot{\wp}_{\phi(i)})}\right)\right)^{w_i}\right), \frac{\sqrt[3]{1-\prod_{i=1}^{n}\left(1-\xi^3_{\dot{\wp}_{\phi(i)}}\right)^{w_i}},}{\sqrt[3]{\prod_{i=1}^{n}\left(1-\xi^3_{\dot{\wp}_{\phi(i)}}\right)^{w_i} - \prod_{i=1}^{n}\left(1-\left(\xi^3_{\dot{\wp}_{\phi(i)}}+\psi^3_{\dot{\wp}_{\phi(i)}}\right)\right)^{w_i}}} \right\rangle \tag{60}$$

Proof. The proof of this theorem is similar to Theorem 4. □

Definition 15. *Let $\wp_i = \left\langle \ell_{\sigma(\wp_i)}, \xi_{\wp_i}, \psi_{\wp_i} \right\rangle$, $(i = 1, 2, \ldots, n)$ be a collection of n FFLNs, the FFL-hybrid geometric (FFLHG) operator of dimension n is a mapping* FFLHG : $\Omega^n \to \Omega$, *that has an associated weight vector $\omega = (\omega_1, \omega_2, \ldots, \omega_n)^T$ such that $\omega_i \in [0,1]$ and $\sum_{i=1}^{n} \omega_i = 1$, then*

$$\text{FFLHG}(\wp_1, \wp_2, \ldots, \wp_n) = \overset{n}{\underset{i=1}{\otimes}} \left(\dot{\wp}_{\phi(i)} \tilde{\wedge} \omega \right), \tag{61}$$

where $\dot{\wp}_{\phi(i)}$ is the ith largest number of the weighted FFLNs $\dot{\wp}_i \left(\dot{\wp}_i = \wp_i \tilde{\wedge} n w_i,\ i = 1, 2, \ldots, n \right)$, $w = (w_1, w_2, \ldots, w_n)^T$ is the weight vector of $\wp_i$ $(i = 1, 2, \ldots, n)$ such that $w_i \in [0,1]$, $\sum_{i=1}^{n} w_i = 1$ and n is the balancing coefficient.

Theorem 11. *Let $\wp_i = \left\langle \ell_{\sigma(\wp_i)}, \xi_{\wp_i}, \psi_{\wp_i} \right\rangle$, $(i = 1, 2, \ldots, n)$ be a collection of FFLNs, then the aggregated value by using the FFLHG operator is also a FFLN and*

$$\text{FFLHG}(\wp_1, \wp_2, \ldots, \wp_n) = \left\langle \begin{array}{c} \varphi^{*-1}\left(1 - \prod_{i=1}^{n}\left(1 - \varphi^{*}\left(\ell_{\sigma(\dot{\wp}_{\phi(i)})}\right)\right)^{w_i}\right), \sqrt[3]{\prod_{i=1}^{n}\left(1 - \psi^3_{\dot{\wp}_{\phi(i)}}\right)^{w_i} - \prod_{i=1}^{n}\left(1 - \left(\xi^3_{\dot{\wp}_{\phi(i)}} + \psi^3_{\dot{\wp}_{\phi(i)}}\right)\right)^{w_i}}, \\ \sqrt[3]{1 - \prod_{i=1}^{n}\left(1 - \psi^3_{\dot{\wp}_{\phi(i)}}\right)^{w_i}} \end{array} \right\rangle., \tag{62}$$

Proof. The proof of this theorem can be obtained similar to Theorem 4. □

Note that similar to the FFLOWA and the FFLOWG operators, the FFLHA and FFLHG operators follow the idempotent, bounded, monotonic and commutative properties.

Remark 1. *If $\omega = \left(\frac{1}{n}, \frac{1}{n}, \ldots, \frac{1}{n}\right)^T$, then FFLHA and FFLHG operators become the FFLWA operator and FFLWG operator, respectively;*

Remark 2. *If $w = \left(\frac{1}{n}, \frac{1}{n}, \ldots, \frac{1}{n}\right)^T$, then the FFLHA and FFLHG operators are reduced into FFLOWA operator and FFLOWG operator, respectively.*

In the next section, we formulate a new decision-making method to solve MAGDM problems under the Fermatean fuzzy linguistic environment. Then, we consider a real-life supplier selection problem to demonstrate the decision-making steps.

4. An Approach to MAGDM Making with Fermatean Fuzzy Linguistic Information

4.1. MAGDM Problem Description

For a MAGDM problem, let $F = \{F_1, F_2, \ldots, F_m\}$ be a set of alternatives, $A = \{A_1, A_2, \ldots A_n\}$ be an attribute set with the associated weighting vector $(w_1, w_2, \ldots, w_n)^T$, satisfying $w_j \in [0,1]$ and $\sum_{j=1}^{n} w_j = 1$. Assume $E = \{E_1, E_2, \ldots, E_t\}$ is a collection of s experts whose weight vector is $(\omega_1, \omega_2, \ldots, \omega_s)^T$, satisfying $\omega_q \in [0,1]$ and $\sum_{q=1}^{s} \omega_q = 1$. Further, suppose that $\mathfrak{B}^{(q)} = \left(\wp_{ij}{}^{(q)}\right)_{m \times n}$ is a decision matrix, where $\wp_{ij}{}^{(q)} = \left\langle \ell^{(q)}_{\sigma(\wp_{ij})}, \xi^{(q)}_{\wp_{ij}}, \psi^{(q)}_{\wp_{ij}} \right\rangle$ represents an attribute evaluation value, given by the expert E_q, for the alternative $F_i \in F$ concerning the attribute $A_j \in A$ such that $0 \leq \left(\xi^{(q)}_{\wp_{ij}}\right)^3 + \left(\psi^{(q)}_{\wp_{ij}}\right)^3 \leq 1$ and $\ell^{(q)}_{\sigma(\wp_{ij})} \in \widehat{L}_{[0,2t]}$, $i = 1, 2, \ldots, m; j = 1, 2, \ldots, n$. Then, the ranking of the alternatives is required to obtain the best alternative(s).

4.2. Decision Method

The decision method comprises the following steps.

Step 1: To nullify the effect of the different attributes, transform the decision matrices $\mathfrak{B}^{(q)} = \left({\wp_{ij}}^{(q)}\right)_{m\times n}$ into the normalized form $\hat{\mathfrak{B}}^{(q)} = \left({\hat{\wp}_{ij}}^{(q)}\right)_{m\times n} = \left(\left\langle \ell^{(q)}_{\sigma(\hat{\wp}_{ij})}, \xi^{(q)}_{\hat{\wp}_{ij}}, \psi^{(q)}_{\hat{\wp}_{ij}} \right\rangle\right)_{m\times n}$. The elements of the normalized decision matrices $\hat{\mathfrak{B}}^{(q)}$ can be obtained as follows:

$$\hat{\wp}^{(q)}_{ij} = \begin{cases} \left\langle \ell^{(q)}_{\sigma(\wp_{ij})}, \xi^{(q)}_{\wp_{ij}}, \psi^{(q)}_{\wp_{ij}} \right\rangle, & \text{if } A_j \text{ is benefit type attribute} \\ \left\langle \ell^{(q)}_{2t-\sigma(\wp_{ij})}, \psi^{(q)}_{\wp_{ij}}, \xi^{(q)}_{\wp_{ij}} \right\rangle, & \text{if } A_j \text{ is cos t type attribute} \end{cases}, \tag{63}$$

Step 2: Aggregate all the $\hat{\mathfrak{B}}^{(q)} = \left({\hat{\wp}_{ij}}^{(q)}\right)_{m\times n}$ into a collective normalized decision matrix $\breve{\mathfrak{B}} = \left(\breve{\hat{\wp}}_{ij}\right)_{m\times n} = \left(\left\langle \ell_{\sigma(\breve{\hat{\wp}}_{ij})}, \xi_{\breve{\hat{\wp}}_{ij}}, \psi_{\breve{\hat{\wp}}_{ij}} \right\rangle\right)$ by using either FFLOWA operator

$$\breve{\hat{\wp}}_{ij} = \text{FFLOWA}\left({\hat{\wp}_{ij}}^{(1)}, {\hat{\wp}_{ij}}^{(2)}, \ldots, {\hat{\wp}_{ij}}^{(s)}\right) = \left\langle \begin{array}{c} \varphi^{*-1}\left(1-\prod_{q=1}^{s}\left(1-\varphi^{*}\left(\ell_{\sigma(\hat{\wp}^{\phi(q)}_{ij})}\right)\right)^{\omega_q}\right), \sqrt[3]{1-\prod_{q=1}^{s}\left(1-\xi^3_{\hat{\wp}^{\phi(q)}_{ij}}\right)^{\omega_q}}, \\ \sqrt[3]{\prod_{q=1}^{s}\left(1-\xi^3_{\hat{\wp}^{\phi(q)}_{ij}}\right)^{\omega_q} - \prod_{q=1}^{s}\left(1-\left(\xi^3_{\hat{\wp}^{\phi(q)}_{ij}}+\psi^3_{\hat{\wp}^{\phi(q)}_{ij}}\right)\right)^{\omega_q}} \end{array} \right\rangle, \tag{64}$$

or FFLOWG operator

$$\breve{\hat{\wp}}_{ij} = \text{FFLOWG}\left({\hat{\wp}_{ij}}^{(1)}, {\hat{\wp}_{ij}}^{(2)}, \ldots, {\hat{\wp}_{ij}}^{(s)}\right) = \left\langle \begin{array}{c} \varphi^{*-1}\left(\prod_{q=1}^{s}\left(\varphi^{*}\left(\ell_{\sigma(\hat{\wp}^{\phi(q)}_{ij})}\right)\right)^{\omega_q}\right), \sqrt[3]{1-\prod_{q=1}^{s}\left(1-\psi^3_{\hat{\wp}^{\phi(q)}_{ij}}\right)^{\omega_q} - \prod_{q=1}^{s}\left(1-\left(\xi^3_{\hat{\wp}^{\phi(q)}_{ij}}+\psi^3_{\hat{\wp}^{\phi(q)}_{ij}}\right)\right)^{\omega_q}}, \\ \sqrt[3]{1-\prod_{q=1}^{s}\left(1-\psi^3_{\hat{\wp}^{\phi(q)}_{ij}}\right)^{\omega_q}} \end{array} \right\rangle, \tag{65}$$

where $\hat{\wp}^{\sigma(q)}_{ij} = \left\langle \ell^{\phi(q)}_{\sigma(\hat{\wp}_{ij})}, \xi^{\phi(q)}_{\hat{\wp}_{ij}}, \psi^{\phi(q)}_{\hat{\wp}_{ij}} \right\rangle$ is the qth largest value of $\hat{\wp}^{(q)}_{ij}$ and $(\omega_1, \omega_2, \ldots, \omega_t)^T$ represents the associated ordered position weight vector with $\omega_q \in [0,1]$ and $\sum_{q=1}^{s} \omega_q = 1$.

Step 3: Aggregate all the collective preference values $\breve{\hat{\wp}}_{ij}$ $(j = 1, 2, \ldots, n)$ for obtaining the overall assessment values $\widetilde{\wp}_i$ $(i = 1, 2, \ldots, m)$ corresponding to the alternatives $F_i (i = 1, 2, \ldots, m)$, based on either the FFLWA operator

$$\widetilde{\wp}_i = \text{FFLWA}\left(\breve{\hat{\wp}}_{i1}, \breve{\hat{\wp}}_{i2}, \ldots, \breve{\hat{\wp}}_{in}\right) = \left\langle \begin{array}{c} \varphi^{*-1}\left(1-\prod_{j=1}^{n}\left(1-\varphi^{*}\left(\ell_{\sigma(\breve{\hat{\wp}}_{ij})}\right)\right)^{w_j}\right), \sqrt[3]{1-\prod_{j=1}^{n}\left(1-\xi^3_{\breve{\hat{\wp}}_{ij}}\right)^{w_j}}, \\ \sqrt[3]{\prod_{i=1}^{n}\left(1-\xi^3_{\breve{\hat{\wp}}_{ij}}\right)^{w_j} - \prod_{j=1}^{n}\left(1-\left(\xi^3_{\breve{\hat{\wp}}_{ij}}+\psi^3_{\breve{\hat{\wp}}_{ij}}\right)\right)^{w_j}} \end{array} \right\rangle, \tag{66}$$

or FFLWG operator

$$\widetilde{\wp}_i = \text{FFLWA}\left(\breve{\hat{\wp}}_{i1}, \breve{\hat{\wp}}_{i2}, \ldots, \breve{\hat{\wp}}_{in}\right) = \left\langle \begin{array}{c} \varphi^{*-1}\left(\prod_{j=1}^{n}\left(\varphi^{*}\left(\ell_{\sigma(\breve{\hat{\wp}}_{ij})}\right)\right)^{w_j}\right), \sqrt[3]{\prod_{j=1}^{n}\left(1-\psi^3_{\breve{\hat{\wp}}_{ij}}\right)^{w_j} - \prod_{j=1}^{n}\left(1-\left(\xi^3_{\breve{\hat{\wp}}_{ij}}+\psi^3_{\breve{\hat{\wp}}_{ij}}\right)\right)^{w_j}}, \\ \sqrt[3]{1-\prod_{j=1}^{n}\left(1-\psi^3_{\breve{\hat{\wp}}_{ij}}\right)^{w_j}} \end{array} \right\rangle, \tag{67}$$

Step 4. According to Definition 8, we obtain the order of the overall aggregated values $\widetilde{\wp}_i$ $(i = 1, 2, \ldots, m)$.

Step 5. Rank all the alternatives F_i $(i = 1, 2, \ldots, m)$ and hence select the most desirable one(s).

4.3. Numerical Example

In order to illustrate the application of the developed approach in practice, we consider a real-life decision problem about searching the global supplier with Fermatean fuzzy linguistic information.

Example 5. *Supplier selection is one of the most important processes to accomplish an effective supply chain because a supplier comprehensively contributes to the overall supply chain performance. Due to the involvement of a group of persons and many factors, supplier selection is typically considered a MAGDM problem. In the last few years, the supplier selection problem has received a considerable amount of attention from researchers working in different parts of the globe.*

A Chilean company specializing in commercialized computer and office materials wants to select a suitable material supplier to assign the raw materials' optimum order. After preliminary screening, five potential global suppliers $\{F_1, F_2, F_3, F_4, F_5\}$ were shortlisted for further evaluation. The company invites four experts $\{E_1, E_2, E_3, E_4\}$ to evaluate the shortlisted suppliers concerning five attributes: (i) overall cost of the product A_1; (ii) service performance of the supplier A_2; (iii) reputation of the supplier A_3; (iv) quality of the product A_4; (v) delivery time of the product A_5. The attribute weight vector is given as $w = (0.20, 0.15, 0.25, 0.25, 0.15)^T$. The experts provide their evaluation information corresponding to each attribute in terms of FFLNs based on the following LTS:

$$L = \left\{ \begin{array}{l} \ell_0 = \text{EP(extremly poor)}, \ell_1 = \text{VP(very poor)}, \ell_2 = \text{P(poor)}, \\ \ell_3 = \text{SP(slightly poor)}, \ell_4 = \text{F(fair)}, \ell_5 = \text{SG(slightly good)}, \\ \ell_6 = \text{G(good)}, \ell_7 = \text{VG(very good)}, \ell_8 = \text{EG(extremly good)} \end{array} \right\}.$$

The experts provide the following Fermetean fuzzy linguistic decision matrices $\mathfrak{B}^{(q)} = \left(\wp_{ij}{}^{(q)}\right)_{5\times 5}$ $(q = 1, 2, 3, 4)$, as listed in Tables 3–6, respectively.

Table 3. Decision matrix $\mathfrak{B}^{(1)}$.

	A_1	A_2	A_3	A_4	A_5
F_1	$\langle \ell_3, 0.8, 0.3 \rangle$	$\langle \ell_1, 0.5, 0.5 \rangle$	$\langle \ell_4, 0.6, 0.1 \rangle$	$\langle \ell_1, 0.2, 0.3 \rangle$	$\langle \ell_5, 0.4, 0.6 \rangle$
F_2	$\langle \ell_5, 0.7, 0.2 \rangle$	$\langle \ell_4, 0.6, 0.4 \rangle$	$\langle \ell_7, 0.7, 0.3 \rangle$	$\langle \ell_6, 0.8, 0.1 \rangle$	$\langle \ell_4, 0.5, 0.7 \rangle$
F_3	$\langle \ell_4, 0.4, 0.7 \rangle$	$\langle \ell_2, 0.2, 0.8 \rangle$	$\langle \ell_3, 0.4, 0.6 \rangle$	$\langle \ell_2, 0.6, 0.6 \rangle$	$\langle \ell_5, 0.5, 0.1 \rangle$
F_4	$\langle \ell_1, 0.7, 0.5 \rangle$	$\langle \ell_3, 0.4, 0.5 \rangle$	$\langle \ell_4, 0.3, 0.4 \rangle$	$\langle \ell_4, 0.2, 0.1 \rangle$	$\langle \ell_2, 0.6, 0.2 \rangle$
F_4	$\langle \ell_3, 0.3, 0.1 \rangle$	$\langle \ell_4, 0.7, 0.1 \rangle$	$\langle \ell_1, 0.8, 0.5 \rangle$	$\langle \ell_5, 0.5, 0.8 \rangle$	$\langle \ell_4, 0.9, 0.1 \rangle$

Table 4. Decision matrix $\mathfrak{B}^{(2)}$.

	A_1	A_2	A_3	A_4	A_5
F_1	$\langle \ell_2, 0.5, 0.2 \rangle$	$\langle \ell_3, 0.7, 0.6 \rangle$	$\langle \ell_5, 0.2, 0.4 \rangle$	$\langle \ell_5, 0.3, 0.9 \rangle$	$\langle \ell_7, 0.4, 0.3 \rangle$
F_2	$\langle \ell_4, 0.6, 0.1 \rangle$	$\langle \ell_7, 0.9, 0.5 \rangle$	$\langle \ell_6, 0.8, 0.4 \rangle$	$\langle \ell_8, 0.9, 0.3 \rangle$	$\langle \ell_3, 0.8, 0.3 \rangle$
F_3	$\langle \ell_5, 0.9, 0.3 \rangle$	$\langle \ell_4, 0.5, 0.2 \rangle$	$\langle \ell_3, 0.4, 0.2 \rangle$	$\langle \ell_2, 0.4, 0.5 \rangle$	$\langle \ell_1, 0.7, 0.1 \rangle$
F_4	$\langle \ell_7, 0.5, 0.4 \rangle$	$\langle \ell_2, 0.5, 0.1 \rangle$	$\langle \ell_4, 0.6, 0.7 \rangle$	$\langle \ell_5, 0.2, 0.8 \rangle$	$\langle \ell_5, 0.5, 0.3 \rangle$
F_4	$\langle \ell_5, 0.2, 0.5 \rangle$	$\langle \ell_1, 0.6, 0.8 \rangle$	$\langle \ell_1, 0.9, 0.6 \rangle$	$\langle \ell_7, 0.1, 0.7 \rangle$	$\langle \ell_2, 0.2, 0.2 \rangle$

Table 5. Decision matrix $\mathfrak{B}^{(3)}$.

	A_1	A_2	A_3	A_4	A_5
F_1	$\langle \ell_1, 0.7, 0.2 \rangle$	$\langle \ell_4, 0.6, 0.1 \rangle$	$\langle \ell_3, 0.8, 0.3 \rangle$	$\langle \ell_1, 0.6, 0.5 \rangle$	$\langle \ell_2, 0.8, 0.0 \rangle$
F_2	$\langle \ell_2, 0.6, 0.4 \rangle$	$\langle \ell_8, 0.9, 0.2 \rangle$	$\langle \ell_6, 0.6, 0.1 \rangle$	$\langle \ell_7, 0.9, 0.6 \rangle$	$\langle \ell_3, 0.7, 0.0 \rangle$
F_3	$\langle \ell_4, 0.9, 0.6 \rangle$	$\langle \ell_4, 0.6, 0.7 \rangle$	$\langle \ell_2, 0.4, 0.4 \rangle$	$\langle \ell_4, 0.1, 0.8 \rangle$	$\langle \ell_5, 0.6, 0.2 \rangle$
F_4	$\langle \ell_3, 0.4, 0.4 \rangle$	$\langle \ell_5, 0.7, 0.0 \rangle$	$\langle \ell_6, 0.2, 0.5 \rangle$	$\langle \ell_5, 0.6, 0.8 \rangle$	$\langle \ell_7, 0.1, 0.4 \rangle$
F_4	$\langle \ell_7, 0.3, 0.9 \rangle$	$\langle \ell_3, 0.8, 0.3 \rangle$	$\langle \ell_1, 0.7, 0.6 \rangle$	$\langle \ell_6, 0.3, 0.5 \rangle$	$\langle \ell_1, 0.8, 0.6 \rangle$

Table 6. Decision matrix $\mathfrak{B}^{(4)}$.

	A_1	A_2	A_3	A_4	A_5
F_1	$\langle \ell_2, 0.7, 0.1 \rangle$	$\langle \ell_4, 0.7, 0.0 \rangle$	$\langle \ell_3, 0.6, 0.6 \rangle$	$\langle \ell_4, 0.8, 0.2 \rangle$	$\langle \ell_5, 0.2, 0.9 \rangle$
F_2	$\langle \ell_3, 0.6, 0.9 \rangle$	$\langle \ell_6, 0.5, 0.3 \rangle$	$\langle \ell_7, 0.9, 0.2 \rangle$	$\langle \ell_8, 0.9, 0.4 \rangle$	$\langle \ell_5, 0.7, 0.1 \rangle$
F_3	$\langle \ell_4, 0.3, 0.4 \rangle$	$\langle \ell_3, 0.6, 0.9 \rangle$	$\langle \ell_4, 0.2, 0.5 \rangle$	$\langle \ell_5, 0.4, 0.7 \rangle$	$\langle \ell_4, 0.2, 0.6 \rangle$
F_4	$\langle \ell_3, 0.3, 0.5 \rangle$	$\langle \ell_1, 0.3, 0.4 \rangle$	$\langle \ell_3, 0.7, 0.4 \rangle$	$\langle \ell_3, 0.8, 0.3 \rangle$	$\langle \ell_2, 0.6, 0.7 \rangle$
F_4	$\langle \ell_5, 0.6, 0.4 \rangle$	$\langle \ell_4, 0.4, 0.8 \rangle$	$\langle \ell_1, 0.5, 0.5 \rangle$	$\langle \ell_2, 0.4, 0.7 \rangle$	$\langle \ell_4, 0.5, 0.6 \rangle$

Step 1: Since A_1 is a cost-type attribute while A_2, A_3, A_4 and A_5 are benefit-type attributes, so the normalized decision matrices $\hat{\mathfrak{B}}^{(q)}(q = 1, 2, 3, 4)$ are obtained using Equation (63) as follows (see Tables 7–10).

Table 7. Normalized decision matrix $\hat{\mathfrak{B}}^{(1)}$.

	A_1	A_2	A_3	A_4	A_5
F_1	$\langle \ell_5, 0.3, 0.8 \rangle$	$\langle \ell_1, 0.5, 0.5 \rangle$	$\langle \ell_4, 0.6, 0.1 \rangle$	$\langle \ell_1, 0.2, 0.3 \rangle$	$\langle \ell_5, 0.4, 0.6 \rangle$
F_2	$\langle \ell_3, 0.2, 0.7 \rangle$	$\langle \ell_4, 0.6, 0.4 \rangle$	$\langle \ell_7, 0.7, 0.3 \rangle$	$\langle \ell_6, 0.8, 0.1 \rangle$	$\langle \ell_4, 0.5, 0.7 \rangle$
F_3	$\langle \ell_4, 0.7, 0.4 \rangle$	$\langle \ell_2, 0.2, 0.8 \rangle$	$\langle \ell_3, 0.4, 0.6 \rangle$	$\langle \ell_2, 0.6, 0.6 \rangle$	$\langle \ell_5, 0.5, 0.1 \rangle$
F_4	$\langle \ell_7, 0.5, 0.7 \rangle$	$\langle \ell_3, 0.4, 0.5 \rangle$	$\langle \ell_4, 0.3, 0.4 \rangle$	$\langle \ell_4, 0.2, 0.1 \rangle$	$\langle \ell_2, 0.6, 0.2 \rangle$
F_5	$\langle \ell_5, 0.1, 0.3 \rangle$	$\langle \ell_4, 0.7, 0.1 \rangle$	$\langle \ell_1, 0.8, 0.5 \rangle$	$\langle \ell_5, 0.5, 0.8 \rangle$	$\langle \ell_4, 0.9, 0.1 \rangle$

Table 8. Normalized decision matrix $\hat{\mathfrak{B}}^{(2)}$.

	A_1	A_2	A_3	A_4	A_5
F_1	$\langle \ell_6, 0.2, 0.5 \rangle$	$\langle \ell_3, 0.7, 0.6 \rangle$	$\langle \ell_5, 0.2, 0.4 \rangle$	$\langle \ell_5, 0.3, 0.9 \rangle$	$\langle \ell_7, 0.4, 0.3 \rangle$
F_2	$\langle \ell_4, 0.1, 0.6 \rangle$	$\langle \ell_7, 0.9, 0.5 \rangle$	$\langle \ell_6, 0.8, 0.4 \rangle$	$\langle \ell_8, 0.9, 0.3 \rangle$	$\langle \ell_3, 0.8, 0.3 \rangle$
F_3	$\langle \ell_3, 0.3, 0.9 \rangle$	$\langle \ell_4, 0.5, 0.2 \rangle$	$\langle \ell_3, 0.4, 0.2 \rangle$	$\langle \ell_2, 0.4, 0.4 \rangle$	$\langle \ell_1, 0.7, 0.1 \rangle$
F_4	$\langle \ell_1, 0.4, 0.5 \rangle$	$\langle \ell_2, 0.5, 0.1 \rangle$	$\langle \ell_4, 0.6, 0.7 \rangle$	$\langle \ell_5, 0.2, 0.8 \rangle$	$\langle \ell_5, 0.5, 0.3 \rangle$
F_5	$\langle \ell_3, 0.5, 0.2 \rangle$	$\langle \ell_1, 0.6, 0.8 \rangle$	$\langle \ell_1, 0.9, 0.6 \rangle$	$\langle \ell_7, 0.1, 0.7 \rangle$	$\langle \ell_2, 0.2, 0.2 \rangle$

Table 9. Normalized decision matrix $\hat{\mathfrak{B}}^{(3)}$.

	A_1	A_2	A_3	A_4	A_5
F_1	$\langle \ell_7, 0.2, 0.7 \rangle$	$\langle \ell_4, 0.6, 0.1 \rangle$	$\langle \ell_3, 0.8, 0.3 \rangle$	$\langle \ell_1, 0.6, 0.5 \rangle$	$\langle \ell_2, 0.8, 0.0 \rangle$
F_5	$\langle \ell_6, 0.4, 0.6 \rangle$	$\langle \ell_8, 0.9, 0.2 \rangle$	$\langle \ell_6, 0.6, 0.1 \rangle$	$\langle \ell_7, 0.9, 0.6 \rangle$	$\langle \ell_3, 0.7, 0.0 \rangle$
F_3	$\langle \ell_4, 0.6, 0.9 \rangle$	$\langle \ell_4, 0.6, 0.7 \rangle$	$\langle \ell_2, 0.4, 0.4 \rangle$	$\langle \ell_4, 0.1, 0.8 \rangle$	$\langle \ell_5, 0.6, 0.2 \rangle$
F_4	$\langle \ell_5, 0.4, 0.4 \rangle$	$\langle \ell_5, 0.7, 0.0 \rangle$	$\langle \ell_6, 0.2, 0.5 \rangle$	$\langle \ell_5, 0.6, 0.8 \rangle$	$\langle \ell_7, 0.1, 0.4 \rangle$
F_4	$\langle \ell_1, 0.9, 0.3 \rangle$	$\langle \ell_3, 0.8, 0.3 \rangle$	$\langle \ell_1, 0.7, 0.6 \rangle$	$\langle \ell_6, 0.3, 0.5 \rangle$	$\langle \ell_1, 0.8, 0.6 \rangle$

Table 10. Normalized decision matrix $\mathfrak{B}^{(4)}$.

	A_1	A_2	A_3	A_4	A_5
F_1	$\langle \ell_6, 0.1, 0.7\rangle$	$\langle \ell_4, 0.7, 0.0\rangle$	$\langle \ell_3, 0.6, 0.6\rangle$	$\langle \ell_4, 0.8, 0.2\rangle$	$\langle \ell_5, 0.2, 0.9\rangle$
F_2	$\langle \ell_5, 0.9, 0.6\rangle$	$\langle \ell_6, 0.5, 0.3\rangle$	$\langle \ell_7, 0.9, 0.2\rangle$	$\langle \ell_8, 0.9, 0.4\rangle$	$\langle \ell_5, 0.7, 0.1\rangle$
F_3	$\langle \ell_4, 0.4, 0.3\rangle$	$\langle \ell_3, 0.6, 0.9\rangle$	$\langle \ell_4, 0.2, 0.5\rangle$	$\langle \ell_5, 0.4, 0.7\rangle$	$\langle \ell_4, 0.2, 0.6\rangle$
F_4	$\langle \ell_5, 0.5, 0.3\rangle$	$\langle \ell_1, 0.3, 0.4\rangle$	$\langle \ell_3, 0.7, 0.4\rangle$	$\langle \ell_3, 0.8, 0.3\rangle$	$\langle \ell_2, 0.6, 0.7\rangle$
F_5	$\langle \ell_3, 0.4, 0.6\rangle$	$\langle \ell_4, 0.4, 0.8\rangle$	$\langle \ell_1, 0.5, 0.5\rangle$	$\langle \ell_2, 0.4, 0.7\rangle$	$\langle \ell_4, 0.5, 0.6\rangle$

Step 2: First, we calculate the experts' weighting vector $\omega = (0.1550, 0.3450, 0.3450, 0.1550)^T$ based on the normal distribution method [62]. Then, utilizing the FFLOWA operator mentioned in Equation (64) (without loss of generality, we have taken the linguistic scaling function $\varphi^* = \varphi_2^*(\theta = 1.4)$ to obtain the collective normalized decision matrix $\breve{\mathfrak{B}} = \left(\breve{\wp}_{ij}\right)_{5\times 5}$. Using Equation (8), we obtain

$$\mathfrak{S}\left(\hat{\wp}_{11}{}^{(1)}\right) = \varphi_2^*(\ell_5) \times \left(\frac{0.3^3+1-0.8^3}{2}\right) = 0.1469,\ \mathfrak{S}\left(\hat{\wp}_{11}{}^{(2)}\right) = \varphi_2^*(\ell_6) \times \left(\frac{0.2^3+1-0.5^3}{2}\right) = 0.2953,$$
$$\mathfrak{S}\left(\hat{\wp}_{11}{}^{(3)}\right) = \varphi_2^*(\ell_7) \times \left(\frac{0.2^3+1-0.7^3}{2}\right) = 0.2683,\ \mathfrak{S}\left(\hat{\wp}_{11}{}^{(4)}\right) = \varphi_2^*(\ell_6) \times \left(\frac{0.1^3+1-0.7^3}{2}\right) = 0.2201.$$

Since $\mathfrak{S}\left(\hat{\wp}_{11}{}^{(2)}\right) > \mathfrak{S}\left(\hat{\wp}_{11}{}^{(3)}\right) > \mathfrak{S}\left(\hat{\wp}_{11}{}^{(4)}\right) > \mathfrak{S}\left(\hat{\wp}_{11}{}^{(1)}\right)$, therefore $\hat{\wp}_{11}{}^{(2)} \succ \hat{\wp}_{11}{}^{(3)} \succ \hat{\wp}_{11}{}^{(4)} \succ \hat{\wp}_{11}{}^{(1)}$.

$$\breve{\wp}_{11} = FFLOWA\left(\hat{\wp}_{11}{}^{(1)}, \hat{\wp}_{11}{}^{(2)}, \hat{\wp}_{11}{}^{(3)}, \hat{\wp}_{11}{}^{(4)}\right)$$
$$= \left\langle \begin{array}{c} \varphi_2^{*-1}\left(1-(1-\varphi_2^*(\ell_6))^{0.1550} \times (1-\varphi_2^*(\ell_7))^{0.3450} \times (1-\varphi_2^*(\ell_6))^{0.3450} \times (1-\varphi_2^*(\ell_5))^{0.1550}\right), \\ \sqrt[3]{1-(1-0.2^3)^{0.1550} \times (1-0.2^3)^{0.3450} \times (1-0.1^3)^{0.3450} \times (1-0.3^3)^{0.1550}}, \\ \sqrt[3]{\begin{array}{c} (1-0.2^3)^{0.1550} \times (1-0.2^3)^{0.3450} \times (1-0.1^3)^{0.3450} \times (1-0.3^3)^{0.1550} \\ -(1-(0.2^3+0.5^3))^{0.1550} \times (1-(0.2^3+0.7^3))^{0.3450} \times (1-(0.1^3+0.7^3))^{0.3450} \times (1-(0.3^3+0.8^3))^{0.1550} \end{array}} \end{array} \right\rangle$$
$$= \langle \ell_{6.3636}, 0.2046, 0.7016\rangle.$$

Similarly, we can calculate other collective values. Table 11 presents the collective normalized decision matrix.

Table 11. Collective normalized decision matrix $\breve{\mathfrak{B}}$ based on FFLOWA operator.

	A_1	A_2	A_3	A_4	A_5
F_1	$\langle \ell_{6.3636}, 0.2046, 0.7016\rangle$	$\langle \ell_{3.0842}, 0.6463, 0.4778\rangle$	$\langle \ell_{4.0947}, 0.5943, 0.3966\rangle$	$\langle \ell_{1.9102}, 0.6272, 0.5882\rangle$	$\langle \ell_{4.8442}, 0.6262, 0.5809\rangle$
F_2	$\langle \ell_{4.9662}, 0.5876, 0.6750\rangle$	$\langle \ell_{8.0000}, 0.8048, 0.4686\rangle$	$\langle \ell_{6.6072}, 0.3266, 0.3266\rangle$	$\langle \ell_{8.000}, 0.8892, 0.5234\rangle$	$\langle \ell_{3.4637}, 0.7244, 0.3855\rangle$
F_3	$\langle \ell_{3.8309}, 0.4735, 0.8315\rangle$	$\langle \ell_{3.2911}, 0.5571, 0.8364\rangle$	$\langle \ell_{3.1444}, 0.2951, 0.5097\rangle$	$\langle \ell_{2.6951}, 0.3791, 0.6367\rangle$	$\langle \ell_{4.0135}, 0.4683, 0.4152\rangle$
F_4	$\langle \ell_{5.1312}, 0.3942, 0.5286\rangle$	$\langle \ell_{2.5714}, 0.5054, 0.3709\rangle$	$\langle \ell_{4.1499}, 0.5602, 0.5041\rangle$	$\langle \ell_{4.4243}, 0.5652, 0.6810\rangle$	$\langle \ell_{4.4155}, 0.5367, 0.4497\rangle$
F_5	$\langle \ell_{2.9330}, 0.6195, 0.4349\rangle$	$\langle \ell_{3.0842}, 0.6778, 0.6322\rangle$	$\langle \ell_{0.9998}, 0.7717, 0.6001\rangle$	$\langle \ell_{5.9625}, 0.3895, 0.7325\rangle$	$\langle \ell_{2.7125}, 0.6724, 0.4952\rangle$

Step 3: Utilize the FFLWA operator given in Equation (66) with $w = (0.20, 0.15, 0.25, 0.25, 0.15)^T$ to derive the overall Fermetean fuzzy linguistic preference values $\widetilde{\wp}_i$ $(i = 1,2,3,4,5)$ corresponding to each alternative $F_i (i = 1,2,3,4,5)$. Using the expression mentioned in Equation (66), we obtain

$$\widetilde{\wp}_1 = FFLWA\left(\breve{\wp}_{11}, \breve{\wp}_{12}, \breve{\wp}_{13}, \breve{\wp}_{14}, \breve{\wp}_{15}\right)$$

$$= \left\langle \begin{array}{l} \varphi_2^{*-1}\left(1-(1-\varphi_2^*(\ell_{6.3636}))^{0.20} \times (1-\varphi_2^*(\ell_{3.0842}))^{0.15} \times (1-\varphi_2^*(\ell_{4.0947}))^{0.25} \times (1-\varphi_2^*(\ell_{1.9102}))^{0.25} \times (1-\varphi_2^*(\ell_{4.8442}))^{0.15}\right), \\ \sqrt[3]{1-(1-0.2046^3)^{0.20} \times (1-0.6463^3)^{0.15} \times (1-0.5943^3)^{0.25} \times (1-0.6272^3)^{0.25} \times (1-0.6262^3)^{0.15}}, \\ \sqrt[3]{\begin{array}{l} (1-0.2046^3)^{0.20} \times (1-0.6463^3)^{0.15} \times (1-0.5943^3)^{0.25} \times (1-0.6272^3)^{0.25} \times (1-0.6262^3)^{0.15} \\ -(1-(0.2046^3+0.7016^3))^{0.20} \times (1-(0.6463^3+0.4778^3))^{0.15} \times (1-(0.5943^3+0.3966^3))^{0.25} \\ \times (1-(0.6272^3+0.5882^3))^{0.25} \times (1-(0.6262^3+0.5809^3))^{0.25} \end{array}} \end{array} \right\rangle$$

$$= \langle \ell_{4.3017}, 0.5831, 0.5647 \rangle.$$

The overall Fermetean fuzzy linguistic preference values $\widetilde{\wp}_i$ $(i = 1,2,3,4,5)$ are recorded in Table 12.

Table 12. The overall FFL preference values $\widetilde{\wp}_i$ based on the FFLWA operator.

F_1	F_2	F_3	F_4	F_5
$\langle \ell_{4.3017}, 0.5831, 0.5647 \rangle$	$\langle \ell_{8.0000}, 0.7473, 0.5436 \rangle$	$\langle \ell_{3.2991}, 0.4379, 0.7336 \rangle$	$\langle \ell_{4.2602}, 0.5254, 0.5559 \rangle$	$\langle \ell_{3.2791}, 0.6571, 0.6108 \rangle$

Step 4: According to Definition 8, we have

$$\mathfrak{S}(\widetilde{\wp}_1)= 0.2641,\ \mathfrak{S}(\widetilde{\wp}_2)= 0.6284,\ \mathfrak{S}(\widetilde{\wp}_3)= 0.1562,\ \mathfrak{S}(\widetilde{\wp}_4)= 0.2511,\ \mathfrak{S}(\widetilde{\wp}_5)= 0.2385$$

Step 5: The final ranking order of the suppliers following the score values $\mathfrak{S}(\widetilde{\wp}_i)$ is $F_2 \succ F_1 \succ F_4 \succ F_5 \succ F_3$, thus, the most desirable supplier is F_2.

Additionally, if we use the FFLOWG operator in Step 2 and the FFLWG operator in Step 3 instead of FFLOWA and FFLWA operators, respectively, in the developed method, then the procedure steps are as follows:

Step 1: Same as above.

Step 2: Utilizing the FFLOWG operator to aggregate all the normalized decision matrices $\mathfrak{B}^{(q)} (q = 1,2,3,4)$, the obtained results corresponding to each alternative are shown in Table 13.

Table 13. Aggregated normalized decision matrix $\breve{\mathfrak{B}}$ based on FFLOWG operator.

	A_1	A_2	A_3	A_4	A_5
F_1	$\langle \ell_{6.2263}, 0.2137, 0.7007 \rangle$	$\langle \ell_{2.7656}, 0.6538, 0.4637 \rangle$	$\langle \ell_{3.9865}, 0.5937, 0.3980 \rangle$	$\langle \ell_{1.4768}, 0.5857, 0.6112 \rangle$	$\langle \ell_{3.9815}, 0.5743, 0.6318 \rangle$
F_2	$\langle \ell_{4.7577}, 0.6489, 0.6190 \rangle$	$\langle \ell_{6.4552}, 0.8239, 0.4017 \rangle$	$\langle \ell_{6.5188}, 0.3211, 0.3211 \rangle$	$\langle \ell_{7.3788}, 0.9050, 0.4721 \rangle$	$\langle \ell_{3.3857}, 0.7149, 0.4160 \rangle$
F_3	$\langle \ell_{3.8103}, 0.6273, 0.7881 \rangle$	$\langle \ell_{3.1929}, 0.6306, 0.7975 \rangle$	$\langle \ell_{3.0632}, 0.3571, 0.5091 \rangle$	$\langle \ell_{2.4951}, 0.4715, 0.6414 \rangle$	$\langle \ell_{3.4022}, 0.5068, 0.4347 \rangle$
F_4	$\langle \ell_{4.1466}, 0.4034, 0.5233 \rangle$	$\langle \ell_{2.2839}, 0.5001, 0.3805 \rangle$	$\langle \ell_{3.9398}, 0.5654, 0.5041 \rangle$	$\langle \ell_{4.3441}, 0.5767, 0.6729 \rangle$	$\langle \ell_{3.3720}, 0.5447, 0.4377 \rangle$
F_5	$\langle \ell_{2.6262}, 0.6119, 0.4495 \rangle$	$\langle \ell_{2.7656}, 0.6350, 0.6754 \rangle$	$\langle \ell_{0.9998}, 0.7958, 0.5559 \rangle$	$\langle \ell_{5.3982}, 0.4159, 0.7244 \rangle$	$\langle \ell_{2.3979}, 0.6756, 0.4893 \rangle$

Step 3: The overall Fermetean fuzzy linguistic preference values $\widetilde{\wp}_i$ $(i = 1,2,3,4,5)$ of each alternative $F_i (i = 1,2,3,4,5)$ using the FFLWG operator are summarized in Table 14.

Table 14. The overall Fermetean fuzzy linguistic preference values $\widetilde{\wp}_i$ based on the FFLWG operator.

F_1	F_2	F_3	F_4	F_5
$\langle \ell_{3.1520}, 0.5552, 0.5861 \rangle$	$\langle \ell_{6.0409}, 0.7785, 0.4727 \rangle$	$\langle \ell_{3.0867}, 0.5716, 0.6739 \rangle$	$\langle \ell_{3.6215}, 0.5375, 0.5460 \rangle$	$\langle \ell_{2.3249}, 0.6565, 0.6115 \rangle$

Step 4: The score values $\mathfrak{S}(\widetilde{\wp}_i)$ of the overall Fermetean fuzzy linguistic preference values obtained during Step 3 are calculated as

$$\mathfrak{S}(\widetilde{\wp}_1)= 0.2143,\ \mathfrak{S}(\widetilde{\wp}_2)= 0.4602,\ \mathfrak{S}(\widetilde{\wp}_3)= 0.1923,\ \mathfrak{S}(\widetilde{\wp}_4)= 0.2363,\ \mathfrak{S}(\widetilde{\wp}_5)= 0.1934$$

Step 5. Since $\mathfrak{S}(\widetilde{\wp}_2) \succ \mathfrak{S}(\widetilde{\wp}_4) \succ \mathfrak{S}(\widetilde{\wp}_1) \succ \mathfrak{S}(\widetilde{\wp}_5) \succ \mathfrak{S}(\widetilde{\wp}_3)$, therefore we obtain the final ranking order of the suppliers as $F_2 \succ F_4 \succ F_1 \succ F_5 \succ F_3$. Hence, F_2 is the most desirable supplier.

It is worth noting that a decision-maker can choose the appropriate aggregation operator based on his/her behavior towards the aggregation procedure. If a decision-maker has optimistic behavior towards the aggregation of experts' preference information and pessimistic behavior towards the final decision, then he/she uses the FFLOWA and FFLWG operators in Step 2 and Step 3, respectively, of the developed approach. A complete analysis has been conducted to analyze the effect of the decision-maker's behavioral attitude on the final ranking. The results are summarized in Table 15, along with the suppliers' ranking order. The results shown in Table 15 indicate that when we use the FFLOWA (or the FFLOWG) operator in Step 2 and the FFLWA (or FFLHA) operator in Step 3 then the ranking order of the alternatives is always $F_2 \succ F_1 \succ F_4 \succ F_5 \succ F_3$. On the other hand, if we use the FFLOWA (or the FFLOWG) operator in Step 2 and the FFLWG (or FFLHG) operator in Step 3 then the ranking order of the alternatives is obtained as $F_2 \succ F_4 \succ F_1 \succ F_5 \succ F_3$, which is slightly different from the previous ones. It shows the effect of the nature of varying aggregation operators on the final ranking order of the alternatives.

Table 15. The score values $\mathfrak{S}(\widetilde{\wp}_i)$ and ranking order of the suppliers.

The Operator Used in Step 2	The Operator Used in Step 3	Score Values					Ranking of the Suppliers
		$\mathfrak{S}(\widetilde{\wp}_1)$	$\mathfrak{S}(\widetilde{\wp}_2)$	$\mathfrak{S}(\widetilde{\wp}_3)$	$\mathfrak{S}(\widetilde{\wp}_4)$	$\mathfrak{S}(\widetilde{\wp}_5)$	
FFLOWA	FFLWA	0.2641	0.6284	0.1562	0.2511	0.2385	$F_2 \succ F_1 \succ F_4 \succ F_5 \succ F_3$
	FFLWG	0.2407	0.4832	0.1679	0.2501	0.2030	$F_2 \succ F_4 \succ F_1 \succ F_5 \succ F_3$
	FFLHA	0.2618	0.6245	0.1568	0.2513	0.2235	$F_2 \succ F_1 \succ F_4 \succ F_5 \succ F_3$
	FFLHG	0.2427	0.5334	0.1704	0.2484	0.2165	$F_2 \succ F_4 \succ F_1 \succ F_5 \succ F_3$
FFLOWG	FFLWA	0.2408	0.4812	0.1765	0.2369	0.2228	$F_2 \succ F_1 \succ F_4 \succ F_5 \succ F_3$
	FFLWG	0.2143	0.4602	0.1923	0.2363	0.1934	$F_2 \succ F_4 \succ F_1 \succ F_5 \succ F_3$
	FFLHA	0.2385	0.4665	0.1804	0.2366	0.2151	$F_2 \succ F_1 \succ F_4 \succ F_5 \succ F_3$
	FFLHG	0.2125	0.4236	0.1873	0.2282	0.1899	$F_2 \succ F_4 \succ F_1 \succ F_5 \succ F_3$

Apart from the above analysis, to examine the influence of the different LSFs on the alternatives' ranking order, we have employed different LSFs in the calculation process of the developed decision-making approach. Then, after applying the steps, the corresponding results are summarized in Table 16.

From Table 16, it has been observed that although the score values of the alternatives are entirely different when we use different LSFs; however, the best alternative is always F_2 for the considered problem. Note that the use of different LSFs shows an influence on the final ranking order of the alternatives. It is also worth noting that, in other real-life decision problems, the best alternative may be different depending on the use of different aggregation operators. Our developed method provides an ability to the DMs for choosing the appropriate LSF according to his/her personal choice and the actual semantic environment.

Table 16. The score values $\mathfrak{S}(\tilde{\wp}_i)$ and ranking order of the suppliers based on different LSFs.

LSF	The Operator Used in Step 2	The Operator Used in Step 3	Score Values					Ranking of the Suppliers
			$\mathfrak{S}(\tilde{\wp}_1)$	$\mathfrak{S}(\tilde{\wp}_2)$	$\mathfrak{S}(\tilde{\wp}_3)$	$\mathfrak{S}(\tilde{\wp}_4)$	$\mathfrak{S}(\tilde{\wp}_5)$	
$\varphi^* = \varphi_1^*$	FFLOWA	FFLWA	0.2813	0.6283	0.1610	0.2616	0.2414	$F_2 \succ F_1 \succ F_4 \succ F_5 \succ F_3$
		FFLWG	0.2531	0.4785	0.1702	0.2564	0.1797	$F_2 \succ F_4 \succ F_1 \succ F_5 \succ F_3$
		FFLHA	0.2905	0.6120	0.1602	0.3027	0.2336	$F_2 \succ F_4 \succ F_1 \succ F_5 \succ F_3$
		FFLHG	0.2523	0.4719	0.1686	0.2516	0.1813	$F_2 \succ F_1 \succ F_4 \succ F_5 \succ F_3$
	FFLOWG	FFLWA	0.2368	0.5157	0.1629	0.2309	0.2074	$F_2 \succ F_1 \succ F_4 \succ F_5 \succ F_3$
		FFLWG	0.2002	0.4793	0.1752	0.2265	0.1629	$F_2 \succ F_4 \succ F_1 \succ F_3 \succ F_5$
		FFLHA	0.2373	0.5013	0.1638	0.2500	0.1929	$F_2 \succ F_4 \succ F_1 \succ F_5 \succ F_3$
		FFLHG	0.2000	0.4386	0.1722	0.2373	0.1560	$F_2 \succ F_4 \succ F_1 \succ F_3 \succ F_5$
$\varphi^* = \varphi_3^*$ $(\rho = \tau = 0.8)$	FFLOWA	FFLWA	0.2913	0.6283	0.1591	0.3061	0.2448	$F_2 \succ F_4 \succ F_1 \succ F_5 \succ F_3$
		FFLWG	0.2554	0.5060	0.1669	0.2891	0.1695	$F_2 \succ F_4 \succ F_1 \succ F_5 \succ F_3$
		FFLHA	0.2905	0.6120	0.1602	0.3027	0.2336	$F_2 \succ F_4 \succ F_1 \succ F_5 \succ F_3$
		FFLHG	0.2569	0.4772	0.1661	0.2779	0.1718	$F_2 \succ F_4 \succ F_1 \succ F_5 \succ F_3$
	FFLOWG	FFLWA	0.2398	0.5270	0.1537	0.2319	0.2009	$F_2 \succ F_1 \succ F_4 \succ F_5 \succ F_3$
		FFLWG	0.1931	0.4864	0.1650	0.2274	0.1901	$F_2 \succ F_4 \succ F_1 \succ F_5 \succ F_3$
		FFLHA	0.2412	0.5124	0.1554	0.2337	0.1907	$F_2 \succ F_1 \succ F_4 \succ F_5 \succ F_3$
		FFLHG	0.1942	0.4455	0.1640	0.2232	0.1481	$F_2 \succ F_4 \succ F_1 \succ F_3 \succ F_5$

4.4. Sensitivity Analysis

The decision-making approach developed in this paper uses various AOs with different LSFs to aggregate information data as provided by decision-makers. This section discusses the influence of these AOs and LSFs on the decision result.

A sensitivity analysis has been conducted to better understand the impact of the various AOs on the ranking order of the alternatives with different LSFs. Figures 5–10 have been plotted, portraying the sensitivity of the results based on various AOs taking different LSFs. As shown in Figures 5–10, changes in the AOs and LSFs significantly influence the ranking of alternatives.

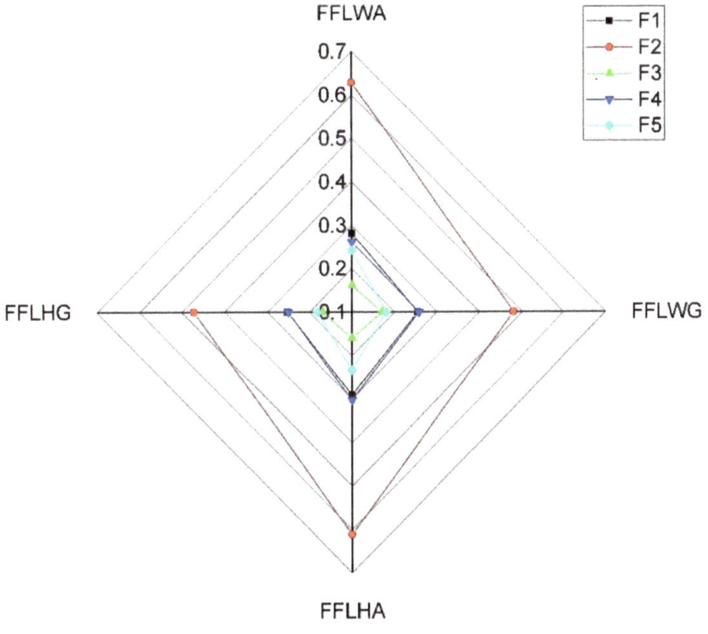

Figure 5. Sensitivity analysis for the alternatives based on FFLOWA operator in step 2 with $\varphi^* = \varphi_1^*$.

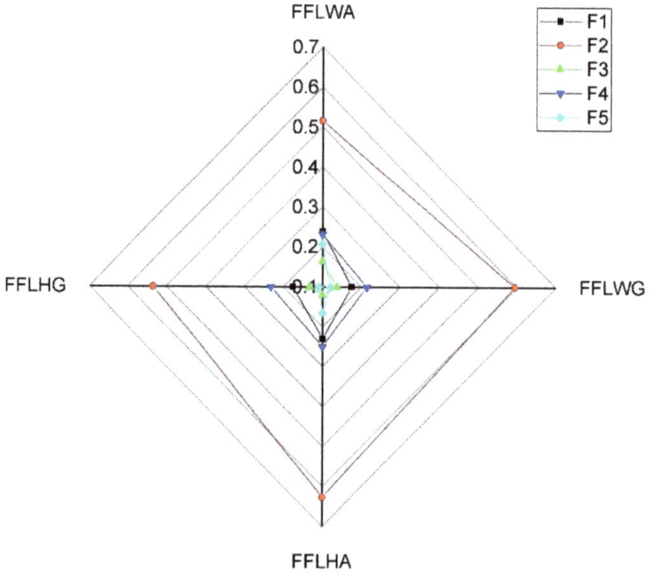

Figure 6. Sensitivity analysis for the alternatives based on FFLOWG operator in step 2 with $\varphi^* = \varphi_1^*$.

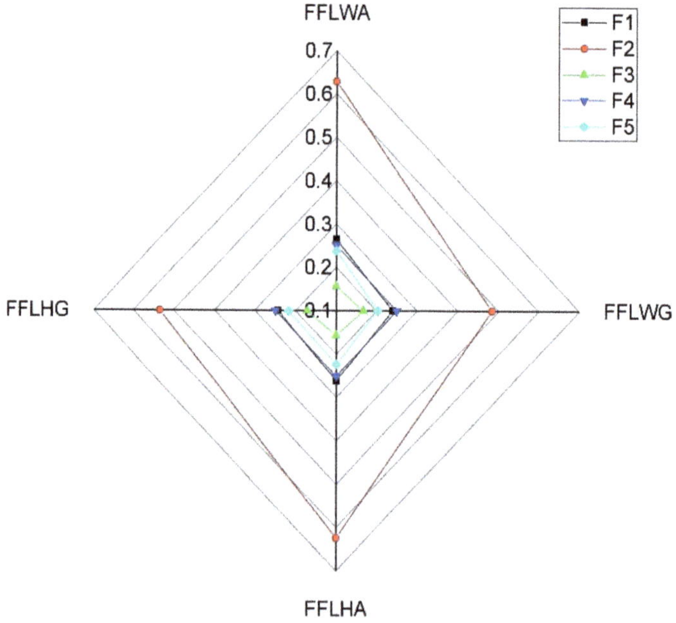

Figure 7. Sensitivity analysis for the alternatives based on FFLOWA operator in step 2 with $\varphi^* = \varphi_2^*$.

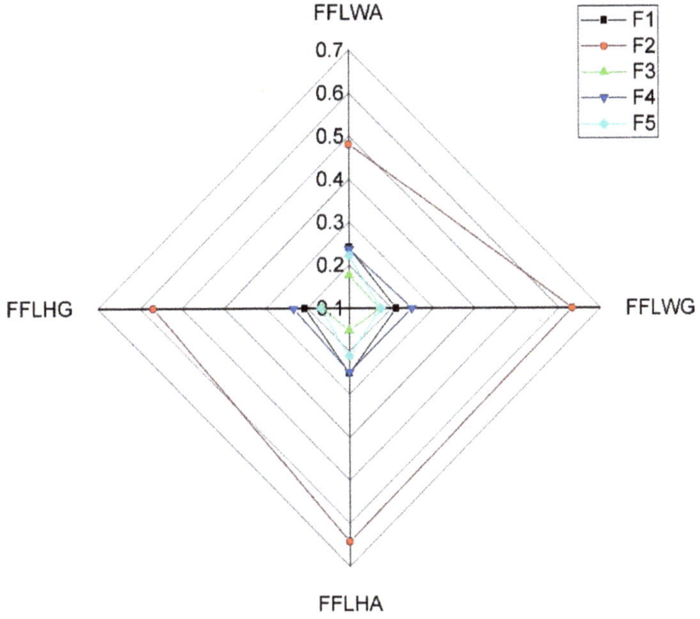

Figure 8. Sensitivity analysis for the alternatives based on FFLOWG operator in step 2 with $\varphi^* = \varphi_2^*$.

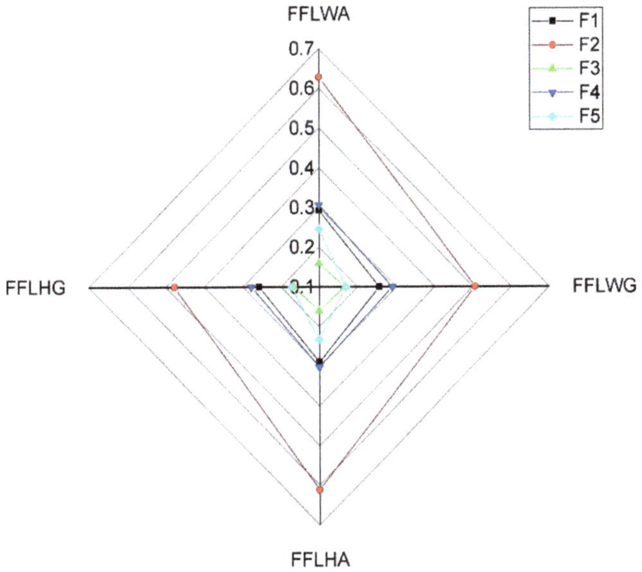

Figure 9. Sensitivity analysis for the alternatives based on FFLOWA operator in step 2 with $\varphi^* = \varphi_3^*$.

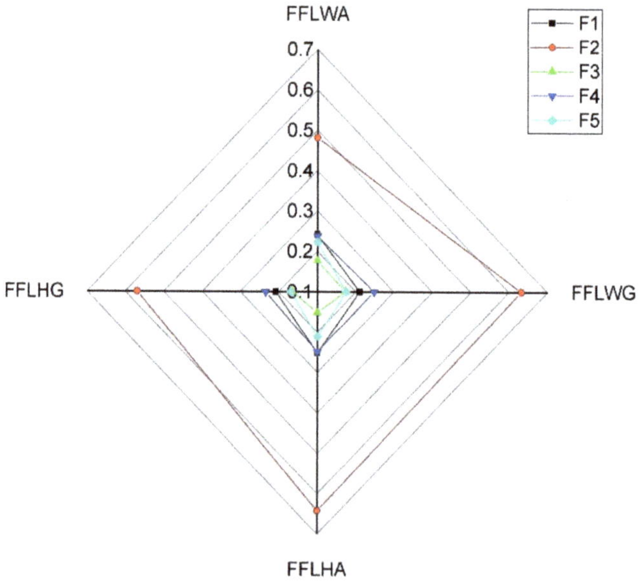

Figure 10. Sensitivity analysis for the alternatives based on FFLOWG operator in step 2 with $\varphi^* = \varphi_3^*$.

4.5. A Comparative Overview of the Results Based on Different AOs

In order to compare the performance of the developed AOs with existing ones, this paper uses the AOs and decision method formulated by Li et al. [53] to solve the above considered MAGDM problem. The obtained values of the closeness coefficient and ranking order of the suppliers are summarized in Table 17.

Table 17. The values of the closeness coefficient $\mathfrak{C}(\widetilde{\wp}_i)$ and ranking order of the suppliers.

Aggregation Operator Used	The Closeness Coefficient Values					Ranking of the Suppliers
	$\mathfrak{C}(\widetilde{\wp}_1)$	$\mathfrak{C}(\widetilde{\wp}_2)$	$\mathfrak{C}(\widetilde{\wp}_3)$	$\mathfrak{C}(\widetilde{\wp}_4)$	$\mathfrak{C}(\widetilde{\wp}_5)$	
FFLWA	0.3803	0.6109	0.2222	0.3317	0.3529	$F_2 \succ F_1 \succ F_5 \succ F_4 \succ F_3$
FFLWG	0.3942	0.5856	0.2063	0.3396	0.3412	$F_2 \succ F_1 \succ F_5 \succ F_4 \succ F_3$

From Table 17, it is inferred that the best alternative obtained by the proposed approach agrees with the method formulated by Li et al. [53] which confirms the consistency of the proposed operators. It is also clear from the results summarized in Table 17 that the best alternative (F_2) and the worst alternative (F_3) are the same by all the approaches. However, the complete ranking order of the suppliers is slightly different from our ranking order because of the use of different aggregation operators for aggregating the preference information of the decision-makers.

In addition, Spearman's rank correlation test [63] is used for the subsequent analyses to identify the differences between the ranking orders of the alternatives obtained by using different AOs in the formulated approach. Spearman's rank correlation measures the strength of association of two variables. It can be defined as follows:

$$r_{SRC} = 1 - \frac{6\sum_{j=1}^{m} d_j^2}{m(m^2-1)},$$

where m is the number of alternatives and d denotes the ranking difference of alternative F_j between two different rankings. According to [63], r_{SRC} lies between -1 to +1. $r_{SRC} = +1$

indicates a perfect positive relationship between the two sets of rankings and $r_{SRC} = -1$ implies a perfect negative relationship between the two sets of rankings. The closer r_{SRC} is to ±1, the stronger the relationship between the two rankings. Tables 18–20 summarize Spearman's rank correlation coefficient values between different rankings obtained based on different AOs and LSFs.

From Tables 18 and 19, we can easily see that the ranking orders obtained using FFLOWA+ FFLWA and FFLOWG+ FFLWA have a perfect positive relationship. Similarly, Tables 19 and 20 show that the rankings obtained by the FFLOWA+ FFLWG and FFLOWA+ FFLHG also have a perfect positive relationship.

Table 18. Results of Spearman's rank correlation with $\varphi^* = \varphi_1^*$.

$\varphi^* = \varphi_1^*$	FFLOWA+ FFLWA	FFLOWA + FFLWG	FFLOWA + FFLHA	FFLOWA + FFLHG	FFLOWG + FFLWA	FFLOWG + FFLWG	FFLOWG + FFLHA	FFLOWG + FFLHG
FFLOWA+ FFLWA	1	0.1	0.1	1	1	−0.3	0.1	−0.3
FFLOWA+ FFLWG	0.1	1	1	0.1	0.1	0.6	1	0.6
FFLOWA+ FFLHA	0.1	1	1	0.1	0.1	0.6	1	0.6
FFLOWA+ FFLHG	1	0.1	0.1	1	1	−0.3	0.1	−0.3
FFLOWG+ FFLWA	1	0.1	0.1	1	1	−0.3	0.1	−0.3
FFLOWG+ FFLWG	−0.3	0.6	0.6	−0.3	−0.3	1	0.6	1
FFLOWG+ FFLHA	0.1	1	1	0.1	0.1	0.6	1	0.6
FFLOWG+ FFLHG	−0.3	0.6	0.6	−0.3	−0.3	1	0.6	1

Table 19. Results of Spearman's rank correlation with $\varphi^* = \varphi_2^*$.

$\varphi^* = \varphi_1^*$	FFLOWA+ FFLWA	FFLOWA + FFLWG	FFLOWA + FFLHA	FFLOWA + FFLHG	FFLOWG + FFLWA	FFLOWG + FFLWG	FFLOWG + FFLHA	FFLOWG + FFLHG
FFLOWA+ FFLWA	1	0.1	1	0.1	1	0.1	1	0.1
FFLOWA+ FFLWG	0.1	1	0.1	1	0.1	1	0.1	1
FFLOWA+ FFLHA	1	0.1	1	0.1	1	0.1	1	0.1
FFLOWA+ FFLHG	0.1	1	0.1	1	0.1	1	0.1	1
FFLOWG+ FFLWA	1	0.1	1	0.1	0.1	0.1	1	0.1
FFLOWG+ FFLWG	0.1	1	1	1	0.1	1	0.1	1
FFLOWG+ FFLHA	1	0.1	1	0.1	1	0.1	1	0.1
FFLOWG+ FFLHG	0.1	1	0.1	1	0.1	1	0.1	1

Table 20. Results of Spearman's rank correlation with $\varphi^* = \varphi_3^*$.

$\varphi^* = \varphi_1^*$	FFLOWA+ FFLWA	FFLOWA+ FFLWG	FFLOWA + FFLHA	FFLOWA+ FFLHG	FFLOWG+ FFLWA	FFLOWG+ FFLWG	FFLOWG+ FFLHA	FFLOWG+ FFLHG
FFLOWA+ FFLWA	1	1	1	1	0.1	1	0.1	0.6
FFLOWA+ FFLWG	1	1	1	1	0.1	1	0.1	0.6
FFLOWA+ FFLHA	1	1	1	1	0.1	1	0.1	0.6
FFLOWA+ FFLHG	1	1	1	1	0.1	1	0.1	0.6
FFLOWG+ FFLWA	0.1	0.1	0.1	0.1	0.1	0.1	1	−0.3
FFLOWG+ FFLWG	1	1	1	1	0.1	1	0.1	0.6
FFLOWG+ FFLHA	0.1	0.1	0.1	0.1	1	0.1	1	−0.3
FFLOWG+ FFLHG	0.6	0.6	0.6	0.6	−0.3	0.6	−0.3	1

4.6. Some Advantages and Limitations of the Proposed Approach

1. The formulated approach can solve decision-making problems with qualitative information data in terms of FFLNs very efficiently.
2. We can also apply this method to solve many existing decision problems with intuitionistic fuzzy linguistic and Pythagorean fuzzy linguistic information [48–50].
3. The main limitation of this study is that it cannot handle the situations in which the attributes have some interaction and prioritization relationship between them.
4. The developed study opens a new door for further research under a qualitative information environment.
5. There can be some adverse situations in which the defined operational laws for FFLNs may not work. Then, we will need to undertake a further detailed investigation of the operational laws of FFLNs.

5. Conclusions

In this paper, we studied the MAGDM problems under a Fermatean fuzzy linguistic environment. To overcome the shortcomings of the existing operational laws of FFLNs, the paper has defined four new algebraic operational laws for FFLNs based on the idea of LSF. Several mathematical properties of the proposed operational laws have been studied in detail. Next, we formulated some AOs, including the FFLWA operator, the FFLWG operator, the FFLOWA operator, the FFLOWG operator, the FFLHA operator, and the FFLHG operator to aggregate different FFLNs. Furthermore, the work has proved many important properties of the proposed AOs, such as idempotency, monotonicity, commutativity, and boundedness, to establish their applicability in different areas. Utilizing the proposed AOs, the paper has developed a new decision-making approach to solve MAGDM problems with Fermatean fuzzy linguistic information. Finally, a real-life supplier selection problem has been considered to illustrate the steps of the proposed method.

In the future, we will employ the proposed AOs to solve some other decision-making problems such as medical diagnosis, pattern recognition, and image processing. Further, we will also develop some new aggregation operators such as Bonferroni mean operator, Heronian mean operator, and Hamy mean operator to aggregate the correlative Fermatean fuzzy linguistic information in future work.

Funding: This research was funded by the Chilean Government (Conicyt) through the Fondecyt Postdoctoral Program (Project Number 3170556).

Institutional Review Board Statement: Not applicable.

Informed Consent Statement: Not applicable.

Acknowledgments: The author is very grateful to the anonymous reviewers for their valuable comments and constructive suggestions that greatly improved the quality of this paper.

Conflicts of Interest: The author declares that he has no conflict of interest.

References

1. Atanassov, K.T. Intuitionistic fuzzy sets. *Fuzzy Sets Syst.* **1986**, *20*, 87–96. [CrossRef]
2. Zadeh, L.A. Fuzzy sets. *Inf. Control* **1965**, *8*, 338–353. [CrossRef]
3. Xu, Z. Intuitionistic fuzzy aggregation operators. *IEEE Trans. Fuzzy Syst.* **2007**, *15*, 1179–1187. [CrossRef]
4. He, Y.; Chen, H.; Zhou, L.; Liu, J.; Tao, Z. Intuitionistic fuzzy geometric interaction averaging operators and their application to multi-criteria decision making. *Inf. Sci.* **2014**, *259*, 142–159. [CrossRef]
5. Ma, Z.M.; Yang, W. Symmetric intuitionistic fuzzy weighted mean operators based on weighted Archimedean t-norms and t-conorms for multi-criteria decision making. *Informatica* **2020**, *31*, 89–112. [CrossRef]
6. Zou, X.Y.; Chen, S.M.; Fan, K.Y. Multiple attribute decision making using improved intuitionistic fuzzy weighted geometric operators of intuitionistic fuzzy values. *Inf. Sci.* **2020**, *535*, 242–253. [CrossRef]
7. He, Y.; He, Z.; Chen, H. Intuitionistic fuzzy interaction Bonferroni means and its application to multiple attribute decision making. *IEEE Trans. Cyber.* **2015**, *45*, 116–128. [CrossRef]
8. Verma, R. Generalized Bonferroni mean operator for fuzzy number intuitionistic fuzzy sets and its application to multiattribute decision making. *Int. J. Intell. Syst.* **2015**, *30*, 499–519. [CrossRef]
9. Liu, P.; Liu, J.; Chen, M.S. Some intuitionistic fuzzy Dombi Bonferroni mean operators and their application to multi-attribute group decision making. *J. Oper. Res. Soc.* **2018**, *69*, 1–24. [CrossRef]
10. Liu, P.; Gao, H. Some intuitionistic fuzzy power Bonferroni mean operators in the framework of Dempster–Shafer theory and their application to multicriteria decision making. *Appl. Soft Comput.* **2019**, *85*, 105790. [CrossRef]
11. Verma, R.; Sharma, B.D. Intuitionistic fuzzy Einstein prioritized weighted average operators and their application to multiple attribute group decision making. *Appl. Math. Inf. Sci.* **2015**, *9*, 3095–3107. [CrossRef]
12. Ai, Z.; Xu, Z. Intuitionistic fuzzy double integrals and their fundamental properties. *IEEE Trans. Fuzzy Syst.* **2018**, *26*, 3782–3792. [CrossRef]
13. Ai, Z.; Xu, Z. Line integrals of intuitionistic fuzzy calculus and their properties. *IEEE Trans. Fuzzy Syst.* **2018**, *26*, 1435–1446. [CrossRef]
14. Ai, Z.; Xu, Z. Multiple definite integrals of intuitionistic fuzzy calculus and isomorphic mappings. *IEEE Trans. Fuzzy Syst.* **2018**, *26*, 670–680. [CrossRef]
15. Zhang, H.; Yu, L. New distance measures between intuitionistic fuzzy sets and interval-valued fuzzy sets. *Inf. Sci.* **2013**, *245*, 181–196. [CrossRef]
16. Ngan, R.T.; Son, L.H.; Cuong, B.C.; Ali, M. H-max distance measure of intuitionistic fuzzy sets in decision making. *Appl. Soft Comput. J.* **2018**, *69*, 393–425. [CrossRef]
17. Mahanta, J.; Panda, S. A novel distance measure for intuitionistic fuzzy sets with diverse applications. *Int. J. Intell. Syst.* **2021**, *36*, 615–627. [CrossRef]
18. Hao, Z.; Xu, Z.; Zhao, H.; Zhang, R. The context-based distance measure for intuitionistic fuzzy set with application in marine energy transportation route decision making. *Appl. Soft Comput.* **2021**, *101*, 107044. [CrossRef]
19. Song, Y.; Wang, X.; Quan, W.; Huang, W. A new approach to construct similarity measure for intuitionistic fuzzy sets. *Soft Comput.* **2019**, *23*, 1985–1998. [CrossRef]
20. Boran, F.E.; Akay, D. A biparametric similarity measure on intuitionistic fuzzy sets with applications to pattern recognition. *Inf. Sci.* **2014**, *255*, 45–57. [CrossRef]
21. Raji-Lawal, H.Y.; Akinwale, A.T.; Folorunsho, O.; Mustapha, A.O. Decision support system for dementia patients using intuitionistic fuzzy similarity measure. *Soft Comput. Lett.* **2020**, *2*, 100005. [CrossRef]
22. Singh, A.; Kumar, S. A novel dice similarity measure for IFSs and its applications in pattern and face recognition. *Expert Syst. Appl.* **2020**, *149*, 113245. [CrossRef]
23. Verma, R.; Sharma, B.D. Exponential entropy on intuitionistic fuzzy sets. *Kybernetika* **2013**, *49*, 114–127.
24. Verma, R.; Sharma, B.D. On intuitionistic fuzzy entropy of order-α. *Adv. Fuzzy Syst.* **2014**, 1–8. [CrossRef]
25. Verma, R.; Sharma, B.D. R-norm entropy on intuitionistic fuzzy sets. *J. Intell. Fuzzy Syst.* **2015**, *28*, 327–335. [CrossRef]
26. Thao, N.X. Some new entropies and divergence measures of intuitionistic fuzzy sets based on Archimedean t-conorm and application in supplier selection. *Soft Comput.* **2021**, *25*, 5791–5805. [CrossRef]
27. Verma, R.; Sharma, B.D. On generalized intuitionistic fuzzy divergence (relative information) and their properties. *J. Uncertain Syst.* **2012**, *6*, 308–320.

28. Verma, R.; Sharma, B.D. Intuitionistic fuzzy Jensen-Rényi divergence: Applications to multiple-attribute decision making. *Informatica* **2013**, *37*, 399–409.
29. Mishra, A.R.; Singh, R.K.; Motwani, D. Intuitionistic fuzzy divergence measure-based ELECTRE method for performance of cellular mobile telephone service providers. *Neural Comput. Appl.* **2020**, *32*, 3901–3921. [CrossRef]
30. Verma, R.; Sharma, B.D. A new measure of inaccuracy with its application to multi-criteria decision making under intuitionistic fuzzy environment. *J. Intell. Fuzzy Syst.* **2014**, *27*, 1811–1824. [CrossRef]
31. Yager, R.R. Pythagorean fuzzy subsets. In Proceedings of the Joint IFSA World Congress and NAFIPS Annual Meeting, Edmonton, AB, Canada, 24–28 June 2013; pp. 57–61.
32. Yager, R.R.; Abbasov, A.M. Pythagorean membership grades, complex numbers, and decision making. *Int. J. Intell. Syst.* **2013**, *28*, 436–452. [CrossRef]
33. Zhang, X.; Xu, Z. Extension of TOPSIS to multiple criteria decision making with Pythagorean fuzzy sets. *Int. J. Intell. Syst.* **2014**, *29*, 1061–1078. [CrossRef]
34. Yager, R.R. Pythagorean membership grades in multicriteria decision making. *IEEE Trans. Fuzzy Syst.* **2014**, *22*, 958–965. [CrossRef]
35. Wei, G.; Lu, M. Pythagorean fuzzy power aggregation operators in multiple attribute decision making. *Int. J. Intell. Syst.* **2018**, *33*, 169–186. [CrossRef]
36. Yang, Y.; Chin, K.; Ding, H.; Lv, H.; Li, Y. Pythagorean fuzzy Bonferroni means based on T-norm and its dual T-conorm. *Int. J. Intell. Syst.* **2019**, *34*, 1303–1336. [CrossRef]
37. Akram, M.; Ilyas, F.; Al-Kenani, N.A. Two-phase group decision-aiding system using ELECTRE III method in Pythagorean fuzzy environment. *Arab. J. Sci. Eng.* **2021**, *46*, 3549–3566. [CrossRef]
38. Ejegwa, P.A. Modified Zhang and Xu's distance measure for Pythagorean fuzzy sets and its application to pattern recognition problems. *Neural Comput. Appl.* **2020**, *32*, 10199–10208. [CrossRef]
39. Molla, M.U.; Giri, B.C.; Biswas, P. Extended PROMETHEE method with Pythagorean fuzzy sets for medical diagnosis problems. *Soft Comput.* **2021**, *25*, 4503–4512. [CrossRef]
40. Bakioglu, G.; Atahan, A.O. AHP integrated TOPSIS and VIKOR methods with Pythagorean fuzzy sets to prioritize risks in self-driving vehicles. *Appl. Soft Comput.* **2021**, *99*, 106948. [CrossRef]
41. Senapati, T.; Yager, R.R. Fermatean fuzzy sets. *J. Ambient Intell. Humaniz. Comput.* **2019**. [CrossRef]
42. Senapati, T.; Yager, R.R. Some new operations over Fermatean fuzzy numbers and application of Fermatean fuzzy WPM in multiple criteria decision making. *Informatica* **2019**, *30*, 391–412. [CrossRef]
43. Senapati, T.; Yager, R.R. Fermatean fuzzy weighted averaging/geometric operators and its application in multi-criteria decision-making methods. *Eng. Appl. Artif. Intell.* **2019**, *85*, 112–121. [CrossRef]
44. Aydemir, S.B.; Yilmaz Gunduz, S. Fuzzy TOPSIS method with Dombi aggregation operators and its application in multi-criteria decision making. *J. Intell. Fuzzy Syst.* **2020**, *39*, 851–869. [CrossRef]
45. Mishra, A.R.; Rani, P.; Pandey, K. Fermatean fuzzy CRITIC-EDAS approach for the selection of sustainable third-party reverse logistics providers using improved generalized score function. *J. Ambient. Intell. Humaniz. Comput.* **2021**, *1*, 1. [CrossRef]
46. Zadeh, L.A. The concept of a linguistic variable and its application to approximate reasoning—II. *Inf. Sci.* **1975**, *8*, 301–357. [CrossRef]
47. Zadeh, L.A. The concept of a linguistic variable and its application to approximate reasoning-III. *Inf. Sci.* **1975**, *9*, 43–80. [CrossRef]
48. Wang, J.B.; Li, H.B. Multi-criteria decision-making method based on aggregation operators for intuitionistic linguistic fuzzy numbers. *Control Decis.* **2010**, *25*, 1571–1574.
49. Liu, P. Some generalized dependent aggregation operators with intuitionistic linguistic numbers and their application to group decision making. *J. Comput. Syst. Sci.* **2013**, *79*, 131–143. [CrossRef]
50. Liu, P.; Wang, Y. Multiple attribute group decision making methods based on intuitionistic linguistic power generalized aggregation operators. *Appl. Soft Comput. J.* **2014**, *17*, 90–104. [CrossRef]
51. Su, W.; Li, W.; Zeng, S.; Zhang, C. Atanassov's intuitionistic linguistic ordered weighted averaging distance operator and its application to decision making. *J. Intell. Fuzzy Syst.* **2014**, *26*, 1491–1502. [CrossRef]
52. Yu, S.; Wang, J.; Wang, J. An extended TODIM approach with intuitionistic linguistic numbers. *Int. Trans. Oper. Res.* **2018**, *25*, 781–805. [CrossRef]
53. Liu, D.; Liu, Y.; Chen, X. Fermatean fuzzy linguistic set and its application in multicriteria decision making. *Int. J. Intell. Syst.* **2019**, *34*, 878–894. [CrossRef]
54. Liu, D.; Liu, Y.; Wang, L. Distance measure for Fermatean fuzzy linguistic term sets based on linguistic scale function: An illustration of the TODIM and TOPSIS methods. *Int. J. Intell. Syst.* **2019**, *34*, 2807–2834. [CrossRef]
55. Herrera, F.; Martínez, L. A model based on linguistic 2-tuples for dealing with multigranular hierarchical linguistic contexts in multi-expert decision-making. *IEEE Trans. Syst. Man Cybern. Part B Cybern.* **2001**, *31*, 227–234. [CrossRef]
56. Xu, Z. Intuitionistic preference relations and their application in group decision making. *Inf. Sci.* **2007**, *177*, 2363–2379. [CrossRef]
57. Wang, J.Q.; Wu, J.T.; Wang, J.; Zhang, H.Y.; Chen, X.H. Interval-valued hesitant fuzzy linguistic sets and their applications in multi-criteria decision-making problems. *Inf. Sci.* **2014**, *288*, 55–72. [CrossRef]

58. Liao, H.; Qin, R.; Gao, C.; Wu, X.; Hafezalkotob, A.; Herrera, F. Score-HeDLiSF: A score function of hesitant fuzzy linguistic term set based on hesitant degrees and linguistic scale functions: An application to unbalanced hesitant fuzzy linguistic MULTIMOORA. *Inf. Fusion* **2019**, *48*, 39–54. [CrossRef]
59. Yager, R.R. On ordered weighted averaging aggregation operators in multicriteria decision making. *IEEE Trans. Syst. Man Cybern.* **1988**, *18*, 183–190. [CrossRef]
60. Chiclana, F.; Herrera, F.; Herrera-Viedma, E. The ordered weighted geometric operator: Properties and application in MCDM problems. In Proceedings of the 8th Conference Information Processing and Management of Uncertainty in Knowledge based Systems (IPMU), Madrid, Spain, 3–7 July 2000; pp. 985–991.
61. Xu, Z.; Da, Q.L. An overview of operators for aggregating information. *Int. J. Intell. Syst.* **2003**, *18*, 953–969. [CrossRef]
62. Xu, Z. An overview of methods for determining OWA weights. *Int. J. Intell. Syst.* **2005**, *20*, 843–865. [CrossRef]
63. Parkan, C.; Wu, M.L. Decision-making and performance measurement models with applications to robot selection. *Comput. Ind. Eng.* **1999**, *36*, 503–523. [CrossRef]

axioms

MDPI

Article

An Intelligent System for Allocating Times to the Main Activities of Managers

Efrain Solares *, **Liliana Guerrero**, **Alberto Aguilera**, **Juana María Hernández**, **Sandra Rodríguez** and **Víctor De-León-Gómez**

Faculty of Accounting and Administration, Universidad Autónoma de Coahuila, Torreón 27000, Mexico; dralilianaclases@gmail.com (L.G.); alberto.aguilera@uadec.edu.mx (A.A.); juana_hernandez@uadec.edu.mx (J.M.H.); rodriguez.sandra@uadec.edu.mx (S.R.); v.gomez@uadec.edu.mx (V.D.-L.-G.)
* Correspondence: efrain.solares@uadec.edu.mx

Abstract: Correctly allocating times to the main activities of a manager is a crucial task that directly affects the possibility of success for any company. Decision support based on state-of-the-art methods can lead to better performance in this activity. However, allocating times to managerial activities is not straightforward; the decision support should provide a flexible recommendation so the manager can make a final decision while ensuring robustness. This paper describes and assesses a novel approach where a search for the best distribution of the manager's time is performed by an intelligent decision support system. The approach consists of eliciting manager preferences to define the value of the manager's main activities and, by using a portfolio-like optimization based on differential evolution, obtaining the best time allocation. Aiming at applicability in practical scenarios, the approach can deal with many activities, group decisions, cope with imprecision, vagueness, ill-determination, and other types of uncertainty. We present evidence of the approach's applicability exploiting a real case study with the participation of several managers. The approach is assessed through the satisfaction level of each manager.

Keywords: time allocation; decision support system; computational intelligence; uncertainty management

MSC: 68T20

Citation: Solares, E.; Guerrero, L.; Aguilera, A.; Hernández, J.M.; Rodríguez, S.; De-León-Gómez, V. An Intelligent System for Allocating Times to the Main Activities of Managers. *Axioms* **2021**, *10*, 104. https://doi.org/10.3390/axioms10020104

Academic Editors: Goran Ćirović, Dragan Pamučar and Faith-Michael E. Uzoka

Received: 25 March 2021
Accepted: 20 May 2021
Published: 25 May 2021

1. Introduction

Time management is an issue that occupies the attention of individuals and society in general. So much importance is attached to time management that several countries have national surveys to measure it [1]. In Mexico, the National Survey on the use of time provides statistical information on the measurement of paid and unpaid work to make visible the importance of domestic work.

Managers' expert knowledge is often the main way how time is allocated to activities. These decision makers usually dominate most of the relevant information that, implicitly and holistically, allows them to make the required set of judgments. Furthermore, expert knowledge from other managers belonging to similar contexts could imply even better decisions. However, managers often dedicate most of their time to the most urgent issues, that is, day-to-day operations. This situation has the consequence that issues with the greatest impact on strategy and the increase in business competitiveness, as time allocation, are being relegated.

A poor time allocation by the manager of an organization can affect the person, the organization, and society in general. That is why various proposals recognize the importance of this managerial ability, but it is still an unsolved problem for many managers. Stephen Covey proposed a time management matrix in 1996, in which he placed important and urgent activities in the first quadrant, important but not urgent tasks in quadrant

2, and, in the last quadrant, activities that are neither important nor urgent, but that by habit the individual performs them and unconsciously steals a large amount of time [2]. "The development of time management is often divided into four generations. In the first generation, what needs to be done (answer the question of what to do) is mainly solved. The second generation adds the question of when it is necessary to do it. The third generation extends the previous two by adding the question of how to perform the task. Finally, the fourth generation focuses mainly on man, self-knowledge and management". The complexity of current times requires the use of information technology in this area of knowledge [3].

Computational intelligence, defined as the technology that allows to exploit computational power to solve "hard" problems, has seen a significant increment in the number of applications within many different fields during the last decades. Undoubtedly, computational intelligence has become a current of thought that has characteristics to help support in the problem of deciding how managers should allocate their time.

Improvements through computational tools help with the reduction of processing times and with optimization [4]. Tools provided by computational intelligence are useful in problems with vital impacts, such as ranging transport models of medical emergency services, prediction of meteorological data to minimize its economic impact, and problems where the result is the recommendations of tourist attractions, for example [4–6].

In most cases, the manager is not able/willing to determine precise proportions of his/her time to perform routine activities. However, the manager may wish to define minimum and maximum acceptable proportions of time. It is also possible that, originating in vagueness or imprecision within the manager's mind, this minimum acceptable value is not well defined and/or the manager does not feel comfortable in expressing it as a precise value. Therefore, a decision support system that exploits computational intelligence to recommend plausible proportions of time to allocate to the diverse manager's activities must be prepared to deal with such situations of uncertainty.

There are several ways to introduce uncertainty into modeling. Fuzzy numbers are a plausible way to model the situation where a number x is not precisely known, but the range where it lies and its distribution are known. This type of numbers is used in many areas, from robotics to finance. In [7] they evaluated the risk associated with investments and in [8] to rank alternatives. There is another way to introduce uncertainty that is potentially simpler than fuzzy numbers, interval numbers. Interval numbers characterize the range where an unknown quantity may be by using uniform distributions. Interval theory allows to determine if a given interval number is greater than or equal to another interval number in a straightforward and intuitive manner [9]. In [10], interval numbers were used to assess risks based on the probability of fails. In [11], a drought risk model is built and evaluated through interval numbers. Solares et al. [12] exploited the ordering properties of interval numbers to characterize and compare investment portfolios. Similarly, Fernandez et al. [13–15] not only characterized investment portfolios through interval numbers, but also the preferences of the investors. Interval numbers are remarkably related to fuzzy numbers [16–18].

Another important issue addressed in this paper is the modelling of preferences. Modelling of preferences has been used in different ways, such as in [19], where a fuzzy technique is applied for order preference and ranking of the alternatives concerning the reverse logistic problem; or by [20] where preference modelling is used to generate individualized interactive narratives based on the preferences of users to improve user satisfaction and experience. One way to model preferences is by using value functions. These types of functions are the result of a very well-studied and well-known theory (see e.g., [21–23]). Recently, value functions have been used to assess project portfolios [24], providers [25], and market segmentations [26], for example. There have been important efforts in creating effective methods to elicit the parameter values of value functions [27–30].

On the other hand, a very effective tool for optimization problems whose decision variables are continuous is differential evolution (DE). This is a tool commonly used for solving engineering problems and it has become very popular among computer scientists and practitioners [31]. Recently, this technique has been introduced in other areas such as finance, marketing, and customer segmentation, as in [15,32].

Regarding the case study of this work, namely the time allocation for managers' activities, some researchers have intended to analyze the impact and importance of this issue, such as in [33], where it is shown how time allocation for sales managers affects the sales team performance. Their findings underscore the importance of effective time management for sales managers across a core set of leader behaviors. Moreover, they argue that when managing more (less) experienced teams, managers should focus on spending more time on managing people (customer interaction). In [34], the influence of entrepreneurs' individual entrepreneurial orientation (IEO) on their time allocation behavior is studied. The findings indicate that proactiveness and risk-taking are associated with specific time allocation behaviors. In [35], it is identified that a core micro-foundation of dynamic managerial capabilities is the ability of the manager to allocate their own time; and it is illustrated that failure to allocate time to capability enactment can lead to capability vulnerability. In [36], it is said that time management practice can facilitate productivity and success, contributing to work effectiveness, maintaining balance, and job satisfaction. Furthermore, the decision support provided to managers must offer flexible recommendations such that the manager can make a final decision according to his/her specific context, but without affecting the approach's effectiveness. In this work, we intend to achieve all these goals.

To the best of our knowledge, there are not published methods that explicitly allocate times to managerial activities. This is likely due to the difficulty for managers to follow strict schedules in ever-changing environments. The problem is, of course, that neglecting the support of recent advances in technology and modeling is discouraged. Traditional approaches to this type of problem consist of mathematical models exploited by exhaustive optimization methods that lead to precise output values where strict schedules are recommended. The manager is not given the option to make a final decision where his/her expert knowledge and that of other managers is used. The recommendation also does not have the flexibility to adapt to unexpected situations. This implies a lack of robustness of traditional approaches. Therefore, in this work, we aim not only to propose a time allocation that best suits the manager (from the perspective of a given objective function), but also to provide sufficient flexibility for the manager to adapt to real-world situations such as considering group decisions and uncertainties. We present a novel way to hybridize some state-of-the-art methods from some theories of the literature (see Section 2).

The paper is structured as follows. In Section 2, we describe the materials and methods used in this work. Section 3 presents the methodology of the proposed approach and details the design of experiments. Section 4 presents and discusses the obtained results. Finally, Section 5 concludes this paper.

2. Materials and Methods

We propose using value functions to model the preferences of the managers (i.e., what the value of each activity is), interval numbers to encompass the uncertainty related to such preferences and to the ideal solution (i.e., on what range the ideal time allocation is), and differential evolution to determine such an ideal solution.

2.1. Value Functions

Value functions [37] can be used to represent the preferences of the managers over a set of decision alternatives regarding time allocation. Value functions are a simple yet effective and very useful way of modeling preferences. This paradigm is particularly relevant here because of the difficulty of defining a mathematical function whose inputs are the times allocated to the activities. It is not straightforward to define tangible impacts on the organizations' objectives for such function. Therefore, the expert opinion of the managers regarding what they consider most convenient is valuable. Value functions are therefore used to represent such opinions by defining "how desirable it is to spend time on a given activity" from the perspective of experts.

The main goal of this type of function is to build a way of relating a real number with each alternative, such that an order on the alternatives can be produced that is consistent with the decision maker's preferences. To achieve it, the theory of value functions assumes the existence of a real-valued function representing the preferences of the decision maker. This function is used to transform the attributes of each alternative into a real number.

2.2. Interval Numbers

An interval number (see [38,39]) represents a numerical quantity whose exact value is not well defined, that is, it is not exactly known. However, it is known that the quantity is within a range of numbers. Let r be a real value lying between r^- and r^+. The interval number representing r is therefore $\boldsymbol{R} = [r^-, r^+]$. A real number s can be represented by an interval number as $[s, s]$. For clarity purposes, we use bold italic font to denote an interval number.

Notice how the nature of the uncertainty modeled by interval numbers is different from that modeled by fuzzy logic. In the former, knowing that the quantity is within a range of numbers is the only known information; in the latter, usually more information about the quantity and range are stated. Therefore, fuzzy logic could handle the proposed approach information in a more sophisticated way than interval theory. However, such sophistication comes at a price, complexity. For example, it is straightforward to determine if an interval number is greater than or equal to another (see function *Poss* below), which usually is not the case for fuzzy numbers. Here we focus on the scenario where the interval numbers are sufficient to model the problem and defer the modeling of such information through fuzzy logic to future research work where the authors are already working.

Basic arithmetic operations that can be performed using interval numbers are addition, subtraction, and multiplication. Let $\boldsymbol{A} = [a^-, a^+]$, $\boldsymbol{B} = [b^-, b^+]$ be two interval numbers. The arithmetic operations between these numbers are defined by:

$$\boldsymbol{A} + \boldsymbol{B} = [a^- + b^-, a^+ + b^+],$$

$$\boldsymbol{A} - \boldsymbol{B} = [a^- - b^+, a^+ - b^-],$$

$$\boldsymbol{A} \times \boldsymbol{B} = [\min\{a^-b^-, a^-b^+, a^+b^-, a^+b^+\}, \max\{a^-b^-, a^-b^+, a^+b^-, a^+b^+\}].$$

Evidently, it is not possible to precisely define the order of two interval numbers when there is overlap between them. Thus, a possibility function was defined in [9] to determine the "credibility that one of the interval numbers is at least as great as the another". The possibility function is defined as:

$$Poss(\boldsymbol{A} \geq \boldsymbol{B}) = \begin{cases} 1 & \text{if } \; p_{AB} > 1, \\ p_{AB} & \text{if } \; 0 \leq p_{AB} \leq 1, \\ 0 & \text{if } \; p_{AB} < 0 \end{cases}$$

where $p_{AB} = \frac{a^+ - b^-}{(a^+ - a^-) + (b^+ - b^-)}$.

When $a^+ = a^- = a$ and $b^+ = b^- = b$, $P(\boldsymbol{A} \geq \boldsymbol{B}) = \begin{cases} 1 \text{ if } a \geq b, \\ 0 \text{ otherwise.} \end{cases}$.

In [13,14], the value $Poss(\boldsymbol{A} \geq \boldsymbol{B})$ is interpreted as "the credibility of a being greater than or equal to b, where a and b are two *realizations* from $\boldsymbol{A}$ and $\boldsymbol{B}$", where a *realization* is a given real number within the interval number.

2.3. Differential Evolution

Differential evolution [40] is an optimization tool highly effective and efficient when addressing optimization problems whose decision variables are continuous. It is characterized by approximating the optimal solution by improving multiple possible solutions at the same time. Differential evolution (DE) is especially convenient when the optimization problem does not satisfy the requirements of exhaustive mathematical optimization methods. However, it does not ensure to find the overall best solution, but only suboptimal solutions. The found solutions are generally good enough to be accepted by the user.

DE uses a generational improvement that simulates biological evolution. At any given moment it deals with a set of potential solutions called individuals or agents; the set of individuals is called population. The parameters used by DE consist of a crossover probability, $CR \in [0, 1]$, a differential weight, $F \in [0, 2]$, and a number of individuals in the population, $P_{size} \geq 4$. Each individual in the population is represented by a real-valued vector $z = [z_1, z_2, \ldots, z_m]^T$, where z_i is the value assigned to the ith decision variable and m is the number of decision variables.

Let $y \in \mathbb{R}^m$ be a temporary solution. DE must perform the following steps:

1. Initialize individuals placing them in a random position within the search space. This means that a random value must be assigned to each decision variable respecting the constraints associated with the variable.
2. Perform the following steps until a termination criterion is reached. This criterion is defined here as a number of iterations, $N_{iterations}$.
    a. Perform the following steps for each individual z in the population
        i. Let a, b, c be individuals from the population chosen randomly such that z, a, b, c are all different.
        ii. Randomly define $r \in \{1, \ldots, m\}$
        iii. Perform the following steps for each $i \in \{1, \ldots, m\}$
            1. Randomly define $u \in [0, 1]$.
            2. If $u < CR$ or $i = r$, set $y_i = a_i + F(b_i - c_i)$, otherwise set $y_i = z_i$.
        iv. If $f(z) \leq f(y)$, then replace z for y in the population. $f(\cdot)$ is a given fitness function (see Equation (1) below).
3. Select the individual z of the population with the best performance $f(z)$.

3. Methodology

Assume the existence of a set of activities, $A = \{a_1, a_2, \ldots, a_n\}$, relevant for the manager of a given company. Let x_i denote the proportion of time allocated to $a_i \in A$; $\sum_{i=1}^{n} x_i = 1$ and $x_i = t_i/T$, where t_i is the time assigned to a_i and T is the total time that the manager assigns to the activities in A. An approach based on computational intelligence that is focused on determining the precise value of x_i is unrealistic since day-to-day operations and urgent issues may alter scheduled activities; moreover, the manager may not feel comfortable with the advised values of x_i. However, such unprevented operations and issues usually imply significant deviations from the ideal allocation of the manager's time. Therefore, we describe here a hybrid approach based on computational intelligence and multicriteria decision aid that exploits interval theory to propose a flexible allocation of the manager's time.

The idea is to provide the manager with the flexibility to choose, among a set of plausible values of x_i, the most convenient one according to his/her specific context and preferences. Let $\boldsymbol{x}_i = [x_i^-, x_i^+]$ denote an interval number representing the set of plausible values from which the manager can choose what he/she considers the most convenient one. In order to define a plausible set of values of x_i, we perform an elicitation of preferences based on multicriteria decision aid that ensures the maximization of the manager's preferences.

The proposed approach consists of four main stages:

1. Determine the set of activities in A.
2. Assign a relative value v_i to each $a_i \in A$; this value represents "how desirable it is to spend time on activity a_i".
3. Determine the set of constraints imposed to the time allocation.
4. Optimize the total value of the performed activities by defining x_i, $i = 1, \ldots, n$.

3.1. Determining the Set of Activities in A

On a preliminary survey of both expert opinions and literature, we found out that activities commonly performed by managers can be assigned to, at least, the following classes:

- Supplier Management
- Marketing and Sales Management
- Strategic Planning
- General administration (Internal processes)
- Inventory Management
- Financial Capital Management (Cash Flow)
- Strategy Management
- Quality and Service Management
- Human Capital Management

Evidently, the specific context of the manager would determine if a different set of activities is considered during the decision-making process. Therefore, a particular analysis of the context handled should be carried out.

3.2. Assigning a Relative Value v_i to Each $a_i \in A$

During this stage, a value representing "how desirable it is to spend time on activity a_i" is defined relatively to the values assigned to the rest of activities in A. Different techniques can be followed to determine such values (cf. [41,42]). The chosen technique must define cardinal values as opposed to ordinal ones that some elicitation procedures define (e.g., [43]). A plausible way to assign such values is then through an elicitation procedure, such as the Swing method [27,28], where the preferences of the manager (or a group of managers from the same sector, region or expertise) are properly defined. If a group of managers is consulted to define the value of the ith activity, then multiple values will be surely determined. To deal with this imprecision, the value of the activity can be defined as an interval number $\boldsymbol{v}_i = [v_i^-, v_i^+]$ where v_i^- and v_i^+ are the minimum and maximum values assigned to the ith activity by the group of managers.

3.3. Determining the Set of Constraints Imposed to the Time Allocation

Common constraints considered when scheduling the time of managers are:

- avoid spending too little time on some activities
- avoid spending too much time on some activities
- avoid spending too much time on all the considered activities
- avoid spending too little time on all the considered activities
- address a maximum number of activities
- address at least a certain number of activities

The previous constraints can be formalized, respectively, as follows:

$$\boldsymbol{x}_i \geq \boldsymbol{l}_i y_i$$

$$\boldsymbol{x}_i \leq \boldsymbol{u}_i y_i$$

$$\sum_{i=1}^{n} \boldsymbol{x}_i \leq \boldsymbol{U}$$

$$\sum_{i=1}^{n} \boldsymbol{x}_i \geq \boldsymbol{L}$$

$$\sum_{i=1}^{n} y_i \leq N^+$$

$$\sum_{i=1}^{n} y_i \geq N^-$$

$$y_i = \{0, 1\}$$

where $\boldsymbol{l}_i$ and $\boldsymbol{u}_i$ are the lowest and highest proportions of time that the manager is willing to allocate to ith activity. $\boldsymbol{L}$ and $\boldsymbol{U}$ are the lowest and highest proportions of time that the manager is willing to allocate to all the considered activities. N^- and N^+ are the minimum and maximum number of activities to which the manager allocates some of his/her time. Additionally, $y_i = 1$ if the manager allocates some time to the ith activity and $y_i = 0$ otherwise. Note how $\boldsymbol{l}_i$, $\boldsymbol{u}_i$, $\boldsymbol{L}$, and $\boldsymbol{U}$ are all defined as interval numbers, providing the manager with additional flexibility when defining the optimization model.

3.4. Defining an Objective Function

Let $X = (x_1, x_2, \ldots, x_n)$ and $V = (v_1, v_2, \ldots, v_n)$ be the sequences of time proportions and activity values, respectively; and let $f(X, V)$ be a function that determines the total value of the time allocation made by the manager. Then, solving the following general statement implies finding the best time allocation:

$$\underset{x_1,\, x_2,\, \ldots,\, x_n}{\text{maximize}} f(X, V) \tag{1}$$

Subject to

$$x_i \geq \boldsymbol{l}_i y_i$$
$$\sum_{i=1}^{n} x_i \leq \boldsymbol{U}$$
$$\sum_{i=1}^{n} x_i \geq \boldsymbol{L}$$
$$\sum_{i=1}^{n} y_i \leq N^+$$
$$\sum_{i=1}^{n} y_i \geq N^-$$
$$y_i = \{0, 1\}$$

We propose to define $f(X, V)$ as a weighted sum, that is:

$$f(X, V) = \sum_{i=1}^{n} v_i x_i$$

We also propose to use differential evolution to address Equation (1).

3.5. Optimizing the Total Value of the Performed Activities

Multiple alternative techniques can be used to optimize Equation (1). However, given the interval-based feature of such equation (necessary in the approach to provide the required flexibility) and its definition as an NP-problem (cf. [44]), a metaheuristic optimization technique should be used. Metaheuristics are optimization techniques of the area of computational intelligence that have shown to be reliable when addressing hard problems and that can be flexible to adapt to situations as the stated above. It has been proved that differential evolution (DE) (e.g., [45]), a highly efficient metaheuristic, often outperforms other optimization techniques when addressing problems similar to that stated in previous sections; particularly, when the optimization problem is mono-objective and with real-valued decision variables. Therefore, we use here differential evolution to define the most convenient values associated to the manager's activities.

3.6. Experimental Design

To assess the proposed approach, we have applied the methodology to a set of nine micro, small and medium-sized organizations in the commerce sector. Each of the five steps in the methodology described above was applied to the organizations, creating a single case study.

The application of the proposal to this case study is twofold. On the one hand, it will allow us to show how the proposed approach can work with a group of decision makers, and how each of them can take advantage of the other decision makers' expert knowledge. On the other hand, the assessment will shed light on the performance of the proposed approach, and we will be able to determine how the proposed approach's recommendations satisfied each manager's preferences. The performance of the proposed approach, assessed through the satisfaction level of each manager, is compared to the performance of a benchmark.

4. Results and Discussions

This section provides (i) the general recommendations provided to the managers in the case study, and (ii) a comparison of each manager's satisfaction between the recommendations provided by the proposed approach and an approach from the literature.

4.1. Results Obtained by the Proposed Approach

The results of the first stage of the methodology described in the previous section showed that the managers in the case study determined the following activities as the ones that should be prioritized when allocating resources:

1. Supplier Management
2. Marketing and Sales Management
3. Strategic Planning
4. General Administration (internal processes)
5. Inventory Management
6. Financial Capital Management (cash flow)
7. Strategy Management
8. Quality and Service Management
9. Human Resource Management

A wide description of these activities is presented in Appendix A.

Regarding stage two of the methodology, we used the so-called Swing method to elicit from the managers the values in the additive value function denoted by Equation (1) (See [27,46], to see a more in-depth description of the method). The results obtained are shown in Table 1.

Table 1. Values assigned by the managers to the activities regarding "how desirable it is to spend time on activity a_i".

Activity	Manager 1	Manager 2	Manager 3	Manager 4	Manager 5	Manager 6	Manager 7	Manager 8	Manager 9
Supplier Management	7%	22%	0%	9%	0%	5%	13%	11%	13%
Marketing and Sales Management	23%	2%	10%	14%	21%	5%	12%	19%	19%
Strategic Planning	10%	18%	32%	1%	19%	53%	14%	11%	9%
General administration (internal processes)	3%	16%	6%	29%	0%	5%	13%	21%	11%
Inventory Management	7%	9%	3%	3%	0%	5%	13%	17%	10%
Financial Capital Management (cash flow)	14%	7%	26%	3%	0%	11%	14%	14%	11%
Strategy Management	16%	2%	10%	3%	20%	11%	13%	0%	9%
Quality and Service Management	10%	11%	10%	19%	20%	3%	7%	0%	9%
Human Resource Management	10%	13%	3%	19%	20%	3%	0%	7%	11%

After defining the weights that each manager assigned to the activities regarding "how desirable it is to spend time on activity a_i", we intend to embrace the whole set of preferences by defining a unique interval number for each activity whose boundaries are set by the minimum and maximum weights provided by the managers, as shown in Table 2. The goal of this aggregation of the managers' preferences is to deal with the whole set of organizations (with similar characteristics in very similar contexts) as a single case study; thus, implying that the combined experience of the managers is convenient to dictate how the organizations' managers should allocate their times.

Table 2. Values assigned by the managers to the activities.

Activity	Minimum Value (%)	Maximum Value (%)
Supplier Management	5	22
Marketing and Sales Management	2	23
Strategic Planning	1	53
General administration (internal processes)	3	29
Inventory Management	3	17
Financial Capital Management (cash flow)	3	26
Strategy Management	2	20
Quality and Service Management	3	20
Human Resource Management	3	20

Stage three of the methodology in Section 3 requires determining the constraints that the managers want to impose to the problem in Equation (1). For the case study carried out here, we found that the managers are only interested in defining boundaries to the proportion of times allocated to the activities. This is originated in the idea none of the nine fundamental activities mentioned above should be performed during very short or very long periods of time. The constraints established by the managers are shown in Table 3.

Table 3. Lowest and highest proportions of time allowed per activity.

Activity	Lowest Proportion (%)	Highest Proportion (%)
Supplier Management	2	25
Marketing and Sales Management	4	8
Strategic Planning	8	17
General administration (internal processes)	4	21
Inventory Management	2	8
Financial Capital Management (cash flow)	4	12
Strategy Management	4	8
Quality and Service Management	8	25
Human Resource Management	12	25

Finally, an effective optimization tool based on metaheuristics, differential evolution, was used to determine the best allocation of times. Common parameter values were assigned to this optimizer. The crossover probability, CR, was set to 0.9; the differential weight, F, was set to 0.8; the population size, P_{size}, was set to 200; and the number of iterations, $N_{iterations}$, was set to 100. Table 4 shows the results obtained when exploiting the proposed approach regarding the case study.

Table 4. Recommendations of the system. If the manager spends a proportion of time indicated by the corresponding interval on a given activity, the manager would be maximizing the total value of the time allocation.

Activity	Best Time Recommended (%)
Supplier Management	[12, 21]
Marketing and Sales Management	[4, 6]
Strategic Planning	[10, 13]
General administration (internal processes)	[15, 18]
Inventory Management	[6, 7]
Financial Capital Management (cash flow)	[4, 9]
Strategy Management	[6, 7]
Quality and Service Management	[19, 25]
Human Resource Management	[15, 17]

As can be seen from Table 4, the summatory of lowest values is lower than 100%, that is, $\sum v_i^- < 100$. Similarly, the summatory of highest values is greater than 100%, that is, $\sum v_i^+ > 100$. This is a desirable feature of the proposed approach regarding pragmatism. When exploiting a decision support system, it is convenient for the manager to have a sufficiently flexible recommendation to generate the final decision. Furthermore, such final decision still must ensure robustness. Through recommendations provided in the form of ranges, where 100% of the time dedicated by the manager to the activities is within the recommended boundaries, the proposed approach satisfies both requirements allowing the manager to decide the precise times dedicated to the activities.

4.2. Comparison with a Benchmark Approach

Once the proposed approach outputted general recommendations for the group of managers (Table 4), the recommendations and the individual preferences stated in Table 1 are used to create a "satisfaction level" per manager by exploiting Equation (1). Such satisfaction level is compared to that obtained by an optimizer from the literature addressing a simplified version of the problem. (Note that there are not published methods that can address the whole complexity of the problem stated in Section 4 in a straightforward manner, so we built a simplified version of the problem so it could be addressed by methods from the literature whose results could be used as a benchmark.) The simplified version of the problem is defined as follows.

Since, it can be shown that, for any interval numbers **E** and **D**, if e and d are, respectively, the middle points of **E** and **D**, then $\mathbf{E} > \mathbf{D} \Leftrightarrow e > d$ and $\mathbf{D} = \mathbf{E} \Leftrightarrow d = e$ (dictatorship of the middle point), we redefine the problem in the case study so now the values "assigned" by the managers to the activities correspond to the middle points of those actually provided by the managers and shown in Table 2. Such values must be normalized. The new values are shown in Table 5.

Table 5. Simplification of the values assigned by the managers to the activities. The middle points of the original intervals have been normalized.

Activity	Value (%)
Supplier Management	11
Marketing and Sales Management	10
Strategic Planning	21
General administration (internal processes)	13
Inventory Management	8
Financial Capital Management (cash flow)	11
Strategy Management	8
Quality and Service Management	9
Human Resource Management	9

The original set of activities and constraints are maintained to ensure fairness. The objective function and the decision variables are now precise; that is, they are real-valued.

Applying the Simplex method to this simplified version of the problem provides the recommendations shown in Table 6.

We now compare the satisfaction level of each manager produced by the recommendations in Tables 4 and 6. This comparison will shed light on the performance of the proposed approach to encompass and exploit the expert knowledge of a group of decision makers from the perspective of each manager. With this purpose, the value function in Equation (1) is used to aggregate the value assigned by each manager in Table 1 with the recommendations of Table 4 first (to create the satisfaction level produced by the proposed approach), and with the recommendations of Table 6 later (to create the satisfaction level produced by the benchmark approach). Such satisfaction levels are shown in Table 7 (note that, since the recommendations provided by the proposed approach consist of interval numbers, the satisfaction levels are given also as interval numbers).

Table 6. Best solution found by a benchmark approach to a simplified version of the problem.

Activity	Best Time Recommended (%)
Supplier Management	25
Marketing and Sales Management	4
Strategic Planning	17
General administration (internal processes)	21
Inventory Management	2
Financial Capital Management (cash flow)	7
Strategy Management	4
Quality and Service Management	8
Human Resource Management	12

Table 7. Satisfaction level of each manager regarding the recommendations provided by the benchmark and proposed approaches.

Manager	Benchmark	Proposal
1	8.76	[8.55, 11.76]
2	15.19	[11.9, 16.32]
3	10.54	[8.67, 12.1]
4	12.26	[13.03, 16.75]
5	8.87	[10.74, 13.53]
6	13.42	[9.27, 12.51]
7	11.16	[8.84, 12.44]
8	11.95	[8.96, 12.3]
9	11.22	[9.81, 13.46]

From Table 7, we can see that each satisfaction level provided by the benchmark approach is contained within the corresponding satisfaction level provided by the proposed approach (except for Managers 4 and 6). This means that the recommendations of the proposed approach combined with good final decisions by the manager could imply better satisfaction levels for him/her. Of course, this combination could also imply worse satisfaction levels. So, here is where the synergy between the expert knowledge of each manager and the advances in computational intelligence and decision support systems can take place. The proposed approach exploits the experience of the group through computational intelligence and gives the opportunity for each manager to provide a final decision where his/her particular knowledge and preferences could lead to better results.

Finally, note how the simplified version of the problem is unrealistic. The managers would never be satisfied following recommendations of strict schedules; so, an approach that depends on the managers following such schedules would lack pragmatism.

Since the paper's goal is to present a novel approach to deal with the realistic problem through the exploitation of a computational intelligence-based system for the first time, it is out of the scope of this work to perform in situ experiments to capture indicators of the organizations.

5. Conclusions

This work presents a novel idea to allocate the times of managers to their main activities. The idea exploits the so-called computational intelligence within a decision support system that provides recommendations about how managers should allocate their times.

Even when computational intelligence has been widely exploited in a plethora of fields, to the best of our knowledge, it has never been applied to the problem of supporting organization managers to allocate their times. We believe this is due to the "hardness" often imposed to models that would represent this problem. That is, models based on computational intelligence usually provide strict recommendations that would not allow the manager to deviate from such recommendations with robustness of effectivity. This is not ideal since managers usually make decisions on the progress of the activities. Therefore, here, a novel hybrid approach that integrates value function theory, interval theory and evolutionary algorithms, intends to give the manager flexibility regarding the times that he/she should dedicate to his/her activities. Furthermore, we ensure that the effectiveness of the approach is maintained as long as the actual allocated times remain within the recommended slack.

The proposed approach was applied in a case study to the managers of nine micro, small and medium-size organizations that participated during the whole process of the methodology described in Section 3. Tables 1–3 show the information provided by the managers that worked as inputs to our approach. Table 4 provides the results obtained. Such results proved to fulfill the constraints imposed by the managers and to maximize the total value of time allocated to the activities from the perspective of group decision. Tables 5–7 show a comparison between the results of our approach and those of a method from the literature. Since the benchmark method is not able to deal with the whole complexity of the case study's problem, a simplified version of the problem was created. The results of both approaches are assessed from the perspective of each manager within the group. The comparison shed light on how the proposed approach could provide a higher satisfaction level to the managers if they make a convenient final decision. Therefore, we conclude that the proposed approach could be of pragmatical relevance to support the decisions of the managers; at least of those in charge of micro-, small- and medium-sized organizations.

Future research lines include (i) provide more in-depth analysis of the approach's impact by assessing the organizations' performances before and after implanting the approach; (ii) use more sophisticated techniques to model the manager's preferences, for example, exploiting the so-called outranking approach (see [47]) and Fuzzy Logic [48]; (iii) follow a statistical procedure to define the parameter values of the approach.

Author Contributions: E.S.: Conceptualization, Investigation, Methodology, Project administration, Writing—original draft; L.G.: Conceptualization, Investigation, Methodology, Supervision, Writing—review & editing; A.A.: Data curation, Formal analysis, Resources, Software, Visualization; J.M.H.: Software, Validation, Visualization, Writing—review & editing; S.R.: Software, Validation, Visualization, Writing—review & editing; V.D.-L.G.: Software, Validation, Visualization, Writing—review & editing. All authors have read and agreed to the published version of the manuscript.

Funding: This research received no external funding.

Data Availability Statement: Not applicable.

Conflicts of Interest: The authors declare no conflict of interest.

Appendix A. Complete Descriptions of the Activities Selected by the Managers

Appendix A.1. Supplier Management

The certainty that a trading company has that its products will be sold are based on the conditions negotiated with its suppliers, which include:

- **The Purchase Price**: Obtaining the best purchase price in the market guarantees the trading company that its sales price will not only be competitive, but also will get the widest Margin on sales, giving them a competitive advantage. If eventually there is a need for a price reduction, this can be done more easily than its competition.

- **The Selling Margin**: By obtaining the best purchase price, the best selling margin is obtained.

- **Credit**: Obtaining the longest credit term provides room for maneuver if the trading company grants the necessary credentials required by the market.

- **Quality**: The trading company must review and confirm that the supplier has implemented qualities systems that guarantees that it complies with the technical specifications of the product offered, guarantee supply, and meets delivery times by reviewing its sources of supply or at least an investigation that shows that the raw materials used are available in time and form in the market.

- **Supply**: This means that the supplier must have the capacity to supply the quantities required by the trading company promptly to avoid the damage caused by losing the sale due to shortages in the customer's inventory.

- **Warranty and Service**: The supplier must offer immediate response to customer claims for defects in the product, the replacement of the same, and bear all costs of handling and freight in the process of return and replacement of products.

- **Marketing**: Nowadays, all suppliers, manufacturers, and distributors have in their budget a sufficient amount to support their customers with financial resources, and in-kind for marketing actions, since these represent the indispensable distribution channel to move their products making them reach the final consumer.

The money support can go from the rent of spaces, for exhibition, or preferential positions, payment of advertising, exclusivity, etc., in-kind can be with promoters personnel to restock the sales floor with merchandise, demonstration-saleswomen to move the merchandise, POP material, exhibitors, promotional campaigns, and others.

- **Strategic Alliances**: This is the highest level that can be reached in the relationship with suppliers, it is reached when the purchase volumes of the commercial company represent an important percentage of the supplier's sales in such a way that if the supplier were to lose the client, this would cause disruptions in its operation that would eventually translate into losses.

The benefits of an alliance for the commercial company includes: preferential prices, guaranteed supply, free replacement of merchandise, promotional and advertising support, cashing-kind payments, prizes and incentives, exclusivity in product lines, and market territories, etc. They are frequently formalized with the signing of the corresponding contracts, which are renewable from time to time.

Appendix A.2. Marketing and Sales Management

- **Sales Management**: The sales generate the income of the commercial enterprise, the security to a great extent that these are given, has its origin in the quality of the negotiation with suppliers, but the other part is complemented with a deep knowledge of the product, the market, and the competition. Among the most important points that the general manager must attend to are the following:

- **In-Depth Knowledge of the Wants and Needs of His Customers**: There are multiple software tools known as CRM (Customer Relationship Management) that provide all the information regarding the tastes, needs, frequency, and buying habits of the customers in addition to providing complementary valuable and personal information about them such as, names, birth dates, anniversaries, number, and ages of children, etc., which facilitates the company to have personal and close communication with its customers.

- **Sales Force**: To create, develop, and maintain the quantity and quality of elements necessary for the generation of sales is a fundamental task of the general manager, whether it is a linear or pyramidal structure, on-site or virtual, must maintain permanent attention to the performance of each and every one of its members, always taking care, not only to cover the established objectives but also to meet the needs expressed by its members, through adequate dynamic retribution of performance that includes the granting of incentives to maintain high motivation and satisfaction for their work.

The permanent training in the sales technique, the method and work plan whose objective is the increasing attention of prospects and the coverage of the sales quota must be permanently attended by the General Manager.

- **Marketing**: The general manager must know and define the customer and consumer profile, what it is like, where is located, where it moves, what places frequents, what is it socioeconomic level, this leads to identifying the target market and to quantify potential market with which will be able to implement.

- **The Communication Plan**: The target market must know the existence of the commercial company, its products, offer, and service it provides. The quantity, quality, frequency, and intensity of the messages received by the target market will largely determine the level of response to the offer provided by the commercial company, which is translated into: traffic of potential customers (prospects) to the company's sales floor, phone calls, emails, and other digital media, requesting information and quotations, increasing acceptance of visits from the company's salesperson, increase in orders and consequently higher sales.

The implementation of a CRM in the company is of great help for the success of the communication plan.

- **Media Plan**: The selection of the media to be used for communication is very important, so the general manager must apply himself to investigate which are the ones that have a greater impact on the target market depending on the objective of the communication, which may be to provoke immediate sales, increase traffic on the sales floor, fix the commercial brand in the customer's mind, create loyalty, etc.

Traditional media; press, radio, television, billboards, specialized magazines, flyers, direct mail, tabloids.

Digital Media; websites, social networks, web search engines, influencers, sales chats, and others.

- **Competitor Analysis**: Daily monitoring of the competition will allow the general manager to know promptly the commercial and promotional actions which will allow him to react adequately to avoid the loss of customers and eventually anticipate better actions, counteracting its main competitors.

- **The Selling Price**: The determination of the selling price is fundamental for the commercial company as it fixes its competitive position in the market since it can be a low price, equal to or higher than the competition, it impacts directly on the volume of sales and the most important part, it contributes to the gross profit margin that must be sufficient to cover its operating expenses and provide the profit desired by the company.

Appendix A.3. Strategic Planning

The company define well its goals, its aspirations, and how far it wants to go in the medium–long term. It is up to the general manager to visualize the scope, coverage, growth, the position it wishes to have in the market, and the time frame in which it wishes to achieve it.

Setting the direction, determining the objectives, formulating the strategies, allocating the resources, executing the action plan, and inspiring the team is the role of the general manager.

Appendix A.4. General Management

In the broadest sense, the general manager applies the administrative process of planning, organization, direction, and control in all areas of the company implicit in the value chain in what Michael Porter defines as primary activities and costs, as well as the support activities and their costs. The common thread is represented by its internal processes, which must be formulated in a clear, complete, and updated manner at all times.

- **The Value Chain**: Every commercial enterprise shares the same value chain, starting in the suppliers' market for the purchase and supply of the goods to be sold, the transportation of the products to the company's warehouses and the inherent logistics, the safekeeping, rotation, and, if necessary, the movement to the sales floor for display, sale, invoicing and collection, packaging, physical delivery to the sales floor or home delivery and the corresponding logistics, to conclude with warranty support and after-sales service.

In the whole chain, there are several activities that the general manager must be personally involved in, some of them being executed in their totality and permanently, that is to say, they cannot be delegated, for example, the negotiation with the suppliers, while some roles can be delegated, he cannot stop being personally involved.

In each of the processes derived from these activities, the general manager must be involved by executing, delegating, or supervising their correct and timely application.

Appendix A.5. Inventory Management

The commercial enterprise must deliver to the customer a quality product, the product must be at the beginning of its life period, whether it is of short duration such as perishables or long life such as furniture, machinery, and capital goods.

Some long-life products, however, only have a short period of time to be sold, as in the case of fashion items or those that are replaced by the next year's model, as in the case of automobiles.

Long stays in warehouses or on the sales floor makes them obsolete and discontinued, in addition to the natural deterioration due to the passage of time.

The constant review of rotation, proper management of inventories, and their replenishment to maintain adequate levels and avoid shortages that cause loss of sales is an obligatory function of the general manager.

Appendix A.6. Financial Capital Management (Cash Flow)

The company must have at all times the availability of financial resources to meet its operating needs, the timely payment even in advance to suppliers, the emergency purchase of assets such as the replacement of computer equipment or the repair of transportation equipment, the payment of taxes, personnel settlements and similar require having the liquid capital on hand to cover any requirement; therefore, the planning, collection, application, and control of resources is a daily task of the general manager.

- **Operating Expenses**: These are disbursements intended to keep the company in operation; they enable the various activities and daily operations to be carried out, without which it would not be possible to achieve the company's objectives.

The expense is necessary and unavoidable and the resources necessary for this purpose come from the margin provided by sales, so the higher the expense, the lower the margin, hence the importance of maintaining strict control and vigilance in the amount and destination of the expense.

Appendix A.7. Strategy Management

The strategy is how the company decides to compete in the market, it represents the specific actions it takes to serve the market, face the competition, and offer greater value to the customer.

How is it going to differentiate itself from the competition, how is it going to make the market perceive greater value when selecting its offer, how is it going to obtain a competitive advantage?

The strategy for a company as such does not exist, it is created, it is the result of the creativity, ingenuity, knowledge, and experience of the general manager who many times is the same entrepreneur. Of course, many managers decide to imitate the actions of the market leaders, but that makes them followers, places them always behind the competition, and generally in last place.

The planning, design, and implementation of the strategy is a very personal function of the general manager.

Appendix A.8. Quality and Service Management

Delivering quality products implies impeccable execution in every process along the value chain. It is the general manager's role to ensure that he and his team of collaborators carry out the assigned activities promptly. Planning, process implementation, resource allocation, and close supervision is the task of the general manager.

Appendix A.9. Human Capital Management

The company is its people, the customer deals with people who represent the company and are responsible for fulfilling the company's promise to the customer by exceeding their expectations.

This is only possible if the team of collaborators is kept at a high level of motivation, committed, and willing to provide solutions.

The primary need is the perception of adequate and sufficient remuneration, but it is not the only one, it also seeks to satisfy the needs of professional development, belonging to a team, recognition, and security of permanence, and growth in the company, among others.

The general manager must create working conditions that meet the expectations of all employees, motivate them, inspire them, and focus on the vision.

References

1. Bengoa, C.C. El tiempo más allá del reloj: Las encuestas de uso del tiempo revisitadas. *Cuad. Relac. Labor.* **2016**, *34*, 357. [CrossRef]
2. Salazar, D.A. La gestión del tiempo como factor clave en las habilidades directivas aplicadas al sector turístico. *Gran Tour Rev. Investig. Tour.* **2017**, *15*, 26–42.
3. Chlebikova, D. Influence of time management on performance of managers. In *Economic and Social Development: Book of Proceedings, Proceedings of the 56th International Scientific Conference on Economic and Social Development, Aveiro, Portugal, 2–3 July 2020*; Varazdin Development and Entrepreneurship Agency (VADEA): Varazdin, Croatia, 2020; pp. 155–162.
4. Bermudez, G.M.T.; Mozo, I.J.V.R. Model of transport of medical emergency services using VANET networks in urban areas and implemented with computer intelligence. In Proceedings of the 2020 15th Iberian Conference on Information Systems and Technologies (CISTI), Seville, Spain, 24–27 June 2020.
5. Acosta, A.; Barzola, K.; Guarda, T. Eclectic System of Information Filtering in Computational Intelligence for the Recommendation of Tourist Attraction. In Proceedings of the 2019 14th Iberian Conference on Information Systems and Technologies (CISTI), Coimbra, Portugal, 19–22 June 2019.
6. Coutinho, E.R.; Silva, R.M.; Delgado, A.R.S. Utilização de Técnicas de Inteligência Computacional na Predição de Dados Meteorológicos. *Rev. Bras. Meteorol.* **2016**, *31*, 24–36. [CrossRef]
7. Guerra, M.; Sorini, L. Value at Risk Based on Fuzzy Numbers. *Axioms* **2020**, *9*, 98. [CrossRef]
8. Jaini, N.I.; Utyuzhnikov, S.V. A Fuzzy Trade-Off Ranking Method for Multi-Criteria Decision-Making. *Axioms* **2017**, *7*, 1. [CrossRef]
9. Shi, J.R.; Liu, S.Y.; Xiong, W.T. A new solution for interval number linear programming. *Syst. Eng. Theory Pract.* **2005**, *2*, 101–106. [CrossRef]
10. Bhattacharjee, P.; Dey, V.; Mandal, U.K. Risk assessment by failure mode and effects analysis (FMEA) using an interval number based logistic regression model. *Saf. Sci.* **2020**, 104967. [CrossRef]
11. Liu, X.; Guo, P.; Tan, Q.; Xin, J.; Li, Y.; Tang, Y. Drought risk evaluation model with interval number ranking and its application. *Sci. Total Environ.* **2019**, *685*, 1042–1057. [CrossRef]
12. Solares, E.; Coello, C.A.C.; Fernandez, E.; Navarro, J. Handling uncertainty through confidence intervals in portfolio optimization. *Swarm Evol. Comput.* **2019**, *44*, 774–787. [CrossRef]
13. Fernández, E.; Figueira, J.; Navarro, J. An interval extension of the outranking approach and its application to multi-ple-criteria ordinal classification. *Omega* **2019**, *84*, 189–198. [CrossRef]
14. Fernandez, E.; Navarro, J.; Solares, E.; Coello, C.C. A novel approach to select the best portfolio considering the preferences of the decision maker. *Swarm Evol. Comput.* **2019**, *46*, 140–153. [CrossRef]
15. Fernandez, E.; Navarro, J.; Solares, E.; Coello, C.C.; Eduardo, F.; Jorge, N.; Efrain, S.; Carlos, C.C. Using evolutionary computation to infer the decision maker's preference model in presence of imperfect knowledge: A case study in portfolio optimization. *Swarm Evol. Comput.* **2020**, *54*, 100648. [CrossRef]
16. Guégan, G.; Knauer, K.; Rollin, J.; Ueckerdt, T. The interval number of a planar graph is at most three. *J. Comb. Theory Ser. B* **2021**, *146*, 61–67. [CrossRef]
17. Stefanini, L.; Guerra, M.L.; Amicizia, B. Interval Analysis and Calculus for Interval-Valued Functions of a Single Variable. Part I: Partial Orders, gH-Derivative, Monotonicity. *Axioms* **2019**, *8*, 113. [CrossRef]
18. Stefanini, L.; Sorini, L.; Amicizia, B. Interval Analysis and Calculus for Interval-Valued Functions of a Single Variable—Part II: Extremal Points, Convexity, Periodicity. *Axioms* **2019**, *8*, 114. [CrossRef]
19. Wang, C.-N.; Dang, T.-T.; Nguyen, N.-A.-T. Outsourcing Reverse Logistics for E-Commerce Retailers: A Two-Stage Fuzzy Optimization Approach. *Axioms* **2021**, *10*, 34. [CrossRef]
20. De Lima, E.S.; Feijó, B.; Furtado, A.L. Adaptive storytelling based on personality and preference modeling. *Entertain. Comput.* **2020**, *34*, 100342. [CrossRef]
21. Jacquet-Lagreze, E.; Siskos, J. Assessing a set of additive utility functions for multicriteria decision-making, the UTA method. *Eur. J. Oper. Res.* **1982**, *10*, 151–164. [CrossRef]
22. Pekelman, D.; Sen, S.K. Mathematical Programming Models for the Determination of Attribute Weights. *Manag. Sci.* **1974**, *20*, 1217–1229. [CrossRef]
23. Srinivasan, V.; Shocker, A.D. Estimating the weights for multiple attributes in a composite criterion using pairwise judgments. *Psychometrika* **1973**, *38*, 473–493. [CrossRef]

24. Frej, E.A.; Ekel, P.; de Almeida, A.T. A benefit-to-cost ratio based approach for portfolio selection under multiple criteria with incomplete preference information. *Inf. Sci.* **2021**, *545*, 487–498. [CrossRef]
25. Segura, M.; Maroto, C. A multiple criteria supplier segmentation using outranking and value function methods. *Expert Syst. Appl.* **2017**, *69*, 87–100. [CrossRef]
26. Liu, J.; Liao, X.; Huang, W.; Liao, X. Market segmentation: A multiple criteria approach combining preference analysis and segmentation decision. *Omega* **2019**, *83*, 1–13. [CrossRef]
27. Clemen, R.T.; Reilly, T. *Making Hard Decisions with DecisionTools*; Cengage Learning: Boston, MA, USA, 2013.
28. Dieter, G.E.; Schmidt, L.C. *Engineering Design*; McGraw-Hill Higher Education: Boston, MA, USA, 2009; pp. 18–20.
29. Blavatskyy, P. A simple non-parametric method for eliciting prospect theory's value function and measuring loss aversion under risk and ambiguity. *Theory Decis.* **2021**. [CrossRef]
30. Kadziński, M.; Ghaderi, M.; Dąbrowski, M. Contingent preference disaggregation model for multiple criteria sorting problem. *Eur. J. Oper. Res.* **2020**, *281*, 369–387. [CrossRef]
31. Neri, F.; Tirronen, V. Recent advances in differential evolution: A survey and experimental analysis. *Artif. Intell. Rev.* **2009**, *33*, 61–106. [CrossRef]
32. Krishna, G.J.; Ravi, V. Mining top high utility association rules using Binary Differential Evolution. *Eng. Appl. Artif. Intell.* **2020**, *96*, 103935. [CrossRef]
33. Rapp, A.A.; Petersen, J.A.; Hughes, D.E.; Ogilvie, J.L. When time is sales: The impact of sales manager time allocation decisions on sales team performance. *J. Pers. Sell. Sales Manag.* **2020**, *40*, 132–148. [CrossRef]
34. Piva, E. Time allocation behaviours of entrepreneurs: The impact of individual entrepreneurial orientation. *Econ. Polit. Ind.* **2018**, *45*, 493–518. [CrossRef]
35. Kevill, A.; Trehan, K.; Harrington, S.; Kars-Unluoglu, S. Dynamic managerial capabilities in micro-enterprises: Stability, vulnerability and the role of managerial time allocation. *Int. Small Bus. J. Res. Entrep.* **2020**. [CrossRef]
36. Chanie, M.G.; Amsalu, E.T.; Ewunetie, G.E. Assessment of time management practice and associated factors among primary hospitals employees in north Gondar, northwest Ethiopia. *PLoS ONE* **2020**, *15*, e0227989. [CrossRef] [PubMed]
37. French, S. (Ed.) *Decision Theory: An Introduction to the Mathematics of Rationality*; Halsted Press: New York, NY, USA, 1986; p. 130.
38. Moore, W.E. *The Conduct of the Corporation*; Random House: New York, NY, USA, 1962; Volume 62.
39. Sunaga, T. Theory of an interval algebra and its application to numerical analysis [reprint of res. assoc. appl. geom. mem. 2 (1958), 29–46]. *Jpn. J. Ind. Appl. Math.* **2009**, *26*, 125–143. [CrossRef]
40. Storn, R.; Price, K. Differential Evolution—A Simple and Efficient Heuristic for global Optimization over Continuous Spaces. *J. Glob. Optim.* **1997**, *11*, 341–359. [CrossRef]
41. De Almeida, A.T.; Duarte, M. A multi-criteria decision model for selecting project portfolio with consideration being given to a new concept for synergies. *Pesqui. Oper.* **2011**, *31*, 301–318. [CrossRef]
42. Doumpos, M.; Zopounidis, C. Preference disaggregation for multicriteria decision aiding: An overview and per-spectives. In *New Perspectives in Multiple Criteria Decision Making*; Springer: Cham, Switzerland, 2019; pp. 115–130.
43. Doumpos, M.; Marinakis, Y.; Marinaki, M.; Zopounidis, C. An evolutionary approach to construction of outranking models for multicriteria classification: The case of the ELECTRE TRI method. *Eur. J. Oper. Res.* **2009**, *199*, 496–505. [CrossRef]
44. Bienstock, D. Computational study of a family of mixed-integer quadratic programming problems. *Math. Program.* **1996**, *74*, 121–140. [CrossRef]
45. Rocca, P.; Oliveri, G.; Massa, A. Differential Evolution as Applied to Electromagnetics. *IEEE Antennas Propag. Mag.* **2011**, *53*, 38–49. [CrossRef]
46. Design-Decisions. Swing Weighting. 2009. Available online: https://wiki.ece.cmu.edu/ddl/index.php/Swing_weighting (accessed on 23 March 2021).
47. Roy, B. The Outranking Approach and the Foundations of Electre Methods. In *Readings in Multiple Criteria Decision Aid*; Bana e Costa, C.A., Ed.; Springer: Berlin/Heidelberg, Germany, 1990; pp. 155–183. [CrossRef]
48. Zadeh, L.A. Fuzzy sets. *Inf. Control* **1965**, *8*, 338–353. [CrossRef]

axioms

Article

The Ordered Weighted Average Human Development Index

Ernesto Leon-Castro [1,*], Fabio Blanco-Mesa [2], Alma Montserrat Romero-Serrano [3] and Marlenne Velázquez-Cazares [3]

[1] Faculty of Economics and Administrative Sciences, Universidad Católica de la Santísima Concepción, Concepción 4070129, Chile
[2] Facultad de Ciencias Económicas y Administrativas, Universidad Pedagógicay Tecnológica de Colombia, Tunja 150003, Colombia; fabio.blanco01@uptc.edu.co
[3] Unidad Regional Culiacán, Universidad Autónoma de Occidente, Culiacán 80200, Mexico; montserrat.romero@live.com (A.M.R.-S.); marlenne.velazquez@uadeo.mx (M.V.-C.)
* Correspondence: eleon@ucsc.cl

Abstract: The main aim is to propose a new method for estimating the Human Development Index using ordered weighted average. To develop this method, ordered weighted geometric average (OWGA), induced OWGA prioritized OWA (POWA) operator are studied. Using Human Development Index formulation in combination to aggregations operators presented above is proposed the prioritized induced ordered weighted geometric average (PIOWGA) operator. A mathematical application is carried out to estimate the Human Development Index and compare it with the traditional method and other existing methods. Finally, it is noted that decision makers have an influence on the order given in the ranking by its attitude and criterion, and method can capture the subjective information prioritized by them.

Keywords: human development index; OWA operators; prioritized; subjectivity

MSC: 03B52; 90B50

check for updates

Citation: Leon-Castro, E.; Blanco-Mesa, F.; Romero-Serrano, A.M.; Velázquez-Cazares, M. The Ordered Weighted Average Human Development Index. *Axioms* **2021**, *10*, 87. https://doi.org/10.3390/axioms10020087

Academic Editors: Hans J. Haubold and Hsien-Chung Wu

Received: 23 February 2021
Accepted: 30 April 2021
Published: 7 May 2021

1. Introduction

Human Development Index (HDI) is a social-economic indicator that shows the status of the countries in terms of progress and human development [1]. This index was proposed by Mahub ul Haq [1], and functions as a social-economic indicator that allows us to observe the status of countries in terms of progress and human development. However, before this index, economist Amartya Sen X presented a more inclusive method that defines it as development as freedom. This index takes an approach related to the inequality of capabilities, which prioritizes people as the real wealth of a nation and their capabilities for assessing its development [2]. Although the two proposals may seem distant, they have a common element of aggregating information and obtaining averages that allow for ranking of countries. As the HDI is accepted by the international community, it emphasizes that people, their capabilities and expending human choices should be the ultimate criteria for assessing the development of a country, not only economic progress (UNIDP, 2020)

HDI is composed of three key dimensions; human development, long and healthy life, knowledge, and a decent standard of living, which consider several indicators and are measured between maximum and minimum values, and it is calculated through the geometric mean of normalized indices for each of the three key dimensions of human development. This index is apparently reliable but still needs to be improved, as inequalities and development are different from one nation to another. Thus, the index is susceptible to improvement as there are components that change over time, where dominant positions are reinforced, and new inequalities are emerging. This becomes a challenge to generate new ways of assessing the changes, inequality and inequity faced in the new context.

One of the problems that can be seen in the formulation of the HDI is in the way the index considers each key dimension. The results of each country are based on a geometric average where the relative importance of each component is the same ($1/n$). Due to that, the analysis that has been conducted with the data is limited. Based on that, there is a possibility of generating different analyses using the same information but considering a different relative importance for each of the components, based on the realities experienced by each of the countries or the expectations of different decision makers or experts. The purpose is to be able to visualize how the ranking behaves using different data analysis, allowing us, in turn, to generate new positions in the countries and thus be able to confirm whether they have a high or low human development.

Based on the above, with the development of information science and mathematics, new ways of making closer approximations to reality have emerged. Of these advances, aggregation operators stand out, which allow information from different sources and types to be aggregated to obtain a single significant value [3]. Of all the methodologies proposed, the Ordered Weighted Average Operator (OWA) stands out [4]. This operator has the characteristic of taking into account the attitude of the decision maker (subjective information) [5]. Among its developments are the following operators: OWA Induced [6], OWA Heavy [7], OWA Prioritized [8], OWA Probabilistic [9], OWA Bonferroni [10], OWA Logarithmic [11], OWA Pythagorean [12], etc. Applications have also been developed in entrepreneurship [13], finance [14–17], management [18–20], as well as proposals for indices such as transparency [21,22]. In this sense, using these new methodologies can improve the index by being able to include more variables to generate a better assessment.

The main aim is to propose a new method for estimating the Human Development Index using ordered weighted average. For this purpose, we study the characteristics and properties of the following aggregation operators: ordered weighted geometric average (OWGA), and induced OWGA prioritized OWA (POWA) operator. In combination of the studied operators and the formula for determining the Human Development Index, a new method is proposed, called the prioritized induced ordered weighted geometric average (PIOWGA) operator. Using this new method, a mathematical application is made to estimate the Human Development Index and compare it with the traditional method and other existing methods. Finally, it is noted that decision makers have an influence on the order given in the ranking by its attitude and criterion, since they prioritize the three elements according to different resources, different developments and more or less stable political and economic systems throughout the subjective information prioritized by them.

This work is structured as follows: Section 2 presents in a concrete way the theoretical concepts related to the Human Development Index. Section 3 reviews the aggregation operators that will be useful to construct the proposed method. Section 4 presents the mathematical application of the HDI. Finally, the conclusions are presented in Section 5.

2. Theoretical Framework

The following are the most important aspects of the Human Development Index and the definitions of the three variables used for its calculation.

2.1. *Human Development Index*

For a long time, and during the last few years of the 20th century, economists and policymakers debated and questioned the so "classical" theory of economic development, where the Gross National Income (GNI) per capita as the only measure for national and social development, as it fails to capture the distribution of the benefits of economic growth [23], and key social outcomes for humans. For this matter, and since 1990, the United Countries Development Program (UNDP) uses the Human Development Index (HDI), developed and guided by the economist Mahub ul Haq [1], as a social-economic indicator that shows the status of the countries in terms of progress and human development

The economist Amartya Sen developed a new approach to human development, with inequalities and people's capabilities [24] and presented the concept of development as freedom [2]. Sen´s work argues about the freedom and capability to make life choices as fundamental for human development. In this sense, Sen´s approach for inequality of capabilities, the Human Development Index (HDI) prioritizes people as the real wealth of a nation and their capabilities for assessing its development. In other words, human development is a "process of enlarging people´s choices" [1], and its main purpose is to ensure an enabling environment for people to enjoy long, healthy, productive, and creative lives, to be educated and to have easy access to resources for a decent standard of living. Additionally, there are some valued choices as social, economic and political freedom, protection of human rights, security, environmental sustainability, self-esteem, gender equity, among others [25,26].

HDI is a composite index that summarized and measures the average achievements in three key dimensions of human development; long and healthy life, knowledge, and a decent standard of living. In the first dimension, the health dimension is determined by life expectancy at birth. The second dimension is knowledge or education attainment and is assessed by two criteria: expected years of schooling for children of school entering age and average of years of adult schooling (25 years and more). The third dimension, the standard of living or income dimension, is estimated by GNI per capita on a natural logarithmic scale, to reflect the diminishing importance of income with increasing GNI. Thus, each dimension has its indicator as it is shown in Figure 1. The three HDI dimension indices are aggregated into a composite index as a geometric mean of normalized indices [27].

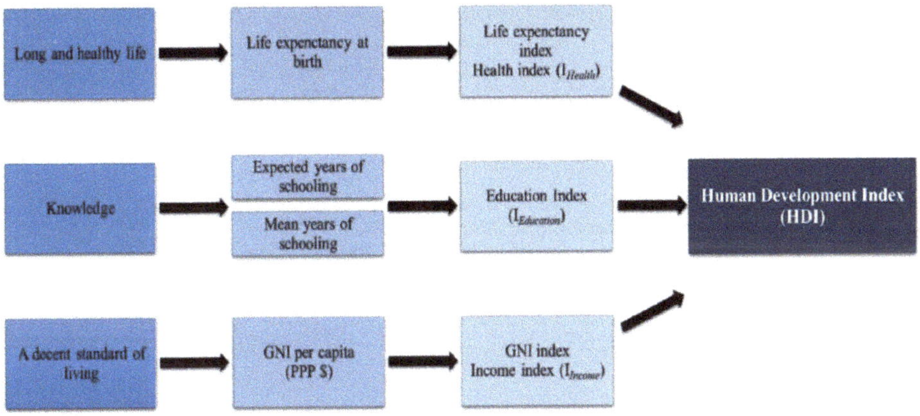

Source: Based on UNDP [27]

Figure 1. Graphical presentation of the Human Development Index (HDI).

A long and healthy life is undeniably a very valuable capacity; in this sense, a high life expectancy of birth indicator represents a significant measure of human development, which leads to guaranteed physical and mental health, a healthy environment and lifestyle. Access to knowledge allows individuals´ freedom and self-sufficiency. A person without a good education these days finds it more difficult to have security, self-determination, opportunities and a productive life that human development demands. As income increases, people have access to shelter, medical care, food, education, and a higher standard of life. Improvement in HDI is correlated with economic growth and the incrementation of a healthy and educated populations, leading to a virtuous cycle [28].

The Human Development Report Office (HDRO) has been using HDI to rank countries every year since 1990, as an objective metric for human development that relies on indicators that can be compared independently from the development of the countries. Since its creation the HDI has had important adjustments in its methods and has been criticized by some authors because of its formula or calculation [29], its limitations as the absence of sustainability indicator [30,31], social and freedom dimension [28,31], and of these dimensions are the top priority for the 2030 Agenda on Sustainable Development Goals (SDGs) [30].

As mentioned before, HDI has evolved and has gradually been improved for more realistic measures [32], and the main changes in calculation technicalities were made in 2010 and 2015. For example, the index aggregation formula has changed from the arithmetic mean to the geometric mean of the three-dimension indices, and equally assigns weightings to each dimension. Furthermore, the HDI is a simple index that captures only a part of human development. Therefore, there are more Human Development Indices developed by UNDP that broader proxy on some more key aspects of human development such as inequality, gender disparity, and poverty [32]: Inequality-adjusted Human Development Index (IHDI) [33], Gender Development Index (GDI), Gender Inequality Index (GII) [34], and Multidimensional Poverty Index (IMPI) [35].

Human Development Index has become the internationally most prominent and widely used composite indicator for human development [30]. Human development creates fair opportunities, freedom and improves human welfare, allowing people to lead the kind of life they choose and value the most. For this matter, the HDI emphasizes that people, their capabilities and expending human choices should be the ultimate criteria for assessing the development of a country, not only economic progress (UNIDP, 2020). HDI is a starting point to understand how countries respond to different social, economic, and environmental challenges. This index can be used for national policy analysis, identifying countries with the same level of income per capita but with a large discrepancy in human development outcomes, stimulating political and priorities changes, benchmarking and evaluating country´s progress through time [36].

There is a notable improvement in all HDI components over time on average, which seems to highlight the idea that the world is becoming less unequal; in other words, more people have escaped poverty and disease, and have progressed to better living standards. Nevertheless, inequalities and disparities remain or even have increased within countries, hurting society, economy, and the environment, and preventing people from reaching their full potential. For this reason, the last HDI report in 2019 emphasizes that human development goes beyond income, averages and time. The key message in this report is that disparity remains widespread and extreme deprivations have decreased; new inequalities are emerging, and the old ones accumulate through life, reinforcing the demand for a revolution in measurement to assessed and responded to this inequalities and changes, and finally be able to act now (UNPD, 2019).

2.2. HDI Calculation

The current HDI is the geometric mean of normalized indices for each of the three key dimensions of human development: a long and healthy life, access to knowledge and a decent standard of living.

The normalizing parameters scale component indices (Table 1), mapping the three statistics in the unit interval (0, 1). They also debunk any part of a statistic that is above its prescribed range. It is not necessary to scale each component since it affects the classification, and it is not necessary that any subscript falls in the unit interval [32].

Table 1. Variables and parameters of the most recent Human Development Index HDI.

Dimension	Indicator	Minimum	Maximum
Health	Life expectancy (years)	20	85
Education	Expected years of schooling (years)	0	18
	Mean years of schooling (years)	0	15
Standard of living	Gross national income per capita (2011 PPP $)	100	75,000

Source: Based on UNDP [27].

2.2.1. Life Expectancy at Birth

Life expectancy at birth contributes to human development without any upper limit ("having a long and healthy life").

Progress in many factors such as lifestyle, nutrition, social equality, advancement in the medical sciences, accident prevention, etc., should, in the not too distant future, make it possible for most people in advanced countries live beyond the age that is now the highest life expectancy at birth, more than 80 years, aimed at reaching a level of 100 years and more [37].

Based on historical evidence, it is observed that no 20th century country has a life expectancy below the age of 20 years, which is why it is used as a natural zero in this indicator [38]. For the maximum value of life expectancy, 85 years of age are defined, which is a realistic goal for many economies worldwide due to constant improvements in living conditions and health [27].

2.2.2. Education: Expected Years of Schooling Mean Years of Schooling

The expected years of schooling is defined as the "number of years of schooling that a child of school entrance age can expect to receive if prevailing patterns of age specific enrolment rates persist throughout the child's life" [27]. Education and income have no upper limits and will always contribute to "human development".

The mean years of schooling is the "average number of years of education received by people ages 25 and older, converted from education attainment levels using official durations of each level" [27].

There are societies that can subsist without formal education, and 0 years is defined as the lower limit in the item expected years of schooling (years); as the upper limit, we have 18 years, which is equivalent to the years of formal education if a graduate degree is obtained. For the item mean years of schooling (years), the lower limit is defined as 0 years and the upper limit is 15 years, which is the average number of years that formal education is received in most countries [27].

2.2.3. Gross National Income

To justify the upper limit on the income variable, Anand and Sen [37] states "that there is virtually no gain in human development" beyond USD 75,000. Kahneman and Deaton [39] studied two aspects of well-being: emotional well-being and life evaluation. They conclude that high income buys life satisfaction but not happiness, and that low income is associated both with low life evaluation and with low emotional well-being. The low minimum value for gross national income (GNI) per capita, USD 100, is justified by the considerable amount of unmeasured subsistence and nonmarket production in economies close to the minimum, which is not captured in the official data.

Once we have defined the minimum and maximum values, the dimension indices are calculated as:

$$Dimension\ index = \frac{actual\ value - minimum\ value}{maximum\ value - minimum\ value}$$

3. Methodology

3.1. Basic Formulations

This section explains the different formulations that will be used in the paper. The first one to be explained will be the actual formula that use UNPD (2019) to calculate the final score for each country that is based on a geometric mean. The definition is as follows:

Definition 1. The HDI is the geometric mean of three-dimensional indices as follows.

$$\mathrm{HDI} = \left(\mathrm{I}_{\mathrm{Health}} \cdot \mathrm{I}_{\mathrm{Education}} \cdot \mathrm{I}_{\mathrm{Income}}\right)^{1/3} \quad (1)$$

where HDI is Human Development Index, I_{Health} is health index, $I_{Education}$ is education index and I_{Income} is income index. It is important to note that the formulation can be change its representation to include a weight associated to each value as follows.

$$HDI = \left(I_{Health}^{\frac{1}{3}} \cdot I_{Education}^{\frac{1}{3}} \cdot I_{Income}^{\frac{1}{3}} \right). \quad (2)$$

The actual formulation of HDI index will be expanded using the OWA operator (Yager, 1988). The main idea is to include the knowledge and expectations of the decision maker in the results through the weighting vector and by adding a reordering step generate the minimum and the maximum scenario [40,41]. As the formulation is based geometric means, the extension of the OWA operator that will be used is the ordered weighted geometric average (OWGA) operator [42]. The definition is as follows

Definition 2. A OWGA operator of dimension n is a mapping $R^{+^n} \rightarrow R^+$ that has associated with it a weighting vector $w = (w_1, \ldots, w_n)^T$, with $w_i \in [0,1]$ and $\sum_{i=1}^{n} w_i = 1$, such that.

$$OWGA(\alpha_1, \ldots, \alpha_n) = \prod_{j=1}^{n} b_j^{w_j}, \quad (3)$$

where b_j is the *jth* largest of the α_i $(i = 1, 2, \ldots, n)$.

Another extension that will be used is the induced OWGA (IOWGA) operator [43]. The main idea of this operator is that the reordering step will be done based on induced variables determined by the decision maker, by doing this, is possible to add some weights to certain attributes instead of only taking into account the value of the attribute. The formulation is as follows.

Definition 3. An induced OWGA (IOWGA) operator is defined as.

$$IOWGA(\langle u_1, \alpha_1 \rangle, \ldots, \langle u_n, \alpha_n \rangle) = \prod_{j=1}^{n} b_j^{w_j}, \quad (4)$$

where $w = (w_1, \ldots, w_n)^T$ is the associated exponential weighting vector such that $w_j \in [0,1]$, $\sum_{j=1}^{n} w_j = 1$, and b_j is a value of $\langle u_i, a_i \rangle$ having the *jth* largest u value. The term u_i is referred as the ordered inducing variable and a_i is referred as the argument variable.

An extension that will be also included in the paper is the prioritized OWA (POWA) operator. This operator is important in group decision making when not all the decision makers have the same importance in the decision. Usually, this operator is important when different experts are questioned about the situations and each of them give different values and to everyone to be included in the results each one of them are given a weight based on their experience and importance in the decision [44,45]. The formulation is as follows.

Definition 4. Assume that we have a collection of criteria portioned into q distinct groups, $H_1, H_2, \ldots, H_q$ for which $H_i = (C_{i1}, C_{i2}, \ldots, C_{in})$ denotes the criteria of the ith category (i = 1, ... ,q) and n_i is the number of criteria in the class. Furthermore, we have a prioritization between the groups as $H_1 > H_2 > \ldots > H_q$. That is, the criteria in the category H_i have a higher priority than those in H_k for all $i < k$ and $i, k \in (1, \ldots, q)$. Denote the total set of criteria as $C = \cup_{i=1}^{q} H_i$ and the total number of criteria as $n = \sum_{i=1}^{q} n_i$. Additionally, suppose $X = (x_1, \ldots, x_m)$ indicates the set of alternatives. For a given alternative x, let $C_{ij}(x)$ measure the satisfaction of the jth criteria in the ith group by alternative $x \in X$, for each $i = 1, \ldots, q$, $j = 1, \ldots, i_i$. The formula is as follows:

$$POWA\left(C_{(x)}\right) = \sum_{i=1}^{q} \sum_{j=1}^{n_i} w_{ij} C_{ij}(x), \quad (5)$$

where w_{ij}, is the corresponding weight of the jth criteria in the ith category, $i = 1, \ldots, q$, $j = 1, \ldots, i_i$. If $w_i = 1/n$ for all i, the PrOWA becomes the prioritized average (PrA).

3.2. Prioritized Induced Ordered Weighted Geometric Average

The paper introduces a new extension of the OWGA operator that includes in the same formulation the idea of a reordering step based on induced value of the IOWGA operator and includes the contribution of the POWA operator for group decision making where not all the decision makers have the same importance in the result. This new operator is called the prioritized induced ordered weighted geometric average (PIOWGA) operator. The formulation is as follows.

Definition 5. Assume that we have a collection of criteria portioned into q distinct groups, $H_1, H_2, \ldots, H_q$ for which $H_i = (C_{i1}, C_{i2}, \ldots, C_{in})$ denotes the criteria of the ith category (i = 1, … ,q) and n_i is the number of criteria in the class. Furthermore, we have a prioritization between the groups as $H_1 > H_2 > \ldots > H_q$. That is, the criteria in the category H_i have a higher priority than those in H_k for all $i < k$ and $i, k \in (1, \ldots, q)$. Denote the total set of criteria as $C = U_{i=1}^{q} H_i$ and the total number of criteria as $n = \sum_{i=1}^{q} n_i$. Additionally, suppose $X = (x_1, \ldots, x_m)$ indicates the set of alternatives. For a given alternative x, let $C_{ij}(x)$ measure the satisfaction of the jth criteria in the ith group by alternative $x \in X$, for each $i = 1, \ldots, q,\ j = 1, \ldots, i_i$. The formula is as follows:

$$\text{PIOWGA}\left(C_{(x)}\right) = \sum_{i=1}^{q} \prod_{j=1}^{n_i} b_j{}^{w_j} C_{ij}(x), \tag{6}$$

where $w = (w_1, \ldots, w_n)^T$ is the associated exponential weighting vector such that $w_j \in [0, 1]$, $\sum_{j=1}^{n} w_j = 1$, and b_j is the a value of $\langle u_i, a_i \rangle$ having the jth largest u value. The term u_i is referred as the ordered inducing variable and a_i is referred as the argument variable.

Additionally, note that if the induced values are $u_i = 1/n$ the PIOWGA operator becomes the POWGA operator and its formulation is the following.

Definition 6. Assume that we have a collection of criteria portioned into q distinct groups, $H_1, H_2, \ldots, H_q$ for which $H_i = (C_{i1}, C_{i2}, \ldots, C_{in})$ denotes the criteria of the ith category (i = 1, … ,q) and n_i is the number of criteria in the class. Furthermore, we have a prioritization between the groups as $H_1 > H_2 > \ldots > H_q$. That is, the criteria in the category H_i have a higher priority than those in H_k for all $i < k$ and $i, k \in (1, \ldots, q)$. Denote the total set of criteria as $C = U_{i=1}^{q} H_i$ and the total number of criteria as $n = \sum_{i=1}^{q} n_i$. Additionally, suppose $X = (x_1, \ldots, x_m)$ indicates the set of alternatives. For a given alternative x, let $C_{ij}(x)$ measure the satisfaction of the jth criteria in the ith group by alternative $x \in X$, for each $i = 1, \ldots, q,\ j = 1, \ldots, i_i$. The formula is as follows:

$$\text{POWGA}\left(C_{(x)}\right) = \sum_{i=1}^{q} \prod_{j=1}^{n_i} b_j{}^{w_j} C_{ij}(x), \tag{7}$$

where b_j is the jth largest of the α_i $(i = 1, 2, \ldots, n)$.

The PIOWGA operator is monotonic, bounded, and idempotent (Blanco-Mesa et al., 2019; 2020).

Theorem 1 (Monotonicity). Assume f is the PIOWGA operator; if $a_i \geq e_i$, for all a_i, then

$$f(\langle u_1, a_1 \rangle, \ldots, \langle u_n, a_n \rangle) \geq f(\langle u_1, e_1 \rangle, \ldots, \langle u_n, e_n \rangle), \tag{8}$$

Theorem 2 (Boundedness). Assume f is the PIOWGA operator; then,

$$\min(a_i) \leq f(\langle u_1, a_1 \rangle, \ldots, \langle u_n, a_n \rangle) \leq \max(a_i), \tag{9}$$

Theorem 3 (Idempotency). Assume f is the PIOWGA operator; if $a_i = a$, for all a_i, then

$$f(\langle u_1, a_1 \rangle, \ldots, \langle u_n, a_n \rangle) = a, \tag{10}$$

3.3. Numerical Example

As the paper will use the PIOWGA operator in calculating the HDI value for 189 countries in the world, the numerical example will serve as an example of how the calculus are done and how it is different from the traditional formulation. The country that will be used to make the example will be Norway (see Table 2). The data for this country is the following.

Table 2. Information for calculating HDI index for Norway.

Country	Life Expectancy at Birth	Expected Years of Schooling	Mean Years of Schooling	Gross National Income (GNI) per Capita
Norway	82.3	18.1	12.6	68,059

The formula to calculate I_{Health}, $I_{Education}$ and I_{Income} we used the information provided by [27] and explained in Section 2 of the paper. Note that in calculating the HDI value, expected years of schooling is capped at 18 years and GNI per capita is capped at USD 75,000.

The results are the following.

$$I_{Health} = \frac{82.3 - 20}{85 - 20} = 0.9580$$

$$I_{Education} = \frac{18 - 0}{18 - 0} + \frac{12.60 - 0}{15 - 0} = 0.9189$$

$$I_{Income} = \frac{\ln(68059 - \ln(100)}{\ln(75000) - \ln(100)} = 0.9853$$

With the use of the traditional formulation (Definition 1) the result is $HDI = 0.9580^{\frac{1}{3}} \cdot 0.9189^{\frac{1}{3}} \cdot 0.9580^{\frac{1}{3}} = 0.9537$.

For the use of the PIOWGA operator and other operators the information provided by one expert will be used. In this case, the weights that the expert provided are $W = (0.40, 0.30, 0.030)$, the induced values are $U = (5, 10, 15)$ and for the prioritized operators the results of the traditional formulation and the expert will be unified by traditional = 40% and expert = 60%. With this information, the results are the following:

$$OWGA = \left(0.9853^{0.40} \cdot 0.9580^{0.30} \cdot 0.9189^{0.30}\right) = 0.9572$$

$$IOWGA = \left(0.9580^{0.40} \cdot 0.9853^{0.30} \cdot 0.9189^{0.30}\right) = 0.9541$$

$$POWGA = (0.9537 \cdot 0.40) + (0.9572 \cdot 0.60) = 0.9558$$

$$IPOWGA = (0.9537 \cdot 0.40) + (0.9541 \cdot 0.60) = 0.9539$$

As can be seen with the different results, the importance of each index can drastically change the result of the HDI. A further analysis of the results and the importance of the use of aggregation operators instead of traditional ones will be discussed at the end of results section.

4. The Human Development Index by Using PIOWGA Operator

Having presented the arguments on the Human Development Index and using the aggregation operators for the development of the new methodological proposal for its calculation called prioritized induced ordered weighted geometric average, we proceed to apply it to the calculation of the HDI. To carry out the application of the new HDI estimation method, a 4-step process is established, which is explained below:

Step 1. Initially taken into account is the information of I_{Health}, $I_{Education}$ and I_{Income}, which is obtained by UNDP [46], then the experts must be selected. In this step, the experts will be determined based on their experience in the topic. It is recommended that they have worked in different governmental organizations that work in the different fields that the HDI considers, that is, health, education, and income, and that also have experience in public policy making. These two aspects are very important because in that way they will know at first-hand how the different elements of how HDI works and how public policies are enacted to improve in that field.

Step 2. In this step, the weighting vector, induced and prioritized values are established. For the weighting vector, for expert 1 $W = 0.40,\ 0.30,\ 0.20$, expert 2 $W = 0.25,\ 0.25,\ 0.50$ and expert 3 $W = 0.30,\ 0.40,\ 0.30$. In the case of the induced values, for expert 1 $U = 5, 10, 15$, expert 2 $U = 10, 15, 5$ and expert 3 $U = 10, 5, 15$. Finally, the prioritized importance of each experts is $e_1 = 0.30$, $e_2 = 0.50$ and $e_3 = 0.20$. These last values are determined based on the expertise and research time in the field.

Step 3. The calculations are done for each country following the same process explained in Section 3.3. All the results for the OWGA, IOWGA, POWGA and PIOWGA operator are found in Appendix A.

Step 4. All results are obtained. To present the results, three different tables were produced, organized into the Top 10 countries (evaluation from position 1 to 10, see Table 3), Middle 10 countries (evaluation from position 91 to 100, see Table 4) and Worst 10 (evaluation from position 180 to 189, see Table 5). As can be seen, with the analysis made from Top 10, Middle 10, and Worst 10 is possible to visualize how much the ranking can change depending in the weights assigned to each dimension of the HDI calculation.

Table 3. Top 10 countries.

R	T	$OWGA_{e1}$	$OWGA_{e2}$	$OWGA_{e3}$	$IOWGA_{e1}$	$IOWGA_{e2}$	$IOWGA_{e3}$	POWGA	IPOWGA
1	NOR	NOR	NOR	NOR	NOR	NOR	NOR	NOR	NOR
2	CHE	CHE	SGP	SGP	CHE	SGP	DEU	FIN	AUS
3	IRL	SGP	CHE	CHE	HKG	CHE	IRL	NLD	SWE
4	HKG	IRL	HKG	HKG	IRL	HKG	CHE	DNK	DEU
5	DEU	HKG	IRL	IRL	AUS	IRL	AUS	SWE	LIE
6	ISL	ISL	LIE	LIE	ISL	LIE	ISL	ISL	ISL
7	AUS	DEU	ISL	ISL	SWE	ISL	SWE	AUS	IRL
8	SWE	AUS	DEU	SWE	DEU	DEU	DNK	CHE	HKG
9	SGP	SWE	SWE	NLD	SGP	SWE	NLD	IRL	CHE
10	NLD	NLD	NLD	LUX	NLD	NLD	FIN	DEU	SGP

Source: Own elaboration. R: Rank; T: Traditional; NOR: Norway; CHE: Switzerland; IRL: Ireland; HKG: Hong Kong, China (SAR); DEU: Germany; ISL: Iceland; AUS: Australia; SWE: Sweden; SGP: Singapore; NLD: The Netherlands; LIE: Liechtenstein; LUX: Luxembourg, DNK: Denmark; FIN: Finland.

Table 4. Middle 10 countries.

R	T	$OWGA_{e1}$	$OWGA_{e2}$	$OWGA_{e3}$	$IOWGA_{e1}$	$IOWGA_{e2}$	$IOWGA_{e3}$	POWGA	IPOWGA
91	TUN	TUN	TUN	ARM	TUN	TUN	TON	MNG	TUN
92	MNG	LBN	LBN	TUN	LBN	MNG	DOM	FJI	BWA
93	LBN	BWA	MDV	BWA	DMA	UKR	LCA	TON	LEB
94	VCT	MNG	UKR	PRY	MNG	VCT	VEN	VEN	MDV
95	BWA	MDV	MNG	VCT	JAM	LBN	BWA	BWA	MNG
96	VEN	VCT	VCT	DMA	VCT	TKM	ZAF	TUN	VCT
97	JAM	PRY	TKM	TKM	MDV	SUR	TUN	JAM	PRY
98	PRY	DMA	PRY	SUR	PRY	PRY	JAM	VCT	SUR
99	DMA	SUR	SUR	UKR	JOR	MDV	VCT	SUR	TKM
100	FJI	VEN	DMA	MNG	VEN	GAB	SUR	JOR	DMA

Source: Own elaboration. R: Rank; T: Traditional; TUN: Tunisia; MNG: Mongolia; LBN: Lebanon; VCT: Saint Vincent and the Grenadines; BWA: Botswana; VEN: Venezuela; JAM: Jamaica; PRY: Paraguay; DMA: Dominica; FJI: Fiji; MDV: Maldives; SUR: Suriname; UKR: Ukraine; TKM: Turkmenistan; ARM: Armenia; JOR: Jordan; GAB: Gabon; TON: Tonga; DOM: Dominican Republic; LCA: Saint Lucia; ZAF: South Africa.

Table 5. Worst 10 countries.

R	T	$OWGA_{e1}$	$OWGA_{e2}$	$OWGA_{e3}$	$IOWGA_{e1}$	$IOWGA_{e2}$	$IOWGA_{e3}$	POWGA	IPOWGA
180	MOZ	ZAR	BFA	LBR	MOZ	ERI	MOZ	MOZ	BFA
181	SLE	BFA	MLI	MLI	ERI	BFA	YDR	YEM	MLI
182	ERI	MOZ	MOZ	MOZ	BFA	SLE	BDI	BDI	COD
183	BFA	MLI	ZAR	ZAR	SLE	MOZ	BFA	BFA	MOZ
184	MLI	SLE	SLE	SLE	MLI	ZAR	MLI	MLI	SLE
185	BDI	BDI	SSD	SSD	BDI	SSD	ERI	ERI	SSD
186	SSD	SSD	TCD	TCD	SSD	TCD	SSD	SSD	TCD
187	TCD	TCD	BDI	BDI	TCD	BDI	TCD	TCD	BDI
188	CAF	NER	NER	NER	NER	NER	CAF	CAF	NER
189	NER	CAF	CAF	CAF	CAF	CAF	NER	NER	CAF

Source: Own elaboration. R: Rank; T: Traditional; MOZ: Mozambique; SLE: Sierra Leone; ERI: Eritrea; BFA: Burkina Faso; MLI: Mali; BDI: Burundi; SSD: South Sudan; TCD: Chad; CAF: Central African: NER: Niger: ZAR; LBR: Liberia; COD: Congo; YDR: Yemen.

The first analysis is performed based on Top 10 countries. With this information, it is possible to detect that Norway is the country with the highest score even when different aggregation operators were used. After that, Switzerland and Singapore are usually between number 2 and 3 in many of the operators. An interesting case can be Germany because in the traditional formulation, its position is number 5 and within the $IOWGA_{e3}$ it is number 2. Additionally, Liechtenstein is not considered in the traditional Top 10 but can be in the ranking according to the $OWGA_{e2}$, $OWGA_{e3}$, $IOWGA_{e2}$ or $POWGA$ operators. Hence, it is possible to visualize that even when the weights of the dimension are changed, Norway is always number 1, but after that, some important changes in the ranking can be seen.

In the Middle 10 countries, it is possible to find some notorious changes, for example, Fiji is presented in the traditional and IPOWGA operator only. Botswana presents important changes, being in position 95 in the traditional score and number 91 in the POWGA operator. Another example can be Jamaica, which is just presented in 4 of the 9 operators that are being compared. The ranking with more changes is Middle 10. This is because the ranking in that section is sensitive to changes, and because of that, if a dimension has more weight than another one, the results can change drastically. Additionally, we observe the ultimate idea that the aggregation operators, such as the IPOWGA operator, can help to generate new scenarios.

Finally, the Worst 10 countries is the ranking that present fewer changes. In the case of position 188–189, there is always Niger or Central Africa; Chad goes from rank 187–186, South Sudan from 186–185 and in some cases, for example, Congo can be in or out of the ranking. The Worst 10 presented the least changes in comparison to another two rankings because even when the weights to each dimension are changed, they are usually the lowest score in all of them. In this sense, it is a must that the politics that are assigned to these countries and the help that they receive from other ones improve, in a general way, the three dimensions.

The following figures show a graphical comparison of the results obtained from the traditional ranking (T) and the rankings generated by the proposed POWGA and IPOWGA operators (see Figures 2–4). Initially, the radials for all methods show a spiral shape and their desiccant sequence is clockwise. Secondly, it is observed that the results for the proposed operators have two main changes; the order of the ranking where they change position and enter and leave countries according to their results; the distance of the results as their distances are wider and the spirals are steeper. The results for the POWGA and IPOWGA operators show that the countries within the ranking vary according to the traditional one. The shape of the graph is easier to see these changes, as it differs at different points, showing lower results in a more concave manner and higher results in a more convex manner, while the traditional graph has straighter aspects. Likewise, the lowest scores are even more pronounced in the 10 worst-ranked countries. These changes are due to the amount of information that is aggregated. Here, in the proposed methods, the shape of the radial marks a more pronounced spiral, which indicates that the distances between each of the countries' results. Hence, the influence that the different criteria of those evaluated can have on the levels of development of the countries is evident.

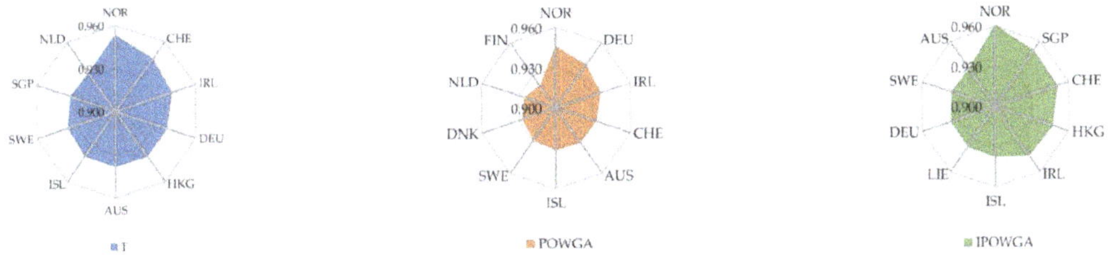

Figure 2. Comparison of the proposed methods for the top 10 countries.

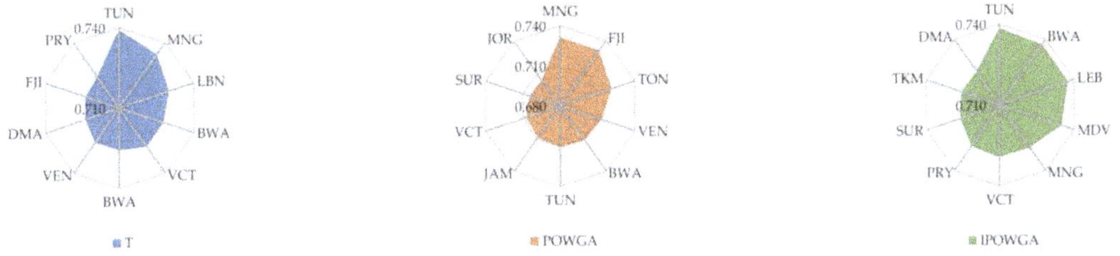

Figure 3. Comparison of the proposed methods for the middle 10 countries.

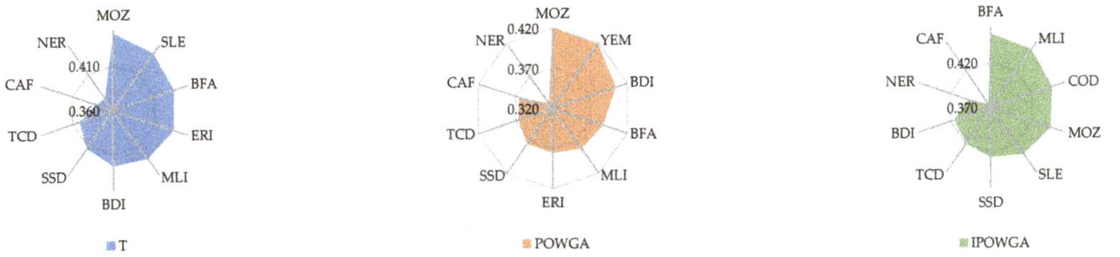

Source: Own elaboration

Figure 4. Comparison of the proposed methods for Worst 10 countries.

These results lead us to address aspects related to the notion of average. The mean is most commonly understood as the average value of a set of numerical data, which is calculated by dividing the sum of the set of values by the amount of data. For the topic under discussion, the geometric mean is used, which is the calculation of the *n-th* root of a joint product, and its characteristic is to have positive numbers. For our proposal, we take into account the ordered weighted average (OWA) as an operator that provides a parameterized family of aggregation operators between maximum and minimum values, allowing us to over or underestimate the information according to the attitude of the decision maker in the studied problem [4,5,47]. This operator has the versatility to allow aggregation of those degrees of truth or optimism in a formal method, i.e., it has the ability to model in a linguistic way through instructions that aggregate subjective information to obtain a single representative value [4].

In this sense, averaging and geometric averaging allow you to efficiently measure the data you aggregate in your operation, although it is quite complicated to give meaning to a broad mass valuation to a mere numerical value. With the OWA operator being able to follow subjective instructions for the aggregation of arguments, it has a greater versatility in responding to situations in the environment that link individual's reasoning and situations that deserve to be explained in terms of their meaning [48]. Likewise, it allows us to propose wider extensions that help to take into account data that is not possible with traditional methods. Comparing the three methods, it is evident that the OWA operator has more advantages by being able to add in its formulation soft aspects (approximate reasoning and degrees of truth) that have an influence on the final result. Thus, the two proposed methods contain the characteristics of the mean, geometric mean and OWA operator and additionally, the characteristics of the induced and prioritized variables. The latter two aspects are closely related to the judgement and subjectivity of the individuals. Finally, the figures presented show those nuances, some more prominent than others, but which can help to give meaning to the information by the origin of the data, i.e., one can always turn to the expert or individual who provided the initial judgement (soft information).

Based on the above, the main idea of the HDI is to generate a vision to each country and that in results can improve and generate new politics, but not all the countries have the same amount of resources to make changes in all three dimensions at the same time and, because of that, a ranking based on dimensions that have different weights will make them visualize if the politics that are being implemented are changing their position in the ranking and, also, not all the countries have the same problems and, because of that, the prioritization of one dimension above another is something that has to be taken into account.

It is important to note that this type of operator has some limitations. First, the weighting vector is proposed by the experts or decision makers and, because it is an essential element for the calculation, if different weights are proposed, the results can vary. Additionally, this flexibility has a positive effect because the results can change depending on the attitude and expectations of the decision maker. Second, these operators are useful when the relative importance of each of the variables that compose the HDI is not the same, if the expert considers that each variable should weight $\frac{1}{n}$ there is no reason to use the different aggregation operators. Finally, with the use of these operators, different results can be obtained and, because of that, it is not possible to assume that only one result is correct, because each result is based on the weighting vector proposed, and if there is not a consensus, it is possible to obtain as many different results as there are decision makers, making it difficult to achieve only one result; however, the idea of this type of operator is that they produce different scenarios based on the aptitude, expectations and knowledge of the decision makers that can be considered in the decision making process, and, with that, there is a better understating and general vision of the phenomenon to study.

Another limitation of the paper is that the study is based on the OWA operator and its extensions, but there are many other operators whose formulation is interesting and can be useful in this type of analysis of information. Such is the case of the Hami means that are used to aggregate values, simultaneously including mutual correlation among multiple arguments [49,50], Bonferroni means that are an averaging aggregation function that allows capturing the interrelationship between arguments [51,52], the use of different Dombi operators [53–55], among others.

5. Conclusions

This paper has reviewed the main aspects of the Human Development Index and its components. By revising the general formula for determining the HDI, a new method is proposed using the aggregation operators [3]. The proposed method is called the prioritized induced ordered weighted geometric average (PIOWGA) operator. The main idea of this operator is that the reordering step will be performed based on induced variables determined by the decision maker, and allows for considering different values and to everyone to be included in the results. Each one of them are given a weight based on their experience and importance in the decision [44,45]. Thus, by having induced variables and decision-prioritizing aspects in a group of experts, it is possible to consider both the information derived from the data and the opinions of the decision makers in group decisions.

The mathematical application developed follows a 4-stage process that considers objective input information on education, health and standard of living and subjective information that allows different scenarios to be considered to observe the usefulness and applicability of the methodological proposal. In this sense, three different levels, Top 10, Middle 10 and Worst 10 are shown. For the Top 10, comparing the traditional method with IPOWGA, there are significant variations in general, and the ten countries only move a little in the ranking from position 5 to position 10. For Middle 10, changes are evident, such as Fiji being present in the traditional and IPOWGA operator only. Botswana presents important changes, being in position 95 in the traditional score and position 91 in the POWGA operator. Ranking in this section is sensitive to changes, because it is a dimension that has more weight than another one; therefore, the results can change drastically. For Worst 10, the rankings show no major alterations, only a change of positions in the country of Niger, Central Africa, Chad, and South Sudan. This smaller variation is because when the weight to each dimension is changed, they are usually the lowest score in all of them. In addition, looking at the results graphically, it can be seen that the proposed new method leads to changes in the rankings, the order of countries and the exit and entry of countries in the three boundaries presented. These changes are due to the amount of information that is aggregated. Hence, the influence that the different criteria of those evaluated can have on the levels of development of the countries is evident. Thus, with these results, it can be assumed that the valuation given by the different decision makers has an influence on the order given in the ranking, either by extreme positions of pessimism or optimism. This can occur because of how decision makers prioritize the three elements that make up the HDI, given that each country has different resources, different developments, and more or less stable political and economic systems. Hence, the proposed method brings us closer to the reality that each country has in terms of human development because of the importance given to the subjective information prioritized by decision makers.

Additionally, it is important to visualize the different applications that the IPOGWA operator can has, because any problem that is analyzed by the geometric average (GA) and where the relative importance of each variable that compose the GA is considered by the decision maker that should not be the same these operators can be done. For example, The OGWA operator can be used when only one decision maker is considered, and the weights are ordered based on maximum or minimums; the IOGWA operator is useful when the ordering between weights and attributes want to be induced by specific values and the POWGA operator can be used when more than one decision maker is considered and their importance in the results is not the same. Additionally, the IPOWGA operator is used when the complexity of the problem requires it, that is, in a group decision making problem where the problem is analyzed by a geometric average where the variables that compose it do not have the same relative importance and the reordering of the weights is based on induced values. Thus, the two proposed methods contain the characteristics of the mean, geometric mean and OWA operator and additionally, the characteristics of the induced and prioritized variables. The latter two aspects are closely related to the judgement and subjectivity of the individuals. Finally, the figures presented show those nuances, some more prominent than others, but which can help to give meaning to the information by the origin of the data, i.e., one can always turn to the expert or individual who provided the initial judgement (soft information).

Finally, the research provides a different vision of how to approach the evaluation of the different indices that measure and provide reliable information for decision making at the governmental level in each country. In addition, it shows the usefulness of aggregation operators to consider different types of information. For future lines of research, new proposals can be made with indices such as the happiness, GINI, or competitiveness indices. Likewise, in the development of methodological proposals, these tools can be improved by complementing them with Bonferroni means [56], multi-person aggregation [57], soft multi-set [58], among others.

Author Contributions: Conceptualization, E.L.-C.; methodology, F.B.-M.; formal analysis, M.V.-C.; writing—original draft preparation, A.M.R.-S. All authors have read and agreed to the published version of the manuscript.

Funding: This research was funded by Universidad Pedagogica y Tecnologica de Colombia, grant number SGI 3134 and Chilean Government through FONDECYT initiation, grant number 11190056.

Institutional Review Board Statement: The study was conducted according to the guidelines of the Universidad Católica de Santísima Concepción.

Informed Consent Statement: All subjects gave their informed consent for inclusion before they participated in the study. The study was conducted in accordance with the Declaration of Helsinki.

Acknowledgments: Author Leon-Castro acknowledges support from the Chilean Government through FONDECYT initiation grant No. 11190056.

Conflicts of Interest: Declare conflicts of interest or state "The authors declare no conflict of interest."

Appendix A

Table A1. Results of the HDI index using different aggregation operators.

R	Traditional	$OWGA_{e1}$	$OWGA_{e2}$	$OWGA_{e3}$	$IOWGA_{e1}$	$IOWGA_{e2}$	$IOWGA_{e3}$	POWGA	PIOWGA
1	Norway	0.9537	0.9572	0.9619	0.9638	0.9541	0.9615	0.9462	0.9609
2	Switzerland	0.9459	0.9484	0.9512	0.9553	0.9492	0.9506	0.9326	0.9512
3	Ireland	0.9425	0.9439	0.9457	0.9476	0.9438	0.9456	0.9362	0.9455
4	Germany	0.9388	0.9379	0.9364	0.9362	0.9390	0.9364	0.9400	0.9368
4	Hong Kong, China (SAR)	0.9388	0.9433	0.9472	0.9540	0.9443	0.9457	0.9171	0.9474
6	Australia	0.9384	0.9368	0.9340	0.9365	0.9418	0.9337	0.9318	0.9353
6	Iceland	0.9385	0.9380	0.9368	0.9393	0.9413	0.9367	0.9315	0.9377
8	Sweden	0.9366	0.9364	0.9358	0.9382	0.9393	0.9356	0.9294	0.9364
9	Singapore	0.9348	0.9439	0.9533	0.9602	0.9389	0.9507	0.9104	0.9519
10	The Netherlands	0.9335	0.9342	0.9350	0.9375	0.9357	0.9348	0.9258	0.9353
11	Denmark	0.9299	0.9305	0.9313	0.9321	0.9305	0.9313	0.9273	0.9312
12	Finland	0.9252	0.9240	0.9219	0.9237	0.9276	0.9218	0.9207	0.9229
13	Canada	0.9221	0.9221	0.9214	0.9248	0.9257	0.9211	0.9122	0.9223
14	New Zealand	0.9209	0.9177	0.9123	0.9140	0.9243	0.9119	0.9178	0.9143
15	United Kingdom	0.9204	0.9188	0.9162	0.9175	0.9225	0.9160	0.9174	0.9172
16	United States	0.9199	0.9239	0.9293	0.9296	0.9185	0.9289	0.9172	0.9277
17	Belgium	0.9188	0.9191	0.9190	0.9217	0.9215	0.9188	0.9109	0.9196
18	Liechtenstein	0.9167	0.9276	0.9396	0.9448	0.9182	0.9369	0.8967	0.9371
19	Japan	0.9147	0.9157	0.9144	0.9215	0.9221	0.9130	0.8941	0.9162
20	Austria	0.9138	0.9156	0.9175	0.9212	0.9169	0.9171	0.9020	0.9177
21	Luxembourg	0.9087	0.9190	0.9291	0.9368	0.9133	0.9260	0.8818	0.9276
22	Israel	0.9062	0.9044	0.9001	0.9046	0.9121	0.8993	0.8944	0.9023
22	Korea (Republic of)	0.9058	0.9054	0.9032	0.9085	0.9118	0.9024	0.8910	0.9050
24	Slovenia	0.9016	0.8991	0.8945	0.8970	0.9055	0.8941	0.8960	0.8964
25	Spain	0.8928	0.8940	0.8925	0.9001	0.9008	0.8908	0.8708	0.8944
26	Czechia	0.8908	0.8888	0.8855	0.8865	0.8928	0.8854	0.8890	0.8867
26	France	0.8911	0.8947	0.8967	0.9043	0.8979	0.8950	0.8677	0.8976
28	Malta	0.8853	0.8868	0.8864	0.8935	0.8924	0.8849	0.8644	0.8879
29	Italy	0.8826	0.8861	0.8867	0.8958	0.8914	0.8844	0.8553	0.8884
30	Estonia	0.8815	0.8799	0.8771	0.8782	0.8835	0.8770	0.8794	0.8782
31	Cyprus	0.8730	0.8746	0.8749	0.8812	0.8790	0.8738	0.8543	0.8761
32	Greece	0.8720	0.8698	0.8637	0.8698	0.8799	0.8622	0.8562	0.8667

Table A1. *Cont.*

R	Traditional	$OWGA_{e1}$	$OWGA_{e2}$	$OWGA_{e3}$	$IOWGA_{e1}$	$IOWGA_{e2}$	$IOWGA_{e3}$	POWGA	PIOWGA
32	Poland	0.8718	0.8697	0.8663	0.8680	0.8746	0.8661	0.8678	0.8677
34	Lithuania	0.8693	0.8685	0.8672	0.8655	0.8681	0.8671	0.8747	0.8673
35	United Arab Emirates	0.8664	0.8832	0.8998	0.9070	0.8687	0.8942	0.8383	0.8962
36	Andorra	0.8568	0.8714	0.8819	0.8941	0.8657	0.8756	0.8162	0.8812
36	Saudi Arabia	0.8570	0.8667	0.8784	0.8810	0.8559	0.8762	0.8451	0.8754
36	Slovakia	0.8569	0.8580	0.8592	0.8621	0.8594	0.8589	0.8476	0.8594
39	Latvia	0.8539	0.8528	0.8509	0.8498	0.8534	0.8508	0.8579	0.8513
40	Portugal	0.8502	0.8535	0.8531	0.8627	0.8598	0.8504	0.8218	0.8551
41	Qatar	0.8484	0.8755	0.8963	0.9095	0.8558	0.8840	0.8001	0.8927
42	Chile	0.8469	0.8452	0.8401	0.8459	0.8543	0.8387	0.8316	0.8428
43	Brunei Darussalam	0.8446	0.8680	0.8900	0.8977	0.8458	0.8810	0.8129	0.8850
43	Hungary	0.8447	0.8452	0.8454	0.8482	0.8474	0.8451	0.8362	0.8459
45	Bahrain	0.8378	0.8477	0.8575	0.8646	0.8418	0.8545	0.8127	0.8560
46	Croatia	0.8373	0.8368	0.8343	0.8394	0.8432	0.8334	0.8231	0.8360
47	Oman	0.8338	0.8429	0.8513	0.8591	0.8389	0.8483	0.8073	0.8503
48	Argentina	0.8301	0.8259	0.8185	0.8198	0.8340	0.8176	0.8286	0.8210
49	Russian Federation	0.8240	0.8252	0.8267	0.8254	0.8222	0.8266	0.8275	0.8260
50	Belarus	0.8171	0.8135	0.8072	0.8074	0.8193	0.8066	0.8187	0.8091
50	Kazakhstan	0.8172	0.8171	0.8169	0.8170	0.8174	0.8169	0.8170	0.8170
52	Bulgaria	0.8157	0.8141	0.8114	0.8134	0.8186	0.8112	0.8107	0.8126
52	Montenegro	0.8159	0.8133	0.8078	0.8116	0.8215	0.8069	0.8066	0.8102
52	Romania	0.8156	0.8177	0.8193	0.8242	0.8199	0.8185	0.8003	0.8198
55	Palau	0.8142	0.8107	0.8044	0.8035	0.8154	0.8038	0.8192	0.8061
56	Barbados	0.8133	0.8109	0.8034	0.8102	0.8224	0.8012	0.7962	0.8070
57	Kuwait	0.8084	0.8399	0.8653	0.8767	0.8126	0.8508	0.7637	0.8600
57	Uruguay	0.8078	0.8085	0.8064	0.8136	0.8155	0.8048	0.7872	0.8085
59	Turkey	0.8065	0.8122	0.8157	0.8243	0.8139	0.8132	0.7795	0.8164
60	Bahamas	0.8055	0.8116	0.8185	0.8229	0.8076	0.8172	0.7900	0.8173
61	Malaysia	0.8042	0.8111	0.8170	0.8245	0.8097	0.8147	0.7796	0.8167
62	Seychelles	0.8014	0.8055	0.8103	0.8137	0.8033	0.8095	0.7893	0.8095
63	Serbia	0.7993	0.7962	0.7900	0.7939	0.8051	0.7890	0.7902	0.7927
63	Trinidad and Tobago	0.7990	0.8062	0.8141	0.8188	0.8012	0.8124	0.7820	0.8127
65	Iran (Islamic Republic of)	0.7975	0.7978	0.7958	0.8021	0.8044	0.7946	0.7795	0.7977
66	Mauritius	0.7964	0.8001	0.8034	0.8091	0.8010	0.8021	0.7782	0.8035
67	Panama	0.7951	0.7997	0.8004	0.8104	0.8047	0.7972	0.7650	0.8022
68	Costa Rica	0.7935	0.7941	0.7875	0.7979	0.8057	0.7836	0.7656	0.7916
69	Albania	0.7914	0.7880	0.7778	0.7849	0.8016	0.7748	0.7747	0.7823
70	Georgia	0.7864	0.7797	0.7646	0.7631	0.7901	0.7608	0.7960	0.7688
71	Sri Lanka	0.7801	0.7764	0.7667	0.7726	0.7890	0.7642	0.7665	0.7708
72	Cuba	0.7777	0.7716	0.7527	0.7584	0.7895	0.7460	0.7687	0.7595
73	Saint Kitts and Nevis	0.7768	0.7880	0.7974	0.8063	0.7829	0.7932	0.7464	0.7963
74	Antigua and Barbuda	0.7762	0.7854	0.7905	0.8015	0.7855	0.7860	0.7412	0.7912
75	Bosnia and Herzegovina	0.7692	0.7688	0.7626	0.7713	0.7797	0.7596	0.7459	0.7662
76	Mexico	0.7674	0.7715	0.7731	0.7812	0.7750	0.7709	0.7427	0.7742
77	Thailand	0.7646	0.7693	0.7691	0.7796	0.7751	0.7654	0.7335	0.7712
78	Grenada	0.7634	0.7608	0.7559	0.7585	0.7675	0.7553	0.7575	0.7579
79	Brazil	0.7612	0.7625	0.7600	0.7684	0.7702	0.7576	0.7374	0.7624
79	Colombia	0.7609	0.7621	0.7574	0.7672	0.7719	0.7541	0.7340	0.7608
81	Armenia	0.7600	0.7550	0.7432	0.7475	0.7681	0.7403	0.7518	0.7476
82	Algeria	0.7590	0.7612	0.7581	0.7679	0.7696	0.7548	0.7312	0.7610

Table A1. *Cont.*

R	Traditional	$OWGA_{e1}$	$OWGA_{e2}$	$OWGA_{e3}$	$IOWGA_{e1}$	$IOWGA_{e2}$	$IOWGA_{e3}$	POWGA	PIOWGA
82	North Macedonia	0.7594	0.7595	0.7552	0.7633	0.7686	0.7529	0.7375	0.7581
82	Peru	0.7591	0.7593	0.7539	0.7628	0.7695	0.7510	0.7351	0.7573
85	China	0.7576	0.7636	0.7643	0.7755	0.7684	0.7601	0.7242	0.7663
85	Ecuador	0.7579	0.7555	0.7459	0.7538	0.7688	0.7424	0.7383	0.7503
87	Azerbaijan	0.7539	0.7558	0.7564	0.7624	0.7596	0.7552	0.7358	0.7574
88	Ukraine	0.7497	0.7435	0.7299	0.7300	0.7546	0.7267	0.7541	0.7340
89	Dominican Republic	0.7446	0.7490	0.7504	0.7590	0.7527	0.7479	0.7185	0.7517
89	Saint Lucia	0.7449	0.7461	0.7413	0.7510	0.7559	0.7379	0.7184	0.7447
91	Tunisia	0.7392	0.7406	0.7347	0.7453	0.7513	0.7306	0.7107	0.7386
92	Mongolia	0.7347	0.7323	0.7281	0.7296	0.7376	0.7277	0.7316	0.7296
93	Lebanon	0.7301	0.7375	0.7333	0.7484	0.7460	0.7255	0.6878	0.7376
94	Botswana	0.7278	0.7330	0.7385	0.7433	0.7308	0.7372	0.7116	0.7378
94	Saint Vincent and the Grenadines	0.7279	0.7292	0.7276	0.7347	0.7354	0.7259	0.7074	0.7295
96	Jamaica	0.7257	0.7227	0.7123	0.7196	0.7361	0.7088	0.7086	0.7169
96	Venezuela (Bolivarian Republic of)	0.7258	0.7230	0.7160	0.7211	0.7331	0.7143	0.7134	0.7191
98	Dominica	0.7238	0.7278	0.7205	0.7342	0.7392	0.7136	0.6871	0.7254
98	Fiji	0.7237	0.7202	0.7138	0.7120	0.7242	0.7129	0.7310	0.7153
98	Paraguay	0.7243	0.7279	0.7265	0.7365	0.7345	0.7232	0.6956	0.7289
98	Suriname	0.7237	0.7254	0.7249	0.7315	0.7304	0.7234	0.7043	0.7263
102	Jordan	0.7234	0.7214	0.7123	0.7202	0.7341	0.7089	0.7038	0.7166
103	Belize	0.7202	0.7167	0.7047	0.7121	0.7312	0.7005	0.7035	0.7098
104	Maldives	0.7187	0.7317	0.7314	0.7483	0.7352	0.7215	0.6693	0.7349
105	Tonga	0.7174	0.7109	0.6946	0.6951	0.7236	0.6897	0.7216	0.6996
106	Philippines	0.7119	0.7112	0.7074	0.7134	0.7190	0.7060	0.6956	0.7097
107	Moldova (Republic of)	0.7115	0.7068	0.6953	0.6998	0.7196	0.6924	0.7027	0.6997
108	Turkmenistan	0.7101	0.7186	0.7272	0.7328	0.7130	0.7247	0.6902	0.7258
108	Uzbekistan	0.7105	0.7053	0.6927	0.6964	0.7184	0.6894	0.7041	0.6972
110	Libya	0.7076	0.7132	0.7142	0.7244	0.7173	0.7104	0.6770	0.7159
111	Indonesia	0.7069	0.7105	0.7110	0.7194	0.7150	0.7085	0.6818	0.7126
111	Samoa	0.7068	0.7020	0.6876	0.6934	0.7172	0.6828	0.6953	0.6931
113	South Africa	0.7049	0.7068	0.7090	0.7067	0.7019	0.7087	0.7112	0.7078
114	Bolivia (Plurinational State of)	0.7028	0.6988	0.6888	0.6937	0.7110	0.6862	0.6922	0.6928
115	Gabon	0.7016	0.7097	0.7189	0.7226	0.7025	0.7169	0.6870	0.7169
116	Egypt	0.6997	0.7042	0.7046	0.7141	0.7089	0.7014	0.6716	0.7064
117	Marshall Islands	0.6976	0.6925	0.6736	0.6797	0.7097	0.6660	0.6875	0.6805
118	Viet Nam	0.6927	0.6926	0.6812	0.6924	0.7071	0.6748	0.6649	0.6869
119	Palestine, State of	0.6900	0.6869	0.6724	0.6809	0.7028	0.6664	0.6715	0.6784
120	Iraq	0.6888	0.7031	0.7127	0.7238	0.6971	0.7061	0.6515	0.7121
121	Morocco	0.6764	0.6853	0.6797	0.6958	0.6936	0.6702	0.6323	0.6846
122	Kyrgyzstan	0.6742	0.6686	0.6453	0.6481	0.6849	0.6345	0.6750	0.6528
123	Guyana	0.6703	0.6718	0.6689	0.6772	0.6793	0.6663	0.6471	0.6714
124	El Salvador	0.6667	0.6713	0.6662	0.6788	0.6804	0.6602	0.6322	0.6703
125	Tajikistan	0.6560	0.6511	0.6320	0.6375	0.6677	0.6238	0.6478	0.6388
126	Cabo Verde	0.6507	0.6573	0.6529	0.6666	0.6653	0.6457	0.6126	0.6570
126	Guatemala	0.6510	0.6626	0.6604	0.6765	0.6672	0.6507	0.6052	0.6643
126	Nicaragua	0.6511	0.6540	0.6424	0.6558	0.6675	0.6338	0.6175	0.6485
129	India	0.6469	0.6507	0.6486	0.6587	0.6574	0.6447	0.6180	0.6513
130	Namibia	0.6450	0.6512	0.6578	0.6620	0.6472	0.6562	0.6298	0.6566

Table A1. *Cont.*

R	Traditional	$OWGA_{e1}$	$OWGA_{e2}$	$OWGA_{e3}$	$IOWGA_{e1}$	$IOWGA_{e2}$	$IOWGA_{e3}$	POWGA	PIOWGA
131	Timor-Leste	0.6259	0.6371	0.6397	0.6528	0.6380	0.6325	0.5860	0.6416
132	Honduras	0.6230	0.6320	0.6211	0.6383	0.6425	0.6084	0.5789	0.6278
132	Kiribati	0.6232	0.6208	0.6097	0.6172	0.6341	0.6052	0.6060	0.6145
134	Bhutan	0.6173	0.6392	0.6448	0.6623	0.6329	0.6308	0.5631	0.6466
135	Bangladesh	0.6137	0.6192	0.6092	0.6238	0.6306	0.5996	0.5763	0.6151
135	Micronesia (Federated States of)	0.6142	0.6120	0.6009	0.6087	0.6253	0.5962	0.5960	0.6058
137	Sao Tome and Principe	0.6086	0.6076	0.5922	0.6024	0.6232	0.5837	0.5859	0.5989
138	Congo	0.6085	0.6115	0.6118	0.6189	0.6154	0.6097	0.5872	0.6132
138	Eswatini (Kingdom of)	0.6081	0.6184	0.6296	0.6329	0.6079	0.6266	0.5942	0.6269
140	Lao People's Democratic Republic	0.6041	0.6144	0.6164	0.6290	0.6158	0.6095	0.5660	0.6183
141	Vanuatu	0.5968	0.5973	0.5817	0.5932	0.6126	0.5721	0.5711	0.5887
142	Ghana	0.5957	0.5943	0.5887	0.5944	0.6030	0.5868	0.5811	0.5915
143	Zambia	0.5915	0.5886	0.5806	0.5855	0.5988	0.5783	0.5803	0.5840
144	Equatorial Guinea	0.5884	0.6225	0.6492	0.6567	0.5887	0.6319	0.5551	0.6427
145	Myanmar	0.5843	0.5968	0.5994	0.6128	0.5967	0.5912	0.5434	0.6013
146	Cambodia	0.5815	0.5882	0.5803	0.5947	0.5975	0.5711	0.5438	0.5856
147	Kenya	0.5786	0.5783	0.5679	0.5773	0.5908	0.5624	0.5560	0.5729
147	Nepal	0.5795	0.5834	0.5696	0.5834	0.5967	0.5586	0.5465	0.5765
149	Angola	0.5745	0.5804	0.5848	0.5912	0.5796	0.5824	0.5534	0.5847
150	Cameroon	0.5627	0.5599	0.5545	0.5563	0.5662	0.5538	0.5595	0.5565
150	Zimbabwe	0.5631	0.5589	0.5484	0.5516	0.5698	0.5454	0.5575	0.5522
152	Pakistan	0.5604	0.5782	0.5813	0.5972	0.5750	0.5693	0.5124	0.5835
153	Solomon Islands	0.5573	0.5662	0.5476	0.5648	0.5788	0.5296	0.5184	0.5567
154	Syrian Arab Republic	0.5489	0.5634	0.5527	0.5718	0.5697	0.5360	0.5003	0.5598
155	Papua New Guinea	0.5431	0.5517	0.5506	0.5631	0.5555	0.5435	0.5071	0.5534
156	Comoros	0.5378	0.5390	0.5295	0.5396	0.5505	0.5232	0.5127	0.5344
157	Rwanda	0.5360	0.5417	0.5263	0.5409	0.5543	0.5129	0.5022	0.5339
158	Nigeria	0.5341	0.5417	0.5503	0.5524	0.5335	0.5484	0.5248	0.5482
159	Tanzania (United Republic of)	0.5283	0.5360	0.5306	0.5441	0.5428	0.5220	0.4918	0.5350
159	Uganda	0.5282	0.5259	0.5104	0.5177	0.5402	0.5025	0.5139	0.5165
161	Mauritania	0.5271	0.5419	0.5428	0.5578	0.5413	0.5321	0.4830	0.5456
162	Madagascar	0.5207	0.5229	0.5022	0.5135	0.5377	0.4872	0.4987	0.5107
163	Benin	0.5198	0.5192	0.5097	0.5178	0.5306	0.5048	0.5004	0.5142
164	Lesotho	0.5180	0.5188	0.5199	0.5203	0.5180	0.5198	0.5163	0.5196
165	Côte d'Ivoire	0.5157	0.5212	0.5245	0.5313	0.5215	0.5219	0.4943	0.5249
166	Senegal	0.5138	0.5359	0.5343	0.5534	0.5324	0.5168	0.4596	0.5386
167	Togo	0.5127	0.5096	0.4944	0.5000	0.5232	0.4872	0.5028	0.5001
168	Sudan	0.5075	0.5321	0.5361	0.5538	0.5236	0.5192	0.4537	0.5384
169	Haiti	0.5027	0.5050	0.4917	0.5030	0.5175	0.4820	0.4767	0.4979
170	Afghanistan	0.4960	0.5019	0.4902	0.5038	0.5122	0.4791	0.4629	0.4965
171	Djibouti	0.4954	0.5256	0.5282	0.5484	0.5141	0.5065	0.4357	0.5314
172	Malawi	0.4854	0.4878	0.4682	0.4789	0.5016	0.4536	0.4644	0.4762
173	Ethiopia	0.4698	0.4880	0.4792	0.4980	0.4897	0.4609	0.4213	0.4856
174	Gambia	0.4657	0.4715	0.4609	0.4737	0.4809	0.4506	0.4343	0.4667
174	Guinea	0.4655	0.4793	0.4773	0.4920	0.4801	0.4661	0.4240	0.4809
176	Liberia	0.4647	0.4698	0.4505	0.4630	0.4822	0.4341	0.4392	0.4588
177	Yemen	0.4627	0.4778	0.4652	0.4833	0.4829	0.4468	0.4187	0.4726

Table A1. *Cont.*

R	Traditional	$OWGA_{e1}$	$OWGA_{e2}$	$OWGA_{e3}$	$IOWGA_{e1}$	$IOWGA_{e2}$	$IOWGA_{e3}$	POWGA	PIOWGA
178	Guinea-Bissau	0.4614	0.4632	0.4557	0.4648	0.4725	0.4502	0.4383	0.4598
179	Congo (Democratic Republic of the)	0.4587	0.4604	0.4360	0.4423	0.4728	0.4173	0.4518	0.4446
180	Mozambique	0.4460	0.4498	0.4364	0.4478	0.4608	0.4255	0.4200	0.4427
181	Sierra Leone	0.4385	0.4378	0.4309	0.4372	0.4467	0.4276	0.4231	0.4342
182	Burkina Faso	0.4335	0.4515	0.4477	0.4643	0.4503	0.4323	0.3878	0.4521
182	Eritrea	0.4336	0.4642	0.4583	0.4802	0.4553	0.4323	0.3753	0.4644
184	Mali	0.4272	0.4464	0.4469	0.4624	0.4418	0.4328	0.3822	0.4499
185	Burundi	0.4229	0.4298	0.4057	0.4165	0.4404	0.3832	0.4052	0.4151
186	South Sudan	0.4128	0.4255	0.4220	0.4359	0.4269	0.4107	0.3745	0.4258
187	Chad	0.4012	0.4149	0.4173	0.4290	0.4119	0.4080	0.3656	0.4189
188	Central African Republic	0.3807	0.3812	0.3692	0.3768	0.3916	0.3615	0.3645	0.3743
189	Niger	0.3766	0.4017	0.3904	0.4104	0.3975	0.3654	0.3280	0.3978

References

1. UNDP. *Human Development Report 1990;* Concept and Measurament of Human Development, United Nations: New York, NY, USA, 1990. Available online: http://www.hdr.undp.org/en/reports/global/hdr1990 (accessed on 27 June 2017).
2. Sen, A. *Development as Freedom*, 2nd ed.; Oxford University Press: New York, NY, USA, 2001.
3. Blanco-Mesa, F.; León-Castro, E.; Merigó, J.M. A bibliometric analysis of aggregation operators. *Appl. Soft Comput.* **2019**, *81*, 105488. [CrossRef]
4. Yager, R.R. On ordered weighted averaging aggregation operators in multicriteria decisionmaking. *IEEE Trans. Syst. Man Cybern.* **1988**, *18*, 183–190. [CrossRef]
5. Baez-Palencia, D.; Olazabal-Lugo, M.; Romero-Muñoz, J. Toma de decisiones empresariales a través de la media ordenada ponderada. *Inquietud Empresarial* **2019**, *19*, 11–23.
6. Yager, R.R. Induced aggregation operators. *Fuzzy Sets Syst.* **2003**, *137*, 59–69. [CrossRef]
7. Yager, R.R. Heavy OWA operators. *Fuzzy Optim. Decis. Mak.* **2002**, *1*, 379–397. [CrossRef]
8. Yager, R.R. Prioritized aggregation operators. *Int. J. Approx. Reason.* **2008**, *48*, 263–274. [CrossRef]
9. Merigó, J.M. Probabilities in the OWA operator. *Expert Syst. Appl.* **2012**, *39*, 11456–11467. [CrossRef]
10. Yager, R.R. On generalized Bonferroni mean operators for multi-criteria aggregation. *Int. J. Approx. Reason.* **2009**, *50*, 1279–1286. [CrossRef]
11. Alfaro-García, V.G.; Merigó, J.M.; Gil-Lafuente, A.M.; Kacprzyk, J. Logarithmic aggregation operators and distance measures. *Int. J. Intell. Syst.* **2018**, *33*, 1488–1506. [CrossRef]
12. Yager, R.R. Pythagorean membership grades in multicriteria decision making. *IEEE Trans. Fuzzy Syst.* **2013**, *22*, 958–965. [CrossRef]
13. Blanco-Mesa, F.; Gil-Lafuente, A.M.; Merigó, J.M. New aggregation operators for decision-making under uncertainty: An applications in selection of entrepreneurial opportunities. *Technol. Econ. Dev. Econ.* **2018**, *24*, 335–357. [CrossRef]
14. León-Castro, E.; Avilés-Ochoa, E.; Merigó, J.M. Induced heavy moving averages. *Int. J. Intell. Syst.* **2018**, *33*, 1823–1839. [CrossRef]
15. León-Castro, E.; Espinoza-Audelo, L.F.; Merigó, J.M.; Herrera-Viedma, E.; Herrera, F. Measuring volatility based on ordered weighted average operators: Agricultural products prices case of use. *Fuzzy Sets Syst.* **2020**, *395*, 197–198. [CrossRef]
16. Fonseca-Cifuentes, G.; León-Castro, E.; Blanco-Mesa, F. Predicting the future price of a commodity using the OWMA operator: An approximation of the interest rate and inflation in the brown pastusa potato price. *J. Intell. Fuzzy Syst.* **2021**, *40*, 1970–1981.
17. Espinoza-Audelo, L.F.; Olazabal-Lugo, M.; Blanco-Mesa, F.; León-Castro, E.; Alfaro-Garcia, V. Bonferroni Probabilistic Ordered Weighted Averaging Operators Applied to Agricultural Commodities' Price Analysis. *Mathematics* **2020**, *8*, 1350. [CrossRef]
18. Blanco-Mesa, F.; Rivera-Rubiano, J.; Patino-Hernandez, X.; Martinez-Montana, M. The importance of enterprise risk management in large companies in Colombia. *Technol. Econ. Dev. Econ.* **2019**, *25*, 600–633. [CrossRef]
19. Blanco-Mesa, F.; León-Castro, E.; Merigó, J.M. Bonferroni induced heavy operators in ERM decision-making: A case on large companies in Colombia. *Appl. Soft Comput.* **2018**, *72*, 371–391. [CrossRef]
20. Mariño-Becerra, G.; Blanco-Mesa, F.; León-Castro, E. Pythagorean membership grade distance aggregation: An application to new business ventures. *J. Intell. Fuzzy Syst.* **2021**, *40*, 1827–1836. [CrossRef]
21. Avilés-Ochoa, E.; León-Castro, E.; Perez-Arellano, L.A.; Merigó, J.M. Government transparency measurement through prioritized distance operators. *J. Intell. Fuzzy Syst.* **2018**, *34*, 2783–2794. [CrossRef]
22. Perez-Arellano, L.A.; Leon-Castro, E.; Blanco-Mesa, F.; Fonseca-Cifuentes, G. The ordered weighted government transparency average: Colombia case. *J. Intell. Fuzzy Syst.* **2020**, *40*, 1837–1849. [CrossRef]
23. Kelley, A.C. The human development index: "Handle with care". *Popul. Dev. Rev.* **1991**, *17*, 315–324. [CrossRef]

24. Sen, A. Equality of what? *Tann. Lect. Hum. Values* **1980**, *1*, 197–220.
25. Yakunina, R.P.; Bychkov, G.A. Correlation analysis of the components of the human development index across countries. *Procedia Econ. Financ.* **2015**, *24*, 766–771. [CrossRef]
26. Zirogiannis, N.; Krutilla, K.; Tripodis, Y.; Fledderman, K. Human development over time: An empirical comparison of a Dynamic Index and the standard HDI. *Soc. Indic. Res.* **2019**, *142*, 773–798. [CrossRef]
27. UNDP. *Human Development Report 2019*; UNDP: New York, NY, USA, 2019.
28. Ranis, G.; Stewart, F. Success and failure in human development, 1970–2007. *J. Hum. Dev. Capab.* **2012**, *13*, 167–195. [CrossRef]
29. Chaaban, J.; Irani, A.; Khoury, A. The composite global well-being index (CGWBI): A new multi-dimensional measure of human development. *Soc. Indic. Res.* **2016**, *129*, 465–487. [CrossRef]
30. Hickel, J. The sustainable development index: Measuring the ecological efficiency of human development in the anthropocene. *Ecol. Econ.* **2020**, *167*, 106331. [CrossRef]
31. Biggeri, M.; Mauro, V. Towards a more 'sustainable' human development index: Integrating the environment and freedom. *Ecol. Indic.* **2018**, *91*, 220–231. [CrossRef]
32. Lind, N. A development of the human development index. *Soc. Indic. Res.* **2019**, *146*, 409–423. [CrossRef]
33. Kovacevic, M. Measurement of inequality in Human Development–A review. *Measurement* **2010**, *35*, 1–65.
34. Gaye, A.; Klugman, J.; Kovacevic, M.; Twigg, S.; Zambrano, E. Measuring key disparities in human development: The gender inequality index. *Hum. Dev. Res. Pap.* **2010**, *46*, 1–37.
35. Alkire, S.; Jahan, S. *The New Global MPI 2018: Aligning with the Sustainable Development Goals 2018*; University of Oxford: Oxford, UK, 2018.
36. Sayed, H.; Hamed, R.; Hosny, S.H.; Abdelhamid, A.H. Avoiding ranking contradictions in human development index using goal programming. *Soc. Indic. Res.* **2018**, *138*, 405–442. [CrossRef]
37. Anand, S.; Sen, A. The income component of the human development index. *J. Hum. Dev.* **2000**, *1*, 83–106. [CrossRef]
38. Maddison, A. *Historical Statistics of the World Economy*; OECD Publishing: Paris, France, 2003. [CrossRef]
39. Kahneman, D.; Deaton, A. High Income Improves Evaluation of Life but not Emotional Well-being. *Proc. Natl. Acad. Sci. USA* **2010**, *107*, 16489–16493. [CrossRef] [PubMed]
40. Merigó, J.M. Fuzzy decision making with immediate probabilities. *Comput. Ind. Eng.* **2010**, *58*, 651–657. [CrossRef]
41. Olazabal-Lugo, M.; Leon-Castro, E.; Espinoza-Audelo, L.F.; Maria Merigo, J.; Gil Lafuente, A.M. Forgotten effects and heavy moving averages in exchange rate forecasting. *Econ. Comput. Econ. Cybern. Stud. Res.* **2019**, *53*, 79–96.
42. Xu, Z.S.; Da, Q.-L. The uncertain OWA operator. *Int. J. Intell. Syst.* **2002**, *17*, 569–575. [CrossRef]
43. Xu, Z.; Da, Q.-L. An overview of operators for aggregating information. *Int. J. Intell. Syst.* **2003**, *18*, 953–969. [CrossRef]
44. Avilés-Ochoa, E.; Perez-Arellano, L.A.; León-Castro, E.; Merigó, J.M. Prioritized induced probabilistic distances in transparency and access to information laws. *Fuzzy Econ. Rev.* **2017**, *22*, 45–55. [CrossRef]
45. Pérez-Arellano, L.A.; León-Castro, E.; Avilés-Ochoa, E.; Merigó, J.M. Prioritized induced probabilistic operator and its application in group decision making. *Int. J. Mach. Learn. Cybern.* **2019**, *10*, 451–462. [CrossRef]
46. UNDP. *Human Development*; UNDP: New York, NY, USA, 2018.
47. Merigo, J.M. *La Media Ponderada Ordenada Probabilística: Teoría y Aplicaciones*; Fundación Universitaria ESERP: Barcelona, Spain, 2014.
48. Blanco-Mesa, F.; Merigó, J.M.; Gil-Lafuente, A.M. Fuzzy decision making: A bibliometric-based review. *J. Intell. Fuzzy Syst.* **2017**, *32*, 2033–2050. [CrossRef]
49. Hara, T.; Uchiyama, M.; Takahasi, S.-E. A refinement of various mean inequalities. *J. Inequalities Appl.* **1998**, *1998*, 932025. [CrossRef]
50. Sinani, F.; Erceg, Z.; Vasiljević, M. An evaluation of a third-party logistics provider: The application of the rough Dombi-Hamy mean operator. *Decis. Mak. Appl. Manag. Eng.* **2020**, *3*, 92–107.
51. Bonferroni, C. Sulle medie multiple di potenze. *Boll. dell'Unione Mat. Ital.* **1950**, *5*, 267–270.
52. Blanco-Mesa, F.; León-Castro, E.; Merigó, J.M.; Xu, Z. Bonferroni means with induced ordered weighted average operators. *Int. J. Intell. Syst.* **2019**, *34*, 3–23. [CrossRef]
53. Dombi, J. Basic concepts for a theory of evaluation: The aggregative operator. *Eur. J. Oper. Res.* **1982**, *10*, 282–293. [CrossRef]
54. Dombi, J. The Generalized Dombi Operator Family and the Multiplicative Utility Function. In *Soft Computing Based Modeling in Intelligent Systems*; Springer: Berlin/Heidelberg, Germany, 2009; pp. 115–131.
55. Pamucar, D. Normalized weighted Geometric Dombi Bonferoni Mean Operator with interval grey numbers: Application in multicriteria decision making. *Rep. Mech. Eng.* **2020**, *1*, 44–52. [CrossRef]
56. Blanco-Mesa, F.; Merigó, J.M. Bonferroni distances and their application in group decision making. *Cybern. Syst.* **2020**, *51*, 27–58. [CrossRef]
57. Blanco-Mesa, F.; Gil-Lafuente, A.M.; Merigó, J.M. Subjective stakeholder dynamics relationships treatment: A methodological approach using fuzzy decision-making. *Comput. Math. Organ. Theory* **2018**, *24*, 441–472. [CrossRef]
58. Riaz, M.; Çagman, N.; Wali, N.; Mushtaq, A. Certain properties of soft multi-set topology with applications in multi-criteria decision making. *Decis. Mak. Appl. Manag. Eng.* **2020**, *3*, 70–96. [CrossRef]

axioms

Article

A Spherical Fuzzy Analytic Hierarchy Process (SF-AHP) and Combined Compromise Solution (CoCoSo) Algorithm in Distribution Center Location Selection: A Case Study in Agricultural Supply Chain

Phan Thuy Kieu [1], Van Thanh Nguyen [2,*], Viet Tinh Nguyen [2,*] and Thanh Phong Ho [3]

1 School of Business, International University, Vietnam National University, Ho Chi Minh 723000, Vietnam; phanthuykieu2006@gmail.com
2 Faculty of Commerce, Van Lang University, Ho Chi Minh 723000, Vietnam
3 Department of Logistics and Supply Chain Management, Hong Bang International University, Ho Chi Minh 723000, Vietnam; phonght@gmail.com
* Correspondence: jenny9121989@gmail.com (V.T.N.); tinh.nv@vlu.edu.vn (V.T.N.)

Abstract: Logistics is an important service sector, contributing to improving the competitiveness of the economy. Therefore, along with increasing the application of technology and effective business models, it is necessary to increase the connectivity of the infrastructure systems of industrial parks, roads, and seaports of regions and the country. Over the past decades, Vietnamese businesses have been step-by-step going through many stages from production, packaging, quality, hygiene, and safety to grasping new stages in the domestic and global value chain. In many industries, businesses are increasing the content of their own designs, exploiting brands, and approaching consumption networks in the target market. The role of the distribution center is becoming more and more important in ensuring a seamless and flawless supply chain. In particular, the distribution center is the most sensitive contact point between supply and demand in each enterprise. Therefore, the key mission of a distribution center is to reconcile supply and demand requirements. Distribution center location selection problems usually involve multiple quantitative and qualitative criteria that the decision maker must take into account for assessing the symmetrical impact of the criteria to reach the most accurate result. In this study, the authors propose a hybrid MCDM model based on Spherical Fuzzy Analytic Hierarchy Process (SF-AHP) and Combined Compromise Solution (CoCoSo) Algorithm to support the distribution location selection problem of perishable agricultural products. The proposed model is then applied to the numerical case study of the sweet potato product of the Mekong Delta region of Vietnam to demonstrate the feasibility of the model. The contribution of this research is to propose an MCDM model for improving the efficiency of the agricultural supply chain through selecting a location distribution center. This proposed model can be applied to the agricultural supply chain around the world.

Keywords: multicriteria decision making model (MCDM); location selection; Spherical Fuzzy Analytic Hierarchy Process (SF-AHP); Combined Compromise Solution (CoCoSo); distribution center

Citation: Kieu, P.T.; Nguyen, V.T.; Nguyen, V.T.; Ho, T.P. A Spherical Fuzzy Analytic Hierarchy Process (SF-AHP) and Combined Compromise Solution (CoCoSo) Algorithm in Distribution Center Location Selection: A Case Study in Agricultural Supply Chain. *Axioms* **2021**, *10*, 53. https://doi.org/10.3390/axioms10020053

Academic Editor: Goran Ćirović

Received: 3 March 2021
Accepted: 31 March 2021
Published: 3 April 2021

1. Introduction

Most perishable supply chains in the Mekong Delta Region of Vietnam are inefficient, which contributes to low production and productivity of the agricultural sector of the region as a whole. Among many agriculture products of the region, sweet potato is considered as one of the major products. However, the majority of sweet potato growers are small-scale farmers who are not able to produce and distribute their produce efficiently due to the inefficiency of the current supply chain [1]. One of the reasons is the lack of a proper distribution center to service the largest domestic market region and international logistics gateway of the country—the metropolitan part of the South East region of Vietnam [2]. As the local government has put a focus on improving the livelihood of the small-scale farmers by improving the inefficiency, by improving the design of the current supply chain, the problem of choosing the optimal location for a dedicated distribution center is becoming an important question to solve in order to improve these farmers' livelihood, as well as the overall profitability of the whole sweet potato supply chain. Multiple criteria in both quantitative and qualitative forms must be considered in a systematic approach in order to ensure the efficiency of the final design of the supply chain. Therefore, the distribution center location selection problem can be considered as a multicriteria decision-making problem under uncertain environments. Mekong Delta Region and South East Region of Vietnam is shown in Figure 1.

Figure 1. Mekong Delta Region and South East Region of Vietnam [3].

Distribution center location selection problems usually involve multiple quantitative and qualitative criteria. A feasible approach to such problems is the use of multicriteria decision-making (MCDM) methods to develop specialized MCDM models. These models differ from each other by having different criteria or employing different MCDM methods. There are multiple MCDM methods that can be employed to support the decision makers such as Analytical Hierarchy Process (AHP), Analytical Network Process (ANP), Multicriteria Optimization and Compromise Solution (VIKOR), Technique for Order Preference Similarity to the Ideal Solution (TOPSIS), etc. In the cases where the decision-making problem involves an uncertain decision-making environment, fuzzy theory is employed in combination with MCDM methods to create fuzzy MCDM models to effectively solve the problems. In this study, the authors propose a hybrid MCDM model based on Spherical Fuzzy Analytic Hierarchy Process (SF-AHP) and Combined Compromise Solution (CoCoSo) Algorithm to support the distribution location selection problem of perishable agricultural products. The proposed model is then applied to the numerical case study of the sweet potato product of the Mekong Delta region of Vietnam to demonstrate the feasibility of the model.

2. Literature Review

Over the years, many decision support systems based on MCDM methods have been developed to assist decision makers in solving complex decision-making problems in different sectors, such as computer science, environmental science, manufacturing engineering, energy and fuels, etc. Among these, supply chain management is an increasingly frequent topic of research with numerous MCDM models developed to support the optimization of different supply chains. Common decision-making problems in the supply chain management field include sustainable supplier selection, sustainable innovation selection, facility location selection, and many more.

Supplier selection is one of the most demanding multicriteria decision-making problems, especially in cases where sustainability is a concern. Fallahpour et al. [4] proposed a fuzzy AHP-TOPSIS method to support the supplier ranking and selection process. The author applied the fuzzy preference programming technique to calculate the relative fuzzy weights of the ranking criteria, while fuzzy TOPSIS is employed to determine the ranking of the potential suppliers. Govidan et al. [5] introduced the fuzzy TOPSIS-based MCDM model to support the sustainable supplier evaluation process. Dai and Blackhurst [6] utilized the AHP and Quality Function Deployment (QFD) methods to develop a MCDM model for the sustainable supplier selection problem. Luthra et al. [7] introduced a sustainable supplier selection method based on AHP and VIKOR methods. The proposed model has 22 criteria for the three pillars of sustainability. Wang et al. [8] developed a hybrid fuzzy ANP-PROMETHEE II to assist the supplier evaluation and selection process in the textile industry. The selection criteria of the proposed model are based on the popular Supply Chain Operation Reference (SCOR) model.

Sustainable innovation is also an important part of supply chain management where MCDM models are frequently employed. Gupta and Sarkis [9] introduced a Best-Worst Method based theoretical framework for ranking sustainable assessment criteria. Entezaminia et al. [10] developed an AHP-based decision support system to assist the evaluation of potential products of the supply chain based on sustainability criteria. Facility location selection is another aspect of supply chain management where MCDM methods are frequently applied to support the decision makers. Chien et al. [11] proposed a hybrid fuzzy ANP-TOPSIS model to support the location selection problem of hydroelectric plant projects. The model is applied to a hydroelectric plant development project in Vietnam to verify its feasibility. Tadić et al. [12] utilized the Delphi method, AHP, and Combinative Distance-based Assessment (CODAS) to develop a decision support system under grey environment to support the location selection process of a dry port terminal. Budak et al. [13] utilized Interval-valued Intuitionistic Fuzzy sets theory in combination with the Decision-Making Trial and Evaluation Laboratory (DEMATEL) method to create a real-time location system (RTLSs) to support the asset location management problem of humanitarian relief efforts. Deveci et al. [14] combined a fuzzy COPRAS-based MCDM model with Geographical Information Systems (GIS) to solve a factory location selection problem. In order to solve a stacker's selection problem in a logistics system, Ulutaş et al. [15] employed correlation coefficient and the standard deviation to determine the objective weights of criteria, the Indifference Threshold-based Attribute Ratio Analysis (ITARA) method to calculate the semi-objective weights of criteria. Finally, the compromise solution method (MARCOS) is applied to calculate the alternative ranking. The proposed model provided a comprehensive and easy approach to the problem. Ulutaş et al. [16] developed a novel MULTIMOOSRAL approach to the supplier selection problem. Ulutaş [17] developed a grey MCDM model based on grey Step-wise Weight Assessment Ratio Analysis (SWARA) and Multi-Objective Optimization Method by Ratio Analysis (MOORA) to evaluate the logistics performance of transition economies. The model suggests that the most influential criterion is "infrastructure" and Serbia is the country with the best logistics performance among the transition economies.

There are multiple literatures on the development of MCDM models supporting distribution center (DC) location selection problems. Yilmaz and Kabak [18] developed a type—2 fuzzy AHP-TOPSIS approach to identify the criteria for a disaster response distribution center. Liu and Li [19] developed a MCDM model utilizing 2-dimensional linguistic (2DL) information to ensure the effective decision-making process under uncertain environments to support a DC location selection problem. Quynh et al. [20] developed a fuzzy TOPSIS-based model to assist the DC location selection process. Kuo [21] introduced a utilized fuzzy AHP/ANP and fuzzy DEMATEL to support the international DC selection problem. The proposed approach is employed to solve an international DC selection problem in Pacific Asia to demonstrate the model and its feasibility. Yang et al. [22] proposed a novel MCDM-based approach to solve the logistics center location selection process for FMCG supply chains in China.

While the application of MCDM methods in solving DC selection problems of various supply chains has been studied in multiple literatures, only a few focus on solving the problem under uncertain decision-making environments by incorporating fuzzy theory to existing MCDM methods. Among these models, none are dedicated to the DC selection problem of agriculture perishable supply chains. Therefore, this research aims to develop a comprehensive MCDM model to support the DC selection process of agricultural supply chains under uncertain decision-making environments. The proposed model is based on a hybrid SF-AHP and CoCoSo approach and is applied to a real-world case study of sweet-potato produced in the Mekong Delta Region of Vietnam.

3. Methodology

3.1. Research Graph

Distribution center location selection is an important decision-making issue that has a profound impact on the performance of any supply chains. However, the decision-making process usually involves not only quantitative criteria but also qualitative ones, which increases the complexity of the process. Thus, fuzzy set theory is frequently integrated into MCDM models, which allows the ambiguity of the decision-making process to be reflected. While there are multiple methods to calculate the weighting of the criteria, such as BWM, LBWA, FAHP, FUCOM, and FANP. There are few applications of three dimensions fuzzy sets on the developments of MCDM modes. Therefore, this paper aims to create a hybrid MCDM model based on SF-AHP and CoCoSo methods to solve the DC location selection problem.

The application of the proposed approach includes four steps shown in Figure 2 below:

Step 1: Analyzing the current statuses of the product distribution system. Next, the decision-making criteria set, and sub-criteria set are established based on the relevant literatures and industry expert interviews.

Step 2: Applying the SF-AHP method to calculate the weights of the criteria. The weight of the criteria is also the input data of CoCoSo method in Step 4.

Step 3: Checking the consistency of the results of the SF-AHP model.

Step 4: Employing the CoCoSo method to calculate the ranking of the alternatives based on the criteria weights calculated using the SF-AHP model.

3.2. Theoretical Basis

3.2.1. Spherical Fuzzy Sets Theory

The spherical fuzzy sets theory has been applied in multiple MCDM models. Sharaf [23] applied spherical fuzzy sets in combination with the VIKOR method to solve a supplier selection problem. The implementation of spherical fuzzy sets provides the decision makers with a larger preference domain [23]. Otay and Atik [24] created an MCDM model to solve a real-world oil station location evaluation problem using spherical fuzzy sets and the WASPAS method. Sensitivity analysis showed that the proposed model is robust [24]. Gül [25] developed a spherical fuzzy extension of the DEMATEL method. The proposed model was applied to a building contractor selection problem [25]. In this research, a hybrid SF-AHP and CoCoSo approach is developed to solve a DC location selection problem.

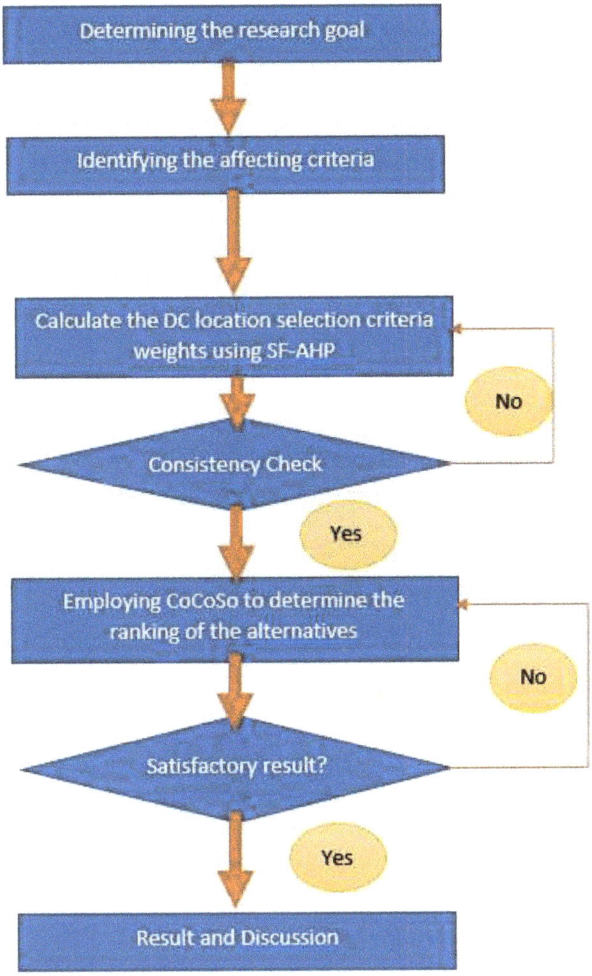

Figure 2. Research Graph.

Spherical fuzzy sets theory was introduced recently by Gundogdu and Kahraman [26] as a synthesis of Pythagorean fuzzy sets [27] and Neutrosophic sets theories [28]. Pythagorean fuzzy sets' membership functions are defined by membership, non-membership, and hesitancy parameters; Neutrosophic fuzzy sets membership functions are also composed of truthiness, falsity, and indeterminacy parameters. Spherical fuzzy sets theory is based on the idea that by defining a membership function on a spherical surface, decision makers can generalize different types of fuzzy sets [26].

The membership function of a spherical fuzzy set is defined by three parameters: the degree of membership, the degree of non-membership, and the degree of hesitancy. Each of these parameters can have a value between 0 and 1 independently and the sum of the squared values of these parameters is at most 1.

A spherical fuzzy set $\widetilde{A}_S$ of the universe of U_1 is defined as:

$$\widetilde{A}_S = \left\{x,\ \left(\mu_{\widetilde{A}_S}(x),\ v_{\widetilde{A}_S}(x),\ \pi_{\widetilde{A}_S}(x)\right)|x\epsilon U_1\right\} \quad (1)$$

with:

$$\mu_{\tilde{A}_S}(x) : U_1 \to [0,1],\ v_{\tilde{A}_S}(x) : U_1 \to [0,1],\ \text{and}\ \pi_{\tilde{A}_S}(x) : U_1 \to [0,1]$$

and

$$0 \le \mu^2_{\tilde{A}_S}(x) + v^2_{\tilde{A}_S}(x) + \pi^2_{\tilde{A}_S}(x) \le 1 \tag{2}$$

with $\forall x \in U_1, \mu_{\tilde{A}_S}(x)$ as the degree of membership, $v_{\tilde{A}_S}(x)$ as the degree of non-membership, and $\pi_{\tilde{A}_S}(x)$ as the hesitancy of x to $\tilde{A}_S$.

Basic arithmetic operations—such as union, intersection, addition, multiplication, and power—of spherical fuzzy sets are defined and demonstrated in the work of Gundogdu and Kahraman [29]. For these spherical fuzzy sets $\tilde{A}_S = (\mu_{\tilde{A}_S}, v_{\tilde{A}_S}, \pi_{\tilde{A}_S})$ and $\tilde{B}_S = (\mu_{\tilde{B}_S}, v_{\tilde{B}_S}, \pi_{\tilde{B}_S})$, basic arithmetic operations are performed as follows:

$$\tilde{A}_S \cup \tilde{B}_S = \left\{ max\left\{\mu_{\tilde{A}_S}, \mu_{\tilde{B}_S}\right\}, min\left\{v_{\tilde{A}_S}, v_{\tilde{B}_S}\right\}, min\left\{ \left[1 - \left(\left(max\left\{\mu_{\tilde{A}_S}, \mu_{\tilde{B}_S}\right\}\right)^2 + \left(min\left\{v_{\tilde{A}_S}, v_{\tilde{B}_S}\right\}\right)^2\right)\right]^{0.5}, max\left\{\pi_{\tilde{A}_S}, \pi_{\tilde{B}_S}\right\}\right\}\right\} \tag{3}$$

- Intersection of $\tilde{A}_S$ and $\tilde{B}_S$:

$$\begin{aligned}\tilde{A}_S \cap \tilde{B}_S = &\left\{ min\left\{\mu_{\tilde{A}_S}, \mu_{\tilde{B}_S}\right\}, max\left\{v_{\tilde{A}_S}, v_{\tilde{B}_S}\right\}, max\{[1 \right. \\ &\left. - \left(\left(min\left\{\mu_{\tilde{A}_S}, \mu_{\tilde{B}_S}\right\}\right)^2 + \left(max\left\{v_{\tilde{A}_S}, v_{\tilde{B}_S}\right\}\right)^2\right)]^{0.5}, min\left\{\pi_{\tilde{A}_S}, \pi_{\tilde{B}_S}\right\}\}\right\}\end{aligned} \tag{4}$$

- Addition of $\tilde{A}_S$ and $\tilde{B}_S$:

$$\tilde{A}_S + \tilde{B}_S = \left\{ \left(\mu^2_{\tilde{A}_S} + \mu^2_{\tilde{B}_S} - \mu^2_{\tilde{A}_S}\mu^2_{\tilde{B}_S}\right)^{0.5}, v_{\tilde{A}_S}v_{\tilde{B}_S}, \left(\left(1 - \mu^2_{\tilde{B}_S}\right)\pi^2_{\tilde{A}_S} + \left(1 - \mu^2_{\tilde{A}_S}\right)\pi^2_{\tilde{B}_S} - \pi^2_{\tilde{A}_S}\pi^2_{\tilde{B}_S}\right)^{0.5} \right\} \tag{5}$$

- Multiplication of $\tilde{A}_S$ and $\tilde{B}_S$:

$$\tilde{A}_S \times \tilde{B}_S = \left\{ \mu_{\tilde{A}_S}\mu_{\tilde{B}_S}, \left(v^2_{\tilde{A}_S} + v^2_{\tilde{B}_S} - v^2_{\tilde{A}_S}v^2_{\tilde{B}_S}\right)^{0.5}, \left(\left(1 - v^2_{\tilde{B}_S}\right)\pi^2_{\tilde{A}_S} + \left(1 - v^2_{\tilde{A}_S}\right)\pi^2_{\tilde{B}_S} - \pi^2_{\tilde{A}_S}\pi^2_{\tilde{B}_S}\right)^{0.5} \right\} \tag{6}$$

- Multiplication of $\tilde{A}_S$ and a scalar $(\lambda > 0)$:

$$\lambda \times \tilde{A}_S = \left\{ \left(1 - \left(1 - \mu^2_{\tilde{A}_S}\right)^{\lambda}\right)^{0.5}, v^{\lambda}_{\tilde{A}_S}, \left(\left(1 - \mu^2_{\tilde{A}_S}\right)^{\lambda} - \left(1 - \mu^2_{\tilde{A}_S} - \pi^2_{\tilde{A}_S}\right)^{\lambda}\right)^{0.5} \right\} \tag{7}$$

- Power of $\tilde{A}_S$, with $\lambda > 0$:

$$\tilde{A}^{\lambda}_S = \left\{ \mu^{\lambda}_{\tilde{A}_S}, \left(1 - \left(1 - v^2_{\tilde{A}_S}\right)^{\lambda}\right)^{0.5}, \left(\left(1 - v^2_{\tilde{A}_S}\right)^{\lambda} - \left(1 - v^2_{\tilde{A}_S} - \pi^2_{\tilde{A}_S}\right)^{\lambda}\right)^{0.5} \right\} \tag{8}$$

3.2.2. Spherical Fuzzy Analytic Hierarchy Process (SF-AHP) Model

The SF-AHP method is introduced by Gundogdu and Kahraman [29] is an extension of AHP with spherical fuzzy sets. In this paper, SF-AHP is employed to determine the DC selection criteria weights. The SF-AHP method has seven steps [29]:

Step 1: Build the model hierarchical structure.

A hierarchical structure with three levels is constructed. Level 1 is the goal of the model based on a score index. The score index is determined with n criteria, which is represented in Level 2 of the structure. A set of m alternative A ($m \ge 2$), is defined in Level 3 of the structure.

Step 2: Build pairwise comparison matrices of the criteria using spherical fuzzy judgement based on linguistic terms (Table 1):

Table 1. Linguistic measures of importance [29].

Definition	(μ, v, π)	Score Index
Absolutely more importance (AM)	(0.9, 0.1, 0.0)	9
Very high importance (VH)	(0.8, 0.2, 0.1)	7
High importance (HI)	(0.7, 0.3, 0.2)	5
Slightly more importance (SM)	(0.6, 0.4, 0.3)	3
Equally importance (EI)	(0.5, 0.4, 0.4)	1
Slightly lower importance (SL)	(0.4, 0.6, 0.3)	1/3
Low importance (LI)	(0.3, 0.7, 0.2)	1/5
Very low importance (VL)	(0.2, 0.8, 0.1)	1/7
Absolutely low importance (AL)	(0.1, 0.9, 0.0)	1/9

Equation (9) and (10) are applied to calculate the score indices (SI) of each alternative.

$$\mathrm{SI} = \sqrt{\left|100 * \left[\left(\mu_{\tilde{A}_s} - \pi_{\tilde{A}_s}\right)^2 - \left(v_{\tilde{A}_s} - \pi_{\tilde{A}_s}\right)^2\right]\right|} \tag{9}$$

for AM, VH, HI, SM, and EI.

$$\frac{1}{\mathrm{SI}} = \frac{1}{\sqrt{\left|100 * \left[\left(\mu_{\tilde{A}_s} - \pi_{\tilde{A}_s}\right)^2 - \left(v_{\tilde{A}_s} - \pi_{\tilde{A}_s}\right)^2\right]\right|}} \tag{10}$$

for SL, LI, VL, and AL.

Step 3: Check the consistency of each pairwise comparison matrix.

The classical consistency check is applied with the threshold of the Consistency Ratio (CR) value of 10%:

$$CR = \frac{CI}{RI} \tag{11}$$

With CI as Consistency Index calculated as:

$$CI = \frac{\lambda_{max} - n}{n - 1} \tag{12}$$

where λ_{max} is the maximum eigenvalue of the matrix, and n is the number of criteria.

The Random Index (RI) is determined based on the number of criteria.

Step 4: Obtain the fuzzy weights of criteria and alternatives.

Each alternative's weight with respect to each criterion is obtained using the following equation:

$$\begin{aligned} SWM_w\left(\tilde{A}_{S_{i1}}, \ldots, \tilde{A}_{S_{in}}\right) &= w_1\tilde{A}_{S_{i1}} + \cdots + w_n\tilde{A}_{S_{in}} \\ &=< \left[1 - \prod_{j=1}^{n}\left(1 - \mu^2_{\tilde{A}_{s_{ij}}}\right)^{w_j}\right]^{0.5}, \prod_{j=1}^{n} V^{w_j}_{\tilde{A}_{s_{ij}}}, \left[\prod_{j=1}^{n}\left(1 - \mu^2_{\tilde{A}_{s_{ij}}}\right)^{w_j} - \prod_{j=1}^{n}\left(1 - \mu^2_{\tilde{A}_{s_{ij}}} - \pi^2_{\tilde{A}_{s_{ij}}}\right)^{w_j}\right]^{0.5} > \end{aligned} \tag{13}$$

where $w = 1/n$.

Step 5: Obtain the global weights using hierarchical layer sequencing.

The final ranking of the alternatives is estimated by aggregating the spherical weights at each level of the hierarchical structure. There are two feasible ways to perform the computation at this point.

The first way is using the score function in Equation (14) to defuzzify the criteria weights:

$$S\left(\tilde{w}_j^s\right) = \sqrt{\left|100 * \left[\left(3\mu_{\tilde{A}_s} - \frac{\pi_{\tilde{A}_s}}{2}\right)^2 - \left(\frac{v_{\tilde{A}_s}}{2} - \pi_{\tilde{A}_s}\right)^2\right]\right|} \tag{14}$$

Then, the criteria weights are normalized using Equation (15) and spherical fuzzy multiplication in Equation (16) is applied:

$$\overline{w}_j^s = \frac{S\left(\tilde{w}_j^s\right)}{\sum_{j=1}^{n} S\left(\tilde{w}_j^s\right)}. \tag{15}$$

$$\widetilde{A}_{S_{ij}} = \overline{w}_j^s * \widetilde{A}_{S_i} = < \left(1 - \left(1 - \mu^2_{\widetilde{A}_{S_i}}\right)^{\overline{w}_j^s}\right)^{1/2}, v_{\widetilde{A}_{S_i}}^{\overline{w}_j^s}, \left(\left(1 - \mu^2_{\widetilde{A}_{S_i}}\right)^{\overline{w}_j^s} - \left(1 - \mu^2_{\widetilde{A}_{S_i}} - \pi^2_{\widetilde{A}_{S_i}}\right)^{\overline{w}_j^s}\right)^{1/2} > \tag{16}$$

The final ranking score ($\widetilde{F}$) for each alternative A_i is calculated using Equation (17):

$$\widetilde{F} = \sum_{j=1}^{n} \widetilde{A}_{S_{ij}} = \widetilde{A}_{S_{i1}} + \widetilde{A}_{S_{i2}} + \cdots + \widetilde{A}_{S_{in}} \tag{17}$$

Another option is to continue the calculation without the defuzzification of the criteria weights. The spherical fuzzy global weights are calculated as:

$$\prod_{j=1}^{n} \widetilde{A}_{S_{ij}} = \widetilde{A}_{S_{i1}} * \widetilde{A}_{S_{i2}} * \ldots * \widetilde{A}_{S_{in}} \tag{18}$$

Then, the final ranking score ($\widetilde{F}$) of each alternative is calculated using Equation (17).

3.2.3. Combined Compromise Solution (CoCoSo)

CoCoSo is an MCDM method developed by Yazdani et al. [30], combining simple additive weighting method and exponentially weighted product model. In this research, the CoCoSo method is used to obtain the ranking of the potential DC locations. A typical CoCoSo model with m alternatives and n criteria has 5 steps:

Step 1: Determine the decision-making matrix $X = \left(x_{ij}\right)_{m \times n}$ for the ith alternative and the jth criterion:

$$x_{ij} = \begin{bmatrix} x_{11} & x_{12} & \ldots & x_{1n} \\ x_{21} & x_{22} & \ldots & x_{2n} \\ \ldots & \ldots & \ldots & \ldots \\ x_{m1} & x_{m2} & \ldots & x_{mn} \end{bmatrix} \tag{19}$$

With $i = 1, 2, \ldots, m$ and $j = 1, 2, \ldots, n$.

Step 2: Normalizing the decision-making matrix [30]:

For beneficial criterion:

$$r_{ij} = \frac{x_{ij} - \underset{i}{min} x_{ij}}{\underset{i}{max} x_{ij} - \underset{i}{min} x_{ij}} \tag{20}$$

For non-beneficial criterion:

$$r_{ij} = \frac{\underset{i}{max} x_{ij} - x_{ij}}{\underset{i}{max} x_{ij} - \underset{i}{min} x_{ij}} \tag{21}$$

Step 3: The power weight of comparability (S_i) and the total of the power weight of comparability (P_i) sequence for each alternative is calculated using Equation (22) and (23):

$$S_i = \sum_{j=1}^{n} \left(w_j r_{ij}\right) \tag{22}$$

$$P_i = \sum_{j=1}^{n} \left(r_{ij}^{w_j}\right) \tag{23}$$

Step 4: Calculate three aggregated performance scores. With k_{ia} as the relative performance scores of the ith alternative calculated as the arithmetic mean of sums of S_i and P_i scores:

$$k_{ia} = \frac{P_i + S_i}{\sum_{i=1}^{m} (P_i + S_i)}, \tag{24}$$

k_{ib} is the relative performance scores of the ith alternative calculated as the sum of relative scores of S_i and P_i scores in comparison to the ideal performance values.

$$k_{ib} = \frac{S_i}{\underset{i}{min} S_i} + \frac{P_i}{\underset{i}{min} P_i} \tag{25}$$

k_{ic} is the relative performance scores of the ith alternative calculated as the compromise of S_i and P_i performance scores. In Equation (20), the λ value is selected by the decision makers and has a value between 0 and 1 (usually $\lambda = 0.5$).

$$k_{ic} = \frac{\lambda(S_i) + (1-\lambda)P_i}{\lambda \underset{i}{max} S_i + (1-\lambda)\underset{i}{max} P_i} \tag{26}$$

Step 5: Obtain each alternative's performance score (k_i):

$$k_i = (k_{ia}k_{ib}k_{ic})^{\frac{1}{3}} + \frac{1}{3}(k_{ia} + k_{ib} + k_{ic}) \tag{27}$$

The final ranking of the alternatives is based on the calculated performance scores with the optimal alternative having the highest score.

4. Case Study

4.1. Model Application

In order to increase the objectivity for the determination of the location of the distribution center, as well as to match the actual situation and the socio-economic development of the region, interviews were conducted to ask for opinions of experts, including scientists, managers, and local representative leaders, who are directly involved in the DC development project, for options according to the criteria as well as the importance between the criteria. Then, a list of DC location selection criteria is identified as shown in Table 2:

Table 2. List of DC location selection criteria.

Criteria	Symbol	Sub Criteria
Cost	A	Land Cost (A1)
		Logistics Cost (A2)
Available Infrastructure	B	Proximity to Airport (B2)
		Proximity to Highway (B3)
		Proximity to Railway (B4)
Service Level	C	Transportation Time (C1)
		Distance to Markets (C2)
		Distance to Manufacturers(C3)
Sustainability Factors	D	Distance to forest area (D1)
		Distance to surface water (D2)
		Ethical Factors (D3)

In the first stage of this research, the author applied the Spherical Fuzzy Analytic Hierarchy Process (SF-AHP) for determining the weight of eleven criteria. The results are shown in Table 3.

Table 3. Results from the SF-AHP model.

Spherical Fuzzy Weights			Crisp Weights
Degree of Membership	Degree of Non-Membership	Degree of Hesitancy	
0.433	0.540	0.318	0.067
0.325	0.660	0.254	0.049
0.422	0.589	0.241	0.067
0.443	0.583	0.229	0.071
0.472	0.554	0.229	0.076
0.564	0.459	0.219	0.092
0.634	0.390	0.182	0.106
0.667	0.343	0.202	0.111
0.705	0.302	0.174	0.118
0.707	0.295	0.196	0.118
0.741	0.256	0.177	0.125

Then, Combined Compromise Solution (CoCoSo) Algorithm is applied at this step to calculate the ranking of the potential locations of the DC. The normalized matrix, weighted comparability sequence and Si, and exponentially weighted comparability sequence and Pi, are shown in Tables 4–6.

Table 4. Normalized matrix.

	C1	C2	C3	C4	C5	C6	C7	C8	C9	C10	C11
A1	0.6667	1.0000	1.0000	0.0000	0.3333	0.5000	0.0000	1.0000	0.5000	0.5000	0.8000
A2	1.0000	0.0000	0.5000	0.5000	0.0000	0.0000	0.3333	0.7500	0.0000	0.0000	0.0000
A3	0.0000	0.0000	0.5000	0.5000	1.0000	0.5000	0.6667	0.0000	1.0000	1.0000	0.6000
A4	0.6667	0.5000	0.0000	1.0000	0.3333	1.0000	0.6667	0.2500	0.5000	0.0000	1.0000
A5	1.0000	0.0000	1.0000	1.0000	0.0000	1.0000	1.0000	0.2500	0.5000	0.0000	0.8000

Table 5. Weighted comparability sequence and Si value.

	C1	C2	C3	C4	C5	C6	C7	C8	C9	C10	C11
A1	0.0447	0.0490	0.0670	0.0000	0.0253	0.0460	0.0000	0.1110	0.0590	0.0590	0.1000
A2	0.0670	0.0000	0.0335	0.0355	0.0000	0.0000	0.0353	0.0833	0.0000	0.0000	0.0000
A3	0.0000	0.0000	0.0335	0.0355	0.0760	0.0460	0.0707	0.0000	0.1180	0.1180	0.0750
A4	0.0447	0.0245	0.0000	0.0710	0.0253	0.0920	0.0707	0.0278	0.0590	0.0000	0.1250
A5	0.0670	0.0000	0.0670	0.0710	0.0000	0.0920	0.1060	0.0278	0.0590	0.0000	0.1000

Table 6. Exponentially weighted comparability sequence and Pi values.

	C1	C2	C3	C4	C5	C6	C7	C8	C9	C10	C11
A1	0.9732	1.0000	1.0000	0.0000	0.9199	0.9382	0.0000	1.0000	0.9215	0.9215	0.9725
A2	1.0000	0.0000	0.9546	0.9520	0.0000	0.0000	0.8901	0.9686	0.0000	0.0000	0.0000
A3	0.0000	0.0000	0.9546	0.9520	1.0000	0.9382	0.9579	0.0000	1.0000	1.0000	0.9381
A4	0.9732	0.9666	0.0000	1.0000	0.9199	1.0000	0.9579	0.8574	0.9215	0.0000	1.0000
A5	1.0000	0.0000	1.0000	1.0000	0.0000	1.0000	1.0000	0.8574	0.9215	0.0000	0.9725

In the final stage, an aggregated multiplication rule is employed to release the ranking of the alternatives and end the decision process. As the results from Table 7, alternative A_1 (location A_1) is the optimal location. Findings: the authors described a real case of choosing optimal location for distribution center in Mekong Delta, Vietnam from an agricultural supply chain project.

Table 7. Final Aggregation and Ranking.

Alternatives	Ka	Ranking	Kb	Ranking	Kc	Ranking	Ki
A_1	0.2301	1	4.0181	1	0.9969	1	2.7215
A_2	0.1254	5	2.0000	5	0.5435	5	1.4043
A_3	0.2077	4	3.8739	4	0.9001	4	2.5586
A_4	0.2283	2	3.9248	3	0.9892	2	2.6747
A_5	0.2084	3	3.9432	2	0.9031	3	2.5903

4.2. Sensitivity Analysis

In this section, a sensitivity analysis is performed to validate the result of the model. A sensitivity analysis can allow the decision makers to validate the outcome of their decision-making process by changing parameters of the original model. In this study, different λ values between 0 and 1 are used to perform the sensitivity test. The performance scores of each alternative with different λ values are shown in Table 8.

Table 8. Final performance score (Ki) with different λ values.

Alternative	Final Performance Score (Ki)									
	λ = 0.1	λ = 0.2	λ = 0.3	λ = 0.4	λ = 0.5	λ = 0.6	λ = 0.7	λ = 0.8	λ = 0.9	λ = 0.10
A1	2.72	2.72	2.72	2.72	2.72	2.72	2.72	2.72	2.71	2.69
A2	1.41	1.41	1.41	1.41	1.40	1.40	1.40	1.39	1.38	1.33
A3	2.56	2.56	2.56	2.56	2.56	2.56	2.56	2.57	2.57	2.61
A4	2.68	2.68	2.68	2.68	2.67	2.67	2.67	2.67	2.66	2.65
A5	2.59	2.59	2.59	2.59	2.59	2.59	2.60	2.60	2.61	2.63

Based on the result of Table 8, the rankings of each alternative with different λ values are unchanged as shown in Figure 3 below:

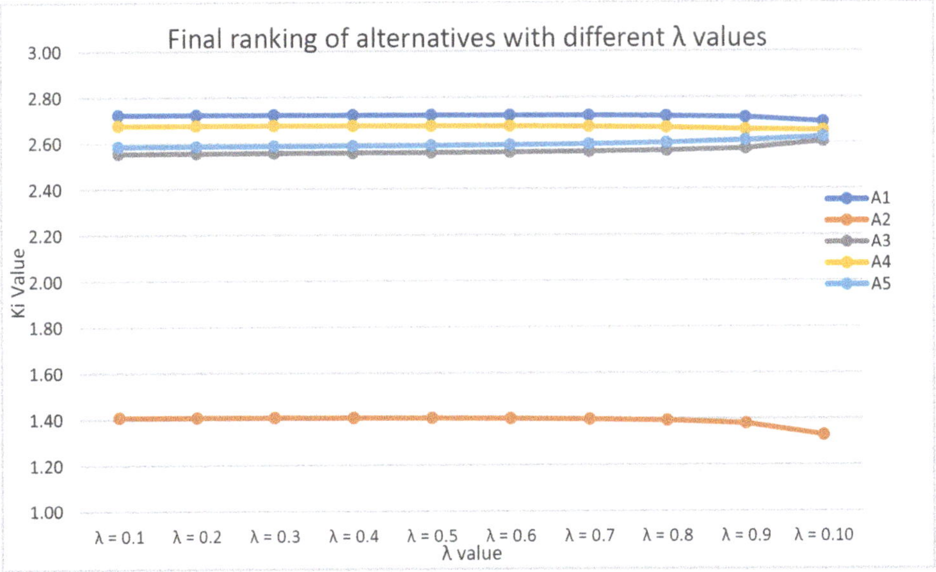

Figure 3. Ranking of the alternatives with different λ values.

According to Table 8 and Figure 3, the result of the proposed model is robust with different values of λ. Alternative 1 (A1) is consistently the optimal location for the given DC selection problem.

Therefore, it can be concluded that the proposed model's performance is adequate and can be applied to real-world cases.

Distribution center (DC) location evaluation and selection process is a crucial issue in modern supply chain design and management. An effective DC location selection method, which allows the decision makers to consider multiple quantitative and qualitative criteria, can help improve the performance of supply chains. In this research, a comprehensive MCDM-based approach is proposed. After the relevant criteria are identified and evaluated, the SF-AHP method is employed to calculate the weights of the criteria. Then, the CoCoSo method is applied to calculate the ranking of the alternative. The proposed model is verified by applying to a DC location selection problem of a sweet potato supply chain in Southern Vietnam. A sensitivity analysis is also performed to verify the reliability of the model. The results show that the optimal location is Alternative 1 (A1) and the model performs consistently with different values of the parameter λ. Therefore, it can be concluded that the proposed model is feasible and can be applied to real-world DC location selection problems.

5. Conclusions

In recent years, the global market has been volatile in order to survive and grow, companies must focus on building business strategies that help reduce costs, continually improve quality, and increase satisfaction customer performance and on-time delivery. Therefore, the identification of an optimal location for the construction of a distribution center is one of the most important decision-making problems. This decision requires achieving all the above objectives. In this research, the authors propose a MCDM-based approach, utilizing spherical fuzzy analytic hierarchy process (SF-AHP) and Combined Compromise Solution (CoCoSo) Algorithm to support the distribution location selection problem of perishable agricultural products.

A real problem of distribution center's assessment in Vietnam is handled to examine the performance of the proposed algorithm. By some comparative analysis and through the evidence, the stability of the CoCoSo algorithm is also approved. The proposed model can be applied to the agricultural supply chain around the world. Implementing and applying this new-born technique not only increases the accuracy of the decision-making system, but also aids company policies, accredits the global objectives, and delivers the beneficial consequences to the management control.

The future scope of this research can be extended by comparing the relative performance of the other MCDM methods, like Multi-attributive Ideal-Real Comparative Analysis (MAIRCA), Complex Proportional Assessment (COPRAS), and Linear Programming Technique for Multi-dimensional Analysis of Preference (LINMAP) while solving the facility location selection problems.

Author Contributions: Conceptualization, P.T.K., V.T.N. (Van Thanh Nguyen), V.T.N. (Viet Tinh Nguyen) and T.P.H.; Data curation, P.T.K., V.T.N. (Van Thanh Nguyen), V.T.N. (Viet Tinh Nguyen) and T.P.H.; Formal analysis, P.T.K., V.T.N. (Van Thanh Nguyen), V.T.N. (Viet Tinh Nguyen) and T.P.H.; Funding acquisition, P.T.K., V.T.N. (Van Thanh Nguyen), V.T.N. (Viet Tinh Nguyen) and T.P.H.; Investigation, P.T.K., V.T.N. (Van Thanh Nguyen) and T.P.H.; Methodology, V.T.N. (Van Thanh Nguyen) and V.T.N. (Viet Tinh Nguyen); Project administration, P.T.K., V.T.N. (Van Thanh Nguyen) and V.T.N. (Viet Tinh Nguyen); Resources, V.T.N. (Viet Tinh Nguyen); Software, V.T.N. (Van Thanh Nguyen); Supervision, V.T.N. (Viet Tinh Nguyen); Writing—original draft, P.T.K., V.T.N. (Van Thanh Nguyen) and V.T.N. (Viet Tinh Nguyen); Writing—review and editing, V.T.N. (Van Thanh Nguyen). All authors have read and agreed to the published version of the manuscript.

Funding: This research received no external funding.

Institutional Review Board Statement: Not applicable.

Informed Consent Statement: Not applicable.

Data Availability Statement: Not applicable.

Conflicts of Interest: The authors declare no conflict of interest.

References

1. Phung, Q.T. Sweet Potato Supply Chain Solutions for Binh Tan District, Vinh Long Province. Master's Thesis, Can Tho University, Can Tho, Vietnam.
2. Available online: http://www.baovinhlong.com.vn/kinh-te/201903/chuoi-cung-ung-khoai-lang-nhin-tu-giai-phap-dong-bo-giao-thong-2937202/ (accessed on 11 November 2020).

3. Google Map, Mekong Delta Region, Vietnam. Available online: https://www.google.com/maps/@10.3424551,106.2414917,8z (accessed on 11 November 2020).
4. Fallahpour, A.; Olugu, E.U.; Musa, S.N.; Wong, K.Y.; Noori, S. A decision support model for sustainable supplier selection in sustainable supply chain management. *Comput. Ind. Eng.* **2017**, *105*, 391–410. [CrossRef]
5. Govindan, K.; Khodaverdi, R.; Jafarian, A. A fuzzy multi criteria approach for measuring sustainability performance of a supplier based on triple bottom line approach. *J. Clean. Prod.* **2013**, *47*, 345–354. [CrossRef]
6. Dai, J.; Blackhurst, J. A four-phase AHP-QFD approach for supplier assessment: A sustainability perspective. *Int. J. Prod. Res.* **2012**, *50*, 5474–5490. [CrossRef]
7. Luthra, S.; Govindan, K.; Kannan, D.; Mangla, S.K.; Garg, C.P. An integrated framework for sustainable supplier selection and evaluation in supply chains. *J. Clean. Prod.* **2017**, *140*, 1686–1698. [CrossRef]
8. Wang, C.N.; Viet, V.T.H.; Ho, T.P.; Nguyen, V.T.; Nguyen, V.T. Multi-Criteria Decision Model for the Selection of Suppliers in the Textile Industry. *Symmetry* **2020**, *12*, 979. [CrossRef]
9. Kusi-Sarpong, S.; Gupta, H.; Sarkis, J. A supply chain sustainability innovation framework and evaluation methodology. *Int. J. Prod. Res.* **2019**, *57*, 1990–2008. [CrossRef]
10. Entezaminia, A.; Heydari, M.; Rahmani, D. A multi-objective model for multi-product multi-site aggregate production planning in a green supply chain: Considering collection and recycling centers. *J. Manuf. Syst.* **2016**, *40*, 63–75. [CrossRef]
11. Chien, F.; Wang, C.N.; Nguyen, V.T.; Nguyen, V.T.; Chau, K.Y. An Evaluation Model of Quantitative and Qualitative Fuzzy Multi-Criteria Decision-Making Approach for Hydroelectric Plant Location Selection. *Energies* **2020**, *13*, 2783. [CrossRef]
12. Tadić, S.; Krstić, M.; Roso, V.; Brnjac, N. Dry Port Terminal Location Selection by Applying the Hybrid Grey MCDM Model. *Sustainability* **2020**, *12*, 6983. [CrossRef]
13. Budak, A.; Kaya, İ.; Karaşan, A.; Erdoğan, M. Real-Time Location Systems Selection by Using a Fuzzy MCDM Approach: An Application in Humanitarian Relief Logistics. *Appl. Soft Comput.* **2020**, *92*, 106322. [CrossRef]
14. Deveci, M.; Akyurt, I.Z.; Yavuz, S. A GIS-Based Interval Type-2 Fuzzy Set for Public Bread Factory Site Selection. *J. Enterp. Inf. Manag.* **2018**, *31*, 820–847. [CrossRef]
15. Ulutaş, A.; Karabasevic, D.; Popovic, G.; Stanujkic, D.; Nguyen, P.; Karaköy, Ç. Development of a Novel Integrated CCSD-ITARA-MARCOS Decision-Making Approach for Stackers Selection in a Logistics System. *Mathematics* **2020**, *8*, 1672. [CrossRef]
16. Ulutaş, A.; Stanujkic, D.; Karabasevic, D.; Popovic, G.; Zavadskas, E.; Smarandache, F.; Brauers, W. Developing of a Novel Integrated MCDM MULTIMOOSRAL Approach for Supplier Selection. *Informatica* **2021**, 145–161. [CrossRef]
17. Ulutaş, A.; Karaköy, Ç. Evaluation of LPI Values of Transition Economies Countries with a Grey MCDM Model. In *Marketing, Customer Relationship Management, and E-Services*; IGI Global: Hershey, PA, USA, 2021; pp. 499–511.
18. Yılmaz, H.; Kabak, Ö. Prioritizing Distribution Centers in Humanitarian Logistics Using Type-2 Fuzzy MCDM Approach. *J. Enterp. Inf. Manag.* **2020**, *33*, 1199–1232. [CrossRef]
19. Liu, P.; Li, Y. Multiattribute Decision Method for Comprehensive Logistics Distribution Center Location Selection Based on 2-Dimensional Linguistic Information. *Inf. Sci.* **2020**, *538*, 209–244. [CrossRef]
20. Quynh, M.P.; Thu, T.L.; Huong, Q.D.; Van, A.P.T.; Van, H.N.; Van, D.N. Distribution Center Location Selection Using a Novel Multi Criteria Decision-Making Approach Under Interval Neutrosophic Complex Sets. *Decis. Sci. Lett.* **2020**, *9*, 501–510. [CrossRef]
21. Kuo, M. Optimal Location Selection for An International Distribution Center By Using A New Hybrid Method. *Expert Syst. Appl.* **2011**, *38*, 7208–7221. [CrossRef]
22. Yang, Y.; Fan, J.; Zhang, L. Study On Location Selection Of FMCG Logistics Centers Based On Fuzzy MCDM Model. *Appl. Mech. Mater.* **2015**, *744*, 1888–1894. [CrossRef]
23. Sharaf, I. Spherical Fuzzy VIKOR With SWAM And SWGM Operators For MCDM. In *Decision Making with Spherical Fuzzy Sets*; Springer: Cham, Switzerland, 2020; pp. 217–240.
24. Otay, I.; Atik, S. Multi-Criteria Oil Station Location Evaluation Using Spherical AHP&WASPAS: A Real-Life Case Study. In *Intelligent Systems and Computing*; Springer: Cham, Switzerland, 2020; pp. 591–598.
25. Gül, S. Spherical Fuzzy Extension of DEMATEL (SF-DEMATEL). *Int. J. Intell. Syst.* **2020**, *35*, 1329–1353. [CrossRef]
26. Gündoğdu, F.; Kahraman, C. Spherical Fuzzy Sets and Spherical Fuzzy TOPSIS Method. *J. Intell. Fuzzy Syst.* **2019**, *36*, 337–352. [CrossRef]
27. Yager, R. Pythagorean fuzzy subsets. In Proceedings of the 2013 Joint IFSA World Congress and NAFIPS Annual Meeting (IFSA/NAFIPS), Edmonton, AB, Canada, 24–28 June 2013; IEEE: Piscataway, NJ, USA, 2013; pp. 57–61.
28. Smarandache, F. *A Unifying Field in Logics Neutrosophy: Neutrosophic Probability, Set and Logic*; American Research Press: Rehoboth, DE, USA, 1999; pp. 1–141.
29. Gündoğdu, F.; Kahraman, C. A Novel Spherical Fuzzy Analytic Hierarchy Process and Its Renewable Energy Application. *Soft Comput.* **2019**, *24*, 4607–4621. [CrossRef]
30. Yazdani, M.; Zarate, P.; Kazimieras Zavadskas, E.; Turskis, Z. A Combined Compromise Solution (Cocoso) Method for Multi-Criteria Decision-Making Problems. *Manag. Decis.* **2019**, *57*, 2501–2519. [CrossRef]

axioms

MDPI

Article

Multiple Optimal Solutions and the Best Lipschitz Constants Between an Aggregation Function and Associated Idempotized Aggregation Function

Hui-Chin Tang * and **Wei-Ting Chen ***

Department of Industrial Engineering and Management, National Kaohsiung University of Science and Technology, Kaohsiung 80778, Taiwan
* Correspondence: tang@nkust.edu.tw (H.-C.T.); I109143103@nkust.edu.tw (W.-T.C.)

Abstract: This paper presents and compares the optimal solutions and the theoretical and empirical best Lipschitz constants between an aggregation function and associated idempotized aggregation function. According to an exhaustive search we performed, the multiple optimal solutions and the empirical best Lipschitz constants are presented explicitly. The results indicate that differences of the multiple optimal solutions exist among the Minkowski norm, the number of steps, and the type of aggregation function. We demonstrate that these differences can affect the theoretical and empirical best Lipschitz constants of an aggregation function.

Keywords: aggregation; Lipschitz; computation; idempotent

MSC: 90C59; 65K05

Citation: Tang, H.-C.; Chen, W.-T. Multiple Optimal Solutions and the Best Lipschitz Constants Between an Aggregation Function and Associated Idempotized Aggregation Function. *Axioms* **2021**, *10*, 52. https://doi.org/10.3390/axioms10020052

Academic Editors: Javier Fernandez and Goran Ćirović

Received: 18 February 2021
Accepted: 30 March 2021
Published: 2 April 2021

1. Introduction

Aggregation functions [1–8] find wide applications in almost all branches of engineering. Typical fields include mathematics and information sciences, especially in decision-making and the fusion of information problems. The aim of an aggregation function is to summarize an n-tuple of information by means of a single representative value. The fundamental axiom of an aggregation function is the non-decreasing monotonicity. Another axiomatic constraint of an aggregation function is that the aggregating of minimal or maximal inputs are, respectively, minimal and maximal outputs.

The prototypical example of aggregation functions is the arithmetic mean, which is the first modern definition of mean. The concept of arithmetic mean seems to have been proposed first by Cauchy in 1821 [9]. Since then, a large variety of aggregation functions have been proposed. The conjunctive, the disjunctive, the internal, and the mixed aggregation functions are four main classes of aggregation functions based on many-valued logics connectives [10]. The algebraic and analytical properties of an aggregation function are proposed and analyzed in the literature [1–8]. Associativity, symmetry, bisymmetry, idempotency, neutral element, and annihilator element are algebraic properties. Continuity, Lipschitzian, and additivity are analytical properties. A first review of papers reporting aggregation function results was undertaken by Xu and Da [8]. More details can be seen in the excellent reviews on the state of the art by Grabisch et al. [3–5], group decision making by Mohd and Abdullah [7] and Del Moral et al. [2], and construction methods by Khameneh and Kilicman [6]. Recently, many papers have been dedicated to an aggregation function in group decision making [11–13], multi-criteria decision making [14], two-side matching decision making [15], and others [16,17].

One characterization of the mean is the Chisini's equation [9], described as follows: a mean M, with respect to the function F, is that each input of F can be replaced with M without changing the overall aggregation. When F is considered as the sum and the product, the solution of Chisini's equation is the arithmetic mean and the geometric mean, respectively. For the analytical properties, an aggregation function, which satisfies the Lipschitz condition is a continuous one. More details can be found in [1,3]. This paper analyzes and compares the Lipschitz behaviors between the sum and the arithmetic mean, and those of the product and the geometric mean. The Lipschitz constants for the sum, the arithmetic mean, the product, and the geometric mean can be obtained analytically by the triangular inequality and the Hölder inequality [1,3]. However, the best Lipschitz constants, which are the greatest lower bound of the Lipschitz constants, may or may not be attainable. The reason is that the feasible region of constraints for the mathematical programming model of the best Lipschitz constant is not compact. To the best knowledge of the authors, such a problem has not been considered in the literature. For the best Lipschitz constant, a mathematical model with non-Archimedean numbers is proposed. We also propose a discrete approximation of the mathematical model. We adopt an exhaustive analysis to empirically find and compare the optimal solutions and the empirical best Lipschitz constants for the sum and the arithmetic mean, and for the product and the geometric mean. The multiple optimal solutions and the empirical best Lipschitz constants are presented explicitly.

The organization of this paper is as follows. Section 2 briefly reviews an aggregation function. We analyze and compare the optimal solutions and the best Lipschitz constants between the sum function and the arithmetic mean in Section 3, and between the product function and the geometric mean in Section 4. Finally, some concluding remarks and future research are presented.

2. An Aggregation Function

We now recall the definition of an aggregation function [1–4,6,7]. Let $\mathbb{I} \subset \mathcal{R}$ be the closed unit interval [0,1], and $\mathbb{I}^n = \{x = (x_1, x_2, \ldots, x_n) | x_i \in \mathbb{I}, i = 1, 2, \ldots, n\}$. Furthermore, $\boldsymbol{x} \leq \boldsymbol{y}$ if and only if $x_i \leq y_i, i = 1, 2, \ldots, n$.

Definition 1. *An n-ary aggregation function $A^{(n)} : \mathbb{I}^n \to \mathbb{I}$ satisfies:*

- $A^{(1)}(x) = x$, *for* $n = 1$ *and* $x \in \mathbb{I}$;
- *If* $\boldsymbol{x} \leq \boldsymbol{y}$, *then* $A^{(n)}(\boldsymbol{x}) \leq A^{(n)}(\boldsymbol{y})$ *for* $\boldsymbol{x}, \boldsymbol{y} \in \mathbb{I}^n$;
- $A^{(n)}(0, 0, \ldots, 0) = 0$ *and* $A^{(n)}(1, 1, \ldots, 1) = 1$.

The generalized inputs $\mathbb{I}$ of an aggregation function are a subdomain of the extended real line $[-\infty, \infty]$. They can be any type (open, closed, ...) of interval. For simplicity, we deal with the closed unit interval [0,1]. An extended aggregation function is a mapping $A : \cup_{n \in \mathcal{N}} \mathbb{I}^n \to \mathbb{I}$ whose restriction to $\mathbb{I}^n$ is the n-ary aggregation function $A^{(n)}$ for any $n \in \mathcal{N}$. When no confusion can arise, we use the convenient notation A to represent $A^{(n)}$.

For $x_i \in \mathbb{I}, i = 1, 2, \ldots, n$, some well-known examples of aggregation functions [1–4,6,7] are as follows:

1. Median Md defined by $\text{Md}(x_1, x_2, \ldots, x_n) = x_{\left(\frac{n+1}{2}\right)}$ if n is odd and $\text{Md}(x_1, x_2, \ldots, x_n) = \frac{1}{2}\left(x_{\left(\frac{n}{2}\right)} + x_{\left(\frac{n}{2}+1\right)}\right)$ if n is even where $x_{(1)} \leq x_{(2)} \leq \cdots \leq x_{(n)}$.
2. Arithmetic mean (AM) $\text{AM}(x_1, x_2, \ldots, x_n) = \frac{1}{n}\sum_{i=1}^{n} x_i$.
3. Weighted arithmetic mean (WAM) $\text{WAM}(x_1, x_2, \ldots, x_n) = \frac{1}{n}\sum_{i=1}^{n} w_i x_i$, where $w_i \in \mathbb{I}$, $i = 1, 2, \ldots, n$, $\sum_{i=1}^{n} w_i = 1$.
4. Geometric mean (GM) $\text{GM}(x_1, x_2, \ldots, x_n) = \left(\prod_{i=1}^{n} x_i\right)^{1/n}$.
5. Harmonic mean (HM) $\text{HM}(x_1, x_2, \ldots, x_n) = \frac{n}{\sum_{i=1}^{n} 1/x_i}$.
6. Minimum (min) $\min(x_1, x_2, \ldots, x_n) = \min_{i=1}^{n} x_i$ and maximum (max) $\max(x_1, x_2, \ldots, x_n) = \max_{i=1}^{n} x_i$.
7. Product function $\prod(x_1, x_2, \ldots, x_n) = \prod_{i=1}^{n} x_i$.
8. Projection function to the kth coordinate $P_k(x_1, x_2, \ldots, x_n) = x_k$.

9. The weakest aggregation function $A_w(x_1, x_2, \ldots, x_n) = \begin{cases} 1, \text{if } (x_1, x_2, \ldots, x_n) = (1, 1, \ldots, 1) \\ 0, \text{else.} \end{cases}$
10. The strongest aggregation function $A_s(x_1, x_2, \ldots, x_n) = \begin{cases} 0, \, if \, (x_1, x_2, \ldots, x_n) = (0, 0, \ldots, 0) \\ 1, \, else. \end{cases}$
11. Operator $A_c(x_1, x_2, \ldots, x_n) = max(0, \min(1, c + \sum_{i=1}^{n}(x_i - c))$ for $c \in \mathbb{I}$.

For all $x_1, x_2, \ldots, x_n \in [0, 1]$, the relationship between the arithmetic mean, the geometric mean, the harmonic mean, the minimum, the maximum, the product function, the weakest aggregation function, and the strongest aggregation function is
$A_w(x_1, x_2, \ldots, x_n) \leq \prod(x_1, x_2, \ldots, x_n) \leq \text{Min}(x_1, x_2, \ldots, x_n) \leq \text{HM}(x_1, x_2, \ldots, x_n) \leq \text{GM}(x_1, x_2, \ldots, x_n) \leq \text{AM}(x_1, x_2, \ldots, x_n) \leq \text{Max}(x_1, x_2, \ldots, x_n) \leq A_s(x_1, x_2, \ldots, x_n)$.

The algebraic and analytical properties of aggregation functions [1–4,6,7] are described as follows:

Definition 2. *An aggregation function* $A : \mathbb{I}^n \to \mathbb{I}$ *is called*

- *having a neutral element* $e \in \mathbb{I}$*, if for* $i = 1, 2, \ldots, n$*, we have* $A(x_1, \ldots, x_{i-1}, e, x_{i+1}, \ldots, x_n) = A(x_1, \ldots, x_{i-1}, x_{i+1}, \ldots, x_n)$.
- *having an annihilator element* $a \in \mathbb{I}$*, if for* $i = 1, 2, \ldots, n$*, we have* $A(x_1, \ldots, x_{i-1}, a, x_{i+1}, \ldots, x_n) = a$.
- *additive, if for any* $\boldsymbol{x}, \boldsymbol{y}, \boldsymbol{x} + \boldsymbol{y} \in \mathbb{I}^n$*, we have* $A(\boldsymbol{x} + \boldsymbol{y}) = A(\boldsymbol{x}) + A(\boldsymbol{y})$.
- *associative, if for all* $(x_1, x_2, x_3) \in \mathbb{I}^3$*, we have* $A(A(x_1, x_2), x_3) = A(x_1, A(x_2, x_3))$.
- *idempotent, if for all* $x \in \mathbb{I}$*, we have* $A(x, x, \ldots, x) = x$.
- *symmetric, if for all* $(x_1, x_2, \ldots, x_n) \in \mathbb{I}^n$ *and for any permutation* σ *of {1, 2, . . . ,n}, we have* $A(x_1, x_2, \ldots, x_n) = A\left(x_{\sigma(1)}, x_{\sigma(2)}, \ldots, x_{\sigma(n)}\right)$.
- *bisymmetric, if for all* $x_{ij} \in \mathbb{I}$, $i, j \in \{1, 2, \ldots, n\}$*, we have* $A(A(x_{11}, x_{12}, \ldots, x_{1n}), \ldots, A(x_{n1}, x_{n2}, \ldots, x_{nn})) = A(A(x_{11}, x_{21}, \ldots, x_{n1}), \ldots, A(x_{1n}, x_{2n}, \ldots, x_{nn}))$.
- *continuous,* $\forall \varepsilon > 0$, $\exists \delta > 0$*, if* $|x_i - y_i| < \delta$ *for* $i \in \{1, 2, \ldots, n\}$*, then* $|A(x_1, x_2, \ldots, x_n) - A(y_1, y_2, \ldots, y_n)| < \varepsilon$.
- *c-Lipschitzian with respect to the norm* $\|.\|$*, if for some constant* $c \in (0, +\infty)$*, we have the Lipschitz condition* $|A(x_1, x_2, \ldots, x_n) - A(y_1, y_2, \ldots, y_n)| \leq c\|(x_1, x_2, \ldots, x_n) - (y_1, y_2, \ldots, y_n)\|$ *for all* $(x_1, x_2, \ldots, x_n), (y_1, y_2, \ldots, y_n) \in \mathbb{I}^n$ *and* $\|.\| : \mathcal{R}^n \to [0, +\infty)$.

The Minkowski norm of order $p \in [1, \infty)$, L_p-norm, defined by

$$\|x\|_p = \left(\sum_{i=1}^{n} |x_i|^p\right)^{1/p}$$

is a well-known norm. When $p = \infty$,

$$\|x\|_\infty = \max_{i=1}^{n} |x_i|$$

is called the Chebyshev norm. Since

$$\max_{i=1}^{n} |x_i - y_i| \leq \left(\sum_{i=1}^{n} |x_i - y_i|^{p+1}\right)^{\frac{1}{p+1}} \leq \left(\sum_{i=1}^{n} |x_i - y_i|^p\right)^{1/p}$$

for all $x_i, y_i \in \mathbb{I}$, $i \in \{1, 2, \ldots, n\}$ and $p \in [1, \infty)$, it follows that each d-Lipschitzian with respect to L_∞-norm implies d-Lipschitzian with respect to L_p-norm, $p \in [1, \infty)$. Additionally, each d-Lipschitzian with respect to L_{p+1}-norm implies d-Lipschitzian with respect to L_p-norm, $p \in [1, \infty)$.

The best Lipschitz constant is the greatest lower bound d of b such that $A(x_1, x_2, \ldots, x_n)$ is d-Lipschitzian but $A(x_1, x_2, \ldots, x_n)$ is not b–Lipschitzian for any $b \in (0, d)$. Two types of best Lipschitz constant are considered: theoretical best Lipschitz constant and empirical best Lipschitz constant. Theoretical best Lipschitz constant is obtained analytically by the triangular inequality and the Hölder inequality [1,3,4]. Empirical best Lipschitz constant is obtained by finding the maximum value of

$$\frac{|A(x_1, x_2, \ldots, x_n) - A(y_1, y_2, \ldots, y_n)|}{\|(x_1, x_2, \ldots, x_n) - (y_1, y_2, \ldots, y_n)\|}$$

for $(x_1, x_2, \ldots, x_n) \neq (y_1, y_2, \ldots, y_n)$, $x_i, y_i \leq 1$ and $x_i, y_i \geq 0, i \in \{1, 2, \ldots, n\}$. For an aggregation function $A(x_1, x_2, \ldots, x_n)$, the mathematical programming model of the empirical best Lipschitz constant with respect to L_p-norm is

$$\begin{aligned} &\text{Maximize } \frac{|A(x_1, x_2, \ldots, x_n) - A(y_1, y_2, \ldots, y_n)|}{\left(\sum_{i=1}^{n}|x_i - y_i|^{p}\right)^{1/p}} \\ &\text{subject to } \left(\sum_{i=1}^{n}|x_i - y_i|^{p}\right)^{1/p} > 0 \\ &x_i, y_i \leq 1, i \in \{1, 2, \ldots, n\} \\ &x_i, y_i \geq 0, i \in \{1, 2, \ldots, n\} \end{aligned} \tag{1}$$

The feasible region of constraints for the mathematical programming model (1) is not compact. The denominator of the objective function is required to be greater than a small positive number ε. Following the data envelopment analysis, this small number ε is called a non-Archimedean number [18]. The mathematical programming model (1) becomes

$$\begin{aligned} &\text{Maximize } \frac{|A(x_1, x_2, \ldots, x_n) - A(y_1, y_2, \ldots, y_n)|}{\left(\sum_{i=1}^{n}|x_i - y_i|^{p}\right)^{1/p}} \\ &\text{subject to } \left(\sum_{i=1}^{n}|x_i - y_i|^{p}\right)^{1/p} \geq \varepsilon \\ &x_i, y_i \leq 1, i \in \{1, 2, \ldots, n\} \\ &x_i, y_i \geq 0, i \in \{1, 2, \ldots, n\} \end{aligned} \tag{2}$$

It follows that the largest objective function of the mathematical programming model (2) is the empirical best Lipschitz constant. If $\left(\sum_{i=1}^{n}|x_i - y_i|^{p}\right)^{1/p} \geq \varepsilon$ is a binding constraint, the value of objective function is dependent of the non-Archimedean number ε. Since the empirical best Lipschitz constants are the actual best Lipschitz constants, the analytical behaviors of the aggregation function can be analyzed by the behaviors of the empirical best Lipschitz constants.

The following definition establishes that a non-idempotent aggregation function can be transformed into an idempotent one [1,3,4].

Definition 3. *Let* $A : \mathbb{I}^n \to \mathbb{I}$ *be an aggregation function such that* $\delta_A(x) = A(x, x, \ldots, x)$ *is strictly increasing and*

$$\{\delta_A(x) | x \in \mathbb{I}\} = \{A(x_1, x_2, \ldots, x_n) | x_i \in \mathbb{I}, i = 1, \ldots, n\},$$

then the idempotent aggregation function is given by $AI(x_1, x_2, \ldots, x_n) = \delta_A^{-1}(A(x_1, x_2, \ldots, x_n))$, which is called idempotized A.

To characterize the mean $M : \mathbb{I}^n \to \mathbb{I}$, the first one is Cauchy's internality property [9]. A mean M is an internal function, i.e., $\text{Min}(x_1, x_2, \ldots, x_n) \leq M(x_1, x_2, \ldots, x_n) \leq \text{Max}(x_1, x_2, \ldots, x_n)$. The second is the Chisini's equation. A mean M with respect to the function $F : \mathbb{I}^n \to \mathbb{I}$ *is a number* M *such that*

$$F(M, M, \ldots, M) = F(x_1, x_2, \ldots, x_n).$$

The Chisini's equation can be rewritten as

$$\delta_F(M) = F(x_1, x_2, \ldots, x_n).$$

Under some constraints, the mean that is obtained from the solution of Chisini's equation can fulfill Cauchy's internality property [1,3,4], described as follows:

Definition 4. *A function* $M : \mathbb{I}^n \to \mathbb{I}$ *is an average associated with F in* $\mathbb{I}^n$ *if there exists a nondecreasing and idempotizable function* $F : \mathbb{I}^n \to \Re$ *satisfying* $\delta_F(M) = F$.

From Definitions 3 and 4, it is implied that M is the idempotized F if and only if M is an average associated with F. When F is considered as the sum and the product, the idempotized F is the arithmetic mean and the geometric mean, respectively. The following sections will analyze and compare the optimal solutions and the best Lipschitz constants between an aggregation function and associated idempotized aggregation function.

3. The Best Lipschitz Constants of the Sum and Arithmetic Mean Functions

This section deals with the sum function $\sum(x_1, x_2, \ldots, x_n) = \sum_{i=1}^{n} x_i$ and the arithmetic mean $\mathrm{AM}(x_1, x_2, \ldots, x_n)$. The arithmetic mean is the idempotized sum function. Additionally, the arithmetic mean is an average associated with the sum function. The domain of the arithmetic mean is [0, 1], so the domain of the sum function is $[0, \infty)$. The arithmetic mean is an aggregation function with minimal Lipschitz constant with respect to L_1-norm, we will show related results for the other L_p-norms. It is evident that the sum function satisfies additive, associative, symmetric, bisymmetric, continuous, and Lipschitzian but non-idempotent. The sum function has neutral element $e = 0$ but no annihilator element [1,3,4].

A variant of the sum function is the bounded sum $\sum_L(x_1, x_2, \ldots, x_n) = \min\left(\sum_{i=1}^{n} x_i, 1\right)$. The bounded sum preserves some properties of the original sum function, such as the associativity, symmetry, bisymmetry, continuity, Lipschitzian, non-idempotency and neutral element $e = 0$. Two different properties exist between $\sum(x_1, x_2, \ldots, x_n)$ and $\sum_L(x_1, x_2, \ldots, x_n)$. The sum function possesses additivity and no annihilator element, while the bounded sum function dissatisfies additive and has annihilator element $a = 1$.

We now present the optimal solutions and the empirical best Lipschitz constant of an aggregation function empirically. This paper conducts some computational experiments to empirically study the influence of the number of variables, the Minkowski norm, the number of steps, and the type of aggregation function on the optimal inputs and the empirical best Lipschitz constant performance.

The first numerical experiment is conducted to find the forms of optimal solutions x and y, and the empirical best Lipschitz constant for $\sum(x_1, x_2, \ldots, x_n)$. For L_p-norm, the mathematical programming model is

$$\begin{aligned} &\text{Maximize } \frac{|\sum(x_1,x_2,\ldots,x_n) - \sum(y_1,y_2,\ldots,y_n)|}{\left(\sum_{i=1}^{n}|x_i - y_i|^p\right)^{1/p}} \\ &\text{subject to } \left(\sum_{i=1}^{n}|x_i - y_i|^p\right)^{1/p} \geq \varepsilon \\ &x_i, y_i \leq 1, i \in \{1,2,\ldots,n\} \\ &x_i, y_i \geq 0, i \in \{1,2,\ldots,n\}. \end{aligned} \tag{3}$$

Since the sum function is a symmetric one, without loss of generality, let $\varepsilon = 1/m$, $m \in \{1000, 10{,}000, 100{,}000\}$, the mathematical programming model (3) becomes

$$\begin{aligned} &\text{Maximize } \frac{|\sum(x_1,x_2,\ldots,x_n) - \sum(y_1,y_2,\ldots,y_n)|}{\left(\sum_{i=1}^{n}|x_i - y_i|^p\right)^{1/p}} \\ &\text{subject to } y_k \geq x_k + \varepsilon, \text{for some } k \in \{1,2,\ldots,n\} \\ &x_i, y_i \leq 1, i \in \{1,2,\ldots,n\} \\ &x_i, y_i \geq 0, i \in \{1,2,\ldots,n\} \end{aligned} \tag{4}$$

Let $m = 1/\varepsilon$ be the number of steps, the discrete approximation of the mathematical programming model (4) is

$$\begin{array}{l} \text{Maximize } \frac{|\sum(x_1,x_2,\ldots,x_n)-\sum(y_1,y_2,\ldots,y_n)|}{\left(\sum_{i=1}^{n}|x_i-y_i|^p\right)^{1/p}} \\ \text{subject to } x_i, y_i \in \left\{0, \frac{1}{m}, \frac{2}{m}, \ldots, 1\right\}, i \in \{1,2,\ldots,n\} \\ (x_1,x_2,\ldots,x_n) \neq (y_1,y_2,\ldots,y_n) \end{array} \quad (5)$$

For the number of variables $n \in \{2,3\}$, L_p-norm, $p \in \{1,2,3,\infty\}$ and the number of steps $m \in \{1000, 10{,}000, 100{,}000\}$, we perform an exhaustive search for all $x_i, y_i \in \left\{0, \frac{1}{m}, \frac{2}{m}, \ldots, 1\right\}$, $i \in \{1,2,\ldots,n\}$ and $(x_1,x_2,\ldots,x_n) \neq (y_1,y_2,\ldots,y_n)$ with the objective function

$$\text{Maximize } \frac{|\sum(x_1,x_2,\ldots,x_n)-\sum(y_1,y_2,\ldots,y_n)|}{\left(\sum_{i=1}^{n}|x_i - y_i|^p\right)^{1/p}}$$

For the two-variable $\sum(x_1,x_2)$ and L_1-norm, the optimal value for the objective function (5) is

$$\frac{|x_1+x_2-(x_1\pm\alpha_1+x_2\pm\alpha_2)|}{\alpha_1+\alpha_2} = 1$$

and is attained at the multiple solutions $x = (x_1,x_2)$ and $y = (x_1\pm\alpha_1, x_2\pm\alpha_2)$, $x_i, \alpha_i, x_i \pm \alpha_i \in [0,1]$, $i = 1,2$. For L_p-norm, $p \in \{2,3,\infty\}$, the multiple optimal solutions $x = (x_1,x_2)$ and $y = (x_1\pm\alpha, x_2\pm\alpha)$, $x_i, \alpha, x_i\pm\alpha \in [0,1]$, $i = 1,2$ yield the largest objective function

$$\frac{|x_1+x_2-(x_1\pm\alpha+x_2\pm\alpha)|}{(\alpha^p+\alpha^p)^{1/p}} = 2^{1-1/p}.$$

These optimal solutions are verified by applying the popular modelling language LINGO [19], which utilizes the power of linear and nonlinear optimization to solve mathematical problems (4). When the Chebyshev norm L_∞, the empirical best Lipschitz constant becomes 2. The empirical best Lipschitz constant $2^{1-1/p}$ will increase as the order p increases.

For the three-variable $\sum(x_1,x_2,x_3)$, the multiple optimal solutions are $x = (x_1,x_2,x_3)$ and $y = (x_1\pm\alpha_1, x_2\pm\alpha_2, x_3\pm\alpha_3)$, $x_i,\alpha_i,x_i\pm\alpha_i \in [0,1]$, $i = 1,2,3$ and $x = (x_1,x_2,x_3)$ and $y = (x_1\pm\alpha, x_2\pm\alpha, x_3\pm\alpha)$, $x_i,\alpha,x_i\pm\alpha \in [0,1]$, $i = 1,2,3$ with the associated empirical best Lipschitz constant 1 and $3^{1-1/p}$ for $p = 1$ and $p \in \{2,3,\infty\}$, respectively. These optimal solutions are verified by applying LINGO with $\varepsilon = 1/m$, $m \in \{1000, 10{,}000, 100{,}000\}$. If $p = \infty$, we find the empirical best Lipschitz constant 3.

Theoretically, applying the triangular inequality and the Hölder inequality, the result of a more general n-ary sum function $\sum(x_1,x_2,\ldots,x_n)$ is described as follows.

Theorem 1. *For the sum function $\sum(x_1,x_2,\ldots,x_n)$, the theoretical best Lipschitz constant is $n^{1-1/p}$ and n for $p \in [1,\infty)$ and $p = \infty$, respectively. The associated optimal solutions are $x = (x_1,x_2,\ldots,x_n)$ and $y = (x_1\pm\alpha_1, x_2\pm\alpha_2,\ldots,x_n\pm\alpha_n)$, $x_i,\alpha_i,x_i\pm\alpha_i \in [0,1]$, $i = 1,2,\ldots,n$ and $x = (x_1,x_2,\ldots,x_n)$ and $y = (x_1\pm\alpha, x_2\pm\alpha,\ldots,x_n\pm\alpha)$, $x_i,\alpha,x_i\pm\alpha \in [0,1]$, $i = 1,2,\ldots,n$ for $p = 1$ and $p \in [2,\infty]$,* respectively.

Proof of Theorem 1. From the triangular inequality, we have

$$\left|\sum_{i=1}^{n} x_i - \sum_{i=1}^{n} y_i\right| = \left|\sum_{i=1}^{n}(x_i - y_i)\right| \leq \|x-y\|_1$$

for $x_i, y_i \in [0,1]$, $i = 1,2,\ldots,n$ [2,3,5]. From the Hölder inequality, for $\frac{1}{p}+\frac{1}{q} = 1$, $p,q \in [1,\infty)$, we obtain

$$\left|\sum_{i=1}^{n} x_i - \sum_{i=1}^{n} y_i\right| \leq \|x-y\|_1 \leq (1,1,\ldots,1)_q \times x - y_1 = n^{1-1/p}\|x-y\|_p$$

It follows that the theoretical best Lipschitz constant is $n^{1-1/p}$. The theoretical best Lipschitz constants of the solutions $x = (x_1, x_2, \ldots, x_n)$ and $y = (x_1 \pm \alpha_1, x_2 \pm \alpha_2, \ldots, x_n \pm \alpha_n)$, $x_i, \alpha_i, x_i \pm \alpha_i \in [0,1]$, $i = 1,2,\ldots,n$ and $x = (x_1, x_2, \ldots, x_n)$ and $y = (x_1 \pm \alpha, x_2 \pm \alpha, \ldots, x_n \pm \alpha)$, $x_i, \alpha, x_i \pm \alpha \in [0,1]$, $i = 1,2,\ldots,n$, are 1 and $n^{1-1/p}$ for $p = 1$ and $p \in [2,\infty]$, respectively. Therefore, these solutions are the optimal ones. □

From Theorem 1, it is implied that the theoretical best Lipschitz constants are the same as those of the empirical best Lipschitz constants. Therefore, the theoretical and empirical best Lipschitz constant of the sum function is $n^{1-1/p}$. The best Lipschitz constant $n^{1-1/p}$ increases with increases in either the order p, or the number of variables n. Moreover, our numerical experiment indicates that the optimal solutions are multiple and the theoretical best Lipschitz constants are attainable.

According to the experiment we perform on a bounded sum function, the empirical best Lipschitz constants and associated optimal solutions x and y of the sum function and those of the bounded sum function coincide.

For the arithmetic mean $\mathrm{AM}(x_1, x_2, \ldots, x_n)$, it is evident that AM fulfills additive, idempotent, symmetric, bisymmetric, continuous, and Lipschitzian, but non-associative and has no neutral element and no annihilator element.

We now present the optimal values of x and y and the empirical best Lipschitz constant of $\mathrm{AM}(x_1, x_2, \ldots, x_n)$. Since

$$\text{Maximize} \frac{|\mathrm{AM}\,(x_1, x_2, \ldots, x_n) - \mathrm{AM}\,(y_1, y_2, \ldots, y_n)|}{\left(\sum_{i=1}^{n} |x_i - y_i|^{p}\right)^{1/p}} = \text{Maximize} \frac{1}{n} \frac{|\sum(x_1, x_2, \ldots, x_n) - \sum(y_1, y_2, \ldots, y_n)|}{\left(\sum_{i=1}^{n} |x_i - y_i|^{p}\right)^{1/p}} \quad (6)$$

for $(x_1, x_2, \ldots, x_n) \neq (y_1, y_2, \ldots, y_n)$, $x_i, y_i \leq 1$ and $x_i, y_i \geq 0$, $i \in \{1,2,\ldots,n\}$. The result of $\mathrm{AM}\,(x_1, x_2, \ldots, x_n)$ are directly linked to related results of the sum function described as follows.

For the $\mathrm{AM}(x_1, x_2, \ldots, x_n)$, the theoretical best Lipschitz constant is $n^{-1/p}$ and 1 for $p \in [1,\infty)$ and $p = \infty$, respectively. The associated multiple optimal solutions are $x = (x_1, x_2, \ldots, x_n)$ and $y = (x_1 \pm \alpha_1, x_2 \pm \alpha_2, \ldots, x_n \pm \alpha_n)$, $x_i, \alpha_i, x_i \pm \alpha_i \in [0,1]$, $i \in \{1,2,\ldots,n\}$ and $x = (x_1, x_2, \ldots, x_n)$ and $y = (x_1 \pm \alpha, x_2 \pm \alpha, \ldots, x_n \pm \alpha)$, $x_i, \alpha, x_i \pm \alpha \in [0,1]$, $i \in \{1,2,\ldots,n\}$ for $p = 1$ and $p \in [2,\infty]$, respectively.

It implies that the theoretical best Lipschitz constants, which are the same as those of the empirical best Lipschitz constants. Therefore, the theoretical and empirical best Lipschitz constant is $n^{-1/p}$. The best Lipschitz constant $n^{-1/p}$ increases for either the number of variables n increasing or the order p increasing. Moreover, the optimal solutions are multiple and the theoretical best Lipschitz constants are attainable.

We compare the algebraic and analytical properties of $\sum(x_1, x_2, \ldots, x_n)$ and $\mathrm{AM}(x_1, x_2, \ldots, x_n)$ head to head. The differences of both kinds of aggregation functions exist among the idempotency, associativity, and neutral element. The sum function satisfies associative and non-idempotent, and has neutral element $e = 0$. While the arithmetic mean satisfies non-associative and idempotent and has no neutral element. For the sum and arithmetic mean functions, the associated multiple optimal solutions of the empirical best Lipschitz constants are identical and are $x = (x_1, x_2, \ldots, x_n)$ and $y = (x_1 \pm \alpha_1, x_2 \pm \alpha_2, \ldots, x_n \pm \alpha_n)$, $x_i, \alpha_i, x_i \pm \alpha_i \in [0,1]$, $i \in \{1,2,\ldots,n\}$ and $x = (x_1, x_2, \ldots, x_n)$ and $y = (x_1 \pm \alpha, x_2 \pm \alpha, \ldots, x_n \pm \alpha)$, $x_i, \alpha, x_i \pm \alpha \in [0,1]$, $i \in \{1,2,\ldots,n\}$ for $p = 1$ and $p \in [2,\infty]$, respectively. For L_p-norm, $p \in [1,\infty]$, the empirical best Lipschitz constant is $n^{1-1/p}$ for the sum function and $n^{-1/p}$ for the arithmetic mean, which are the same as those of analytical method. The ratio of the best Lipschitz constant of the sum to that of the arithmetic mean is n, which is independent of p. Moreover, our numerical experiments indicate that the optimal solutions are multiple, and the theoretical best Lipschitz constants are attainable. The multiple optimal solutions can be expected, since $\sum(x_1, x_2, \ldots, x_n)$ and $\mathrm{AM}\,(x_1, x_2, \ldots, x_n)$ satisfy symmetry. More precisely, if $(x_1, x_2, \ldots, x_n)$ and $(y_1, y_2, \ldots, y_n)$ is an optimal solution, then $\left(x_{\sigma(1)}, x_{\sigma(2)}, \ldots, x_{\sigma(n)}\right)$ and $\left(y_{\sigma(1)}, y_{\sigma(2)}, \ldots, y_{\sigma(n)}\right)$ is also an optimal solution for any permutation σ of $\{1, 2, \ldots, n\}$. The $\mathrm{AM}(x_1, x_2, \ldots, x_n)$ is a kernel aggregation function, which is a maximally stable aggregation function with respect to possible input errors [20]. The theoretical best Lipschitz constants of $\mathrm{AM}(x_1, x_2, \ldots, x_n)$ and associated $\sum(x_1, x_2, \ldots, x_n)$ are attainable.

4. The Best Lipschitz Constants of the Product and Geometric Mean Functions

This section is devoted to the product function $\prod(x_1, x_2, \ldots, x_n)$ and the geometric mean GM $(x_1, x_2, \ldots, x_n)$. The geometric mean is the idempotized product function. Additionally, the geometric mean is an average associated with the product function. The domains of the product function $\prod(x_1, x_2, \ldots, x_n)$ and the geometric mean GM $(x_1, x_2, \ldots, x_n)$ are $[0,1]^n$. Evidently, the product function satisfies associative, symmetric, bisymmetric, continuous and Lipschitzian, but non-additive and non-idempotent. The product function has neutral element $e = 1$ and annihilator element $a = 0$.

The second experiment is concerned with an exhaustive search for a product function $\prod(x_1, x_2, \ldots, x_n)$, with the objective of maximizing the empirical Lipschitz constant performance. For the number of variables $n \in \{2,3\}$, L_p-norm, $p \in \{1,2,3,\infty\}$ and the number of steps $m \in \{1000, 10{,}000, 100{,}000\}$, we perform an exhaustive search for all $x_i, y_i \in \left\{0, \frac{1}{m}, \frac{2}{m}, \ldots, 1\right\}$, $i \in \{1,2,\ldots,n\}$ and $(x_1, x_2, \ldots, x_n) \neq (y_1, y_2, \ldots, y_n)$ to find the optimal value of the objective function

$$\text{Maximize } \frac{\left|\prod(x_1, x_2, \ldots, x_n) - \prod(y_1, y_2, \ldots, y_n)\right|}{\left(\sum_{i=1}^{n}|x_i - y_i|^{p}\right)^{1/p}} \tag{7}$$

Consider the two-variable programming problem. For L_1-norm, the optimal value of the objective function (7) is

$$\frac{|x_1 - y_1|}{|x_1 - y_1|} = 1$$

and the associated multiple optimal solutions are $x = (x_1, 1)$ and $y = (y_1, 1)$, $x_1, y_1 \in [0,1]$. For L_p-norm, $p \in \{2,3,\infty\}$, the unique optimal solution $x = \left(1 - \frac{1}{m}, 1 - \frac{1}{m}\right)$ and $y = (1,1)$, $m \in \{1000, 10{,}000, 100{,}000\}$, yields the largest objective function

$$\frac{\left|\left(1 - \frac{1}{m}\right)\left(1 - \frac{1}{m}\right) - 1\right|}{\left(\left(\frac{1}{m}\right)^{p} + \left(\frac{1}{m}\right)^{p}\right)^{1/p}} = 2^{1-1/p} - \frac{2^{-1/p}}{m}.$$

These optimal solutions are verified by adopting LINGO with $\varepsilon = 1/m$, $m \in \{1000, 10{,}000, 100{,}000\}$. The limit of the largest objective function is equal to $2^{1-1/p}$ as the number of steps m approaches ∞. Since $2^{1-1/p} - \frac{2^{-\frac{1}{p}}}{m} < 2^{1-1/p}$, $m \in \mathcal{N}$, the limit of the empirical best Lipschitz constant $2^{1-1/p}$ is unattainable. The value of $2^{1-1/p}$ grows with increases in p. When $p = 1$, the limit value 1 is the same as that of L_1-norm. Furthermore, if $p = \infty$, the limit of the empirical best Lipschitz constant becomes 2.

For the three-variable product function $\prod(x_1, x_2, x_3)$, we get the multiple optimal solutions $x = (x_1, 1, 1)$, $y = (y_1, 1, 1)$, $x_1, y_1 \in [0,1]$ and the unique optimal solution $x = \left(1 - \frac{1}{m}, 1 - \frac{1}{m}, 1 - \frac{1}{m}\right)$, $y = (1,1,1)$, $m \in \{1000, 10{,}000, 100{,}000\}$ with the associated empirical best Lipschitz constant 1 and $3^{1-1/p} - \frac{3^{1-\frac{1}{p}}}{m} + \frac{3^{-1/p}}{m^2}$ for $p = 1$ and $p \in \{2,3,\infty\}$, respectively. These optimal solutions are verified by adopting LINGO with $\varepsilon = 1/m$, $m \in \{1000, 10{,}000, 100{,}000\}$. For $p \in \{2,3,\infty\}$, we can make the empirical best Lipschitz constant as close to $3^{1-1/p}$ as we please, provided we choose m sufficiently close to ∞. When $p = 1$, the limit of the empirical best Lipschitz constant becomes 1, which is the same as that of L_1-norm. Furthermore, if $p = \infty$, the limit of the empirical best Lipschitz constant is 3.

By induction on n, the empirical best Lipschitz constant is 1 and $n^{1-1/p} + n^{-1/p}\sum_{i=2}^{n} C_i^n\left(-\frac{1}{m}\right)^{i-1}$ for $p = 1$ and $p \in (1,\infty]$, respectively. The associated optimal solutions are

$x = (x_1, 1, \ldots, 1)$ and $y = (y_1, 1, \ldots, 1)$, $x_1, y_1 \in [0,1]$ and $x = \left(1-\frac{1}{m}, 1-\frac{1}{m}, \ldots, 1-\frac{1}{m}\right)$ and $y = (1,1,\ldots,1)$, $m \in \mathcal{N}$ for $p = 1$ and $p \in (1,\infty]$, respectively. The empirical best Lipschitz constant of $p \in (1,\infty]$ can be made close to $n^{1-1/p}$ by taking m sufficiently close to ∞.

Theoretically, the result of a more general n-ary product function $\prod(x_1, x_2, \ldots, x_n)$ is presented as follows.

Theorem 2. *For an n-ary product function $\prod(x_1, x_2, \ldots, x_n)$, the theoretical best Lipschitz constant is $n^{\,1-1/p}$ for $p \in [1,\infty]$.*

Proof of Theorem 2. From the triangular inequality, the Hölder inequality and $x_i, y_i \in [0,1]$, $i = 1, 2, \ldots, n$, we have

$$\begin{aligned} |x_1x_2\ldots x_n - y_1y_2\ldots y_n| &= |x_n(x_1x_2\ldots x_{n-1} - y_1y_2\ldots y_{n-1}) + y_1y_2\ldots y_{n-1}(x_n - y_n)| \\ &\le |x_1x_2\ldots x_{n-1} - y_1y_2\ldots y_{n-1}| + |x_n - y_n| \\ &= |x_{n-1}(x_1x_2\ldots x_{n-2} - y_1y_2\ldots y_{n-2}) + y_1y_2\ldots y_{n-2}(x_{n-1} - y_{n-1})| + |x_n - y_n| \\ &\le |x_1x_2\ldots x_{n-2} - y_1y_2\ldots y_{n-2}| + |x_{n-1} - y_{n-1}| + |x_n - y_n| \\ &\le \|x-y\|_1 \le n^{\,1-1/p}\|x-y\|_p. \end{aligned}$$

It follows that the theoretical best Lipschitz constant is $n^{\,1-1/p}$. □

From Theorem 2, the theoretical best Lipschitz constant $n^{\,1-1/p}$ increases for either the number of variables n increasing or the order p increasing. The theoretical best Lipschitz constant coincides with the limit of the empirical best Lipschitz constant. However, our numerical experiment indicates that the theoretical best Lipschitz constant $n^{\,1-1/p}$, $p \in (1,\infty]$, is unattainable because $n^{\,1-1/p} + n^{-1/p}\sum_{i=2}^{n} C_i^n\left(-\frac{1}{m}\right)^{i-1} < n^{\,1-1/p}$ for all $m \in \mathcal{N}$. Therefore, the actual best Lipschitz constant of the product function is 1 and $n^{\,1-1/p} + n^{-1/p}\sum_{i=2}^{n} C_i^n\left(-\frac{1}{m}\right)^{i-1}$ for $p = 1$ and $p \in (1,\infty]$, respectively.

The geometric mean GM $(x_1, x_2, \ldots, x_n)$ satisfies idempotent, symmetric, bisymmetric, and continuous, but non-associative, non-additive, and non-Lipschitzian. The geometric function has annihilator element $a = 0$ but no neutral element.

The third computational experiment is empirically studying the empirical best Lipschitz constant of GM $(x_1, x_2, \ldots, x_n)$. For the number of variables $n \in \{2,3\}$, L_p-norm, $p \in \{1,2,3,\infty\}$, and the number of steps $m \in \{1000, 10{,}000, 100{,}000\}$, we perform an exhaustive search for all $x_i, y_i \in \left\{0, \frac{1}{m}, \frac{2}{m}, \ldots, 1\right\}$, $i \in \{1,2,\ldots,n\}$, and $(x_1, x_2, \ldots, x_n) \neq (y_1, y_2, \ldots, y_n)$ with the objective of maximizing the Lipschitz constant

$$\text{Maximize } \frac{|\text{GM}(x_1, x_2, \ldots, x_n) - \text{GM}(y_1, y_2, \ldots, y_n)|}{\left(\sum_{i=1}^{n}|x_i - y_i|^p\right)^{1/p}} \tag{8}$$

For the two-variable GM (x_1, x_2), the optimal value for the objective function (8) is $\sqrt{m}$. For L_p-norm, $p \in \{1,2,3\}$, the associated unique optimal solution is $x = (0,1)$ and $y = \left(\frac{1}{m}, 1\right)$, $m \in \{1000, 10{,}000, 100{,}000\}$. For L_∞-norm, the associated multiple optimal solutions are $x = (0,1)$, $y = \left(\frac{1}{m}, 1\right)$ and $x = \left(0, 1-\frac{1}{m}\right)$, $y = \left(\frac{1}{m}, 1\right)$, $m \in \{1000, 10{,}000, 100{,}000\}$. These optimal solutions are verified by applying LINGO with $\varepsilon = 1/m$, $m \in \{1000, 10{,}000, 100{,}000\}$. The empirical best Lipschitz constant $\sqrt{m}$ tends to infinity as m takes on arbitrarily large positive value. Therefore, the two-variable GM(x_1, x_2) does not satisfy the Lipschitz condition.

For the three-variable GM(x_1, x_2, x_3), the unique optimal solution $x = (0, 1,\ 1)$ and $y = \left(\frac{1}{m}, 1,\ 1\right)$, $m \in \{1000, 10{,}000, 100{,}000\}$, has the largest Lipschitz constant $m^{\,2/3}$ for

L_p-norm, $p \in \{1,2,3\}$. For L_∞-norm, the multiple optimal solutions are $x = (0,1,\ 1)$, $y = \left(\frac{1}{m}, 1,\ 1\right)$, and $x = \left(0, 1 - \frac{1}{m}, 1 - \frac{1}{m}\right), y = \left(\frac{1}{m}, 1,\ 1\right)$, $m \in \{1000, 10{,}000, 100{,}000\}$ with associated empirical best Lipschitz constant $m^{\ 2/3}$. These optimal solutions are verified by applying LINGO with $\varepsilon = 1/m$, $m \in \{1000, 10{,}000, 100{,}000\}$. For $p \in \{1,2,3,\infty\}$, we can make the empirical best Lipschitz constant $m^{\ 2/3}$ as close to ∞ as we please, provided we choose m sufficiently close to ∞. It implies that the three-variable GM (x_1, x_2, x_3) does not fulfill the Lipschitz condition.

By induction on n, the empirical best Lipschitz constant of an n-ary geometric mean function GM $(x_1, x_2, \ldots, x_n)$ is $m^{\ 1-1/n}$ for all $p \in [1,\infty]$. The associated optimal solutions are $x = (0,1,\ldots,\ 1)$, $y = \left(\frac{1}{m}, 1, \ldots,\ 1\right)$, $m \in \mathcal{N}$ for $p \in [1,\infty]$ and $x = (0,1,\ldots,\ 1)$, $y = \left(\frac{1}{m}, 1, \ldots, 1\right)$ and $x = \left(0, 1 - \frac{1}{m}, \ldots, 1 - \frac{1}{m}\right), y = \left(\frac{1}{m}, 1, \ldots,\ 1\right)$, $m \in \mathcal{N}$ for $p = \infty$. For $n \geq 2$ and L_p-norm $p \in [1,\infty]$, the best Lipschitz constant $m^{\ 1-1/n}$ approaches plus infinity as m approaches plus infinity. This can be expected since GM $(x_1, x_2, \ldots, x_n)$, $n \geq 2$, is not differentiable at $x = (0,0,\ldots,\ 0)$. Additionally, GM $(x_1, x_2, \ldots, x_n)$, $n \geq 2$, is not uniformly continuous on $[0,1]^{\ n}$. Note that the best Lipschitz constant, $m^{\ 1-1/n}$ is independent of order p.

Comparing the algebraic and analytical properties of $\prod(x_1, x_2, \ldots, x_n)$ and GM $(x_1, x_2, \ldots, x_n)$, the differences of the adopted properties exist among the associativity, idempotency, Lipschitzian, and neutral element. The product function satisfies associative, non-idempotent, Lipschitzian, and has neutral element $e = 1$. While the geometric mean satisfies non-associative, idempotent, non-Lipschitzian, and has no neutral element. The associated optimal solutions of the product function and those of the geometric mean function are different. The associated optimal solutions of the product function are $x = (x_1, 1, \ldots, 1)$, $y = (y_1, 1, \ldots, 1)$, $x_1, y_1 \in [0,1]$ and $x = \left(1 - \frac{1}{m}, 1 - \frac{1}{m}, \ldots, 1 - \frac{1}{m}\right)$, $y = (1,1,\ldots,1)$, $m \in \mathcal{N}$ for $p = 1$ and $p \in (1,\infty]$, respectively. The associated optimal solutions of the geometric mean function are $x = (0,1,\ldots,\ 1)$, $y = \left(\frac{1}{m}, 1, \ldots,\ 1\right)$, $m \in \mathcal{N}$ for $p \in [1,\infty)$ and $x = (0,1,\ldots,\ 1)$, $y = \left(\frac{1}{m}, 1, \ldots,\ 1\right)$, and $x = \left(0, 1 - \frac{1}{m}, \ldots, 1 - \frac{1}{m}\right)$, $y = \left(\frac{1}{m}, 1, \ldots,\ 1\right)$, $m \in \mathcal{N}$ for $p = \infty$. The empirical best Lipschitz constant of the product function is 1 and $n^{\ 1-1/p} + n^{-1/p} \sum_{i=2}^{n} C_i^n \left(-\frac{1}{m}\right)^{i-1}$ for $p = 1$ and $p \in (1,\infty]$, respectively. The empirical best Lipschitz constant of the geometric mean function is $m^{\ 1-1/n}$ for all $p \in [1,\infty]$. As m approaches infinity, the empirical best Lipschitz constant approaches $n^{\ 1-1/p}$ and infinity for the product function and the geometric mean function, respectively. Moreover, our numerical experiments indicate that the limits of the empirical best Lipschitz constants of the product and geometric mean functions are unattainable as m approaches infinity. The reason is because the non-kernel aggregation functions of the product and geometric mean functions. Moreover, the product function do not fulfill the Lipschitz condition.

5. Conclusions and Future Research

This paper analyzes and compares the optimal solutions and the theoretical and empirical best Lipschitz constants between an aggregation function and associated idempotized aggregation function. We conduct some computational experiments to empirically study the influence of the number of variables, the Minkowski norm, the number of steps and the type of aggregation function on the optimal solutions and the theoretical and empirical best Lipschitz constant performance.

For the sum function and the arithmetic mean, the differences of the adopted algebraic and analytical properties exist among the idempotency, associativity, and neutral element. Our numerical experiments indicate that for both sum and arithmetic mean functions, the associated optimal solutions are multiple and identical. For L_p-norm, $p \in [1,\infty]$, the theoretical and empirical best Lipschitz constant is $n^{\ 1-1/p}$ for the sum function and $n^{\ -1/p}$ for the arithmetic mean. These theoretical best Lipschitz constants are attainable. The ratio of the best Lipschitz constant of the sum to that of the arithmetic mean is n, which is independent of p.

For the product function and geometric mean, the differences exist among the associativity, idempotency, Lipschitzian, and neutral element. Our numerical experiments indicate that the associated optimal solutions of the product function and those of the geometric mean are different and dependent of m. The empirical best Lipschitz constant of the product function is 1 and $n^{1-1/p} + n^{-1/p} \sum_{i=2}^{n} C_i^n \left(-\frac{1}{m}\right)^{i-1}$ for $p = 1$ and $p \in (1, \infty]$, respectively. The empirical best Lipschitz constant of the geometric mean function is $m^{1-1/n}$ for all $p \in [1, \infty]$. As the number of steps m approaches ∞, the empirical best Lipschitz constant approaches $n^{1-1/p}$ and ∞ for the product function and the geometric mean function, respectively. These limits of the empirical best Lipschitz constants are unattainable.

For an aggregation function and associated idempotized aggregation function, the differences of the adopted algebraic and analytical properties always exist among the associativity, idempotency, and neutral element. However, the associated optimal solutions of the best Lipschitz constant for the product function and those of the geometric mean are different. It follows that the product function satisfies Lipschitzian, but the geometric mean do not. While the optimal solutions of the sum and arithmetic mean functions are multiple and identical. Both sum and arithmetic mean functions satisfy Lipschitzian and attain the theoretical best Lipschitz constant.

The results of this paper can be considered to apply in group decision making or two-sided decision making matching problems. For a group decision making problem, a group of experts are usually required to express preference information over a set of alternatives according to their knowledge and experience. By adopting the results of this paper, we aggregate the individual preference information to obtain collective preference information. Then, a solution is obtained. By considering the leadership and bounded confidence levels of experts, Zhang et al. [13] proposed a new consensus reaching algorithm for social network group decision making problems with interval fuzzy preference relations. For a two-sided matching decision making (TSMDM) problem, people aim to find an appropriate matching between two sets of objects, such as marriage matching, colleges admissions, person–job matching, and knowledge service matching. Due to the imprecise knowledge of matching objects and the different culture of decision makers, TSMDM problems with different preference structures are proposed. It is natural that matching objects will provide linguistic assessments. Aggregation of the linguistic assessments is the main process, especially for the multi-criteria TSMDM problems with multi-granular hesitant fuzzy linguistic term sets and incomplete criteria weight information [15].

In the future, we will analyze the best Lipschitz constants for all aggregation functions theoretically and empirically. In particular, the theoretical and empirical analysis can be extended to the conjunctive, the disjunctive, and the mixed aggregation functions. Thus, the Lipschitz analysis for the conjunctive, the disjunctive, and the mixed aggregation functions is a subject of considerable ongoing research.

Author Contributions: H.-C.T. analyzed the method and wrote the paper. W.-T.C. performed the experiments. All authors have read and agreed to the published version of the manuscript.

Funding: This research received no external funding.

Institutional Review Board Statement: Not applicable.

Informed Consent Statement: Not applicable.

Data Availability Statement: Not applicable.

Conflicts of Interest: The authors declare that they have no competing interests.

References

1. Calvo, T.; Kolesárová, A.; Komorníková, M.; Mesiar, R. Aggregation operators: Properties, classes and construction methods. In *Aggregation Operators: New Trends and Applications*; Physica: Heidelberg, Germany, 2002; pp. 3–104.

2. del Moral, M.J.; Chiclana, F.; Tapia, J.M.; Herrera-Viedma, E. A comparative study on consensus measures in group decision making. *Int. J. Intell. Syst.* **2018**, *33*, 1624–1638. [CrossRef]
3. Grabisch, M.; Marichal, J.L.; Mesiar, R.; Pap, E. Encyclopedia of Mathematics and its Applications. In *Aggregation Functions;* Cambridge University Press: Cambridge, UK, 2009; Volume 127.
4. Grabisch, M.; Marichal, J.L.; Mesiar, R.; Pap, E. Aggregation functions: Means. *Inf. Sci.* **2011**, *181*. [CrossRef]
5. Grabisch, M.; Marichal, J.L.; Mesiar, R.; Pap, E. Aggregation functions: Construction methods, conjunctive, disjunctive and mixed classes. *Inf. Sci.* **2011**, *181*, 23–43. [CrossRef]
6. Khameneh, A.Z.; Kilicman, A. Some Construction Methods of Aggregation Operators in Decision-Making Problems: An Overview. *Symmetry* **2020**, *12*, 694. [CrossRef]
7. Mohd, R.; Abdullah, L. Aggregation methods in group decision making: A decade survey. *Informatica* **2017**, *41*, 71–86.
8. Xu, Z.S.; Da, Q.L. An Overview of operators for aggregating information. *Int. J. Intell. Syst.* **2003**, *18*, 953–969. [CrossRef]
9. Bullen, P.S. Mathematics and its Applications. In *Handbook of Means and Their Inequalities;* Kluwer Academic Publishers, Group: Dordrecht, The Netherlands, 2003; Volume 560.
10. Gottwald, S. *A Treatise on Many-Valued Logics;* Studies in Logic and Computation Research Studies Press Ltd.: Baldock, UK, 2001; Volume 9.
11. Irvanizam, I.; Zi, N.N.; Zuhra, R.; Amrusi, A.; Sofyan, H. An extended MABAC method based on triangular fuzzy neutro-sophic numbers for multiple-criteria group decision making problems. *Axioms* **2020**, *9*, 104. [CrossRef]
12. Jamil, M.; Abdullah, S.; Khan, M.Y.; Smarandache, F.; Ghani, F. Application of the Bipolar Neutrosophic Hamacher Averaging Aggregation Operators to Group Decision Making: An Illustrative Example. *Symmetry* **2019**, *11*, 698. [CrossRef]
13. Zhang, Z.; Gao, Y.; Li, Z. Consensus reaching for social network group decision making by considering leadership and bounded confidence. *Knowl. Based Syst.* **2020**, *204*, 106240. [CrossRef]
14. Tian, C.; Peng, J.J. A Multi-Criteria Decision-Making Method Based on the Improved Single-Valued Neutrosophic Weighted Geometric Operator. *Mathematics* **2020**, *8*, 1051. [CrossRef]
15. Zhang, Z.; Gao, J.; Gao, Y.; Yu, W. Two-sided matching decision making with multi-granular hesitant fuzzy linguistic term sets and incomplete criteria weight information. *Expert Syst. Appli.* **2021**, *168*, 114311. [CrossRef]
16. Špirková, J.; Beliakov, G.; Bustince, H.; Fernandez, J. Mixture functions and their monotonicity. *Inf. Sci.* **2019**, *481*, 520–549. [CrossRef]
17. Khameneh, A.Z.; Kilicman, A. A fuzzy majority-based construction method for composed aggregation functions by using combination operator. *Inf. Sci.* **2019**, *505*, 367–387. [CrossRef]
18. Charnes, A.; Cooper, W.W. The non-Archimedean CCR ratio for efficiency analysis: A rejoinder to Boyd and Färe. *Euro. J. Oper. Res.* **1984**, *15*, 333–334. [CrossRef]
19. LINDO System Inc. *LINGO User's Guide;* LINDO System Inc.: Chicago, IL, USA, 1999.
20. Kolesárová, A.; Mordelová, J.; Muel, E. Kernel aggregation operators and their marginals. *Fuzzy Sets Syst.* **2004**, *142*, 35–50. [CrossRef]

axioms

Article

Outsourcing Reverse Logistics for E-Commerce Retailers: A Two-Stage Fuzzy Optimization Approach

Chia-Nan Wang [1,*], Thanh-Tuan Dang [1,2,*] and Ngoc-Ai-Thy Nguyen [1,*]

1 Department of Industrial Engineering and Management, National Kaohsiung University of Science and Technology, Kaohsiung 80778, Taiwan
2 Department of Logistics and Supply Chain Management, Hong Bang International University, Ho Chi Minh 723000, Vietnam
* Correspondence: cn.wang@nkust.edu.tw (C.-N.W.); tuandang.ise@gmail.com (T.-T.D.); thy.logistics@gmail.com (N.-A.-T.N.)

Abstract: On the heels of the online shopping boom during the Covid-19 pandemic, the electronic commerce (e-commerce) surge has many businesses facing an influx in product returns. Thus, relevant companies must implement robust reverse logistics strategies to reflect the increased importance of the capability. Reverse logistics also plays a radical role in any business's sustainable development as a process of reusing, remanufacturing, and redistributing products. Within this context, outsourcing to a third-party reverse logistics provider (3PRLP) has been identified as one of the most important management strategies for today's organizations, especially e-commerce players. The objective of this study is to develop a decision support system to assist businesses in the selection and evaluation of different 3PRLPs by a hybrid fuzzy multicriteria decision-making (MCDM) approach. Relevant criteria concerning the economic, environmental, social, and risk factors are incorporated and taken into the models. For obtaining more scientific and accurate ranking results, linguistic terms are adopted to reduce fuzziness and uncertainties of criteria weights in the natural decision-making process. The fuzzy analytic hierarchy process (FAHP) is applied to measure the criteria's relative significance over the evaluation process. The fuzzy technique for order preference by similarity to an ideal solution (FTOPSIS) is then used to rank the alternatives. The prescribed method was adopted for solving a case study on the 3PRLP selection for an online merchant in Vietnam. As a result, the most compatible 3PRLP was determined. The study also indicated that "lead time," "customer's voice," "cost," "delivery and service," and "quality" are the most dominant drivers when selecting 3PLRLs. This study aims to provide a more complete and robust evaluation process to e-commerce businesses and any organization that deals with supply chain management in determining the optimized reverse logistics partners.

Keywords: reverse logistics; recycling; outsource; e-commerce; triangular fuzzy number; FAHP; FTOPSIS; decision making; sustainability

MSC: 90B50; 03E72; 74P05; 74P20; 90B06

Citation: Wang, C.-N.; Dang, T.-T.; Nguyen, N.-A.-T. Outsourcing Reverse Logistics for E-Commerce Retailers: A Two-Stage Fuzzy Optimization Approach. *Axioms* **2021**, *10*, 34. https://doi.org/10.3390/axioms10010034

Academic Editor: Goran Ćirović

Received: 10 February 2021
Accepted: 11 March 2021
Published: 14 March 2021

1. Introduction

In recent years, reverse logistics has become a key component of any successful streamlined supply chain. Today's global value chains require greater resilience and efficiencies in the flow of goods between and within countries. Sustainability in the supply chain has become a strategic intent for almost all businesses, and reverse logistics practice is key to the effort. In maximizing the value recovery and safe disposal of waste, reverse logistics expands products at the end of their life cycles through some activities such as resell, refurbish, remanufacture, and recycle, to name a few [1]. Besides optimizing value and sustainability for businesses, the reverse logistics issue that directly impacts supply chains the most is to manage the return of products from the end consumer back to the manufacturer. With online shopping becoming increasingly prevalent, the reverse loop has never been so prominent in global supply chains. In an e-commerce-focused era in which customers are returning products at an increasing rate in various industry sectors, e-merchants and other retailers are at a critical juncture, as any continued lack of focus on reverse logistics will be unsustainable. Online purchases are being returned three times more often than store purchases [2]. This statistic means reverse logistics supply chain management has become a necessity for online merchants to maintain a balanced inventory turn and operating expenses. Additionally, the unprecedented crisis by the Covid-19 pandemic has brought inexorable growth to the e-commerce sector, which is expected to lead to an even higher volume of returned goods. Undoubtedly, this trend will endure in a post-Covid-19 world. Accordingly, reverse logistics has a significant effect on customer relationships and, most significantly, leads to sustainability and long-term profitability of business operations.

Expected to reach 603.9 billion USD by 2025 [3], reverse logistics, when optimized, can increase customer satisfaction and return on investment (ROI). Simply put, reverse logistics in e-commerce refers to the return process, which is the collection of all activities of goods that move in the reverse direction, i.e., from their point of consumption back to the business. The most critical processes are customer support, physical movement of goods, warehousing, triage, repairs, and after-sales support [4]. An easy and hassle-free return process can gain customer engagement and loyalty. As a result, functional and efficient reverse logistics has become a pivotal element for e-commerce businesses. However, most companies are not able to manage their reverse logistics networks. Due to the complicated process and resource constraints, more and more businesses choose to outsource third-party companies to handle their reverse e-commerce services and optimize the return process. Third-party reverse logistics providers (3PRLP) are delegated to help companies productively manage returned currents of products at optimal cost. Hence, evaluating and selecting the best 3PRLP is an imperative and complicated task that must be undertaken prudently [5] for businesses, especially e-commerce merchants and other retailers, to facilitate an effective reverse logistics process and retain customers.

Given the abovementioned importance of reverse logistics outsourcing to the industries, the relevant literature on potential sectors in developing countries is sparse, taking the e-commerce sector in Vietnam as a good example. This gap has formed our research motivation. The current study aims to address this gap by investigating reverse logistics outsourcing practices in Vietnam. According to Google, Vietnam is ranked the second-fastest-growing e-commerce market in Southeast Asia, following Indonesia [6]. Vietnam's e-commerce has been growing from about 28 percent in 2017 to nearly half of the population in 2020 [7]. It is also forecast that the country's e-commerce market will hit 15 billion USD by 2025 [8]. While e-commerce giants in Vietnam such as Tiki, Lazada, and Grab have already developed their own logistics sector (warehousing, packing, shipping, and reverse logistics), most other online merchants (including some major players like Shopee and Sendo) are not able to operate an in-house logistics, therefore opt to delegate these activities to third-party logistics providers. Thus, it creates great opportunities and a promising market for e-commerce logistics. According to the 2017 logistics report of the Ministry of Industry and Trade, Vietnam has about 50 enterprises providing e-logistics services [9]. With the need for fast, immediate, and on-demand delivery from customers who shop online, more and more e-logistics startups have entered this market. Providing the volume of e-commerce transactions increasing, logistics providers have to handle large volumes of returned goods. In Vietnam, wrong shipping addresses (especially in rural areas) and unsuccessful orders are daunting challenges faced by both e-commerce retailers and e-logistics businesses. Moreover, competition in terms of delivery speed and costs are factors that can distinguish the best third-party logistics providers.

Moreover, the literature on outsourcing 3PRLP is still limited because of its recent emergence and demand from stakeholders. This lack, therefore, attracted our attention. In this paper, the authors aim to efficiently assist the decision-makers in evaluating and selecting the most sustainable 3PRLP by proposing a robust hybrid multicriteria decision-making (MCDM) approach. Among MCDM methods, the analytic hierarchy process (AHP) and the technique for order preference by similarity to an ideal solution (TOPSIS) are two classical and most commonly used techniques. Conventional AHP and TOPSIS have been combined in different ways and investigated in many studies. In these methods, the criteria weights are often determined by AHP, and TOPSIS ranks the alternatives. Some exemplary studies are as follows. In the basic combination of the AHP-TOPSIS approach, the evaluations about criteria and alternatives are all supposed to be deterministic numbers [10]. In the integration of AHP and the fuzzy TOPSIS method applied in [11], the criteria weights determined by AHP are real numbers, and the evaluations of alternatives with respect to different criteria are in linguistic terms. Meanwhile, linguistic terms are adopted to evaluate criteria, and real numbers are used to assess alternatives in [12]. As a further improvement to the existing literature of reverse logistics outsourcing in terms of methodologies, this paper combines fuzzy AHP (FAHP) and fuzzy TOPSIS (FTOPSIS), by which linguistic terms in evaluations of both criteria and alternatives are adopted. This adoption's motive is that experts are often reluctant or unable to assign accurate values during the decision-making process. Thus, they prefer to provide their evaluations in linguistic terms, reflecting their uncertain, ambiguous, and vague judgment. In light of this, fuzzy set theory is a useful method for dealing with uncertainty. The decision model may include unknown, incomplete, and inaccessible information and partially ignorant data. During the whole evaluation process, the linguistic terms are converted into triangular fuzzy numbers.

The research procedure is described as follows. In the first stage, FAHP is applied for determining the fuzzy preference weights of the criteria. The evaluation process's criteria concern economic factors (quality, cost, lead time, delivery and service, R&D capability), environmental factors (recycle, disposal, reproduction, and reuse, green technology, CO_2 emissions), social factors (health and safety, customer's voice, reputation), and risk factors (operation risk, financial risk). In the next stage, FTOPSIS is used to rank all alternatives, offering the optimized 3PRLPs. An application of selecting 3PRLPS for an e-commerce business in Vietnam is presented, simultaneously demonstrating the suggested method. In doing so, this study makes novel contributions to the field by providing a complete and robust evaluation process for 3PRLP selection in the e-commerce sector for a developing country in Asia which is almost neglected in the literature. As a result, this paper provides a holistic framework for businesses with theoretical and managerial implications as a robust decision support system in solving the reverse logistics outsourcing problem.

The paper unfolds as follows. In the next section, a literature review on reverse logistics outsourcing is reviewed. Section 3 summarizes the materials and methods of FAHP and FTOPSIS used in the paper. Result analysis of a case study in Vietnam is shown in Section 4. Finally, Section 5 offers the managerial insights and conclusions of the paper.

2. Literature Review

Concerning the well-developed status of research on outsourcing 3PRLP, multiple criteria decision-making (MCDM) techniques that simultaneously consider various desired selection criteria in different dimensions have appeared to be promising for this task. Literature and practice show that economic, environmental, and social factors are dominant decision-making variables in selecting a sustainable provider of reverse logistics services [13–15]. Sustainable development (economic, environmental, and social aspects) lead organizations to reverse logistics practices (Figure 1) [16]. To determine a qualified provider in the outsourcing process, the proposed evaluation approach and the set of criteria are two quintessential parts [17]. Many notable studies have applied various MCDM techniques that consider different criteria to evaluate and select the best 3PRLP. For example, Tavana et al. [18] proposed an integrated intuitionistic fuzzy AHP and SWOT method for solving the reverse logistics outsourcing problem faced by a company. Their findings indicated that when delegating reverse logistics activities to 3PRLPs, it is the most significant priority for a firm to focus on its core business; meanwhile, reducing costs constitutes one of its least important priorities. In the study of Zarbakhshnia et al. [5], a multiple attribute decision making (MADM) model to rank and select the sustainable third-party reverse logistics providers in the presence of risk factors was proposed, and a realistic case study in the automotive industry was applied to demonstrate the model's effectiveness. Bai and Sarkis [19] first introduced the use of neighborhood rough set, TOPSIS, and VIKOR as a proper and realistic modeling approach for 3PRLPs evaluation and selection using economic/business, environmental, and social (sustainability) factors.

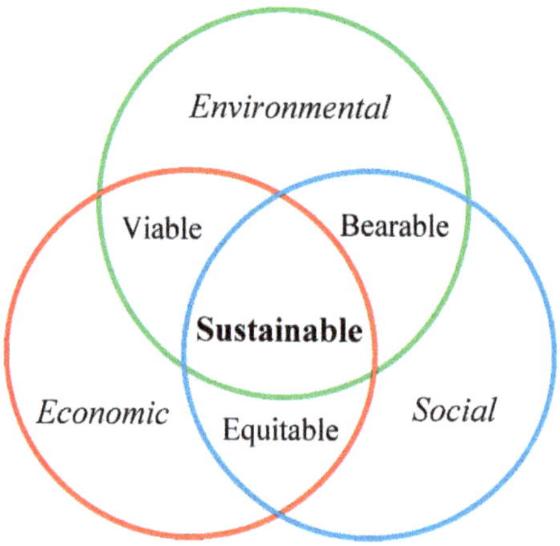

Figure 1. Three pillars of sustainable development [16].

In the management science and decision-making literature, discussing reverse logistics outsourcing issues has become an increasingly important topic. Various criteria and approaches have been considered in the literature. In terms of criteria, businesses traditionally examine cost, quality, and flexibility [19]. For organizations that seek long-term resilience of reverse supply chains, social and environmental concerns are considered sustainability factors [20–22]. Regarding methodologies, numerous evaluation models based on MCDM techniques for outsourcing 3PRLP have been introduced ranging from analytical hierarchy process (AHP) [23–27], fuzzy AHP [28,29], analytic network process (ANP) [30–32], fuzzy ANP [33], technique for order preference by similarity to ideal solution (TOPSIS) [19,27,34,35], fuzzy TOPSIS [36], visekriterijumska optimizacija i kompromisno resenje (VIKOR) method [19,31,33,37], step-wise weight assessment ratio analysis (SWARA) [38,39], quality function deployment (QFD) model [28,40], data envelopment analysis (DEA) [26,35,41,42], other MCDM methods [30–34,38,39,43], exact methods (mathematical programming) [26,37,43–45], and statistical approaches [40,46–48]. Table 1 presents a summary of the literature review on proposed approaches for 3PRLP selection and evaluation problems.

Table 1. Summary of method approaches in reverse logistics provider's selection.

No.	Authors [Citation]	Year	Methodologies										Problems		
			AHP	ANP	TOPSIS	VIKOR	SWARA	QFD	Other MCDM	DEA	Mathematical Model	Statistical Approach	Deterministic	Uncertain	Reverse Logistics
1	Korpela and Tuominen [23]	1996	x										x		
2	Moberg and Speh [46]	2004										x	x		
3	Sinkovics and Roath [47]	2004										x	x		
4	Thakkar et al. [30]	2005		x					x				x		x
5	So et al. [24]	2006	x										x		
6	Bottani and Rizzi [36]	2006			x									x	
7	Sahay et al. [44]	2006									x		x		
8	Göl and Çatay [25]	2007	x										x		
9	Yang et al. [48]	2008										x	x		
10	Zhou et al. [41]	2008								x			x		
11	Hamdan and Rogers [42]	2008								x			x		
12	Kannan et al. [34]	2009			x				x				x		
13	Liu and Wang [45]	2009									x			x	
14	Liou et al. [31]	2010		x		x			x				x		
15	Sasikumar and Haq [37]	2011				x					x		x		x
16	Ho et al. [28]	2012	x					x						x	
17	Falsini et al. [26]	2012	x							x	x		x		
18	Hsu et al. [32]	2013		x					x				x		
19	Perçin and Min [40]	2013						x				x		x	
20	Jayant et al. [27]	2014	x		x								x		x
21	Tadić et al. [33]	2014		x		x			x					x	
22	Ilgin [29]	2017	x											x	x
23	Zarbakhshnia et al. [38]	2018					x		x				x		
24	Bai and Sarkis [19]	2019			x	x							x		x
25	Govindan et al. [43]	2019							x		x		x		x
26	Wang et al. [35]	2019			x					x			x		x
27	Agarwal et al. [39]	2020					x		x					x	x
28	This paper	2021	x		x									x	x

Note: analytical hierarchy process (AHP), analytical network process (ANP), technique for order of preference by similarity to ideal solution (TOPSIS), visekriterijumska optimizacija i kompromisno resenje (VIKOR), step-wise weight assessment ratio analysis (SWARA), quality function deployment (QFD), multi-criteria decision making (MCDM), data envelopment analysis (DEA).

Given several methodologies used in the evaluation and selection of 3PRLPs, it can be observed that AHP and TOPSIS methods are the two typical and most commonly used due to their applicability. The foundation of the AHP is a set of axioms that carefully delimits the scope of the problem environment [49]. Among mathematical weighting methods, the pairwise comparison method in the AHP is an effective procedure to determine the importance of different attributes to the objective. Its understandability in theory, simplicity in application, and robustness of its outcomes have been proven in practice and validated by a diverse range of decision-making problems. The TOPSIS method, first introduced in [50], is one of the most well-known classical MCDM methods. Simply stated, in a geometrical sense, the TOPSIS method simultaneously considers the distance to the ideal solution and negative-ideal solution of each alternative and choosing the closest relative to the ideal solution as the best alternative [27]. In this paper, the authors aim to solve the fuzzy information during the whole evaluation and selection process by considering linguistic terms in both criteria and alternatives, which thereby are converted into triangular fuzzy numbers using the fuzzy set theory. Thus, the gaps in the existing literature are addressed in this paper as follows: (1) methodologically, this is the first study to suggest a hybrid fuzzy decision support system that combines the fuzzy AHP (FAHP) and the fuzzy TOPSIS (FTOPSIS) for the field of reverse logistics outsourcing; (2) in terms of applications, the prescribed approach is used for a case study in Vietnam to support an e-commerce business determining their compatible and sustainable partners for reverse logistics among eight candidates; (3) the managerial implications of this paper provide a comprehensive insight that enables decision analysts to better understand the complete evaluation and selection process of 3PRLPs considering well-rounded aspects. From a broader standpoint, this study can assist e-commerce businesses or any organization to expedite their reverse logistics strategies in this era.

3. Materials and Methods

3.1. Research Process

Decision-making in real-world problems, especially in the evaluation and selection of third-party reverse logistics providers (3PRLP), involves not only quantitative criteria (i.e., cost, lead time) but also quantitative criteria (i.e., the voice of customers, reputation). Fuzzy set theory is useful for handling complex decision-making problems with numerous associated factors. In this paper, among many MCDM models, FAHP and FTOSPS are chosen to select the most efficient providers among alternatives because they are available in decision-making software and allow decision-makers to practice effectively. The process of the paper includes two stages, as can be seen in Figure 2.

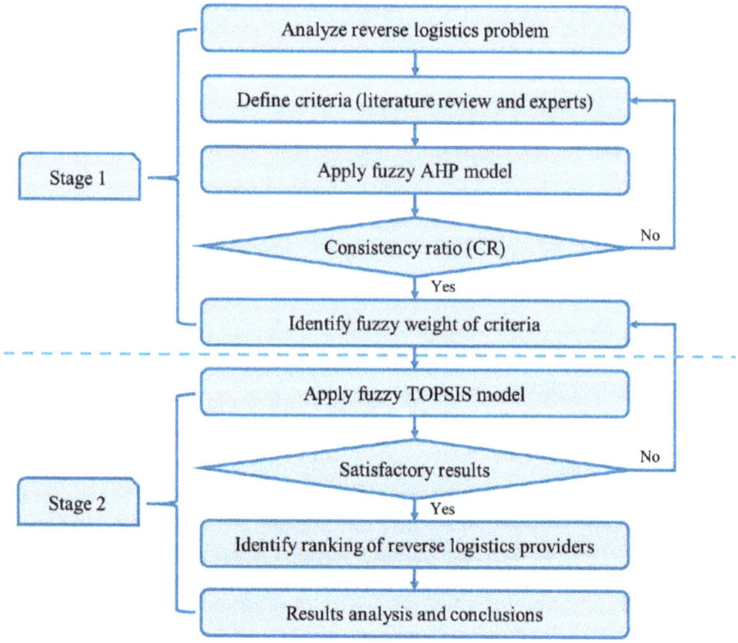

Figure 2. Research process.

In the first stage, FAHP is applied to identify fuzzy preference weights of criteria in the outsourcing reverse logistics problem. The list of criteria used in this paper is selected from the relevant literature review (Table 2) and industrial experts' survey. There are four main criteria and 15 criteria including economic (quality, cost, lead time, delivery and service, R&D capability), environment (recycle, disposal, reproduction and reuse, green technology, CO_2 emissions), social (health and safety, customer's voice, reputation), and risk (operational risk, financial risk). In the second stage, FTOPSIS is applied to rank all alternatives. This paper proposed a hybrid approach by combining two MCDM models that can improve the decision-making process. Besides, the problem of outsourcing reverse logistics for e-commerce retailers is addressed under uncertainty environment using fuzzy theory that can enhance the robust results.

Table 2. List of criteria used in reverse logistics provider's selection.

Main Criteria	Criteria	Target	Authors [Citation]
Economic (C1)	C11. Quality	Max	Bottani and Rizzi [36], Spencer et al. [51], Tsai et al. [52], Zarbakhshnia et al. [38], Mavi et al. [53], Govindan et al. [43], Sasikumar and Haq [37]
	C12. Cost	Min	Bottani and Rizzi [36], Spencer et al. [51], Tsai et al. [52], Zarbakhshnia et al. [38], Mavi et al. [53], Govindan et al. [43], Sasikumar and Haq [37], Efendigil et al. [54]
	C13. Lead time	Min	Zarbakhshnia et al. [38], Mavi et al. [53], Govindan et al. [43], Efendigil et al. [54]
	C14. Delivery and service	Max	Bottani and Rizzi [36], Spencer et al. [51], Tsai et al. [52], Zarbakhshnia et al. [38], Mavi et al. [53], Govindan et al. [43], Sasikumar and Haq [37], Efendigil et al. [54]
	C15. R&D capability	Max	Bottani and Rizzi [36], Goebel et al. [55], Ni et al. [56]
Environment (C2)	C21. Recycle	Max	Zarbakhshnia et al. [38], Mavi et al. [53], Sasikumar and Haq [37], Guimarães and Salomon [57]
	C22. Disposal	Max	Zarbakhshnia et al. [38], Mavi et al. [53], Sasikumar and Haq [37]
	C23. Reproduction and reuse	Max	Goebel et al. [55], Zarbakhshnia et al. [38], Mavi et al. [53], Sasikumar and Haq [37]
	C24. Green technology	Max	Zarbakhshnia et al. [38], Sasikumar and Haq [37], Guimarães and Salomon [57]
	C25. CO_2 emissions	Min	Zarbakhshnia et al. [38], Govindan et al. [43]
Social (C3)	C31. Health and safety	Max	Zarbakhshnia et al. [38], Govindan et al. [43], Mavi et al. [53]
	C32. Customer's voice	Max	Zarbakhshnia et al. [38], Mavi et al. [53], Efendigil et al. [54]
	C33. Reputation	Max	Spencer et al. [51], Mavi et al. [53], Efendigil et al. [54]
Risk (C4)	C41. Operational risk	Min	Zarbakhshnia et al. [38], Mitra et al. [58], Mavi et al. [53]
	C42. Financial risk	Min	Bottani and Rizzi [36], Tsai et al. [52], Ni et al. [56], Mavi et al. [53]

Note: identified by the researchers.

3.2. Triangular Fuzzy Number (TFN)

Fuzzy set theory was introduced by Zadeh [59] to deal with uncertainty problems. A triangular fuzzy number (TFN) is defined as (a, b, c) which denotes pessimistic, most likely, and optimistic values, as shown in Equation (1), and as can be seen in Figure 3.

$$\mu\left(\frac{x}{\widetilde{F}}\right) = \begin{cases} (x-a)/(b-a), & a \leq x \leq b \\ (c-x)/(c-b), & b \leq x \leq c \\ 0, & otherwise \end{cases} \tag{1}$$

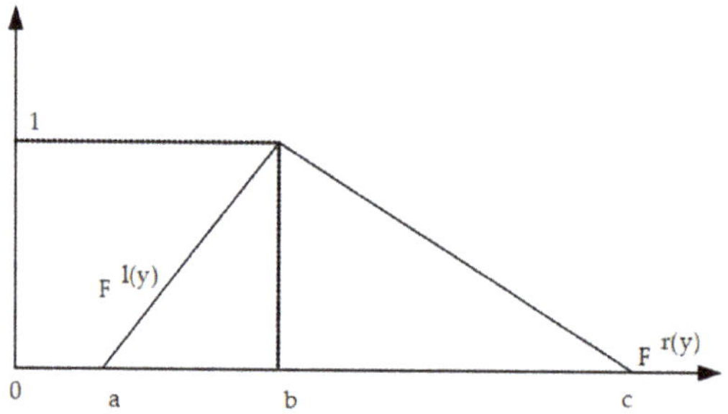

Figure 3. The membership function of triangular fuzzy number (TFN).

The representative of each level of membership function is denoted, as can be seen in Equation (2).

$$\widetilde{F} = (F^{l(y)}, F^{r(y)}) = [a + (b-a)y,\ c + (b-c)y], y \in [0,\ 1] \tag{2}$$

where $F^{l(y)}$, $F^{r(y)}$ denote two sides of the fuzzy number.

3.3. Fuzzy Analytical Hierarchy Process (FAHP)

FAHP is an extension of AHP, which overcomes the drawbacks of AHP, and solves such problems under fuzzy environment. The linguistic expression for fuzzy scale and allocated TFN is shown in Table 3. The procedure of FAHP includes six steps as follows [60].

Table 3. Linguistic rating level and allocated TFN in the fuzzy AHP (FAHP) model.

Fuzzy Number	Linguistics Rating Level	Allocated TFN
1	Equal importance	(1, 1, 1)
2	Weak importance	(1, 2, 3)
3	Not bad	(2, 3, 4)
4	Preferable	(3, 4, 5)
5	Importance	(4, 5, 6)
6	Fairly importance	(5, 6, 7)
7	Very important	(6, 7, 8)
8	Absolute	(7, 8, 9)
9	Perfect	(8, 9, 10)

Step 1: Build a fuzzy pairwise comparison matrix, as can be seen in Equation (3).

$$\widetilde{M^k} = \begin{pmatrix} \widetilde{e^k_{11}} & \widetilde{e^k_{12}} & \cdots & \widetilde{e^k_{1n}} \\ \widetilde{e^k_{21}} & \cdots & \cdots & \widetilde{e^k_{2n}} \\ \cdots & \cdots & \cdots & \cdots \\ \widetilde{e^k_{n1}} & \widetilde{e^k_{n2}} & \cdots & \widetilde{e^k_{nn}} \end{pmatrix} \tag{3}$$

where $\widetilde{e_{ij}^k}$ denotes the important level from kth decision-maker with respect to the ith criterion over the jth criterion using TFN membership function.

Step 2: Assume that a decision group has K experts. An integrated fuzzy pairwise comparison matrix can be calculated as Equation (4).

$$\widetilde{M^k} = \begin{pmatrix} \widetilde{e_{11}} & \widetilde{e_{12}} & \cdots & \widetilde{e_{1n}} \\ \widetilde{e_{21}} & \cdots & \cdots & \widetilde{e_{2n}} \\ \cdots & \cdots & \cdots & \cdots \\ \widetilde{e_{n1}} & \widetilde{e_{n2}} & \cdots & \widetilde{e_{nn}} \end{pmatrix} \text{ such that } \widetilde{e_{ij}} = \frac{\sum_{k=1}^{K} \widetilde{e_{ij}^k}}{K} \quad (4)$$

Step 3: The fuzzy geometric mean of each criterion is calculated as Equation (5), as follows.

$$\widetilde{r_i} = \left(\prod_{j=1}^{n} \widetilde{e_{ij}} \right)^{1/n} \text{ such that } i = 1,\ 2,\ \ldots, n \quad (5)$$

where $\widetilde{r_i}$ denotes the fuzzy geometric mean and $\widetilde{e_{ij}}$ denotes the important level from group of decision-maker with respect to the ith criterion over the jth criterion.

Step 4: Calculate the fuzzy weights of each criterion using Equation (6).

$$\widetilde{w_i} = \widetilde{r_i}\ (\times)\ (\widetilde{r_1}\ (+)\ \widetilde{r_2}\ (+) \ldots (+)\ \widetilde{r_n})^{-1} \quad (6)$$

Step 5: Defuzzify the fuzzy weight using the average weight criteria M_i, as can be seen in Equation (7).

$$M_i = \frac{\widetilde{w_1}\ (+)\ \widetilde{w_2}\ (+) \ldots (+)\ \widetilde{w_n}}{n} \quad (7)$$

Step 6: Calculate the normalized weight criteria N_i as Equation (8).

$$N_i = \frac{M_i}{\sum_{i=1}^{n} M_i} \quad (8)$$

3.4. Fuzzy Technique for Order of Preference by Similarity to Ideal Solution (FTOPSIS)

FTOPSIS is a very useful MCDM model, which is applied to rank different alternatives based on the distance between the fuzzy positive ideal solution (FPIS) and the fuzzy negative ideal solution (FNIS). The process of FTOPSIS includes seven steps below [61].

Step 1: Identify the fuzzy weights of criteria.

In FTOPSIS model, the fuzzy weights of criteria are obtained from FAHP model.

Step 2: Based on the linguistic rating value in Table 4, develop the fuzzy decision matrix, as can be seen in Equations (9) and (10).

$$\widetilde{M} = \begin{bmatrix} \widetilde{x}_{11} & \widetilde{x}_{11} & \cdots & \widetilde{x}_{11} \\ \widetilde{x}_{21} & \widetilde{x}_{22} & \cdots & \widetilde{x}_{2n} \\ \vdots & \vdots & \vdots & \vdots \\ \widetilde{x}_{m1} & \widetilde{x}_{m2} & \cdots & \widetilde{x}_{mn} \end{bmatrix} \text{ such that } i = 1,\ 2, \ldots, m;\ j = 1,\ 2, \ldots, n \quad (9)$$

$$\widetilde{x}_{ij} = \frac{1}{k}\left(\widetilde{x}_{ij}^1\ (+)\ \widetilde{x}_{ij}^2\ (+) \ldots (+)\ \widetilde{x}_{ij}^k\right) \quad (10)$$

where $\widetilde{x}_{ij}^k$ denotes the fuzzy rating of alternative A_i with respect to criteria C_j by kth expert, and $\widetilde{x}_{ij}^k = \left(a_{ij}^k, b_{ij}^k, c_{ij}^k\right)$.

Step 3: In this step, the fuzzy decision matrix is normalized, as shown in Equations (11)–(13).

$$\widetilde{S} = \left[\widetilde{s}_{ij}\right]_{m \times n} \text{ such that } i = 1,\ 2, \ldots, m; j = 1,\ 2, \ldots, n \quad (11)$$

$$\tilde{s}_{ij} = \left(\frac{a_{ij}}{c_j^*}, \frac{b_{ij}}{c_j^*}, \frac{c_{ij}}{c_j^*}\right), c_j^* = max_i\{c_{ij} | i = 1, 2, \ldots, m\} \text{ for benefit criteria} \quad (12)$$

$$\tilde{s}_{ij} = \left(\frac{a'_j}{c_{ij}}, \frac{a'_j}{b_{ij}}, \frac{a'_j}{a_{ij}}\right), a'_j = min_i\{a_{ij} | i = 1, 2, \ldots, m\} \text{ for cost criteria} \quad (13)$$

Step 4: Construct the weighted normalized fuzzy decision matrix $\tilde{u}_{ij}$, Equations (14) and (15).

$$\tilde{U} = [\tilde{u}_{ij}]_{m \times n} \text{ such that } i = 1, 2, \ldots, m; j = 1, 2, \ldots, n \quad (14)$$

$$\tilde{u}_{ij} = \tilde{s}_{ij} \ (\times) \ \tilde{w}_j \quad (15)$$

Step 5: Determine fuzzy positive ideal solution (FPIS) Q^* and fuzzy negative ideal solution (FNIS) Q' based on Equations (16) and (17).

$$Q^* = \left(\tilde{u}_1^*, \ldots, \tilde{u}_j^*, \ldots, \tilde{u}_n^*\right) \quad (16)$$

$$Q' = \left(\tilde{u}'_1, \ldots, \tilde{u}'_j, \ldots, \tilde{u}'_n\right) \quad (17)$$

where $\tilde{u}_j^* = (1, 1, 1), \tilde{u}'_j = (0, 0, 0), j = 1, 2, \ldots, n$.

Step 6: Calculate the distance ($\tilde{D}_i^*$ and $\tilde{D}'_i$) of each alternative from FPIS and FNIS, as can be seen in Equations (18) and (19).

$$\tilde{D}_i^* = \sum_{j=1}^{n} d\left(\tilde{u}_{ij}, \tilde{u}_j^*\right), i = 1, 2, \ldots, m \quad (18)$$

$$\tilde{D}'_i = \sum_{j=1}^{n} d\left(\tilde{u}_{ij}, \tilde{u}'_j\right), i = 1, 2, \ldots, m \quad (19)$$

Step 7: Calculate the closeness coefficient (i.e., relative gaps-degree) of each alternative, Equation (20). The optimal alternative is closer to the FPIS and farther from the FNIS as $\widetilde{CC}_i$ approaches to 1.

$$\widetilde{CC}_i = \frac{\tilde{D}'_i}{\tilde{D}_i^* + \tilde{D}'_i} = 1 - \frac{\tilde{D}_i^*}{\tilde{D}_i^* + \tilde{D}'_i}, i = 1, 2, \ldots, m \quad (20)$$

where $\frac{\tilde{D}'_i}{\tilde{D}_i^* + \tilde{D}'_i}$ is fuzzy satisfaction degree, $\frac{\tilde{D}_i^*}{\tilde{D}_i^* + \tilde{D}'_i}$ is fuzzy gap degree which presents how fuzzy gaps can be improved to obtain the aspiration levels of decision-makers.

Table 4. Linguistics rating level of alternatives in the fuzzy TOPSIS (FTOPSIS) model.

Linguistics Rating Level	Allocated TFN
Very poor (VP)	(0, 0, 1)
Poor (P)	(0, 1, 3)
Medium poor (MP)	(1, 3, 5)
Fair (F)	(3, 5, 7)
Medium good (MG)	(5, 7, 9)
Good (G)	(7, 9, 10)
Very good (VG)	(9, 10, 10)

4. Numerical Application and Results Analysis

4.1. Problem Description

Amid the Covid-19 online sales boom, the e-commerce industry has accelerated in every corner of the world [62], including in Vietnam. For this country, the e-commerce industry is rapidly expanding, thanks to increasing foreign investments, a favorable regulatory environment, and enhanced internet access. Investment and development of logistics are among the premises for the expansion and resilience of e-commerce. Among key strategies, outsourcing logistics has been the first choice. Selecting the most suitable partner is the most convenient and economical solution for any e-commerce merchant in Vietnam.

In this paper, a numerical application of an e-commerce business in Vietnam is used to test the effectiveness of the proposed fuzzy MCDM model. After preliminary evaluation, eight potential third-party reverse logistics providers (3PRLP) were selected based on the requirements of the company in order to select a compatible 3PRLP and to ensure a long-term healthy relationship between the two firms. The list of criteria was selected from the relevant literature review and industrial experts' survey. In the numerical application, a total of 10 experts (head of logistics and relevant departments in this e-commerce business) were consulted by interviews to assess the effect of these criteria on the 3PRLP selection. All experts had more than 10 years' working experiences in the area of logistics and supply chain. Figure 4 presents the decision hierarchy for outsourcing reverse logistics including all criteria and the list of eight potential 3PRLP. There are four main criteria and 15 criteria including economic (quality, cost, lead time, delivery and service, R&D capability), environment (recycle, disposal, reproduction and reuse, green technology, CO_2 emissions), social (health and safety, customer's voice, reputation), and risk (operational risk, financial risk).

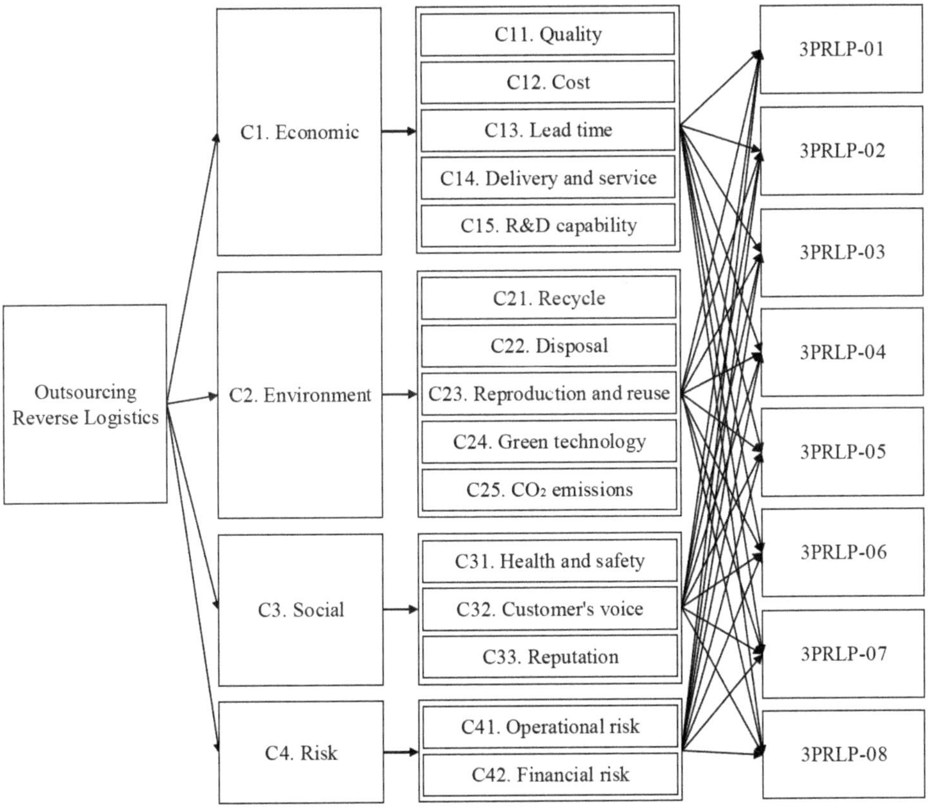

Figure 4. The decision hierarchy for outsourcing reverse logistics.

4.2. Results of Fuzzy AHP

The following FAHP procedure shows an example of the calculation of the four main criteria (economic, environment, social, risk). Other criteria are calculated using the same procedures. The initial and integrated fuzzy comparison matrix of the main criteria are presented in Tables 5 and 6, respectively.

Table 5. Initial comparison matrix of the main criteria.

Criteria	Linguistics Rating Level																	Criteria
	(8, 9, 10)	(7, 8, 9)	(6, 7, 8)	(5, 6, 7)	(4, 5, 6)	(3, 4, 5)	(2, 3, 4)	(1, 2, 3)	(1, 1, 1)	(1, 2, 3)	(2, 3, 4)	(3, 4, 5)	(4, 5, 6)	(5, 6, 7)	(6, 7, 8)	(7, 8, 9)	(8, 9, 10)	
C1							x											C2
C1						x												C3
C1							x											C4
C2								x										C3
C2										x								C4
C3											x							C4

Note: economic (C1), environment (C2), social (C3), risk (C4).

Table 6. Integrated fuzzy comparison matrix of the main criteria.

Criteria	Economic (C1)	Environment (C2)	Social (C3)	Risk (C4)
Economic (C1)	(1, 1, 1)	(2, 3, 4)	(3, 4, 5)	(2, 3, 4)
Environment (C2)	(1/4, 1/3, 1/2)	(1, 1, 1)	(1, 2, 3)	(1/3, 1/2, 1)
Social (C3)	(1/5, 1/4, 1/3)	(1/3, 1/2, 1)	(1, 1, 1)	(1/4, 1/3, 1/2)
Risk (C4)	(1/4, 1/3, 1/2)	(1, 2, 3)	(2, 3, 4)	(1, 1, 1)

Note: identified by the researchers.

In order to check the consistency ratio (CR) of the rating score, the fuzzy number is converted to a real number using lower bound (pessimistic value) and upper bound (optimistic value) values of the fuzzy comparison matrix [60,63,64]. Table 7 shows the non-fuzzy comparison matrix of the main criteria.

Table 7. Non-fuzzy comparison matrix of the main criteria.

Criteria	Economic (C1)	Environment (C2)	Social (C3)	Risk (C4)
Economic (C1)	1	2.8284	3.8730	2.8284
Environment (C2)	0.3536	1	1.7321	0.5774
Social (C3)	0.2582	0.5774	1	0.3536
Risk (C4)	0.3536	1.7321	2.8284	1
Sum	1.9653	6.1378	9.4335	4.7593

Note: calculated by the researchers.

To get the priority vector of the main criteria, the normalized matrix of pairwise comparison is calculated by dividing each number in a column of the comparison matrix by its column sum. In addition, the priority vector is determined by averaging the row entries in the normalized matrix, which are shown in Table 8.

Table 8. Normalized comparison matrix of the main criteria.

Criteria	Economic (C1)	Environment (C2)	Social (C3)	Risk (C4)	Priority Vector
Economic (C1)	0.5088	0.4608	0.4106	0.5943	0.4936
Environment (C2)	0.1799	0.1629	0.1836	0.1213	0.1619
Social (C3)	0.1314	0.0941	0.1060	0.0743	0.1014
Risk (C4)	0.1799	0.2822	0.2998	0.2101	0.2430
Sum	1	1	1	1	1

Note: calculated by the researchers.

In this step, the largest eigenvector (λ_{max}) is calculated to determine the consistency index (CI), the random index (RI), and the consistency ratio (CR), as follows.

$$\begin{bmatrix} 0.5088 & 0.4608 & 0.4106 & 0.5943 \\ 0.1799 & 0.1629 & 0.1836 & 0.1213 \\ 0.1314 & 0.0941 & 0.1060 & 0.0743 \\ 0.1799 & 0.2822 & 0.2998 & 0.2101 \end{bmatrix} \times \begin{bmatrix} 0.4936 \\ 0.1619 \\ 0.1014 \\ 0.2430 \end{bmatrix} = \begin{bmatrix} 2.0318 \\ 0.6524 \\ 0.4083 \\ 0.9849 \end{bmatrix}$$

$$\begin{bmatrix} 2.0318 \\ 0.6524 \\ 0.4083 \\ 0.9849 \end{bmatrix} / \begin{bmatrix} 0.4936 \\ 0.1619 \\ 0.1014 \\ 0.2430 \end{bmatrix} = \begin{bmatrix} 4.1161 \\ 4.0291 \\ 4.0253 \\ 4.0530 \end{bmatrix}$$

This paper considers four main criteria. Hence, we get $n = 4$. Consequently, λ_{max} and CI are calculated as follows.

$$\lambda_{max} = \frac{4.1161 + 4.0291 + 4.0253 + 4.0530}{4} = 4.0559$$

$$CI = \frac{\lambda_{max} - n}{n - 1} = \frac{4.0559 - 4}{4 - 1} = 0.0186$$

where $n = 4$, we get $RI = 0.9$, and the consistency ratio (CR) is calculated as follows:

$$CR = \frac{CI}{RI} = \frac{0.0186}{0.9} = 0.0207$$

From the result, $CR = 0.0207 < 0.1$, therefore, the pairwise comparison matrix is consistent, and the results are satisfactory. Consequently, other criteria are calculated using the same methodology. The integrated fuzzy comparison matrix of 15 criteria is presented in Table A1 (Appendix A).

The results of the fuzzy weights of all criteria from the FAHP model are calculated based on the fuzzy geometric mean concept, shown in Table 9. Each fuzzy weight includes three values, which are pessimistic value (the lowest weight), most likely value (the middle weight), and optimistic value (the highest weight). For example, the fuzzy weight of criteria quality (C11), has the pessimistic weight at 0.0357, the most likely weight of 0.0750, and the most optimistic weight of 0.1545. The remaining criteria have the same demonstration. These fuzzy preference weights will be used in the next stage of the FTOPSIS model.

Table 9. Results of fuzzy weights from the FAHP model.

Main Criteria	Criteria	Target	Fuzzy Geometric Mean			Fuzzy Weights		
Economic (C1)	C11. Quality	Max	0.7654	1.1409	1.6597	0.0357	0.0750	0.1545
	C12. Cost	Min	0.8479	1.2247	1.7031	0.0395	0.0805	0.1585
	C13. Lead time	Min	0.8834	1.2901	1.8245	0.0412	0.0848	0.1698
	C14. Delivery and service	Max	0.7785	1.1502	1.6611	0.0363	0.0756	0.1546
	C15. R&D capability	Max	0.6999	0.9744	1.3549	0.0326	0.0640	0.1261
Environmental (C2)	C21. Recycle	Max	0.6329	0.8985	1.2983	0.0295	0.0591	0.1208
	C22. Disposal	Max	0.5795	0.8318	1.2241	0.0270	0.0547	0.1139
	C23. Reproduction and reuse	Max	0.7801	1.0897	1.4672	0.0364	0.0716	0.1366
	C24. Green technology	Max	0.7869	1.0865	1.4525	0.0367	0.0714	0.1352
	C25. CO_2 emissions	Min	0.6196	0.8559	1.2218	0.0289	0.0563	0.1137
Social (C3)	C31. Health and safety	Max	0.5680	0.7661	1.0838	0.0265	0.0504	0.1009
	C32. Customer's voice	Max	0.9029	1.2784	1.7677	0.0421	0.0840	0.1645
	C33. Reputation	Max	0.6239	0.8631	1.2284	0.0291	0.0567	0.1143
Risk (C4)	C41. Operational risk	Min	0.5917	0.8153	1.1728	0.0276	0.0536	0.1092
	C42. Financial risk	Min	0.6831	0.9483	1.3387	0.0318	0.0623	0.1246

Note: calculated by the researchers.

Figure 5 depicts the influence levels of criteria. As can be seen, "lead time", "customer's voice", "cost", "delivery and service", and "quality" criteria have the most influence percentages, at 8.4559%, 8.3087%, and 7.9628%, 7.6185%, and 7.58%, respectively. Regarding economic factors in choosing 3PRLPs in the e-commerce sector, the results recommend that "lead time" is more critical in experts' evaluation than other cost and quality issues. For e-commerce businesses, lead times are a significant measure when figuring out inventory management strategy, which is the primary estimator for when the managers reorder stock. It is also an especially concerning factor when adding new product lines to the online store. The new products will have their lead times that may be separate from regularly scheduled deliveries. "Customer's voice" (as a social criterion) is also positioned second in the expert ranking. This result shows that information sharing, and customer engagement are key determinants of reverse logistics in the e-commerce industry [5]. In the booming e-commerce market of Vietnam, e-commerce businesses are attempting to survive and thrive by focusing more on economic aspects. However, green and resilient strategies towards sustainable development have come into focus. In order to enhance the competitiveness of Vietnamese businesses, the government encourages enterprises to participate effectively in the global value chain by embracing and integrating sustainable business strategies [65]. Thus, the criteria ranking results indicate that economic criteria were ranked high, but the other criteria from the three pillars of sustainable development (social and environmental factors) were also noteworthy. Among environmental factors, "reproduction and reuse" and "green technology" ranked sixth (6.9908%) and seventh (6.9550%) among 15 criteria. These figures elaborate that social and environmental drivers are of tremendous importance in reverse logistics systems besides economic aspects.

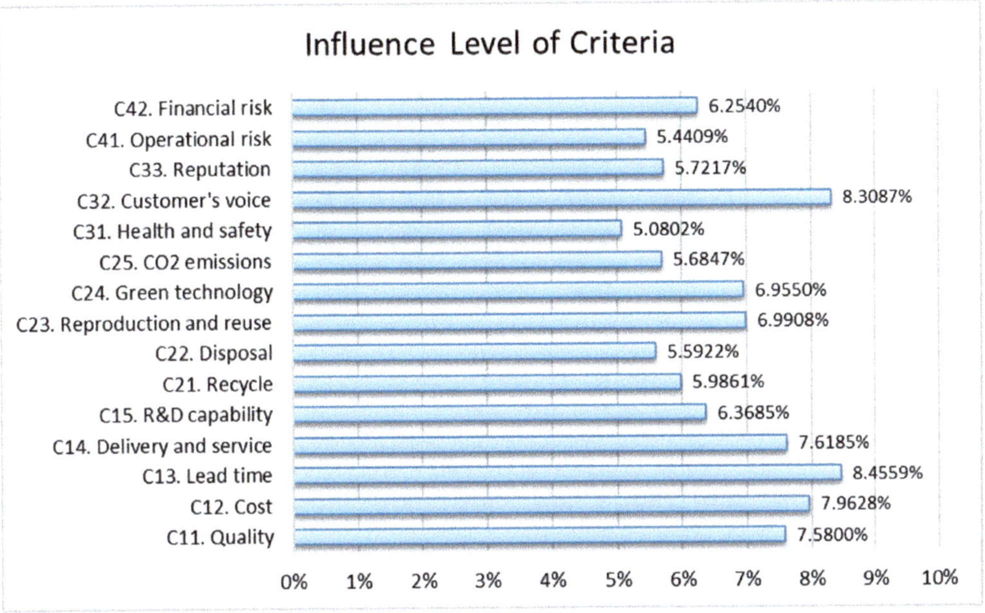

Figure 5. Influence level of criteria from FAHP model.

4.3. Results of Fuzzy TOPSIS

In FTOPSIS model, the fuzzy preference weights of criteria are obtained from FAHP model. According to the FTOPSIS process in Section 3.4, fuzzy normalized decision matrix and fuzzy weighted normalized decision matrix are shown in Tables A2 and A3 (Appendix A). Table 10 and Figure 6 show the top three potential third-party reverse logistics providers, which are 3PRLP-05, 3PRLP-07, and 3PRLP-01, ranked first, second, and third with scores of 0.0590, 0.0506, and 0.0513, respectively.

Table 10. Closeness coefficient of each alternative.

3PRLP	D_i^*	$D_i^{'}$	Gap Degree	Satisfaction Degree	Rank
3PRLP-01	14.3560	0.7756	0.9487	0.0513	3
3PRLP-02	14.5155	0.6184	0.9591	0.0409	6
3PRLP-03	14.4158	0.7260	0.9521	0.0479	4
3PRLP-04	14.5380	0.5851	0.9613	0.0387	8
3PRLP-05	14.2550	0.8943	0.9410	0.0590	1
3PRLP-06	14.5211	0.6152	0.9594	0.0406	7
3PRLP-07	14.3579	0.8446	0.9444	0.0556	2
3PRLP-08	14.5020	0.6222	0.9589	0.0411	5

Note: calculated by the researchers.

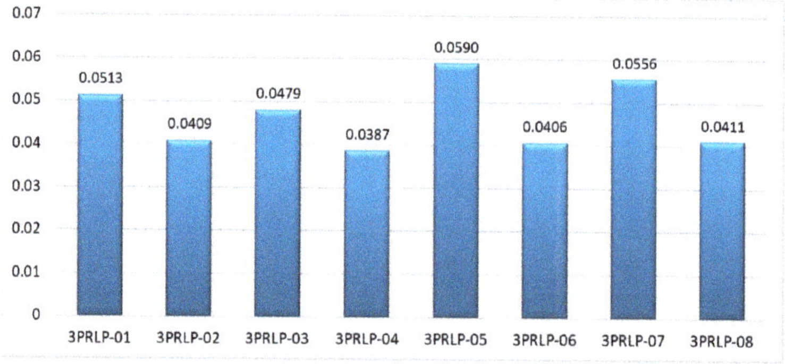

Figure 6. Final ranking of the FTOPSIS model.

5. Discussion and Conclusions

As online shopping volumes grow, so do return volumes. Product return rates are rising in the e-commerce industry. The cost of doing e-commerce business is facilitating a simple and seamless return processes as part of the increase in customer expectations. This is where reverse logistics comes into its unique role, which is to handle many inevitable situations regarding e-commerce transactions, including deliveries of incorrect products, customer behaviors, damaged products, delays in order fulfillment, to name just a few [66]. It cannot be failed to mention that reverse logistics systems, in essence, provide businesses with numerous opportunities to integrate the three drivers of sustainable development, such as remanufacturing, repair, recycle, and disposal. There is no question that proficient reverse logistics not only handles the e-commerce returns problem but also enables any business to gain customer retention, reduced costs, and higher achievement of sustainability goals. However, managing reverse logistics in-house means the supply chain of moving goods must be amplified, which leads companies to significant issues. For this reason, more and more e-commerce retailers consider reverse logistics outsourcing as an inevitable part of their business. Thus, the evaluation and selection problem of 3PRLP has never been so prominent in this era.

Methodologically, the authors elaborate that in using the proposed hybrid MCDM approach (combining FAHP and FTOPSIS), this has so far been the first study to fill the gap of the existing literature that lacks 3PRLP evaluation and selection practices for several industries within a developing countries context, and especially to address the increased demand of reverse logistics outsourcing in the e-commerce sector. The use of linguistic expressions for the whole evaluation process will mitigate the risk of fuzzy and uncertain judgment when weighing criteria, as well as improving the robustness of the ranking results and the overall computation efficiency. Proper transformations of linguistic terms also ensures that the approach has a broad range of applications.

E-commerce has been on the rise in Vietnam. By 2025, e-commerce purchases are projected to be used by over 70 percent of the 100 million population. Regarding the e-commerce logistics sector, it has contributed to approximately 20–25% of the GDP of Vietnam, according to Vietnam Logistics Business Association [67]. This industry is also predicted to grow by roughly 12 percent every year. Thus, more and more logistics companies and investors are flooding into this untapped potential market. On the other hand, the dilemma of outsourcing logistics services and the decision to select a provider based on quality management and financial performance criteria are sure to be a headache facing e-commerce retailers. Within this context, our paper aims to provide significant insights for online merchants on the methods of evaluation and selection of 3PRLP. In doing so, the proposed approach is applied to illustrate a case study of the reverse logistics outsourcing problem in Vietnam. From the FAHP stage, results show that "lead time," "cost," "delivery and service," and "quality" (economic factors) and "customer's voice" (social factor) are the most impactful criteria according to expert evaluation. Environmental drivers such as "reproduction and reuse" and "green technology" were also ranked high, indicating the other aspect from the three pillars of sustainable development were noteworthy in reverse logistics outsourcing of e-commerce in Vietnam. In the next stage, FTOPSIS indicates that 3PRLP-05 was the optimized partner with the final ranking score of 0.059. For practical implications, these findings can help e-commerce businesses or any firms to gain a better understanding of the 3PRLP selection process. Thus, the companies can devise their strategies accordingly to better control their reverse logistics activities.

For future studies involving qualitative and quantitative criteria, new factors concerning today's situation (i.e., post-Covid-19 world) should be upgraded to obtain well-rounded results. Regarding theoretical limitations, this paper calculated the consistency ratio using lower bound (pessimistic value) and upper bound (optimistic value) values of the fuzzy comparison matrix, hence, future studies should approach the procedure of defuzzification according to the derivate fuzzy AHP [68]. Moreover, future studies should target other MCDM techniques (i.e., VIKOR, PROMETHEE II) for ranking alternatives and compare the results using ranking similarity reference coefficients [69], and/or combine with the exact methods [70]. In terms of applications, further studies might therefore investigate reverse logistics outsourcing practices in other countries than Vietnam to improve the findings' external validity. Moreover, the procedure and criteria presented in this paper can also be considered in other related industries, such as supplier selection or any decision-making problems.

Author Contributions: Conceptualization, C.-N.W. and T.-T.D.; Data curation, T.-T.D.; Formal analysis, T.-T.D. and N.-A.-T.N.; Funding acquisition, C.-N.W.; Investigation, T.-T.D. and N.-A.-T.N.; Methodology, C.-N.W. and T.-T.D.; Project administration, C.-N.W.; Software, T.-T.D. and N.-A.-T.N.; Validation, C.-N.W. and T.-T.D.; Writing—original draft, T.-T.D. and N.-A.-T.N.; Writing—review and editing, C.-N.W. and N.-A.-T.N. All authors have read and agreed to the published version of the manuscript.

Funding: This research was partly supported by the National Kaohsiung University of Science and Technology, and MOST 109-2622-E-992-026 from the Ministry of Sciences and Technology in Taiwan.

Institutional Review Board Statement: Not applicable.

Informed Consent Statement: Not applicable.

Data Availability Statement: Not applicable.

Acknowledgments: The authors appreciate the support from the National Kaohsiung University of Science and Technology, Ministry of Sciences and Technology in Taiwan.

Conflicts of Interest: The authors declare no conflict of interest.

Appendix A

Table A1. Integrated fuzzy comparison matrix of 15 criteria (FAHP).

Criteria		C11			C12			C13			C14	
C11	1	1	1	1.0592	1.6632	2.4208	0.7192	1.0414	1.5337	0.5234	0.7800	1.2457
C12	0.4131	0.6012	0.9441	1	1	1	0.9883	1.4902	2.1074	0.9221	1.4310	2.0477
C13	0.6520	0.9603	1.3904	0.4745	0.6711	1.0118	1	1	1	1.2671	1.9896	2.7808
C14	0.8027	1.2821	1.9105	0.4884	0.6988	1.0845	0.3596	0.5026	0.7892	1	1	1
C15	0.5086	0.7490	1.1623	0.4745	0.6711	1.0118	0.5086	0.7490	1.1623	0.2928	0.4131	0.6520
C21	0.4131	0.6012	0.9441	0.4131	0.5610	0.8459	0.4131	0.6012	0.9441	0.4131	0.6012	0.9441
C22	0.4131	0.6012	0.9441	0.4131	0.5610	0.8459	0.4131	0.6012	0.9441	0.4131	0.6012	0.9441
C23	0.5086	0.7490	1.1623	0.4745	0.6711	1.0118	0.9221	1.4310	2.1550	1.7617	2.6531	3.4783
C24	0.9221	1.4310	2.1550	0.7892	1.0592	1.3653	0.2131	0.2732	0.3854	0.5086	0.7490	1.1623
C25	0.5086	0.7490	1.1623	0.8262	1.2457	1.8346	0.2928	0.4131	0.6520	0.5086	0.7490	1.1623

Table A1. *Cont.*

Criteria	**C11**			**C12**			**C13**			**C14**		
C31	0.9221	1.4310	2.1550	0.3596	0.4690	0.7071	0.2378	0.2928	0.3854	0.5086	0.7490	1.1623
C32	0.5086	0.7490	1.1623	0.8262	1.2457	1.8346	0.9221	1.4310	2.1550	0.9221	1.4310	2.1550
C33	0.5086	0.7490	1.1623	0.8262	1.2457	1.8346	0.9221	1.4310	2.1550	0.5086	0.7490	1.1623
C41	0.5086	0.7490	1.1623	0.4745	0.6711	1.0118	0.9221	1.4310	2.1550	0.5086	0.7490	1.1623
C42	0.9221	1.4310	2.1550	0.4745	0.6711	1.0118	0.5086	0.7490	1.1623	0.2928	0.4131	0.6520
Criteria	**C15**			**C21**			**C22**			**C23**		
C11	0.8604	1.3351	1.9663	1.0592	1.6632	2.4208	1.0592	1.6632	2.4208	0.8604	1.3351	1.9663
C12	0.9883	1.4902	2.1074	1.1822	1.7826	2.4208	1.1822	1.7826	2.4208	0.9883	1.4902	2.1074
C13	0.8604	1.3351	1.9663	1.0592	1.6632	2.4208	1.0592	1.6632	2.4208	0.4640	0.6988	1.0845
C14	1.5337	2.4208	3.4154	1.0592	1.6632	2.4208	1.0592	1.6632	2.4208	0.2875	0.3769	0.5676
C15	1	1	1	0.6988	1.0718	1.5971	0.6988	1.0718	1.5971	2.1074	2.7922	3.4154
C21	0.6261	0.9330	1.4310	1	1	1	0.9221	1.3351	1.8346	0.2875	0.3769	0.5676
C22	0.6261	0.9330	1.4310	0.5451	0.7490	1.0845	1	1	1	1.5337	2.4208	3.4154
C23	0.2928	0.3581	0.4745	1.7617	2.6531	3.4783	0.2928	0.4131	0.6520	1	1	1
C24	0.2928	0.3581	0.4745	1.7617	2.6531	3.4783	1.7617	2.6531	3.4783	0.5086	0.6520	0.9330
C25	0.6261	0.8706	1.2821	0.4973	0.7277	1.1161	0.9221	1.4310	2.1550	0.9221	1.2457	1.7299
C31	0.6261	0.8706	1.2821	0.4884	0.7117	1.0845	0.5086	0.7490	1.1623	0.5086	0.6520	0.9330
C32	1.6917	2.4307	3.0837	0.5234	0.7800	1.2457	0.5086	0.7490	1.1623	0.9221	1.2457	1.7299
C33	0.6261	0.8706	1.2821	0.6335	0.8604	1.1623	0.5086	0.7490	1.1623	0.2928	0.3854	0.5842
C41	0.6261	0.8706	1.2821	0.2928	0.4131	0.6520	0.9221	1.4310	2.1550	0.5086	0.6520	0.9330
C42	1.0718	1.4727	1.9744	0.5086	0.7490	1.1623	0.9221	1.4310	2.1550	0.9221	1.2457	1.7299
Criteria	**C24**			**C25**			**C31**			**C32**		
C11	0.4640	0.6988	1.0845	0.8604	1.3351	1.9663	0.4640	0.6988	1.0845	0.8604	1.3351	1.9663
C12	0.7325	0.9441	1.2671	0.5451	0.8027	1.2104	1.4142	2.1324	2.7808	0.5451	0.8027	1.2104
C13	2.5946	3.6606	4.6932	1.5337	2.4208	3.4154	2.5946	3.4154	4.2049	0.4640	0.6988	1.0845
C14	0.8604	1.3351	1.9663	0.8604	1.3351	1.9663	0.8604	1.3351	1.9663	0.4640	0.6988	1.0845
C15	2.1074	2.7922	3.4154	0.7800	1.1487	1.5971	0.7800	1.1487	1.5971	0.3243	0.4114	0.5911
C21	0.2875	0.3769	0.5676	0.8960	1.3741	2.0107	0.9221	1.4051	2.0477	0.8027	1.2821	1.9105
C22	0.2875	0.3769	0.5676	0.4640	0.6988	1.0845	0.8604	1.3351	1.9663	0.8604	1.3351	1.9663
C23	1.0718	1.5337	1.9663	0.5781	0.8027	1.0845	1.0718	1.5337	1.9663	0.5781	0.8027	1.0845
C24	1	1	1	1.0718	1.5337	1.9663	0.5781	0.8027	1.0845	1.0718	1.5337	1.9663
C25	0.5086	0.6520	0.9330	1	1	1	0.7490	1.0718	1.4902	0.4640	0.6084	0.8706
C31	0.9221	1.2457	1.7299	0.6711	0.9330	1.3351	1	1	1	0.4040	0.5086	0.7277
C32	0.5086	0.6520	0.9330	1.1487	1.6438	2.1550	1.3741	1.9663	2.4754	1	1	1
C33	0.4040	0.5451	0.8123	0.6711	0.9330	1.3351	1.1487	1.6438	2.1550	0.6711	0.9330	1.3351
C41	0.4040	0.5451	0.8123	0.6711	0.9330	1.3351	0.6711	0.9330	1.3351	0.4040	0.5451	0.8123
C42	0.6711	0.9330	1.3351	1.1487	1.6438	2.1550	0.6711	0.9330	1.3351	0.2732	0.3517	0.5086
Criteria	**C33**			**C41**			**C42**					
C11	0.8604	1.3351	1.9663	0.8604	1.3351	1.9663	0.4640	0.6988	1.0845			
C12	0.5451	0.8027	1.2104	0.9883	1.4902	2.1074	0.9883	1.4902	2.1074			
C13	0.4640	0.6988	1.0845	0.4640	0.6988	1.0845	0.8604	1.3351	1.9663			
C14	0.8604	1.3351	1.9663	0.8604	1.3351	1.9663	1.5337	2.4208	3.4154			
C15	0.7800	1.1487	1.5971	0.7800	1.1487	1.5971	0.5065	0.6790	0.9330			
C21	0.8604	1.1623	1.5784	1.5337	2.4208	3.4154	0.8604	1.3351	1.9663			
C22	0.8604	1.3351	1.9663	0.4640	0.6988	1.0845	0.4640	0.6988	1.0845			
C23	1.7118	2.5946	3.4154	1.0718	1.5337	1.9663	0.5781	0.8027	1.0845			
C24	1.2311	1.8346	2.4754	1.2311	1.8346	2.4754	0.7490	1.0718	1.4902			
C25	0.7490	1.0718	1.4902	0.7490	1.0718	1.4902	0.4640	0.6084	0.8706			
C31	0.4640	0.6084	0.8706	0.7490	1.0718	1.4902	0.7490	1.0718	1.4902			
C32	0.7490	1.0718	1.4902	1.2311	1.8346	2.4754	1.9663	2.8435	3.6606			
C33	1	1	1	0.4640	0.6084	0.8706	0.7490	1.0718	1.4902			
C41	1.1487	1.6438	2.1550	1	1	1	0.4640	0.6084	0.8706			
C42	0.6711	0.9330	1.3351	1.1487	1.6438	2.1550	1	1	1			

Note: calculated by the researchers.

Table A2. Fuzzy normalized decision matrix of all alternatives (FTOPSIS).

3PRLP	Quality			Cost			Lead Time			Delivery and Service		
3PRLP-01	0.5054	0.6882	0.8280	0.0800	0.0952	0.1277	0.0779	0.0938	0.1277	0.4409	0.6237	0.7957
3PRLP-02	0.1505	0.2796	0.4731	0.1500	0.2500	0.4286	0.1579	0.3000	0.7500	0.1720	0.3011	0.4839
3PRLP-03	0.3441	0.5376	0.7419	0.0923	0.1250	0.1875	0.1017	0.1500	0.2727	0.3656	0.5591	0.7527
3PRLP-04	0.1505	0.2796	0.4516	0.1429	0.2308	0.4286	0.1429	0.2308	0.4286	0.1505	0.2796	0.4516
3PRLP-05	0.6237	0.8387	1.0000	0.0645	0.0769	0.1034	0.0645	0.0769	0.1034	0.6237	0.8387	1.0000
3PRLP-06	0.0645	0.1613	0.3441	0.1875	0.4000	1.0000	0.1875	0.4000	1.0000	0.0645	0.1613	0.3441
3PRLP-07	0.5161	0.7097	0.8817	0.0732	0.0909	0.1250	0.0732	0.0909	0.1250	0.5161	0.7097	0.8817
3PRLP-08	0.2688	0.4409	0.6452	0.1000	0.1463	0.2400	0.1000	0.1463	0.2400	0.2688	0.4409	0.6452

3PRLP	R&D Capability			Recycle			Disposal			Reproduction and Reuse		
3PRLP-01	0.5269	0.6989	0.8280	0.5054	0.6882	0.8280	0.5054	0.6882	0.8280	0.5165	0.7033	0.8462
3PRLP-02	0.1505	0.2796	0.4731	0.1505	0.2796	0.4731	0.1505	0.2796	0.4731	0.1538	0.2857	0.4835
3PRLP-03	0.3656	0.5484	0.7419	0.3441	0.5376	0.7419	0.3441	0.5376	0.7419	0.3516	0.5495	0.7582
3PRLP-04	0.1505	0.2796	0.4516	0.1505	0.2796	0.4516	0.1505	0.2796	0.4516	0.1538	0.2857	0.4615
3PRLP-05	0.6237	0.8387	1.0000	0.6237	0.8387	1.0000	0.6237	0.8387	1.0000	0.6154	0.8352	1.0000
3PRLP-06	0.0645	0.1613	0.3441	0.0645	0.1398	0.3011	0.0645	0.1398	0.3011	0.0220	0.1209	0.3077
3PRLP-07	0.5161	0.7097	0.8817	0.5161	0.7097	0.8817	0.5161	0.7097	0.8817	0.4835	0.6813	0.8571
3PRLP-08	0.2688	0.4409	0.6452	0.2688	0.4301	0.6237	0.2688	0.4301	0.6237	0.1648	0.3407	0.5495

3PRLP	Green Technology			CO_2 Emissions			Health and Safety			Customer's Voice		
3PRLP-01	0.5402	0.7356	0.8851	0.0779	0.0938	0.1277	0.5281	0.7191	0.8652	0.5949	0.8101	0.9747
3PRLP-02	0.1609	0.2989	0.5057	0.1364	0.2308	0.4286	0.1573	0.2921	0.4944	0.1772	0.3291	0.5570
3PRLP-03	0.3678	0.5747	0.7931	0.0870	0.1200	0.1875	0.3596	0.5618	0.7753	0.4051	0.6329	0.8734
3PRLP-04	0.1839	0.3218	0.5057	0.1429	0.2308	0.4286	0.1011	0.2360	0.4270	0.3797	0.5316	0.7089
3PRLP-05	0.5977	0.8276	1.0000	0.0645	0.0723	0.0882	0.6180	0.8315	1.0000	0.3291	0.5823	0.8228
3PRLP-06	0.1149	0.2184	0.4138	0.1875	0.4000	1.0000	0.2022	0.4045	0.6292	0.1772	0.2911	0.4810
3PRLP-07	0.5287	0.7356	0.9195	0.0732	0.0938	0.1364	0.4270	0.5730	0.7416	0.6076	0.8354	1.0000
3PRLP-08	0.3563	0.5402	0.7586	0.1000	0.1463	0.2400	0.1910	0.3596	0.5843	0.4684	0.6709	0.8481

3PRLP	Reputation			Operational Risk			Financial Risk		
3PRLP-01	0.5054	0.6882	0.8280	0.1818	0.2188	0.2979	0.1818	0.2188	0.2979
3PRLP-02	0.1505	0.2796	0.4731	0.3182	0.5385	1.0000	0.2857	0.4118	0.6364
3PRLP-03	0.3441	0.5376	0.7419	0.2029	0.2800	0.4375	0.1918	0.2414	0.3500
3PRLP-04	0.1505	0.2796	0.4516	0.3333	0.5385	1.0000	0.2500	0.3333	0.4667
3PRLP-05	0.6237	0.8387	1.0000	0.2414	0.3684	0.6087	0.2154	0.3043	0.5385
3PRLP-06	0.1613	0.2903	0.4731	0.2090	0.2545	0.3415	0.3684	0.6087	1.0000
3PRLP-07	0.2903	0.4516	0.6237	0.1707	0.2121	0.2917	0.1772	0.2121	0.2917
3PRLP-08	0.0860	0.2258	0.4301	0.1892	0.2456	0.3590	0.2090	0.2642	0.3784

Note: calculated by the researchers.

Table A3. Fuzzy weighted normalized decision matrix (FTOPSIS).

3PRLP	Quality			Cost			Lead Time			Delivery and Service		
3PRLP-01	0.0180	0.0516	0.1279	0.0032	0.0077	0.0202	0.0032	0.0079	0.0217	0.0160	0.0471	0.1230
3PRLP-02	0.0054	0.0210	0.0731	0.0059	0.0201	0.0679	0.0065	0.0254	0.1274	0.0062	0.0228	0.0748
3PRLP-03	0.0123	0.0403	0.1146	0.0036	0.0101	0.0297	0.0042	0.0127	0.0463	0.0133	0.0423	0.1164
3PRLP-04	0.0054	0.0210	0.0698	0.0056	0.0186	0.0679	0.0059	0.0196	0.0728	0.0055	0.0211	0.0698
3PRLP-05	0.0222	0.0629	0.1545	0.0025	0.0062	0.0164	0.0027	0.0065	0.0176	0.0226	0.0634	0.1546
3PRLP-06	0.0023	0.0121	0.0532	0.0074	0.0322	0.1585	0.0077	0.0339	0.1698	0.0023	0.0122	0.0532
3PRLP-07	0.0184	0.0532	0.1362	0.0029	0.0073	0.0198	0.0030	0.0077	0.0212	0.0187	0.0537	0.1363
3PRLP-08	0.0096	0.0331	0.0997	0.0040	0.0118	0.0380	0.0041	0.0124	0.0408	0.0098	0.0333	0.0997

3PRLP	R&D Capability			Recycle			Disposal			Reproduction and Reuse		
3PRLP-01	0.0172	0.0448	0.1044	0.0149	0.0406	0.1001	0.0136	0.0376	0.0943	0.0188	0.0504	0.1156
3PRLP-02	0.0049	0.0179	0.0597	0.0044	0.0165	0.0572	0.0041	0.0153	0.0539	0.0056	0.0205	0.0660
3PRLP-03	0.0119	0.0351	0.0936	0.0101	0.0317	0.0897	0.0093	0.0294	0.0845	0.0128	0.0394	0.1035
3PRLP-04	0.0049	0.0179	0.0570	0.0044	0.0165	0.0546	0.0041	0.0153	0.0515	0.0056	0.0205	0.0630

Table A3. *Cont.*

3PRLP	R&D Capability			Recycle			Disposal			Reproduction and Reuse		
3PRLP-05	0.0203	0.0537	0.1261	0.0184	0.0495	0.1208	0.0168	0.0459	0.1139	0.0224	0.0598	0.1366
3PRLP-06	0.0021	0.0103	0.0434	0.0019	0.0083	0.0364	0.0017	0.0076	0.0343	0.0008	0.0087	0.0420
3PRLP-07	0.0168	0.0455	0.1112	0.0152	0.0419	0.1066	0.0139	0.0388	0.1005	0.0176	0.0488	0.1171
3PRLP-08	0.0088	0.0282	0.0814	0.0079	0.0254	0.0754	0.0073	0.0235	0.0711	0.0060	0.0244	0.0750
3PRLP	**Green Technology**			**CO_2 Emissions**			**Health and Safety**			**Customer's Voice**		
3PRLP-01	0.0198	0.0525	0.1197	0.0023	0.0053	0.0145	0.0140	0.0362	0.0873	0.0250	0.0681	0.1604
3PRLP-02	0.0059	0.0213	0.0684	0.0039	0.0130	0.0487	0.0042	0.0147	0.0499	0.0075	0.0277	0.0916
3PRLP-03	0.0135	0.0410	0.1072	0.0025	0.0068	0.0213	0.0095	0.0283	0.0782	0.0170	0.0532	0.1437
3PRLP-04	0.0067	0.0230	0.0684	0.0041	0.0130	0.0487	0.0027	0.0119	0.0431	0.0160	0.0447	0.1166
3PRLP-05	0.0219	0.0591	0.1352	0.0019	0.0041	0.0100	0.0164	0.0419	0.1009	0.0138	0.0489	0.1354
3PRLP-06	0.0042	0.0156	0.0559	0.0054	0.0225	0.1137	0.0054	0.0204	0.0635	0.0075	0.0245	0.0791
3PRLP-07	0.0194	0.0525	0.1243	0.0021	0.0053	0.0155	0.0113	0.0289	0.0748	0.0256	0.0702	0.1645
3PRLP-08	0.0131	0.0386	0.1026	0.0029	0.0082	0.0273	0.0051	0.0181	0.0589	0.0197	0.0564	0.1395
3PRLP	**Reputation**			**Operational Risk**			**Financial Risk**					
3PRLP-01	0.0147	0.0390	0.0947	0.0050	0.0117	0.0325	0.0058	0.0136	0.0371			
3PRLP-02	0.0044	0.0159	0.0541	0.0088	0.0289	0.1092	0.0091	0.0257	0.0793			
3PRLP-03	0.0100	0.0305	0.0848	0.0056	0.0150	0.0478	0.0061	0.0150	0.0436			
3PRLP-04	0.0044	0.0159	0.0516	0.0092	0.0289	0.1092	0.0080	0.0208	0.0581			
3PRLP-05	0.0181	0.0476	0.1143	0.0067	0.0197	0.0664	0.0069	0.0190	0.0671			
3PRLP-06	0.0047	0.0165	0.0541	0.0058	0.0136	0.0373	0.0117	0.0379	0.1246			
3PRLP-07	0.0084	0.0256	0.0713	0.0047	0.0114	0.0318	0.0056	0.0132	0.0363			
3PRLP-08	0.0025	0.0128	0.0492	0.0052	0.0132	0.0392	0.0067	0.0165	0.0471			

Note: calculated by the researchers.

References

1. Sahay, B.S.; Srivastava, S.K.; Srivastava, R.K. Managing Product Returns for Reverse Logistics. *Int. J. Phys. Distrib. Logist. Manag.* **2006**, *36*, 524–546.
2. E-Commerce Product Return Rate. Available online: https://www.invespcro.com/blog/ecommerce-product-return-rate-statistics/ (accessed on 5 February 2021).
3. Reverse Logistics Market. Available online: https://www.alliedmarketresearch.com/press-release/reverse-logistics-market.html#:~:text=According%20to%20a%20recent%20report,reach%20%24603.9%20billion%20by%202025%2C (accessed on 5 February 2021).
4. The Importance of Reverse Logistics for E-Commerce. Available online: https://www.thebalancesmb.com/what-is-reverse-logistics-and-why-is-it-important-1141742 (accessed on 5 February 2021).
5. Chen, Z.S.; Zhang, X.; Govindan, K.; Wang, X.J.; Chin, K.S. Third-party reverse logistics provider selection: A computational semantic analysis-based multi-perspective multi-attribute decision-making approach. *Expert Syst. Appl.* **2021**, *166*, 114051. [CrossRef]
6. E-Commerce SEA 2019. Available online: https://www.blog.google/documents/47/SEA_Internet_Economy_Report_2019.pdf (accessed on 5 February 2021).
7. E-Commerce on an Upward Trajectory. Available online: https://www.vietnam-briefing.com/news/why-you-should-invest-vietnams-e-commerce-industry.html/#:~{}:text=E%2Dcommerce%20has%20been%20on,be%20using%20e%2Dcommerce%20transactions (accessed on 5 February 2021).
8. Thriving E-Commerce Market in Vietnam. Available online: https://www.cekindo.vn/blog/e-commerce-logistics-vietnam (accessed on 5 February 2021).
9. E-Commerce Market in Vietnam 2020. Available online: https://blog.tomorrowmarketers.org/toan-canh-ve-thi-truong-e-logistics-tai-viet-nam/ (accessed on 5 February 2021).
10. Lin, M.C.; Wang, C.C.; Chen, M.S.; Chang, C.A. Using AHP and TOPSIS Approaches in Customer-Driven Product Design Process. *Comput. Ind.* **2008**, *59*, 17–31. [CrossRef]
11. Solangi, Y.A.; Tan, Q.; Mirjat, N.H.; Valasai, G.D.; Khan, M.W.A.; Ikram, M. An Integrated Delphi-AHP and Fuzzy TOPSIS Approach Toward Ranking and Selection of Renewable Energy Resources in Pakistan. *Processes* **2019**, *7*, 118. [CrossRef]
12. Musaad, O.A.S.; Zhuo, Z.; Siyal, Z.A.; Shaikh, G.M.; Shah, S.A.A.; Solangi, Y.A.; Musaad, O.A.O. An Integrated Multi-Criteria Decision Support Framework for the Selection of Suppliers in Small and Medium Enterprises Based on Green Innovation Ability. *Processes* **2020**, *8*, 418. [CrossRef]
13. Qian, X.; Fang, S.C.; Yin, M.; Huang, M.; Li, X. Selecting green third-party logistics providers for a loss-averse fourth party logistics provider in a multi-attribute reverse auction. *Inf. Sci.* **2021**, *548*, 357–377. [CrossRef]

14. Stekelorum, R.; Laguir, I.; Gupta, S.; Kumar, S. Green supply chain management practices and third-party logistics providers' performances: A fuzzy-set approach. *Int. J. Prod. Econ.* **2021**, *235*, 108093. [CrossRef]
15. Tosarkani, B.M.; Amin, S.H. A multi-objective model to configure an electronic reverse logistics network and third party selection. *J. Clean. Prod.* **2018**, *198*, 662–682. [CrossRef]
16. Garetti, M.; Taisch, M. Sustainable manufacturing: Trends and research challenges. *Prod. Plan. Control* **2012**, *23*, 83–104. [CrossRef]
17. Zarbakhshnia, N.; Wu, Y.; Govindan, K.; Soleimani, H. A Novel Hybrid Multiple Attribute Decision-Making Approach for Outsourcing Sustainable Reverse Logistics. *J. Clean. Prod.* **2020**, *242*, 118461. [CrossRef]
18. Tavana, M.; Zareinejad, M.; Di Caprio, D.; Kaviani, M.A. An Integrated Intuitionistic Fuzzy AHP and SWOT Method for Outsourcing Reverse Logistics. *Appl. Soft Comput.* **2016**, *40*, 544–557. [CrossRef]
19. Bai, C.; Sarkis, J. Integrating and Extending Data and Decision Tools for Sustainable Third-Party Reverse Logistics Provider Selection. *Comput. Oper. Res.* **2019**, *110*, 188–207. [CrossRef]
20. Bai, C.; Sarkis, J.; Dou, Y. Corporate Sustainability Development in China: Review and Analysis. *Ind. Manag. Data Syst.* **2015**, *115*, 5–40. [CrossRef]
21. Govindan, K.; Cheng, T.C.E. Sustainable Supply Chain Management. *Comput. Oper. Res.* **2015**, *54*, 177–179. [CrossRef]
22. Centobelli, P.; Cerchione, R.; Esposito, E. Environmental Sustainability in the Service Industry of Transportation and Logistics Service Providers: Systematic Literature Review and Research Directions. *Transp. Res. Part D Transp. Environ.* **2017**, *53*, 454–470. [CrossRef]
23. Korpela, J.; Tuominen, M. A Decision Aid in Warehouse Site Selection. *Int. J. Prod. Econ.* **1996**, *45*, 169–180. [CrossRef]
24. So, S.H.; Kim, J.; Cheong, K.; Cho, G. Evaluating the Service Quality of Third-Party Logistics Service Providers Using the Analytic Hierarchy Process. *JISTEM J. Inf. Syst. Technol. Manag.* **2006**, *3*, 261–270.
25. Göl, H.; Çatay, B. Third-Party Logistics Provider Selection: Insights from a Turkish Automotive Company. *Int. J. Supply Chain Manag.* **2007**, *12*, 379–384. [CrossRef]
26. Falsini, D.; Fondi, F.; Schiraldi, M.M. A Logistics Provider Evaluation and Selection Methodology Based on AHP, DEA and Linear Programming Integration. *Int. J. Prod. Res.* **2012**, *50*, 4822–4829. [CrossRef]
27. Jayant, A.; Gupta, P.; Garg, S.K.; Khan, M. TOPSIS-AHP Based Approach for Selection of Reverse Logistics Service Provider: A Case Study of Mobile Phone Industry. *Procedia Eng.* **2014**, *97*, 2147–2156. [CrossRef]
28. Ho, W.; He, T.; Lee, C.K.M.; Emrouznejad, A. Strategic Logistics Outsourcing: An Integrated QFD and Fuzzy AHP Approach. *Expert Syst. Appl.* **2012**, *39*, 10841–10850. [CrossRef]
29. Ilgin, M.A. An Integrated Methodology for the Used Product Selection Problem Faced by Third-Party Reverse Logistics Providers. *Int. J. Sustain. Eng.* **2017**, *10*, 399–410. [CrossRef]
30. Thakkar, J.; Deshmukh, S.G.; Gupta, A.D.; Shankar, R. Selection of Third-Party Logistics (3PL): A Hybrid Approach Using Interpretive Structural Modeling (ISM) and Analytic Network Process (ANP). *Int. J. Supply Chain Forum* **2005**, *6*, 32–46. [CrossRef]
31. Liou, J.J.; Chuang, Y.T. Developing a Hybrid Multi-Criteria Model for Selection of Outsourcing Providers. *Expert Syst. Appl.* **2010**, *37*, 3755–3761. [CrossRef]
32. Hsu, C.C.; Liou, J.J.; Chuang, Y.C. Integrating DANP and Modified Grey Relation Theory for the Selection of an Outsourcing Provider. *Expert Syst. Appl.* **2013**, *40*, 2297–2304. [CrossRef]
33. Tadić, S.; Zečević, S.; Krstić, M. A Novel Hybrid MCDM Model Based on Fuzzy DEMATEL, Fuzzy ANP and Fuzzy VIKOR for City Logistics Concept Selection. *Expert Syst. Appl.* **2014**, *41*, 8112–8128. [CrossRef]
34. Kannan, G.; Pokharel, S.; Kumar, P.S. A Hybrid Approach Using ISM and Fuzzy TOPSIS for the Selection of Reverse Logistics Provider. *Resour. Conserv. Recycl.* **2009**, *54*, 28–36. [CrossRef]
35. Wang, Z.; Hao, H.; Gao, F.; Zhang, Q.; Zhang, J.; Zhou, Y. Multi-Attribute Decision Making on Reverse Logistics Based on DEA-TOPSIS: A Study of the Shanghai End-of-Life Vehicles Industry. *J. Clean. Prod.* **2019**, *214*, 730–737. [CrossRef]
36. Bottani, E.; Rizzi, A. A Fuzzy TOPSIS Methodology to Support Outsourcing of Logistics Services. *Int. J. Supply Chain Manag.* **2006**, *11*, 294–308. [CrossRef]
37. Sasikumar, P.; Haq, A.N. Integration of Closed Loop Distribution Supply Chain Network and 3PRLP Selection for the Case of Battery Recycling. *Int. J. Prod. Res.* **2011**, *49*, 3363–3385. [CrossRef]
38. Zarbakhshnia, N.; Soleimani, H.; Ghaderi, H. Sustainable Third-Party Reverse Logistics Provider Evaluation and Selection Using Fuzzy SWARA and Developed Fuzzy COPRAS in the Presence of Risk Criteria. *Appl. Soft Comput.* **2018**, *65*, 307–319. [CrossRef]
39. Agarwal, S.; Kant, R.; Shankar, R. Evaluating Solutions to Overcome Humanitarian Supply Chain Management Barriers: A Hybrid Fuzzy SWARA–Fuzzy WASPAS Approach. *Int. J. Disaster Risk Reduct.* **2020**, *51*, 101838. [CrossRef]
40. Perçin, S.; Min, H. A Hybrid Quality Function Deployment and Fuzzy Decision-Making Methodology for the Optimal Selection of Third-Party Logistics Service Providers. *Int. J. Logist. Res. Appl.* **2013**, *16*, 380–397. [CrossRef]
41. Zhou, G.; Min, H.; Xu, C.; Cao, Z. Evaluating the Comparative Efficiency of Chinese Third–Party Logistics Providers Using Data Envelopment Analysis. *Int. J. Phys. Distrib. Logist. Manag.* **2008**, *38*, 262–279. [CrossRef]
42. Hamdan, A.; Rogers, K.J. Evaluating the Efficiency of 3PL Logistics Operations. *Int. J. Prod. Econ.* **2008**, *113*, 235–244. [CrossRef]
43. Govindan, K.; Jha, P.C.; Agarwal, V.; Darbari, J.D. Environmental Management Partner Selection for Reverse Supply Chain Collaboration: A Sustainable Approach. *J. Environ. Manag.* **2019**, *236*, 784–797. [CrossRef] [PubMed]
44. Sahay, B.S.; Kumar, M.; Vrat, P.; Shankar, R. A Multi–Objective 3PL Allocation Problem for Fish Distribution. *Int. J. Phys. Distrib. Logist. Manag.* **2006**, *36*, 702–715.

45. Liu, H.T.; Wang, W.K. An Integrated Fuzzy Approach for Provider Evaluation and Selection in Third-Party Logistics. *Expert Syst. Appl.* **2009**, *36*, 4387–4398. [CrossRef]
46. Moberg, C.R.; Speh, T.W. Third–Party Warehousing Selection: A Comparison of National and Regional Firms. *Am. J. Bus.* **2004**, *19*, 71–76. [CrossRef]
47. Sinkovics, R.R.; Roath, A.S. Strategic Orientation, Capabilities, and Performance in Manufacturer—3PL Relationships. *J. Bus. Logist.* **2004**, *25*, 43–64. [CrossRef]
48. Yang, J.; Wang, J.; Wong, C.W.; Lai, K.H. Relational Stability and Alliance Performance in Supply Chain. *Omega* **2008**, *36*, 600–608. [CrossRef]
49. Saaty, T.L. *The Analytic Hierarchy Process*; McGraw-Hill International: New York, NY, USA, 1980.
50. Tzeng, G.H.; Huang, J.J. *Multiple Attribute Decision Making: Methods and Applications*; CRC Press-Taylor & Francic Group: New York, NY, USA, 2011.
51. Spencer, M.S.; Rogers, D.S.; Daugherty, P.J. JIT Systems and External Logistics Suppliers. *Int. J. Oper. Prod. Manag.* **1994**, *14*, 60–74. [CrossRef]
52. Tsai, M.C.; Wen, C.H.; Chen, C.S. Demand Choices of High-Tech Industry for Logistics Service Providers—An Empirical Case of an Offshore Science Park in Taiwan. *Ind. Mark. Manag.* **2007**, *36*, 617–626. [CrossRef]
53. Mavi, R.K.; Goh, M.; Zarbakhshnia, N. Sustainable Third-Party Reverse Logistic Provider Selection with Fuzzy SWARA and Fuzzy MOORA in Plastic Industry. *Int. J. Adv. Manuf. Technol.* **2017**, *91*, 2401–2418. [CrossRef]
54. Efendigil, T.; Önüt, S.; Kongar, E. A Holistic Approach for Selecting a Third-Party Reverse Logistics Provider in the Presence of Vagueness. *Comput. Ind. Eng.* **2008**, *54*, 269–287. [CrossRef]
55. Goebel, P.; Reuter, C.; Pibernik, R.; Sichtmann, C. The Influence of Ethical Culture on Supplier Selection in the Context of Sustainable Sourcing. *Int. J. Prod. Econ.* **2012**, *140*, 7–17. [CrossRef]
56. Ni, J.; Chu, L.K.; Yen, B.P. Coordinating Operational Policy with Financial Hedging for Risk-Averse Firms. *Omega* **2016**, *59*, 279–289. [CrossRef]
57. Da Silveira Guimarães, J.L.; Salomon, V.A.P. ANP Applied to the Evaluation of Performance Indicators of Reverse Logistics in Footwear Industry. *Procedia Comput. Sci.* **2015**, *55*, 139–148. [CrossRef]
58. Mitra, S.; Karathanasopoulos, A.; Sermpinis, G.; Dunis, C.; Hood, J. Operational Risk: Emerging Markets, Sectors and Measurement. *Eur. J. Oper. Res.* **2015**, *241*, 122–132. [CrossRef]
59. Zadeh, L.A. Fuzzy Sets. *Inf. Control* **1965**, *8*, 338–358. [CrossRef]
60. Sun, C.C. A Performance Evaluation Model by Integrating Fuzzy AHP and Fuzzy TOPSIS Methods. *Expert Syst. Appl.* **2010**, *37*, 7745–7754. [CrossRef]
61. Chen, C.T. Extensions of the TOPSIS for Group Decision-Making Under Fuzzy Environment. *Fuzzy Sets Syst.* **2000**, *114*, 1–9. [CrossRef]
62. Wang, C.-N.; Dang, T.-T.; Nguyen, N.-A.-T.; Le, T.-T.-H. Supporting Better Decision-Making: A Combined Grey Model and Data Envelopment Analysis for Efficiency Evaluation in E-Commerce Marketplaces. *Sustainability* **2020**, *12*, 10385. [CrossRef]
63. Chou, Y.C.; Yen, H.Y.; Dang, V.T.; Sun, C.C. Assessing the Human Resource in Science and Technology for Asian Countries: Application of Fuzzy AHP and Fuzzy TOPSIS. *Symmetry* **2019**, *11*, 251. [CrossRef]
64. Buckley, J.J. Ranking Alternatives Using Fuzzy Numbers. *Fuzzy Sets Syst.* **1985**, *15*, 21–31. [CrossRef]
65. Green Business in Vietnam. Available online: https://nangluongsachvietnam.vn/d6/vi-VN/news/Doanh-nghiep-huong-toi-phat-trien-xanh-ben-vung-6-1954-6822 (accessed on 8 March 2021).
66. Wang, C.-N.; Dang, T.-T.; Le, T.Q.; Kewcharoenwong, P. Transportation Optimization Models for Intermodal Networks with Fuzzy Node Capacity, Detour Factor, and Vehicle Utilization Constraints. *Mathematics* **2020**, *8*, 2109. [CrossRef]
67. E-Commerce Logistics: Emerging Opportunities in Vietnam. Available online: https://www.vietnam-briefing.com/news/e-commerce-logistics-emerging-opportunities-vietnam.html/ (accessed on 5 February 2021).
68. Tang, Y.-C.; Beynon, M.J. Application and Development of a Fuzzy Analytic Hierarchy Process within a Capital Investment Study. *J. Econ. Manag.* **2005**, *1*, 207–230.
69. Shekhovtsov, A.; Kozlov, V.; Nosov, V.; Sałabun, W. Efficiency of Methods for Determining the Relevance of Criteria in Sustainable Transport Problems: A Comparative Case Study. *Sustainability* **2020**, *12*, 7915. [CrossRef]
70. Wang, C.-N.; Nhieu, N.-L.; Chung, Y.-C.; Pham, H.-T. Multi-Objective Optimization Models for Sustainable Perishable Intermodal Multi-Product Networks with Delivery Time Window. *Mathematics* **2021**, *9*, 379. [CrossRef]

axioms

Article

Integrating the EBM Model and LTS(A,A,A) Model to Evaluate the Efficiency in the Supply Chain of Packaging Industry in Vietnam

Chia-Nan Wang [1,*], Quynh-Ngoc Hoang [1,*] and Thi-Kim-Lien Nguyen [2,*]

[1] Department of Industrial Engineering and Management, National Kaohsiung University of Science and Technology, Kaohsiung 80778, Taiwan
[2] Scientific Research—International Cooperation, Thanh Dong University, Hai Duong 171967, Vietnam
* Correspondence: cn.wang@nkust.edu.tw (C.-N.W.); quynhngoc.hoang3011@gmail.com (Q.-N.H.); lienntk@thanhdong.edu.vn (T.-K.-L.N.)

Abstract: In recent decades, Vietnamese labeling and packaging has been widely recognized as being one of the fastest developing industries in Vietnam, supported by the tremendous demand of domestic production and the exportation of its packaged goods. The emerging packaging technology trends and the participation of foreign direct investment (FDI) companies have led to fierce competition between all packaging enterprises in Vietnam. This paper aims to calculate the productivity performance of 10 packaging companies in Vietnam from the past to the future by combining the additive Holt-Winters (LTS(A,A,A)) model to predict key variables in the financial statement for the next 4 years (2020–2023) and an epsilon-based measure of efficiency (EBM) model of data envelopment analysis (DEA) to define the developing trend, efficiency, and ranking of packaging operations. The empirical results will assist packaging enterprises to identify their positions, suggest feasible solutions to overcome shortcomings and catch up with the global trends, and propose superior partnerships for manufacturers, which have packaging service demands and support investment decisions for investors. Overall, all the enterprises in the packaging industry have high productivity. In particular, SIVICO JSC is identified as the most efficient packaging company in Vietnam, as it continuously maintains the first ranking over the observation time, followed by Agriculture Printing & Packing JSC and Bien Hoa Packaging Company. In the past, Tan Dai Hung Plastic JSC was identified as the most unproductive unit, while in the future term, the inefficient decision-making units (DMUs) are Tan Tien Plastic Packaging JSC, Sai Gon Packaging JSC, Dong A JSC, and PetroVietnam Packaging JSC. The suggestion for incompetent enterprises is changing the value of inputs proportionally to optimize for better performance.

Keywords: data envelopment analysis (DEA); additive Holt-Winters model (LTS(A,A,A)); epsilon-based measurement (EBM); packaging industry

MSC: 60K10; 62-07; 62P20

Citation: Wang, C.-N.; Hoang, Q.-N.; Nguyen, T.-K.-L. Integrating the EBM Model and LTS(A,A,A) Model to Evaluate the Efficiency in the Supply Chain of Packaging Industry in Vietnam. *Axioms* **2021**, *10*, 33. https://doi.org/10.3390/axioms10010033

Academic Editor: Goran Ćirović

Received: 9 February 2021
Accepted: 8 March 2021
Published: 12 March 2021

1. Introduction

Although packaging is an auxiliary industry for many manufacturing industries, it plays a key role, contributing significantly to the development of the economy. It is also widely considered to be one of the most important parts of logistic systems. The purpose of the earliest and most basic packaging was containing products, serving the stages of transportation, preservation, and display. The second benefit of packaging is protecting products from damage, deformation, theft, or reduction of quality due to external and environmental impacts such as air, humidity, water, and light. Furthermore, providing information on products on stamps, labels, or the cover is a legal requirement for packaging to help consumers better understand the product before making a purchasing decision.

Furthermore, packaging has long been recognized as the silent salesperson and has been the focus of much recent regulation [1]. It contributes to product positioning and brand identity. It is also a marketing and sales support tool. Product packaging with innovative designs and unique colors outstanding and suitable for brand identity publications will easily impress consumers and help them associate and remember products and brands more. Research and packaging design is a vital part of the product development strategy of most businesses that cannot be replaced.

Understanding the important role of packaging, as stated by the Vietnam Packaging Association (VINPAS), over the last 10 years, the packaging industry has been recognized as one of the fastest growing economic sectors in both size and the number of enterprises established in Vietnam [2]. Currently, Vietnam has more than 900 packaging factories, and the numbers of companies is still increasing, about 70% of which are concentrated in the southern provinces [3]. The Association of Vietnam Retailers (AVR) explained the first reason behind this development. The population of Vietnam is over 97 million, leading to the rise of domestic demand in the food and beverage industry, as well as for industrial and pharmaceutical product packaging [4]. The Vietnamese food market is on an upward trend and is expected to grow annually by 13.05% (compound annual growth rate (CAGR) 2021–2025) [5]. Besides that, Vietnam is one of the 17 countries with the highest pharmaceutical growth rate in the world, with a market size of about USD 5.1 billion (as stated by IMS Health) [6]. Specifically, in the packaging industry, the proportion of food packaging is approximately one third to a half, while the percentage for electronics packaging is 5–10% and pharmaceutical and chemistry packaging is estimated to be 5–10% [4].

Moreover, recently, the urbanization process has been developing quickly, along with the appearance of a series of foreign supermarkets that invested in Vietnam such as Big C, Aeon, and Lotte Mart. In addition, the habit of using packaged products has given the packaging industry many development opportunities. In addition, the high export market requirement in packing services is stimulating the development of this industry. The Vietnam packaging industry has a high average growth rate of 15–20% per year [5]. In recent years, the attractiveness of the packaging industry in Vietnam has been proven, as many overseas manufacturers have selected Vietnam as an ideal destination to supply machines, devices, and goods and to invest in building factories. The market for packaging materials can be divided into a series of main segments, including paper and cardboard, plastic, metal, glass, wood, textiles, and other suitable materials such as foam and leather. Based on the statistical data from Thongke [7], Figure 1 summarizes the levels of some imported input materials for packaging production in Vietnam from 2010 to 2019.

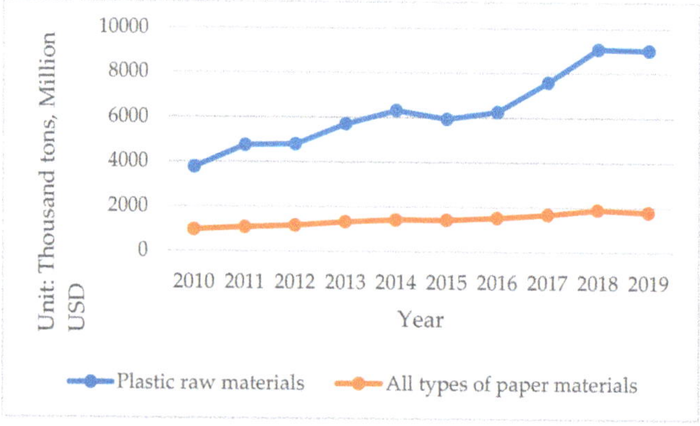

Figure 1. Import levels of some input materials for packaging production in Vietnam in 2010–2019 (Source: thongke.idea.gov.vn [7]).

In addition, in 2015, greenhouse gas (GHG) emissions from plastics accounted for 3.5 percent of the global annual GHG emissions [8], and in 2018, Laura Parker emphasized that around 40 percent of the plastic created was for the packaging industry, which means this industry would also be responsible for the world's pollution [9]. Particularly, plastic packaging in Vietnam achieved a growth rate of 25 percent per year and accounted for the highest proportion in structural plastic (38–39%) [10]. In 2019, the total consumption of paper material reached 3818 million tons, while the percentage of paper packaging production attained was over 80% [10].

The packaging industry is undoubtedly considered a potential industry with high growth rate in Vietnam, but according to the National Steering Committee for Clean Water—Ministry of Natural Resources and Environment [11], the paper manufacturing industry that includes the paper packaging industry is one of the most serious environmental polluting industries today, especially for water resources.

To face concerns about environmental pollution with a high amount of plastic waste, the global packaging operation is looking forward to producing active, intelligent [12], and green packaging in the future. Some preliminary work was carried out in 2001, showing that various executives perceive how influential a strategy on how associated social responsibility affects the social and financial performance of an enterprise [13]. Following the global trend, Vietnamese consumers are gradually switching to using green packaging to ensure their health and safety.

These packaging technologies are also known as the trend of environmentally friendly and sustainable development packaging. The solutions are integrating packaging with Internet of things (IoT) technology, recycling materials, reusable packaging products, and using fast decomposition packaging. All these actions aim to reduce hazardous waste in the environment, sustain materials, expand product storage life, and improve safety, management, and cost-effectiveness. At the same time, governments have been aware of and set out regulations to improve the environment. These commitments were agreed upon by worldwide governments. This tendency enhances tough technological competition among all enterprises in the packaging industry. Therefore, the biggest challenge now for this industry is not only finding customers but also investing in technological innovation that has the minimum impact on the environment by using eco-friendly materials and manufacturing processes to compete and catch up with the ever-growing production and sustain business. When the production process is not optimized, the waste of raw materials, fuel, and emissions will also create significant environmental impacts.

Moreover, in the new development context, Vietnam joined the World Trade Organization (WTO) in 2007 and attracted many foreign companies and corporations to come to Vietnam to seek investment opportunities. At this time, the Vietnam government has also allowed 100% foreign-owned companies to operate in the packaging industry [14]. Considering some aspects of competitiveness and production materials, foreign direct investment (FDI) enterprises have shown superiority. Their machines and technology are very modern, have closed production lines, are mostly automated so their costs are low, and their productivity is very high. Vietnamese packaging enterprises also revealed many shortcomings, such as a lack of vision, unclear long-term strategy, poor governance, low productivity, lack of high-quality human resources, weak financial positions, and so on. In addition, the market still requires businesses in the industry to constantly research and create unique and more effective personalization and interaction. There is a major concern that the profit margins of packaging companies will be reduced more than before due to the increase in production costs, and the obstacle to technology transfer is one factor that inhibits the development of the green packaging market. Besides that, the number of consumers aware of the need to use green packaging is still not in the majority, so it is not enough for packaging companies to completely switch to supplying green packaging. If packaging enterprises do not utilize their competitive advantages and update the technology to adapt to growth trends, they will go backward and lose customers. To initiate a sustainable strategy in an operation, different administration systems, such as commodity expense, capital budgeting, information, and performance assessment, must be composed and defined [13].

According to all these facts mentioned above, the purpose of this study is to identify and evaluate the performance and ranking of 10 packaging companies in Vietnam in each period from 2012 to 2023, by integrating the additive Holt-Winters (LTS(A,A,A)) forecasting model in Tableau and an epsilon-based measure of efficiency (EBM) in data envelopment analysis (DEA). Due to the fact that financial reporting plays an important role in the process of strategic decision-making, specifically decisions of an investment nature [15], while all the packaging companies are trying to meet the market demands and sustain development and increase their competitive advantages or minimize weaknesses, the financial performance forecasting analysis in this study can show how financial variables change over time and hence support packaging companies to make strategic decisions, whether they should align their budgets or determine expenses to invest in new technology, materials, processes, and consultancy to adapt to global trends, because green supply chain management (GSCM) practices in the packaging industry contain the risks of high investment costs and low returns [16]. Besides that, the results will also assist manufacturers, which need packaging services to find the most suitable partners and investors, who need to make investment decisions in this industry. This investigation is expected to add substantially to the understanding of applying EBM to DEA, the model which can give the score and ranking for each decision-making unit (DMU) performance in the experiment years and its implementation, contributing to the specific solution to improve the efficiency for the identified company.

There are five parts in this paper, and they are as follows. Section 1 is an overview of the study that includes the packaging industry background, motivation, objectives, and the process of the research. Section 2 reviews the literature of the packaging industry, the additive Holt-Winters model (LTS(A,A,A)), and an epsilon-based measure of efficiency (EBM) in DEA, proposes the data sources and figures out the input and output that would be applied for the methods. Section 3 presents the empirical results, indicates assessed values, and calculates and discusses the outcomes. Section 4 provides the conclusions, describes some elements that may affect the findings, and recommends future studies.

2. Theoretical Foundations and Methodology

2.1. Literature Review

As mentioned above, packaging plays an important role in every industry. It is not only the thing that is protecting the products, but also the tool that is supporting overall sales. Package design has a huge impact on the decision-making stage of customers. Nielsen demonstrated that more than 60% of buyers try a new product just because the package attracts their eye, and over 40% will consume a product continuously because of its impressive design [17]. Nowadays, traditional packaging is not sufficient to meet the need of the development of consumer experience expectations over time and increasing product complexity. Moreover, recently, national and international have aimed to promote a circular economy and reduce the carbon footprint of manufactured products [18]. Hence, with the growth trend of smart packaging in the Industry 4.0 era, in 2018, Dirk Schaefer and Wai M. Cheung conducted a general overview of smart packaging and defined its underlying base technologies with opportunities and challenges, hence finding out the solutions for smart packaging to minimize its shortcomings and to get its full potential [19]. Gareth R.T. White et al. investigated the decision's complication around the interorganizational green packaging design in an automotive manufacturer. The author noticed that despite the enterprise generating considerable attempts to enhance its environmental effectiveness, the most important aspects in the form of packaging are the operational matters [20]. In this study, the performance of packaging companies in Vietnam is measured by integrating the LTS(A,A,A) model and the EBM model.

The Holt-Winters (HW) theory was one of the favorable variants of the exponential smoothing (ES) forecasting method variations, first introduced by Holt [21]. It is a well-known concept that is used to predict the future data value and performance of an undefined system in diversified interdisciplinary fields, capable of accommodating the changing trends and seasonal adjustments based on a selection of time interval data [22]. The HW model includes mathematical equations that are calculated to create accurate forecasts. It divides into two forms based on the nature of the seasonal element. The first variant is the additive method, suitable for obtaining the seasonality changes in data that are stable during the series, and the second is the multiplicative method which, on the contrary, is suitable for catching up the seasonality changes in data that are raised all over the observation time [23]. For example, in 2015, Eimutis Valakevicius and Mindaugas Brazenas used the seasonal Holt-Winters model to forecast the exchange rate volatility [24]. Vicky Chrystian Sugiarto et al. applied the HW method to predict goods demands from consumers for enterprise resource planning at a sales and distribution module [25]. Furthermore, Maciej Szmit and Anna Szmit proposed a modified HW version to forecast the anomaly detection of network traffic [26]. The HW method is integrated and can be used in Tableau, an analytic forecasting platform that was created from a computer science project at Stanford in 2003 [27]. Tableau is a beneficial business intelligence (BI) platform that supports analysis and gives data visualization for organizations from diverse fields and countries to utilize their decision-making procedures. Tableau accommodates with most data forms and gives out-of-the-box combinations with a diversified range of big data platforms, including Hadoop. Tableau integrates with R, the BI statistical language that many data experts manipulate for progressive analytics [28]. There are different Tableau manners that have been introduced for linear and branching time point-based temporal logics [29]. One of the most practical functions in Tableau is predicting future data by applying exponential smoothing throughout the past statistics. It contains multiplicative and additive methods and enables highly precise results [30]. Its application was reported in the study of Anita S. Harsoor and Anushree Patil, who proposed sales forecasting for Walmart by using the Holt-Winters method in Tableau [30]. In order to forecast the future value of all subjects, this research will conduct the additive Holt-Winters method (LTS (A,A,A)) in the Tableau software.

Data envelopment analysis (DEA) is a decision-making support method that was first introduced in 1978 by Charnes, Cooper, and Rhodes [31], based on the fundamental theory of the nonparametric method for assessing the technical efficiency of Farrel [32], whose domain of inquiry is a group of decision-making units (DMUs) which can obtain multiple inputs and declare multiple outputs [33]. Over four decades, DEA was developed for various models and was utilized by a large number of worldwide researchers and scholars in multiple fields. Since the first Charnes, Cooper, and Rhodes (CCR) model was introduced, there have been many upgraded DEA models which shortened the limitations of previous models, such as the variable returns-to-scale Banker, Charnes, and Cooper (BBC) model (1984) [34], which improved the shortcomings of the constant returns to scale of the CCR model, the slacks-based measure (SBM) considering the change in proportion between the inputs and outputs, and directly dealing with the slacks gap (Tone, 2001) [35]. A highlighted case study confirmed the usefulness of the fuzzy analytic network process (FANP) and data envelopment analysis (DEA), which includes the CCR model, BCC model, and SBM model in order to rank and evaluate the suppliers in the rice supply chain, through the efforts of Wang, C.N et al. in 2018 [36]. DEA normally has two assessments of technical efficiency with different attributes: radial and nonradial [37]. To solve the issue related to radial and nonradial models concerning the proportionality between the input and output changes, the epsilon-based measure (EBM) model was invented in 2010 by K. Tone and M. Tsutsui [37], which has both radial and non-radial attributes in an undetermined structure. In 2018, Chia-Nan Wang, Jen-Der Day, and Thi-Kim-Lien Nguyen used the EBM model and gray forecasting to assess the efficiency of 10 third-party logistics providers [38]. Li Yang, Ke-Liang Wang, and Ji-Chao Geng assessed China's regional ecological energy efficiency and energy saving and pollution abatement potentials with the exploited EBM model [39]. QiangChen et al. applied the EBM model for marketization and calculated the water resource utilization efficiency based on provincial panel data in China during the span of 2008–2013 [40].

2.2. *Method of Research*

2.2.1. Research Process

This research applied the additive Holt-Winters model to predict the future values of performance indicators in financial statements and the EBM model to estimate the performance of each DMU. The final analysis results show the efficiency and inefficiency of 10 packaging companies for every year during the period from 2012 to 2023. The process was divided into even stages, shown in Figure 2:

- Stage 1: With the background knowledge about the packaging industry, the authors defined the importance of assessing the performance of packaging companies and identified the research objectives, target, and scope;
- Stage 2: Based on the overview of the background of previous studies of the packaging industry and the LTS(A,A,A) and EBM methods, the authors found that the research topic was new and necessary. Hence, the researcher established the methodology of the study;
- Stage 3: All suitable packaging companies were chosen from Vietstock [41] to meet the research target, and the models were designed after reviewing the theory of the additive Holt-Winters method and the EBM model. The study collected ten packaging companies;
- Stage 4: Input and output factors were selected to assess the performance of packaging companies. If the input and output indicators were not appropriate, they would be replaced by other factors;
- Stage 5: The study used the series of historical collected data to forecast the future values by using the additive Holt-Winters model. The results of the forecasting data would be examined by the mean absolute percent error (MAPE) indicator. If the MAPE index was accurate and appropriate, the next step would be applied, but if not, the data and factors would need to be retested;
- Stage 6: Following the previous step, an epsilon-based measurement model in DEA would be conducted to measure the performance of 10 enterprises from 2012 to 2023. The Pearson's coefficient would be tested to define the correlation among the input and output variables. According to the EBM model, the Pearson's coefficient was adjusted and formulated by the values of affinity and diversity. The suitable index would need to be between 0 and +1;
- Stage 7: The authors analyzed the performance and ranking of all DMUs from the past to the future. The recommendations for unproductive units to improve their effectiveness based on the EBM model results would be represented. Then, the empirical results and conclusions would be discussed.

2.2.2. Data Sources

There are many companies in the packaging industry, and each company has different sizes, technology, and target products. It is quite difficult to access all companies' data when not all of them provide public financial reports. Firms that have negative values in their financial statements were also not selected for this study. This research aims to calculate the productivity performance of packaging industry companies in Vietnam. Therefore, the authors collected 10 packaging companies in Vietnam that were listed in Vietstock [41] from 2012 to 2019. The name of each DMU is shown in Table 1.

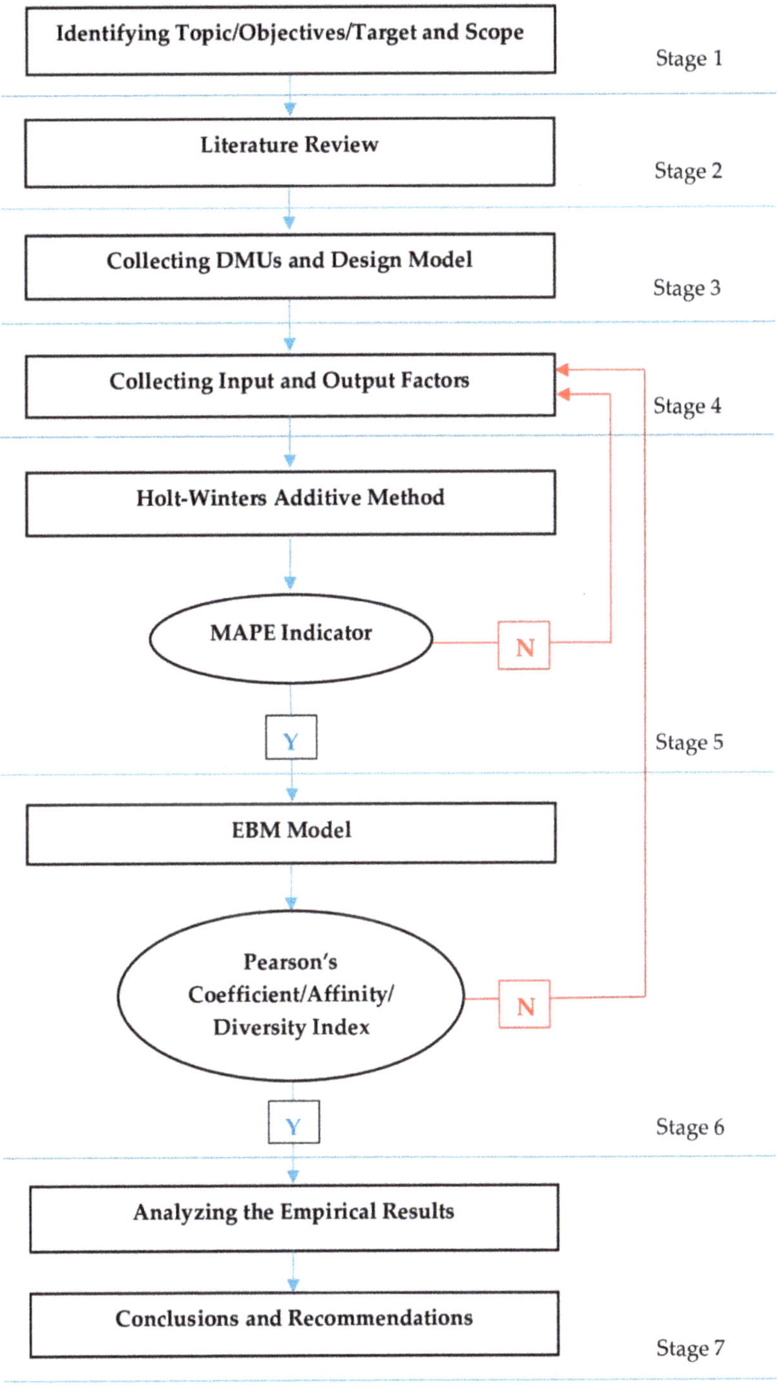

Figure 2. Research framework.

Table 1. List of packaging companies.

DMUs	Company Name	Headquarters
DMU1	Agriculture Printing & Packing Joint Stock Company	Hanoi, Vietnam
DMU2	Tan Tien Plastic Packaging JSC	Ho Chi Minh City, Vietnam
DMU3	Sai Gon Packaging Joint Stock Company	Ho Chi Minh City, Vietnam
DMU4	Bien Hoa Packaging Company	Dong Nai Province, Vietnam
DMU5	SIVICO JSC	Hai Phong City, Vietnam
DMU6	Tan Dai Hung Plastic Joint Stock Company	Ho Chi Minh City, Vietnam
DMU7	Dam Phu My Packaging Joint Stock Company	Vung Tau City, Vietnam
DMU8	Dong A Joint Stock Company	Khanh Hoa Province, Vietnam
DMU9	Do Thanh Technology Corporation	Ho Chi Minh City, Vietnam
DMU10	PetroVietnam Packaging JSC	Bac Lieu City, Vietnam

Source: Vietstock.vn [41].

Finding the input and output factors plays an important role for applying DEA. One of the most beneficial features of DEA is allowing users to choose the variable inputs and outputs. However, these elements must correspond. Experiments on the pricing strategy in the European packaging industry were performed in 2017 by Niklas L.Hallberg, which revealed how asset specificity and routines impacted the pricing strategy and finally enterprise effectiveness [42]. In an economic value-added tree, according to Pohlen and Goldsby, performance indicators including the cost of goods sold, expenses, net profit, sales, fixed assets, and working capital were affected by supply chain activities [43]. Besides that, Roland T. Rust et al. highlighted that the cost determination focused on the efficiency of the operation's processes [44].

Regarding the purpose of the research, this study selected input and output factors for 10 packaging companies during the period from 2012 to 2019 to estimate their performance as mentioned below.

Input variables:

The total assets (TA) was defined as the total amount of assets owned by a person, group, or operation.

The cost of goods sold (CGS) presented the direct costs attributable to the production of the goods sold in a company.

The operating expenses (OE), also called operating expenditures or opex, were the ongoing costs for running a product, business, or system.

Output variables:

The revenue (RE) was the income that a business had from its normal business activities, usually from the sale of goods and services to customers.

The gross profit (GP) was the profit that an operation made after subtracting the cost of goods sold from its revenue.

2.3. *Mathematical Modeling*

2.3.1. Additive Holt-Winters Method

The additive Holt-Winters method is one of the most favorable forecasting tools among the HW methods, in which the seasonal component is indicated in constant terms in the scale in the time series. The LTS(A,A,A) method has been widely adopted by researchers due to its ease of comprehension, moderate data storage conditions, and ability to be effortlessly automated [22]. This research will exploit the Tableau software to obtain the additive Holt-Winters prediction values for 10 packaging companies in Vietnam from 2020 to 2023, based on the historical data from 2012 to 2019.

Let us indicate that X_0 is the units of packaging enterprises, calculated by applying the primary time series $T_1, T_{t+1}, \ldots, T_{t+n}$ (with $t = 0, 1, 2, \ldots n$) and the evaluated prediction values $P_1, P_{t+1}, \ldots, P_{t+n}$ (with $t = 0, 1, 2, \ldots n$).

The sequence of examination for the primary time series and forecasting values begins at $t = 0$ as the first period. The standard formula for exponential smoothing is formulated by

$$\begin{aligned} P_0 &= T_0 \\ P_1 &= \alpha \times T_1 + (1-\alpha) \times P_{t-1} \\ 0 &\leq \alpha \leq 1 \end{aligned} \tag{1}$$

In the additive Holt-Winters method, the overall approach form is described as

$$\begin{aligned} P_1 &= \alpha \times (T_t - S_{t-k}) + (1-\alpha) \times (P_{t-1} + R_{t-1}) \\ R_t &= \beta \times (P_1 - P_{t-1}) + (1-\beta) \times R_{t-1} \\ S_t &= \gamma \times (T_t - P_t) + (1-\gamma) \times S_{t-k} \end{aligned} \tag{2}$$

The forecasted value of the data elements T_t is given by

$$T_t = P_{t-1} + R_{t-1} + S_{t-k} \tag{3}$$

The prediction for the next period n is identified by

$$T_t(n) = P_t + n \times R_t + S_{t+n-k} \tag{4}$$

where α, β, and γ correspond to the smoothing constants for the level of the series $(0 \leq \alpha \leq 1, 0 \leq \beta \leq 1, 0 \leq \gamma \leq 1)$, k is the rate of occurrence span of the seasonality, T_t is the particular value at the past time series t, P_t is the approximate smoothing of the deseasonalized level at the termination of span t, R_t is the approximate smoothing of the trend factor at the termination of span t, S_t is the approximate smoothing of the seasonal factor at the termination of span t, n is the number of spans in the forecasting lead time, and t is the time indicator.

Actually, the gap between the predicted data value and the actual data value always remains. As proposed by Stekler [45,46], an ideal forecast can be sorted out through calculation of the root mean square errors (RMSEs) and mean absolute percentage errors (MAPEs). Both are the most favorable prediction estimation measures used [47,48]. The RMSE is the square root of the second sample moment of the differences between the forecasted and observed values [49] and is non-negative. The lower the RMSE, the better the regression model is. The RMSE and is defined by [50]

$$RMSE = \sqrt{\frac{1}{n}\sum_{t=1}^{n}(P_t - T_t)^2} \tag{5}$$

The mean absolute percent error (MAPE) is an index that is used to define the accuracy of the forecasting values. It gives an intuitive interpretation in terms of the relative error and can be commonly used in many cases [48,51]. It expresses the accuracy as a percentage. The MAPE indicator is interpreted as

$$MAPE = \frac{100}{n}\sum_{t=1}^{n}\left|\frac{T_t - P_t}{T_t}\right| \tag{6}$$

where: T_t is the actual value in time t and P_t is the forecasted value in the time t.

The forecasting values estimated by the additive Holt-Winters method must be examined by the MAPE indicator. If the MAPE index is lower than 50%, it means the predicted value is appreciable. Conversely, if it is higher than 50%, it means the forecasting values have a lot of noise, and then another forecasting model can be retested. The MAPE index was divided into four categories as presented in Table 2.

Table 2. The parameters of the mean absolute percent error (MAPE).

MAPE Value	Ranking
MAPE < 10%	Excellent
10% < MAPE < 20%	Good
20% < MAPE < 50%	Reasonable
MAPE > 50%	Poor

2.3.2. An Epsilon-Based Measure (EBM) Model

An Epsilon-Based Measure of Efficiency

According to DEA, there are two different measurement types for technical efficiency: radial and nonradial. The radial measurement only focuses on the proportionate change of the input or output and ignores the appearance of slacks. In contrast, the nonradial measurement faces slacks directly and is not concerned with the proportion of inputs and outputs changing. As a result, both can lead to inappropriate evaluation in some cases. The epsilon-based measure (EBM) was invented as a solution for this shortcoming. The model combines both radial and nonradial features. Two parameters, one scalar and one vector, are contained in this framework, determined by affinity index with regards to the inputs and outputs. These two parameters are defined to integrate the radial and nonradial models into a unified model to assess the efficiency of DMUs.

By indicating the input-oriented EBM (EBM I-C) for $DMU_0 = (x_0, y_0)$, we then calculate it as

$$\gamma^* = \min_{\theta,\lambda,s^-} \theta - \varepsilon_x \sum_{i=1}^{s} \frac{w_i^- s_i^-}{x_{i0}} \tag{7}$$

This is subject to

$$\theta x_0 - X\lambda - s^- = 0$$
$$Y\lambda \geq y_0, \lambda \geq 0, s^- \geq 0$$

where the weight (relative importance) of input (i) is w_i^- and $\sum_{i=1}^{s} w_i^- = 1(w_i^- \geq 0 \forall i)$ and ε_x is the parameter that integrates the radial θ and nonradial slacks terms.

Diversity Index and Affinity Index

Generally, in DEA, the Pearson's correlation plays an essential role in clarifying the relationship between two variables. It translates the initial data to estimate the correlation. If the Pearson's index is high, it means the two variables associate with each other. On the other side, if the correlation coefficient is low, it means the input and output relation is unappropriated. The value of the Pearson's correlation coefficient ranges from −1 to +1.

In addition, the weight is also one of the most important factors in DEA. The weight determines how much the input will impact the output [52]. If the weight is close to 0, it shows that there is no change in the output even if the input changes. Nonpositive weights indicate the opposite relationship between the input and output, such that if the input grows, the output will decline.

Regarding the EBM model, the values of $_x$ and w_i have a major impact on estimating the efficiency of DMUs. However, instead of using the Pearson's correlation coefficient as another model, the EBM model will use the affinity index between two vectors.

Let $a \in R_+^n$ and $b \in R_+^n$ be two non-negative vectors with a dimension n. They display the examined values for a definite input component in n DMUs. S (a,b) is the affinity index between two vectors a and b with the following features:

$S(a, a) = 1(\forall_a)$ Identical

$S(a, b) = S(a, b)$ Symmetric

$S(ta, b) = S(a, b)/(\forall t > 0)$ Units-invariant

$$1 \geq S(a, b) \geq 0/(\forall a, b)$$

Let us define

$$\begin{gathered} c_j = \ln \frac{b_j}{a_j} \; (j = 1, \ldots, n) \\ \bar{c} = \frac{1}{n} \sum_{j=1}^{n} c_j \\ c_{max} = \begin{matrix} max \\ j \end{matrix} \{c_j\}, c_{min} = \begin{matrix} min \\ j \end{matrix} \{c_j\} \end{gathered} \tag{8}$$

The diversity index of vectors (*a*,*b*) as the deviation of $\{c_j\}$ from the average $\bar{c}$ will be identified as follows:

$$\begin{gathered} D(a,b) = \frac{\sum_{j=1}^{n} |c_j - \bar{c}\,|}{n(c_{max} - c_{min})} = 0 \; if \; c_{max} = c_{min} \\ \text{And}: \; 0 \leq D(a,b) = D(b,a) \leq \tfrac{1}{2} \end{gathered} \tag{9}$$

$D(a,b) = 0$ only if vector *a* and vector *b* are proportional.

If we denote the affinity index between vector *a* and vector *b* as *S*(*a*,*b*), then

$$S(a,b) = 1 - 2D(a,b) \tag{10}$$

If $1 \geq S(a,b) \geq 0$, *S*(*a*,*b*) is accomplished with properties (7) and (8).

In DEA, the Pearson's correlation coefficient (*P*(*a*,*b*)) will be calculated by the following equation:

$$P(a,b) = \frac{\sum_{j=1}^{n} (a_j - \bar{a})(b_j - \bar{b})}{\sum_{j=1}^{n} (a_j - \bar{a})^2 (b_j - \bar{b})^2} \tag{11}$$

where: $\bar{a}$ and $\bar{b}$ are the average of a_j and b_j, respectively.

However, in the EBM model, the affinity index will replace the Pearson's correlation coefficient (*P*(*a*,*b*)). As mentioned above, the Pearson's index range is $-1 \leq P(a,b) \leq 1$. Thus, when analyzing the fundamental factor, there is no assurance for the principal vector only including positive components. Therefore, it will be adjusted to $0 \leq P(a,b) \leq 1$.

3. Results

3.1. *Additive Holt-Winters Forecasting*

3.1.1. Forecasting's Results

In this section, through the data of 10 packaging companies from the period of 2012–2019 that were collected, the additive Holt-Winters additive model in Tableau will be applied to calculate the future data from 2020 to 2023. From the past data sequence, in applying the method, forecasting values for the inputs and outputs of all 10 DMUs from 2012 to 2023 are described in Tables A1 and A2.

3.1.2. Forecasting Accuracy

According to the additive Holt-Winters forecasting model, there is a difference that exists between the predicted data value and the actual data value. In this research, the authors utilized the root mean square error (RMSE) and mean absolute percent error (MAPE) to calculate the accuracy of the forecasting values.

Table 3 illustrates the RMSE index per DMU. It can be seen from the table that all RMSE results were positive values and could be accepted.

As mentioned in Table 2, for the MAPE parameter, if the MAPE index was under 20%, it meant the accuracy of the forecasted value was highly appreciable. Table 4 identifies the average MAPE of each DMU.

It is apparent from Table 4, all DMUs had MAPE indexes under 36%, and their mutual average was 10.56%. As such, all DMU predicted values had good accuracy and were close to the actual values. Furthermore, all predicted values for all DMUs from 2020 to 2023 in Table A2 were non-negative values and acceptable to use in EBM analysis.

Table 3. Root mean square error of the decision-making units (DMUs).

DMU	TA	COGS	OE	RV	GP
DMU10	9299	22,475	1142	24,231	3622
DMU9	4583	9399	1183	10,882	3641
DMU8	15,812	8755	2242	10,464	2786
DMU7	23,760	42,656	2533	45,992	3609
DMU6	48,677	28,471	5974	30,089	7180
DMU5	13,996	12,353	1833	18,976	8786
DMU4	49,316	107,923	4705	93,504	31,286
DMU3	19,964	25,163	3066	29,994	6167
DMU2	176,835	139,673	24,194	114,024	36,453
DMU1	42,930	53,109	13,693	61,806	13,769

Table 4. The average MAPEs of the DMUs.

DMU	TA	CGS	OE	RE	GP
DMU10	8.30%	16.90%	7.40%	16.20%	14.80%
DMU9	2.40%	8.10%	9.30%	7.80%	36.00%
DMU8	11.20%	3.20%	9.80%	3.20%	6.60%
DMU7	15.60%	15.50%	7.70%	13.90%	6.90%
DMU6	6.80%	3.40%	10.90%	3.40%	11.90%
DMU5	12.00%	7.90%	10.90%	8.30%	14.70%
DMU4	5.90%	7.50%	4.10%	6.10%	13.60%
DMU3	12.10%	13.10%	9.50%	12.10%	14.50%
DMU2	17.10%	9.40%	15.60%	6.60%	18.30%
DMU1	9.20%	8.00%	15.80%	8.10%	10.20%
Average			10.56%		

3.1.3. Smoothing Coefficients

According to the condition of smoothing coefficients in the additive Holt-Winters method, an acceptable α, β, γ index ranged from 0 to 1. The three smoothing constants were applied to forecast the future performance of packaging enterprises. The results of the alpha, beta and gamma that are shown in Table A3 confirmed our data were appreciable when their values were accounted for from 0 to 0.5.

3.2. *Assessing the Performance of DMUs*

In this part, the EBM-I-C (input-oriented under constant returns-to-scale assumption) in DEA will be applied to assess the efficiency of each packaging company, based on the historical data (2012–2019) in Table A1 and forecasted data (2020–2023) in Table A2 obtained from the additive Holt-Winters forecasting results. The efficiency of each year will be presented in Tables 8 and 9 below.

One of the biggest concerns before assessing the efficiency of the DMUs through EBM was defining whether the data value was positive. Besides that, the relation between the input and output data was isotonic. The correlation coefficient would be used to define the relationship among two variables, and it would be ranged from -1 to $+1$. If the index was near $+1$, it meant the two variables had a strong correlation. In contrast, if the correlation coefficient was close to -1, it meant the input and output correspondence was low. Table A4 presents the Pearson's correlation coefficient of the DMUs for each year. As can be observed from the results, the correlation coefficient minimum was 0.6889. This means all the data variables were closely connected and acceptable to run EBM.

As stated in the EBM model, two parameters that combine the radial and nonradial models were established by an affinity index. The affinity index between two vectors was calculated to replace the Pearson's correlation coefficient. Their appropriated values had to meet the requirement $0 \leq P(a,b) \leq 1$.

The diversity index of the vectors was determined as the deviation of variables and $0 \leq D(a,b) = D(b,a) \leq 1/2$. It was only equal to 0 when the two vectors were proportional. Both the affinity and diversity indicators were utilized to assure that the correspondence of the input and output variables was suitable for evaluating the efficiency of the DMUs with

EBM. It can be seen from Tables 5 and 6 the data variables satisfied the condition of the EBM model.

Table 5. Affinity index.

	TA	CGS	OE	TA	CGS	OE
Year		2012			2013	
TA	1	0.56183	0.50585	1	0.69466	0.54117
COGS	0.56183	1	0.62592	0.69466	1	0.69653
OPEX	0.50585	0.62592	1	0.54117	0.69653	1
Year		2014			2015	
TA	1	0.58307	0.58106	1	0.58916	0.64542
COGS	0.58307	1	0.66894	0.58916	1	0.3793
OPEX	0.58106	0.66894	1	0.64542	0.3793	1
Year		2016			2017	
TA	1	0.46081	0.41815	1	0.51481	0.43663
COGS	0.46081	1	0.50503	0.51481	1	0.54862
OPEX	0.41815	0.50503	1	0.43663	0.54862	1
Year		2018			2019	
TA	1	0.43808	0.36851	1	0.49053	0.58637
COGS	0.43808	1	0.61053	0.49053	1	0.55946
OPEX	0.36851	0.61053	1	0.58637	0.55946	1
Year		2020			2021	
TA	1	0.40351	0.4343	1	0.42414	0.30355
COGS	0.40351	1	0.47663	0.42414	1	0.55016
OPEX	0.4343	0.47663	1	0.30355	0.55016	1
Year		2022			2023	
TA	1	0.38145	0.42825	1	0.46037	0.36986
COGS	0.38145	1	0.46722	0.46037	1	0.57605
OPEX	0.42825	0.46722	1	0.36986	0.57605	1

Table 6. Diversity index.

	TA	CGS	OE	TA	CGS	OE
Year		2012			2013	
TA	0	0.21908	0.24708	0	0.15267	0.22941
COGS	0.21908	0	0.18704	0.15267	0	0.15173
OPEX	0.24708	0.18704	0	0.22941	0.15173	0
Year		2014			2015	
TA	0	0.20847	0.20947	0	0.20542	0.17729
COGS	0.20847	0	0.16553	0.20542	0	0.31035
OPEX	0.20947	0.16553	0	0.17729	0.31035	0
Year		2016			2017	
TA	0	0.26959	0.29092	0	0.2426	0.28168
COGS	0.26959	0	0.24749	0.2426	0	0.22569
OPEX	0.29092	0.24749	0	0.28168	0.22569	0
Year		2018			2019	
TA	0	0.28096	0.31574	0	0.25473	0.20681
COGS	0.28096	0	0.19473	0.25473	0	0.22027
OPEX	0.31574	0.19473	0	0.20681	0.22027	0
Year		2020			2021	
TA	0	0.29824	0.28285	0	0.28793	0.34823
COGS	0.29824	0	0.26168	0.28793	0	0.22492
OPEX	0.28285	0.26168	0	0.34823	0.22492	0
Year		2022			2023	
TA	0	0.30928	0.28588	0	0.26981	0.31507
COGS	0.30928	0	0.26639	0.26981	0	0.21198
OPEX	0.28588	0.26639	0	0.31507	0.21198	0

The weight of the inputs and outputs and the epsilon indicator played an essential role in eliminating the EBM score for each DMU. A weight index defines the proportional effect the input will have on the output. Table 7 indicates that the entirety of the weight indexes were positive. In this case, this means that changing the input factors would have an impact on the outputs, and if the values of the input increased, the values of the output would grow.

Table 7. Weight to input or output.

Year	TA	CGS	OE
2012	0.32093	0.34465	0.33442
2013	0.32474	0.35017	0.32509
2014	0.32246	0.33894	0.3386
2015	0.36319	0.31142	0.32539
2016	0.32258	0.34353	0.3339
2017	0.32247	0.34689	0.33063
2018	0.29778	0.35773	0.34448
2019	0.33084	0.32498	0.34418
2020	0.32334	0.33465	0.34201
2021	0.29858	0.36348	0.33795
2022	0.32227	0.33315	0.34458
2023	0.30633	0.35596	0.3377

The results of the epsilon for the EBM through the years in Table A5 satisfied the condition $0 \leq$ epsilon index ≤ 1. The efficiencies of 10 packaging enterprises were obtained based on the factors of weight and epsilon for EBM. Tables 8 and 9 indicate the efficiency scores for the DMUs from the past to the future.

Table 8. The efficiency scores for DMUs in the past years (2012–2019).

DMUs	2012	2013	2014	2015	2016	2017	2018	2019
DMU1	0.89705	0.96757	0.9784	0.99872	1	1	1	0.93651
DMU2	1	1	0.87235	0.92132	1	1	1	1
DMU3	0.86749	0.90359	0.89433	0.87861	0.89172	0.91656	0.92816	0.88593
DMU4	0.88807	0.8649	0.94419	0.99352	1	1	1	1
DMU5	1	1	1	1	1	1	1	1
DMU6	0.77576	0.82786	0.95611	0.89414	0.98359	0.97447	0.8957	0.86206
DMU7	0.85263	0.85531	0.99586	1	1	1	0.95107	0.87843
DMU8	1	1	1	1	1	0.95604	0.93866	0.91156
DMU9	0.68077	0.73016	0.821	0.77799	0.85843	0.842	0.87313	0.86069
DMU10	0.77112	0.8618	0.94475	0.92874	0.91311	0.92236	0.9592	0.89168

Table 9. The efficiency scores for DMUs in the prediction years (2020–2023).

DMUs	2020	2021	2022	2023
DMU1	1	1	1	1
DMU2	1	0.96085	0.94435	0.95079
DMU3	0.96805	0.91031	0.99711	0.93022
DMU4	1	1	1	1
DMU5	1	1	1	1
DMU6	0.88965	0.91612	0.88826	0.91979
DMU7	0.92741	0.93248	0.91575	0.92693
DMU8	0.91389	0.91726	0.8986	0.91106
DMU9	0.93047	0.93126	0.97919	0.96635
DMU10	0.92496	0.93115	0.91512	0.92765

In general, all the enterprises in the packaging industry had high productivity, while there was no company with an efficiency score below 0.681 in the observation time from

2012 to 2023. As reported by Tables 8 and 9, there were five DMUs with efficiency scores increasing over time from the past to the future. Specifically, they were DMU1, DMU4, DMU5, and DMU9. In contrast, only DMU8 showed a downward trend compared with the first period; however, its efficiency index remained high. Other DMUs presented the fluctuation trend over the same time span. Figure 3 indicates the ranking positions of all companies from past to future (2012–2023).

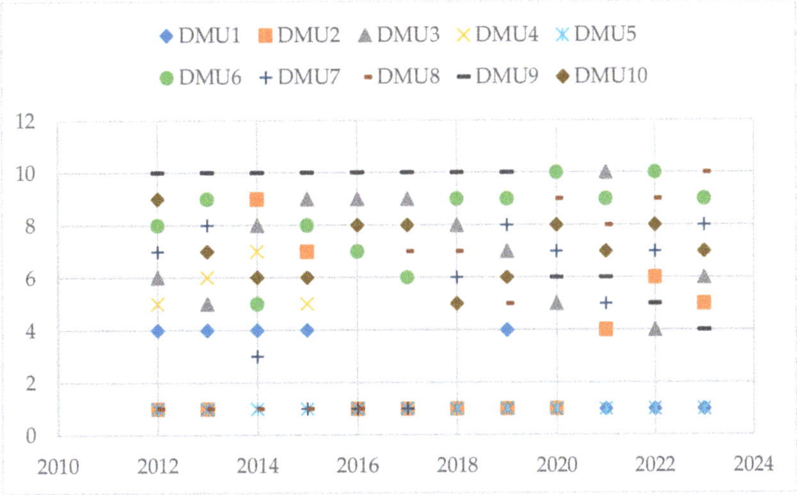

Figure 3. Ranking positions of the DMUs.

Once a DMU gained the first ranking, that meant its theta index (θ) needed to be equal or closest to one, and all slacks for each variable needed to be the lowest and nearest to zero. Conversely, if the slack was high and the theta index was far from one, the DMU could not reach a high position. In the case where θ was higher than one, this meant the DMU was inefficient, and the values of the inputs needed to change accordingly to increase the efficiency and values of the outputs. Table A6 describes theta (θ) and slack (s) in the solution for each unit.

It is interesting to note that in the past data sequence, DMU6 was the most inefficient unit, even with high efficiency scores of 0.95611 (in 2014), 0.98359 (in 2016), and 0.97447 (in 2017) while compared with the efficient unit (score = 1). Particularly, DMU6 had the theta $\theta = \{1.044; 1.064; 1.005\}$ (>1) in 2014, 2016, and 2017, respectively. The input value, theta and slack (s1, s2, and s3) indicators of DMU6 in 2014 in Tables A1 and A6 were picked as a sample for the ideal suggestion emphasized for the inefficient unit. All input indexes were multiplied by $\theta = 1.044$ without the slack. Furthermore, the total assets was reduced by the slack s1 = 384,480. The estimated input for the total assets was $650{,}097 \times 1.044 - 384{,}480 = 294{,}221.268$. Calculated accordingly, the optimal cost of goods sold was $692{,}997 \times 1.044 - 71{,}033.5 = 652{,}455.368$, and $47{,}851 \times 1.044 - 0 = 49{,}956.444$ for the operating expenses. DMU6 was advised to reduce the amount of total assets from 650,097 to 294,221.268 and the cost of goods sold from 692,997 to 652,455.368 and increase the operating expenses from 47,851 to 49,956.444 to have better performance.

It is apparent from Table A6 that the incompetent DMUs in each period were different. Except for DMU6 mentioned above, DMU7 was unproductive in 2014, and so was DMU4 in 2015. In the future term, DMU2, 3, 8 and 10 were predicted to be inefficient. With a few exceptions, the years 2015, 2016, and 2017 illustrated that DMU7 got pretty good scores and rankings. In another year, DMU7 showed fluctuating results in its efficiency score, ranking around the fifth to eighth positions. DMU2 showed a high performance, but it was unstable. In 2012 and 2013, it had the highest rank at first with the score also being one. One year later, its position dropped significantly to ninth and seventh in 2014 and 2015. Between 2016 and 2010, it gained the first ranking with a score of one again. From 2021 to 2023, with its forecast value, it was predicted to fall to the fourth, sixth, and fifth positions, respectively. As can be seen from Tables 8 and 9 and Figure 3, compared with the other DMUs, based on the efficiency score and ranked in the order of DMU3, DMU6, and DMU10, these three DMUs were determined to be the most ineffective enterprises. In the same period, three companies' scores fluctuated below one, and their ranks stayed around the last positions. As opposed to the developing companies, DMU8 was the most efficient enterprise from the initial years. It obtained the first position with the highest point of one in the first five years (2012–2016). Nevertheless, they could not remain stable from 2017 to 2023. It was predicted to be in the last group of low efficiency, with DMU8 falling to the last two positions—the ninth and tenth ranking—in 2022 and 2023 with scores of 0.8986 and 0.9110, respectively. The projected input values that were recommended for each inefficient DMU would not be the same based on the efficiency score, theta, and slack index calculations. However, in general, following the estimated instructions as with DMU6, we can see the common solutions for these DMUs were lowering the input values' total assets and operating expenses to improve the values of the outputs, including the revenue and gross profit.

Overall, DMU5 started with the highest score of one, and it ranked first in 2012 and continuously maintained the same the same level until 2023. Its theta was always equal to one and the slacks were zero. DMU5 was defined as the most efficient unit over time. Following that, DMU1 presented steady growth for the whole time. Its position was fourth from 2012 to 2015. One year after, it increased rapidly to be the first leader among the DMUs. In 2019, its position fell to the fourth ranking again with a score of 0.9365. Then, it reversed positions to first with the highest score for the next four years. DMU4 denoted a slight change in its score and position for the first four years, from 2012 to 2015. Noticeably, its beginning position was fifth with a score of 0.888 and ranked sixth, seventh, and fifth in 2013, 2014, and 2015, respectively. It was even mentioned that it was inefficient in 2015 based on the theta and slack indexes. However, starting from 2016, it climbed to the dominant position together with DMU5 with an efficiency score of one and a ranking of first.

DMU9's score substantially grew within 12 years, but due to it having the lowest score (0.6807) from the beginning, it still held the last ranking (tenth) among ten packaging companies between the year 2012 and 2019. Their position only changed from sixth to fourth, with a score from 0.9312 to 0.9663 from 2020 to 2023, respectively.

3.3. Discussion

The development potential of the packaging industry is expanding. However, Vietnamese packaging companies are facing a lot of pressure and great competition from many FDI enterprises. Specifically, following the global packaging trends combined with high technology and eco-friendly practices together with the COVID-19 pandemic, packaging enterprises need to deal with changes in consumer behavior. When customers turn to attain their fundamental priorities, which are food, shelter, water, and healthcare and pharmaceutical products, they are not focused on luxury order desires [53]. In terms of the packaging materials, packaging companies all faced common difficulties under the impact of the crisis, such as breaking the supply chain in business, difficulty in approaching new customers, and not being able to implement a sales plan. However, packaging businesses also have many opportunities such as Vietnam's e-commerce scale, which will continue to grow [54]. Under the EU–Vietnam Free Trade Agreement (EVFTA), the import tax on Vietnam's plastic bags into the EU market will be removed, creating a significant competitive advantage for the packaging industry [55].

To have a deeper understanding not only of the investment and cooperation opportunities, but also the performance effectiveness of each firm in the packaging industry in

Vietnam, based on the historical financial statements of 10 determined packaging companies from 2012 to 2019, this research evaluated the developing trends from the past, present, and future of all units by integrating the additive Holt-Winters model and epsilon-based measurement (EBM) of DEA. Throughout the analysis, manufacturer managers can find the most suitable company to collaborate with to sustain their business strategy and catch up with global trends. According to the empirical results, generally, all packaging companies had productivity from medium to high. DMU1, DMU4, and DMU5 were evaluated as the three most efficient units and ideal suppliers which reached the first rank and remained at it over time. In contrast, DMU3, DMU6, and DMU8 presented fluctuations and a downward trend and kept the last positions. Formulated on the calculation of feasible solutions of EBM, the inefficient and unstable units could change the input value for better performance of the output value. Besides that, they should have policies to improve their competitiveness in quality, reduce waste in the production process, attach value to maintaining long-term relationships with large customers, strengthen after-sales and customer care services, adjust the selling prices reasonably while ensuring profit, and finally invest in technical machinery and equipment to meet the strict requirements from the market.

This section may be divided by subheadings. It should provide a concise and precise description of the experimental results, their interpretation, as well as the experimental conclusions that can be drawn.

4. Conclusions

The packaging industry has an important role in a developing economy, especially in Vietnam, where the demand for producing products is increasing day by day, leading to an increase in the need for packaging. Packaging's values are not only protecting products, but also its role as a sales and marketing tool. Along with the Fourth Industrial Revolution and high customer requirements, packaging companies are under pressure to deal with challenges to improve their core competencies through technology and associated services as suppliers. However, to adapt with the growth trends, which are being fast, flexible, convenient, good, cheap, and environmentally friendly, changing technology will be a big task for companies when it requires strong capital ability. With uncertain circumstances, financial forecasting and performance evaluation are necessary for packaging companies.

This research aimed to construct the efficiency and developing trends of 10 packaging operations from the past to the future by integrating the additive Holt-Winters model, an extended variation of Holt's exponential smoothing that captures seasonality in Tableau and the EBM of DEA. Based on the collected original data from 2012 to 2019 for the packaging companies, the LTS(A,A,A) approach was employed to forecast the value of the data for the next four years (2019–2023), with the chosen inputs and outputs being total assets, cost of goods sold, operating expenses, revenues, and gross profit. The mean absolute percent error (MAPE) estimated the accuracy of the forecasting values. With the MAPE under 10.56%, the predicted data value in this research had good accuracy. Subsequently, the EBM model was applied to assess the decision-making unit (DMU) productivity by giving efficiency scores with rankings and then providing suggestions through the calculation of the theta and slack indexes for incompetent companies in order to improve their performance. The empirical results will first assist packaging company's managers in defining their positions in the market and making long-term sustainable advancement decisions. Secondly, it will be valuable support for investors and manufacturers for choosing the best supplier for their business and making investment decisions. This finding also validates the usefulness of the Holt-Winters forecasting model and epsilon-based measure of efficiency (EBM) in data envelopment analysis (DEA), as the model can measure the performance of a decision-making unit (DMU) and contribute solutions for companies over the observation period, specifically for cases in the packaging industry. These frameworks' combination can be adopted in multiple fields and different projects.

Although the research was successful, some limitations still remain. Since a company's strategic decision-making process and performance can be defined and affected by diversified variations, including internal and external factors not be presented in a financial statement such as human resources and environmental factors, the study estimated the efficiency of packaging companies based on input and output indicators in financial reports. Accordingly, future investigations can address greater clarity on the links between other factors and their effects on the performance of the industry. The research models that were applied in this study are not the only methods for predicting and assessing the productivity of decision-making units. Future research can employ other frameworks and models to achieve their objectives and have a comparative measurement. Besides that, because many firms have not published their financial reports, the sample size was limited and less comparative. Hence, future studies can expand the research target and scope in other regions and other industries.

Author Contributions: C.-N.W. directed the research, offered analysis software, and edited the content; T.-K.-L.N. designed the research structure, reviewed the content, and guided the method; Q.-N.H. collected data, analyzed the empirical results, and wrote the paper. All authors contributed to issuing the final result. All authors have read and agreed to the published version of the manuscript.

Funding: This research was partly supported by the National Kaohsiung University of Science and Technology and MOST 109-2622-E-992-026 from the Ministry of Sciences and Technology in Taiwan.

Institutional Review Board Statement: Not applicable.

Informed Consent Statement: Not applicable.

Data Availability Statement: Not applicable.

Acknowledgments: The authors would like to express their gratitude to the National Kaohsiung University of Science and Technology's Ministry of Sciences and Technology in Taiwan.

Conflicts of Interest: The authors declare no conflict of interest.

Appendix A

Table A1. Historical data of all DMUs from 2012 to 2019.

DMUs	TA	CGS	OE	RE	GP	TA	CGS	OE	RE	GP
			2012					2013		
1	225,416	340,331	38,933	416,943	76,612	274,489	464,002	40,906	560,700	96,698
2	668,890	1,395,761	54,114	1,492,420	96,659	1,056,549	1,380,548	74,396	1,502,907	122,358
3	160,851	259,660	26,390	298,989	39,329	158,167	263,520	37,208	311,871	48,350
4	549,662	728,958	65,569	851,749	122,791	610,872	854,393	81,818	1,003,373	148,980
5	52,861	94,134	9817	124,178	30,044	74,832	108,153	8925	143,966	35,813
6	613,666	575,399	52,258	607,377	31,978	659,919	639,476	48,231	697,931	58,455
7	85,926	112,173	19,925	139,762	27,589	117,109	153,832	23,847	187,198	33,367
8	85,821	195,900	16,682	224,146	28,246	98,168	199,944	16,068	228,837	28,892
9	130,541	61,722	8149	63,934	2212	135,051	89,090	7923	93,198	4107
10	75,970	63,329	10,801	74,106	10,777	90,478	121,727	11,578	142,961	21,233
			2014					2015		
1	341,105	519,131	50,759	627,524	108,392	397,805	629,962	58,670	762,977	133,015
2	1,178,560	1,349,670	124,823	1,514,504	164,834	813,781	1,199,197	127,930	1,392,908	193,711
3	154,407	195,163	23,177	227,823	32,660	128,275	185,389	25,771	213,096	27,707
4	669,385	975,754	85,333	1,130,701	154,947	758,795	1,170,064	93,132	1,341,383	171,319
5	114,886	115,157	11,523	154,670	39,513	153,226	152,150	18,119	219,307	67,156
6	650,097	692,997	47,851	741,824	48,827	534,730	658,109	53,171	707,016	48,907
7	109,409	190,702	26,730	228,455	37,752	124,503	253,216	29,901	294,832	41,616
8	99,367	220,428	16,878	250,700	30,272	130,624	247,714	20,324	283,429	35,715
9	147,895	96,769	8907	107,445	10,676	149,944	102,962	13,251	123,154	20,193
10	94,615	133,418	12,483	156,913	23,496	85,418	120,657	14,001	144,477	23,820

Table A1. *Cont.*

DMUs	TA	CGS	OE	RE	GP	TA	CGS	OE	RE	GP
			2016					2017		
1	491,379	714,851	82,110	882,745	167,894	554,368	804,222	79,506	978,153	173,931
2	925,723	1,176,364	90,554	1,405,264	228,901	1,089,353	1,300,812	83,663	1,459,899	159,087
3	125,184	146,857	26,553	179,511	32,654	136,676	155,664	29,137	194,254	38,590
4	749,980	1,199,774	95,752	1,381,740	181,966	936,962	1,370,666	107,416	1,554,386	183,719
5	164,648	119,490	16,115	167,652	48,161	199,119	140,997	18,421	196,151	55,153
6	599,823	649,998	42,523	702,107	52,109	643,818	674,064	41,945	735,337	61,273
7	142,893	245,138	28,506	286,394	41,255	196,875	347,340	35,998	396,111	48,770
8	156,247	263,115	24,429	303,369	40,255	196,681	277,142	27,955	324,829	47,688
9	157,994	104,988	12,415	125,975	20,987	158,356	104,128	13,035	122,352	18,224
10	116,449	125,837	17,292	153,299	27,461	121,774	159,485	18,877	186,927	27,442
			2018					2019		
1	653,755	976,249	94,511	1,164,601	188,352	792,415	1,073,852	135,016	1,309,529	235,677
2	1,247,892	1,566,783	90,360	1,704,119	137,337	1,348,780	1,536,620	101,103	1,763,523	226,903
3	154,904	168,339	24,290	204,135	35,796	184,592	176,278	27,793	216,420	40,142
4	922,925	1,594,683	113,093	1,780,171	185,488	904,496	1,404,516	112,349	1,703,555	299,039
5	218,140	149,617	17,891	194,421	44,804	227,599	143,197	22,743	195,523	52,326
6	662,377	645,763	53,968	713,685	67,922	666,365	710,317	57,558	781,061	70,744
7	237,719	396,920	40,416	447,932	51,012	219,920	312,037	38,074	356,255	44,218
8	212,062	292,097	33,075	340,094	47,998	214,670	314,913	33,194	364,964	50,052
9	177,527	124,191	13,163	143,492	19,301	168,725	140,759	16,597	166,938	26,179
10	135,686	204,770	20,944	236,603	31,833	138,740	196,867	20,361	223,738	26,870

Table A2. Forecasting data of all DMUs from 2020 to 2023.

			2020					**2021**		
DMU	TA	CGS	OE	RE	GP	TA	CGS	OE	RE	GP
DMU1	850,040	1,196,789	138,220	1,440,914	245,096	950,126	1,281,480	147,732	1,558,944	267,450
DMU2	1,374,361	1,597,270	105,622	1,823,640	204,782	1,368,105	1,554,814	117,317	1,821,797	232,070
DMU3	175,830	129,146	19,810	168,189	32,505	188,005	126,189	26,516	167,267	34,539
DMU4	996,251	1,637,435	118,693	1,876,436	260,157	1,066,083	1,780,077	129,827	2,038,766	288,901
DMU5	261,082	156,042	22,871	204,316	48,378	288,472	181,496	25,529	246,528	65,084
DMU6	680,308	706,044	54,344	780,796	65,853	645,751	720,639	54,991	808,669	78,104
DMU7	251,207	405,412	41,817	458,543	53,231	274,346	453,014	44,925	510,812	57,963
DMU8	241,088	331,934	37,875	384,130	54,348	262,890	347,643	38,781	406,668	57,687
DMU9	181,861	135,863	16,041	164,526	29,677	184,060	150,650	17,949	184,694	35,383
DMU10	153,283	207,356	23,097	239,495	35,705	155,938	226,242	24,245	263,363	34,249
			2022					2023		
DMU1	1,007,751	1,404,417	163,168	1,690,329	286,882	1,007,751	1,489,108	172,680	1,808,358	309,237
DMU2	1,484,175	1,651,786	116,115	1,902,359	228,986	1,477,920	1,609,330	127,809	1,900,516	256,274
DMU3	179,243	99,386	17,891	136,472	30,548	191,418	96,429	24,597	135,549	32,582
DMU4	1,096,442	1,838,949	129,923	2,110,224	295,616	1,166,274	1,981,591	141,057	2,272,553	324,360
DMU5	308,559	171,025	26,133	224,616	53,591	335,949	196,478	28,791	266,828	70,297
DMU6	689,501	729,578	56,184	812,369	71,837	654,944	744,173	56,830	840,242	84,088
DMU7	293,641	470,269	46,726	528,806	58,764	316,780	517,871	49,834	581,076	63,496
DMU8	281,545	365,746	43,462	426,143	61,167	303,347	382,355	44,367	448,680	64,505
DMU9	193,144	150,899	18,021	185,439	36,204	195,343	165,686	19,929	205,607	41,910
DMU10	171,279	235,558	26,251	271,358	40,154	173,935	254,475	27,399	295,226	38,698

Table A3. Forecasting parameters of all DMUs from 2020 to 2023.

DMU	TA			CGS			OE			RE			GP		
	α	β	γ	α	β	γ	α	β	γ	A	β	γ	α	β	γ
DMU10	0.5	0	0	0.1	0.5	0	0.5	0	0	0.1	0.5	0	0	0	0.5
DMU9	0.2	0.5	0	0.2	0.5	0	0.1	0.5	0	0.1	0.5	0	0	0.2	0
DMU8	0.5	0	0	0.5	0	0.1	0.5	0	0.5	0.5	0	0.2	0.5	0	0
DMU7	0.5	0	0	0.1	0.5	0	0.2	0.4	0	0.1	0.5	0	0	0.5	0
DMU6	0.1	0	0	0	0	0	0.3	0	0	0	0	0	0.1	0.5	0
DMU5	0.2	0.4	0	0	0.5	0	0.1	0.5	0	0	0	0	0	0	0
DMU4	0.1	0.5	0	0.1	0.5	0	0.1	0.5	0	0.2	0.4	0	0.2	0	0.1
DMU3	0.5	0	0.5	0	0	0	0	0	0	0.5	0	0	0.1	0	0
DMU2	0.1	0.5	0	0.5	0	0.2	0	0	0	0.5	0	0.4	0	0.1	0
DMU1	0.5	0	0.5	0.5	0	0.5	0.5	0	0.1	0.5	0	0.5	0.5	0	0

Table A4. Pearson's correlation coefficient from 2012 to 2020.

	TA	CGS	OE	RE	GP	TA	CGS	OE	RE	GP
Year			2012					2013		
TA	1	0.8995	0.9214	0.8983	0.6889	1	0.9765	0.8682	0.9682	0.7643
COGS	0.8995	1	0.8203	0.9984	0.7635	0.9765	1	0.9108	0.9986	0.8525
OPEX	0.9214	0.8203	1	0.8389	0.8564	0.8682	0.9108	1	0.9267	0.9441
REV	0.8983	0.9984	0.8389	1	0.7983	0.9682	0.9986	0.9267	1	0.8792
GP	0.6889	0.7635	0.8564	0.7983	1	0.7643	0.8525	0.9441	0.8792	1
Year			2014					2015		
TA	1	0.9795	0.9572	0.9716	0.8403	1	0.9852	0.9584	0.9809	0.8849
COGS	0.9795	1	0.9861	0.9989	0.9175	0.9852	1	0.9742	0.9986	0.9208
OPEX	0.9572	0.9861	1	0.9896	0.9445	0.9584	0.9742	1	0.9775	0.9317
REV	0.9716	0.9989	0.9896	1	0.9349	0.9809	0.9986	0.9775	1	0.9400
GP	0.8403	0.9175	0.9445	0.9349	1	0.8849	0.9208	0.9317	0.9400	1
Year			2016					2017		
TA	1	0.9719	0.9023	0.9687	0.8896	1	0.9758	0.8901	0.9701	0.8555
COGS	0.9719	1	0.9614	0.9983	0.9261	0.9758	1	0.9615	0.9989	0.9163
OPEX	0.9023	0.9614	1	0.9710	0.9641	0.8901	0.9615	1	0.9709	0.9696
REV	0.9687	0.9983	0.9710	1	0.9463	0.9701	0.9989	0.9709	1	0.9342
GP	0.8896	0.9261	0.9641	0.9463	1	0.8555	0.9163	0.9696	0.9342	1
Year			2018					2019		
TA	1	0.9587	0.8824	0.9522	0.8058	1	0.9717	0.8562	0.9619	0.8640
COGS	0.9587	1	0.9599	0.9990	0.8972	0.9717	1	0.9187	0.9986	0.9431
OPEX	0.8824	0.9599	1	0.9701	0.9716	0.8562	0.9187	1	0.9307	0.9491
REV	0.9522	0.9990	0.9701	1	0.9161	0.9619	0.9986	0.9307	1	0.9595
GP	0.8058	0.8972	0.9716	0.9161	1	0.8640	0.9431	0.9491	0.9595	1
Year			2020					2021		
TA	1	0.9624	0.8729	0.9599	0.8710	1	0.9596	0.9141	0.9634	0.9185
COGS	0.9624	1	0.9367	0.9993	0.9484	0.9596	1	0.9497	0.9991	0.9629
OPEX	0.8729	0.9367	1	0.9472	0.9789	0.9141	0.9497	1	0.9597	0.9811
REV	0.9599	0.9993	0.9472	1	0.9588	0.9634	0.9991	0.9597	1	0.9716
GP	0.8710	0.9484	0.9789	0.9588	1	0.9185	0.9629	0.9811	0.9716	1
Year			2022					2023		
TA	1	0.9543	0.8796	0.9540	0.8892	1	0.9475	0.8951	0.9518	0.9145
COGS	0.9543	1	0.9365	0.9994	0.9598	0.9475	1	0.9459	0.9992	0.9689
OPEX	0.8796	0.9365	1	0.9465	0.9761	0.8951	0.9459	1	0.9562	0.9782
REV	0.9540	0.9994	0.9465	1	0.9685	0.9518	0.9992	0.9562	1	0.9769
GP	0.8892	0.9598	0.9761	0.9685	1	0.9145	0.9689	0.9782	0.9769	1

Table A5. Epsilon for the EBM in each year.

Year	2012	2013	2014	2015	2016	2017	2018	2019	2020	2021	2022	2023
Epsilon Indicator	0.43475	0.35458	0.3885	0.45829	0.53821	0.49927	0.52371	0.45406	0.56151	0.57004	0.57388	0.52865

Table A6. Theta and slack(s) index of inputs for all DMUs.

	θ	s1	s2	s3	θ	s1	s2	s3	θ	s1	s2	s3
DMUs		TA	CGS	OP		TA	CGS	OP		TA	CGS	OP
	2012				2013				2014			
DMU1	0.929	31,857.3	0	3195.4	0.976	0	0	3041.67	0.995	0	0	6376.4
DMU2	1	0	0	0	1	0	0	0	0.879	61674.2	0	0
DMU3	0.880	13,990.3	0	0	0.950	0	0	14,933.2	0.922	0	0	4962.6
DMU4	0.924	141,796	0	0	0.882	17,388.9	0	9979.64	0.945	0	0	717.87
DMU5	1	0	0	0	1	0	0	0	1	0	0	0
DMU6	0.833	250,021	0	0	0.859	176,739	0	0	1.044	384,480	71,033.5	0
DMU7	0.945	21,662.3	0	7770.2	0.914	9755.52	0	10,195.4	1.067	0	12,693.5	12,587
DMU8	1	0	0	0	1	0	0	0	1	0	0	0
DMU9	0.785	75,288.1	0	1344.4	0.786	57,690.6	0	448.829	0.872	60,551.9	0	0
DMU10	0.887	35,843.9	0	3722.6	0.882	5517.84	0	1352.41	0.953	0	0	749.08
	2015				2016				2017			
DMU1	1	0	0	503.37	1	0	0	0	1	0	0	0
DMU2	0.938	0	0	14,575	1	0	0	0	1	0	0	0
DMU3	0.922	0	0	7567.8	0.990	23,990.9	0	9586.41	1	9019.53	0	12,853
DMU4	1.034	163,592	40128	0	1	0	0	0	1	0	0	0
DMU5	1	0	0	0	1	0	0	0	1	0	0	0
DMU6	0.953	184,021	9580	0	1.064	175,678	103,835	0	1.005	98,118.2	21,995.2	0
DMU7	1	0	0	0	1	0	0	0	1	0	0	0
DMU8	1	0	0	0	1	0	0	0	0.964	5435.88	0	536.3
DMU9	0.830	38,383	0	821.22	1	73,793.2	0	4178.29	0.863	20,932.3	0	0
DMU10	0.953	0	0	2306	1	24,775.6	0	4807.43	0.964	11,407.2	0	2997.1
	2018				2019				2020			
DMU1	1	0	0	0	1	57,216.4	0	45,477.8	1	0	0	0
DMU2	1	0	0	0	1	0	0	0	1	0	0	0
DMU3	1	17,622	0	7283.9	1	54,888.6	0	12,343	1.051	45,456.5	0	3759.5
DMU4	1	0	0	0	1	0	0	0	1	0	0	0
DMU5	1	0	0	0	1	0	0	0	1	0	0	0
DMU6	0.990	285,762	0	8089.8	0.907	189,408	0	669.823	0.965	241,965	0	3054.2
DMU7	1	2253.92	0	10,630	0.941	17,857.2	0	12,343.9	0.987	4486.41	0	12,268
DMU8	0.976	16,061.5	0	4681.9	0.955	11,340.6	0	7647.54	1.005	36,412.6	0	12,651
DMU9	0.969	91393.4	0	1104.2	0.978	76344	0	5219.01	0.994	63710.1	0	0
DMU10	1	7665.27	0	3713.5	0.937	11,205.9	0	4322.7	0.992	20,175.1	0	5160.4
	2021				2022				2023			
DMU1	1	0	0	0	1	0	0	0	1	0	0	0
DMU2	1.023	446,999	0	4009.5	1.009	508,648	8349.4	0	1.030	546,525	0	13,645
DMU3	1.061	54,696.9	0	13,954	1.066	26,314.5	0	3772.2	1.066	57,073.2	0	12,006
DMU4	1	0	0	0	1	0	0	0	1	0	0	0
DMU5	1	0	0	0	1	0	0	0	1	0	0	0
DMU6	0.980	209,830	0	2383.2	0.970	246,953	0	4501.22	0.985	213,602	0	3797.4
DMU7	0.985	2990.18	0	11,701	0.980	12,985.1	0	13,230.1	0.978	11,725.8	0	12,690
DMU8	1.021	55,483.7	0	13,686	1.010	59,100.6	0	15,919	1.021	78,770.5	0	16,905
DMU9	1.002	39,098.6	0	3220	0.993	14,513	0	0	0.997	11,595.1	0	2335.1
DMU10	1.016	20,777	0	7871.2	0.991	23,287.3	0	6794.24	1.012	24,443	0	9392.2

References

1. Imiru, G.A. The Effect of Packaging Attributes on Consumer Buying Decision Behavior in Major Commercial Cities in Ethiopia. *Int. J. Mark. Stud.* **2017**, *9*, 43–54. [CrossRef]
2. Tiem Nang Cua Nganh Cong Nghiep Bao Bi Viet Nam. Available online: https://hhbb.vn/xu-huong-bao-bi/tiem-nang-cua-nganh-cong-nghiep-bao-bi-viet-nam-54.html (accessed on 20 July 2020).
3. Vietnam Economic News. Packaging Industry Ahead of Good Opportunities. Available online: http://ven.vn/packaging-industry-ahead-of-good-opportunities-20720.html (accessed on 20 July 2020).
4. VN's Processing and Packaging Industry: Many Encouraging Signals. Available online: http://news.gov.vn/Home/VNs-processing-and-packaging-industry-Many-encouraging-signals/201910/37847.vgp (accessed on 31 August 2020).
5. Mordor Intelligence. Vietnam Food Service Market—Growth, Trends, Covid-19 Impact, and Forecasts (2021–2026). Available online: https://www.mordorintelligence.com/industry-reports/Vietnam-Food-Service-Market (accessed on 20 February 2020).
6. Viet Nam La Thi Truong Duoc Pham Lon Thu 2 Dong Nam A. Available online: https://vietnamnet.vn/vn/suc-khoe/viet-nam-la-thi-truong-duoc-pham-lon-thu-2-dong-nam-a-603838.html (accessed on 20 February 2020).
7. Thongke. Available online: http://thongke.idea.gov.vn/ (accessed on 28 September 2020).
8. Zheng, J.; Suh, S. Strategies to reduce the global carbon footprint of plastics. *Nat. Clim. Chang.* **2019**, *9*, 374–378. [CrossRef]
9. National Geographic. Fast Facts About Plastic Pollution. Available online: https://www.nationalgeographic.com/ (accessed on 10 January 2021).
10. Top 10 Cong Ty Bao Bi Uy Tin 2020. Available online: https://vietnamnet.vn/vn/kinh-doanh/vef/top-10-cong-ty-bao-bi-uy-tin-nam-2020-677358.html (accessed on 16 October 2020).
11. Giam Thieu Su Dung Giay De Bao Ve Moi Truong. Available online: http://nioeh.org.vn/tin-tuc/giam-thieu-su-dung-giay-de-bao-ve-moi-truong (accessed on 20 October 2020).
12. Realini, C.E.; Marcos, B. Active and intelligent packaging systems for a modern society. *Meat Sci.* **2014**, *98*, 404–419. [CrossRef] [PubMed]
13. Epstein, M.J.; Roy, M.J. Sustainability in Action: Identifying and Measuring the Key Performance Drivers. *Long Range Plan.* **2001**, *34*, 585–604. [CrossRef]
14. Trungtamwto. Available online: https://trungtamwto.vn/upload/files/wto/7-/25-van-kien/Tai-lieu-cam-ket-ve-dich-vu-khi-gia-nhap-wto-binh-luan-cua-nguoi-trong-cuoc-pdf.pdf (accessed on 20 October 2020).
15. Papadakis, V.; Lioukas, S.; Chambers, D. Strategic decision-making processes: The role of management and context. *Strateg. Manag. J.* **1998**, *19*, 115–147. [CrossRef]
16. Wang, Z.; Mathiyazhagan, K.; Xu, L.; Diabat, A. A decision making trial and evaluation laboratory approach to analyze the barriers to Green Supply Chain Management adoption in a food packaging company. *J. Clean. Prod.* **2016**, *117*, 19–28. [CrossRef]
17. Design Audit Series Wine. Available online: https://labelprintingportland.com (accessed on 22 October 2020).
18. Cheung, W.M.; Leong, J.T.; Vichare, P. Incorporating lean thinking and life cycle assessment to reduce environmental impact of plastic injection moulded products. *J. Clean. Prod.* **2017**, *167*, 759–775. [CrossRef]
19. Schaefer, D.; Cheung, W.M. Smart Packaging: Opportunities and Challenges. *Procedia CIRP* **2018**, *72*, 1022–1027. [CrossRef]
20. White, G.R.T.; Wang, X.J.; Li, D. Inter-organisational green packaging design: A case study of influencing factors and constraints in the automotive supply chain. *Int. J. Prod. Res.* **2015**, *53*, 6551–6566. [CrossRef]
21. Holt, C.C. Forecasting seasonals and trends by exponentially weighted moving averages. *Int. J. Forecast.* **2004**, *20*, 5–10. [CrossRef]
22. Goodwin, P. The Holt-Winters Approach to Exponential Smoothing: 50 Years Old and Going Strong. *Foresight* **2010**, *19*, 30–33.
23. Hyndman, R.J.; Athanasopoulos, G. *Forecasting: Principles and Practice*, 1st ed.; Otexts: Melbourne, Australia, 2013.
24. Valakevicius, E.; Brazenas, M. Application of the Seasonal Holt-Winters Model to Study Exchange Rate Volatility. *Inžinerinė Ekonomika* **2015**, *26*, 384–390.
25. Sugiarto, V.C.; Sarn, R.; Sunaryono, D. Sales forecasting using Holt-Winters in Enterprise Resource Planning at sales and distribution module. In Proceedings of the 2016 International Conference on Information & Communication Technology and Systems (ICTS), Surabaya, Indonesia, 12 October 2016; pp. 8–13.
26. Szmit, M.; Szmit, A. Usage of Modified Holt-Winters Method in the Anomaly Detection of Network Traffic: Case Studies. *J. Comput. Netw. Commun.* **2012**, *2012*, 192913. [CrossRef]
27. Tableau. Available online: https://www.tableau.com/why-tableau/what-is-tableau (accessed on 21 February 2020).
28. Jena, B. An Approach for Forecast Prediction in Data Analytics Field by Tableau Software. *IJIEEB Int. J. Inf. Eng. Electron. Bus.* **2019**, *11*, 19–26. [CrossRef]
29. Goranko, V.; Montanari, A.; Sala, P.; Sciavicco, G. A general tableau method for propositional interval temporal logics: Theory and implementation. *J. Appl. Log.* **2006**, *4*, 305–330. [CrossRef]
30. Harsoor, A.S.; Patil, A.; Tech, M. Forecast of sales of Walmart store using big data applications. *Int. J. Res. Eng Technol.* **2015**, *4*, 51–59.
31. Charnes, A.A.; Cooper, W.W.; Rhodes, E. Measuring the efficiency of decision-making units. *Eur. J. Oper. Res.* **1978**, *2*, 429–444. [CrossRef]
32. Farrell, M.J. The measurement of productivity efficiency. *J. R. Stat. Soc.* **1957**, *120*, 449–513.
33. Wang, C.N.; Lin, H.S.; Hsu, H.P.; Le, V.T.; Lin, T.F. Applying Data Envelopment Analysis and Grey Model for the Productivity Evaluation of Vietnamese Agroforestry Industry. *Sustainability* **2016**, *8*, 1139. [CrossRef]

34. Banker, R.D.; Charnes, A.; Cooper, W.W. Some models for estimating technical and scale inefficiencies in data envelopment analysis. *Manag. Sci.* **1984**, *30*, 1078–1092. [CrossRef]
35. Tone, K. A slacks-based measure of efficiency in data envelopment analysis. *Eur. J. Oper. Res.* **2001**, *130*, 498–509. [CrossRef]
36. Wang, C.N.; Nguyen, V.T.; Duong, D.H.; Do, H.T. A Hybrid Fuzzy Analytic Network Process (FANP) and Data Envelopment Analysis (DEA). Approach for Supplier Evaluation and Selection in the Rice Supply Chain. *Symmetry* **2018**, *10*, 221. [CrossRef]
37. Tone, K.; Tsutsui, M. An epsilon-based measure of efficiency in DEA—A third pole of technical efficiency. *Eur. J. Oper. Res.* **2010**, *207*, 1554–1563. [CrossRef]
38. Wang, C.N.; Day, J.D.; Nguyen, T.K.L. Applying EBM Model and Grey Forecasting to Assess Efficiency of Third-Party Logistics Providers. *J. Adv. Transp.* **2018**, *2018*, 1212873. [CrossRef]
39. Yang, L.; Wang, K.L.; Geng, J.C. China's regional ecological energy efficiency and energy saving and pollution abatement potentials: An empirical analysis using epsilon-based measure model. *J. Clean. Prod.* **2018**, *194*, 300–308. [CrossRef]
40. Chen, Q.; Ai, H.; Zhang, Y.; Hou, J. Marketization and water resource utilization efficiency in China. *Sustain. Comput. Inform. Syst.* **2019**, *22*, 32–43. [CrossRef]
41. Vietstock. Available online: http://en.vietstock.vn/ (accessed on 8 July 2020).
42. Hallberg, N.L. The micro-foundations of pricing strategy in industrial markets: A case study in the European packaging industry. *J. Bus. Res.* **2017**, *76*, 179–188. [CrossRef]
43. Pohlen, T.L.; Goldsby, T.J. VMI and SMI programs. How economic value added can help sell the change. *Int. J. Phys. Distrib. Logist. Manag.* **2003**, *33*, 565–581. [CrossRef]
44. Rust, R.T.; Moorman, C.; Dickson, P.R. Getting Return on Quality: Revenue Expansion, Cost Reduction, or Both? *J. Mark.* **2002**, *66*, 7–24. [CrossRef]
45. Stekler, H.O. Macroeconomic forecast evaluation techniques. *Int. J. Forecast.* **1991**, *7*, 375–384. [CrossRef]
46. Stekler, H.O. Are economic forecasts valuable? *J. Forecast.* **1994**, *13*, 495–505. [CrossRef]
47. Mohammed, E.A.; Naugler, C. Open-source Software for Demand Forecasting of Clinical Laboratory Test Volumes Using Time-series Analysis. *J. Pathol. Inform.* **2017**, *8*, 7.
48. Wang, C.N.; Day, J.D.; Nguyen, T.K.L.; Luu, Q.C. Integrating the Additive Seasonal Model and Super-SBM Model to Compute the Efficiency of Port Logistics Companies in Vietnam. *Sustainability* **2018**, *10*, 2782. [CrossRef]
49. Arum, K.C.; Ugwu, C.L.J.; Ugwuowo, F.I.; Oranye, H.E.; Agu, P.I. Time Series Model Comparative Approaches in Analyzing Accident and Emergency Departmental Demand in Eastern Nigeria. *Afr. J. Math. Stat. Stud.* **2020**, *3*, 55–62.
50. Hussain, A.; Rahman, M.; Memon, J.A. Forecasting electricity consumption in Pakistan: The way forward. *Energy Policy* **2016**, *90*, 73–80. [CrossRef]
51. Hansun, S.; Charles, V.; Indrati, C.R.; Subanar, S.S. Revisiting the Holt-Winters' Additive Method for Better Forecasting. *Int. J. Enterp. Inf. Syst.* **2019**, *15*, 43–57. [CrossRef]
52. Wei, C.-K.; Chen, L.-C.; Li, R.-K.; Tsai, C.-H.; Huang, H.-L. A study of optimal weights of Data Envelopment Analysis—Development of a context-dependent DEA-R model. *Expert Syst. Appl.* **2012**, *39*, 4599–4608. [CrossRef]
53. Loxton, M.; Truskett, R.; Scarf, B.; Sindone, L.; Baldry, G.; Zhao, Y. Consumer Behaviour during Crises: Preliminary Research on How Coronavirus Has Manifested Consumer Panic Buying, Herd Mentality, Changing Discretionary Spending and the Role of the Media in Influencing Behaviour. *J. Risk Financ. Manag.* **2020**, *13*, 166. [CrossRef]
54. Statistic. Available online: https://www.statista.com/outlook/243/127/ecommerce/Vietnam (accessed on 14 December 2020).
55. EU-Vietnam Free Trade Agreement. Available online: http://evfta.moit.gov.vn/?page=overview&category_id=45745512-6ea1-4740-bcba-15c09e3d994c (accessed on 14 December 2020).

axioms

Article

Comparison of the Sub-Tour Elimination Methods for the Asymmetric Traveling Salesman Problem Applying the SECA Method

Ramin Bazrafshan [1], Sarfaraz Hashemkhani Zolfani [2,*] and S. Mohammad J. Mirzapour Al-e-hashem [1]

1 Department of Industrial Engineering and Management Systems, Amirkabir University of Technology (Tehran Polytechnic), Tehran 15875-4413, Iran; Ramin.bazrafshan88@gmail.com (R.B.); mirzapour@aut.ac.ir (S.M.J.M.A.-e-h.)
2 School of Engineering, Catholic University of the North, Larrondo 1281, Coquimbo 1780000, Chile
* Correspondence: sarfaraz.hashemkhani@ucn.cl

Abstract: There are many sub-tour elimination constraint (SEC) formulations for the traveling salesman problem (TSP). Among the different methods found in articles, usually three apply more than others. This study examines the Danzig–Fulkerson–Johnson (DFJ), Miller–Tucker–Zemlin (MTZ), and Gavish–Graves (GG) formulations to select the best asymmetric traveling salesman problem (ATSP) formulation. The study introduces five criteria as the number of constraints, number of variables, type of variables, time of solving, and differences between the optimum and the relaxed value for comparing these constraints. The reason for selecting these criteria is that they have the most significant impact on the mathematical problem-solving complexity. A new and well-known multiple-criteria decision making (MCDM) method, the simultaneous evaluation of the criteria and alternatives (SECA) method was applied to analyze these criteria. To use the SECA method for ranking the alternatives and extracting information about the criteria from constraints needs computational computing. In this research, we use CPLEX 12.8 software to compute the criteria value and LINGO 11 software to solve the SECA method. Finally, we conclude that the Gavish–Graves (GG) formulation is the best. The new web-based software was used for testing the results.

Keywords: sub-tour elimination constraint (SEC); asymmetric traveling salesman problem (ATSP); multiple-criteria decision making (MCDM); simultaneous evaluation of criteria and alternatives (SECA)

Citation: Bazrafshan, R.; Hashemkhani Zolfani, S.; Mirzapour Al-e-hashem, S.M.J. Comparison of the Sub-Tour Elimination Methods for the Asymmetric Traveling Salesman Problem Applying the SECA Method. *Axioms* **2021**, *10*, 19. https://doi.org/10.3390/axioms10010019

Academic Editor: Goran Ćirović
Received: 29 December 2020
Accepted: 2 February 2021
Published: 8 February 2021

1. Introduction

The traveling salesman problem (TSP) is one of the most well-known combinational optimization problems studied in the operation research literature. It consists of determining a tour that starts and ends at a given base node after visiting a set of nodes exactly once while minimizing the total distance [1]. Solving the TSP problem is crucial because it belongs to the class of non-polynomial (NP)-complete. In this class of problems, no polynomial–time algorithm has been discovered. If someone finds an efficient TSP algorithm, it can be extended to other NP-complete class issues. Unfortunately, to date, no one has been able to do it. The TSP is divided into two categories, symmetric and asymmetric, based on the distance between any two nodes. In asymmetric TSP (ATSP), the distance from one node to another is different from the inverse distance, and in symmetric TSP (STSP), this distance is the same. As previously mentioned, the TSP consists of determining a minimum-distance circuit passing through each vertex once and only once. Such a circuit is known as a tour or Hamiltonian circuit (or cycle) [2].

A large number of exact algorithms have been proposed to solve the TSP problem. In addition to exact algorithms, some heuristic algorithms are used to provide high-quality solutions, but not necessarily optimal. The importance of identifying effective heuristics to solve large-scale TSP problems prompted the '8th DIMACS Implementation Challenge, organized by Johnson et al. [3] and solely dedicated to TSP algorithms [4]. Lin and Kernighan's heuristic algorithm appears so far to be the most effective in terms of solution quality, particularly with the variant proposed by Helsgaun (2000) [5]. Potvin (1996) [6] proposed a genetic algorithm to the TSP, and Aarts et al. (1988) [7] analyzed the TSP problem with the simulated annealing algorithm [8]. All of the traveling salesman problems have a similar structure by one difference. The basic model is as follows:

$$\min \sum_{i=1}^{n} \sum_{j=1}^{n} c_{ij} * y_{ij} \tag{1}$$

subject to Equation (2)

$$\sum_{i=1}^{n} y_{ij} = 1, \qquad i = 1, \ldots, \mathrm{n} \tag{2}$$

$$\sum_{j=1}^{n} y_{ij} = 1, \qquad j = 1, \ldots, \mathrm{n} \tag{3}$$

$$y_{ij} \in \{0,1\}, \qquad i, j = 1, \ldots, \mathrm{n} \tag{4}$$

In this formulation, Equation (1) is the objective function that minimizes the total distance and c_{ij} is distance or weight of arc (i,j), Equations (2) and (3) are the assignment constraint, which ensures that each node is visited and left exactly once, and Equations (4) and (5) indicate that y_{ij} is a binary variable and equals to 1 if arc (i,j) participates in the tours.

The basic model that is mentioned above is not complete because it does not support the Hamiltonian circuit. Suppose there are six nodes and a traveler wants to visit all of them, he can do this in the two ways shown in Figure 1:

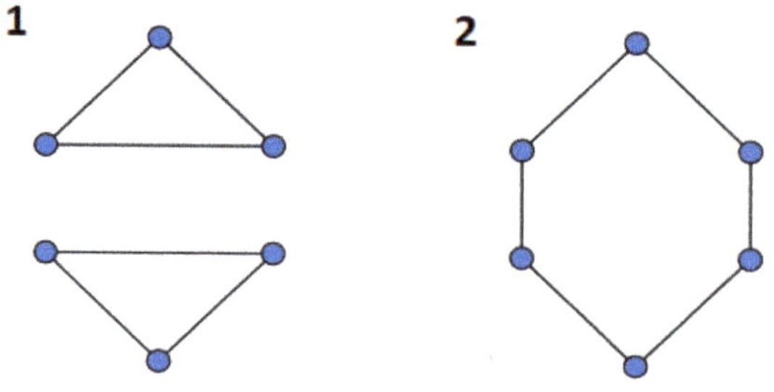

Figure 1. Number (1) does not have a Hamiltonian circuit, and number (2) has a Hamiltonian circuit.

In the above graphs (1 and 2), all of the nodes are visited, but in (1), we do not have a Hamiltonian circuit. This figure indicates that the basic formulation is not complete and should use a constraint that omits graph (1). For that, researchers add a constraint to the basic formulation for eliminating these sub-tours. Researchers have proposed many constraints for sub-tour breaking, but it is not clear which one is better. Therefore, in this research, an attempt has been made to compare the three methods most used in articles. This study used a multi-criteria decision-making method for the evaluation and comparison of these three constraints. Since the purpose of the research is to survey the three formulations, it is proposed to use the simultaneous evaluation of criteria and alternatives (SECA) method for decision making and ranking. One of this method's properties is that it does not need experts' opinions for weighting criteria. The SECA method can compute weights of criteria by mathematical methods.

2. Description of Three Sub-Tour Elimination Constraints (SECs)

2.1. The Danzig–Fulkerson–Johnson (DFJ) Formulation

Danzig, Fulkerson, and Johnson proposed the first integer linear programming (ILP) formulation in 1954 as an SEC [9]. The DFJ constraints are

$$\sum_{i \in Q} \sum_{j \in Q} y_{ij} \leq |Q| - 1 \text{ for all } Q \subset \{1, 2, \ldots, n\} \text{ and } 2 < |Q| \leq n - 1 \tag{5}$$

In each subset Q, sub-tours are prevented, ensuring that the number of arcs selected in Q is smaller than the number of Q nodes [10]. y_{ij} is a binary variable and is equal to 1 when the nodes of i,j are visited. Q is a set of vertices whose cardinalities are between 3 and $n - 1$ because two nodes cannot take a tour, and the minimum number for making a tour is 3.

2.2. The Miller–Tucker–Zemlin (MTZ) Formulation

The earliest known extended formulation of the TSP was proposed by Miller in 1960 [11]. It was initially proposed for a vehicle routing problem (VRP), where each route's number of vertices is limited [12]. The VRP can be simply defined as the problem of designing least-cost delivery routes from a depot to a set of geographically scattered customers, subject to side constraints. This problem is central to distribution management and must be routinely solved by carriers. In practice, several variants of the problem exist because of the diversity of operating rules and constraints encountered in real-life applications [13]. The capacitated vehicle routing problem (CVRP) is one of the variants of the VRP. The CVRP consists, in its basic version, of designing a set of minimum cost-routes for several identical vehicles having a fixed capacity to serve a set of customers with known demands [14]. The MTZ constraints are

$$u_i - u_j + n y_{ij} \leq n - 1 \text{ for all } j \neq 1 \text{ and } i \neq j \tag{6}$$

In this formulation u_i and u_j are integer variables that define the order of vertices visited on a tour. y_{ij} is a binary variable and is equal to 1 when the nodes of i,j are visited. Constraint acts on the basis of node labeling. This means each node receives a number label, and these numbers should be sequential. Figure 2 shows that each number is greater than the previous one except in the last one (1 is not greater than 4). This simple rule helps prevent the TSP from making arc i,l and eliminate taking a tour.

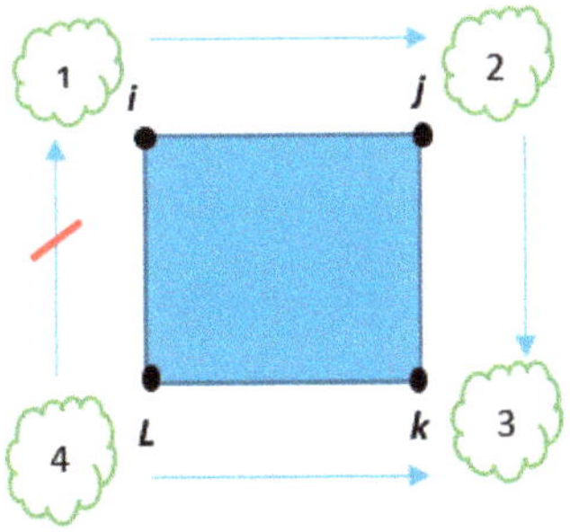

Figure 2. The Miller–Tucker–Zemlin (MTZ) number labeling that does not allow to construct arc i,l.

2.3. The Gavish–Graves (GG) Formulation

A large class of extended ATSP formulations is known as commodity flow formulations, where the additional variables represent commodity flows through the arcs and satisfy additional flow conservation constraints. These models belong to three classes: single-commodity flow (SCF), two-commodity flow (TCF), and multi-commodity flow (MCF) formulations. The earliest SCF formulation is due to Gavish and Graves. The additional continuous non-negative variables z_{ij} describe a single commodity's flow vertex

1 from every other vertex [12]. The GG [15] formulation for a single commodity problem that has sub-tour elimination constraints in it is

$$\sum_{j=1} z_{ij} - \sum_{j\neq 1} z_{ij} = 1 \qquad i = 2, \ldots, n \tag{7}$$

$$z_{ij} \leq (n-1)y_{ij}, \qquad i = 2, \ldots, n \text{ and } j = 1, \ldots, n \tag{8}$$

$$z_{ij} \geq 0 \text{ for all } i, j \tag{9}$$

In this formulation, z is a positive variable. y_{ij} is a binary variable and is equal to 1 when the nodes of i,j are visited. Constraint (7) ensures that the flow variable (Z_{ij}) exists between nodes with one unit following. Constraint (8) assures that a flow is possible when the nodes are connected (y_{ij} = 1).

3. Research Gap

As indicated, there are many SECs of the TSP formulation in literature. Researchers prefer using one of them based on their previous experiences. Consequently, if someone enters this field, they do not know which one is more related to their work. Sometimes new researchers use one method that is not proper for their research. For example, when the number of nodes increases, using the DFJ method is not suitable because it is an exponential growth of constraints that make it complicated for the software to achieve a result. Nevertheless, some researchers use the DFJ method in problems with a high number of nodes. However, there has been no research attending to all aspects or details. Some researchers select SECs just for their lower constraints or variables. Others work on the relaxation to get better answers, which are nearer to the optimum. So far, researchers have not considered all related criteria that impact the selection of SECs. This study attempted to cover the criteria that have the most impact on the selection of SECs. Consider someone who wants to use SECs for sub-tour elimination. He faces DFJ and realizes that DFJ gets an answer nearer to an optimum value, but it has many constraints and needs more time for running, and for the exponential growth of constraints, it needs a more powerful computer. With these properties of DFJ, is its selection suitable or not? The MTZ method gets results comparable to an optimum value, but it generates integer variables and incredibly increases the problem's complexity. The GG method does not get a result near the optimum value, but it has fewer constraints than DFJ and has no integer variable. With these properties, which one of them is better than the others?

Accordingly, it was decided to convey three SECs used more than others in research and determine which of them is better and related to our work.

4. Methodology

The core of operations research is the development of approaches for optimal decision making. A prominent class of such problems is multi-criteria decision making (MCDM) [16]. There are many MCDM methods in the literature. These approaches are classified according to the type of data (deterministic, stochastic, and fuzzy) and to the number of decision-makers (single, group). In the decision-making process, usually three steps are followed for numerical analysis of alternatives:

(1) Specifying the relevant criteria and alternatives
(2) Assigning numerical measures to the criteria under the impact of alternatives
(3) Ranking each alternative

According to these steps, various methods have been proposed. In continuation, some prevalent MCDM methods introduced recently are explained.

The best–worst method (BWM) was proposed by Rezaee (2015). In this method, decision-makers first determine some decision criteria and then identify the best (most desirable) and the worst (least desirable). These criteria (best and worst) are compared to other criteria (pairwise comparison). A maximin problem is then formulated and solved to determine the weights of different criteria [17].

With the aid of some aggregation strategies, Yazdani et al. (2018) introduced a new method, which is a combined compromise decision-making algorithm [18]. They called it CoCoSo, which is an abbreviation of combined compromise solution. This method is used to compromise normalization, which was proposed by Zeleny (1973) [19]. The CoCoSo weight of alternatives is determined by three equations achieved by the aggregated multiplication rule.

Stevic et al. (2019) proposed a new method: measurement alternatives and ranking according to compromise solution (MARCOS). This method is based on defining the relationship between alternatives and reference values (ideal and anti-ideal alternatives). Based on the defined relationships, the utility functions of alternatives are determined and compromise ranking is made in relation to ideal and anti-ideal solutions. Decision preferences are defined on the basis of utility functions. Utility functions represent the position of an alternative concerning an ideal and anti-ideal solution. The best alternative is the one that is closest to the ideal and at the same time furthest from the anti-ideal reference point [20].

This study uses the SECA method for decision making and ranking [21]. One of the reasons for selecting this method is that experts, like most other methods, do not need to allocate weights of criteria. This study compares three mathematical constraints and does not need expert opinion for scoring the criteria. It recommends two reference points (the standard deviation and correlation) and then minimizes the deviation of criteria weights from the reference point. The score of each alternative and the weight of each criterion are determined with software. The SECA model is multi-objective non-linear programming, which uses some techniques for optimization, and the formulation is equal to

$$\max z = \lambda_a - \beta(\lambda_b + \lambda_c) \tag{10}$$

subject to

$$\lambda_a \leq S_i, \quad \forall i \in \{1, 2, \ldots, n\} \tag{11}$$

$$S_i = \sum_{j=1}^{m} w_j {x_{ij}}^N, \quad \forall i \in \{1, 2, \ldots, n\} \tag{12}$$

$$\lambda_b = \sum_{j=1}^{m} \left(w_j - {\sigma_j}^N\right)^2 \tag{13}$$

$$\lambda_c = \sum_{j=1}^{m} \left(w_j - {\pi_j}^N\right)^2 \tag{14}$$

$$\sum_{j=1}^{m} w_j = 1, \tag{15}$$

$$w_j \leq 1, \quad \forall j \in \{1, 2, \ldots, m\} \tag{16}$$

$$w_j \geq \varepsilon \quad \forall j \in \{1, 2, \ldots, m\} \tag{17}$$

where x_{ij} denotes the performance value of i-th alternative on j criterion and w_j is the weight of each unknown criterion. Moreover,σ_j, each vector elements' standard deviation π_j, shows the degree of conflict between j-th criterion and other criteria. In addition, ε, a small positive parameter, is equal to 10^{-3} as a lower bound for criteria weights. The coefficient β is used for minimizing deviation from reference points. In the source paper, it is mentioned that when the values of β are greater than 3 ($\beta \geq 3$), the performance of alternatives is more stable. Therefore, β is taken to be 3 in this study. S_i shows the overall performance score of each alternative.

The SECA method also is used in the evaluation of sustainable manufacturing strategies. In this decision model, SECA is combined with a weighted aggregated sum product assessment (WASPAS) [22].

5. Selection of Related Criteria by Reviewing Articles

Defining related criteria is the essence of using the MCDM methods. The MCDM methods indeed evaluate multiple conflicting criteria, but this does not mean that the criteria are not related to the issue. So, selecting proper criteria is an essential step in decision making. There are two ways to choose criteria. One way is to review some articles and convey on them to select the right criteria. The other way is to consult with experts and use what they opt for. This study used both methods for selecting related criteria. Further research that deals with this issue was undertaken, and a summary is provided in the following content.

ATSP formulations are shown in Table 1, and the order of their variables and constraints will be determined like this [12]:

Table 1. Classification of asymmetric traveling salesman problem (ATSP) formulations.

Category	Formulations	Variables	Constraints
Exponential size	DFJ	O (n^2)	O (2^n)
Miller–Tucker–Zemlin-based	MTZ	O (n^2)	O (n^2)
Single commodity flow	GG	O (n^2)	O (n^2)

DFJ, Danzig–Fulkerson–Johnson; MTZ, Miller–Tucker–Zemlin; and GG, Gavish–Graves.

To complete their comparative study, they tested the LP relaxation of these models. The result of this comparison shows that DFJ is better than GG, and GG is better than MTZ, which means the result of LP relaxation of the DFJ model is closer to the optimal value. Their results are similar to Wong's research [23].

Orman and Williams classified models into four groups: conventional (C), sequential (S), flow-based (F), and time-staged (T) [24]. They extracted the following information:

(1) DFJ is located in the C group, and the combination of the base model with this sub-tour elimination has $2^n + 2n - 2$ constraints and $n(n-1)$ 0–1 variables, because the exponential number of constraints cannot solve this practically.
(2) MTZ is located in the S group, and the combination of the base model with this sub-tour elimination has $n^2 - n + 2$ constraints, $n(n-1)$ 0–1 variables, and $(n-1)$ continuous variables.
(3) GG is located in the F1 group, and the combination of the base model with this sub-tour elimination has $n(n+2)$ constraints, $n(n-1)$ 0–1 variables, and $n(n-1)$ continues variables.
(4) To demonstrate the relative strengths of LP relaxations of these SECs, they provide the following results (Table 2) for 10 cities' TSP.

Table 2. Computational results.

Model	Size	LP.obj	Iterations	Time (s)	IP.obj	Nodes	Time (s)
C	502 × 90	766	37	1	766	0	1
S	92 × 99	773.6	77	3	881	665	16
F1	120 × 180	794.22	148	1	881	449	13

Benhida and Mir [25] compared DFJ and MTZ sub-tour elimination and declared that the DFJ formulation of the TSP contains $n(n-1)$ variables and $2^n + 2n - 2$ constraints. MTZ contains $(n-1)(n+1)$ variables and $n^2 - n + 2$ constraints. To compare this method, they randomly generated 10 complete graphs from 10 to 950 nodes. These nodes were randomly taken between 0 and 99 coordinates. The distances between the nodes are Euclidean distances (d), and they calculated the relaxation value (R) by relaxing the integrality constraints. They reported the results in a table and showed the R values of DFJ and MTZ for 10 to 950 nodes. This final result of the research was that the DFJ relaxation value is better than the MTZ relaxation value, and MTZ is charming because it is easy to implement but gives a low continuous relaxation.

By reviewing the above articles and consulting with experts, six criteria that have a significant impact on the selection of SECs are chosen and listed below:

(1) Number of constraints: when this criterion increases, the time to solve increases, too.
(2) Number of variables: these criteria affect the solution time.
(3) Relaxation value: whatever is closer to an optimum value is better.
(4) Number of nodes: it affects solution time and SEC performance.
(5) Type of variable: integer variables increase the complexity of a problem.
(6) Time in second: the time to find a solution is a significant issue in selecting a method.

6. Computational Results

After defining related criteria, the three sub-tour elimination constraints should be evaluated. In this evaluation, the number of nodes is considered constant in each step of comparison. Optimization software is needed to assess these SECs. This study uses CPLEX 12.8 for coding these three sub-tour eliminations (codes attached in Appendix A). In this code, we calculated the optimal answer for different nodes with a random distance (rand (10) + rand (200)), and we reported the results in Table 3. When the number of nodes increases, the difficulty of a problem also increases. In mathematical optimization, relaxation is a modeling strategy. Solving problems by a relaxation variable provided useful information about the original problem. DFJ relaxation gets the best answer from others because it has one type of variable (binary). MTZ gets the worst solution for its two types of variables (integer and binary).

For relaxation in CPLEX, we changed the type of variable to float+ and added a constraint ($0 \leq y_{ij} \leq 1$).

Table 3. Results reported by CPLEX.

Instances	SEC	Constraints	Variables	Type-V	Time (s)	Vopt	R
Inst-10	DFJ	987	100	B	0	462	462
Inst-10	MTZ	111	100 + 10	B + I	0	462	462
Inst-10	GG	119	100 + 90	B + P	0	462	462
Inst-15	DFJ	32,676	225	B	5	371	371
Inst-15	MTZ	241	225 + 15	B + I	0	371	354.73
Inst-15	GG	254	225 + 210	B + P	0	371	369.57
Inst-16	DFJ	65,430	256	B	11	425	425
Inst-16	MTZ	273	256 + 16	B + I	0	425	425
Inst-16	GG	287	256 + 240	B + P	0	425	425
Inst-17	DFJ	130,951	289	B	34	451	450
Inst-17	MTZ	307	289 + 17	B + I	0	451	416.4
Inst-17	GG	322	289 + 272	B + P	0	451	416.56
Inst-18	DFJ	262,007	324	B	72	352	352
Inst-18	MTZ	343	324 + 18	B + I	0	352	335
Inst-18	GG	359	324 + 306	B + P	0	352	336.76
Inst-19	DFJ	524,134	361	B	-	-	421
Inst-19	MTZ	381	361 + 19	B + I	0	421	394.68
Inst-19	GG	398	361 + 342	B + P	0	421	394.78

Table 3. *Cont.*

Instances	SEC	Constraints	Variables	Type-V	Time (s)	Vopt	R
Inst-20	DFJ	1,048,194	400	B	-	-	-
Inst-20	MTZ	421	400 + 20	B + I	0	399	350.6
Inst-20	GG	439	400 + 380	B + P	0	399	350.68
Inst-50	DFJ	-	-	-	-	-	-
Inst-50	MTZ	2551	2500 + 50	B + I	0	516	502.16
Inst-50	GG	2599	2500 + 2450	B + P	1	516	502.25
Inst-100	DFJ	-	-	-	-	-	-
Inst-100	MTZ	10,100	10,000 + 100	B + I	2	665	656.08
Inst-100	GG	10,119	10,000 + 9900	B + P	8	665	656.08
Inst-500	DFJ	-	-	-	-	-	-
Inst-500	MTZ	250,501	250,000 + 500	B + I	44	1173	1173
Inst-500	GG	250,999	250,000 + 249,500	B + P	115	1173	1173

SEC, sub-tour elimination constraint; B, binary; I, integer; P, positive; S, second; and R, the objective value when variables were relaxed.

7. Using the SECA Method for Ranking Computational Results

With the information in Table 4, which is achieved by comparing the criteria, it is possible to use the MCDM method. As mentioned before, among the decision-making methods, SECA is selected in this research. Now, in this section, we implement the stages of this method. At first, like other MCDM methods, define a decision matrix for a problem and normalize it. In the decision matrix, x_{ij} denotes the performance value of alternatives (*i*) on each criterion column (*j*). Use linear normalization for normalizing. In this, the criteria are divided into two sets, beneficial and non-beneficial. Linear normalization formulation is

$$x_{ij}^N = \begin{cases} \frac{x_{ij}}{\max_k x_{kj}} & If\ j\ ie\ Beneficia \\ \frac{\min_k x_{kj}}{x_{ij}} & If\ j\ ie\ Non- \end{cases} \tag{18}$$

Table 4. Decision matrix.

Nodes = 15	Constraint	Variable	Type	Time	Gap
	NB	NB	NB	NB	NB
DFJ	32,676	225	1	6	1
MTZ	241	240	16	1	16.27
GG	254	435	1	1	1.43

NB, non-beneficial.

After normalization, this formulation should be used to calculate the degree of conflict between the criteria. r_{jl} is the correlation between *j* and *l* vectors.

$$\pi_j = \sum_{l=1}^{m} (1 - r_{jl}) \tag{19}$$

After calculating the standard deviation of the elements of each vector (σ_j), we normalize π_j and σ_j by these formulations:

$$\pi_j{}^N = \frac{\pi_j}{\sum_{l=1}^{m} \pi_l} \tag{20}$$

$$\sigma_j^N = \frac{\sigma_j}{\sum\limits_{l=1}^{m} \sigma_l} \quad (21)$$

In our problem, there are three alternatives and five criteria. The score of the nodes should be calculated for the ranking of alternatives. It should be considered that it is not possible to use $x_{ij} = 0$ in the SECA model. For this reason, the cells that are zero are converted to 1. One may ask why it is allowed to substitute 0 with 1 in the decision matrix. As mentioned above, the minimum amount of x in SECA method is 1 and cannot use a smaller number. The significant number of nodes (100 and 500) in which there are no criteria values less than 1 are calculated to confirm this research result. In the table given below, gap is the difference between the optimal and the relaxed value, and the less the value, the better and beneficial it is. An example of the decision matrix is used to show the case of Node = 15 in Table 4.

After implementing the stages for calculating σ and π (the steps are provided in Appendix B), each alternative's computing score should be calculated using optimization software. This work used LINGO 11 software for coding the SECA optimization model (exist in Appendix C). We got the following results for each node (Table 5). Their ranking is shown in Table 6.

Table 5. Scoring alternatives by LINGO 11.

Node	10	15	16	17	18	19	20	50	100	500
DFJ	0.6655	0.6233	0.37	0.605	0.6	-	-	-	-	-
MTZ	0.6655	0.6233	0.81	0.605	0.6	0.62	0.67	0.64	0.59	0.57
GG	0.84	0.8356	0.88	0.685	0.7	0.85	0.84	0.85	0.69	0.73

Table 6. Ranking of alternatives.

Node	10	15	16	17	18	19	20	50	100	500
DFJ	2	2	3	2	2	-	-	-	-	-
MTZ	2	2	2	2	2	2	2	2	2	2
GG	1	1	1	1	1	1	1	1	1	1

By looking at the ranking table, we understand that GG is the best method between the three SEC formulations. For testing, the SECA method's scoring used the website www.mcdm.app (accessed on 25 December 2020), which has a powerful calculation engine and covers many MCDM methodologies. As seen, the GG method has some features that lead it to the first place. One reason making it better from the MTZ method is the type of variables. GG has no integer variable that increases the complexity of a problem. When the number of nodes increases, the DFJ method's constraints extend exponentially, and an optimum computing value is more challenging for a computer. As we see in the above tables, when the number of nodes is more significant than 19, typically, personal computers will not be able to compute an optimum value for DFJ and to report the result, because estimating this large volume of calculations, personal computers run out of random access memory (RAM). RAM is short-term storage that holds programs and processes running on a computer. Behinda and Mir calculated the DFJ method for many cities, which is in contrast to the paper's result. This may occur for several reasons; for example, they might use powerful computers with high RAM (they do not refer to the system's information). This study uses a usual computer (the system used for this research had an 8 GB RAM and a CPU with seven cores). One of the reasons may be due to the ATSP, because in this type of problem, the route between two cities is different from the return route, and this issue increased the complexity of the solution. Using parallel computing or changing the amount of rand can get an answer for many cities. For these reasons, the codes used in this study are attached in the Appendix C for readers.

Applegate et al. [26] decided to solve various TSP instances and constructed a library named TSPLIB. They used DFJ sub-tour elimination. The size of cities ranged from 17 to 85,900. For the largest, of 85,900 nodes, they used 96 workstations for a total of 139 years of CPU time [8].

8. Conclusions

One of the usual problems for a researcher in using TSP formulation is to select the best sub-tour elimination constraint. As everyone may know, many SEC formulations are presented, but it is not specified which of them is most suited to our work. So, they should be compared to each other to determine which of them is superior. This study analyzes three SECs of the TSP formulation (DFJ, MTZ, and GG), which are used more than others in research. For comparison using MCDM methods, some criteria needed to be introduced. By reviewing research papers, five criteria were concluded: the number of constraints, the number of variables, type of variables, time of solving, and the differences between optimum and relaxed value, and that was the main research gap of the study. These SEC formulations are non-linear. When the number of nodes rises, solving problems with non-linear variables is hard. For this reason, these variables are turned into linear variables, because linear problems are solved quickly. This conversion is named LP relaxation. Therefore, the lower value of the gap is more suitable because the relaxation value is closer to its optimum value. It should be mentioned that the relaxation value gets a lower bound of a problem. Whenever this lower bound is more comparable to an optimum value, the result reaches the optimum by fewer iterations in the optimization software.

This research aimed to analyze the three sub-tour elimination formulations of the ATSP by an MCDM method. This study used the simultaneous evaluation of criteria and alternatives (SECA) method for multiple decision making and ranking the alternatives. The computation of this method shows that GG SEC is better than others. Comparison between DFJ and MTZ does not show a distinct difference, but as shown, the DFJ SEC's computing is time-consuming because, as the number of nodes increases, the constraints grow exponentially. This particular reason drives us to use MTZ SEC in the ATSP problem, especially when the number of nodes increases.

If we look at Table 4, we may ask why GG is better than MTZ, while MTZ has fewer variables and constraints and takes less time to solve. To answer this question, it is better said, as mentioned before, that MTZ has a charming face. One of the criteria considered in this study is the type of variables. MTZ generates integer variables, and as we know, these variables increase the complexity of solving. The real traveling salesman problem could not reach the exact answer in polynomial time because this is an NP_hard problem.

Thus, researchers used heuristic methods to obtain an upper bound and relaxation to earn a lower bound for these problems. They know the answer is in this interval. Relaxation of the MTZ constraint should get two types of variables, binary and integer. Most of the times, the relaxation variable is not an integer, and other methods should be used to convert it into an integer, but GG does not have this problem because it has binary and positive variables and gets a relaxation value that is closer to the optimum value. Therefore, the type of variable is a crucial criterion and significantly affects the ranking of alternatives. So, the main reason for this ranking is this criterion. Covering all aspects, this study proposes that GG is the best sub-tour elimination.

Author Contributions: Conceptualization, R.B. and S.H.Z.; methodology, R.B.; software, S.H.Z.; validation, S.H.Z. and R.B.; formal analysis, S.H.Z. and S.M.J.M.A.-e-h.; investigation, R.B.; data curation, R.B.; writing—original draft preparation, R.B. and S.H.Z.; writing—review and editing, R.B. and S.H.Z.; supervision, S.H.Z. and S.M.J.M.A.-e-h.; project administration, S.H.Z.; funding acquisition, S.H.Z. All authors have read and agreed to the published version of the manuscript.

Funding: There is no external fund for this study.

Acknowledgments: The authors acknowledge, with thanks, Danesh Tabatabaee, the master's student of the Department of Industrial Management Systems and Engineering, Amirkabir University of Technology, for help in software coding.

Conflicts of Interest: There is no conflict of interest.

Appendix A

CPLEX code:

```
DFJ:
//define number of nodes
int nbnode=10;                                      // define parameter
range nodes=1..nbnode;                              // define index

//c is the distance between nodes
float c[i in nodes][j in nodes]=rand(10)+rand(200);

//in this section define set and subset
range ss = 1..ftoi(round(2^nbnode));
{int} sub [s in ss] = {i | i in 1..nbnode: (s div ftoi(2^(i-1))) mod 2 == 1};

//model
dvar boolean y[nodes][nodes];                       // y is decision variable
which
                                                    is binary.
minimize sum(i,j in nodes)c[i][j]*y[i][j];          //objective function
subject
to{                                                 //constraints
forall (j in nodes) sum(i in nodes)y[i][j]==1;
forall (i in nodes) sum(j in nodes)y[i][j]==1;
forall (s in ss: 2<card(sub[s])<nbnode) sum(i, j in sub[s]) y[i][j] <= card(sub[s])-1;

}
MTZ:
//define number of nodes
int nbnode=10;                                      // define parameter
range nodes=1..nbnode;                              // define index

//c is the distance between nodes
float c[i in nodes][j in nodes]=rand(10)+rand(200);

//model
dvar boolean y[nodes][nodes];                       //y is binary variable
dvar int+ u[nodes];                                 // u is integer variable

minimize sum(i,j in nodes)c[i][j]*x[i][j];          //objective function
subject
to{                                                 //constraints
forall (j in nodes) sum(i in nodes)y[i][j]==1;
forall (i in nodes) sum(j in nodes)y[i][j]==1;
forall (i,j in nodes: j!=1) u[i]-u[j]+nbnode*y[i][j]<=nbnode-1;
}
GG:
//define number of nodes
int nbnode=10;                                      // define parameter
range nodes=1..nbnode;                              // define index
```

```
//c is the distance between nodes
float c[i in nodes][j in nodes]=rand(10)+rand(200);


//model
dvar boolean y[nodes][nodes];                    //y is binary variable
dvar float+ z[nodes][nodes];                     //z is positive variable

minimize sum(i,j in nodes)c[i][j]*y[i][j];       //objective function
subject
to{                                              //constraints
forall (j in nodes) sum(i in nodes)y[i][j]==1;
forall (i in nodes) sum(j in nodes)y[i][j]==1;
forall (i in nodes: i>=2 ) sum(j in nodes)z[i][j]-sum(j in nodes: j!=1)z[j][i]==1;
forall (i,j in nodes: i!=1) z[i][j]<=(nbnode-1)*y[i][j];

}
```

Appendix B

Table A1. Normalized decision matrix.

Normalize	Constraint	Variable	Type	Time	Gap
DFJ	0.007375	1	1	0.166667	1
MTZ	1	0.9375	0.0625	1	0.061463
GG	0.948819	0.517241	1	1	0.699301

Table A2. Standard deviation of criteria.

STD	**0.456343**	**0.214367**	**0.441942**	**0.392837**	**0.39131**
STD-N	0.240598	0.113021	0.233006	0.207116	0.206311

Table A3. Correlation of criteria.

r_{ij}	Constraint	Variable	Type	Time	Gap
Constraint	1	−0.5622	−0.53913	0.998951	−0.77613
Variable	−0.56225	1	−0.39336	−0.59953	−0.08508
Type	−0.53913	−0.3933	1	−0.5	0.949517
Time	0.998951	−0.5995	−0.5	1	−0.74644
Gap	−0.77613	−0.0850	0.949517	−0.74644	1

Table A4. Calculate $\pi = \Sigma\,(1 - r_{ij})$.

$1 - r_{ij}$	Constraint	Variable	Type	Time	Gap	Sum Each Row	Πn
Constraint	0	1.562251	1.539128	0.001049	1.77613	4.878559	0.199069
Variable	1.56225	0	1.393365	1.599526	1.085082	5.640223	0.230148
Type	1.53913	1.39336	0	1.5	0.050483	4.482973	0.182927
Time	0.001049	1.59953	1.5	0	1.746444	4.847023	0.197782
Gap	1.77613	1.08508	0.050483	1.74644	0	4.658133	0.190074

Table A5. Ranking of alternatives by score.

	SCORE	Ranking
DFJ	0.6233	2
MTZ	0.6233	2
GG	0.8356	1

Appendix C

Code of SECA in LINGO 11 for node=15:

```
MODEL:

SETS:
AL/1..3/:S;                    #AL is alternatives and s is score
CR/1..5/: W,zig,p;             # CR is criteria
LINK (AL, CR): X;              # X denoted the performance value of
                                 alternatives on each criterion column
ENDSETS

#read data from excel file
DATA:
B=3;                           #B is beta in the SECA method
#zig is the normalization of standard deviation
#p is the normalization of sum (1- correlation) of each row
X, zig, p=@OLE('C:\MATRIX.XLSX','DECISION','SIG','PI');
ENDDATA

@FOR (AL (I):
    s(I)=@SUM (CR(J):W(J)*X(I,J));
    LA <=S (I);
);
@FOR(CR (J):
    W (J) <=1;
    W (J) >=0.001;             # W shouldn't be zero
);

@sum(CR(J):W(J))=1;

LB=@SUM (CR (J):((W (J)- zig (J))^2 ));

LC=@SUM(CR(J):((W (J)- p (J))^2 ));

Z=LA-(B*(LB+LC)); #x2003;      #objective function

@FREE(Z); #x2003;              # Z is free variable

MAX=Z;

END
```

References

1. Campuzano, G.; Obreque, C.; Aguayo, M. Accelerating the Miller–Tucker–Zemlin model for the asymmetric traveling salesman problem. *Expert Syst. Appl.* **2020**, *148*, 113–229. [CrossRef]
2. Laporte, G. The Traveling Salesman Problem: An overview of exact and approximate algorithms. *Eur. J. Oper. Res.* **1992**, *59*, 231–247. [CrossRef]
3. Johnson, D.; McGeoch, L.; Glover, F.; Rego, C. The Traveling Salesman Problem. In *8th DIMACS Implementation Challenge*; DIMACS Center, Rutgers University: Piscataway, NJ, USA, 2000; Available online: http://dimacs.rutgers.edu/archive/Challenges/TSP/about.html (accessed on 25 December 2020).
4. Rego, C.; Gamboa, D.; Glover, F.; Osterman, C. Traveling salesman problem heuristics: Leading methods, implementations and latest advances. *Eur. J. Oper. Res.* **2011**, *211*, 427–441. [CrossRef]
5. Helsgun, K. An effective implementation of the Lin–Kernighan traveling salesman heuristic. *Eur. J. Oper. Res.* **2000**, *126*, 106–130. [CrossRef]
6. Potvin, J. Genetic algorithms for the traveling salesman problem. *Ann. Oper. Res.* **1996**, *63*, 339–370. [CrossRef]
7. Aarts, E.; Korst, J.; Laarhoven, P. A quantitative analysis of the simulated annealing algorithm: A case study for the traveling salesman problem. *J. Stats. Phys.* **1988**, *50*, 189–206. [CrossRef]
8. Hoffman, K.; Padberg, M.; Rinaldi, G. *Traveling Salesman Problem*; Kluwer Academic Publishers: Boston, MA, USA, 2001. [CrossRef]

9. Dantzig, G.; Fulkerson, J.; Johnson, S. Solution of a Large-Scale Traveling-Salesman Problem. *Oper. Res. Soc. Am.* **1954**, *2*, 393–410. [CrossRef]
10. Taccari, L. Integer programming formulations for the elementary shortest path problem. *Eur. J. Oper. Res.* **2016**, *252*, 122–130. [CrossRef]
11. Miller, C.; Tucker, A.; Zemlin, R. Integer programming formulations and travelling salesman problems. *J. Assoc. Comput. Mach.* **1960**, *07*, 326–329. [CrossRef]
12. Öncan, T.; Altınel, I.; Laporte, G. A comparative analysis of several asymmetric traveling salesman problem formulations. *Comput. Oper. Res.* **2009**, *36*, 637–654. [CrossRef]
13. Laporte, G. Fifty Years of Vehicle Routing. *Transp. Sci.* **2009**, *43*, 408–416. [CrossRef]
14. Faiz, S.; Krichen, S.; Inoubli, W. A DSS based on GIS and Tabu search for solving the CVRP: The Tunisian case. *Egypt. J. Remote Sens. Space Sci.* **2014**, *17*, 105–110. [CrossRef]
15. Gavish, B.; Graves, S. *The Travelling Salesman Problem and Related Problems*; Massachusetts Institute of Technology, Operations Research Center: Cambridge, MA, USA, 1978; p. 78.
16. Triantaphyllou, E.; Shu, B.; Sanchez, S.; Ray, T. Multi-Criteria Decision Making: An Operations Research Approach. In *Encyclopedia of Electrical and Electronics Engineering*; John Wiley & Sons: New York, NY, USA, 1998; pp. 175–186.
17. Rezaei, J. Best-worst multi-criteria decision-making method. *Omega* **2015**, *53*, 49–57. [CrossRef]
18. Yazdani, M.; Zarate, P.; Zavadskas, E.; Turskis, Z. A Combined Compromise Solution (CoCoSo) method for multi-criteria decision-making problems. *Manag. Decis* **2018**, *57*. [CrossRef]
19. Zeleny, M. Compromise programming. In *Multiple Criteria Decision Making*; Cocchrane, J.L., Zeleny, M., Eds.; University of South Carolina Press: Columbia, SC, USA, 1973; pp. 262–301.
20. Stević, Z.; Pamučar, D.; Puška, A.; Chatterjee, P. Sustainable supplier selection in healthcare industries using a new MCDM method: Measurement Alternatives and Ranking according to COmpromise Solution (MARCOS). *Comput. Ind. Eng.* **2019**, *140*, 106–231. [CrossRef]
21. Keshavarz-Ghorabaee, M.; Amiri, M.; Zavadskas, E.; Antucheviciene, J. Simultaneous Evaluation of Criteria and Alternatives (SECA) for Multi-Criteria Decision-Making. *Informatica* **2018**, *29*, 265–280. [CrossRef]
22. Keshavarz-Ghorabaee, M.; Govindan, K.; Amiri, M.; Zavadskas, E.; Antuchevičienė, J. An integrated type-2 fuzzy decision model based on WASPAS and SECA for evaluation of sustainable manufacturing strategies. *J. Environ. Eng. Landsc. Manag.* **2019**, *27*, 187–200. [CrossRef]
23. Wong, R. Integer programming formulations of the traveling salesman problem. In *IEEE Conference on Circuits and Computers*; IEEE Press: Piscataway, NJ, USA, 1980; pp. 149–152.
24. Orman, A.; Williams, H. A Survey of Different Integer Programming Formulations of the Travelling Salesman Problem. In *Optimisation, Econometric and Financial Analysis*; Springer: Berlin/Heidelberg, Germany, 2005; pp. 91–104.
25. Benhida, S.; Mir, A. Generating subtour elimination constraints for the Traveling Salesman Problem. *IOSR J. Eng. (IOSRJEN)* **2018**, *8*, 17–21.
26. Applegate, D.; Bixby, R.; Chvátal, V.; Cook, W. *Finding Cuts in the TSP (A Preliminary Report) DIMACS Technical Report 95-05*; Rutgers University: New Brunswick, NJ, USA, 1995.

axioms

MDPI

Article

An Extended MABAC Method Based on Triangular Fuzzy Neutrosophic Numbers for Multiple-Criteria Group Decision Making Problems

Irvanizam Irvanizam [1,*], Nawar Nabila Zi [1], Rahma Zuhra [2], Amrusi Amrusi [3] and Hizir Sofyan [4]

1 Department of Informatics, Universitas Syiah Kuala, Banda Aceh 23111, Indonesia; nawar.nabila2014@gmail.com
2 Department of Mathematics, Universitas Syiah Kuala, Banda Aceh 23111, Indonesia; rahmazuhra@unsyiah.ac.id
3 Department of Economics Education, Universitas Syiah Kuala, Banda Aceh 23111, Indonesia; amrusi@unsyiah.ac.id
4 Department of Statistics, Universitas Syiah Kuala, Banda Aceh 23111, Indonesia; hizir@unsyiah.ac.id
* Correspondence: irvanizam.zamanhuri@unsyiah.ac.id

Received: 15 August 2020; Accepted: 7 September 2020; Published: 10 September 2020

check for updates

Abstract: In this manuscript, we extend the traditional multi-attributive border approximation area comparison (MABAC) method for the multiple-criteria group decision-making (MCGDM) with triangular fuzzy neutrosophic numbers (TFNNs) to propose the TFNNs-MABAC method. In the proposed method, we utilize the TFNNs to express the values of criteria for each alternative in MCGDM problems. First, we briefly acquaint the basic concept of TFNNs and describe its corresponding some operation laws, the functions of score and accuracy, and the normalized hamming distance. We then review two aggregation operators of TFNNs. Afterward, we combine the traditional MABAC method with the triangular fuzzy neutrosophic evaluation and provide a sequence of calculation procedures of the TFNNs-MABAC method. After comparing it with some TFNNs aggregation operators and another method, the results showed that our extended MABAC method can not only effectively handle the conflicting attributes, but also practically deal with incomplete and indeterminate information in the MCGDM problem. Therefore, the extended MABAC method is more effective, conformable, and reasonable. Finally, an investment selection problem is demonstrated as a practice to verify the reasonability of our MABAC method.

Keywords: triangular fuzzy neutrosophic sets (TFNSs); MABAC method; MCGDM problems; TFNNs-MABAC method; invested technology enterprise

1. Introduction

The MABAC (multi-attributive border approximation area comparison) approach has been widely utilized to investigate multiple-criteria group decision-making (MCGDM) problems and has been extensively applied in various case studies by many fabulous researchers. In many existing prestigious pieces of literature, many original MCGDM approaches have been continually discussed, such as the TODIM model [1–3], the PROMETHEE model [4–6], the TOPSIS model [7–9], SAW model [10,11], the ELECTRE model [12,13], the VIKOR model [14], and the EDAS model [15].

In reality, many real-life MCGDM problems cannot easily interpret the criteria and linguistic values with appropriate values as a consequence of the complexity and fuzziness of the alternatives. These values should be described in the form of fuzzy to be more useful, rational, and feasible. The theory of the fuzzy set (FS), initially apprised by Zadeh in [16], has been frequently utilized as a worthy instrument for MCGDM [17,18] problems. This theory can capture objects into members of the set through a degree of membership that can be presented by arbitrary values within the real-number interval from 0 to 1. Atanassov [19] then introduced the intuitionistic fuzzy set (IFS) that characterizes each element of an object not only in the form of a membership degree but also in the term of non-membership. Thus, it can describe the fuzzy information more definitively and specifically than the FS. However, it can only manage uncertainty and incomplete information but not the inconsistent and indeterminacy information that occurs usually in practice. Therefore, Smarandache [20] initiated the neutrosophic, a branch of philosophy, to propose the theory of neutrosophic sets (NSs). To be more helpful for applying the NSs in real-case studies, Wang et al. [21] defined a sub-class of NSs, the single-valued neutrosophic sets (SVNSs), in which each element of an object is depicted by the degrees of truth-membership, indeterminacy-membership, and falsity-membership spreading over in the real-number interval. Ye [22] introduced the simplified neutrosophic sets (SNSs) to solve a multicriteria decision-making (MCDM) problem. Afterward, Ye [23] offered the idea of a single-valued neutrosophic linguistic set (SVNLS) combined with the TOPSIS method. Ye also explored two aggregation operators of SVNLS to an environment of SVNLS. Deli and Braumi [24] exposed the neutrosophic soft matrix (NSM) and investigated their operators to store NSs in computer memory. Deli et al. [25] first developed the concept of NSs by introducing bipolar NSs for MCDM problems. Based on the bipolar NSs, the functions of a score of accuracy can evaluate the values of alternatives and select the best one. Stanujkic et al. [26] proposed a novel MCDM approach based on bipolar NSs and the Hamming distance for assessing the quality of the websites. Stanujkic et al. [27] utilized SVNSs to extend the MULTIMOORA method for handling complex problems through prediction and judgment. Biswas et al. [28] innovated the idea of a triangular fuzzy neutrosophic number (TFNN) by combining the concepts of NS and triangular fuzzy number (TFN). Deli and Şubaş [29] integrated the TFN and triangular intuitionistic fuzzy numbers (TIFN) for reviewing several MCDM problems. Aal et al. [30] explored two ranking means through information system quality under the TFN information. Liu [31] studied the operators of SVNs weighted averaging and SVNs weighted geometric to implement a decision-making problem.

Additionally, many recent MCGDM problems have actively involved a group of decision-makers (DMs) in the process of decision-making to minimize the subjectivity of the DMs' judgment. They tend to have their own different opinions to assess alternatives and criteria and usually give their evaluation opinions using the linguistic variables term. To deal with this, there are some studies of hesitant fuzzy linguistic term sets (HFLTSs) [32] in MCGDM. Zhang et al. [33] introduced three novel algorithms for solving MCGDM problems with multi granular unbalanced hesitant fuzzy linguistic information. The first algorithm was utilized to express a linguistic distribution assessment (LDA) using a hesitant linguistic distribution (HLD). Two others were used to modify an unbalanced HFLTS into a balanced LDA and to modify a balanced LDA into an unbalanced LDA. Yu et al. [34] proposed a novel consensus reaching model in MCGDM with multi-granular HFLTSs. This optimization model was established to minimize the overall adjustment amount of DMs' preference and to be very simpler than the use of HFLTSs.

Many researchers have extensively developed applications of SVNs in MCGDM problem. However, in uncertain and complex situations, the degrees of truth-membership, indeterminacy-membership, and falsity-membership of SVNs cannot be used to delineate an element with precise real-numbers. Meanwhile, TFN can effectively manage fuzzy information rather than the real-number interval. Therefore, the combination of TFN with SVNs, or TFNNs, will be a suitable tool to handle incomplete, indeterminacy, and uncertain information occurring in MCGDM problems.

The MABAC approach was first conveyed by Pamučar and Ćirović [35] in solving a selection problem of transportation and resource distribution at a logistic center. The basic concept of this approach is to look at many ideal attributes respond to criteria located at the border approximation area (BAA). It can consider the conflicting attributes. Consequently, the MABAC takes the advantages of BAA in concerning the inconsistency of decision maker and uncertainty conditions, whereas other traditional decision-making approaches cannot conduct it. Additionally, this approach has an uncomplicated computation procedure and can reveal the decision theory in logical and systematic ways. Later on, Pamučar et al. [36] improved the MABAC by utilizing interval-valued fuzzy-rough numbers (IVFRNs). Pamučar et al. [37] integrated AHP (Analytical Hierarchy Process) and MABAC in developing a software to assess some official university websites. Jia et al. [38] have utilized analytically the concept of FS to develop a new MABAC model for MCGDM based on rough numbers (RNs). Alluding the advantages of interval type-2 fuzzy set (IT2FS), Dorfeshan and Mousavi in [39] developed a novel MABAC to determine the attribute path of beneficial projects under MCGDM process in a case study of aircraft maintenance industries. Yu et al. [40] proposed a MABAC based on an improvement of type-1 fuzzy sets (T1FSs), interval type-2 fuzzy sets (IT2FSs) to handle intrinsic and extrinsic uncertainties. Zhang et al. [41] extended MABAC for MCGDM cases with picture 2-tuple linguistic in evaluating the project of renewable energy power. Mishra et al. [42] utilized interval valued intuitionistic fuzzy sets (IVIFSs) to develop an extension of MABAC method for a programming language assessment.

In recent years, there are several MCGDM methods which can enhance the methods' adaptability. As far as we know, there have been no studies regarding the MABAC approach under TFNNs environment for MCGDM problems. Therefore, we emphasize our attention to enlarging the MABAC method to support the TFNN environment and implement it for evaluating an investment selection problem. Later on, we summarize some contributions and motivations of this study as follows:

1. There are at least two motivations for using TFNNs. Firstly, TFNNs which are adopted by TFN with NSs can effectively support uncertain information. In real practical cases, the same judgment in the form of the linguistic variable may express different meanings for various people. TFNNs provide DMs freedom decisions in defining the membership function and it can better explain and handle inaccurate information. Secondly, TFNNs are a proper instrument to deal with incomplete and indeterminacy information in MCGDM problems.
2. Because the computational complexity of TFNN, especially the loop performance in using some aggregation operators of TFNNs, is relatively a bit slow, we require a simple and uncomplicated method to determine decisions. Compared with some other methods, the MABAC has not only abilities to effectively handle the conflicting attributes, but also logically reveal the decision-making theory with uncomplicated and systematic computation procedures.

The remaining of our paper is managed systematically as follows: Section 2 discusses things related to TFNNs, such as the definition of TFNNs, some operation laws, the functions of score and accuracy, and the normalized hamming distance between two TFNNs. Later on, in Section 2, we also depict the operators of triangular fuzzy neutrosophic number weighted averaging (TFNNWA) and triangular fuzzy neutrosophic number weighted geometric (TFNNWG). Section 3 modifies the original MABAC method to triangular fuzzy neutrosophic environment and shows a sequence of calculation procedures of TFNN-MABAC model. Section 4 demonstrates an illustrative-example to select a possible invested technology enterprise to investigate the proposed MABAC method and performs a comparative analysis between our proposed MABAC and some other aggregation operators. Section 5 recapitulates our paper conclusions and discuses all possible future studies and researches.

2. Preliminaries

In this section, we re-discuss the definition of TFNNs, operation laws of TFNNs, the functions of score and accuracy of TFNNs, and the normalized hamming distance between two arbitrary TFNNs. We also recall the definition of TFNNWA and TFNNWG operators.

2.1. Triangular Fuzzy Number Neutrosophic Sets

Based on the concepts of single-valued neutrosophic sets and triangular fuzzy number intuitionistic fuzzy sets (TFNIFSs), Biswas et al. [28] first developed the triangular fuzzy number neutrosophic

(TFNNSs) by presenting the truth-membership degree (TMD), the indeterminacy-membership degree (IMD), and the falsity-membership degree (FMD) in the form of triangular-fuzzy numbers.

Definition 1 ([28]). Let X be the universal set, the TFNNSs μ can be represented as: $\mu = \{(x, \alpha_\mu(x), \beta_\mu(x), \gamma_\mu(x) | x \in X)\}$ where $\alpha_\mu(x), \beta_\mu(x), \gamma_\mu(x) \in [0,1]$ describe the truth-membership degree, the indeterminacy-membership degree, and the falsity-membership degree respectively that can be formulated by TFNs as follows.

$$\alpha_\mu(x) = \left(\alpha_\mu^L(x), \alpha_\mu^M(x), \alpha_\mu^U(x)\right),\ 0 \le \alpha_\mu^L(x) \le \alpha_\mu^M(x) \le \alpha_\mu^U(x) \le 1 \tag{1}$$

$$\beta_\mu(x) = \left(\beta_\mu^L(x), \beta_\mu^M(x), \beta_\mu^U(x)\right),\ 0 \le \beta_\mu^L(x) \le \beta_\mu^M(x) \le \beta_\mu^U(x) \le 1 \tag{2}$$

$$\gamma_\mu(x) = \left(\gamma_\mu^L(x), \gamma_\mu^M(x), \gamma_\mu^U(x)\right),\ 0 \le \gamma_\mu^L(x) \le \gamma_\mu^M(x) \le \gamma_\mu^U(x) \le 1 \tag{3}$$

For notational convenience, we assume that $\mu = \left(\left(\alpha_\mu^L(x), \alpha_\mu^M(x), \alpha_\mu^U(x)\right), \left(\beta_\mu^L(x), \beta_\mu^M(x), \beta_\mu^U(x)\right), \left(\gamma_\mu^L(x), \gamma_\mu^M(x), \gamma_\mu^U(x)\right)\right)$ is a TFNN, it has to satisfy the condition $0 \le \alpha_\mu^U(x) + \beta_\mu^U(x) + \gamma_\mu^U(x) \le 3$.

Definition 2 ([28]). Let $\mu_1 = \left(\left(\alpha_{\mu_1}^L(x), \alpha_{\mu_1}^M(x), \alpha_{\mu_1}^U(x)\right), \left(\beta_{\mu_1}^L(x), \beta_{\mu_1}^M(x), \beta_{\mu_1}^U(x)\right), \left(\gamma_{\mu_1}^L(x), \gamma_{\mu_1}^M(x), \gamma_{\mu_1}^U(x)\right)\right)$, $\mu_2 = \left(\left(\alpha_{\mu_2}^L(x), \alpha_{\mu_2}^M(x), \alpha_{\mu_2}^U(x)\right), \left(\beta_{\mu_2}^L(x), \beta_{\mu_2}^M(x), \beta_{\mu_2}^U(x)\right), \left(\gamma_{\mu_2}^L(x), \gamma_{\mu_2}^M(x), \gamma_{\mu_2}^U(x)\right)\right)$, and $\mu_3 = \left(\left(\alpha_{\mu_3}^L(x), \alpha_{\mu_3}^M(x), \alpha_{\mu_3}^U(x)\right), \left(\beta_{\mu_3}^L(x), \beta_{\mu_3}^M(x), \beta_{\mu_3}^U(x)\right), \left(\gamma_{\mu_3}^L(x), \gamma_{\mu_3}^M(x), \gamma_{\mu_3}^U(x)\right)\right)$ be three TFNNs, the following mathematical operation laws are satisfied as:

$$\mu_1 \oplus \mu_2 = \left(\begin{array}{c} \left(\alpha_{\mu_1}^L(x) + \alpha_{\mu_2}^L(x) - \alpha_{\mu_1}^L(x)\alpha_{\mu_2}^L(x), \alpha_{\mu_1}^M(x) + \alpha_{\mu_2}^M(x) - \alpha_{\mu_1}^M(x)\alpha_{\mu_2}^M(x), \alpha_{\mu_1}^U(x) + \alpha_{\mu_2}^U(x) - \alpha_{\mu_1}^U(x)\alpha_{\mu_2}^U(x)\right), \\ \left(\beta_{\mu_1}^L(x)\beta_{\mu_2}^L(x),\ \beta_{\mu_1}^M(x)\beta_{\mu_2}^M(x),\ \beta_{\mu_1}^U(x)\beta_{\mu_2}^U(x)\right), \\ \left(\gamma_{\mu_1}^L(x)\gamma_{\mu_2}^L(x),\ \gamma_{\mu_1}^M(x)\gamma_{\mu_2}^M(x),\ \gamma_{\mu_1}^U(x)\gamma_{\mu_2}^U(x)\right) \end{array}\right) \tag{4}$$

$$\mu_1 \otimes \mu_2 = \left(\begin{array}{c} \left(\alpha_{\mu_1}^L(x)\alpha_{\mu_2}^L(x),\ \alpha_{\mu_1}^M(x)\alpha_{\mu_2}^M(x),\ \alpha_{\mu_1}^U(x)\alpha_{\mu_2}^U(x)\right), \\ \left(\beta_{\mu_1}^L(x) + \beta_{\mu_2}^L(x) - \beta_{\mu_1}^L(x)\beta_{\mu_2}^L(x), \beta_{\mu_1}^M(x) + \beta_{\mu_2}^M(x) - \beta_{\mu_1}^M(x)\beta_{\mu_2}^M(x), \beta_{\mu_1}^U(x) + \beta_{\mu_2}^U(x) - \beta_{\mu_1}^U(x)\beta_{\mu_2}^U(x)\right), \\ \left(\gamma_{\mu_1}^L(x) + \gamma_{\mu_2}^L(x) - \gamma_{\mu_1}^L(x)\gamma_{\mu_2}^L(x), \gamma_{\mu_1}^M(x) + \gamma_{\mu_2}^M(x) - \gamma_{\mu_1}^M(x)\gamma_{\mu_2}^M(x), \gamma_{\mu_1}^U(x) + \gamma_{\mu_2}^U(x) - \gamma_{\mu_1}^U(x)\gamma_{\mu_2}^U(x)\right) \end{array}\right) \tag{5}$$

$$\lambda\mu_3 = \left(\begin{array}{c} \left(1 - \left(1 - \alpha_{\mu_3}^L(x)\right)^\lambda,\ 1 - \left(1 - \alpha_{\mu_3}^M(x)\right)^\lambda, 1 - \left(1 - \alpha_{\mu_3}^U(x)\right)^\lambda\right), \\ \left(\left(\beta_{\mu_3}^L(x)\right)^\lambda,\ \left(\beta_{\mu_3}^M(x)\right)^\lambda,\ \left(\beta_{\mu_3}^U(x)\right)^\lambda\right), \\ \left(\left(\gamma_{\mu_3}^L(x)\right)^\lambda,\ \left(\gamma_{\mu_3}^M(x)\right)^\lambda,\ \left(\gamma_{\mu_3}^U(x)\right)^\lambda\right) \end{array}\right), \text{ for} \lambda > 0 \tag{6}$$

$$\mu_3{}^\lambda = \left(\begin{array}{c} \left(\left(\alpha_{\mu_3}^L(x)\right)^\lambda,\ \left(\alpha_{\mu_3}^M(x)\right)^\lambda,\ \left(\alpha_{\mu_3}^U(x)\right)^\lambda\right), \\ \left(1 - \left(1 - \beta_{\mu_3}^L(x)\right)^\lambda,\ 1 - \left(1 - \beta_{\mu_3}^M(x)\right)^\lambda, 1 - \left(1 - \beta_{\mu_3}^U(x)\right)^\lambda\right), \\ \left(1 - \left(1 - \gamma_{\mu_3}^L(x)\right)^\lambda,\ 1 - \left(1 - \gamma_{\mu_3}^M(x)\right)^\lambda, 1 - \left(1 - \gamma_{\mu_3}^U(x)\right)^\lambda\right) \end{array}\right), \text{ for} \lambda > 0 \tag{7}$$

According to the properties of the real-number system, the operators mentioned in Definition 2 has satisfied clearly as all TFNN properties follows.

$$\mu_1 \oplus \mu_2 = \mu_2 \oplus \mu_1,\ \mu_1 \otimes \mu_2 = \mu_2 \otimes \mu_1; \tag{8}$$

$$\lambda(\mu_1 \oplus \mu_2) = \lambda\mu_2 \oplus \lambda\mu_1,\ (\mu_1 \otimes \mu_2)^\lambda = (\mu_1)^\lambda \otimes (\mu_2)^\lambda,\ for\ \lambda > 0 \tag{9}$$

$$\lambda_1\mu_1 \oplus \lambda_2\mu_1 = (\lambda_1 + \lambda_2)\mu_1,\ \mu_1{}^{\lambda_1} \oplus \mu_1{}^{\lambda_2} = \mu_1{}^{(\lambda_1+\lambda_2)},\ for\ \lambda_1, \lambda_2 > 0. \tag{10}$$

Definition 3 ([28]). Let $\mu_1 = \left(\left(\alpha^L_{\mu_1}(x), \alpha^M_{\mu_1}(x), \alpha^U_{\mu_1}(x)\right), \left(\beta^L_{\mu_1}(x), \beta^M_{\mu_1}(x), \beta^U_{\mu_1}(x)\right), \left(\gamma^L_{\mu_1}(x), \gamma^M_{\mu_1}(x), \gamma^U_{\mu_1}(x)\right)\right)$ be a TFNN, the functions of score $S(\mu_1)$ and accuracy $A(\mu_1)$ can be respectively calculated by:

$$\begin{aligned} S(\mu_1) = \tfrac{1}{12}\Big[8 + \left(\alpha^L_{\mu_1}(x) + 2\alpha^M_{\mu_1}(x) + \alpha^U_{\mu_1}(x)\right) - \left(\beta^L_{\mu_1}(x) + 2\beta^M_{\mu_1}(x) + \beta^U_{\mu_1}(x)\right) \\ -\left(\gamma^L_{\mu_1}(x) + 2\gamma^M_{\mu_1}(x) + \gamma^U_{\mu_1}(x)\right)\Big],\ for\ S(\mu_1) \in [0,1] \end{aligned} \tag{11}$$

$$A(\mu_1) = \frac{1}{4}\Big[\left(\alpha^L_{\mu_1}(x) + 2\alpha^M_{\mu_1}(x) + \alpha^U_{\mu_1}(x)\right) - \left(\gamma^L_{\mu_1}(x) + 2\gamma^M_{\mu_1}(x) + \gamma^U_{\mu_1}(x)\right)\Big],\ for\ A(\mu_1) \in [-1,1] \tag{12}$$

Consider two TFNNs in the real-number set: $\mu^- = ((0,0,0),(1,1,1),(1,1,1))$ and $\mu^+ = ((1,1,1),(0,0,0),(0,0,0))$, then the values of score function μ^- and μ^+ are $S(\mu^-) = 0$ and $S(\mu^+) = 1$, respectively. Moreover, the values of accuracy function $A(\mu^-)$ is -1 for the TFNN μ^- and $A(\mu^+)$ is 1 for the TFNN μ^+. The accuracy function $A(\mu_1) \in [-1,1]$ states the discrepancy between truth and falsity [28]. Larger the discrepancy indicates the most affirmative of the TFNNs.

Assume that there are two TFNNs μ_1 and μ_1, then, according to Definition 3, the following conditions reach a true value.

$$\begin{aligned} &if\ S(\mu_1) < S(\mu_2),\ then\ \mu_1 < \mu_2; \\ &if\ S(\mu_1) > S(\mu_2),\ then\ \mu_1 > \mu_2; \\ &if\ S(\mu_1) = S(\mu_2)\ and\ A(\mu_1) < A(\mu_2),\ then\ \mu_1 < \mu_2; \\ &if\ S(\mu_1) = S(\mu_2)\ and\ A(\mu_1) > A(\mu_2),\ then\ \mu_1 > \mu_2; \\ &if\ S(\mu_1) = S(\mu_2)\ and\ A(\mu_1) = A(\mu_2),\ then\ \mu_1 = \mu_2; \end{aligned} \tag{13}$$

Definition 4 ([28]). Let $\mu_j = \left(\left(\alpha^L_{\mu_j}(x), \alpha^M_{\mu_j}(x), \alpha^U_{\mu_j}(x)\right), \left(\beta^L_{\mu_j}(x), \beta^M_{\mu_j}(x), \beta^U_{\mu_j}(x)\right), \left(\gamma^L_{\mu_j}(x), \gamma^M_{\mu_j}(x), \gamma^U_{\mu_j}(x)\right)\right)$ be a TFNNs group and $W = \{w_j\}$ be a set of the weighted criteria for $j = 1,2,3,\ldots,n$ in the group of real-numbers respectively, the operator of TFNNWA notated by $TFNNWA(\mu_1, \mu_2, \mu_3, \ldots, \mu_n)$ is determined by:

$$TFNNWA(\mu_1, \mu_2, \mu_3, \ldots, \mu_n) = w_1\mu_1 \oplus w_2\mu_2 \oplus w_3\mu_3 \oplus \ldots \oplus w_n\mu_n = \bigoplus_{j=1}^{n} w_j\mu_j \tag{14}$$

Theorem 1 ([28]). Let $\mu_j = \left(\left(\alpha^L_{\mu_j}(x), \alpha^M_{\mu_j}(x), \alpha^U_{\mu_j}(x)\right), \left(\beta^L_{\mu_j}(x), \beta^M_{\mu_j}(x), \beta^U_{\mu_j}(x)\right), \left(\gamma^L_{\mu_j}(x), \gamma^M_{\mu_j}(x), \gamma^U_{\mu_j}(x)\right)\right)$ be a TFNNs group in the real-numbers set, the aggregated value of TFNNWA operator is also a TFNN as the form as follows.

$$TFNNWA(\mu_1, \mu_2, \mu_3, \ldots, \mu_n) = \bigoplus_{j=1}^{n} w_j\mu_j = \left(\begin{array}{c} \left(1 - \prod_{j=1}^{n}\left(1-\left(\alpha^L_j\right)^{w_j}\right), 1 - \prod_{j=1}^{n}\left(1-\left(\alpha^M_j\right)^{w_j}\right), 1 - \prod_{j=1}^{n}\left(1-\left(\alpha^U_j\right)^{w_j}\right)\right), \\ \left(\prod_{j=1}^{n}\left(\left(\beta^L_j\right)^{w_j}\right), \prod_{j=1}^{n}\left(\left(\beta^M_j\right)^{w_j}\right), \prod_{j=1}^{n}\left(\left(\beta^U_j\right)^{w_j}\right)\right), \\ \left(\prod_{j=1}^{n}\left(\left(\gamma^L_j\right)^{w_j}\right), \prod_{j=1}^{n}\left(\left(\gamma^M_j\right)^{w_j}\right), \prod_{j=1}^{n}\left(\left(\gamma^U_j\right)^{w_j}\right)\right) \end{array} \right) \tag{15}$$

Definition 5 ([28]). Let $\mu_j = \left(\left(\alpha^L_{\mu_j}(x), \alpha^M_{\mu_j}(x), \alpha^U_{\mu_j}(x)\right), \left(\beta^L_{\mu_j}(x), \beta^M_{\mu_j}(x), \beta^U_{\mu_j}(x)\right), \left(\gamma^L_{\mu_j}(x), \gamma^M_{\mu_j}(x), \gamma^U_{\mu_j}(x)\right)\right)$ be a TFNNs group and $W = \{w_j\}$ be a set of the weighted criteria for $j = 1,2,3,\ldots,n$ in the group of real-numbers respectively, the operator of TFNNWG notated by $TFNNWG(\mu_1, \mu_2, \mu_3, \ldots, \mu_n)$ is presented by:

$$TFNNWG(\mu_1, \mu_2, \mu_3, \ldots, \mu_n) = \mu_1^{w_1} \otimes \mu_2^{w_2} \otimes \mu_3^{w_3} \otimes \ldots \otimes \mu_n^{w_n} = \underset{j=1}{\overset{n}{\otimes}} \mu_j^{w_j} \tag{16}$$

Theorem 2 ([28]). Let $\mu_j = \left(\left(\alpha^L_{\mu_j}(x), \alpha^M_{\mu_j}(x), \alpha^U_{\mu_j}(x)\right), \left(\beta^L_{\mu_j}(x), \beta^M_{\mu_j}(x), \beta^U_{\mu_j}(x)\right), \left(\gamma^L_{\mu_j}(x), \gamma^M_{\mu_j}(x), \gamma^U_{\mu_j}(x)\right)\right)$ be a TFNNs group in the real-numbers set, the aggregated value of TFNNWG operator is also a TFNN as the form as follows:

$$TFNNWG(\mu_1, \mu_2, \mu_3, \ldots, \mu_n) = \underset{j=1}{\overset{n}{\otimes}} \mu_j^{w_j} = \begin{pmatrix} \left(\prod_{j=1}^{n}\left(\left(\alpha^L_j\right)^{w_j}\right), \prod_{j=1}^{n}\left(\left(\alpha^M_j\right)^{w_j}\right), \prod_{j=1}^{n}\left(\left(\alpha^U_j\right)^{w_j}\right)\right), \\ \left(1 - \prod_{j=1}^{n}\left(1 - \left(\beta^L_j\right)^{w_j}\right), 1 - \prod_{j=1}^{n}\left(1 - \left(\beta^M_j\right)^{w_j}\right), 1 - \prod_{j=1}^{n}\left(1 - \left(\beta^U_j\right)^{w_j}\right)\right), \\ \left(1 - \prod_{j=1}^{n}\left(1 - \left(\gamma^L_j\right)^{w_j}\right), 1 - \prod_{j=1}^{n}\left(1 - \left(\gamma^M_j\right)^{w_j}\right), 1 - \prod_{j=1}^{n}\left(1 - \left(\gamma^U_j\right)^{w_j}\right)\right) \end{pmatrix} \tag{17}$$

2.2. The Distance of Normalized Hamming between Any Two TFNNs

In many practical and theoretical issues, once we have two fuzzy sets in the same finite universe of discourse, the way to measure a difference between them can be reflected by a distance. In this paper, we reconsider the normalized Hamming distance for the fuzzy sets in an TFN circumstance for MCGDM problem. The normalized Hamming distance of two TFNNs was initially identified by Wang et al. [43] by adopting the basic concept of Hamming distance for triangular intuitionistic fuzzy numbers (TIFN) [44].

Definition 6 ([43]). Assume that there are two TFNNs: $\mu_1 = \left(\left(\alpha^L_{\mu_1}(x), \alpha^M_{\mu_1}(x), \alpha^U_{\mu_1}(x)\right), \left(\beta^L_{\mu_1}(x), \beta^M_{\mu_1}(x), \beta^U_{\mu_1}(x)\right), \left(\gamma^L_{\mu_1}(x), \gamma^M_{\mu_1}(x), \gamma^U_{\mu_1}(x)\right)\right)$ and $\mu_2 = \left(\left(\alpha^L_{\mu_2}(x), \alpha^M_{\mu_2}(x), \alpha^U_{\mu_2}(x)\right), \left(\beta^L_{\mu_2}(x), \beta^M_{\mu_2}(x), \beta^U_{\mu_2}(x)\right), \left(\gamma^L_{\mu_2}(x), \gamma^M_{\mu_2}(x), \gamma^U_{\mu_2}(x)\right)\right)$; the normalized Hamming distance $H(\mu_1, \mu_2)$ between these two TFNNs can be depicted precisely by:

$$\begin{aligned} H(\mu_1, \mu_2) = {} & \tfrac{1}{9}\Big[\left|\alpha^L_{\mu_1}(x) - \alpha^L_{\mu_2}(x)\right| + \left|\alpha^M_{\mu_1}(x) - \alpha^M_{\mu_2}(x)\right| + \left|\alpha^U_{\mu_1}(x) - \alpha^U_{\mu_2}(x)\right| + \left|\beta^L_{\mu_1}(x) - \beta^L_{\mu_2}(x)\right| + \left|\beta^M_{\mu_1}(x) - \beta^M_{\mu_2}(x)\right| \\ & + \left|\beta^U_{\mu_1}(x) - \beta^U_{\mu_2}(x)\right| + \left|\gamma^L_{\mu_1}(x) - \gamma^L_{\mu_2}(x)\right| + \left|\gamma^M_{\mu_1}(x) - \gamma^M_{\mu_2}(x)\right| + \left|\gamma^U_{\mu_1}(x) - \gamma^U_{\mu_2}(x)\right| \\ & + \left|\gamma^U_{\mu_1}(x) - \gamma^U_{\mu_2}(x)\right|\Big] \end{aligned} \tag{18}$$

3. The Proposed MABAC Method for MCGDM Problems under TFNNs Environment

In recent MCGDM problems, the MABAC model has become one of the prospective decision-making approaches, due to its ability to consider conflicting attributes. It makes many scholars frequently innovate in venturing to utilize it in many fuzzy set circumstances. We also attempt to blend the MABAC model with the TFNNs environment by revealing the assessment values in the term of TFNNs. To be more specific, we provide the calculation procedures for our proposed MABAC method as follows and also show it in Figure 1.

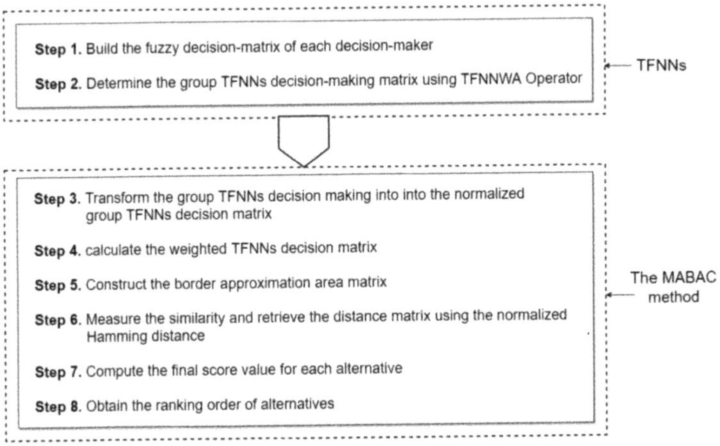

Figure 1. Flow diagram of the calculation procedures for our proposed MABAC method.

Let $\{E_1, E_2, \ldots, E_m\}$ be a number of alternatives, $\{d_1, d_2, \ldots, d_s\}$ be a group of decision makers with weighting-vector for each decision maker being $\{v_1, v_2, \ldots, v_s\}$, and $\{c_1, c_2, \ldots, c_n\}$ be a number of criteria with weighting-vector for each criterion being $\{w_1, w_2, \ldots, w_n\}$, which thus satisfies $w_i \in [0,1]$, $v_k \in [0,1]$, $\sum\limits_{j=1}^{n} w_j = 1$, and $\sum\limits_{k=1}^{s} v_k = 1$.

Step 1. Build the fuzzy decision-matrix $\mu^{(k)} = \left[\mu_{ij}^k\right]_{m\ x\ n}$ of each decision-maker, in which $\mu_{ij}^k = \left(\left(\left(\alpha_{ij}^L\right)^k, \left(\alpha_{ij}^M\right)^k, \left(\alpha_{ij}^U\right)^k\right), \left(\left(\beta_{ij}^L\right)^k, \left(\beta_{ij}^M\right)^k, \left(\beta_{ij}^U\right)^k\right), \left(\left(\gamma_{ij}^L\right)^k, \left(\gamma_{ij}^M\right)^k, \left(\gamma_{ij}^U\right)^k\right)\right)$, and assume that $\left(\left(\alpha_{ij}^L\right)^k, \left(\alpha_{ij}^M\right)^k, \left(\alpha_{ij}^U\right)^k\right) \in [0,1]$ is the TMD, $\left(\left(\beta_{ij}^L\right)^k, \left(\beta_{ij}^M\right)^k, \left(\beta_{ij}^U\right)^k\right) \in [0,1]$ is the IMD, $\left(\left(\gamma_{ij}^L\right)^k, \left(\gamma_{ij}^M\right)^k, \left(\gamma_{ij}^U\right)^k\right) \in [0,1]$ is the FMD, and $0 \leq \left(\alpha_{ij}^U\right)^k + \left(\beta_{ij}^U\right)^k + \left(\gamma_{ij}^U\right)^k \leq 3$ where $i = 1, 2, 3, \ldots, m$, $j = 1, 2, 3, \ldots, n$, and $k = 1, 2, 3, \ldots, s$.

Step 2. Determine the group TFNNs decision-making matrix $F = \left[\left(\left(\alpha_{f_{ij}}^L, \alpha_{f_{ij}}^M, \alpha_{f_{ij}}^U\right), \left(\beta_{f_{ij}}^L, \beta_{f_{ij}}^M, \beta_{f_{ij}}^U\right), \left(\gamma_{f_{ij}}^L, \gamma_{f_{ij}}^M, \gamma_{f_{ij}}^U\right)\right)\right]_{m\ x\ n}$ in which $F = \left[f_{ij}\right]_{m\ x\ n}$ where for TFNNWA Operator

$$f_{ij} = \begin{pmatrix} \left(1 - \prod\limits_{k=1}^{s}\left(1 - \left(\alpha_{ij}^L\right)^k\right)^{v_k}, 1 - \prod\limits_{k=1}^{s}\left(1 - \left(\alpha_{ij}^M\right)^k\right)^{v_k}, 1 - \prod\limits_{k=1}^{s}\left(1 - \left(\alpha_{ij}^U\right)^k\right)^{v_k}\right), \\ \left(\prod\limits_{k=1}^{s}\left(\left(\beta_{ij}^L\right)^k\right)^{v_k}, \prod\limits_{k=1}^{s}\left(\left(\beta_{ij}^M\right)^k\right)^{v_k}, \prod\limits_{k=1}^{s}\left(\left(\beta_{ij}^U\right)^k\right)^{v_k}\right), \\ \left(\prod\limits_{k=1}^{s}\left(\left(\gamma_{ij}^L\right)^k\right)^{v_k}, \prod\limits_{k=1}^{s}\left(\left(\gamma_{ij}^M\right)^k\right)^{v_k}, \prod\limits_{k=1}^{s}\left(\left(\gamma_{ij}^U\right)^k\right)^{v_k}\right) \end{pmatrix} \quad (19)$$

or for TFNNWG Operator

$$f_{ij} = \begin{pmatrix} \left(\prod_{k=1}^{s} \left(\left(\alpha_{ij}^{L} \right)^{k} \right)^{v_k}, \prod_{k=1}^{s} \left(\left(\alpha_{ij}^{M} \right)^{k} \right)^{v_k}, \prod_{k=1}^{s} \left(\left(\alpha_{ij}^{U} \right)^{k} \right)^{v_k} \right), \\ \left(1 - \prod_{k=1}^{s} \left(1 - \left(\beta_{ij}^{L} \right)^{k} \right)^{v_k}, 1 - \prod_{k=1}^{s} \left(1 - \left(\beta_{ij}^{M} \right)^{k} \right)^{v_k}, 1 - \prod_{k=1}^{s} \left(1 - \left(\beta_{ij}^{U} \right)^{k} \right)^{v_k} \right), \\ \left(1 - \prod_{k=1}^{s} \left(1 - \left(\gamma_{ij}^{L} \right)^{k} \right)^{v_k}, 1 - \prod_{k=1}^{s} \left(1 - \left(\gamma_{ij}^{M} \right)^{k} \right)^{v_k}, 1 - \prod_{k=1}^{s} \left(1 - \left(\gamma_{ij}^{U} \right)^{k} \right)^{v_k} \right) \end{pmatrix} \tag{20}$$

Step 3. Transform the group TFNNs decision making $F = \left[f_{ij} \right]_{m \times n}$ into the normalized group TFNNs decision matrix $N = \left[\left(\left(\alpha_{n_{ij}}^{L}, \alpha_{n_{ij}}^{M}, \alpha_{n_{ij}}^{U} \right), \left(\beta_{n_{ij}}^{L}, \beta_{n_{ij}}^{M}, \beta_{n_{ij}}^{U} \right), \left(\gamma_{n_{ij}}^{L}, \gamma_{n_{ij}}^{M}, \gamma_{n_{ij}}^{U} \right) \right) \right]_{m \times n}$ in which $N = \left[n_{ij} \right]_{m \times n}$ where n_{ij} can be reached by using Equation (22) or (23). We then calculate the minimum and the maximum values of TFNNs for each criterion C_j $(j = 1, 2, 3, \ldots, n)$.

$$\begin{gathered} \alpha_{f_{ij}}^{L-} = \min_{1 \le i \le m} \left\{ \alpha_{f_{ij}}^{L} \right\}, \beta_{f_{ij}}^{L-} = \min_{1 \le i \le m} \left\{ \beta_{f_{ij}}^{L} \right\}, \gamma_{f_{ij}}^{L-} = \min_{1 \le i \le m} \left\{ \gamma_{f_{ij}}^{L} \right\}, \alpha_{f_{ij}}^{U+} = \max_{1 \le i \le m} \left\{ \alpha_{f_{ij}}^{U} \right\}, \\ \beta_{f_{ij}}^{U+} = \max_{1 \le i \le m} \left\{ \beta_{f_{ij}}^{U} \right\}, \text{and } \gamma_{f_{ij}}^{U+} = \max_{1 \le i \le m} \left\{ \gamma_{f_{ij}}^{U} \right\}. \end{gathered} \tag{21}$$

If C_j is a benefit criterion, each element of the matrix F can be normalized as follows.

$$n_{ij} = \begin{pmatrix} \left(\frac{\alpha_{f_{ij}}^{L} - \alpha_{f_{ij}}^{L-}}{\alpha_{f_{ij}}^{U+} - \alpha_{f_{ij}}^{L-}}, \frac{\alpha_{f_{ij}}^{M} - \alpha_{f_{ij}}^{L-}}{\alpha_{f_{ij}}^{U+} - \alpha_{f_{ij}}^{L-}}, \frac{\alpha_{f_{ij}}^{U} - \alpha_{f_{ij}}^{L-}}{\alpha_{f_{ij}}^{U+} - \alpha_{f_{ij}}^{L-}} \right) \left(\frac{\beta_{f_{ij}}^{U+} - \beta_{f_{ij}}^{U}}{\beta_{f_{ij}}^{U+} - \beta_{f_{ij}}^{L-}}, \frac{\beta_{f_{ij}}^{U+} - \beta_{f_{ij}}^{M}}{\beta_{f_{ij}}^{U+} - \beta_{f_{ij}}^{L-}}, \frac{\beta_{f_{ij}}^{U+} - \beta_{f_{ij}}^{L}}{\beta_{f_{ij}}^{U+} - \beta_{f_{ij}}^{L-}} \right), \\ \left(\frac{\gamma_{f_{ij}}^{L} - \gamma_{f_{ij}}^{L-}}{\gamma_{f_{ij}}^{U+} - \gamma_{f_{ij}}^{L-}}, \frac{\gamma_{f_{ij}}^{M} - \gamma_{f_{ij}}^{L-}}{\gamma_{f_{ij}}^{U+} - \gamma_{f_{ij}}^{L-}}, \frac{\gamma_{f_{ij}}^{U} - \gamma_{f_{ij}}^{L-}}{\gamma_{f_{ij}}^{U+} - \gamma_{f_{ij}}^{L-}} \right) \end{pmatrix} \tag{22}$$

If C_j is a cost criterion, each element of the matrix F can be normalized as follows.

$$n_{ij} = \begin{pmatrix} \left(\frac{\alpha_{f_{ij}}^{U+} - \alpha_{f_{ij}}^{U}}{\alpha_{f_{ij}}^{U+} - \alpha_{f_{ij}}^{L-}}, \frac{\alpha_{f_{ij}}^{U+} - \alpha_{f_{ij}}^{M}}{\alpha_{f_{ij}}^{U+} - \alpha_{f_{ij}}^{L-}}, \frac{\alpha_{f_{ij}}^{U+} - \alpha_{f_{ij}}^{L}}{\alpha_{f_{ij}}^{U+} - \alpha_{f_{ij}}^{L-}} \right), \left(\frac{\beta_{f_{ij}}^{U+} - \beta_{f_{ij}}^{U}}{\beta_{f_{ij}}^{U+} - \beta_{f_{ij}}^{L-}}, \frac{\beta_{f_{ij}}^{U+} - \beta_{f_{ij}}^{M}}{\beta_{f_{ij}}^{U+} - \beta_{f_{ij}}^{L-}}, \frac{\beta_{f_{ij}}^{U+} - \beta_{f_{ij}}^{L}}{\beta_{f_{ij}}^{U+} - \beta_{f_{ij}}^{L-}} \right), \\ \left(\frac{\gamma_{f_{ij}}^{U+} - \gamma_{f_{ij}}^{U}}{\gamma_{f_{ij}}^{U+} - \gamma_{f_{ij}}^{L-}}, \frac{\gamma_{f_{ij}}^{U+} - \gamma_{f_{ij}}^{M}}{\gamma_{f_{ij}}^{U+} - \gamma_{f_{ij}}^{L-}}, \frac{\gamma_{f_{ij}}^{U+} - \gamma_{f_{ij}}^{L}}{\gamma_{f_{ij}}^{U+} - \gamma_{f_{ij}}^{L-}} \right) \end{pmatrix} \tag{23}$$

Step 4. Utilize Equation (24) to calculate the weighted matrix $P = \left[\left(\left(\alpha_{p_{ij}}^{L}, \alpha_{p_{ij}}^{M}, \alpha_{p_{ij}}^{U} \right), \left(\beta_{p_{ij}}^{L}, \beta_{p_{ij}}^{M}, \beta_{p_{ij}}^{U} \right), \left(\gamma_{p_{ij}}^{L}, \gamma_{p_{ij}}^{M}, \gamma_{p_{ij}}^{U} \right) \right) \right]_{m \times n}$ in which $P = \left[p_{ij} \right]_{m \times n}$ and $\sum_{j=1}^{n} w_j = 1$.

$$p_{ij} = w_j * n_{ij} = \begin{pmatrix} \left(1 - \left(1 - \alpha_{n_{ij}}^{L} \right)^{w_j}, 1 - \left(1 - \alpha_{n_{ij}}^{M} \right)^{w_j}, 1 - \left(1 - \alpha_{n_{ij}}^{U} \right)^{w_j} \right), \\ \left(\left(\beta_{n_{ij}}^{L} \right)^{w_j}, \left(\beta_{n_{ij}}^{M} \right)^{w_j}, \left(\beta_{n_{ij}}^{U} \right)^{w_j} \right), \\ \left(\left(\gamma_{n_{ij}}^{L} \right)^{w_j}, \left(\gamma_{n_{ij}}^{M} \right)^{w_j}, \left(\gamma_{n_{ij}}^{U} \right)^{w_j} \right) \end{pmatrix} \tag{24}$$

Step 5. Based on Equation (25), the border-approximation-area (BAA) matrix $Q = \left[\left(\left(\alpha^L_{q_j}, \alpha^M_{q_j}, \alpha^U_{q_j}\right), \left(\beta^L_{q_j}, \beta^M_{q_{ij}}, \beta^U_{q_{ij}}\right), \left(\gamma^L_{q_j}, \gamma^M_{q_j}, \gamma^U_{q_j}\right)\right)\right]_{1\ x\ n}$ in which $Q = \left[q_j\right]_{1\ x\ n}$ can be constructed and q_j stands for the BAA for criterion j.

$$q_j = \begin{pmatrix} \left(\prod_{i=1}^{m}\left(\left(\alpha^L_{p_{ij}}\right)^{1/m}\right), \prod_{i=1}^{m}\left(\left(\alpha^M_{p_{ij}}\right)^{1/m}\right), \prod_{i=1}^{m}\left(\left(\alpha^U_{p_{ij}}\right)^{1/m}\right)\right), \\ \left(1 - \prod_{i=1}^{m}\left(1 - \left(\beta^L_{p_{ij}}\right)^{1/m}\right), 1 - \prod_{i=1}^{m}\left(1 - \left(\beta^M_{p_{ij}}\right)^{1/m}\right), 1 - \prod_{i=1}^{m}\left(1 - \left(\beta^U_{p_{ij}}\right)^{1/m}\right)\right), \\ \left(1 - \prod_{i=1}^{m}\left(1 - \left(\gamma^L_{p_{ij}}\right)^{1/m}\right), 1 - \prod_{i=1}^{m}\left(1 - \left(\gamma^M_{p_{ij}}\right)^{1/m}\right), 1 - \prod_{i=1}^{m}\left(1 - \left(\gamma^U_{p_{ij}}\right)^{1/m}\right)\right) \end{pmatrix} \quad (25)$$

Step 6. Based on Equation (13) and Definition 6, calculate the distance matrix $D = \left[d_{ij}\right]_{m\ x\ n}$. The element d_{ij} is called the alternatives' distance from BAA and is depicted by using Equation (26).

$$d_{ij} = \begin{cases} H\left(p_{ij}, q_j\right), & if\ p_{ij} > q_j \\ 0, & if\ p_{ij} = q_j \\ -H\left(p_{ij}, q_j\right), & if\ p_{ij} < q_j \end{cases} \quad (26)$$

where $H\left(p_{ij}, q_j\right)$ is the normalized Hamming distance between the alternative p_{ij} and the BAA q_j.

According to the traditional MABAC's principle, we can see that if $d_{ij} = 0$, the alternative E_i will be a part of the border approximation area (G); if $d_{ij} > 0$ (d_{ij} has a positive value), the alternative E_i will be a part of the upper approximation area (G^+); and if $d_{ij} < 0$ (d_{ij} has a negative value), the alternative E_i will be a part of the lower approximation area (G^-).

Since the ideal alternative E_i^+ and the non-ideal alternative E_i^- are spread across the upper approximation border (G^+) and the lower approximation border (G^-), respectively, in order to decide the best alternative, we should have as many the criterion of the alternative as possible located on the upper approximation border (G^+).

Step 7. Compute the final score value $V(E_i)$ by using Equation (27).

$$V(E_i) = \sum_{j=1}^{n} d_{ij}, \quad (i = 1, 2, 3, \ldots, m)\ . \quad (27)$$

Step 8. Based on the value of $V(E_i)$, rank all the alternatives in descending order. In MCGDM problems for a selection case study, the alternative E_i will be the best alterative when the final score value $V(E_i)$ has the highest value.

4. Numerical Example and Discussion

This section separated into two subsections. Firstly, we present calculating steps of the proposed TFNNs-MABAC model for MCGDM, in this case, we illustrate an invest selection problem. Secondly, we compare our proposed TFNNs-MABAC method with TFNNWA Operator, TFNNWG Operator, and VIKOR method.

4.1. Calculating Steps of the Proposed TFNNs-MABAC Method for MCGDM Problems

This sub-section demonstrates an illustrative example for evaluating an invest selection problem under the TFNNs environment to show the proposed MABAC method. Suppose that a growth investor wants to provide a sum of money to invest in one of the five technology enterprise candidates $E_i (i = 1, 2, \ldots, 5)$. The investor has assigned three decision-makers $d_k (k = 1, 2, 3)$ to evaluate these five technology enterprises. Each technology enterprise will be assessed based on four prerequisite criteria $C_j (j = 1,2,3,4)$, which are the market-growth analysis (C_1), the market-risk analysis (C_2), the employee's analysis (C_3), and the environmental impact analysis (C_4), where C_1, C_2, and C_3 are benefit criteria, and C_4 is a cost criterion. The weighting-vector for each criterion $w_j = \{w_1, w_2, w_3, w_4\}$ has been given as $w = \{0.41,\ 0.14,\ 0.25,\ 0.20\}$ and the weighting-vector for each decision-maker $v_k = \{v_1, v_2, v_3\}$ has been determined as $v = \{0.35,\ 0.40,\ 0.25\}$. Based on the decision-makers' experience and knowledge, the evaluation process will be conducted in the form of TFNNs.

In order to determine the best technology enterprise, we present the proposed calculation procedure step by step as follows.

Step 1. Build the fuzzy decision-matrix $\mu^{(k)} = \left[\mu_{ij}^{k}\right]_{m\ x\ n}$ based on the evaluation of the decision makers d_k for each alternative E_i into each criterion C_j that can be illustrated in Tables 1–3.

Step 2. Utilize Equation (19) to determine the group TFNNs decision-making matrix $F = \left[f_{ij}\right]_{m\ x\ n}$ using TFNNWA Operator and the results are presented in Table 4.

Step 3. Use Equation (22) or (23) to transform the group TFNNs decision making $F = \left[f_{ij}\right]_{m\ x\ n}$ into the normalized group TFNNs decision matrix $N = \left[n_{ij}\right]_{m\ x\ n}$ and the results are shown in Table 5.

Step 4. Utilize Equation (24) to calculate the weighted TFNNs matrix $P = \left[p_{ij}\right]_{m\ x\ n}$. The elements of matrix P can be listed sequentially in Table 6.

Step 5. Construct the BAA matrix $Q = \left[q_j\right]_{1\ x\ n}$ by using Equation (25) as seen in Table 7.

Step 6. Determine the distance matrix $D = \left[d_{ij}\right]_{m\ x\ n}$ by using Equation (26) and the elements of matrix D can be seen in Table 8.

Step 7. Calculate $V(E_i)$ by using Equation (27) as listed in Table 9.

Step 8. Based on the results of $V(E_i)$, all alternatives can be sorted in descending order. The alternative E_i that has maximum value is the most possible selected alternative. Obviously, the result in term of the ranking order of those alternatives is $E_1 > E_5 > E_4 > E_2 > E_3$. Thus, the selected technology enterprise in which the investment company invest to is the alternative E_1.

Table 1. TFNNs judgement matrix by the decision maker d_1.

	C_1	C_2	C_3	C_4
E_1	⟨(0.5, 0.7, 0.9), (0.1, 0.2, 0.4), (0.1, 0.2, 0.3)⟩	⟨(0.2, 0.4, 0.6), (0.3, 0.4, 0.5), (0.1, 0.3, 0.4)⟩	⟨(0.4, 0.5, 0.6), (0.1, 0.2, 0.3), (0.1, 0.2, 0.3)⟩	⟨(0.3, 0.6, 0.9), (0.4, 0.5, 0.7), (0.1, 0.3, 0.5)⟩
E_2	⟨(0.4, 0.5, 0.6), (0.3, 0.4, 0.5), (0.2, 0.3, 0.4)⟩	⟨(0.1, 0.3, 0.5), (0.2, 0.4, 0.6), (0.1, 0.2, 0.4)⟩	⟨(0.4, 0.5, 0.9), (0.5, 0.6, 0.7), (0.4, 0.5, 0.6)⟩	⟨(0.3, 0.4, 0.6), (0.2, 0.3, 0.5), (0.4, 0.5, 0.7)⟩
E_3	⟨(0.2, 0.4, 0.5), (0.1, 0.3, 0.4), (0.4, 0.5, 0.7)⟩	⟨(0.1, 0.2, 0.3), (0.3, 0.4, 0.5), (0.5, 0.6, 0.7)⟩	⟨(0.6, 0.7, 0.9), (0.2, 0.4, 0.5), (0.1, 0.3, 0.4)⟩	⟨(0.3, 0.4, 0.7), (0.4, 0.6, 0.9), (0.1, 0.2, 0.3)⟩
E_4	⟨(0.1, 0.4, 0.6), (0.2, 0.5, 0.7), (0.1, 0.2, 0.3)⟩	⟨(0.4, 0.6, 0.7), (0.2, 0.3, 0.4), (0.1, 0.4, 0.6)⟩	⟨(0.3, 0.5, 0.7), (0.2, 0.3, 0.4), (0.1, 0.2, 0.5)⟩	⟨(0.4, 0.6, 0.9), (0.3, 0.5, 0.7), (0.1, 0.2, 0.4)⟩
E_5	⟨(0.6, 0.7, 0.9), (0.1, 0.2, 0.3), (0.1, 0.2, 0.3)⟩	⟨(0.4, 0.6, 0.7), (0.3, 0.4, 0.7), (0.1, 0.3, 0.4)⟩	⟨(0.4, 0.5, 0.6), (0.1, 0.3, 0.4), (0.1, 0.3, 0.5)⟩	⟨(0.2, 0.3, 0.9), (0.1, 0.3, 0.4), (0.1, 0.4, 0.5)⟩

Table 2. TFNNs judgement matrix by the decision maker d_2.

	C_1	C_2	C_3	C_4
E_1	((0.4, 0.6, 0.7), (0.1, 0.2, 0.3), (0.1, 0.2, 0.3))	((0.1, 0.3, 0.5), (0.2, 0.3, 0.4), (0.1, 0.2, 0.3))	((0.3, 0.4, 0.5), (0.1, 0.3, 0.4), (0.2, 0.4, 0.6))	((0.2, 0.4, 0.7), (0.3, 0.4, 0.6), (0.2, 0.3, 0.4))
E_2	((0.3, 0.4, 0.6), (0.2, 0.5, 0.7), (0.3, 0.5, 0.6))	((0.2, 0.3, 0.4), (0.1, 0.3, 0.5), (0.2, 0.3, 0.4))	((0.3, 0.4, 0.6), (0.4, 0.5, 0.9), (0.2, 0.3, 0.5))	((0.1, 0.3, 0.5), (0.1, 0.2, 0.3), (0.1, 0.2, 0.4))
E_3	((0.3, 0.6, 0.9), (0.2, 0.4, 0.7), (0.5, 0.7, 0.9))	((0.1, 0.2, 0.4), (0.1, 0.3, 0.6), (0.4, 0.7, 0.9))	((0.1, 0.3, 0.4), (0.2, 0.4, 0.6), (0.1, 0.3, 0.5))	((0.3, 0.4, 0.6), (0.4, 0.7, 0.9), (0.1, 0.2, 0.5))
E_4	((0.2, 0.3, 0.6), (0.2, 0.6, 0.9), (0.1, 0.3, 0.4))	((0.1, 0.7, 0.9), (0.3, 0.4, 0.5), (0.3, 0.4, 0.6))	((0.4, 0.6, 0.9), (0.2, 0.3, 0.4), (0.1, 0.2, 0.3))	((0.3, 0.4, 0.5), (0.1, 0.2, 0.3), (0.1, 0.2, 0.3))
E_5	((0.4, 0.5, 0.6), (0.1, 0.3, 0.4), (0.1, 0.2, 0.5))	((0.5, 0.6, 0.9), (0.3, 0.4, 0.6), (0.2, 0.3, 0.4))	((0.4, 0.5, 0.7), (0.2, 0.3, 0.4), (0.3, 0.4, 0.5))	((0.2, 0.3, 0.6), (0.1, 0.3, 0.4), (0.1, 0.2, 0.5))

Table 3. TFNNs judgement matrix by the decision maker d_3.

	C_1	C_2	C_3	C_4
E_1	((0.4, 0.5, 0.7), (0.1, 0.2, 0.5), (0.1, 0.2, 0.3))	((0.2, 0.3, 0.5), (0.3, 0.4, 0.6), (0.1, 0.2, 0.3))	((0.3, 0.4, 0.7), (0.2, 0.3, 0.4), (0.2, 0.5, 0.7))	((0.3, 0.5, 0.7), (0.3, 0.5, 0.6), (0.2, 0.3, 0.4))
E_2	((0.3, 0.4, 0.5), (0.4, 0.5, 0.6), (0.4, 0.5, 0.6))	((0.2, 0.3, 0.5), (0.1, 0.3, 0.4), (0.2, 0.3, 0.4))	((0.2, 0.4, 0.6), (0.1, 0.5, 0.9), (0.2, 0.3, 0.6))	((0.2, 0.3, 0.5), (0.1, 0.2, 0.4), (0.1, 0.2, 0.4))
E_3	((0.4, 0.6, 0.7), (0.3, 0.4, 0.6), (0.6, 0.7, 0.9))	((0.1, 0.2, 0.4), (0.1, 0.3, 0.4), (0.4, 0.6, 0.9))	((0.2, 0.3, 0.4), (0.2, 0.3, 0.5), (0.1, 0.3, 0.4))	((0.2, 0.4, 0.6), (0.4, 0.6, 0.9), (0.1, 0.2, 0.3))
E_4	((0.2, 0.3, 0.4), (0.2, 0.7, 0.9), (0.1, 0.3, 0.4))	((0.1, 0.4, 0.7), (0.3, 0.4, 0.9), (0.3, 0.5, 0.6))	((0.4, 0.5, 0.9), (0.2, 0.3, 0.5), (0.1, 0.2, 0.4))	((0.2, 0.4, 0.6), (0.1, 0.2, 0.4), (0.1, 0.2, 0.3))
E_5	((0.4, 0.5, 0.7), (0.1, 0.3, 0.5), (0.1, 0.2, 0.4))	((0.5, 0.6, 0.7), (0.3, 0.4, 0.5), (0.2, 0.3, 0.4))	((0.4, 0.5, 0.6), (0.2, 0.3, 0.5), (0.3, 0.4, 0.6))	((0.2, 0.3, 0.4), (0.1, 0.3, 0.4), (0.1, 0.2, 0.3))

Table 4. The group TFNNs decision matrix F by TFNNWA Operator.

	C_1	C_2	C_3	C_4
E_1	((0.437, 0.6175, 0.7957), (0.1, 0.2, 0.3769), (0.1, 0.2, 0.3))	((0.161, 0.3367, 0.5375), (0.255, 0.3565, 0.4786), (0.1, 0.2304, 0.3317))	((0.3367, 0.437, 0.593), (0.1189, 0.260, 0.3616), (0.1569, 0.3318, 0.4892))	((0.262, 0.5025, 0.7957), (0.3317, 0.4573, 0.633), (0.1569, 0.3, 0.4324))
E_2	((0.3367, 0.437, 0.577), (0.274, 0.4624, 0.5987), (0.2797, 0.4181, 0.5206))	((0.1663, 0.3, 0.4621), (0.1274, 0.3317, 0.504), (0.1569, 0.2603, 0.4))	((0.3142, 0.437, 0.7537), (0.3058, 0.5329, 0.824), (0.2549, 0.3587, 0.5578))	((0.1996, 0.337, 0.5375), (0.1274, 0.230, 0.3854), (0.162, 0.2756, 0.4865))
E_3	((0.2942, 0.539, 0.7688), (0.1736, 0.362, 0.5537), (0.484, 0.6222, 0.8242))	((0.1, 0.2, 0.3667), (0.1468, 0.3317, 0.509), (0.4324, 0.6381, 0.8242))	((0.342, 0.4796, 0.6795), (0.2, 0.3722, 0.5378), (0.1, 0.3, 0.4373))	((0.2762, 0.4, 0.6383), (0.4, 0.6381, 0.9), (0.1, 0.2, 0.368))
E_4	((0.166, 0.3367, 0.5573), (0.2, 0.585, 0.8242), (0.1, 0.2603, 0.3616))	((0.219, 0.6054, 0.8066), (0.260, 0.3616, 0.5356), (0.2042, 0.4229, 0.6))	((0.3667, 0.5426, 0.8531), (0.2, 0.3, 0.4229), (0.1, 0.2, 0.3854))	((0.314, 0.4793, 0.7307), (0.1468, 0.276, 0.4336), (0.1, 0.2, 0.3317))
E_5	((0.479, 0.5818, 0.7708), (0.1, 0.2603, 0.3824), (0.1, 0.2, 0.3954))	((0.467, 0.6, 0.8066), (0.3, 0.4, 0.605), (0.1569, 0.3, 0.4))	((0.4, 0.5, 0.6434), (0.1569, 0.3, 0.4229), (0.2042, 0.3616, 0.5233))	((0.2, 0.3, 0.7275), (0.1, 0.3, 0.4), (0.1, 0.2549, 0.44))

Table 5. The normalized TFNNs decision matrix N.

	C_1	C_2	C_3	C_4
E_1	(0.4301, 0.7168, 1), (0, 0.138, 0.3824), (0, 0.138, 0.2761)	(0.0868, 0.335, 0.6191), (0.267, 0.4796, 0.7353), (0, 0.1801, 0.32)	(0.0417, 0.2279, 0.517), (0, 0.2004, 0.3442), (0.1243, 0.5064, 0.8502)	(0, 0.4918, 0.8961), (0.3334, 0.5533, 0.710), (0.1398, 0.4825, 0.8527)
E_2	(0.2707, 0.430, 0.6525), (0.240, 0.5004, 0.6886), (0.2481, 0.4392, 0.5807)	(0.0938, 0.283, 0.5124), (0, 0.4278, 0.7884), (0.0785, 0.2213, 0.4142)	(0, 0.2779, 0.8156), (0.2649, 0.587, 1), (0.3393, 0.5651, 1)	(0.4331, 0.77, 1), (0.643, 0.8368, 0.9656), (0, 0.5456, 0.8384)
E_3	(0.2032, 0.592, 0.9572), (0.1017, 0.361, 0.6265), (0.5302, 0.721, 1)	(0, 0.1415, 0.3774), (0.0406, 0.4278, 0.798), (0.5491, 0.743, 1)	(0.052, 0.3069, 0.6778), (0.1149, 0.359, 0.5939), (0, 0.4368, 0.7368)	(0.264, 0.6639, 0.8715), (0, 0.3272, 0.625), (0.3066, 0.7412, 1)
E_4	(0, 0.2707, 0.6211), (0.138, 0.6697, 1), (0, 0.2213, 0.3613)	(0.1684, 0.7152, 1), (0.278, 0.4904, 0.8546), (0.1439, 0.4459, 0.6904)	(0.974, 0.4239, 1), (0.1149, 0.2567, 0.431), (0, 0.2184, 0.6235)	(0.109, 0.531, 0.8078), (0.5829, 0.7804, 0.941), (0.4003, 0.7412, 1)
E_5	(0.497, 0.6601, 0.9604), (0, 0.2213, 0.3899), (0, 0.138, 0.4079)	(0.5194, 0.7075, 1), (0.3612, 0.5706, 1), (0.0785, 0.2761, 0.4142)	(0.159, 0.3447, 0.6109), (0.0538, 0.2567, 0.431), (0.2276, 0.5716, 0.9246)	(0.1145, 0.832, 0.9994), (0.625, 0.75, 13), (0.1202, 0.5992, 1)

Table 6. The weighted normalized TFNNs decision matrix P.

	C_1	C_2	C_3	C_4
E_1	(0.2059, 0.4039, 1), (0, 0.444, 0.6743), (0, 0.444, 0.59)	(0.0126, 0.0555, 0.126), (0.831, 0.9022, 0.9578), (0, 0.7866, 0.8525)	(0.0106, 0.063, 0.1664), (0, 0.6691, 0.7659), (0.5938, 0.844, 0.9602)	(0, 0.1266, 0.3642), (0.803, 0.8883, 0.9338), (0.6747, 0.8644, 0.9686)
E_2	(0.1214, 0.2059, 0.3516), (0.5574, 0.7529, 0.8581), (0.5647, 0.7137, 0.8002)	(0.014, 0.0455, 0.0956), (0, 0.8879, 0.9672), (0.7004, 0.8096, 0.8839)	(0, 0.0626, 0.3447), (0.7174, 0.8753, 1), (0.7626, 0.867, 1)	(0.1073, 0.2547, 1), (0.9155, 0.965, 0.993), (0, 0.8859, 0.9653)
E_3	(0.0889, 0.3076, 0.7253), (0.3917, 0.6587, 0.8255), (0.7709, 0.8745, 1)	(0, 0.0211, 0.0641), (0.639, 0.8879, 0.9689), (0.8967, 0.9592, 1)	(0.013, 0.0875, 0.2466), (0.582, 0.7741, 0.8778), (0, 0.8129, 0.9265)	(0.0595, 0.1959, 0.337), (0, 0.7998, 0.9102), (0.7894, 0.9418, 1)
E_4	(0, 0.1214, 0.3283), (0.444, 0.8484, 1), (0, 0.5388, 0.6587)	(0.0255, 0.1612, 1), (0.8359, 0.905, 0.9782), (0.7623, 0.893, 0.9494)	(0.0252, 0.1288, 1), (0.582, 0.7118, 0.8102), (0, 0.6836, 0.8886)	(0.023, 0.1404, 0.2809), (0.8976, 0.952, 0.9879), (0.8327, 0.9418, 1)
E_5	(0.2457, 0.3575, 0.7339), (0, 0.5388, 0.6797), (0, 0.444, 0.6923)	(0.0974, 0.1581, 1), (0.8671, 0.9244, 1), (0.7004, 0.8351, 0.8839)	(0.042, 0.1002, 0.2102), (0.4817, 0.7118, 0.81), (0.6907, 0.8695, 0.9806)	(0.024, 0.2998, 0.7807), (0.9102, 0.944, 1), (0.6546, 0.9026, 1)

Table 7. The TFNNs-BAA matrix $Q[q_j]_{1\,x\,4}$.

	C_1	C_2	C_3	C_4
q_j	(0, 0.2565, 0.5724), (0.316, 0.6815, 1), (0.3694, 0.6517, 1)	(0, 0.0671, 0.2388), (0.7341, 0.9025, 1), (0.7058, 0.8761, 1)	(0, 0.085, 0.3124), (0.5197, 0.7613, 1), (0.5047, 0.8257, 1)	(0, 0.1927, 0.4852), (0.8274, 0.9267, 1), (0.6692, 0.9126, 1)

Table 8. The distance between the matrix N and the matrix Q.

	C_1	C_2	C_3	C_4
E_1	0.294133218	0.135433717	0.13017763	0.044585725
E_2	−0.14492263	0.127541677	−0.073960167	0.17199896
E_3	−0.132228984	−0.070633077	0.096657248	0.156082795
E_4	−0.166411125	0.125660975	0.201853503	−0.064361377
E_5	0.241339491	0.140794649	0.076253482	0.061268628

Table 9. The final score values of alternatives.

	E_1	E_2	E_3	E_4	E_5
$V(E_i)$	0.60433029	0.08065784	0.049877982	0.096741976	0.51965625

4.2. Compare the TFNNs-MABAC Method with Some TFNNs Aggregation Operators and VIKOR Method

This sub-section demonstrates the comparison between our proposed TFNNs-MABAC with TFNNWA operator and TFNNWG operator to examine the effectiveness of our proposed MABAC method in the TFNN environment. Based on the obtained results of Table 4 and weighting-vector for each criterion $w_j = \{0.41, 0.14, 0.25, 0.20\}$, the operators of TFNNWA and TFNNWG can be used to calculate overall f_{ij} to f_i (See Table 10). The use of these two operators aims to fuse overall the weighted input data that are expressed as TFNNs into a single TFNN (see Theorem 1 and 2). In other words, the aggregation result of both TFNNWA or TFNNWG operators is still in terms of fuzzy information. Moreover, to look at an exact number or a crips value representing the aggregation result for each alternative, we will easily find them through the score function value of TFNNs. After calculating the values of the TFNNs score function $S(f_i)$, we can generate the results of alternatives score as presented in Table 11. Afterward, the alternatives' ranking order by these two TFNNs aggregation operators can be seen in Table 13 and Figure 2.

Analyzing the results of our proposed TFNNs-MABAC method with TFNNWA and TFNNWG operators, we confirm that the results of our proposed MABAC method are the same as the results generated by the TFNNWA operator but insignificantly changed with the TFNNWG operator. The proposed TFNNs-MABAC method showed that the alternatives E_1 and E_5, respectively, placed in the first position and the second position, whereas the TFNNWG advised vice versa. Since the results in terms of ranking order provided by both aggregation operators are different, we then investigated further the discrepancy between truth and falsity of the TFNNWA and TFNNWG results for each alternative through the accuracy function of TFNNs. After calculating the accuracy function values of the TFNNs $A(f_i)$ for each aggregation operator, as seen in Table 12, we obtain the accuracy function values for all alternatives determined by TFNNWA have a bit larger than TFNNWG. It indicates that the ranking order suggested by TFNNWA is more affirmative in this aggregate comparison.

Nevertheless, in terms of the computational complexity, those two aggregation operators need relatively shorter computations to obtain decision-making by evaluating overall alternatives with their operators. Considering the abovementioned TFNNWA's advantage and from its result, as shown in Table 4, we then continued to perform the procedures of our proposed TFNNs-MABAC method for selecting the best alternative. The TFNNs-MABAC method evaluates ideal and non-ideal alternatives by spreading as many the criterion of the alternative as possible located on the upper approximation border. Although the TFNNs-MABAC takes a bit more time in returning the decision, it considers the conflicting attribute to avoid the inconsistency and uncertainty of DMs. Therefore, our proposed TFNNs-MABAC can be more scientific and reasonable in real-life MCGDM applications.

Furthermore, comparing our TFNNs-MABAC method with the TFNNs-VIKOR [43] method, as displayed in Table 13 and Figure 2, the best alternative selected by the VIKOR method is similar; however, the result of ranking order is slightly different to our proposed method. The VIKOR method advised the alternative E_3 and the alternative E_2, respectively, placed in the fourth position and the fifth position, whereas the proposed method suggested vice versa. Additionally, the alternatives' evaluation process in the VIKOR method is based on distance measures from the positive and negative ideal solutions in terms of each criterion like set-pair Analysis and TOPSIS. In contrast to other decision-making methods, the VIKOR method chooses an alternative with the lowest final score as the best alternative.

Table 10. The overall alternative values by using some TFNNs aggregation operators.

	f_1	f_2	f_3	f_4	f_5
TFNNWA	$\begin{pmatrix} (0.34, 0.52, 0.72), \\ (0.15, 0.27, 0.42), \\ (0.12, 0.25, 0.36) \end{pmatrix}$	$\begin{pmatrix} (0.28, 0.4, 0.61), \\ (0.21, 0.39, 0.57), \\ (0.22, 0.34, 0.5) \end{pmatrix}$	$\begin{pmatrix} (0.27, 0.45, 0.68), \\ (0.2, 0.4, 0.59), \\ (0.23, 0.41, 0.59) \end{pmatrix}$	$\begin{pmatrix} (0.25, 0.46, 0.72), \\ (0.19, 0.39, 0.57), \\ (0.11, 0.24, 0.38) \end{pmatrix}$	$\begin{pmatrix} (0.41, 0.51, 0.74), \\ (0.13, 0.29, 0.42), \\ (0.12, 0.25, 0.43) \end{pmatrix}$
TFNNWG	$\begin{pmatrix} (0.32, 0.49, 0.69), \\ (0.17, 0.29, 0.45), \\ (0.12, 0.25, 0.38) \end{pmatrix}$	$\begin{pmatrix} (0.27, 0.39, 0.58), \\ (0.23, 0.42, 0.63), \\ (0.23, 0.35, 0.5) \end{pmatrix}$	$\begin{pmatrix} (0.25, 0.42, 0.64), \\ (0.22, 0.42, 0.66), \\ (0.32, 0.49, 0.69) \end{pmatrix}$	$\begin{pmatrix} (0.23, 0.44, 0.68), \\ (0.19, 0.43, 0.65), \\ (0.11, 0.25, 0.4) \end{pmatrix}$	$\begin{pmatrix} (0.38, 0.49, 0.73), \\ (0.14, 0.29, 0.43), \\ (0.13, 0.26, 0.43) \end{pmatrix}$

Table 11. The score function value of alternatives $S(f_i)$.

	$S(f_1)$	$S(f_2)$	$S(f_3)$	$S(f_4)$	$S(f_5)$
TFNNWA	0.6661	0.5566	0.5505	0.6129	0.6641
TFNNWG	0.6476	0.5393	0.5010	0.5868	0.6511

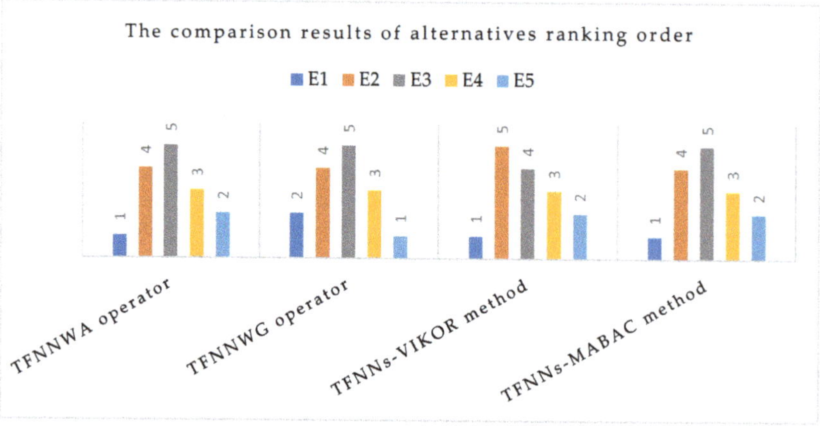

Figure 2. Flow diagram of the calculation procedures for our proposed MABAC method.

Table 12. The accuracy function value of alternatives $S(f_i)$.

	$A(f_1)$	$A(f_2)$	$A(f_3)$	$A(f_4)$	$A(f_5)$
TFNNWA	0.2799	0.0680	0.0546	0.2309	0.2779
TFNNWG	0.2479	0.0480	−0.0603	0.1937	0.2476

Table 13. The results of ranking order of alternatives.

	Ranking Order
TFNNWA	$E_1 > E_5 > E_4 > E_2 > E_3$
TFNNWG	$E_5 > E_1 > E_4 > E_2 > E_3$
TFNNs-VIKOR method [43]	$E_1 > E_5 > E_4 > E_3 > E_2$
TFNNs-MABAC method	$E_1 > E_5 > E_4 > E_2 > E_3$

5. Conclusions

In this article, we proposed the TFNNs-MABAC method based on some fundamental theories in TFNNs and the traditional MABAC model for MCGDM. Firstly, we reviewed the concepts, some essential operators, and operation laws of TFNNs, and then encapsulated the score and accuracy functions of TFNNs. Afterward, we discussed two aggregation operators regarding TFNNs and reviewed the definition of normalized Hamming distance among two TFNNs. Secondly, we developed the TFNNs-MABAC method by integrating the traditional MABAC with TFNNs. We demonstrated the steps of calculating the procedure of our proposed TFNNs-MABAC in detail through a numerical-example for an invest selection problem. Eventually, we performed a comparative-analysis to underline the benefits of the proposed TFNNs-MABAC. The proposed method verified conformity, effectiveness, and reasonableness for implemented to MCGDM problems.

In practice decision-making real-life time, the TFNNs are an effective instrument to solve the impreciseness and incompleteness of DMs. However, there is a limitation of the proposed method. Due to the number of functions for each membership degree of TFNNs, increasingly, the computational complexity in particular to calculate the overall value of some aggregation TFNN operators for a large of TFNNs group will be a bit slower and more complex. Therefore, it needs a high-performance computing technology or a database indexing technique to retrieve the overall aggregated value fast in the decision-making process.

Future works can utilize our proposed TFNNs-MABAC method to risk assessment for MCGDM cases, such as [45–50], many other uncertain and fuzzy circumstances [51–60]. The neutrosophic sets, such as [61–69], can be many possible chances to improve our proposed MABAC method for further studies. Other interesting future studies are to develop a novel decision-making model based on the TFNNs in social network group decision making [70] or apply the model to two-sided matching decision-making problems [71].

Author Contributions: Conceptualization, I.I.; methodology, I.I.; software, I.I. and N.N.Z.; validation, A.A., R.Z. and H.S.; formal analysis, I.I., R.Z. and H.S.; investigation, I.I., A.A. and H.S.; resources, I.I.; data curation, I.I.; writing—original draft preparation, I.I.; writing—review and editing, I.I. and H.S.; visualization, I.I. and N.N.Z.; supervision, I.I. and H.S.; funding acquisition, I.I.; project administration, I.I. All authors have read and agreed to the published version of the manuscript.

Funding: This research received no external funding.

Acknowledgments: All authors wish to acknowledge the Department of Informatics, Universitas Syiah Kuala for material and technical supports so this research has been conducted successfully. In addition, the authors also intend to appreciate the reviewers for their constructive opinions and valuable suggestions.

Conflicts of Interest: The authors declare no conflict of interest.

References

1. Xie, L.; He, J.; Cheng, P.; Xiao, R.; Zhou, X. A Multi-Criteria 2-Tuple Linguistic Group Decision-Making Method Based on TODIM for Cholecystitis Treatments Selection. *IEEE Access* **2019**, *7*, 127967–127986. [CrossRef]
2. Irvanizam, I.; Marzuki, M.; Patria, I.; Abubakar, R. An application for smartphone preference using TODIM decision making method. In Proceedings of the 2018 International Conference on Electrical Engineering and Informatics (ICELTICs), Banda Aceh, Indonesia, 19–20 September 2018; IEEE: Piscataway, NJ, USA, 2018. [CrossRef]
3. Wang, X.-K.; Wang, Y.-T.; Wang, J.-Q.; Cheng, P.-F.; Li, L. A TODIM-PROMETHEE II based multi-criteria group decision making method for risk evaluation of water resource carrying capacity under probabilistic linguistic z-number circumstances. *Mathematics* **2020**, *8*, 1190–1218. [CrossRef]
4. Akram, M.; Shumaiza; Alcantud, J.C.R. An m-polar fuzzy PROMETHEE approach for AHP-assisted group decision-making. *Math. Comput. Appl.* **2020**, *25*, 26. [CrossRef]
5. Akram, M.; Shumaiza; Al-Kenani, A.N. Multi-criteria group decision-making for selection of green suppliers under bipolar fuzzy PROMETHEE process. *Symmetry* **2020**, *12*, 77. [CrossRef]
6. Espinilla, M.; Halouani, N.; Chabchoub, H. Pure linguistic PROMETHEE I and II methods for heterogeneous MCGDM problems. *Int. J. Comput. Intell. Syst.* **2015**, *8*, 250–264. [CrossRef]
7. Adeel, A.; Akram, M.; Koam, A.N.A. Group decision-making based on m-polar fuzzy linguistic TOPSIS method. *Symmetry* **2019**, *11*, 735. [CrossRef]
8. Tehrim, S.T.; Riaz, M. A novel extension of TOPSIS to MCGDM with bipolar neutrosophic soft topology. *J. Intell. Fuzzy Syst.* **2019**, *37*, 5531–5549. [CrossRef]
9. Büyüközkan, G.; Güleryüz, S. Multi criteria group decision making approach for smart phone selection using intuitionistic fuzzy TOPSIS. *Int. J. Comput. Int. Syst.* **2016**, *9*, 709–725. [CrossRef]
10. Irvanizam, I.; Rusdiana, S.; Amrusi, A.; Arifah, P.; Usman, T. An application of fuzzy multiple-attribute decision making model based onsimple additive weighting with triangular fuzzy numbers to distribute the decenthomes for impoverished families. In Proceedings of the SEMIRATA-International Conference on Science and Technology, Medan, Indonesia, 4–6 May 2018; IOP Publishing: Bristol, UK, 2018. [CrossRef]
11. Piasecki, K.; Roszkowska, E.; Łyczkowska-Hanćkowiak, A. Simple additive weighting method equipped with fuzzy ranking of evaluated alternatives. *Symmetry* **2019**, *11*, 482. [CrossRef]

12. You, X.; Chen, T.; Yang, Q. Approach to multi-criteria group decision-making problems based on the best-worst-method and ELECTRE method. *Symmetry* **2016**, *8*, 95. [CrossRef]
13. Hashemi, S.S.; Hajiagha, S.H.R.; Zavadskas, E.K.; Mahdiraji, H.A. Multicriteria group decision making with ELECTRE III method based on interval-valued intuitionistic fuzzy information. *Appl. Math. Model.* **2016**, *40*, 1554–1564. [CrossRef]
14. Wu, Z.; Ahmad, J.; Xu, J. A group decision making framework based on fuzzy VIKOR approach for machine tool selection with linguistic information. *Appl. Soft. Comput.* **2016**, *42*, 314–324. [CrossRef]
15. Fan, J.; Cheng, R.; Wu, M. Extended EDAS methods for multi-criteria group decision-making based on IV-CFSWAA and IV-CFSWGA operators with interval-valued complex fuzzy soft information. *IEEE Access* **2019**, *7*, 105546–105561. [CrossRef]
16. Zadeh, L.A. Fuzzy sets. *Inf. Control.* **1965**, *8*, 338–356. [CrossRef]
17. Bellman, R.; Zadeh, L.A. Decision making in a fuzzy environment. *Manag. Sci.* **1970**, *17*, 141–164. [CrossRef]
18. Yoger, R.R. Multiple object decision-making using fuzzy sets. *Int. J. Man-Mach. Stud.* **1997**, *9*, 375–382. [CrossRef]
19. Atanassov, K.T. Intuitionistic fuzzy sets. *Fuzzy Sets Syst.* **1986**, *20*, 87–96. [CrossRef]
20. Smarandache, F. *A Unifiying Field in Logics: Neutrosophic Logic. Neutrosophy, Neutrosophic Set, Neutrosophic Probability and Statistics*, 3rd ed.; American Research Press: Phoenix, AZ, USA, 2003; pp. 11–12.
21. Wang, H.; Smarandache, F.; Zhang, Y.Q.; Sunderraman, R. Single valued neutrosophic sets. *Multispace Multistruct* **2010**, *4*, 410–413. Available online: http://fs.unm.edu/SingleValuedNeutrosophicSets.pdf (accessed on 1 July 2020).
22. Ye, J.A. Multicriteria decision-making method using aggregation operators for simplified neutrosophic sets. *J. Intell. Fuzzy Syst.* **2014**, *26*, 2459–2466. [CrossRef]
23. Ye, J. An extended TOPSIS method for multiple attribute group decision making based on single valued neutrosophic linguistic numbers. *J. Intell. Fuzzy Syst.* **2015**, *28*, 247–255. [CrossRef]
24. Deli, I.; Braumi, S. Neutrosophic soft matrices and NSM-decision making. *J. Intell. Fuzzy Syst.* **2019**, *37*, 5531–5549. [CrossRef]
25. Deli, I.; Ali, M.; Smarandache, F. Bipolar neutrosophic sets and their application based on multi-criteria decision making problems. In Proceedings of the International conference on advanced mechatronic systems (ICAMechS), Beijing, China, 22–24 August 2015; IEEE: Piscataway, NJ, USA, 2015. [CrossRef]
26. Stanujkic, D.; Karabasevic, D.; Smarandache, F.; Zavadskas, E.K.; Maksimovic, M. An innovative approach to evaluation of the quality of websites in the tourism industry: A novel MCDM approach based on bipolar neutrosophic numbers and the hamming distance. *Transform. Bus. Econ.* **2019**, *18*, 149–162.
27. Stanujkic, D.; Zavadskas, E.K.; Smarandache, F.; Brauers, W.K.; Karabasevic, D. A neutrosophic extension of the MULTIMOORA method. *Informatica* **2017**, *28*, 181–192. [CrossRef]
28. Biswas, P.; Pramanik, S.; Giri, B.C. Aggregation of triangular fuzzy neutrosophic set information and its application to multi-attribute decision making. *Neutrosophic Sets Syst.* **2016**, *12*, 22–40. Available online: https://digitalrepository.unm.edu/nss_journal/vol12/iss1/4/ (accessed on 1 July 2020).
29. Deli, I.; Şubaş, Y. Some weighted geometric operators with SVTrN-numbers and their application to multi-criteria decision making problems. *J. Intell. Fuzzy Syst.* **2017**, *32*, 291–301. [CrossRef]
30. Aal, S.I.A.; Ellatif, M.M.A.A.; Hassan, M.M. Proposed model for evaluating information systems quality based on single valued triangular neutrosophic numbers. *Int. J. Math. Sci. Comput.* **2018**, *4*, 1–14. [CrossRef]
31. Liu, P. The aggregation operators based on archimedean t-Conorm and t-Norm for single-valued neutrosophic numbers and their application to decision making. *Int. J. Fuzzy Syst.* **2016**, *18*, 849–863. [CrossRef]
32. Rodríguez, R.M.; Martínez, L.; Herrera, F. Hesitant fuzzy linguistic term sets for decision making. *IEEE T. Fuzzy Syst.* **2012**, *20*, 109–119. [CrossRef]
33. Zhang, Z.; Yu, W.; Martínez, L.; Gao, Y. Managing multigranular unbalanced hesitant fuzzy linguistic information in multiattribute large-scale group decision making: A linguistic distribution-based approach. *IEEE T. Fuzzy Syst.* **2019**, 1–15. [CrossRef]
34. Yu, W.; Zhang, Z.; Zhong, Q. Consensus reaching for MAGDM with multi-granular hesitant fuzzy linguistic term sets: A minimum adjustment-based approach. *Ann. Oper. Res.* **2019**, *1*, 1–14. [CrossRef]
35. Pamučar, D.; Ćirović, G. The selection of transport and handling resources in logistic centers using multi-attributive border approximation area comparison (MABAC). *Expert Syst. Appl.* **2015**, *42*, 3016–3028. [CrossRef]

36. Pamučar, D.; Petrovic, I.; Ćirović, G. Modificaton of the best-worse and MABAC methods: A novel approach based on interval-valued fuzzy-rough numbers. *Expert Syst. Appl.* **2018**, *91*, 89–106. [CrossRef]
37. Pamučar, D.; Stević, Ž.; Zavadskas, E.K. Integration of interval rough AHP and interval rough MABAC methods for evaluating university web pages. *Appl. Soft. Comput.* **2018**, *67*, 141–163. [CrossRef]
38. Jia, F.; Liu, Y.; Wang, X. An extended MABAC method for multi-criteria group decision making based on intuitionistic fuzzy rough numbers. *Expert Syst. Appl.* **2019**, *127*, 241–255. [CrossRef]
39. Dorfeshan, Y.; Mousavi, S.M. A novel interval type-2 fuzzy decision model based on two new versions of relative preference relation-based MABAC and WASPAS methods (with an application in aircraft maintenance planning). *Neural Comput. Appl.* **2020**, *32*, 3367–3385. [CrossRef]
40. Yu, S.-M.; Wang, J.; Wang, J.-Q. An interval type-2 fuzzy likelihood-based MABAC approach and its application in selecting hotels on a tourism website. *Int. J. Fuzzy Syst.* **2017**, *19*, 47–61. [CrossRef]
41. Zhang, S.; Wei, G.; Alsaadi, F.E.; Hayat, T.; Wei, C.; Zhang, Z. MABAC method for multiple attribute group decision making under picture 2-tuple linguistic environment. *Soft. Comput.* **2020**, *24*, 5819–5829. [CrossRef]
42. Mishra, A.R.; Chandel, A.; Motwani, D. Extended MABAC method based on divergence measures for multi-criteria assessment of programming language with interval-valued intuitionistic fuzzy sets. *Granul. Comput.* **2020**, *5*, 97–117. [CrossRef]
43. Wang, J.; Wei, G.; Lu, M. An extended VIKOR method for multiple criteria group decision making with triangular fuzzy neutrosophic numbers. *Symmetry* **2018**, *10*, 497. [CrossRef]
44. Grzegorzewski, P. Distances between intuitionistic fuzzy sets and/or interval-valued fuzzy sets based on the Hausdor & metric. *Fuzzy Set Syst.* **2004**, *148*, 319–328. [CrossRef]
45. Li, M.; Cao, P. Extended TODIM method for multi-attribute risk decision making problems in emergency response. *Comput. Ind. Eng.* **2019**, *135*, 1286–1293. [CrossRef]
46. Mondal, K.; Pramanik, S.; Giri, B.C.; Smarandache, F. NN-Harmonic mean aggregation operators-based MCGDM strategy in a neutrosophic number environment. *Axioms* **2018**, *7*, 12. [CrossRef]
47. Wu, S.; Wang, J.; Wei, G.; Wei, Y. Research on Construction Engineering Project Risk Assessment with Some 2-Tuple Linguistic Neutrosophic Hamy Mean Operators. *Sustainability* **2018**, *10*, 1536. [CrossRef]
48. Wang, J.; Wei, G.; Lu, M. TODIM method for multiple attribute group decision making under 2-tuple linguistic neutrosophic environment. *Symmetry* **2018**, *10*, 486. [CrossRef]
49. Wei, G.; Gao, H.; Wei, Y. Some q-Rung orthopair fuzzy heronian mean operators in multiple attribute decision making. *Int. J. Intell. Syst.* **2018**, *33*, 1426–1458. [CrossRef]
50. Zhou, H.; Wang, J.; Zhang, H. Stochastic multicriteria decision-making approach based on SMAA-ELECTRE with extended gray numbers. *Int. Trans. Oper. Res.* **2019**, *26*, 2032–2052. [CrossRef]
51. Wei, G.; Lu, M.; Tang, X.; Wei, Y. Pythagorean hesitant fuzzy hamacher aggregation operators and their application to multiple attribute decision making. *Int. J. Intell. Syst.* **2018**, *33*, 1197–1233. [CrossRef]
52. Wei, G.W. Some similarity measures for picture fuzzy sets and their applications. *Iran. J. Fuzzy Syst.* **2018**, *15*, 77–89. [CrossRef]
53. Bozanic, D.; Tešić, D.; Milić, A. Multicriteria decision making model with Z-numbers based on FUCOM and MABAC model. *Decis. Mak. Appl. Manag. Eng.* **2020**, *3*, 19–36. [CrossRef]
54. Li, P.; Ji, Y.; Wu, Z.; Qu, S.-J. A new multi-attribute emergency decision-making algorithm based on intuitionistic fuzzy cross-entropy and comprehensive grey correlation analysis. *Entropy* **2020**, *22*, 768. [CrossRef]
55. Chen, C.-H. A novel multi-criteria decision-making model for building material supplier selection based on entropy-AHP weighted TOPSIS. *Entropy* **2020**, *22*, 259. [CrossRef]
56. Irvanizam, I.; Syahrini, I.; Afidh, R.P.F.; Andika, M.R.; Sofyan, H. Applying fuzzy multiple-attribute decision making based on set-pair analysis with triangular fuzzy number for decent homes distribution problem. In Proceedings of the 2018 6th International Conference on Cyber and IT Service Management (CITSM), Parapat, Indonesia, 7–9 August 2018; IEEE: Piscataway NJ, USA, 2018. [CrossRef]
57. Biswas, S.; Pamučar, D. Facility location selection for b-schools in indian context: A multi-criteria group decision based analysis. *Axioms* **2020**, *9*, 77. [CrossRef]
58. Barukab, O.; Absullah, S.; Ashraf, S.; Arif, M.; Khan, S.A. A new approach to fuzzy TOPSIS method based on entropy measure under spherical fuzzy information. *Entropy* **2019**, *21*, 1231. [CrossRef]
59. Perez-Domínguez, L.; Rodríguez-Picón, L.A.; Alvarado-Iniesta, A.; Luviano Cruz, D.; Xu, Z. MOORA under Pythagorean fuzzy set for multiple criteria decision making. *Complexity* **2018**, *2018*, 2602376. [CrossRef]

60. Irvanizam, I.; Usman, T.; Iqbal, M.; Iskandar, T.; Marzuki, M. An Extended Fuzzy TODIM Approach for Multiple-Attribute Decision-Making with Dual-Connection Numbers. *Adv. Fuzzy. Syst.* **2020**, *2020*, 6190149. [CrossRef]
61. Thong, N.T.; Lan, L.T.H.; Chou, S.; Son, L.H.; Dong, D.D.; Ngan, Y.T. An extended TOPSIS method with unknown weight information in dynamic neutrosophic environment. *Mathematics* **2020**, *8*, 401. [CrossRef]
62. Xue, H.; Yang, X.; Chen, C. Possibility neutrosophic cubic sets and their application to multiple attribute decision making. *Symmetry* **2020**, *12*, 269. [CrossRef]
63. Pramanik, S.; Dey, P.P.; Smarandache, F.; Ye, J. Cross entropy measures of bipolar and interval bipolar neutrosophic sets and their application for multi-attribute decision-making. *Axioms* **2018**, *7*, 21. [CrossRef]
64. Ye, J. Operations and aggregation method of neutrosophic cubic numbers for multiple attribute decision-making. *Soft Comput.* **2018**, *22*, 7435–7444. [CrossRef]
65. Garg, H. Novel single-valued neutrosophic aggregated operators under Frank norm operation and its application to decision-making process. *Int. J. Uncertain. Quantif.* **2016**, *6*, 361–375. [CrossRef]
66. Jun, Y.B.; Kim, S.J.; Smarandache, F. Interval neutrosophic sets with applications in BCK/BCI-algebra. *Axioms* **2018**, *7*, 23. [CrossRef]
67. Jun, Y.B.; Smarandache, F.; Song, S.-Z.; Khan, M. Neutrosophic positive implicative N-ideals in BCK-algebras. *Axioms* **2018**, *7*, 3. [CrossRef]
68. Ali, M.; Dat, L.Q.; Son, L.H.; Smarandache, F. Interval complex neutrosophic set: Formulation and applications in decision-making. *Int. J. Fuzzy Syst.* **2018**, *20*, 986–999. [CrossRef]
69. Khalil, A.M.; Cao, D.; Azzam, A.A.; Smarandache, F.; Alharbi, W. Combination of the single-valued neutrosophic fuzzy set and the soft set with applications in decision-making. *Symmetry* **2020**, *12*, 1361. [CrossRef]
70. Zhang, Z.; Gao, Y.; Li, Z. Consensus reaching for social network group decision making by considering leadership and bounded confidence. *Knowl-Based. Syst.* **2020**, *204*, 106240–106265. [CrossRef]
71. Zhang, Z.; Kou, X.; Yu, W.; Gao, Y. Consistency improvement for fuzzy preference relations with self-confidence: An application in two-sided matching decision making. *J. Oper. Res. Soc.* **2020**, *72*, 1731–1746. [CrossRef]

MDPI
St. Alban-Anlage 66
4052 Basel
Switzerland
Tel. +41 61 683 77 34
Fax +41 61 302 89 18
www.mdpi.com

Axioms Editorial Office
E-mail: axioms@mdpi.com
www.mdpi.com/journal/axioms

www.ingramcontent.com/pod-product-compliance
Lightning Source LLC
LaVergne TN
LVHW070201100526
838202LV00015B/1981
* 9 7 8 3 0 3 6 5 2 8 1 7 5 *